GILTE LEGENDE

VOLUME 2

EARLY ENGLISH TEXT SOCIETY

No. 328

2007

whanne thei rose thei fonde the bodi
in the place that thei had made
borun thedir with auugels and that
was in the kalendes of octobre and
after that longe tyme in that same
day he was sette with all his shri
ne of seluer in a more riche shrine
about the pere of oure lorde cccc
iij and x Here ensithe the liff of
Seint Kenigle And nerst beginnithe
the liff of saint leodegari cap̄ c lsⁱⁱⁱ

Leodegare whiles he
shined in vertues ē
disseruid to the biss
hop of Actus and wha
ebtarie kinge of ffra
unse was dede he was gretli greued
with the cure of the creamme in so
muche that bi the wiff of god and
bi the counsaile of barouns he made

British Library, MS. Egerton 876, f.235ʳ

GILTE LEGENDE

VOLUME 2

EDITED BY

RICHARD HAMER
with the assistance of Vida Russell

Published for
THE EARLY ENGLISH TEXT SOCIETY
by the
OXFORD UNIVERSITY PRESS
2007

OXFORD

UNIVERSITY PRESS

Great Clarendon Street, Oxford OX2 6DP

Oxford University Press is a department of the University of Oxford.
It furthers the University's objective of excellence in research, scholarship,
and education by publishing worldwide in

Oxford New York

Auckland Cape Town Dar es Salaam Hong Kong Karachi
Kuala Lumpur Madrid Melbourne Mexico City Nairobi
New Delhi Shanghai Taipei Toronto

With offices in

Argentina Austria Brazil Chile Czech Republic France Greece
Guatemala Hungary Italy Japan Poland Portugal Singapore
South Korea Switzerland Thailand Turkey Ukraine Vietnam

Oxford is a registered trade mark of Oxford University Press
in the UK and in certain other countries

Published in the United States
by Oxford University Press Inc., New York

British Library Cataloguing in Publication Data

Data available

Library of Congress Cataloging in Publication Data

Data applied for

ISBN 978-0-19-923439-4

1 3 5 7 9 10 8 6 4 2

Typeset by Anne Joshua, Oxford
Printed in Great Britain
on acid-free paper by
The Cromwell Press, Trowbridge, Wiltshire

CONTENTS OF VOLUME 2

PLATES IN VOLUME 2

þe feſt of ſeint marke ¶ And as ſone
as þei hað gres to ſeint marke ⁊
behyȝt him to halowe his feeſte
he drof oute þe peſtilence of þat
contre. And yaf hem grete abundaunce and goode aire and couable
reyne. Narraco ¶

Aboute þe yere of oure lorde a-
þouſan ccc· and xiiij^{ti} þey was
a ffrere of þauye of þe order of frey
prechoo þat was holi and of religious
converſacon ¶ Iulien was his name
borne of ffauentyne young in age
but Auncient in corage· þe which
was ſike vnto þe dethe· And ſent
for his þoup of his house· And
tolde þat his deth was nye ¶ And
ſodenli he appered ful of ioy and
gladneſſe þat he began to ſtreth oute
his hondes. And to gre breþeren·
yeue me place for þuli for þe grete
habundaunce of ioi þat I fele my

British Library, MS. Harley 630, f.112^r

GILTE LEGENDE

Here endithe the liff of Seint Iame, and nexst foluithe the
lyff of Seint Cristofore, Capitulum .iiij^{xx}.xiiij.

Seint Cristofore was of the kynrede of Cananee, and he was of so gret
stature þat he was .xij. cubites longe and hadde right a dredfull visage.
And it is redde in sum gestes that whanne he hadde serued a king of
Canane it fell in his thought þat he wolde seke the grettest prince in the
worlde and duelle withe hym and obeye hym. And so longe he sought 5
that he founde right a gret kynge of whom the renowne was that he was
the grettest of the worlde, and whanne the king seigh hym he receyued
hym gladly and made hym duelle withe hym in his courte.

And in a tyme it fell that a iogelour songe afore the kinge and in
hys songe he named of[t] the deuel, and the kinge that was cristen, 10
whanne he herde that he blessed hym faste. And whan Cristofore
[seigh] hym do so he mervailed hym gretly what signe that | was and   f. 161vb
whi he dede so. He asked, and whanne the kinge wolde not telle
hym, [he saide] but yef [he tolde hym], he wolde neuer serue hym
lengger. And [thanne] the kinge saide hym: 'Euery tyme that I here 15
the fende named I drede leste he take power ouer me and noye me,
and therfor I blesse me withe th[is] signe of the crosse for to defende
me from his power.' Thanne saide Cristofre: 'Yef thou drede the
deuell thanne ys he more myghti and gretter lorde thanne thou,
wherfor I see wel that I am deceiued of my hope, for I wende to 20
haue founde the þe grettest and the myghtyest prince in the worlde.
But now farewell, for I wille seke hym to be my lorde and that I be
his servaunt.'

And thanne he departed from the kinge and went in gret haste to
seke the deuell, and as he went by a gret desert he seigh a gret 25
felawship of knyghtes, amonge whyche ther was a cruell horrible
knyght that come to hym and asked hym whedir he went. And
Cristofre saide: 'I goo to seke my lorde the deuell for to haue hym to
my maister.' And thanne the deuel sayde: 'I am he that thou sekest.'
And thanne was Cristofre ioyfull and gladde and obliged hym to be 30
perpetuelly his servaunt. And thanne as they went togedre by a gret
high waye they founde a crosse sette up, and as sone as the fende seigh
that crosse he was aferde and fledde and lefte the high way and ledde

EH1H2A1A2L; D breaks off after 42 þou art   2 was] add of H1   3 sum] the
same D   10 oft] of EH1   12 seigh] herde E   14 he saide] om. E   he] I EH1
tolde hym] L, mow knowe it E, moost knowe it H1D   15 thanne] om. E, ins. H1
17 this] the ED   21 prince in] of D   22 for] add nowe H1   27 And] A H1

Cr[i]stofre thorugh a sharpe desert, and whanne thei were passed the
35 crosse he brought hym into the high way ayenne. And whanne
Cristofre seigh that, he asked hym what hym ayled that he was so
aferde, and he wolde not tell hym. And thanne saide Cristofre: 'But
f. 162ra yef thou telle me I | shall anone parte from the.' And than the fende
was constreined to telle hym and saide: 'A man that is called Crist was
40 hangged in the crosse, and whan I see that signe I am sore aferde
therof and flee as ferre as y may.' Thanne saide Cristofore: 'Whi, is he
mightier and gretter thanne thou that thou art aferde of hym and his
signe? Now see I well that I [haue labouride] in veyne whan I haue not
founde the grettest lorde, and therfor go thi way, [for] I will no lenger
45 serue the, but I will go seke that Crist.'

And whanne he hadde longe sought and asked who might teche
hym to Crist, at the laste he come into the last ende of a desert and
ther he founde an hermite, the whiche preched to hym of Ihesu Crist
and taught hym diligently in the faithe and saide hym: 'This kinge
50 that thou desirest to serue askethe the seruise of ofte fastinge.' And
Cristofore saide to hym: 'Aske of me sum other thinge, for that may I
not do.' And the hermite saide: 'Thanne thou most wake and saye
many praiers.' And C[r]istofore saide: 'I note what that is, I may do no
suche thingges.' And thanne the hermite saide: 'Knowest thou suche a
55 flode?' And Cristofore saide: 'Ye.' And thanne the hermite saide:
'Miche peple perisshen there, and thou art of gret stature and stronge
and mighti. Yef thou woldest duelle besydes that ryuere and passe
ouer al men that come it shulde be right plesaunt to God, and I truste
fully that he that thou desirest to serue will apere to the.' And thanne
60 Cristofore saide: 'S[uer]ly this seruise may I wel do, and I behote truly
to God that I will do it.'

Thanne went Seint C[r]istofore to that flode and made ther an
habitacle for hym, and he bare a gret perche in his honde in stede of a
f. 162rb staffe | vpon the whiche he lened in the water and bere ouer alle men
65 that wolde come witheoute cesinge, and ther he was mani a day. And
in a tyme as he slepte in his litell hous he herd the voys of a childe that
called hym and saide: 'Cristofore, come oute and bere me ouer.' And
thanne he awoke and come oute, but he founde no creatoure. And
whanne he was ayein in his hous he herde the same voys, and he ranne

34 Cristofre] Crstofre E   37 aferde] affraied D   40 in] on H1D   43 I'] y on
erasure H1   haue labouride] habounde E, labourid on erasure H1   44 for] om. E
60 Suerly] sothely EH1   62 Cristofore] Cistofore E   65 witheoute] add 'eny' H1
66 he'] ins. H1   69 herde] add ayene H1

oute and founde nobodye. The .iij. tyme he was called and come oute, 70
and thanne he founde a childe besydes the brinke of the riuere that
praied hym benignely to helpe hym ouer. And Cristofore toke the
childe vpon his necke and toke [his staffe in his honde] and entered
into the water for to passe ouer. And the water beganne to encrece
litell and litell and the childe beganne to waye greuously as lede, and 75
the further that he went the more the water beganne to encrece and
the childe to weye more vpon his [necke] so ferforthely that Cristofore
[felt a] gret anguisshe and was in gret doute to be drouned.

And whanne he was ascaped withe gret peyne and passed ouer and
sette the childe to the grounde, [he] sayde to hym: 'Childe, thou hast 80
putte me in gret perell and weyed so moche that though I hadde bore
alle the worlde I might not bere no hevier vpon me thanne I dede.'
And the childe ansuered: 'Cristofore, meruaile the not, for thou hast
not only born upon thi shuldres Ihesu Crist thi kinge, that thou
seruest in this werke, but hym that made alle the worlde hast thou 85
bore upon thi shuldres, and for thou shalt wete that I saye sothe,
whanne thou art | passed ouer ayein piche thi staffe in the erthe f. 162va
besides thine hous and thou shalt see tomorw that he shalle bere
floures and fruit.' And anone he vanisshed from his sight. And than
went Cristofore and [f]iched his staffe in the erthe, and whanne he 90
arose in the morutyde he founde it as a palme tree beringe bothe floure
and fruit.

And thanne went Cristofre into the citee of Lyce and he vnderstode
not her langage, and thanne he praied to oure Lorde that he wolde
yeue hym grace to vnderstonde that tunge, and so he dede. And as he 95
was in that praier the iuges wende that he hadde be a fole and lete hym
be, and whanne he vnderstode that langage he couered his visage and
went to the place wher thei martered cristen men and comforted hem
in oure Lorde. And thanne one of the iuges smote hym in the visage,
ande Cristofore saide: 'Yef I were not a cristen man I wolde reuenge 100
anone my wronge.' And after that Cristofore [f]iched his staffe in the
erthe and praied oure Lorde to that ende that the peple might be
conuerted that she might bere floures and fruit, and so it was done,
and thanne ther were conuerted .viij. thousand men.

70 .iij.] .iiij. *del.* thirde H1   73 his . . . honde] in hys honde his perche E
77 necke] backe E   78 felt a] fell in EH1   80 he] and EH1   85 werke] *add* alle
the worlde EH1   87 thi] þe H1   89 vanisshed] *add* awey H2   90 went] *ins.* H1
fiched] L, piched EH1H2   91 as] *ins.* H1   92 and fruit] *ins.* H1   95 tunge]
þinge H1   96 praier] praied *changed to* praier H1   99 the^r] his H1H2
101 anone/my wronge] *trs.* H1   fiched] L, piched EH1H2   104 .viij.] .vij. H2

105   And the kinge sent .CC. knightes for to bringe Cristofore to hym,
and thei founde hym praienge and dredden to saye her massage to
hym. And thanne he sent as many mo, ande whanne thei come to hym
and sene hym thei beganne to praie withe hym. And whanne
Cristofore arose from his praier he saide to hem: 'What seke ye?'
110 And they saide: 'The kynge hathe comaunded us to bringe the to hym
bounden.' And Cristofore saide: 'And I wolde, ye shulde not bringe |

f. 162vb   me to hym bounde nother vnbounde.' And thei saide to hym: 'But the
lust come, go quite wher thou wilt, and we shull saie to the kynge that
we haue not founde the.' 'Nay, it shalle not go so,' saide Cristofore,
115 'but I wille go withe you.' And thanne he conuerted hem in the faithe
and comaunded hem that they shulde bynde his hondes behinde his
backe and lede hym to the kinge.

    And whanne the kinge seigh hym he felle doune of [his] see for
drede of the sight of hym, and his servauntes toke hym up. And
120 thanne the kinge asked hym of his name and of his contrey, and
Cristofore ansuered: 'Before my bapteme my name was Reproued,
and sethe my name is Cristofore.' And than the kynge saide: 'Thou
hast take on þe a folysshe name, that is to wete of the crucifyed God
that profited not to hymselff ne not may to the. A, thou Canenyen
125 withe thi wichecraft, whi wilt not thou sacrifice to oure goddes?' To
whom Cristofore saide: 'Thou art right wysely called Dagarus, for
thou art dethe of the worlde and felawe to the fende, and thi goddes be
so worthy that mennes hondes haue made hem.' And thanne the kinge
said to hym: 'Thou were norisshed amonge wilde bestes and therfor
130 thou spekest so madly, and therfor yef thou wilt sacrifice to oure
goddes I shall geue the gret worshippes, and yef thou wilt not I shalle
waste the awaye bi peynes and gret turmentes.' And whan he wolde in
no wise sacrifye he was ledde into a streite prisone, and the knightes
that he hadde conuerted the kinge made hem to be beheded for the
135 name of Crist.

f. 163ra   And than after that the king made putte .ij. | right faire maydenes to
Cristofore, that one hight Vicine and that other Aquiline, and he
behight hem gret yeftes yef thei might drawe hym to synne withe
hem. And whanne Cristofore sawe that, he gaue hym to praier. And
140 whanne he was constreined bi the clippinge and iapinge of the
maydenes, he rose hym up and saide: 'What seke ye? For what

106 dredden] red H2   109 he] and H1   112 But] *add* 'if' H1, *add* yf H2
118 his] the E   see] *add* that he satte inne E   122 is] was H2   128 hondes] *ins.* H1
134 to] *om.* H1   be] 'be' H1   136 maydenes] maidons *subp.* 'wommen' H1
141 maydenes] maydensnas *subp.* 'wommen' H1

cause be ye come hedir?' And tho that were aferde [for] the clerenesse
of his visage saide: 'Holy seint of God, haue pitee on us so that we
mow leue in that God that thou prechest.' And whanne the kinge wost
it he made hem be putte oute and saide to hem: 'Whi be ye now 145
deseiued? I swere to my goddes that but yef ye sacrifie ye shull
perisshe of euell deth.' And they saide to hym: 'If thou wilt that we
sacrefie, comaunde that the places be clensed and that alle the peple
assemble to the temple.' And whanne that was done thei entered into
the temple and toke her gerdeles and putte hem aboute the neckes of 150
the ydoles and drowe hem to the erth and breke hem alle into peces
and saide to hem that stode ther: 'Go calle the leches that mowe hele
youre goddes.' And thanne by the comaundement of the kinge
Aquil[yn]e was hangged and a gret stone of a rochc haugged atte
her fete so that alle her membres were todrawe. And whanne she was 155
passed to oure Lorde her suster Vicena was cast in a flavme of fere,
but she went oute witheoute any harme, and sethe she was beheded.
    And thanne was Cristofore brought before the kinge, and he
comaunded that he shulde be bete withe yerdes of yren and that
men shulde ordeyne for hym a coyfe of yren hote brennynge and sette 160
it on his hede, | and thanne he dede make hym a gret sege of iren and f. 163rb
made Cristofore be bounde fast therto and sethe sette fere therunder
and caste piche therto, but the sege melted as wexse ande Cristofore
went oute al hole witheoute any harme. And thanne he comaunded
that he shulde be bounde to a stake and that he shulde be shot to and 165
persed thorugh with .xl. knightez. But the arwes of the knightes
hynggen in the eyre and might not touche hym. And thanne the kinge
wende that he hadde be thorughe persed withe arowes of the knyghtes
and dressyd hym to go towarde hym, and an harowe come sodenly
from the heir and turned hym bacwarde and smote the kinge in the 170
eye and made hym blynde. To whom Cristofore saide: 'Thou tyraunt,
I shalle passe tomorw to oure Lorde, and thanne medle my blood
withe the erthe and anoynte thin eyen and thou shalt receiue hele.'
And as he sayd, the morw after he was ledde to be byheded by the
comaundement of the kinge, and there he made his orison and sethe 175
he was beheded. And thanne the kinge toke a litell of his blode and
leyde it vpon hys eye and sayd: 'In the name of oure Lorde and of
Seint Cristofore,' and anone he was hole. And thanne þe kynge leved

---

142 come hedir] her H2   for] of E   clerenesse] chernes H1   146 swere] add now
H1   148 that²] om. H1   149 assemble] assembled H1   154 Aquilyne] L, Aquile
EH1H2   161–2 and . . . therto] ins. H1   168 be] ins. after thorughe H1

in God and comaunded ouer al that hosoeuer blamed God or Seint
180 Cristofore that he shulde be smete withe a suerde.

Ambrose saieth in his Preface of this marter in this wise: 'Lorde,
thou hast yeue to Cristofore so gret plente of vertues and suche grace
of doctrine that he conuerted .xlviij. thousande men of paynyme lawe
to the lawe of cristen faithe by his shynynge miracles; and Vicena and
f. 163ᵛᵃ Aquil[yn]e that longe | tyme hadde be comune atte bordell vnder the
186 stinke of lecherie he conuerted and made hem to lyue in the abite of
chastite and taught hem to haue a crowne of marterdom; and withe
that he was bounde to a chaier of yren and fere putte under and
dradde not the hete; and thorugh a longe day he was bounde to a stake
190 and might not be pershed thorugh withe arowes of al tho knightes.
And withe that, one of the arowes persed the eye of the tyraunt, to
whom the blode of the blessed marter restabled the sight and
enlumyned hym in takinge away the blyndenesse of the body and
gate hym a cristen wille, wher thorugh bi his praiers he hadde grace
195 for to do awey alle maner siknesse.

Here endithe the lyff of Seint Cristofere, and nexst foluithe
the lyff of the .vij. slepers, Capitulum .iiijˣˣ.xv.

The .vij. slepers were born in the citee of Ephesim, and whan Decyen
the emperour came into Ephesim for the persecucion of cristen peple,
he comaunded to edefye the temples in the middel of the citee so that
all might come withe hym to sacrifice to the idoles, and made seke alle
5 the cristen and lete bringe hem bounde, other to deye or to do
sacrifice, so that euery were so aferde of peynes that the frende forsoke
his frende and the sone renied his fader and the fader the sone.

And thanne in that citee were founde .vij. cristen, of whom the
names weren Maximien, Malch, Martinien, Denys, Iohn, Sempion
10 and Constantine, and whan thei sawe this persecucion thei had gret
sorugh. And for thei were the furst in the paleys, despisinge the
f. 163ᵛᵇ sa|crifice of ydoles, thei hidde hem in her hous and weren in fastinge
and in prayer continuelly. And thanne they were accused before
D[e]cyen and came thedir and verrely proued cristen men, and thanne

182 and] add of H1   185 Aquilyne] L, Aquile EH1H2   188 and¹] a H1   putte]
om. H1   under] twice once del. H1   190 and] ins. H1   194 his] þies H

EH1H2A1A2L; D resumes at 114 nothinge; for Decyen H1 has e on erased a till 114,
thereafter e.   1 .vij.] ins. H1   5 other] or H1   6 so²] add sore E
14 Decyen] Dacyen E   verrely] add thei were H2

was ther yeue hem space to repente hem vnto the comynge of Decyen. 15
And in the mene tyme thei spended alle her patrimonie amonge the
pore peple and tokin counsaile ande wenten to the mount Selyon, and
there they ordeyned hem to be more priuely. And there they hidde
hem longe and one of her felawshippe to ordeine for her lyuelode, and
whanne he went into the citee he clothed hym as a begger. 20

And whanne D[e]cyen was comen into the citee he lete seke hem,
and thanne Malk her ministre retourned full of drede to hem and
tolde hem of the cruelte of the emperour. And thanne were they gretly
afraied, but neuertheles Malk sette afore hem the brede that he hadde
brought so that whanne they were well comforted withe mete they 25
myght be strengger to turmentes. And whanne thei hadde take her
refeccion, as they sate in sorugh and wepinge, they fillen sodenly
aslepe as God wolde. And whanne it came to the morw and they
hadde be sought and might not be founde, Decyen was full sori that
he hadde loste so goodly yonge men, and thanne thei were accused 30
how thei hadde yeue al her goodes to pore men and were hydde vnto
that tyme in the mount of Selyon and aboden alway in her cristen
purpos. And thanne D[e]cyen lete calle her kinrede and manased hem
withe dethe but yef they wolde tell alle that they knewe of hem. And
thei accused hem and compleyned on hem, sayeng that they hadde 35
dispended alle her goodes in pore men. And than | Desyen thought f. 164ʳᵃ
what he might do withe hem and ordeyned that they shulde be closed
up in the caue with stones to that ende that they might deye there for
hunger and [for] sorugh. And thanne the werkemen that dede that
and .ij. cristen men, that is to wete Theodore and Ruffyn, wrote her 40
marterdom and putte it sotelly amonge the stones.

And whanne Decyen was dede and al that generacion, .CCC.lxxvij.
yere after, in the .xxx. yere of the empire of Theodesyen, whanne the
heresye of hem that renyed the resureccion of the dede bygunne to
encrese, thanne the right cristen emperour Theodesyen, whanne he 45
sawe the faithe to be so felonisly demened, he was full of sorugh and
clothed hym withe the hayre and was in a secrete place and wepte
euery day. And whanne oure [pitous] Lorde God sawe this thinge, he
wolde comfort the wepers and geue hope of resureccion of the dede,
and opened the tresour of his pitee and arered the forsaide marteres in 50

15 to repente hem] of repentaunce H2   19 longe] *add* tyme H2   21 Decyen]
Dacyen E   22 drede] deede *changed to* drede H1   26 her] *om.* H1   27 sodenly]
so dedli H2   33 Decyen] Dacyen E   39 for] *om.* E   46 faithe] filthe H1
48 pitous] *om.* E

this wise. He gaue wille to a burgeys of Ephesym that he wolde make
in that mountayne a sta[b]le to hys shepardez. And so it fell by
auenture that the masones opened that caue, and the seintes awoke
thanne and bade eche of hem other good morw and wend they hadde
55 slepte but one night, and thanne they recorded her sorugh of the day
before. And Malk that mynistred her necessitees to hem saide what
Decien hadde ordeyned of hem, for he sayde: 'We haue be sought as I
tolde you yestereuen for to sacrifise to the ydoles or ellys to deye.' And
Maxymien saide: 'God wote that we will neuer sacrifye to deye.'

f. 164rb   And whanne he hadde comforted | his felawes, he bade Malke that
61 he shulde go into the citee and beye hem brede, and that he brought
hem more thanne the day before and aspie redely what the emperoure
hadde ordeyned for hem. And thanne Malke toke .v. shyllingges and
went oute of the caue, and whanne he sawe the stones he hadde gret
65 meruayle, but he thought but litell in the stones, he thought moche on
other thinge. And than he come al dredfully to the gates of the citee
and he was al abaisshed, for he sawe the sygne of the crosse sette
theron. And thanne he wente to another gate and [founde] the same
token of the crosse, and thanne he mervayled ouer mesure, for upon
70 euery gate he founde the signe of the crosse, and thanne he blessed
hym and retorned ayein to the furst gate and went to haue dremed.
And thanne he confermed hymselff and hydde hys visage and entered
into the citee, and whanne he come to the selleres of brede and he
herde men speke of God yet was he more abasshed and sayde:
75 'Benedicite, what menithe this? Yesterday there durste no man
speke of Ihesu Crist and today euery man knowlegithe that they be
cristen. I trowe this is not the citee of Ephesim, for she is alle
otherwyse byl[d]ed, I note whiche.' And he asked, and they tolde hym
sykerly that it was Ephesim. Hym thought in hymselff verrely that he
80 hadde maddyd and thought to haue go ayenne to his felawes.

And than he went to hem that solde brede, and whanne he shewed
the money the selleres meruailedin gretly and saide that one to that
other that the yonge man hadde founde sum olde tresour. And
f. 164va whanne Malke | sawe hem speke togederes he dredde hym leste thei
85 wolde lede hym to the emperoure, and praied hem that þei wolde lete
hym goo and kepe hys money stille and the brede also. But thei helde

52 stable] stale E   60 And] L, *add* Maxymien saide EH1H2   62 hem] *om.* H1
the day] he did H2   aspie] espied H2   63 toke] told H1   65–6 on other] more H2
68 to] into H1   founde] *om.* EH1   78 bylded] byled E   I . . . whiche] *om.* H2
80 hadde] *om.* H1

hym faste and saide: 'Whennes art thou? Thou hast founde the tresour[es] of aunsien emperoures. Shewe us wher it is, that we mow be felawes withe þe, and we shulle kepe thi counsaill.' And Malke wost not what to ansuer hem for drede that he hadde, and 90 whanne thei sawe that he helde hys pees thei teyed a corde [aboute his necke] and drowe hym thorughe þe strete into the middes of the citee, and the tydingges went al aboute that a yonge man hadde founde the hidde tresours, so that alle assembeled aboute hym. And whanne euery man meruailed of hym and he wolde in no wyse confesse that he 95 hadde found any tresours, and euery man behelde hym and he was knowe of none, and in that other syde he behelde the peple to loke yef he coude knowe any of hys kynne that he went hadde leved yet and he coude none fynde, wherfor he was nye oute of hymself for this gret meruaile, and thus he stode al mased amonge al the peple of that citee. 100

And whanne Seint Martin the bisshoppe, and Antypater that was consult whiche was new come to the citee, herde this thinge they sent anone that they shulde bryng hym wysely into her presence and þat the money shulde be brought withe hym. And whanne he was brought to the chirche he went verrely that he shulde haue come before the 105 emperour. And thanne the bisshop and the consult meruayled hem of the money and asked hym wher he hadde founde that tresour vnknowen. And he ansuered that he hadde | nothingge founde, but f. 164ᵛᵇ that he hadde cam by hys kynrede. And he ansuered and saide: 'I wote well that I was bore in this citee yef this be the citee of Ephesim.' And 110 thanne the iuge saide to hym: 'How shulde we leue the that this money cam of thi kinrede whanne the scripture of the money shewithe that it is passed .CCC. yere .lxvij. that it was made, for it went in the furst dayes of Decyen the emperour and resemblithe in nothinge to oure money? And how myght it be that thi kynne shulde be of suche 115 age to lyue now? Thou arte but late born and woldest deceyue the wyse and the auncyen of the citee of Ephesim, and therfor I comaunde that thou be demened after the lawes into the tyme that thou hast confessed that thou hast founde.'

And thanne Malcus kneled downe and sayd: 'For Goddes loue, my 120 lordes, telle me one thynge that I shall axse you. Wher is Decyen the emperour that was in this citee, wher is he?' And the bysshop

87 Thou hast] trsp. H2   88 tresoures] tresour EH1   91–2 aboute his necke] L, om. EH1H2   94 hidde] olde H2   99 wherfor] & therefore changed to wherefore H1 100 al] om. H2   109 he ansuered and] also he H2   110 this] add citee EH1 112 money] om. H2   113 .lxvij.] .lxxvij. H2   118 that thou] om. H1   be] om. D 120 my] om. H1

ansuered hym and saide: 'Sone, ther nys none now alyve that hyght
Decyen. There was an emperour that hyght so, many worlde passid.'
125 And thanne Malke sayde: 'Of this I meruayle me gretly and there nys
none that levithe me. But foluithe me and I shalle shewe you my
felawes that be in the mount of Selyon, and thanne I hope ye wille leue
hem, for I wote wel that we fledde us for drede of the emperoure
Decyen, and I wote wel that yesternyght I sawe the emperoure
130 Decyen entre into this citee, yef this be the citee of Ephesim.'
    And thanne the byssopp bethought hymselff and sayde to the iuge
that this was sum vision that God wolde shewe bi this yong man. And
f. 165ʳᵃ thanne they went withe hym and a gret multitude of peple of | the
citee folued hem, and whanne thei came thedir Malke entered furst
135 inne [to his felawes, and the bisshop folued]. And as the bysshop went
he fonde amonge the stones the letteres seled with two selys of siluer,
and thanne he called the peple and redde hem before hem alle, and
alle weren gretly abasshed of the mervaylous heringe. And thanne
they sawe these seintes sittynge ande her visages as fresshe as any
140 floure of rose, wherfor alle the peple glorefyed God.
    And anone the bisshop and the iuge sent to Theodesien the
emperoure, praieng hym that he wolde come see the gret meruayles
that God hadde shewed now late. And whanne the emperoure herde
this message, anone he arose from the erthe and dede awaye the sacke
145 wherinne he wepte, and glorified God and come fro Constantinenople
to Ephesim, and alle went ayeinst hym and come to the mountayne
wher they entered into the caue. And as sone as the seintes sawe the
emperoure her faces shyned as the sonne, and whanne the emperoure
sawe this he glorified God and clipped hem and wepte upon eueriche
150 of hem and saide: 'I beholde you as though I sawe oure Lorde areyse
Lazar from dethe to lyff.' And thanne Maxymyen saide: 'Leue us
truly, Sir emperoure, that for thi loue oure Lorde hathe arered vs
before the day of the resureccion for thou shuldest stedfastly beleue
the resureccion of the dede that be to come. And verrely we be
155 resuscite and lyvin, and right as the childe is in the moderes wombe
witheoute felynge or dysese, right so we haue be here leving and
slepinge witheoute any disese felinge.'

    123 hym] om. D   124 worlde] old dai on erasure H1   130 yef . . . citee²] om. H1
135 to . . . folued] L, om. EH1D   137 he] þe bisshop D   139 as¹] al D
142 come] add and D   143 now] om. D   144 sacke] space for one word D
146 alle] add the cite D   hym] L, add and alle came ayeinst hym EH1D   147 they]
he D   150 of] vppon H1

And whanne they hadde thus sayde they bowed downe her hedys to
þe erthe and gaue up her sperites by the comaundement of God. And
thanne the | emperoure arose and felle vpon hem and wepte and   f. 165rb
cussed hem and went his waye, and comaunded that men shulde   161
ordeyne shrines of golde and syluer to leye hem inne. And that night
they appered to the emperoure and sayd hym that he shulde suffre
hem lye in þe erthe as they hadde done into [the] tyme that God luste
to rere hem ayen. And thanne the emperoure comaunded that the   165
place shulde be arrayed nobly withe stones and that alle bisshoppes
that wolde confesse the resureccion werin assoiled. It is done of that is
sayde that they slepin .CCC.lxxvij. yere, for they arosen the yere
of oure Lorde .CCCC.xlviij., and Decyen regned but one yere only
and .iiij. monthes, and that was in the yere of oure Lorde .CC.lij., and   170
so by this they shulde not slepe but an .C. .iiij.^{xx}. .xiij. yere.

Here endithe the lyff of .vij. slepers, and nexst beginnithe
the lyff of Seint Nazaren, Capitulum .iiij^{xx}.xvj.

Nazarian was sone of Aufrican, a right noble man but he was a Iwe,
and of a right cristen woman Seint Perpetuele whiche was come of the
right noble kinrede of Rome, and she was baptised of Seint Petre the
apostele. And whanne this childe was .ix. yere olde he mervayled
gretly that he sawe his fader and his moder of so diuerse contreye and   5
relygion. And thanne he dredde gretly withe which he might holde,
for eucry of hem laboured to drawe hym to her lawe and religion. But
atte the laste by the will of God he drowe hym to the lawe of his
moder and resseyued baptyme of Seint Lyne that was pope afterward.
And whanne his fader vnderstode it, he dede his power to withe-   10
drawe hym from his holy purpose and tolde hym | bi ordre alle the   f. 165va
turmentes that men deden to cristen, but he might in no wise
withedrawe hym from his holy purpose. And Nazarien liued longe
after his bapteme as it shewithe by that, for he suffered marterdom of
Neiron that crucifyed Seint Petre in the laste yere of his empire, and   15
Lyne was pope after Seint Petre. And as he wolde in no wyse consent
to his fader but preched stedfastly Ihesu Crist, and his kinrede dradde
lest he shuld be slayne and by her praiers they made hym go oute of

160 and¹] and//and H1   162 that] add same D   164 the] om. E   167 is . . .
of that] was done and hit D   169 of oure] afore H1

EH1DH2A1A2   2 come] om. D   6 he¹] þis childe D   12 cristen] add 'men'
H1, so D   18 lest] laste H1

the towne and token .vij. someres charged with richesses withe hym,
20 and he went into Itayle and gaue alle that good as he went to the pore
peple.

   And in the yere that he was parted fro Rome he cam to Plesance and
fro thennes he came to Melayn, and ther he fonde Seint Geruase and
Seint Prothase that were there holde in prison and he went and
25 comforted hem. And whanne it was knowen that he hardied the
forsaide marteres he was anone brought to the prouost, and he
continuelly dured in the confession of Ihesu Crist and was bete
withe staues and dreuen oute of the towne. And as he went from one
place to another, his moder that was passed oute of this worlde appered
30 to hym and comforted her sone and taught hym that he shulde go into
Fraunce. And as he come into a citee of Fraunce that hight Iumylly he
conuerted there moche peple, and a lady offered to hym her sone that
hight Cel[c]e that was a childe of noble stature, and whanne he hadde
baptised hym [ladde] hym withe hym. And whanne the prouost of
f. 165ᵛᵇ Fraunce herde that, he putte hem bothe in prison, the hon|des bounde
36 behynde hem, with a stronge cheyne aboute her necke, for to turmente
hem in the morw. And thanne the wyff of the prouost sent to her
husbonde and saide that it was no rightwysse iugement to sle the
innocentes and after that to require any helpe of the grete goddes, by
40 whiche wordes the prouost [was] corrected, and deliuered the seintes
and defended hem that they shulde preche no more.

   And after that he come to the citee of Treues, and there he was the
furst that preched Ihesu Crist and conuerted moche peple to the
faithe of God and edefyed there a chirche. And whanne Cornelyen
45 that was vyker woste it, he lete Nero to haue knoulage therof and he
sent an hundred knyghtes for to take hym, and they fonde hym in an
oratorie that he hadde made for hymselff, and they toke hym and
bonde his hondes, sayenge: 'The gret Nero hathe sent for the.' And
thanne Nazarien [sayde to] hem: 'The kinge withoute ordenaunce
50 hathe knightes out of ordre. Whi hadde not ye come goodly and sayde:
"Nero wolde haue you," and I wolde haue goo withe you withe good
wylle.' And thanne they drow hym forthe faste bounde and boffeted
the childe Cel[c]e and constreined hym to folowe hem. And whanne
Nero sawe hym he comaunded that he shulde be sette in prison into

---

26 he²] *add* was E   30 comforted] *add* him Hɪ   33 Celce] Celte EHɪ
34 ladde] helde EHɪ   35 the] and her D   40 was] *om.* EHɪ   42 he¹]
Nazarien D   49 sayde to] sent E, *so changed to* seyd 'to' Hɪ   53 Celce] Celte EHɪ
hym] hem D

tyme he wolde make hym to deye. And in the mene tyme Nero sent 55
his hunteres for to hunt for wilde bestes, and the bestes come inne
gret multitude and al tobrake her ordenaunces and entered into the
gardin of Nero, and ther they slow many men so ferforthely that Nero
fledde al afrayed, and he was so wounded in his fote that he laye many
dayes | after in hys bedde for sorugh of that wounde. And atte the laste f. 166ʳᵃ
he remembered hym of Nazarien ande went that the goddes hadde be 61
wrothe withe hym for he hadde suffered hym so longe to lyue. And
thanne by the comaundement of the emperour the knightes bete
Nazarien and the childe and putte hem oute of the prison and brought
hem before the emperour. And whanne Nero sawe [the] visage of hym 65
shyninge as bryght as the sonne, he went to haue be scorned and bade
hym do away his enchauntementes and comaunded hym to sacrifise to
his goddes. And thanne Nazarien was ledde to the temple and he praied
hem alle to go oute, and he praied and alle the goddes were tobroke.
And whanne Nero herde that he comaunded that he shuld be thrawe 70
into the see, comaundynge that yef he ascaped that anone he shulde be
brent in the fyre and throwe the pouudre of h[y]m into the see.

And thanne they putte Nazarien and the chylde Celse in a shippe
and ledde hem into the middes of the see and caste hem bothe
therinne, and thanne a gret tempest arose in the see aboute the shyppe 75
and aboute the seintes and the see was before right pesible. And
thanne men of the shippe dradde hem gretly to retorne and repented
hem of her wyckednesse, and Nazarien and Celse went vpon the water
withe gladde visage and came to hem and they beleued in God. And
thanne by his orison he cesed the tempest and came withe hem to a 80
place that is a .vjC. pace nighe to the citee of Ianys. And there he
preched, and sethe he come to Melane wher he hadde lefte Seint
Geruase and Seint Prothase. And whanne the prouost anone herde
that, he ledde hym into exile and Celse abode withe a | good lady. And f. 166ʳᵇ
thanne Nazarien come to Rome and fonde his fader that was [than] an 85
olde man [and] cristen and asked of hym how he hadde be conuerted,
and he sayde that Seint Peter the apostel appered to hym and bade
hym to folowe hys wyff and his sone that went before hym to Ihesu
Crist.

And after that he was constreyned by the bysshoppes to go to 90

    56 for²] add þe H1   63 the emperour] Nero D   65 the²] his EH1   72 hym]
hem EH1   80 hem] him H1   81 Ianys] so changed to Iamys H1, Iames D
83 anone] om. D   84 ledde hym] sente hem D   abode] add stille D   85 than] om.
EH1   86 and¹] om. EH1   87 that] om. H1

Melayne fro whennes he hadde be sent into exile, and there he was
presented to the prouost anone withe the childe Celse. And there he
made hem be byheded and threw the bodyes to houndes, but the
cristen stale her bodyes and leyde hem in a gardin, and that night they
95 appered to a seint that hight Crato and bade hym that he shulde berie
the bodyes more dipper in his hous for Nero. To whom he sayde:
'Syre, I beseche you that ye hele my doughter furst that is syke in the
palsy.' And anone she was hole, and thanne he toke the bodyes and
beryed hem as he hadde comaunded.

100 And so longe tyme after oure Lorde re[uel]ed her bodies to Seint
Ambrose, and he lefte Celse in his place and fonde Nazarien withe his
blood al fresshe as though he hadde be byheded that same houre, al
hole witheoute any corrupcion, withe berde and al his here and the
sepulcre smellinge of meruaylous suetnesse. And thanne he bare hym
105 to the chirche of the aposteles and beried hym worshipfully. And after
that he toke up Celse and leyde hym in the same chirche. And they
suffered dethe under Nero that beganne aboute the yere of oure Lorde
.lxvij. And of this marter saiethe Ambrose in his Preface: 'O thou
blessed and noble champion of oure Lorde, the whiche amonge the
110 assauutes of the worlde thou gaderedist as a prince multitude of peple |
f. 166ᵛᵃ witheoute nombre to euerlastinge lyff. O thou gret sacrement
vnspekeable, O blessed moder of her children glorified by turmentes,
the whiche ledde hem not to helle by wepinge ne by playninge but
folowed hem goinge to the kyngdom of heuene by perdurable
115 praisinge.' And thus sayeth Ambrose.

Here endithe the lyff of Seint Nazarien, and nexst
beginnithe the lyff of Seint Felix, Cap. .iiijˣˣ.xvij.

Felix was chose to be pope of Lyberien and was ordeyned. In as moche
as Lyberien the pope wolde not consent to the heresye of Ariene he
was [put] into exile of Constancien the sone of Consta[n]tine and
duelled there thre yere. For whiche thynge alle the clergye of Rome
5 haue ordeyned Felix to be pope by the will and consent of Lyberyen.
And this Felix after the counsaile of .xlviij. bisshoppes condempned

96 he] Crato D   100 so] *om.* D   reueled] releued EH1   102 al'] as D
103 any] *om.* D   106 he] Ambrose D   107 aboute] *om.* D

EH1DH2A1A2; in D *pope* is erased throughout, and an excision has affected parts of 12–
end   2 Ariene] the Aryens D   3 put] *om.* EH1   Constantine] Constatine E
4 thynge] thyinge E

Constancien the eretik and Arien and the emperour and .ij. prestes
withe hym that susteyned hym in his heresye. For whiche thinge he
was displesed and chased Felix oute of his bysshopriche and repeled
Lyberien by suche comenaunt only that he shulde be partener withe 10
hym and withe that other that Felix hadde condempned. And
Lyberien, that was turmented withe aney of the exile, su[b]mitted
hym to the wickednesse of the heresye, and so the persecusyon
encresed so moche that many prestes and clerkes weren slayne
witheinne the chirche witheoute that Lyberien defended hem. And 15
Felix, that was caste oute of his bisshopriche, duellyd in his propre
heritage, of whiche he was putte oute and was martered by smytinge
of his hede aboute the yere of oure [Lorde] | .CCC.xl.   f. 166vb

Here endithe the lyff of Seinte Felix, and nexst beginnithe
the lyff of Seint Symplicien, Cap. .iiij^{xx}.xviij.

Simplicien and Faustin bretheren were constreyned to sacrifice to þe
idoles, and for thei refused it thei suffered many turmentes atte Rome
vnder Dyoclucian. And atte the laste ende the sentence was yeue upon
hem ande were be[h]eded and her [bodyes] caste into Tybre, and
Beatrice her suster toke her bodyes up fro the water and beried hem 5
worshipfully.

Lucres that was prouost of Rome went in a tyme disportinge aboute
the heritage of Beatrice and sawe her and lete take her and comaunded
her to do sacrifice, and she refused it. And Lucres sawe that and lete
strangle her by night with his seruauntes, and Lucyne the virgine stele 10
the body and beried it withe her bretherin. And after that Lucres
entered into her heritage, and right as he in this tyme assailed the holy
marteres and made there a gret dynere to alle his frendes, and as they
dyned a litell childe that was in hys moders lappe swathed in clowtis
and suckynge sodenly lepte oute of hys moders lappe and cried, 15
heringe alle, and sayde: 'Lucresse, vnderstonde how that thou hast
slayne and assailed the marteres, wherfor wete thou well that thou art
youen into the power of fendes.' And anone Lucres dredde and
trembeled and was in the same houre rauisshed withe the fende and
was so horribly turmented by thre houres withe the fende that he 20
deyed atte that same dyner. And whanne tho that were there sawe

8 his] this EH1   12 aney] anuye *on erasure* H1   submitted] surmitted E,
surmunted H1   18 Lorde] *om.* E

EH1DH2A1A2   4 beheded] bebeded E   bodyes] hedes EH1D (*corps* P2)

this, they conuerted hem to the faythe and tolden to alle the passion of
f. 167ra Seint Beatrice | the virgine, the whiche was venged atte that dynere.
And they suffered dethe vnder Dioclusian about the yere of oure
25 Lorde .CC.iiij^{xx}.vij..

Here endithe the liff of Seint Symplicien, and nexst
beginnithe the lyff of Seint Martha, Capitulum .iiij^{xx}.xix.

Seint Martha the ostesse of oure Lorde Ihesu Crist was descended of
riall kinrede. Her fader hight Syro and her moder Eukarye. Her fader
was duke of Surie withe alle the parties of that see. And Martha withe
her suster possedid by right heritage of her moder .iij. castelles,
5 Magdalon, Bethanie and a partie of Ierusalem. And it is not redde that
she hadde euer husbonde ne felawship of man. And this noble ostesse
serued oure Lorde withe gret diligence, and her suster wolde do no
suche seruice for her thought herselff not sufficiaunt to do seruice to
so gret an oste.
10   After the passion of oure Lorde whanne the departinge of the
disciples was made, she and her brother the lazar, Marie Magdelein
her suster, and Seint Maxymyan that hadde baptized hem and to
whom they were committed by the holy goste, withe many other that
were sette in a shippe witheoute gouernayle and witheoute sayle,
15 witheoute any sustenaunce of lyvinge by the mysbeleued Iues, and by
the ledinge of the holy goste they come to Marcell. And sethe thei
went to Ays, and there they conuerted the pople to the faithe. And
this blessed Marthe was faire of speche and gracious in the sight of alle
        And that tyme ther was in a wode vnder the Rone betwene Arle and
f. 167rb [Avion] a dragon, halff beste and | halff fisshe, more gretter thanne any
21 oxe and lengger thanne an hors and hadde his wyngges longe and
sharp as a swerde and was horned on eueri syde, and he [hydde] hym
in the water and slow alle tho that passed bi it and drowned the
shippes. And this dragon was come by the see of Galacie and hadde be
25 engendered of Lamecana, a right cruel serpent of the water, and of a
beste that is called snake that the region of Galacie engenderithe. And
whanne he is folued by a sertayne space of tyme he putte oute hys
felthe oute of hys bely as shyninge as a mirrour and brennithe alle

EH1DH2A1A2L; excision of initials on preceding recto affects D 1–10 *whanne the*
14 sette] L, shette E, set *on erasure* H1, *om.* D   16 sethe] seide that D   20 Avion]
space EH1D (*Auignon* P2)   21 an] eny D   22 hydde] dede E   25 Lamecana]
Iamalian D

thinge that it touchithe. And Martha by the praier of the peple went
theder and founde hym etinge a man, and thanne she threw upon hym 30
holy water and shewed hym the signe of the crosse. And he was anone
ouercome and was as meke as any shepe, and Seint Martha teyed hym
withe her gerdill and anone he was slayne withe speres and with
stones. And that dragon was called of hem of the cuntre Carasture or
Taracle, and yet in rememberaunce of that is that place called 35
Tharascon, and before it was called the blacke place for as moche as
there was a shadowynge wode.

In a time as she preched betwene Avion and Rone, a yonge man
And thanne the blessed Seint Marthe by the licence of Maxymian
her maister and of her suster she duelled there fro thennes forwarde
and toke hede witheoute cesinge to fastinge and to praiers. And after 40
that she assembeled a gret companye of women and edefyed a chirche
in the worship of oure Lady the blessed Virgine Marie, and ther they
ledde right a sharpe lyff, and she eschewed | to ete flesche and all fatte, f. 167ᵛᵃ
eyren, chese, botre and wyne. She ete not but ones in the day and she
kneled an .C. tymes in the day and as moche in the night. 45

In a tyme as she preched betwene Avion and Rone, a yonge man
desyred to [here] her sermon and he coude gete no vessell to bringe
hym ouer [the water] an despoiled hymselff for to swymme, but he
was drowned anone by the strengthe of the water. And his body was
vnnethes founde the secounde day after and was presented to the fete 50
of Seint Martha, and she leyde her streite to the grounde in wise of a
crosse and praied in this wise: 'O Adonay, Lorde Ihesu Crist, that thi
frende my brother areredest from dethe to lyff, byholde the faith of
hem that be here and arere this childe.' And thanne she toke hym by
the honde and areised hym al quike, and he receyued bapteme. 55

Eusebie tellithe in the boke of [the Stori] Ecclesiast that sethe that
woman was cured of her maladye, she made an ymage lyknesse of
Ihesu Crist in her court or in her gardyn and made hym frenges as she
hadde sene hym were, and worshipped it gretly. And the herbes þat
growed vnder that image that before were not worthe, as sone as þei 60
hadde touched the frenge of the vestement of the ymage they were of
so grete vertu that they heled many siknesse. And that syke woman
that oure Lorde heled was Martha, as Ambrose tellithe. Seint Ierome
tellithe, and it is wrete in the Storie Parted in Thre, that Iulian

32 as¹] om. H1   39 of] add Magdaleyn D   43 fatte] add 'þing' H1   47 here]
om. EH1   48 the water] om. EH1   52 O] add þou D   53 brother] add þou D
56 the Stori] om. EH1   that²] add Martha þat D   57 ymage] add in D   61 ymage]
add anone D   64 and] as D

65 Apostata toke awaye that image and sette his image in that place, and
it was broken withe a stroke of thunder.

Oure Lorde re[uel]id to Seint Martha her passinge hens a yeer
f. 167vb before her [dethe] | and alle that yere she was seke of the feuer. And
the day before her passinge hennes she herde the felawshippe of
70 aungeles that bare the soule of her suster to heuene, and thanne she
assembled alle the felawshippe of susteres and of bretheren and saide
to hem: 'My felawes that haue be longe norisshed togederes, reioyse
you withe me, for I see the felawship of aungelles bere the soule of my
suster to the blesse of heuene. O my right faire suster and frende, lyue
75 now withe thi maister and myn oste in that blessed sege.' And anone
the blessed Martha that felt her passinge taught her folke to light up
lyght and wake aboute her tyl her passynge oute. And aboute
midnight before her passinge her kepers were gretly greued withe
slomberinge, and in the mene tyme ther entered inne a gret wynde
80 that quenched alle her lyght, and she sawe a gret tourbe of wicked
sperites and beganne to praie and sayde: 'Mi fader, my oste dere, these
traytoures be assembled to deuoure me, holdynge in her hondes my
wicked dedes that I haue done. Now, dere Ely, be not fer fro me, but
entende to my helpe.' And thanne she sawe her suster come to her
85 that helde a bronde in her honde and lyghted ayenne alle the lompes
and torches, and eche called other by her name. And in this mene
tyme Ihesu Crist came and saide: 'My dere ostesse, wher as I am thou
shalt be withe me. Thou receyuedest me in thi hous, and I shall
receyue the in my heuene and I shall enhaunse hem that praie to the
90 for the loue of the.'

And whanne the houre of her passinge oute neighed, she made
herselff to be born oute that she might beholde the heuene, and she
f. 168ra bade that she might be leide | on the erthe in asshes and that men shulde
holde before her the crosse, and thanne she praied in these wordes: 'My
95 dere oste, kepe now thi pore ostesse, and as thou deynedest to be
herborwed withe me, receyue me now into thy heuenly hous.' And
thanne she comaunded that the passion after Seint Luke shulde be
redde before her, and whan he that redde it sayd: 'Fader, into thine
hondes I recomende my sperit,' she yeld up the sperit.

65 that²] þe same H1   67 reuelid] releuid E, *so changed to* reuelid H1   68 dethe]
om. E, *ins.* H1   74 lyue] leve me D   75 thi] my H1   76 passinge] *add* sike D
up] vppon H1   77 lyght] *om.* D   oute] *add* of this wordle D   80 her] *preceding
letter erased* H1   84 sawe] shawe *with* h *subp.* H1   91 oute] hens D   95 as] *om.* D
96 into] in H1   98 into] in H1   98–9 into thine hondes/I recomende] *trs.* D
99 she . . . sperit] *om.* H1   the] her D

And the day folwynge that was on a Sonday, whanne they sayde 100
Laudes, aboute tierce oure Lorde appered atte Peregorke to Seint
Frount that halowed the masse and after þe [pistell], whanne he satte
in his chayer, and saide to hym: 'My frende, yef thou wylt fulfell that
thou hightest a gret while goo to my oste, arise up hastely and folow
me.' And he dede his comaundement and comen bothe to Taraskon 105
and beganne to syngge aboute the body and dede alle the office and the
other ansuered, and sethe they putte the body withe her propre
hondes in the sepulcre. And verrely whanne the songe was ended atte
Peregorke that the deken shulde rede the euuangely and he awoke the
bisshoppe to saye the benison, and whanne he awoke sodenly he 110
ansuered and saide: 'Brother, why awake ye me? Oure Lorde Ihesu
Crist hath led [me to] the body of Marthe his ostesse and we haue
leyde her in her sepulcre. Sendithe anone a massengere for to bringe
me my ringe of golde and my gloues and my crismatorie, for whan I
arrayed me to bery the body I toke hem to the sextayne and for ye 115
hasted me sodenly I forgate hem there.' And thanne there were
massengeres sent and they fonde it right as the bisshop hadde sayde,
and they broughte the ring and one of the gloues only and leffte | that f. 168ʳᵇ
other there in token of this thing, the whiche the sexstayne kepte. And
yet saide Fronte that 'whanne [w]e went oute of the chirche after the 120
sepulture, a wise brother of that place that was a clerke folowed vs and
asked of oure Lorde hou he was called. And he ansuered nothinge but
shewed hym the boke open that he helde in hys hond wherin was
wrete none other thynge but this verse: "Myn ostesse shalle lyue in
euerlastinge mynde and shall not drede her of evell in the last day." 125
And as he turned this boke he fonde this vers wretin ouer all.'

And many a fayre miracle was done atte her tombe. And thanne the
kynge Cloouys, kinge of Fraunce, that was made late cristin of Seint
R[e]my suffered gret turment in his reynes and come to her toumbe
and bare thennes perfite hele. And he enriched the place gretly and 130
gaue hem the space of .iij. myle of londe aboute hem on euery syde
and gaue gret fraunchise to her place.

And Marcell wrote the lyff of his maistresse and after went into
Esclauoyne and ther he preched the gospell of Ihesu Crist. And the .x.

102 pistell] preste EH1   103 My] add dere D   104 to my] om. D
107 sethe] than D   109 that] And than D   111 Lorde] 'lorde' H1   111–
12 Ihesu Crist] om. D   112 me to] om. EH1   116 me] add so H1   forgate] lefte D
120 we] he E   122 hou] whou E, so changed to whom H1   ansuered] add him H1
124 wrete/none other thynge] trs. D   128 made late] trs. H1   129 Remy] Romy
EH1   131 space] place H1

135   yere after the passinge hennes of Martha he rested in oure Lorde in
pees.

Here endithe the lyff of Seint Martha, and nexst beginnithe the lyff of Abdon and Sennes, Cap. .C.

Abdon and Sennes suffered marterdome under the emperour Dacyan.
The emperour hadde surmounted Babiloyne and the other provinces.
He fonde sum cristen witheinne the citee and ledde hem withe hym
bounde to the citee of Cordule, and there he made hem to deye by
f. 168ᵛᵃ   diuerse turmentes. And thanne Abdon and | Sennes, that weren as two
6   gouernours of the cuntre, token the bodies and beried hem, and
thanne they were accused and brought before Dacyen, and he made
hem to be ledde after hym to Rome faste ibounde withe cheynes. And
thanne thei come afore Dacian and before the senatoures, and thei
10   were comaunded to do sacrifice and so to haue alle her goodes pesibly,
or ellys thei shulde be deuoured withe wilde bestes, but they despised
her sacrifices and spettin ayenst the fals images. Thanne were they
drawe to the place of her marterdom and men lete go to hem two
lyones and .iiij. beres, and thei towched in no wise to the seintes but
15   rather kept hem. And they caste speres atte hem, and so atte the laste
they were thorugh smite withe speres, and than they were bounde by
the fete and drawyn thorugh the towne tylle they come before the
idole of the sonne. And whanne they hadde laye there .iij. dayes
Qwiryn that was subdeken toke hem and beried hem in his hous. And
20   they suffered dethe aboute the yere of oure Lorde .CC.liij.

Here endithe the lyves of Abdon and Sennes, and nexst
beginnithe the lyff of Seint Germane, Capitulum .C.j.

Seint Germayne was of noble kinrede, born of the citee of A[uc]erre
and was taught wonder welle in alle the artes lyberall, and atte the
laste he come to Rome for to lerne true kunnynge, and there he
receiued so gret a dignite that the senatoures sent hym into Fraunce to
5   haue the highnesse of the dignite of all Burgoyne. And so as he
f. 168ᵛᵇ   gouerned the citee of Aucer|re more diligentely thanne any other, he

135 yere] 'day' H1

EH1DH2A1A2L; A1 breaks off after 4 *Cor*/   2 The] þat H1   hadde] *om*. D
6 cuntre] courte H1   12 and spettin] in speting H1   13 her] the D   18 idole]
ydollis D

EH1DH2A1A2L   1 Aucerre] Anderre EH1D (*aucerre* P2)

hadde a pyne appell [tree] in the middes of the citee vpon whiche
bowes for to see the meruayles of his huntynge [h]e hangged the hedes
of the bestes that he toke. But whanne Seint Amador that was bisshop
of the citee parceyued that, he vndertoke hym of that vanyte and 10
councelled hym to cutte doune that tree leste any euell occasion felle
therby to the cristen, but he wolde not consent in no wise. And therfor
in a tyme whanne Germayne was oute of the towne the bisshoppe
made cutte downe the tree and lete brenne it, and whanne Germayne
woste it he forgate the relegion of cristen and come withe force and 15
armes to haue slayne the bisshop. And the bisshop knewe by devine
reuelacion that Germayne shuld be hys successour. He gaue place to
his madnesse and went to [Augustinense]. And after, whanne he was
come ayein to Ausuere, he enclosed sotelly Germayne withein the
chirche and sacrid hym there and saide hym that he shulde be his 20
successour in the bysshopriche.

And so it fell, for a litell after Amador deyed goodly, and alle the
peple praied Germayne to be bisshop, and thanne he gaue alle his
goodes to the pore peple and chaunged his wyff vnto his suster and
turmented his body so that in .xxx.ti wynter he ete neuer brede of 25
whete, ne dranke neuer wyne, ne vsed neuer potage, ne in so moche
that he wolde take salt atte any tyme to sauir suche symple mete as he
vsed. And yet .ij. tymes in the yere he drank wyne, that was atte
Cristemasse and atte Ester, but it was so alayed withe water that the
taste of wyne was [vt]terly excluded. And in hys re|feccion he toke f. 169ra
furst of asshes and after he toke brede of barle and fasted euery day 31
and ete not till night. And wynter ne somer he vsed none other
clothinge but the heyre, a cote and a gowne. And yef perauenture he
gaue not hys clothinge to sum pore, he wolde were it so longe till it
were al tobroke. His bedde was all enclosed withe asshin and withe the 35
hayre and withe [the] sacke, and his hede was not lefte up withe no
peloes higher thanne his shuldres, but he wepte alle day and bare
aboute his necke reliques of seintes, neuer oþer clothinge, and full
selde shone and selde gurte. Alle that he dede was ouer mannes pouer.
His lyff was suche that but miracle hadde proued it hit hadde be to 40

7 pyne] peyne *with first* e *del.* H1   tree] *om.* EH1   of] *twice* E   8 he] be EH1
18 Augustinense] L, Seint Austine EH1D   19 Ausuere] answhere H1, answer D
27 take] *add* eny D   30 vtterly] beterly E, bitterly *with* b *changed to* w H1   33 but]
add onli D   yef] ʒit D   perauenture] *add* yf D   34 so longe] solong *with* lo *on erasure*
H1   35 bedde] heed D   36 the sacke] L, sackes EH1D   38 clothinge] *add* but
one maner D

sight incredyble, but he dede so many miracles that yef his merites
hadde not go before it shuld haue be trowed fantasye.

In a tyme he was herborued in a place wher men made redy the
borde for to go to diner after he hadde souped, and he was gretly
45 meruayled and asked for whom the borde was sette ayein. And they
saide hym: 'For the good women that walke be night.' And thanne
Seint Germayne ordeyned that night to be waken. And thanne atte
sertayne houre gret multitude of fendes comyn in to the borde in
lyknesse of men and of women, and he comaunded hem that they
50 shulde not part thennes, and he awoke alle the meyne and asked hem
yef they knewe any of tho persones. And they sayde that it were her
neygheboures, and thanne he sent to her houses and they were founde
alle abedde. And thanne they alle [hadden gret meruayle] and
thoughten wel that it were fendes that hadde so longe scorned hem.

f. 169rb   In | that tyme Seint Lue bisshop of Troyes was beseged by the
56 kynge Attille, and thanne Seint Lowe went vpon the walles and asked
who it was that assayled hem. And the kinge sayd: 'I am Attylle, the
scourge and betinge of God.' And thanne the meke bysshop saide hym
sore wepinge: 'And I am Lowe that haue wasted the bestes of God,
60 [and haue nede of betinge and of chastinge of God.'] And thanne he
comaunded to open the gates, and alle the peple were so blynded by
the wille of God that they passed thorugh alle the gates and sawe no
men of the citee ne mysdede to none. And the blessed Seint
Germayne toke Seint Lowe with hym and went into Bretayne there
65 as were many heresyes, but whanne they were in the see a gret
turment arose, the whiche Seint Germayne apesed anone. And they
were worshipfully receyued of the peple of the cuntre, and the fendes
that Seint Germayne hadde putte oute [of] the bodyes of diuerse men
tolde before of his comynge. And whanne they hadde ouercome the
70 heretykes they retorned ayen to her propre places.

Hit befell that Seint Germayne was full syk in a strete, and that
same strete by caas was take with fyre. And men counceyled hym to be
bore oute of the strete for to eschewe the fyre, and he putte hymselff
ayeinst the fyre and the flawme brent al aboute and touched nothinge
75 the hous that he was inne. Another tyme that he come into Bretayne

43 herborued] herboroued *with* u *changed to* w Hι   49 he] þan Germayn D
50 thennes] *add and del.* And he awoke al þe mayne and asked hem þat þei shulde not parte
thens Hι   51 tho] þe Hι   53 hadden/gret meruayle] *trs.* EHι   55 Lue] lo`w´e
with w *on erasure* Hι, lyne D   56 kynge] L, *add of* EHιD   60 and¹ . . . God] *om.*
EHι   he] Lowe D   61 peple] *add of* Actille D   66 turment] tempest D
68 of¹] *om.* EHι   69 of] *om.* Hι   72 caas] cause *with* u *subp.* Hι

for the heresyes, one of hys disciples folowed hym hastely and fell
syke and deyed by the way. And whanne Seint Germayne retorned
that way he asked whiche was the sepulcre of his disciple and made
open it and | called hym bi his name and asked how he dede and f. 169ᵛᵃ
whedir he wolde any more go withe hym. And he ansuered that he 80
was well and all thingges were esy to hym, wherfor he kept not be
called thennes. And thanne the seint graunted hym that he shulde
abide in rest, and he leyde downe his hede and slepte in oure Lorde.

He preched in a tyme in Bretayne so that the kinge of Bretayne
forbade hym his hous and hys felawshippe, and thanne the kingges 85
cowherde hadde ledde his bestes to pasture. So as the Saxenes faught
ayenst the Bretones and they saw that they were fewe, and as they saw
the seintes passe by the waye they called hem to hem, and thanne
these holy men preched to hem in suche wyse so that they come to
grace of bapteme. And on Ester Day they cast of her armes, and 90
thorugh right brennynge charite of faithe they purposed to fyght. And
whanne that other partie herde it they hasted hem to go ayeinst hem
hastely for that they were dysarmed, but Seint Germayne hidde hym
amonge hem and taught hem that whan he cried: 'Alleluya,' that they
shulde alle ansuere withe one voys: 'Alleluia.' And whanne they hadde 95
cried: 'Alleluya,' so grete fere toke her enemyes that came vpon hem
that they threw her armes awaye, for they went not only that the hilles
hadd falle vpon hem but heuene alle hole, and fledden in gret haste.

In a tyme that Germayne passed by Augustinence he came by the
toumbe of Seint Cassien bisshoppe and enquered hym how it stode 100
withe hym. And he ansuered hym oute of the tombe wher he was and
sayde: 'I am in | right suete rest and abyde the comynge of the f. 169ᵛᵇ
saueoure.' And he saide thanne to hym: 'Reste than stille in pees in
oure Lorde and praie for us deuoutely that we mowe deserue to haue
the holy ioye of the resurreccion.' 105

Whanne Seint Germayne come into Ravenne he was receyued
worshipfully of the quene Placida and of Valentynien her sone. And
atte soper tyme she sent hym right a gret disshe of syluer full of
delicious metes whiche he receyued and gaue the servauntes the mete
and withehelde the disshe of seluer for pore folke. And in stede of that 110
yefte he sent the quene a dysshe of tree and a barly lofe witheinne, the

77 retorned] *add* aȝen D   79 open] opned H1   82 the seint] seint Germayne D
88 seintes] seinte D   hem¹] him D   89 these holy men] þis holi man D   men] *om*. H1
93 hidde hym] come D   95 alle] *om*. D   102 suete] suer H1   103 hym] L,
add ayen EH1D   pees] *add* and thanne he sayd (*add* aȝen D) to hym rest in pees EH1D
110 withehelde] with he`l´de H1

whiche yefte she toke gladly and made that same disshe to be couered withe siluer.

And in a tyme after, the quene prayed hym to dyner, and he
115 graunted her wele and came gladly. And for he was weke of laboure and of fastinge he rode to her vpon an asse, and whiles he was atte dyner his asse deyed. And whanne the quene woste it she made present to the bisshoppe a meruaylous high horse, and whanne he sawe it he saide: 'I praye you brynge me myn owne asse, for he that
120 brought me hedir shall bryngge me home ayen.' And thanne Seint Germayne went to his asse and sayde: 'Aryse thou asse, and go we ayenne home.' And anone the asse arose and shoke herselff as thou her hadde ayled none euell and bare Germayne ayen to his hous. But before he parted from Rauen he sayde that he shulde not longe abyde
125 in this worlde. And a litell while after, he fell seke in the feuer, and in
f. 170ra the .viij. day he passed to oure Lorde | and his body was born into Fraunce lyk as he hadde required the quene, and he passed in the yere of oure Lorde .iiijC. and [.xx.]

And Seint Germayne had behight to Eusebe bysshoppe of
130 [Vercellis] that whanne he retorned ayein he wolde halwen his chirche that he had founded. And whanne Seint Eusebee vnderstode that he was dede, he wolde dedyen his chirche hymselff and made to lyght up torches, but the ofter they light hem the ofter thei weren quenched. And whanne Seint Euseby sawe this he vnderstode that this dedica-
135 cion shulde be do in sum other tyme or elles of sum other bisshoppe. And whanne the body of Seint Germayne was brought to Versayles, as sone as he was entered into the forsayd chirche alle the lyghtes were lyght sodenly by devyne lyght. And thanne Seint Eusebe recorded the promys of Seint Germayne and conceyued that he wolde fulfelle [in]
140 dede the promesse that he hadde made in his lyff. But it is not vnderstonde of the gret Eusebe that was bisshop of Verseilis that this was done in his tyme, for he was dede vnder Valentyne emperour, and fro the dethe of hym into the dethe of Seint Germayne was more thanne .l. yere, but it was another Eusebie vnder the whiche this
145 thinge was done.

114 prayed] bade D   115 wele] her wille D   117–18 made present] presentid D
119 owne] om. D   123 none] no þinge H1   125 And] add withynne D
128 .xx.] .xix. E, so with i erased H1   130 Vercellis] Vrselles EH1   132 was] add
ny3e D   dedyen] edifie D   139 in] om. EH1

Here endithe the lyff of Seint Germayn, and nexst
beginnithe the liff of Seint Eusebe, Capitulum .C.ij.

Eusebe was alwaye virgine, and as he was yet nwe in the faithe he
receiued bapteme and name of Eusebe the pope, in whiche bapteme
men sawe the hondes of aungeles that lefte hym from the font stone. A
lady was ouertake with | the beauute of hym that she wolde haue gone   f. 170rb
to his chaumbre, but aungeles kepte so the dore that she might not   5
come in, and thanne in the morwtyde she kneled downe to his fete and
asked hym mekely mercy. Whanne he was ordeyned to be preste he
shyned withe so gret holynesse that whanne he halowed the sollempnite of the masse the aungeles seruid hym.

And after that the heretik Ariene hadde corrupte alle Itayle, and   10
thanne Constancien emperour was consentant, the pope Iulius sacred
Eusebie bisshop of Versayles, that citee helde among alle that other of
Itayle the lordship. And whanne the heretykes herde that, they made
close the gates of the chirche that was of the blessed Virgine Marie,
and Eusebe kneled downe and opened al the gates by his prayer. And   15
he putte thanne oute Agnicien bisshop of Melan that was corrupte by
the malyce of that eresye and ordeyned in hys place Denys, right a
good man. And in this wyse Eusebe purged alle the chirches of the
occident and Athanase of the orient of the pestilence of heresye. And
that heretyk Arian was a preste of Alysaundre that [meinteyned] and   20
sayde that Ihesu Crist was a p[u]re creatoure, not God, and that he
hadde a begynninge, and that he was made for us so that God shulde
make us by hym right as by an instrument. And therfor Constantine
the Gret made and ordeyned the Counsayle of Nyce wher hys grete
errour was dampned. And after that Arien deyed of euel deth, for he   25
putte oute alle hys boweles benethe forthe as he went a procession.

And Constancien the sone of | Constantine was corrupte withe þat   f. 170va
heresye, for whiche cause this Constancien hadde grete hate to Eusebe
and assembled a Counsaile of many bysshoppes and called Denis ande
sent many lettres to Eusebe, and he wost well that the malice encresed   30
and wolde not come. And the emperour ordeyned ayeinst hys

EH1DH2A2L   1 alwaye] euer D   6 morwtyde] morowe D   she] this ladi D
10 that . . . Ariene] this þe heretikes of Ariens D   11 consentant] add to D   Iulius] add
that D   12 Versayles] add and D   16 thanne oute] trs. H1   18 Athanase] add
here EH1   orient] add hurde D   heresye] add and helde þerwith D   20 meinteyned]
imagenid EH1   21 pure] pore EH1   22 begynninge] benigne ʻmoderʼ H1
24 hys] þis on erasure H1, this D   25 that] add þe D   26 a] in D   29 assembled]
add hym EH1

excusacion that the Counsaile was ordeyned atte Melan that was nigh
hym. And whanne he sawe that Eusebe was not come, he comaunded
to the Arienes that thei shulde write her faithe to the bysshopp Denys
35 of Melan and to [.xxx.^{ti}] bisshopes. And whanne Eusebe herde that,
he went oute of the citee for to go to Melan and tolde well before that
he shulde suffre moch sorugh. And as he come to a ryuer for to go
ouer to Melan and the shippe was fer in that other syde, he called the
shippe and she come anone atte hys comaundement and bare hym
40 ouer and hys felawship witheoute any gouernour. And thanne the
forsayd Denis come ayeinst hym and kneled doune to hys fete and
asked hym foryeuenesse.

And whanne Eusebe myght not be turned nother by yeftes nor by
prayers ne by manaces of the emperour, he sayde before alle: 'Ye sayn
45 that the sone ys lasse than the fader, why haue ye thanne my sone and
my disciple made gretter thanne me? For the disciple is not aboue the
maister ne the sone aboue the fader.' And thanne they were meued by
that reson and shewed hym the wrytinge that they hadde made and
sayden that Denis hadd wretin and bade hym write als. And he saide:
f. 170vb 'I will not wry|te after my sone to whom I am made souerayne by
51 auctorite, but brennithe this and after that I shall write anewe.' And so
by the will of God that syrograff was brent that Denys and .xxix.
bisshopes hadde wrete. And thanne ayen the Aryenes write a new
cirograff and toke it to Eusebe and to the other bysshopes to write the
55 same, and thanne the bisshopes made hardy by Eusebe wolde not
consent in no wyse to her wrytinge, but were fulle gladde that the
writinge wherinne they hadde wretin by constreint was brent.

And thanne was Constancien wrothe and toke Eusebe to the wille
of the Arienes, and anone thei drowe hym fro the bisshopes and beten
60 hym cruelly, and drowe hym fro the higthe of the paleys by the
degrees doune to the lowest and fro the lowest ayenne to the highest,
till hys hede was al tobroste and that the blode ranne oute in gret
plente, and yet he wold in no wise assent to hem. And they bonde a
corde aboute his necke and bonde his hondes byhynde hym, and he
65 gaue thankingges to God and saide that he was redy for to deye for the
confession of the faithe of holy Chirche.

And thanne Constancien the emperour made sende into exile

33 comaunded] come D   35 .xxix.^{ti}] L, .xxx.^{ti} E, xx`ï´x^{ti} H1   36 tolde] *add*
hem D   49 saide] *add* I will not EH1   51 but] wherfore D   54–5 to write . . .
bisshopes] *om.* H1, *add* that were D   57 by constreint/was] *trs.* D   62 al] *om.* D
that] þan H1

Lyberien the pope and Denis with alle the bisshoppes that Eusebe had
made hardy to withestonde her wyckednesse. And the Aryens ledde
Eusebe into Ierapolyn, a citee of Palestyne, and there they closed hym 70
up in a streite place that he was so courbe that he myght not streche
oute hys fete ne turne fro one syde to another ne nothinge remeue of
hym but his hede and his shuldres and hys armes, so fer|forthe the f. 171ʳᵃ
place was streite in lengthe and in brede.

And thanne whan Constancien was dede Iulian succeded after hym 75
that wolde lyke to alle, and comaunded that the bisshoppes that were
in exile were called ayen, and he wolde that the temples of [the]
goddes were repayred and wolde vse the pees under euery lawe that
eueriche wolde holde. And so come Eusebe oute of prison and cam to
Athanase and tolde what he hadde suffered. And thanne Iulien [deyed 80
and] Io[vyn]ien regnid and the Arrienes were alle koy and Eusebe
retorned to Verseyles, and the [peple] rccciucd hym with grct ioye.
And whanne Valentine regned the Arienes resorted ayenne [and were]
in gret strengthe and entered into the hous of Eusebe and stoned hym
withe stones, and so he passed debonairly to oure Lorde and was 85
beried in the chirche that he hadde made. And it is sayde that he asked
that grace of oure Lorde by hys praiers that none heretyk Ariene
might not lyue in that citee. And after the cronicles he lyued .iiijˣˣ.
and .viij. [yeres] atte the lest, and he floured aboute the yere of oure
Lorde .CCC.l. 90

Here endithe the lyff of Euseby, and nexst beginnithe the
lyff of .vij. Machabeus, Capitulum .C.iij.

There were .vij. Machabeus withe her worshipfull moder and Eliazar
preste. They wolde not ete of the flesshe of porke for that thei were
defended it in her lawe, as it is more pleinly conteigned in the secound
chapitre of Makabeus, for they suffered turmentes suche as was neuer
lyke herde. And it is [to] knowe that the Chirche of the orient makithe 5
solempnite of the seintes of | that one and of that other Testament, but f. 171ʳᵇ
the Chirche of the occident makithe no fest of hem of the Olde

68 the] his D   72 fro] om. D   to] fro D   74 in²] om. H1D   77 called] add
home D   temples] temple D   the²] om. EH1   79 eueriche] euer D   80 what] þat
H1   deyed] did E, so changed to ded H1   81 and¹] om. EH1   Iovynien] Ionyvien EH1
82 the] þei H1   peple] om. EH1   83 and were] om. EH1   84 and¹] add come and D
86 hadde] om. D   89 yeres] om. ED, ins. H1 (ans P2)

EH1DH2A2L   3 it¹] om. D   lawe] lawes EH1   4 neuer] add none D
4–5 neuer lyke] trs. H1   5 to] om. EH1

Testament but of the Innocentes, for that the seintes in that tyme
descended into helle, but she makithe feste of the Innocentes for as
10 moche as Ihesu Crist was slayne in eueriche of hem, and also of the
Machabeus.

And .iiij. resones there be whiche the Chirche makithe feste of the
Machabeus, thou it be so that the Chirche make no sollempnite of
hem for as moche as they descended to helle, but for as moche as ther
15 be comyn gret multitude of new, but alwayes is made in these .vij. the
reuerence of alle, for as it is sayde that .vij. is a nombre vniuersell.

The .iij. reson ys for they were as ensaumple for to suffre and thei
be purposed in ensaumple made hardy in the loue of the faithe and for
to suffre for the lawes of the gospell right as they dede for the lawe of
20 Moyses.

The fourthe reson is for the cause of the turmentes that they
suffered for the lawe that they helde to defende as the cristene done
for the lawe of the gospell.

> Here endithe the Machabeus, and nexst beginnithe the *ad*
> *Uincula* of Seint Petre, Capitulum .C.iiij.

The feste of Seint Petre the Apostell that is called *ad Uincula* was
ordeyned for .iiij. causes, that is to saye in the mynde of the
deliueraunce of Seint Peter, in the mynde of the deliueraunce of
Alisaundre, for to destroye the paynyme custume, and for [to gete]
5 absolucion of spirituel bondes.

Furste the cause of [the] deliueraunce of Peter the Apostell, for as it
f. 171ᵛᵃ is sayde in | the Maister of Stories, Herodes Agrippa went to Rome
and was right familyer withe Tyberien the emperour. And in a day as
Herode was in a chayer with Gayen he lefte his hondes to heven and
10 sayde: 'I wolde gladly see the dethe of that olde felawe and see the
lorde of alle the worlde.' And the chare man herd how he saide and
anone he tolde the emperour Tyberien what Herode hadde saide, for
whiche thinge the emperour putte Herode in prison. And as he was in
prison, in a day he loked vpon a tree and he sawe an oule sitte vpon the
15 braunches, and a prisoner that was therin als that knewe dyuine

8 for . . . seintes] *om.* H1   12 whiche] why D   15 but] `but´ þat H1, þat D
18 ensaumple] *add* be H1, *add* to be D   for] that H1D   21 is] *om.* H1D

EH1DH2A2L; in D *pope is erased passim*   2 ordeyned] orde`i´ned H1   3 Seint
. . . of³] *om.* D   4 to gete] L, the gret EH1D   6 the²] L, *om.* EH1D   10 I wolde
gladly] *om.* D   11 man] men H1   and] *om.* H1   12 Herode] *on erasure* H1
15 the braunches] a braunche D   that²] *add* he EH1

thingges saide to Herode: 'Drede the not, for thou shalt sone be
deliuered and thou shalt be so enhaunsed that thy enemyes shull haue
enuye therto and so deye in that prosperite. And wete thou wel that
whanne thou seest a brydde of this maner sitte ouer the, thou shalt
deye witheinne the fythe day.'   20

And thanne a litell tyme after, Tyberyen deyed and Gayen was
made emperour, the whiche delyuered Herodes oute of prison and
lefte hym up glorously and sent hym home kinge of Iudee. And as
sone as he come thedyr he shewed his might and beganne to turment
sum of hem of the Chirche and made slee Iames the brother of Iohn   25
with a suerde the day before Estre. And for that he sawe that it was
agreable to the Iwes, he toke Petre in the Day of Estre and closed hym
up in prison and thought after the Ester to sle hym. But the aungell of
God come merveylously and vnbounde hym of his chaynes and sent
hym al quite | to the scruise of predicacion. And of the felonye of that   f. 171vb
kinge ne suffred not any delacion of vengeaunce, for the day foluinge   31
he made come before hym the kepers for to turment hem withe
diuerse paynes for the fleinge of Petre. But alway he was lette to do
that for that deliueraunce of Peter shulde be [noyinge] to none other,
for he went hastely into Cesare and ther he was smiten withe the   35
aungell and deyed.

And, as Iosephus tellithe in the boke of the .xix. Aunsyens, that
whanne Herodes came into Cesare and alle the men of that prouince
come to hym, whanne the day come that he shulde goo into iugement,
he went clothed withe a clothe of tyssue merveillousment riche. And   40
whanne he was there and the sonne shyn[ed] on his clothinge, the
brightnesse of the sonne made it shyine more gloriously and caused
gret reuerence and drede to the beholders, and therfor the pride of
hym was so grete that he semed beter a man made bi crafte thanne by
mannes nature. And thanne the comune peple beganne to crye and   45
saye: 'We haue saye the vnto this tyme as m[a]n, but now we knowlage
that thou art aboue the nature of man.' And as he was fullfelled withe
worshippes of flateringges and refused not the devine worshyppes, he
loked and behelde ouer hys hede and he sawe the oule sitte aboue hym

18 that] *om.* D   19 whanne] *ins.* H1   20 the . . . day] .v. daies D   21 tyme]
om. DH1   Gayen] Galien H1   22 made] *om.* H1   24 he^1] she *with* s *erased* H1
28 after] *om.* D   30 quite] quiete D   31 kinge] *add* Herode D   32 hem] *so
changed to* hym H1   34 noyinge] neighinge E, ne`y´ghyng H1   37 .xix.] .xx. D
38–9 of that prouince/come to hym] *trs.* D   40 tyssue] Tissell H1   merveillousment]
mervelous D   41 shyned] shyninge EH1   on his clothinge] *om.* H1   44 that] *add*
þat H1   46 man^1] men EH1   but now] *twice once subp.* H1   48 worshippes]
wurship D   49 and behelde . . . hym] *twice* E

50 whiche was messanger of his nigh dethe. And thanne he behelde the
peple and sayde: 'Surely I that am youre lorde shall deye in haste,' for
he knewe by that the devyne hadde tolde hym that he shulde deye

f. 172ra witheinne .v. dayes, and anone he | was smite withe so horrible a
syknesse that wormes ete all his boweles and so he deyed. And this

55 sayethe Iosephus. And therfore in the rememberaunce of the
[delyueraunce of the] prince of aposteles oute of his cheynes and of
veniaunce done to the tyraunt anone after foluynge, the Chirche
halowithe the [feste] of Saint Petre withe his cheynes. And it is wrete
in the pistell of the masse in what this deliueraunce is wytnesse to

60 haue be done.

The secounde cause of the ordenaunce was for that the pope
Alisaundre, which was the .vj. after Petre, and Hermes that was
prouost of Rome, whiche Hermes was conuerted to the fayth by that
same Alisaundre, were hold in diuerse [places] of prisone by Quirin

65 the iuge. And thanne saide Quirin the iuge to Hermen the prouost: 'I
meruayle me gretly that thou that were so wyse a man hast lefte the
worshippe of thi prouost[e] and goste dremynge another lyff.' And
Hermes saide to hym: 'Afore this tyme I despised alle these thingges
and went ther hadde be but this only lyff.' And Quiren ansuered and

70 sayde: 'Make proef before me that ther ys another lyff and I shall
anone come to thi faithe.' To whom Hermes saide: 'Alisaundre that
thou holdest in prison can tell the beter thanne I.' Thanne Quirin
cursed Alisaundre and saide; 'I haue bode the that thou shuldest preue
this thinge, and thou sendest me to Alisaundre that I holde in prisone

75 for hys wyckednesse. Now truly I shall double the prison vpon the
and vpon hym and sette good kepers ouer you, and yef it so be that I
fynde hym withe the or the withe hym I shall geue faithe to thi
w[ord]es and to hys.'

f. 172rb   And | thanne he sette sure warde vpon hem and lete Alisaundre

80 haue knoulage hereof. And thanne Seint Alisaundre praied and an
aungell come to hym and ledde hym into the prisoune to Hermen, and
thanne Quirin fonde hem togedre and was gretly meruayled. And
whanne Hermen had tolde to Quirin how Alysaundre had heled his
sone and reysed hym fro dethe to lyff Quirin sayde to Alysaundre: 'I

85 haue a doughter that hight Balbyne and she is syke of the gowte, and I

56 delyueraunce . . . the³] *om.* EH1   and of] of the D   57 anone after foluynge]
folowinge aftre H1   58 feste] chirche E, *so del.* 'feste' H1   64 places] L, bondes
EH1D   65 And . . . iuge] *ins.* H1   Quirin] Everyn D   66 lefte] lost D
67 prouoste] prouost EH1D (*preuoste* P2)   78 wordes] werkes EH1D (*paroles* P2)
80 Seint] *om.* D   81 to] of D

behight the that yef thou mayst gete hele to my doughter þat I shall
receyue thi faithe.' To whom Alisaundre saide: 'Goo anone and bringe
her to my prisone.' And Quirin saide: 'How shulde I fynd the in [thi]
prison whanne thou art here?' And Alisaundre saide to hym: 'Goo
anone, for he that brought me hedyr canne sone bringe me there.' And 90
thanne Quirin brought his doughter to the prisone of Alisaundre and
fond hym there, and thanne he kneled downe atte his fete. And his
doughter cussed the cheynes of Seint Alisaundre for to receiue her
hele therby. And Alisaundre saide to her: 'Doughter, cusse not my
cheynes, but [seke] the fetheres of Seint Petre and cusse hem by 95
deuocion and thou shalt resseyue thin hele' And thanne Quirin made
seke withe grete diligence the fethres of Seint Peter in the prison
where Petre hadde bene, and whanne thei were founde he made hys
doughter to cusse hem and anone she was perfitely hole. And than
Quirin asked foryeuenesse and putte oute Alisaundre of prisone and 100
he receiued baptime and his wyff and his [meyne] and many other.
And thanne Alisaundre ordeined | this feste to be halowed in August f. 172ᵛᵃ
and made a chirche in worshippe of Seint Peter the Apostell wherin
he putte hys cheynes, and to that sollempnite come moche peple and
kessyd there the cheynes. 105

The .iij. cause of the ordenaunce of this fest after Bede is this.
Antonye and Octauian were so ioyned togederes by affynite that they
departed betwene hem the empire of alle the world, and Octauian
hadde in [the] occident Italye, Fraunce and Spayne, and Antonie
hadde [in] the orient Asie, Pont and Aufrike. And Antonie was wylde 110
and a ribauude of his body, and hadde wedded the suster of Octauian
and lefte her and toke Cleopatre, quene of Egipte. And therfor
Octauian had despite of his gouernaunce ande went withe strengthe
of armes ayeinst Antonie into Asye and ouercome hym in alle thinge.
And than Antonie and Cleopatre fledde away and slowe hemselff 115
sorufully. And Octauyan destroyed the rewme of Egipte and made it
of the prouince of Rome. And fro thennes he went into Alysaundre
and despoiled it of alle hys richesse and brought it to Rome and
encresed so gretly the profit of Rome and of the comune that men

85 behight] be`s'hight H1   that] *om.* H1D   88 saide] L, *add* hym EH1D   thi] *om.*
EH1   90 there] thider D   93 the . . . Alisaundre] his cheynes D   her] *om.* D
94 her] his D   95 seke] L, kesse EH1D   fetheres] feheris *changed* to feteres H1
97 fethres] feheris *changed to* feteres H1   100 Alisaundre] *add* oute EH1   101 his
meyne] L, alle his housholde EH1D   103 in] *add* þe H1   105 there] *om.* D
109 in] *ins.* D   the] *om.* EH1   110 in] *om.* EH1   114 into] *ins.* H1
119 comune] comens D

120 gaue gladly for a peny that before was yeue for .iiij. And for that Rome
was gretly wasted byfore by batayles, he renewed it ayenne and saide:
'I fonde the of tyle and I shalle leue the of marble.' And for that he so
gretly encresed the profite of Rome and of the comune he was the
furst emperour that euer was called Augustus, and of hym bene alle
125 the other called Augustus, tho that after hym succeded in the empire,
f. 172ᵛᵇ right [as] | after his vncle Iulius Cesar the thother were called
Cesariens. And than that monthe of August that was before called
Sextillys he entitelyd it of his name and called it August, in
rememberaunce and in victorie of the emperoure that he hadde the
130 furst day of that monthe. And alle the Romaynes made that day of the
yere a gret sollempnitee and this they vsed vnto the tyme of the
emperour Theodesyen that beganne to regne the yere of oure Lorde
.CCCC.xxvij.

And thanne Eudesie doughter of the saide emperour, wyff of
135 Valentynien, went to Ierusalem by a vowe and there a Iwe gaue her
for a gret yefte the cheynes that Seint Petre hadde be bounde with
vnder Herodes. And whanne she come ayenne to Rome and saw how
the Romaynes halowed the kalendes of August in the worship of a
paynime emperoure, she was full sory that she sawe suche worship
140 done to a dampned man and thought her that lyghtly they myght not
be withdraw fro that custume, and in thenkinge hereon she ordeyned
that the same custume shulde not be vsed so, but it shulde be vsed in
the worshyppe of Seint Petre withe cheynes. And thanne that same
day she helde collacion with Seint Pelagien the pope and brought the
145 peple therto withe fayre and softe wordes that the rememberaunce of
the prince of Romaynes were foryete and the rememberaunce of the
prince of the aposteles were halowed, and it lyked wel to alle. And
thanne she brought forthe the cheynes that she hadde brought from
Ierusalem and shewed hem to the peple. And than the pope brought
f. 173ʳᵃ forthe that cheyne | that he hadde be bounde withe vnder Nero, and as
151 sone as they come togederes alle th[re] ioyned togedre as one cheyne

120 .iiij.] add pens D   Rome] Rewme D   121 by] þe Hı   122 of tyle] a title
with second t subp. Hı   of²] a Hı   123 comune] comens D   124 Augustus] add þe
þat del. Hı   124–5 and . . . Augustus] om. D   125 Augustus] August Hı
126 as] L, om. EHı, and D   128 it²] his changed to hit Hı   August] Augustus E
129 of the] add victorie of the EHı   135 Valentynien] Valentyne D   vowe] add made
to Ierusalem D   140 they myght] twice once del. Hı   142 so . . . vsed] ins. Hı
vsed²] worshipid D   144 helde] had D   147 alle] þe peple D   150 that cheyne]
þe cheynes D   he] Petre D   bounde] fetered del. 'bounde' Hı   151 thre] they EHıD
(.iij. P2)

by miracle. And than the pope and the quene putte these cheynes in the chirche of Seint Peter in Cheynes and the quene gaue gret possessiones and gret yeftes to the chirche and gate her gret preuileges and ordeyned that day to be holde holy ouer alle. And this saiethe 155 Bede, and Sigebert saiethe the same.

And of how gret vertu these cheynes be, it appered wel in the yere of oure Lorde .CCCC.xliiij. Ther was an erle that was nygh to the emperoure Othoni, the whiche the fende hadde so cruelly rauisshed hym byfore all folke that he al torent hymselff withe his tethe. And 160 thanne by the comaundement of the emperour he was ledde to the pope Iohn for that he shulde do hangge aboute his necke the cheynes of Seint Petre, but he dede aboute his necke another cheyne that dede hym no good, and what meruaile was yt for that cheyne hadde no vertu. And atte the laste the verray cheyne of Seint Petre was brought 165 and hangged aboute the necke of the wode man, and the fende might not suffre the burdon of so grete vertu but went his waye anone, crienge before alle the peple. And thanne Theodorik toke that cheyne in his honde and saide he wolde neuer leue it but [yef] they cutte of his honde. And thanne ther was gret descencion betwene the pope and 170 the bisshopp and the other clerkes, but the emperour atte the laste apesed al that contekt and asked of the pope to haue a lynke of the cheyne.

Milet tellithe in his Cronicle, and also hit in the Storie Parted in Thre tellith | the same, that in that tyme ther was a gret dragon that f. 173rb appered in Epiron and the bisshoppe before named made the sygne of 176 the crosse byfore his mouthe and thorughe vertu therof he spette the dragon in the mouthe and he deyed anone, the whiche dragon was so gret that .vij. couple of oxen might not draw hym thennes to the place wher he was brent for that he shulde not corrupte the eyre bi his 180 stinke. And also it is sayde in the same Storie that the fende apered in Crete in lyknesse of Moyses and assembeled the Iues before hym ouer alle and ledde hem withe hym vpon the toppe of an high hyll and behight hem to lede hem drye fote ouer the see into the Londe of Beheste. And men suppose that the fende dede this for euell wille of 185 þe Iwes that hadde geue the cheynes to the quene wher thorugh the

157 appered] appereth H1   158 Ther] D starts new paragraph with major initial
159 fende] feendis D   165 cheyne] cheynes D   166 the'] his D   of . . . man] om. D
169 leue] bileue D   yef] L, om. EH1D   171 bisshopp] bisshopes D   174 hit] add
is H1D   182 Crete] Grece D   184 fote] footid D   185 dede this] deide D
wille] om. D

feste of Octauian was cesyd. And whanne he hadde hem alle there he
drowned a gret hepe of hem.

The .iiij. cause of the ordenaunce of this feste may be assygned in
190 this wyse, for oure Lorde delyueringe Seint Petre bi miracle gaue hym
pouer to bynde and vnbinde, and we be alle bounde and holde in the
bondes of synne and haue nede to be assoyled. And therfor in the
sollempnite that is sayde 'of bondes' we worship hym that, right as he
deseruid to be vnbounde of bondes and receiued might and power of
195 oure Lorde to assoyle, that he us assoile fro the bondes of synne. And
this last cause may be lightly perceiued for bothe hys pistelles and his
gospell rehersin the power that he hathe to assoyle soules bounden in
synne.

Here endithe the feste of the bondes of Seint Petre, and
nexst beginnithe the Inuencion of the holi body of Seint
Stephen, | Capitulum .C.v.^m

f. 173va The findinge of the holy body of Seint Stephen the furst marter was
made in the yere of oure Lorde .CCCC.xvij. in the .xvij. yere of
Honere the prince, and in suche wise. Ther was a preste that hight
Lucien of the contre of Ierusalem, the whiche Gerarde acountithe
5 hym amonge holy men and this he writethe of hym, that in a Fryday
as he was in his bedde and slepte not faste, an auncien man of noble
stature and of faire visage withe a longe berde, clothed withe a white
mantell wherinne there were litell precious stones and wrought
thorugh with litell crosses of golde and helde a rodde of golde in
10 his honde and touched hym and sayde hym: 'Go anone with gret
diligence and open oure toumbes, for we lye vnhonestely and in a
place of despite, and go a Thoursday to the bisshop of Ierusalem and
tell hym that he sette us in more worshipfull place, and for that
drought and tribulacion is now thorugh the worlde God hathe
15 ordeyned to be mercyfull to the worlde thorugh oure praiers.'

And thanne Lucien sayde to hym: 'Good Sire, what art thou?' 'I am,'
he sayde, 'Gamalyell that norisshed the apostell Paule and taught hym
the lawe. And he that lyethe withe me is Seint Stephen that was stoned
for Goddes loue of the Iues and caste out of the citee for to be deuoured

190 oure] ou`r´e H1   191 vnbinde and] *om.* H1   193 that²] *om.* D

EH1DH2A2L; H2 breaks off after 21 *varienge and*; in D *pope* has been erased
5 this] thus D   11 lye vhonestely and] be vnhonestly leide D   vnhonestely]
vnesely H1   17 norisshed] noresheth *with* eth *subp.* `id´ H1

withe bestes. But he kepte hym to whom he hadde kepte [his] faithe 20
witheoute varienge and I gadered h[y]m with gret diligence and beried
h[y]m in my newe toumbe. And that other that lyethe with me is
Nichodemus my nevew that went by night to Ihesu and receyued
bapteme | of Petre and of Iohn, and therfor the princes of prestes were f. 173vb
wrothe withe hym and wolde haue slayne hym, ne hadde be the drede 25
of us. And notwithstonding they toke away all hys substaunce and
putte hym downe of hys prinsehode and betin hym sore and lefte hym
for dede. And after that I hadde brought hym to myn hous he lyued but
a while, and whanne he was dede I made berie hym atte the fete of Seint
Stephen. 30

'And the thridde that is withe me is Abybas my sone that receyued
bapteme withe me in the .xv.^e yere of his age and was a virgine and
lerned the lawe of God with Paule my disciple. And Ethea my wyff
and Selencyas my sone that wolde not receiue bapteme ne the faithe of
Ihesu Crist were not worthy of oure sepulture, thou shalt fynde hem 35
beried ellwhere and her toumbes be full voyde.' And whanne he
hadde all this sayd Seint Gamalyel vanisshed away, and thanne
Lucyan awoke and praied to God [that] yef this visyon were true,
that it shulde be shewed ayenne the secound tyme and the thridde.

And the Fryday folwinge [he] appered to hym as he dede before 40
and sayde to hym: 'Why haste thou disdeyne for to do that I haue
required the?' And he saide: 'Lorde, I haue not dysdeyne but I haue
praied God that yef this come from hym that he wolde shewe it to me
ayenne.' And thanne Gamalyel saide hym: 'For that thou hast thought
in thi herte that, yef thou mightest fynde [vs] oute, hou thou myght 45
deuyde the relqyues of eueriche, I shall shewe the of euery by
symilitude to knowe the toumbes and the reliques of eueryche.'
And thanne he shewyd hym .iij. panyers of golde and the fourthe
of syluer, of whiche that one was full of rede roses, the other two of
white rosez, and the fourthe that was of syluer was full | of saferon. f. 174ra
And thanne Gamaliel said to hym: 'These paniers be oure toumbes 51
and these roses be oure reliques. The furste that is full of rede roses is
the toumbe of Seint Stephen, the whiche only decerued before us alle

20 he², his] L, they, her ED, þei, `here' H1   21 witheoute] add eny D   I gadered]
igadered E   witheoute] add eny D   hym] L, hem EH1D   22 hym] L, hem EH1D
23 Ihesu] Iohn with o subp. H1   29 while] add after D   31 is¹] lithe D
33 lerned] biried del. `lernyd' H1      38 that yef] this yef E, `þat ʒif' H1   39 be] ins.
H1   thridde] add tyme D   40 he¹] om. EH1   42 he] add ansuerid and D
45 mightest] myʒt eft H1   vs] L, om. EH1D   48 panyers] pan`y'ers H1   49 two]
add full H1D   51 paniers] parteners del. `panyers' H1   53 decerued] add to be D

to receiue the crowne of marterdom. That other two withe white roses
55 be the toumbez of me and of Nichodeme that perseuereden withe
clene hert in the confession of Ihesu Crist. And the fourthe that is
syluer was Abybas my sone that shyned by whitenesse of virginite and
went pure oute of this worlde.' And whanne this was saide he
vanisshed away.

60   And the Fryday after the woke foluynge he apered to hym alle
wrothe and blamed hym gretly of hys delayenge and of his
neclygence. And than anone Lucyen went to Ierusalem and tolde
alle by ordre to the bisshopp Iohn. And he called other bisshopes with
hym and went to the place that had be shewed to Lucyene, and
65 whanne they hadde begonne to digge and that the erthe was meued, a
right suete smell was felt. And for the meruaylous sauour that was felt
of that sote smell and by the merites of the seintes, .lxx. seke men were
deliuered fro diuerse siknesses, and so these relyques were bore to the
chirche of Syon that ys in Ierusalem, in the whiche Seint Stephen
70 hadde vsed the office of archedeken, and there they were ordeyned for
full worshipfully. In that same houre there descended from heuen a
grete reyne. And of this vision and inuencion of Seint Stephen Bede
makithe mencion in his Cronicle.

And this inuencion was made that same day that his passyon was
75 halowed, and his passion as men sayen was done in that day. But the
festes be chaunged by the ordenaunce of the Chirche for double
f. 174rb resones. The furste | is for that Ihesu Crist was bore in erthe for man
shulde be bore in heuene. So þat it apertenithe thanne that [to] the
natiuite of Ihesu Crist the natiuite of Seint Stephen that was born into
80 heuene by marterdom [shulde folowe nexst, for he was the furste that
suffred marterdom], and therfor it is songe of hym: 'Ihesu Crist was
yesterday born in erthe for Seint Stephen shulde be bore this day in
[heuene]'.

The secounde reson is for that the fest of the Inuencion was more
85 sollempnely halowed thanne the feste of his passyon, and that ys only
for the reuerence of the natiuite of oure Lorde, notwithestondinge
that God hathe shewed many gret myracles in his inuencion. But for

54 to receiue] by D   two] *add* that be D   56 hert] *add* and H1   57 whitenesse]
witnes D   60 the woke] he awoke H1   63 by] *add* the EH1   to] of *changed to* to H1
68 siknesses] sikenesse H1   75 halowed] *add* 'of' H1   78 to] L, *om.* EH1D
79 Crist] *add* and D   80 nexst] *om.* D   80–1 shulde . . . marterdom] *om.* E, *ins.*
omitting nexst H1   82 be bore/this day] *trs.* H1   83 heuene] erthe EH1   84 is]
om. H1   86 for] of *changed to* for H1   reuerence of the] *ins.* H1   natiuite] *twice once*
ins. H1   87 many] *om.* D

his passyon ys more worthi thanne hys inuencion therfor it shulde be
more sollempne, and therfor the Chirche ordeyned hys passyon in
suche tyme in whiche he might haue gret[test] reuerence.   90

And as Seint Austine sayethe, the translacion of hym was in this
wyse: Alisaundre senatour of Constantinople and his wyff wente to
Ierusalem and made a faire oratorie to Seint Stephen the furst marter,
and after hys dethe he beried hymselff by hym. And .vij. yere after
that Iulyane hys wyff wolde turne ayenne into hys contre for that the   95
princes deden her wronge, and she wolde haue withe her the body of
her husbonde. And whanne she hadde required the bisshop therof by
many prayers, the bisshop shewyd her .ij. toumbes of syluer and sayde
to her: 'I wote not whiche is of [thyn] husbonde.' And she sayde: 'I
wote fulle well.' And thanne she went in gret haste and enbrased the   100
body of Seint Stephen. And so by cause of fortune, whanne she went
[to] haue take the body of her husbonde, she toke the body of the
marter.

And whanne she | was gone into [thc] shippe withe the body, there   f. 174ᵛᵃ
was herde ympnes and songges of aungeles, and right suete sauour   105
was felt, and the fendes cryeden and made gret tempestes and sayde:
'Alas, alas, the furst marter passithe hereby and betithe us cruelly
withe fire.' And as the shipmen dredden the peryle, they called to
Seint Stephen and anone he apered to hem and sayde: 'I am here,
drede you not.' And anone gret pees was made in the see. And thanne   110
[w]as the voys of fendes herde cryenge: 'Thou felon pr[inc]e, brenne
this shippe, for Stephen oure aduersarie ys therinne.' And thanne the
prince of fendes sent .v. fendes for to brenne the shyppe, but the
aungell of oure Lorde plunged hem in the deppest of the see. Ande
whanne they come into Calcidoigne the fendes cryed and sayde: 'The   115
servaunt of God comithe that was stoned of the Iwes.' And thanne
they come alle into Constantinople and there was the body of Seint
Stephen sette withe gret reuerence in a chirche. And this saiethe Seint
Austine.

The coniunccion of the body of Seint Stephen withe the body of   120
Seint Laurens was made by this ordenaunce. Hit felle that the
doughter of Theodesyen the emperour was greuously turmented

---

90 grettest] L, gret EH1D   91 as] *ins.* H1   this] suche DH1   92 Alisaundre]
Alisandre *with* is *on erasure* H1   wyff] *add* withe hym EH1   93 furst] *om.* D   94 by
hym] *ins.* H1   94–5 And . . . that¹] *twice* E   96 her wronge] wronge to her H1D
99 thyn] her EH1   102 to] *om.* EH1   103 marter] *add* seinte stephen D
104 the¹] her EH1   111 was] vas E   prince] L, prve EH1, *om.* D
120 coniunccion] conuencion H1

withe the fende. And whanne it was tolde to her fader that was in
Constantinople, he comaunded that hys doughter shulde be brought
125 thedir that she myght touche the holy reliques of the right holy marter
Seint Stephen. And than the enemy cried witheinne her and saide:
'But yef Stephen come to Rome I will not go oute, for it is the will of
the aposteles.' And whanne the emperour herde this thynge he
f. 174vb   pray|ed the clergie and the peple of Constantinople that they wolde
130 geve to þe Romaynes the body of Seint Stephen and they shulde haue
the body of Seint Laurens. And the emperoure wrote therfor to the
pope that hyght Pelagien, and thanne the pope withe the counsaile of
the cardinalles consented to the request of the emperoure. And thanne
went the cardinalles to Constantinople and brought to Rome the body
135 of Seint Stephen, and the Grekes come to haue the body of Seint
Laurens.

The body of Seint Stephen was receyued in Capuenne and the
peple of that contre by her devoute prayers hadde the right arme of
Seint Stephen and made the chirche of Metropolytan, that is to saye
140 the see of the ershebissop, in the worshypp of hym. And whanne the
Romaynes were come to Rome they wolde haue bore the body to the
chirche of Seint Petre withe Chaynes, but tho that bare hym myght go
no further, and the fende that was in the mayde cryed withe houge
voys and sayde: 'Ye trauayle you in vayne for he shall not be here, but
145 withe Laurens his brother where he hathe chosyn his place.' And
thanne was the body brought thedyr and this mayde touched the body
and receyued parfyt hele. And Seint Laurence right as for reioysinge
of his brother and laughynge turned hym into that other parte of the
sepulcre and made hym place and lefte hym halff the place of the
150 sepulcre. And whanne the Grekes settyn hondes for to haue take
Laurens, they felle to the erthe as dede, and thanne the pope and alle
the peple praied for hem and yet unnethe they came to hemselff atte
f. 175ra   even, and notwithestondinge they were alle dede withe|in .x. dayes.
And the Lumbardes and alle tho that consented therto were take
155 withe a frensy and myght not be heled till the two bodyes were in one
toumbe togederes. And than ther was herde a voys from heuen that
sayde: 'O thou blessed Rome, that hast enclosed in one toumbe the
glorious weddes, the body of Seint Laurens of Spayne and of Seint

125 holy¹] body *changed to* holy H1   right] *om.* D   126 enemy] *add* the feende D
132 that] and *del.* `þat' H1   that hyght] *om.* D   139 Seint Stephen] Steven the seynt
H1   141 wolde] shuld H1   142 tho] thei H1D   143 houge] hie H1
144 he] ye H1   145 his¹] *ins.* H1   153 and] *add* ȝit D   158 and] *add* þe bodi D

Stephen of Ierusalem.' This ioyning was made aboute the yere of oure
Lorde .ixC.xxv.   160
    Seint Austin tellithe in the .xxij. boke of the Citee of God that .vj.
dede bodyes were areysed from dethe to lyff by the merites of Seint
Stephen. That is to wete that there was one that laye dede and the
name of Seint Stephene was called vpon hym and anone he was
areysed from dethe to lyff. And a childe that was slayne withe a carte, 165
the whiche childe the moder bare to the chirche of Seint Stephen and
anone he receyued lyff and hele. And a no[nne] that was atte her laste
ende was bore to the chirche of Seint Stephen and there she deyed,
and after þat arered ayen by miracle. And after a mayde of Iponence,
of whiche her fader bare her cote to the chirche of Seint Stephen, and 170
he leyde it on the bodye of the dede and she arose anone to lyve.
Another yonge man of Iponence de[i]de, as sone as his body was
anoynted withe the oyle of Seint Stephen he was restablid to his hele.
Another childe was born al dede to the chirche of Seint Stephen and
was anone turned to lyff.   175
    And of this precious marter saiethe Seint Austine: 'Gamaliel
maister of scole shewed furst this ma[r]ter, Saule dispoiled stoned
hym, Ihesu Crist wrapped in pore clothes made hym furst riche and
crowned hym withe his precious blode. In Seint | St[e]phen there   f. 175rb
shyned beauute of body, floure of age, fayre spekynge withe reson, 180
wisdom of holy thought and werke of dyuinitee. He was a stronge
piler of faithe and of God, for whanne he was take and holde withe a
maner of tongges betwene the hondes of the stoners, in the furneys of
the fere of the faithe he was destreyned, smiten harde, demened and
beten, and yet his faithe encresed and was not ouercome. And Austin 185
saiethe ellyswhere vpon this auctorite of hys mightynesse of vigour:
'Beholde Stephen thi felawe, he was a man as thou art and of the same
gobet of synne as thou and bought withe suche a pris as thou. He was
dekene and redde the gospell as thou redest or herest redde, and there
thou fyndest wreten 'loue your enemyes'. And this same Seint   190
Stephen lerned in redynge and profited in obeysinge or obeyenge.'

161 .xxij.] .xij. H1D   167 a nonne] L, another EH1D   169 þat] was D
170 and] add than whan he come home aȝen she was ded and than D   171 he] she EH1
it] the cote D   172 deide] dede EH1   173 Stephen] add anone D   restablid]
restablisshid D   hele] add aȝen D   176 Austine] add and D   177 marter] mater
EH1   dispoiled] add him and D   179 there] om. H1   182 faithe . . . God] the feithe
of God D   184 smiten] add and D   185 encresed] add more D   188 suche]
om. D   190 wreten] om. D   And this] the D   191 obeysinge or] om. D

Here endithe the Inuencion of Seint Stephene, and nexst
begynnithe the lyff of Seint Domenik, Capitulum .C.vj.^m

Domenik was duke of the Ordre of Prechoures and a noble fader, of
the parties of Spayne of a towne that hyght Caloriga of the diocise of
Exonience, and his fader hyght Felix and his moder Ione, of which
he come as after the flesshe. And hys moder before that he was born
5 sawe in slepinge that she bare a lytelle whelpe in her wombe that
bare a bronde of fyre in hys mouthe, and whanne he was gone oute
of her wombe he brent alle the worlde. And hit semed to a lady that
lefte hym of the funts[t]on that the blessyd Domenik hadde a clere
f. 175va sterre in hys | forhede that enlumined alle the worlde. And whanne
10 he was yet a child and in the kepinge of his norice, men founde hym
often tymes levynge his bedde and lyenge in the naked erthe.

And after that, whanne he was sent to Palence for to lerne science
he tasted neuer in .x. yere wyne. And after that, whanne he sawe that
ther was gret famyne there, he solde his bokes and alle his substaunce
15 and gaue the pris to the pore. And whanne the renome of his bounte
encresed, he was made a seculer chanon of the bysshop of Meomense
in his chirche, and after that he was a mirrour of lyff and was ordeyned
supprioure of the chanones. And nyght and day he entended to rede
and to praie, in prayenge [to God] continuelly that he wolde geue hym
20 grace that in alle hys werkes he might profit to his [euene] cristen. In
the boke of Collaciones of Faderes he redde curiously and toke therof
gret perfeccion.

And whanne he wente to Tholete withe the bisshopp he vndertoke
hys oste of laughynge and conuerted hym to the faithe of Ihesu Crist
25 and presented hym to oure Lorde right as an handefull of the furst
nouelte of plente [of] cornes that were to come.

Hit is redde in the dedes of the erle of Monfort that in a day as
Seint Domenik prechyd ayeinst the eretykes he put in wrytinge the
auctoritees that he purposed and toke it [to] an eretyk to argue ayeinst
30 hys obiecciones. And þat night the heretikes assembled hem togederes
by the fyre and there he shewed hem the scrowe. And they sayd hym
that he shulde caste it into the fyre and yef it brenned his faythe was

EH1DA2; D breaks off after 284 *duell*   8 of] at D   funtston] funtson E, fumptsone
del. `fontstone' H1   10 yet . . . and] and *del.* D   11 in the/naked] *trs.* D   13–
14 that ther was] þere D   15 the²] *ins.* H1   bounte] beaute H1   16 made] *om.* D
17 his] this EH1   after] afore *del.* `aftyr' H1   ordeyned] made D   19 to God] *om.* E,
`god' H1   20 euene] eme EH1   24 hys oste] him ofte D   24–5 to . . . hym] *twice* E
25 right] *om* D   26 of] or E   29 to] *om.* E, `to' Hl

not, and yef it brenned not than | was hys faithe good and he preched   f. 175vb
the verray faithe of the Chirche of Rome. And thanne was the scrowe
caste into the fere, and whanne she hadde abydde a while there she   35
lepte oute alle hole. And than one that was more hardyer thanne
another sayde; 'Caste it ayenne onys and we shulle proue it beter and
more pleinly the trouthe.' And thanne it was caste ayenne, and it come
oute ayenne witheoute any brennynge. And thanne the same sayde:
'Late it be caste ayenne the .iij. tyme, and witheoute fayle thanne   40
shulle we knowe the issue of this thing.' And she was caste ayenne the
.iij. tyme and come oute ayenne witheoute any harmynge. And yet the
heretykes abydinge in her harde malice suore amonge hem right
suerly that they shulde publysshe this thinge in no wyse. But alway as
yt happed there was a knight there present whiche was sumwhat   45
enclyned to oure faithe, and he discouered this myracle.

And men sayen that lykly thing felle in the hylle of Victorien in the
temple of Iovis ther was a dispituson ordeyned amonge the heretikes;
so as the syknesse of the wickednesse of heresye encresed in the
parties of Dawngeoys, this solempne disputuson was in the temple of   50
Iovis, and there were ordeyned iuges of other parte to whiche men
shulde take to in writinge the afferminge of euery faithe that eueryche
affermed, so that the litell book of Seint Domenik was chosen and
presented amonge other. And thanne was there stryff and contencion
amonge the iuges, so atte the laste it was ordeigned that the bokes of   55
bothe parties shulde be caste in the fyre, and that boke that might not
brenne witheoute any fayle conteygned the verray faith. And thanne
were the bokes caste in a grete brennynge fyre and the bokes of | the
eretykes were brent anone and the boke of Seint Domenik not only   f. 176ra
was not brent but sodenly lepte oute of the fyre witheoute any   60
harmynge. And thanne secoundely he was caste in ayenne and he
lepte oute witheoute any harmynge or brenninge.

And thanne that other cristen peple went home to her propre places
and the bysshop of Exonience deyed, and Seint Domenik abode allone
ayeinst the eretykes withe fewe of the Chirche that anounced sadly the   65
worde of God. And the aduersaries of holy Chirche scorned hym and
spitte on hym and caste filthe on hym and knitte behynde hym wyspes

38 ayenne] *add* the seconde tyme D   39 sayde] se῾i῾de *del.* ῾seyde῾ H1
43 abydinge] *add* stille D   45 there²] *om.* D   47 that] *ins.* H1
50 this] *begins new paragraph in* D   51 of] *add* þat D   parte] partie H1
52–3 that . . . affermed/so] *trs.* D   55 iuges] iues H1D   59 boke] bokes D
59–60 not . . . was] were D   61 secoundely] sodenly H1, þe seconde tyme D   he was]
þei were D   he²] þei D   62 oute] *add* aȝen D   64 Seint] se῾i῾nt H1

of strawe in despite of hym. And whan they manaced hym he
ansuered withoute drede: 'I am not worthy marterdom ne I haue
70 not deserued that glorious dethe,' and therfor he passed hardely
thorugh the places there men aspied hym and sangge and walked
merily. And the same meruayled and sayden: 'Hast thou not drede of
dethe? What woldest thou haue do yef that we hadde take the?' 'I
wolde haue prayed you,' saide he, 'that ye wolde not haue slayne me
75 sodenly, but that ye wolde haue dismembrid me membre from
membre and thanne leyde my membres before my syght, and atte
the laste that ye hadde putte oute myn eyen and so lefte my body al
tohewen halff quicke wamelynge in his owne bloode, or elles that ye
wold haue slayne me atte youre owne luste.'

80   In a tyme he fonde a man that for the gret pouerte that he suffered
he was ioyned to the eretykes, and Seint Domenik seinge this
ordeyned hymselff to be solde and that the pris that shulde be gove
for hym were goue to the pore man to helpe hym of his | pouertee and
f. 176ʳᵇ for to beye hym oute of the foul errour that he was inne. And in
85 trouthe he hadde be solde yef the devine purueaunce hadde not
purueyed for that other pore man.

      Another tyme a woman come to compleyne to hym that her brother
was taken and holde in chetifeson in the power of Sarisenes and that
she coude no counsayle of his deliueraunce. And this holy man anone
90 was meuyd withe pite of hert and ordeigned hymselff to be solde for
the redempcion of that other, but God that knewe hym more
profitable for gostely redempcion of many one that were in gret
thraldom ne suffered not.

      In a tyme he was herborwed in the parties of Tholose fast by sum
95 ladyes that by occasyon of relygion hadden be deceyued of heretykes,
and he seynge this, for sorugh and compassion he fast alle the Lent
brede and water, and his felaw also, that by the shadowe of his
relygion he myght take hem oute of her errour. And the nightes that
he woke, as sone as necessite of slepe toke, he leyde hym doune vpon
100 an harde borde witheoute any other thinge, and so it fell by his good
ensaumple these women were brought to the knowlage of trouthe.

69 withoute] add eny D   71 aspied] aspised del. ʿdispisedʾ H1   72 same] add
aduersaries D   73 take the] add I wold haue do yef that we hadde take the del. H1
73–4 I wolde . . . you/saide he] trs. D   75 haue] om. marked for insertion H1
78 tohewen halff] to heven al D   82–3 that² . . . for] of D   85 yef] ne D
purueaunce] add of god D   88 and²] add seide D   89 counsayle] comforte D
91 that other] this oþer man D   93 thraldom] thˋrˊaldome H1   96 this] add and
EH1   98–9 that he] þat we H1, in þe D

And thanne he beganne to thenke of the ordenaunce of the Ordre and of what office he myght be to go and preche thorugh the worlde and for to enhaunce the faithe of holy Chirche ayeinst the heretykes. And whanne he hadde duelled .x. yere in the parties of Tholose fro 105 the dethe of the bisshop of Exouience into the tyme that the Councell shulde be holde atte Lateran, he went to the Councell Generall withe Fouke the bisshop of Tholose for to aske of the pope Innocence the Ordre that was saide of the Prechoures | and that it might be f. 176 va confermed by hym and by his successours. And as the pope made 110 hym stronge to acord in all to this mater, in a night as he laye in his bedde he sawe in vision that the chirche [of] Lateran was sodenly manased for to falle. And as he loked dredfully theron he sawe in that one parte the seruaunt of God Domenik rennynge ayeinst it and susteyned her mightly that she fell not. And thanne he awoke and 115 vnderstode this visyon and receiued gladly the peticion of the seruaunt of God and bade hym that he ande his bretheren shulde loke sum rule that was preued and he wolde conferme it atte his owne will. And thanne he come to his bretheren and tolde hem as the pope hadde saide and they were atte that tyme but .xvj. freres. And thanne 120 thei besought helpe of oure Lorde and chosin the rule of blessed Austin prechour and noble doctour, and they wolde alle withe one wille duelle togedre alle precheoures, and ordeyned amonge hem more streite custumes of lyvinge thanne they hadde before and behight to kepe hem truly. And in the mene tyme Innocent pope 125 deyed and Honore was made pope, and thanne he asked confirmacion of hys Ordre of that Honore in the yere of oure Lorde .M^l.CC.xvj.

And as this holy man praied atte Rome in the chirche of Seint Petre for the encresynge of hys Ordre, he sawe cominge to hym the glorious princes of the aposteles Petre and Paule, and it semed hym that Seint 130 Petre toke hym furst a staffe and Seint Paule toke hym a boke and saide to hym; 'Go preche, for thou art called of God to that ocupacion.' And in a moment of tyme | it semed hym that he sawe his sones departed f. 176vb thorugh alle the worlde and went two and two prechinge the peple the worde of oure Lorde, for whiche thinge he come to Tholose and 135 departed his bretheren and sent sum of hem into Spayne, the thother to Paris, and other .ij. to Boloyne and went hymselff to Rome.

103 be to go] go to D   112 of] om. EH1   119 come] add aȝen D   his] add owne H1D   126 he] Dominik D   128 man] ins. H1   133 moment] monument D sones] bretheren D   135 of] add god subp. H1   136 Spayne] add `&' H1   thother] Broþer with Br del. H1   137 and^1] add þe H1

A monke before the ordenaunce of this Ordre sayde that he was all
rauisshed in sperit and sawe the blessed Virgine Marie knelynge afore
140 her sone holdynge up her hondes prayeng besyly for mankynde. And
he ofte tymes werned her, but atte the laste he said to her that
continued in her praier: 'Good moder, what shall I or may I do more
for hem? Haue I not sent my patriarkes and my profites and they be
litell amended, and I come to hem myselff. After, I haue sent aposteles
145 and they haue slayne hem. I haue sent marteres and confessours and
they will not therof. But for as moche as it is not reson that I werne
the, I shalle geue hem my precheoures by whiche they mowe be
lyghtned and clensed, and yef they will not amende hem I shall come
myselff ayeinst hem.'

150 A Frere Menour that longe tyme hadde be felowe to Seint
Fraunceys tolde to many bretheren of the Ordre of Precheoures
that whanne Seint Domenik was atte Rome for the confirmacion of
hys Ordre to haue of the pope, he sawe in a night Ihesu Crist in the
eyre and .iij. speris braundisshinge ayeinst the worlde. And hys
155 blessed moder ranne hastely ayeinst hym and asked what he wolde
do. And he saide: 'Alle the worlde is full of [.iij. vices], of pride, of
luxurie, and of auarice. And therfor I will dystroye her withe these
f. 177ra thre | speres.' And thanne the blessed Virgine fell downe to his fete
and sayd: 'Dere sone, haue pitee and attempre thi rightwisnesse withe
160 thi mercy.' And Ihesu Crist saide: 'See ye not, moder, how many
iniuries thei do me?' And she saide: 'Sone, attempre thi w[r]atthe and
abyde a while. I haue a true seruaunt and a noble fighter that shalle
renne ouer alle and wynne the worlde and putte it fully vnder thi
lordshipp. And I shall geue hym another seruaunt in helpe that shal
165 fight withe hym.' And the sone sayde: 'I am apesed and receyue thi
prayer, but I wolde knowe hym that ye wolde sende in so gret an
office.' And thanne she presented to hym Seint Domenik. And Ihesu
Crist saide: 'Verrely this is a good and a noble champion and he shall
do full curiously that ye haue saide.' And thanne she offered hym
170 Seint Fraunceys and he praysed hym as he dede the furst. And thanne
Seint Domenik considered diligentely his felawe in that vision, for he
hadde neuer saien hym before, and he fonde hym in the morw in the
chirche and knewe hym by that he hadde sayen hym in the vision
withoute any other shewynge, and began to cusse hym and saide:

141 that] for she D   146 not¹] om. D   148 yef] twice H1   156 Alle] om. D
worlde] word H1   .iij. vices] trs. E, so marked for trs. H1   157 her] hem DH1
161 wratthe] watthe E   170 Fraunceys] add for þat other D   praysed] prai's'ed H1

'Thou art my felawe, we shull renne togederes and ther shall none 175
aduersitee ouercome us.' And he tolde hym by ordre alle his avision,
and fro thennes forwarde were they made one hert and one wille in
oure Lorde and alle tho that shulde come after hym for euer.

In a tyme as this holy man Domenik woke in his chirche atte
Boloigne, the fende apered to hym in lyknesse of a frere, and Seint 180
Domenik that went it hadde be a frere made hym sygne that he |
shulde go to his bedde withe other of his bretheren. And the fende f. 177rb
made hym sygnes ayenne as in scorninge hym. And thanne Seint
Domenik wolde haue knowlage what he was that dispised his
comaundement and light his candell atte the lampe and behelde 185
hym in the visage, and anone he confessed hym that he was a fende.
And whanne he hadde blamed hym gretly, the fende reioysed hym
that he hadde made hym breke his silence, and [Seint Domenik] saide
that he might speke wel inow for he was maister of the freres. And
thanne he constreyned the fende to telle hym wherof he tempted the 190
freres in the quere. And he saide: 'I make hem to come to late inne and
to go oute to sone.' And thanne he ledde hym into the dortre and
asked hym wherof he tempted the freres there. And he saide: 'I make
hem slepe to moche and rise to late, and so they abyde to longe from
her seruice.' And after that he ledde hym into the froitour and asked 195
the fende wherof he tempted hem there. And thanne the fende lepte
vp and doune vpon the bordes, and whan he asked hym what he ment
he ansuered and saide: 'Here I tempte the freres, sum to ete to lytell
and sum to ete to moche, so that I make hem vnmyghty and vnable to
Goddes seruice and in kepinge her observaunce[s] of her Ordre.' And 200
thanne he ledde hym to the parlour and asked hym wherof he tempted
hem there. Thanne the fende putte oute his tunge and iangelyd faste
and made an horrible noyse of confusyon. And the seint asked hym
what he ment therby, and he saide: 'This place is alle myn, for whanne
the freres be assembeled here to speke | togedre I tempte hem thanne f. 177va
to iangle faste and wordes witheoute profit and that none abide others 206
reson.' And thanne Seint Domenik ledde hym into the chapitre, but
whanne he come before the dore he wolde not entre in no wyse and
saide: 'I wille not come ther for no thinge, for that is a cursed place
and fast shet to me, for there I lese as moche as I wynne in other 210

186 hym in the] his D   189 Seint Domenik] om. EH1D (saint Dominique P2)
192 he] the feende D   195 he] seinte Dominik D   196 the fende'] him D   hem]
him changed to hem H1   197 he'] Dominik D   198 tempte] temptid D
200 observaunces] observaunce EH1   205 be] add alle D   206 faste and] of D
207 Seint . . . hym] seyde Dominik I wil lede the D   chapitre] add hous D

places. For whanne I haue made any frere to synne by any maner
neclygence, he purgithe hym anone of that defauute in that place and
accusithe hym before alle the bretheren. And there thei bene so
taught, confessed, accused, beten and assoiled that I lese there as
215 moche as I reioysed me to haue wonne before in other place.' And
whanne he hadde saide this he vanisshed awaye.

And in the ende whanne the terme of his pilgrimage neighed, he
was atte Boloigne and beganne to langoure by gret syknesse of body.
And the departinge fro his body was shewed hym by a vision, for he
220 sawe right a faire yonge man that called hym by these wordes and
saide: 'Come my frende into ioye, come.' And thanne he assembeled
.xij. freres of the couent of Boloigne, and for he wolde not leue hem
disherited and orphelyens he made his testament and saide: 'These be
the thingges that I shalle yeue you in possession bi right heritage as to
225 my sones, that is to saye, perfite charite, to kepe humilite and to
possede wilfull pouerte. And I forbede you aboue al thinge possession
of any propre erthely good, prayeng to God that whosumeuer
presumithe to defoule the Ordre of Prechoures withe any temporall
richesse that he may haue the curse of God almighty and myn.' And
f. 177ᵛᵇ the freres were full | sori of his departinge and he comforted hem
231 suetly and saide hem: 'Lete not my bodely departinge trouble you for
drede les[t] ye shull haue me more profitable dede thanne quicke.'

And he came to his last houre the yere of oure Lorde .Mⁱ.CC.xxj.
and slepte in Ihesu Crist. The passing of whom was shewed that
235 same day to Frere Galle that was than prioure of the Frere Prechoures
of Brixe and was after bisshopp of Celetre and in this wise. For as he
slepte a lyght slumber, his hede enclined to the wall, he sawe the
heuene open and .ij. white ladderes cominge oute therof of which
Ihesu Crist helde that one ende and hys moder helde that other, and
240 aungeles wentyn downe and come up ayenne by these laddres
synginge and making moche ioye. And in one of the laddres ther
was a sege and a man sittinge in that sege his hede couered and was a
frere, and Ihesu Crist and his moder drewe the ladder up an high till
he that satte there was drawen up to heuen and anone the openinge of
245 heuene closed. And thanne that frere come to Boloigne and knewe
well that atte that day and that houre he deyed.

213 hym] himselfe D   215 reioysed] reioyse HₘD   216 heⁱ] the feende D
221 into] add my D   come] om. D   222 hem] him changed to hem Hₘ
227 propre] om. D   erthely] erth by Hₘ   232 drede lest] dredeles E   ye] I del. `ye' Hₘ
238 white] om. D   of] ins. Hₘ   240 up] om. D   242 andⁱ . . . sege] ins. Hₘ
244 he] ins. Hₘ   245 frere] add Galle D   246 he] Dominik D

A frere that hight Raude that was atte Tybour in that day and in that houre that the holy fader passed. He went to syngge his masse, and whanne he herde that he was seke atte Boloigne and he [come in the] canon in that place wher men shulde make mencion of the quicke 250 and he wolde haue praied for his hele, he was sodenly rauisshed in exces of mynde and [sawe] the servaunt of God Domenik crowned with a crowne of golde shyninge withe meruailous lyght, and felaweshiped withe .ij. worshipfull men in eche syde of hym and went oute of Boloigne by the riall waye. And thanne he | assigned the f. 178ra houre and the tyme and fonde that the seruaunt of God Domenik was 256 passed to God.

And whan the body of hym hadde layne longe tyme under the erthe and miracles were done witheoute cesynge so that hys holinesse might not be hidde, the deuocion of good men sawe that it were gretly 260 worthi that his body were layed in higher place. And whanne hys beryels were broke withe gret strengthe and opin, the sauour of right suete smelle came oute so solempnely that it semed that al the sepulcre and alle the place were full of the sauour of aromatis and more suetter thanne is the sauour of any aromates. And this suetnesse 265 was not only in the bones ne in the body nor in the pouder but in al the erthe aboute hym, so that the erthe of his graue was bore into many diuerse cuntreyes for the meruaile therof. And that same savour abode in the hondes of the freres that hadden touched the holy relyques that neither water ne rubbinge might take the sauour aweye. 270

Maister Alisaundre, bisshop of Bendom, tellithe in his pisteles upon this vers: *Misericordia et ueritas obuiauerunt sibi*, that ther was a scoler duellinge atte Boloigne whiche was gretly ab[andon]ed to wrechidnesse and to vanitees of the worlde, whiche clerke sawe in a vision þat hym semed he was in a gret felde and how a gret tempest 275 fell vpon hym. And he as moche as he might fledde the tempest and come before an hous and founde it shette, and he knocked atte the dore for to haue come in. And the ostesse ansuered: 'I am Ryghtwisnesse that duelle here, and this hous is myn and thou art not rightfull and therfor thou maist not duell | therinne.' And thanne he wepte f. 178rb bitterly for these wordes and went to another hous that he sawe 281 beyende þat and required that he might be herborughed therinne for

249 he^3] he *del.* `yn heigh' H1, *om.* D   249–50 come in the] *om.* EH1   in the canon] *om.* D   252 sawe] *om.* EH1D (*vit* P2)   Domenik] *add* was D   253 lyght] ly3tis D 254 felaweshiped] in felaushp D   eche] euery D   264 and^2] þat is D   265 is . . . aromates] eny savour D   268 savour] laboure *changed to* `f'lavoure (?) H1 273 abandoned] abounded EH1D (*habandonne* P2)

the tempeste. And she that was witheinne ansuered and saide: 'I am
Pees that duell here, and withe felones ther nys no pees but only withe
285 men of good will. And therfor I thenke the thoughtes of pees, I shall
yeue the good counsaile: my suster duellithe here byyend me, the
whiche yeuithe helpe to wrechys. Go to her and do as she wille
counsaile the.' And thanne he went to that hous and she that was
withinne ansuered: 'I am Mercy that duellithe here. Yef thou wylt be
290 saued from this tempest, go to the hous of the Frere Prechoures of
Boloigne and there thou shalt fynde the stable of mercy, the crache of
continence and the pastures of doctrine, and witheinne the crache
of scripture thou shalt fynde the asse of discrecion and the oxe of
sympelnesse, and Marie that shalle enlumyne the and Iosep that shall
295 profite the, and the childe Ihesus that shall saue the.' And whanne this
scoler awoke he went to the hous of Freres and tolde his vision by
ordre and required the habite and hadde it.

Seint Domenik the ordenaunce of his Ordre sawe Ihesu Crist that
helde .iij. dartes in his honde and manaced the worlde *etc.* For I Frere
300 Iohn of Benyngnay translatour of this boke will no more putte here of
that vision, for she is before in the same chapitre. And thus endith this
glorious lyff of Seint Domenik the furst fader and techer of the Frere
Prechoures, notwithestondinge that I haue not fully drawe oute alle
f. 178va the glorious miracles that hys | blessed lyff makithe mension of for
305 shortnesse of tyme, but hoso luste to rede hem or to here hem he may
clerely and plenteuously se hem in *Legenda Aurea*, and oure blessed
Lorde thorugh his praiers yeue us part of his holy merites. Amen.

Here endithe the lyff of Seint Domenik, and nexst
beginnithe the lyff of Seinte Sixte, Capitulum .C.vij.^m

Sixte the pope was of the nacion of Athenes and he was furst
philosofer and sethe he was disciple of Ihesu Crist and was made
souerain bisshopp, and afterwarde he was presented to Valerian and to
Decyen emperoures, and .ij. of his disciples Felix and Agapit. And
5 whanne Dacien might not encline hem in no manere, he made hym to
be ledde to þe temple of Mart for to sacrifice or to be putte in her
prisone of Mamentyn. And as he hadde refused to sacrifice and was
ledde into the prisone of Mamentyn the blessed Laurens cried after
hym sayenge: 'Fader, whedyr goest thou witheoute thi sone? Preest,

295 and . . . saue the] *om.* H1   saue] salue E   300 here of] hereof EH1
EH1A2   5 hem] *add* to subp. H1   in no] *ins.* H1

whedir goest thou witheoute thi mynistre?' To whom Sixte sayd: 10
'Sone, I leue the not, for gretter batailes shull be do to the. Thou, sone
dekene, witheinne thre dayes shall folowe thi preest, but in the mene
tyme take the tresours of the chirche and departe hem wher the lust.'
And whanne he hadde departed hem to the pore cristen, Valerian
ordeyned that Sixte shulde be ayenne ledde for to sacrifice in the 15
temple of Mars, and yef he refused it that he shulde haue anone his
hede smite of. And as he was ledde to his dethe, the blessed Laurens
cried | after hym sayenge: 'Fader forsake me not, for I haue dispended f. 178ᵛᵇ
alle the tresour[s] of the chirche.' And whanne the knightes herde
hym saye so thei helde hym faste. And thanne they behe[ded] Seint 20
Sixte and Felice and Agapit.

And in that same day is the Transfiguracion of our Lorde, and in
sum chirches men sacren the blood of oure Lorde withe nwe wyne or
elles with a ripe grape. And in that day be grapes in many places
blessed and the peple taken hem as holy breed. And þe reson is this, 25
for that oure Lorde in his cene saide to his disciples: 'I shal no more
drinke withe you of this growynge of the vyne before that I shall
drinke it newe in the rewme of my fader.' And that transfiguracion of
oure Lorde in that it is saide new representithe the glorious newynge
that Ihesu Crist hadde after the resureccion, and therfor in that day of 30
the transfiguracion, the whiche representithe the resureccion, men
sekin the nwe wyne. And it is to knowe that it is saide that the
transfiguracion was made aboute the begynninge of Veer, but the
disciples kepte it priue in as moche as oure Lorde had defended hem
that they shulde not open it in tho dayes, but they shewed it after in 35
that day.

Here endithe the lyff of Seint Sixte and nexst foluithe lyff
of Seint Donat, Capᵐ. .C.viij.ᵐ

Seint Donat was norysshed and taught of Iulien the emperour, and
whanne he was enhaunsed so to that estate he slow the fader and the
moder of Seint Donat. And Donat fledde hym into the citee of Arate
and duelled there withe the monke [Hylla]ry and dede there gret 4
myra|cles. For the prouost of the towne had a sone [v]exed withe a f. 179ʳᵃ

17 as] *om.* H1   19 tresours] tresoure E   20 so] *om.* H1   beheded] behelde
EH1 (*decolerent* P2)   27 vyne] wyne *with one loop of* w *subp.* H1   35 in tho] in
two H1

EH1A2; D resumes at 79 *and constreined*   2 to] þo *subp.* `to' H1   4 Hyllary]
Ybory E, Yvory H1 (*Hilaire* P2)   5 vexed] wexed E, *so with one loop of* w *subp.* H1

fende, and he was brought to the blessed Donate and the wicked
sperit beganne to crye and saide: 'In the name of oure Lorde Ihesu
Crist, do me none harme ne late me not go oute of myn hous. O thou
Donat, whi constreinest thou me to go oute withe turmentes?' But he
10 was deliuered oute anone as Donat praied.

A man hight Eustas, whiche resseiued in Tuskanie the revenues of
the prince, lefte in kepinge of his wiff that hight Eufrosyne the
money that he hadde receyued, but for the sorugh that she hadde of
the enemyes that wasted the cuntre she hydd the money and ended
15 her lyff. And whanne her husbonde come and coude not fynde the
money, he shulde haue be ledde to prison, bothe he and his sone, and
anone he fledde to Seint Donat. And thanne went Donat withe hym
to the sepulcre of hys wyff and made his orison and sayde withe a
clere voys: 'Eufrosine, I coniure the by the vertu of the holy gost that
20 thou saye to us wher thou hast sette this money.' And she ansuered:
'Atte the entre of the hous wher I hidd it under erthe.' And thanne
they went and fonde it as she hadde saide.

And thanne witheinne a fewe dayes after the bysshop Satyr deyed,
and alle the peple chase Donat to be bisshop in hys stede and so he
25 was. In a daye, as Seint Gregori tellithe in his Dyaloges, as Donat
hoseled the peple after masse and the deken ministred to hym the
holy body of oure Lorde, sodenly the deken felle by the prees of
paynemes that came vpon h[y]m and the chalice brake. And that was
gret sorugh to hym and to hem alle, ande thanne Donat gadered
f. 179rb togedre the bro|ken peces of the chalice and made hys orison and
31 sette it in hys furste fourme. And a litell pece was hydde by the fende
that fayled in the chalys, and that chalice is yet in that chirche in
token of this miracle.

Ther was a welle that was so corrupte that whoeuer dranke therof
35 anone he was dede. And Seint Donat went anone thedir upon his asse
for to praie and to hele the water, and thanne an horrible dragon come
oute of the water and wrapped hys tayle aboute Donat assis fete and
dressed hym upright ayeinst Donat. And Donat smote hym withe hys
staffe, or after that sum sayen he spette in his mouthe and he deyed
40 anone. And thanne he praied oure Lorde that he wolde chace away alle
the venim of that welle. Another tyme he and his felawes were opressed
and he made to springe up a we[lle] before hem.

9 me] *add* here H1   17 And ... Donat] 'and seynt donat went' H1   21 the¹]
'þe' H1   22 she] he *changed to* she H1   24–5 in ... was] *om.* H1   26 hym] hem H1
28 hym] hem EH1   30 broken] bro//broken E   39 that] as H1   42 welle] wey
EH1 (*fontaine* P2)

The doughter of Theodesyen the emperour was sore turmented of
a fende and was brought to Seint Donat and he saide: 'Thou foule
sperit, go oute and duelle no more here in this place that is formed 45
after God.' And the fende saide: 'Yeue me passage that I may go oute
and by what place I shall goo and whedir I shalle go.' And Donat
saide: 'Fro whennes came thou hedir?' And he saide: 'Fro the
desert.' And Donat sayd: 'Thanne go theder ayenne.' And the
fende sayde: 'I see in the the token of the crosse, wherof the fyre 50
smitethe so sore ayeinst me that for the fere therof I dare not goo
oute. Wherfor I praie the that thou wilt geue me place to goo oute.'
And Donat sayde: 'See here that thou hast issue, retorne ayen fro
whennes thou comyst.' And thanne he made alle the | hous to f. 179ᵛᵃ
tremble and went his waye. 55

Men baren a dede body to be beried, and there came a man that
brought a chartre in his honde and saide that the dede man owed
hym .x. *libri* and tille that he were paicd he wolde not suffre hym to
be beryed in no wyse. And thanne his wyff that was wedue come to
Seint Donat and shewed hym this mater al wepinge and sayde that 60
he hadde receyued alle his money. And thanne Seint Donate went
thedir and touched the dede body and saide: 'Arise up and loke what
thou wilt do to this man þat wille not suffre the to be beried.' The
man satte up and ouercome hym before alle men of the payement of
his dette and toke the chartre of hys honde and al tocutte it. And 65
thanne he sayde to Seint Donate; 'Syr, comaunde that I reste in
pees.' And he saydc: 'Sone, go to thi reste fro hennes forwarde.'

In that tyme it hadd not reyned in thre yere, and the erthe was alle
bareyne and mighte bringe forthe no fruit, the paynimes come to the
emperoure Theodesyan requiringe hym that he wolde delyuer to 70
hem hym that hadde wrought this by his art magike. But, atte the
request of the emperour, Donat came and praied to oure Lorde that
he of his grace wolde geue hem reyne. And oure Lorde of his
habundaunt grace anone sent suche a reyne that they were alle wete
sauf only Donate that went drye to his hous. 75

In that tyme the Gothis wasted Itaile and that miche peple were
wasted from the faithe of oure Lorde. And Dasyan the prouost was
reproued of apostasye bi Seint Donat and Seint Hylarin. He thanne
toke hem bothe and constreined hem to do sacrifice | to Iubiter, and f. 179ᵛᵇ

43 Theodesyen] theOdesyen *with* the *on erasure* H1   46 Yeue] If H1
49 Thanne] *om.* H1   50 wherof] wherfore H1   67 to] þo *changed to* to H1
68 thre] þe H1   71 wrought] broȝt *changed to* wroȝt H1   79 and²] but D

80 thei refused it pleinly. Thanne he made Hyllari to be bete al naked til
he gaue up the sperit to God. And he putte Donat in prison and
sethe made hym to be beheded the yere of oure Lorde .CCC. and
.iiij^{xx}.

Here endithe the lyff of Seint Donate, and nexst begin-
nuthe the lyff of Seint Syriake, Capitulum .C ix.^m

Syriake was ordeyned deken by the pope Marcell, and after that he
was take and brought to the emperoure Maxymien ande hit was
comaunded that he and hys felawes shulde digge the erthe and bere
it on her shuldres to the place wher men made the caues, and ther
5 was Seint Saturien, an olde m[a]n, þe whiche Ciriake and Sysymian
halpe hem for to bere. And sethe was Ciriake enclosed up in prison
and atte the laste he was presented to the provost. And as Apynien
ledde hym thedir, he sawe sodenly a lyght come from heuene and
herde a voys that saide: 'Comithe the blessed of my fader *etc.*' And
10 thanne Apinien beleued in God and receiued bapteme and came to
the prouost and confessed Ihesu Crist. To whom the prouost saide:
'Thou art not made cristen as I trowe.' And he ansuered: 'Allas, I
haue loste alle my dayes.' And the prouost saide to hym: 'Verily thou
shalt lese thi dayes,' ande thanne he comaunded that he were
15 beheded. And whanne Saturnyn and Sysimian wolde not sacrifice,
they were turmented by diuerse turmentes and atte the laste
beheded.

And whan the doughter of Dyoclysyan, Arthemye by name, was
sore vexed and turmented withe a fende, the same fende cryed
20 witheinne her and sayde: 'I wil not goo oute before that Ciriake the |
f. 180ra deken come.' And thanne was Ciriake brought forthe to the same,
and than the fende sayde to hym: 'Yef thou wylt that I go oute, yeue
me place wherin I shall entre.' And thanne Ciriake ansuered: 'See
here my body, entre yef thou maist.' And he sayde: 'In thy vessell I
25 may not entre, for it is sygned and closed in alle parties, wherfor I
telle the that yef thou make me goo hennes, I shall ordeyne for the
that thou shalt hastely goo into Babyloyne.' And whanne Ciriake
hadde constreyned hym to go oute, Arthemye cried and sayd: 'I see

82 .CCC.] .CCCC. D

EH1DA2   4 made] make D   5 an . . . man] and olde men EH1   whiche] chirch
del. 'whiche' H1   9 the] 3e D (*les* P2)   *etc.*] *om.* D   12 ansuered] *add* and seide D
14 lese] *add* alle D   24 he] þe feende D   28 hym] the feende

the God that Ciriake prechithe.' And whanne he hadde baptised her,
and by the grace of Dyoclusyan and of Serve his wyff he duelled and 30
leued suerly in an hous that they hadde yeue hym, and thanne came
there a messenger from the kinge of Pers to Dyoclusyan praienge
hym that he wolde send hym Ciriake, for his doughter was vexed
withe a fende.

And so by the prayer of Dyoclusyan, Ciriake went thedir gladly 35
withe Large and Synaracke and baren withe hem alle her necessitees.
And whanne they come to the doughter of the kynge of Pers, the
fende cryed by the mouthe of the mayde and sayde: 'O thou Ciriake,
how thou art wery of trauaile.' And he ansuered and saide: 'I am not
wery, for I am alway gouerned by the helpe of oure Lorde.' Ande 40
thanne the fende sayde: 'Yet haue I alwaye brought the there as I
wolde.' And Ciriake saide: 'Ihesu Crist comaundithe the that thou go
oute of this body.' And thanne the fende went oute and sayde: 'O
thou dredfull name, how thou constreynest me sore.' And thus was
the mayde heled and was baptised withe her fader and moder and 45
moche other peple. And thanne they offered to hym gret yeftes, but
he wold | none receyue, and there he duelled withe hem .xlv. dayes in f. 180ʳᵇ
fastinge bred and water, and after that he went ayein to Rome.

And thanne two monthes after that deyed Dyoclucian, and
Maxymien succeded after hym in the empire and was wrothe 50
withe Arthemy his suster, and toke Ciriake and bonde hym withe
chaynes and made hym to be drawe after hys chare. And Maxymien
was sayde Valerian and he might as moche be called the sone of
Dyoclusyan, for he succeded after hym in the empire and wedded his
doughter that hight Valery. And after that he comaunded Harpas his 55
viker that he shulde constreyne Ciriake and his felawship to do
sacrifice or elles to slee hem by diuerse turmentes. And thanne was
Ciriake take withe alle hys felawship and hanged on the turment that
ys called in Frenshe eculee, and they poured boyled pyche upon his
hede, and after that they beheded hym withe alle his felawshipp 60
aboute the yere of oure Lorde thre hundred.

And whanne Carpas hadde asked the hous of Ciriake and in
despite of Ciriake he hadde made a batthe of the place that Ciriake
was wont to baptise inne, and there he bathid hymselff and made a

29 he] Ciriak D   30 Serve] Sorbee D   36 and Synaracke] *om.* D   43 oute²]
om. D   44 how] *om.* D   48 ayein] *om.* D   49 thanne] withynne D
53 moche] wel D   55 that hight] *om.* D   58 the] a Hı D   59 boyled] boylinge D
64 bathid] baptized Hı

65 feste there to .xix. felawes and alle were dede sodenly, and for that
cause the batthe was closed up and the paynimes beganne to loue and
to drede cristen men.

Here endithe the lyff of Seint Ciriake, and nexst beginnithe the lyff of Seint Laurence, Cap^m. .C.x.^m

Seint Laurence the holy marter and subdekene of the kynrede of
f. 180va Spayne the which Seint Sixte brought | oute of that cuntree so as
Maister Iohan Belet saiethe and in this wise. I[n] a tyme as Seint
Sixte wente into Spayne he fonde there .ij. yonge men of whiche that
5 one hyght Laurence and that other Vincent, whiche were cosenes,
whiche .ij. yonge men were full vertuous and full of alle good
condiciones. And Seint Sixte ledde hem withe hym to Rome, and
Laurens duelled withe hym stille and Vincent his cosyn retorned into
Italye, and there he ended hys lyff by glorious marterdom. But to
10 this reson of misterie Iohn Belette contrariethe the tyme of marterdom of that one and of that other, for it is redde that Seint Laurens
was vnder Dacyen, and Vincent vnder Dioclusyan and Dacyene. But
betwene Dioclusyan and Dasyan was nighe .xl.^ti wynter and there
were .vij. emperoures in the mene tyme, so that Vincent might not
15 be thanne.
And the blessed Sixte ordeined Laurence to be his erchedeken.
And in that tyme Phelip emperour and Phelip his sone receyued the
faithe of Ihesu Crist, and whanne thei were cristened thei entended
gretly to [enhaunse] the Chirche. And this emperoure was the furst
20 that receyued the faithe of Ihesu, the whiche as sum men sayen
Origenes conuertid to the faithe, though it be so that ower elles it is
redde that Seint Ponciane had conuerted hym. And he regned in the
yere a .M^l. that the citee of Rome was made, so that same yere of a
thousande was [rather] sayd of Crist thanne of idoles. And that [yere]
25 was halowed of the Romaynes withe gret array of games and of playes.
And ther was thanne a knight withe the emperour Phelip | that
f. 180vb hight Decyen that was gretly renomed in armes. And so as Fraunce

EH1T1DA2L; D breaks off after 216 *Laurence*; H2 resumes at 81 *disese*; A1 resumes at
285 *the Office*; for LgA *Decius* H1 mostly changes *Decien* to *Dacien*, but from 128–140 *Dacien*
is original, and 145 *Dacien* is changed to *Decien*; D has *Dacian   Rubric* .C.x.] C.ix. E
3 In] I E   5 were] *add* .ij. D   6 whiche . . . men] and D   yonge] *om.* H1   8 his]
on erasure H1   10 contrariethe] contraiheth H1   12 and Dacyene] *del.* H1
19 enhaunse] L, ensaumple of EH1D   22 Ponciane] Potencian D   23 that¹] aftir D
24 rather] *om.* EH1   yere] day EH1

rebelled ayeinst the same emperour he sent theder Decyen for to
sowde and submitte Fraunce to the empire of Rome. And Decyen
theder sent, dede alle these thingges well and submitted Fraunce to 30
Rome and hadde the victorie. And whanne the emperour herde his
comynge he thought to worshipp hym more hily and went ayeinst
hym [fro] Rome [into Veron], but for that that of so moche as the
wicked fele[th] hymselff more worshipped, so moche the more be
they bolnyd withe pride, and thanne Dacyen lefte up in pride 35
beganne to coueyte the empire, and as he knew that the emperoure
slepte in his parlour he entered witheinne priuely and cutte the
throte of his lorde slepinge. And thanne he drowe to hym by yeftes
and by praiers alle tho of the oste that the emperour hadde brought
withe hym and went anone to the citee of Rome. 40

   And whanne Phelip the yonge herde this thingge he dradde hym
gretly. And as Sicard saiethe in his Cronicle, he toke al the tresour of
his fader and of hys to Seint Sixte and to Seint Laurence, so that yef
it felle that he were slayne of Decyen that they shulde geue that
tresour to the Chirche and to pore men. And wondre not for that 45
that the tresoures that Laurens gaue to the pore be not called the
tresours of the emperour but of the Chirche, for it is trwe that withe
tho tresoures of the emperour he yaue the tresour of the Chirche. Or
perauenture they were sayde the tresour of the Chirche for Phelip
hadde lefte hem for to be dispended in the chirche. And whanne this 50
was done Phelip fledde for drede of Decyen, and thanne the
sena|tours went ayeinst Decyen and confermed hym in the empire. f. 181ʳᵃ
And for þat he wolde not be sayne that he had slayne his lorde in
treson but for the loue that he hadde ren[y]ed his idoles, he beganne
right cruelly to do persecusyon vpon the cristene and comaunded 55
that they were all distroyed withoute any mercy. And many thousand
marteres were slayne, amonge the whiche Phelip was crowned withe
marterdom.

   And thanne after Decyen made enquere of the tresour of his lorde,
and thanne was Sixte brought to hym as he that worshypped Ihesu 60

28 rebelled] rebelleth H1   29 Decyen] *add* was D   31–2 his comynge] þis D
32 and went] *om*. D   33 fro] L, into E, ʾinʾto H1, to D   into Veron] L, *om*. EH1D
that¹ . . . so] as D   34 feleth] feled EH1   the] ʾþeʾ H1   36 as] in a tyme whan D
38 he] Dacian D   39 by] *om*. H1D   tho of] *om*. D   43 hys] *add* and toke hit D
45–6 that that] that D   47 emperour] emperouris D   48 tresoures] resones *changed
to* tresours H1   tresour] tresours D   48–9 Or . . . Chirche] *om*. L   49 tresour]
tresours D   53 sayne] slayne *changed to* sayne H1, *add* for H1D   54 renyed] rened
E, renʾyʾed H1   57 marteres] maʾrʾteres H1   59 after] aftirward D   tresour]
tresours D

Crist and hadde the tresours of the emperour. Thanne Dacyen comaunded that he were putte in prison so longe that by turmentes he shulde renie God and shewe the tresours. And the blessed Laurence folowed hym and cried after hym and saide: 'Wheder
65 goest thou, fader, witheoute thi sone? Prest, whedir goest thou witheoute thi ministre? Thou art not acustumed to sacrifie witheoute thi ministre. What is in me that hathe displesed to thy faderhode? Hast thou preued me to go oute of kynde or forlingne? Preue me that hast chose me couenable to dispense the blood of oure Lorde.' To
70 whom blessed Sixte sayde: 'I leue the not, ne will not leue the, but gretter bataile is due to the for the faithe of Ihesu Crist. We haue take vpon us as olde men the cours of the moste lyghtest batayle, and the moste glorious abidethe to the as to the most yonge, and thou shalt haue victorie of the tyraunt and folowe me withinne thre dayes.'
75 And thanne he deliuered hym alle the tresour, comaundynge hym that he shulde [yeue hem alle] to [the] chirches and to pore folke.

f. 181rb And thanne the blessed Laurence soughte | diligentely the pore night and day, and gaue to eueriche as hem nedid. And thanne he come to the hous of a pore woman that hadde hidde in her hous
80 many cristen men, and this woman hadde be longe tyme suffered gret disese in her hede. And thanne Seint Laurence leide his honde vpon her hede and heled her anone, and thanne he wysshe the fete of the pore and to eueryche of hem gaue almesse. And that same night he went to the hous of a cristen and fonde witheinne a blynde man
85 and gaue hym syght withe the sygne of the crosse.

And as the blessed Sixte wolde not obeye to Decyen ne sacrifye to the idoles, he comaunded that he shulde be ledde to be byheded. And the blessed Laurence ranne after hym and sayde: 'Holy Seint, leue me not, for I haue dispended the tresours that thou toke me.'
90 And whanne the knightes herde speke of the tresours thei token Laurence and after toke hym to the prouost Valerian. And the prouost deliuered hym to Dacyen, and thanne Dycien Cesar saide to hym: 'Wher be the tresours of the Chirche that we knowe well [that] thou hast hidd?' And he ansuered nothinge. Than he toke hym to
95 Valeryan prouost so that he shulde shewe the tresours and do

63 renie] reyne H1   shewe] *so with first* e *on erasure* H1   68 forlingne] forlyvinge D, forlinge H1L   70 ne] *add* I H1D   71 is due] shal be done D   72 lyghtest] hiest H1D   73 glorious] *add* bataile D   76 yeue hem/alle] *trs.* EH1   the] *om.* EH1 chirches] chirch D   78 as hem] of hem as him D   81 disese] di's'ese H1 90 herde] *add* him D   91 And the prouost] *twice* D   93 that²] *om.* EH1   94 he¹] laurence D

sacrifice to the idoles or ellys þat he made hym deye by diuerse
turmentes. And Valerian toke hym to another prouost that hight
Ypolyte for to putte hym in prison, and so he was enclosed in prison
withe many other. And so amonge other ther was a paynime in
prison that hyght Lucille, the whiche hadde loste his syght in   100
wepinge. And Seint Laurence behight hym to restore hym his
syght yef he wold beleue in Ihesu Crist and receiue | bapteme, and f. 181ᵛᵃ
he anone [desired] bapteme. And thanne Seint Laurence toke water
and saide hym: 'Alle thingges be wasshe in confession.' And whanne
he hadde diligentely taught hym in the artycles of the faithe and that 105
he had confessed that he beleued hem alle, he shedde the water vpon
his hede and baptised hym in the name of Ihesu Crist, and anone he
that was blynde receyued his syght. And for that cause ther come to
hym many blynde þe whiche receyued her syght by hym.
   Thanne sayde Ipolite to hym: 'Shewe me the tresours.' To whom 110
Seint Laurens sayde: 'O Ipolite, yef thou wilt beleue in oure Lorde
Ihesu Crist, I shalle shewe the the tresours and behyght the
euerlastinge lyff.' And Ypolite sayd: 'Yef thou do that thou sayest,
I shalle fulfell that thou requirest.' And in þat same houre Ipolite
beleued and resseiued bapteme and alle hys meyne. And whanne he 115
was baptised he sayd: 'I haue sene the soules of innocentes gladly
reioysinge hem.' And thanne after this Valerian sent to Ipolite that
he shulde bringe hym Laurence. And Laurence sayde: 'Goo we
bothe togederes, for the glorie and ioye is ar[ai]ed for me and for
the.' And thanne he came ayenne into iugement and he was ayenne 120
enquered of the tresours, and Laurence asked dilacion or space of .iij.
dayes, and Valerian graunted hym vnder the plegge of Ipolyte. And
than Laurens in these .iij. dayes gadered togedre alle the pore, lame
and blynde and presented hem before Decyen in the palays of
Salustien and saide: 'These here bene the euerlastinge tresoures 125
that neuer shull fayle but encrece, and be departed in eueriche by
h[y]mselff, and be founde in alle. The hondes of these here haue
born the tresours | into heuene. Thanne Valerian, present Dacyen, f. 181ᵛᵇ
sayde: 'What goest thou variaunt in many thingges? Do sacrifice

98 and . . . prison] *ins. with* closed *for* enclosed H1, *om.* D   100 prison] *add* with
meny othir D, *so del.* H1   103 desired] L, receiued EH1D   104 confession]
confusion *changed to* confession *in different hand* D   119 araied] L, arered EH1D
120 he¹] laurence D   121 enquered] required D, *so changed to* 'en'quired H1   or] of
H1D   125 here] *om.* D   126 be] *ins.* H1   127 hymself] hemself EH1   here]
add and D   128 Valerian] *add* was D   present] *add* bifore D   Dacyen] L, *add* and
EH1D   129 sayde] *add* to laurence D   thou] *add* so D

130 anone and putte awaye thin art magyke.' And thanne Seint Laurens
sayde to hym: 'Whiche aught beter to be worshipped, eyther [he] that
made, or he that ys made?' And thanne Dacyen was wrothe and
comaunded that he shulde be bete with scourges and that alle maner
turmentes were brought before hym, and saide to hym that he shulde
135 do sacrifice to eschewe th[o] turmentes. And he ansuered: 'Thou
cursed wreche, I haue alwaye desired suche metes.' Than Decyen
sayde: 'Yef thei be metes, shewe me thi cursed felawshippe that they
mowe dyne togederes withe the.' To whom Laurence saide: 'Thei haue
now yeue her names into heuene and thou art not worthi to see hem.'
140   And than by the comaundement of Dycien he was bete al naked
withe yerdes and withe staues, and peces of brenninge iren were sette
faste to hys sydes. And thanne Laurens saide: 'Lorde Ihesu Crist, the
sone of God, haue pitee of thy servaunt that hathe be accused and
hath not renyed the, and whanne I haue be asked I haue knouleged
145 the my Lorde.' Thanne sayde Dycien to hym: 'I wote well that thou
despisest the turmentes be thine art magike, but thou mayst not
despise me. Wherfor I suere by my goddes and [by] my goddesses
that, but thou sacryfie, I shall punisshe the with diuerse turmentes.'
And thanne he comaunded that he shulde ryght long be bete withe
150 pelotes of lede, and than Seint Laurence praied sayenge: 'Lorde
God, receyue my sperit.' And thanne a voyce sayde from heuene,
heringe Decyen, 'Many turmentes be dewe to the yet.' And thanne
Decyen fulfelled withe felonye saide: 'Ye men of Rome, haue ye | not
f. 182ʳᵃ herde how the fendes comforte this cursed that neyther dredithe
155 oure goddes ne worshippithe hem, ne dredithe not the turmentes ne
the wrathe of princes?' And thanne he comaunded ayenne that he
shulde be bete withe scourges. Thanne Seint Laurens in smylynge
gave thankyngges to God and praied for hem that were there. And in
that houre a knight that hight [Romanus] beleued in God and sayde
160 to the blessed Seint Laurence: 'I see [stond] before the right a fayre
yonge man wypinge thi woundes and thi membres with a lynen
clothe, and I coniure the in the name of oure Lorde that thou leue
me not, but that thou haste the that I were baptised.' Thanne saide
Dycien to Valerian: 'I trowe that we be ouercome by this art magike.'

130 magyke] *add* or ellis þou shalt deie D   131 he] *om.* E, *ins.* H1   132 or] *add*
ellis D   or . . . made] *ins.* H1   135 tho] the EH1   he] than laurence D   137 they]
ȝe D   138 withe the] *om.* D   the] me *del.* `the' H1      145 the] by *del.* `the' H1
146 the] þi H1D   147 by²] *om.* E   149 he'] Dacian D   152 Decyen] *so changed*
to Dacyen *del.* `Laurence' H1   dewe] *om.* D   154 cursed] *add* man D
159 Romanus] L, Laurence EH1D   160 stond] L, *om.* EH1D

And than he comaunded that he shulde be vnbounde and putte in 165
the prison of Ipolyte, and thanne the Romayne brought an erthen
potte of water and leyd hym atte the fete of Seint Laurence and
receiued bapteme of hym. And whan Dycien woste it, he comaunded
that þe Romayne were bete withe yerdes, and he sayde that he was
frely a cristen man, and thanne Dycien made hym to be byheded. 170
  And that night was Seint Laurence brought to Dycien, and Ipolite
sawe that. He beganne to wepe and wolde haue sayde that he was
cristen, and Seint Laurence saide to hym: 'Hyde Ihesu Crist witheinne the, and whan I crye, here and come thedyr.' And than alle
maner turmentes were brought before Dycien. And thanne sayde 175
Dacycn to Seint Laurence: 'Either thou shalt sacrifye to [oure]
goddes or elles this night shall alle be dyspended in turmentynge
the.' Thanne sayde Seint Laurence: 'My night hathe no derkenesse,
but alle thingges shynen in my lyght.' And | thanne sayde Dacyen: f. 182rb
'Bringe forthe a bedde of iren that this wreched Laurence may reste 180
hym witheinne.' And thanne the ministres dispoiled hym and
strechid hym oute vpon a gredyren and putte under brenninge
coles and turned hym to and fro withe fyre forkes. And thanne
sayde Laurence to Valerian: 'Vnderstonde, thou cursed wreche, and
see how the coles yeue me refresshinge, and to the euerlasting 185
turment, and oure Lorde knowithe that I haue be accused and
haue not renyed hym, and whanne I haue be examyned I haue
confessed Ihesu Crist, and I, rosted, yelde thankingges to oure Lorde
Ihesu Crist.' And sethe he sayd to Dacyen: 'Thou cursed, thou hast
rosted that one syde, turne that other and ete it.' And thanne in 190
yeldinge thankyngges he sayde: 'Lorde, I thankke the that I haue
deserued to entre withinne thi gates.' And therwithe he gaue up his
blessed sperit. And thanne Dacyen went al confused to the palays
Tyberien withe Valerian and lefte the body up[on] the fyre, and
Ipolyte rauisshed the body in the morwtyde and beried it withe 195
Iustine the preste and anointed hym withe precious oynementes and
putte hym in the feled Beren. And the cristen that beryed hym
wokyn hym thre dayes and .iij. nightes wepinge and cryenge.
  Gregori putte in hys boke of Dyologes that ther was a nonne in
Sabyne that was a ful chast woman of her body, but she eschued not 200

167 the] ins. H1   176 oure] om. EH1   179 lyght] si3te D   184 wreche] add
come H1, add and come D   the] þi D   187 renyed] revied D   191 he] I H1D
192 thi] þe H1   193 palays] add of D   194 upon] up EH1   196 the] there H1
197 feled Beren] space D   199 in¹] ins. H1   boke] bokes D   in²] þat hy3t D

wel the iangelynge of her tongge. And she deyed and was beryed in
the chirche of the blessed marter Seint Laurence before the auuter,
and than was she take of the fendes and cutte even atwayne, and that
f. 182va one parte saued al hole and that other partie | al brent, as it appered
205 in the morw to alle visibly.

And Gregori of Toures saiethe that [as] a prest repaired the
chirche of Seint Laurence and one of the bemes was to shorte, he
required Seint Laurence that, as he hadde norisshed the pore peple
bi hys charite, that he wolde now helpe to hys pouert. And sodenly
210 the beme encresed so that ther lefte a gret partie, and the prest cutte
that partye in smal peces and heled many seke folke therwithe. And
this witnessithe the blessed Fortunat. Hit befell atte Brioras, a castell
of Itayle, that a man was strongly syke in the tethe and he touched
his teth withe that tree and was hole anone.

215 A preest that hight Sabatyn, as Seint Gregori witnessithe in hys
Dyaloges, repaired a chirche of Seint Laurence that hadde be brent
withe Lumbardes, and hered many werkemen. And he hadde not
atte one tyme to yeue hem mete, and than he made his prayer and
sethe he behelde in hys panier and fonde a right white loef, but it
220 semed hym that it wolde vnnethes suffice to one dyner for .iij.
persones, but Seint Laurens that wolde not fayle to hys werkemen
made that loef so to multeplye that hys werkemen were susteyned
therwithe .x. dayes.

In the chirche of Seint Laurens atte Mylen ther was a wonder
225 fayre chalice of cristall. And as the deken bare it in a solempne day
towarde the auuter it fell of hys hondes to the erthe and was al
tobroke. And thanne the deken wepinge gadered the peces togedre
and leyde hem on the auuter and besought that blessed marter Seint
f. 182vb Laurence that by his merites he woulde ressoude | that broken
230 chalice, and anone it was founde al hole.

It is redde in the Miracles of the blessed Virgine Marie how that
there was a iuge that hight Stephen atte Rome and toke gladly yeftes
and turned vpsodoune hys iugementes. This iuge toke awaye with
force .iij. houses that were of the chirche of Seint Laurens and a
235 gardeyne of Seint Anneis and helde hem with wronge. And so it fell
that this iuge deyed and was brought to iugement byfore God. And

201 wel] *om.* D   203 of] vp bi D   205 morw] morwe tyde D   206 as] *om.*
EH1   207 to] so H2   shorte] *add* that H2   209 hys²] this H2   210–11 and . . .
partye] *ins.* H1, *om.* H2   211 and] *add* there were H2   213–14 and . . . teth] *ins.* H1
219 behelde] behe`l´de H1, loked H2   right] *om.* H2   222 made . . . werkemen] *om.* H2
230 chalice] *add* ayen H2

whanne Seint Laurence sawe hym he went to hym by gret despite
and streyned his arme thre tymes right harde and turmented hym
right sore. And Seint Anneis withe other virgines deyned not to
beholde hym but turned her face from hym. And thanne the iuge 240
yeuinge sentence ayeinst hym saide: 'For that he hathe withedrawe
the goodes of other and taken yeftes and solde the trouthe, be he
sette in the place of Iudas the traytour.' And than Seint Proiect, the
whiche this Stephen hadde gretly loued in his lyff, came to blessed
Seint Laurence and to Seint Anneis and asked mercy for hym. And 245
thanne the blessed Virgine Marie and they praied to God for hym,
and it was graunted hem that the soule shulde come into the body
ayenne and do penaunce ,xxx. dayes. And that most blessed Virgine
Marie comaunded hym that as longe as he lyved he shulde saye this
psalme: *Beati immaculati.* And whanne he was come ayenne to his 250
body the arme of hym was so blewe and broyled as though he hadde
suffered the hurte in his body, and this sygne was in hym as long as
he lyued. And thanne he yelded ayenne that he hadde take withe
wrong and dede penaunce, and in the .xxx.^{ti} day | he passyd to oure f. 183ra
Lorde. 255

Hit is redde in the lyff of Seint Herry the emperoure that he and
hys wyff Ragonde lyued togederes in virginite, and so by entisinge of
the fende he hadde suspecion betwene a knight and his wyff and made
her go [barfote] .xv. paes vpon brenninge coles. And as she went
theron she saide; 'Right as I am vncorrupte [fro] Harri and from alle 260
other, Ihesu Crist helpe me.' And thanne Harri was ashamed and
gaue her a bofet vnder the cheke, and withe that ther was a voys that
sayde: 'The blessed Virgine Marie shall deliuer the, virgine.' And
thanne she went witheoute any harme vpon the brenninge irnes.

And whanne the emperoure was dede, there passed gret multitude 265
of fendes before the celle of an holy hermite, and he opened his
wyndow and asked of the laste what they were. And he saide: 'A
legion of fendes that gone to the dethe of the emperour to wete yef we
mowe finde any propre thingges of oures in hym.' And he coniured
hem to come ayenne by hym, and thanne they retorned [and] saiden: 270
'We haue nothinge profyted, for whanne that fals suspecion of hys

239 Anneis] *add* come H2   virgines] *add* and H2   249 lyved] *add* aftir H2
250 *immaculati*] *add in* H1   his] þis H1   253 ayenne] *add* al H2   254 dede] *add*
gret H2   in] *om.* H1H2   day] *add* aftir H2   257 wyff] *add* that hyghte H2
259 barfote] L, *om.* EH1H2   260 fro] L, to EH1H2   264 went] *add* forthe H2
irnes] colis H2   265 whanne] *add* Harry H2   270 thanne] whan H2   they] *add* that
EH1   and²] *om.* EH1, *add* come ayen thei H2

wyff and al good and euell were brought togederes in a balaunce, that
broyled Laurence brought a potte of [golde of] gret wyght in that
other syde so that she p[ey]sed doune al that other partie, and I was
275 wrothe and brake an ere of the potte.' And that was a chalys that the
emperoure hadde geue to the chirche of Seint Laurence and it was so
grete that it hadde .ij. eres. And it was founde that the emperoure
passed atte þat tyme and that the ere of the chalys was broke.

Gregorie tellithe in hys Registre that hys predecessour | coueited
f. 183ʳᵇ to amende sum thingges that were aboute the blessed body of Seint
281 Laurence, but how it felle that the blessed body of Seint Laurence
was vnheled by ignoraunce, but alle tho that were there present as
well monkes as other were dede in .ix. dayes.

Seint Laurens amonge other marteres hathe .iij. priuileges as
285 touching to the Office. Of the furste is that he hathe Uigile
amonge the other marteres. But in these dayes the Vigile of seintes
be turned into fastinge be many ordenaunces, for as Iohn Belet
tellithe it was sumtyme vsed of custume that men withe her wyues
and with her children went into chirches in [the] solempnite of festes
290 and there they woke al night withe torches and withe lyghtes, but for
as moche as ther felle many straunge auentures atte the[se] Vigiles it
was ordeigned that the Vigiles shulde be turned into fastingges, and
yet alwaye the olde name of Vigile abidethe. The secounde is in vtas;
for he and Steven haue oeptas only amonge other marteres, right as
295 Seint Martin amonge the other confessours. The thridde is in
takinge ayen the antemes, the whiche Seint Paule hath only, but
Paule hathe hem for the excellence of his predicacion, and this holy
Seint Laurence hathe hem for the excellence of his passion.

Here endithe the lyff of the blessed Seint Laurence, and
nexst beginnithe the lyff of Seint Ipolite, Capᵐ. .C.xj.ᵐ

Whanne Seint Ipolite hadde beried the body of Seint Laurence he
came to his hous and gaue pees to alle hys seruauntes and hoseled
f. 183ᵛᵃ alle hys meyni | withe the sacrement that Iustine the preste hadde
halowed. And the borde was sette, but before that they might take

273 golde of] L, om. EH1H2   274 peysed] L, pressed EH1H2   275 ere] L,
here EH1, hole H2   278 and that] whan H2A2   279 predecessour] predecessours
EH1   285 hathe] add a H2   289 with] om. H2   the] L, om. EH1H2
290 lyghtes] add brennynge H2   291 these] L, the E, 'thes' H1, om. H2   293 in]
the H2   294 haue] had H2   other] alle the H2   295 other] om. H2

EH1T1H2A1A2; H1 writes Dacien to 25, Decyen from 60   4 that] or H1H2

any mete the knightes come and toke hym and ledde hym to the 5
cesar. And whanne Dacyen sawe hym he smiled and saide to hym:
'Art thou now made an enchauntour that haste beried the body of
Laurence?' And Ipolite ansuered and sayde: 'That I haue do, not as
an enchauntour but as a true cristen man.' And thanne Dacyen
fulfelled withe wodenesse comaunded that he shulde be dispoiled of 10
his habite þat he vsed as a cristen man and that his mouthe were bete
withe stones. Thanne saide Ipolite to Dacyen: 'Thou hast not
dispoiled me, but thou hast beter clothed me.' Thanne saide
Dacyen: 'How is it that thou art made so grete a fole that thou art
not ashamed of thi nakednesse? Now sacrifie anone that thou 15
perisshe not withe thy Laurence.' And Ipolite ansuered and saide:
'Wolde God I were worthi to take ensaumple of Laurens, the whiche
thou manacest withe thi defoulyd mouth.'

And thanne Dacien made hym al torent withe staues and withe
hokes of iren, and he confessed withe clere voys to be cristen. And 20
whanne he hadde dispised the turmentes he made hym to be clothed
withe the clothinge of a knight whiche he hadde vsed before,
techinge hym that he shulde kepe hys frenship and hys furste
knighthode. And Ipolyte saide that he was only the knight of
Ihesu Crist, and Dacyen fulfelled withe wrathe delyuered hym to 25
Valerian the prouost and that he shulde take alle hys goodez and sle
hym by diuerse turmentez. And thanne he fonde that alle hys meyni
were cristened and alle were brought | before hym. And whanne they f. 183ᵛᵇ
shulde be constreined to sacrifie, Concorde that was norice of Ipolite
ansuered before alle: 'We loue beter to deye chastely with oure Lorde 30
thanne to lyue wickedly.' And thanne Valerian, Ipolite present,
comaunded that she shulde be so bete withe balles of lede that she
shulde putte oute the sperit. And thanne Ipolite sayde: 'Lorde, I
yelde the thankinge of that thou hast sent my norice before the syght
of thi seintes.' 35

And after that Valerian made lede Ipolite withe hys meyne to the
gate of Tyburtyne, and Ypolite comforted hem alle and [sayde]:
'Bretheren, drede you not, for ye and I haue [one] only God.' And
thanne Valerian comaunded that alle they shulde be byheded before
Ipolite, and thanne he made Ipolite to be bounde hondes and fete and 40

14 made] om. H2   18 manacest] del. 'nomyste' H1   19 hym] add be H2
21 dispised] dispoiled del. 'dispisyd' H1, be dispoiled with H2   24 that he was] I am
H2   26 take] lese H2   31 Valerian] add seide and H2   Ipolite] add was H2
35 thi] þe II1   37 sayde] om. E, ins. H1   38 one] om. EH1

teyed hym faste to wylde horses, and they wodely alle todrowe hym
amonge breres and thornes till he yalde up the sperit aboute the yere of
oure Lorde .CC.lxvj. And thanne the good preste Iustine stale hym and
beried hym besydes the body of Seint Laurence, but he coude in no
45 wyse fynde the body of Seint Concorde, for it was caste in a priuey.
  A knight that hight P[or]fire wende that Concorde hadde hadde
golde or precious stones aboute her in her clothinge, came to a
gangefermour that hyght Yreneus þat was priuely a cristen man and
saide to hym: 'Loke thou kepe wel my counsayle and drawe oute the
50 body of Concorde oute of the prevy, for I suppose that she haue in
her clothes golde or precious stones.' And he sayde hym: 'Shew me
the place and I shall kepe well thi counsayle and telle the what I
fynde.' And thanne he drowe oute the body and fonde nothinge, and
f. 184ra thanne the knight fledde awaye anone, and Yre|neus called to hym a
55 cristen man that hight Habond and barin the body to Seint Iustin,
and he toke it deuoutely and beried it besydes the body of Seint
Ipolyte withe other. And whanne Valerian herde that, he made to
take Ireneus and Habond and slowe hem bothe in the same privey,
and Iustin rauisshed the bodyes and beried hem withe the thother.
60   After these thyngges Dacien and Valerian went vp into a chayre
for to turment the cristen. And Dacyen was rauisshed with the fend
and cried: 'O, Ipolite hathe rauisshed me withe sharpe cheynes and
ledith me.' And Valerian cried also: 'O Laurens, how thou drawest
me bounden withe cheynes.' And in that same hour deyed Valerian,
65 and Dacyen turned to his hous and was .iij. dayes turmented with
the fende and cried: 'Laurence, cese a lytell of thi turmentes, I
coniure the', and so he deyed. And whanne Trifone his wyff that was
full cruell saw this thinge, she lefte alle and came with Sirille her
doughter to Iustine and made her to be baptised withe many other.
70 And the nexste day after as Trifone praied, she gaue vp her sperit to
oure Lorde, and the blessed preste Iustyne beryed her body fast by
Seint Ipolite. And whanne .xlvij. of her knightes herde that the
quene ande her doughter were cristened they with her wyves came to
Iustine for to receyue bapteme, the whiche [that] Seint Denys that
75 succeded Seint Sixt baptised hem alle. And Claudyan, thanne

43 hym] add by nyghte H2   46 Porfire] Profire EH1, Porphyry T1, Porferie H2
(*Porphire* P2)   47 in her] *om.* H2   58 bothe] *add* and caste hem H2   60 a
chayre] Achayre E   63 ledith] beteth H1H2   O] *add* þu H1H2   67 deyed] *add*
wrecchidly H2   68 with] to Iustine she and H2   69 her . . . baptised] him to baptise
hem H2   70 day] nyght H2   71–2 by Seint] bisides H1   73 cristened] baptised
H2   they] *add* alle H2   74 that¹] alle EH1   75 succeded] *add* aftir H2

emperoure, [made] cutte the throte of Sirille for she wolde not do sacrifice, and made alle the other knightez to be byheded, and were beryed with other in the feld of Beren.

Of this marter saiethe Seint Ambrose in his Preface: 'The blessed marter Ipolite | consydered that Ihesu Crist was a verray duke and f. 184rb desired to be his knight, the whiche duke to preue his knight[hode] 81 put Seint Laurence in his kepinge. And this knight not only pursued Seint Laurence but rather mekely folowed hym. And whanne he discuted the tresour of the Chirche he fonde a tresour not suche as the tyrauntes might take awaye fro hym but as pitee hadde 85 possession of, for he fonde that tresour wherinne verray richesse is required and asked. And he despised the fauour of the tyraunt for to preue the grace of the euerlastinge kinge. He fledde not to be dismembred, for he wolde not [in no wise] be dysmembered withe euerlasting bondes.'   90

Here endithe the lyff of Seint Ipolite, and nexst beginnithe the blessed Assumpcion of oure Lady, Cap. .C.xij.^{m}

We fynde in a boke that is sent to Seint Iohn Euuangelist in what manere the assumpcion of oure Lady that blessed Virgine was made. He saiethe how the apposteles were departed and gone into diuerse cuntreyes by cause of predicacion, and that blessed Virgine was in her hous besydes the mount of Syon and visited withe gret deuocyon 5 as longe as she leued alle the places, that is to saye of the bapteme of her sone, of his fastinge, of his passyon, of his sepulture, of hys resureccion and of hys assencion. And after that Epiphanys sayethe, she lyued .xxiiij. yere after the assencion of her sone. And also he sayethe that whanne the Virgine conceyued Ihesu Crist she was of 10 the age of .xiiij. yere and bare hym in her .xv. yere and duelled with hym .xxxiij. yere, and after the dethe of | Ihesu Crist she lyued f. 184va .xxiiij. yere, and after this whanne she passed hennes she was two

76 made] _om._ E   77 beryed] caried H2   81 knighthode] knight E
83 Laurence] _add_ in his kepinge H2   84 discuted] did dicute H2   89 in no wise]
_om._ E

EH1H2A1A2T2L; D resumes at 86 _saiethe_, breaks off after 365 _he_ (_this clerke_ D), resumes at 502 _moder_, breaks off after 637 _vnto_, and resumes at 775 _of her lyght_; H2 breaks off after 827 _lyue it is_ and resumes at 951 _he is_; A1 breaks off after 288 _reson_ and resumes at 606 _not_   Rubric beginnithe] _add_ the lyff of _marked for deletion_ E   1 fynde] rede H2T2
is] was H2   sent] sent _changed to_ set H1   Iohn] _ins._ H1, _add_ the H2   2 Lady] _add_ oure
blessid T2   Virgine] _add_ Marie H2   3 He] that H2, _om._ T2   5 her] _om._ T2
7 sepulture] _add_ and E   9 yere] wynter H2   10 Virgine] blessid virgyn Marie H2

and seventy yere. But it is more prouable thinge that is saide in other
15 places wher it [is] said that she ouerlyued her sone .xij. yere and so
she hadde .lx. yere.

And in a day as the herte of the Virgine was gretly sette afyre with
the desyre of her sone, and her brenninge corage was gretly meued
and braste oute in gret habundaunce of teres, for as moche as she
20 hadde not egally the custumable comfort of her sone whiche were
[fore]drawe for a tyme, and as she satte in this longinge an aungell
appered before her in gret lyght and salowed her worshipfully as
moder of hys Lord and sayde: 'Hayle blessed Marie full of grace,
receiue the blessinge of hym that sent the gretingges to Iacob. See
25 here a bowe of palme that I haue brought you, Lady, oute of paradys,
the whiche thou shalt comaunde to bere before thi bere, for thou
shalt be take oute of body the thridde day for thi sone abidethe þe,
worshipfull moder.' To whom she ansuered: 'Yef I haue founde
grace before thin eyen, I praie the that thou telle me thy name, but
30 yet I praie the more hertly that my sone and my bretheren the
aposteles mow be assembeled byfore me so that before that I deye I
may see hem withe my bodely eyen and, hem present, that I may
yelde up my sperit to God and that I may be beried of hem. And also
I praie the [of more] grace that my sperit goyng oute of the body
35 ne see no horrible spirites and that no power of the enemy come
ayeinst me.'

f. 184vb And thanne saide the aungell to her: 'Whi desire | ye to knowe my
name that is dredfull and meruailous? Alle the aposteles shulle be
assembled this day befor þe and shull do to the noble seruice at youre
40 passinge hennes, and in the presens of hem ye shulle yelde up youre
sperit to God. For he that brought the profete from Iude into
Babyloigne may witheoute doute sodenly and in a moment bringe the
aposteles to you. And whi drede ye, blessed Ladye, to see wicked
sperites, sethe thou haste alle bowed doun hys hede and dispoyled
45 hym of hys empire? But alwayes youre wyll be fulfelled that ye see
hem not.' And this thinge saide, the aungell stied up into heven
withe gret lyght, and the palme shined wonderly bryght and the tree
therof was al grene, but the leues therof shyned as morted sterres.

15 is] *om.* E   17 the] *add* blessid H2   20 sone] *add* blessed E, *so and marked for*
trs. H1   21 foredrawe] withedrawe E   24 sent] gaffe H2   25 a bowe of] aboue a
H2T2   32 hem²] *om.* T2   34 of more] *trs.* E   35 enemy] ennemyes T2
41 profete] parfiȝt H2   43 to you] *om.* T2   blessed] *om.* H2   Ladye] ladies *with es*
erased H1   46 aungell] *add* and than H2   47 palme] *add* that he brought H2
48 morted] mor'ow'tide H1, morveretide *changed to* morwetide H2, morowetide T2

And as it thundered sodenly in heven and Seint Iohn preched in
Ephasim, a white cloude toke hym up and brought hym before the 50
gate of the blessed Uirgine and he knocked atte the dore and came
inne and the virgine gret the Virgine worshipfully. The whiche the
blessed Virgine behelde and abasshed her gretly for ioye and might
not witheholde her from wepinge and saide: 'Iohn, sone, remembre
the of the worde of thi master that recomaundi[d] the to me as my 55
sone and me to the as moder. I am called to oure Lorde to paye the
dette of mannes condicion and therfor withe besy cure I recomaunde
to the my body. For I haue herde saye that the Iues sayne and haue
take counsaile in this wise: "Late us abyde till she that bare Ihesu
Crist be dede and thanne we shull take her body and brenne it." And 60
thy|selff make this palme to be bore before my bere whanne ye bere f. 185ʳᵃ
my body to the sepulcre.' And thanne sayd Seint Iohn: 'A, wolde
God that alle my bretheren were here now, so that we might do the
now couenable seruice and worthi praisingges.' And as he saide that,
alle the apposteles were rauisshed in clowdes fro alle the places ther 65
they preched, and were brought before the dore of the blessed
Virgine Marie. And whanne they saw hem ther assembeled togederes
thei meruayledin gretly and sayden: 'What cause is this that oure
Lorde hathe in this wise assembeled us alle hedyr togederes?' And
thanne Seint Iohn come oute and wolcomed hem and told hem how 70
oure Lady shulde passe oute of this worlde, and saide to hem:
'Bretheren, whanne that she is passed, loke that none of us wepe ne
sorughe leste the peple were troubeled therwith and wolde say: "Lo
here tho that dreden [the] dethe and preche the resureccion."'
And Denis the disciple of Paule affermith this same thinge in the 75
boke of Deuine Names, that is to wete that alle the apposteles were
assembeled atte the assumpcion and atte the passing of oure Lady
and weren togederes there, and eche of hem made hys sermon there
betwene hem to the praysinge of Ihesu Crist and of that blessed
Virgine. And Denis in speking to Timothee saieth in this wise: 80
'Thiselff and we [so] as thou knowest and many other of oure holy

49 Iohn] *om.* T2   50 white] *om.* H2   51 the blessid Uirgine] *add* Marie H2
dore] yate T2   52 the virgine] *add* seinte Iohn H2, he T2   Virgine] *add* Marie H2
54 sone] *om.* H2   55 master] masster E   recomaundid] recomaundithe E
56 called] *add* nowe H2   57 recomaunde] *add* me T2   61 ye] thei T2   62 sayd]
twice T2   64 that] *add* worde H2   66 preched] pleched T2   74 here] *add* be
H2T2   that] *add* wolde T2   the¹] *om.* E   preche the] precheth H1T2   75 this] the
T2   76 of] *add* the H1L   77 and . . . passing] *om.* T2   80 Virgine] *add* Marie
H2   to] of T2   81 so] *om.* EH2

bretheren assembled to the visyon of the body of the moder of the
prince of lyff that receiued God, and Iames the brother of God was
there and Petre and right noble soueraignite of the the[olo]giens.
85 And after that it semed me that alle the ierarchie of aungeles preised |
f. 185rb her after her vertu witheoute ende.' And this saiethe Seint Denis.

And whanne the blessed Virgine sawe alle the aposteles assembeled before her, she blessed oure Lorde and sate in the myddes of
hem alle wher ther brenned lyghtes and laumpes. And aboute the
90 thridde oure of the night Ihesu Crist came withe songe, withe the
orderes of aungeles, the felawshipp of patriarkes and of marteres, the
couent of confessours, the karoll of virgines, the karolles of seintes
were ordeyned and sunge ryght suete songe.

And as it is sayde in the forsaide boke that is set to Seinte Iohn in
95 what wyse the ob[s]eques of the blessed Virgine Marie were halowed
and sayden. For Ihesu Crist beganne and sayde: 'Come my chosen,
and I shall sette the in my sege, for I haue coueited thi beauute.' And
she beganne to saye: 'Lorde, myn hert is redy.' And thanne alle tho
that were come withe Ihesu Crist made a suete so[nge] sayenge:
100 'This is she þat neuer touched the bedde of mariage in delite, and
she hathe fruit in refeccion of holy soules.' And she song of herselff
seyenge: 'Alle generacion sayen that I am blessed, for he that is
mighti hathe done to me grete thingges and the name of hym is
holy.' And the chauntour of chauntours sownyd more excellentely
105 aboue hem alle and saide: 'My spouse, come fro Liban, for thou shalt
be crowned.' And she ansuered: 'I come, for it is wretin of me in the
hede of the boke that I shall do thi wille, Lorde God, for my sperit is
reioysed in God my saueoure.'

And so in the morwtyde the soule went oute of the body and flye
f. 185va into the armes of her sone. And she was also straunge | for sorugh of
111 the flesshe as she was clene fro corrupcion, and thanne saide oure
Lorde to the aposteles: 'Bere ye the body of my moder and Virgine
into the vale of Iosephath and laye her in a newe monument that ye
shull fynde there, and abide me there .iij. dayes til I come ayenne to

83 of lyff] And he H2, *add* and H1T2   84 and . . . soueraignite] the right noble
souereyne H2   soueraignite] soueraignes T2   theologiens] the legiens E, the logiens
H1H2T2 (*thiologiens* P2)   85 it semed me] *om.* H1   that²] *om.* H1T2   of] and T2
86 her after] *om.* H1, there T2   87 Virgine] virgynes D   89 brenned] brennesse T2
91 and] *om.* H1T2D   92 karolles] karokles H1   94 is set] was sente D, is sent T2
95 obseques] L, obieques EH1T2, obeiques D   96 For] *om.* D   99 songe] sowne E
101 fruit] frute *with* u *on erasure* H1   102 sayen] seynge T2   106 she] he T2
109 soule] spirit D   110 for] fro *on erasure* H1   112 Bere ye] burie ȝe D, bery T2

you.' And anone she all bewrapped withe roses that is the ruddy 115
felawship of marteres, withe the lelyes of valees that bene the
felawship of aungelles, of confessours, and of virgines. And the
aposteles crieden after her, sayenge: 'Right wise Virgine, wheder
goest thou? Lady remembre the on us.' And thanne the felawship of
seintes that were abyden were waked withe the soun of the songe of 120
hem that styeden vp and came ayenne. And they sawe a kyng bere in
his propre armes the soule of a woman and sawe that same soule was
ioyned to hym, and they ware abaysshed and beganne to crye sayeng:
'What is she that stiethe up fro desert, flowynge in delyces, ioyned to
her loue?' And tho that were in her felawship ansuered and sayde: 125
'This is she that is the fayrest amonge alle the doughteres of
Ierusalem, and right as ye sawe her full of charite and of loue, so
is she ioyfull receiued into heuenes and she is sette in the sege of
glorie in the right syde of her sone.' And the aposteles sawe the soule
of her so white that none erthely yee myght beholde it [ne no bodely 130
tonge telle it.]

Thre virgines thanne that were there, whan they hadde dispoiled
the body for to wasshe it, behelde and sawe how þat the body shyned
withe so gret a lyght that they might not see it, notwithstondinge that
they feled it, and þat lyght shyned ther as longe as they | were aboute f. 185ᵛᵇ
to wasshe the body. And thanne the aposteles toke the body 136
worshipfully and leyde it on the bere, and Seint Iohn saide to
Petre: 'Bere this palme before the bere, for oure Lorde hath
ordeigned the ouer us and made the sheparde and prince ouer his
shepe.' To whom Peter saide: 'It longithe beter to the to bere hit, for 140
thou art virgine of oure Lorde, so that it is most sittinge that the
virgine bere the palme of the Virgine. And also thou deseruedest to
slepe on the breste of oure Lorde, and there thou lernedest more of
grace and of wysdom thanne any other, and therfor me thinkithe that
it ys most sittynge sethe thou haste receyued more yeftes of grace 145
that thou do more of worship to the Virgine. Thou aughttest bere
this palme of lyght to the obsequies of chastite and of holynesse,

115 she] add was D, add and T2   120 soun] so`u´nne H1   121 styeden] stode D
122 sawe] om. D   124 flowynge] folowinge T2   128 ioyfull] ioifully H1DT2   into
heuenes] yn þe he`ve´nes with to above þe and s del. H1, in the bemes T2   130 ne no] L,
`ne´ H1, ne T2, om. D   bodely] add ne D   130–1 ne . . . it] om. E   132 Thre] The
H1T2D   133 how] om. H1DT2   139 ouer²] ouercome DT2, so with come del. H1
142 virgine] add of oure lord D   bere . . . Virgine] om. T2   Virgine] add Marie D
143 lernedest] lernest H1   144 wysdom] add more subp. D   me thinkithe] we þenke D
147 lyght] riȝt D   of²] add the T2

sethe thou drankest the drinke of the welle of euerlastinge clerenesse,
and I shalle bere the holy body with the bere, and the other aposteles
150 oure bretheren shull goo aboute the body yelding thankyngges to
God.' And thanne saide Paule: 'I that am the leste amonge you alle
shall helpe bere her withe you.' And Peter and Paule lefte up the
bere and Seint Petre beganne to synge and saye: 'Israel is gone oute
of Egipte', and the other aposteles performed the songge. And oure
155 Lorde couered the bere withe a clowde so that thei were not sayen,
but the voys of hem was herde alonly. And the aungelles were withe
the aposteles synginge and fulfellynge alle the erthe by the sowne of
meruaylous suetnesse.

      And thanne alle the peple was meued withe so mervaylous a
160 suetnesse and so suete a melodye and wenten oute of the citee in gret
haste and enquered what it might be. And thanne there were sum
f. 186ʳᵃ that | saide to hem: 'Marie that woman ys dede, and the disciples of
her sone Ihesus beren her to berie and make this melodye aboute her
that ye here.' And than they ranne alle to her armes and stered eche
165 other sayenge: 'Goo we and slee we all the disciples and brenne her
in the fire, the body that bare that traitour.' And whanne the prince
of prestes sawe that, he was abaisshed and full of wratthe and sayde:
'Se here the tabernacle of hym that hathe troubled alle oure kinrede,
lo what worship she receiuithe.' And in that sayenge he sette his
170 honde vpon the bere and wolde haue thrawe it downe to the erthe.
And thanne sodenly his hondes dreied up and weren so fastened to
the bere that he might not remeue hem thennes, and so he hynge by
the hondes and was gretly turmented and wepte sore and cried, and
the aungelles that were than in the clowdes blynded so alle that other
175 peple that they sawe right not. And thanne the prince of prestes
sayde: 'Seint Petre, dispise me not in this tribulacion, and I praie the
make for me praier to oure Lorde for thou shuldest haue in
rememberaunce by the chaumbrere that was vssher and how I
excused the.' And Petre saide: 'We be so lette now by the seruice
180 of oure Lady that we mowe not now entende to hele the, but yef
thou wilt beleue in oure Lorde Ihesu Crist and in this lady here that
bare hym, I hope and wene that thou shalt anone haue hele.' And he

149 I] *om.* T2   153 saye] seid T2   155 were not] *om.* T2   157 sowne] sonne
changed to sovne H1   160 a] *om.* H1DT2   161 enquered] quered T2
163 make] made H1T2   164 that ye here] *om.* H1DT2   165 we²] *om.* H1D
168 kinrede] kynne D   169 worship] lordshippe T2   170 thrawe] drawe D
177 shuldest] woldest H1T2   178 chaumbrere] chaumberer *with 2 minims subp.* H1
180 now] *om.* DT2

ansuered: 'I beleue that he is the verray sone of God and that this here
is hys right holy moder.' And anone hys hondes were vnbounde of the
bere, but the drinesse abode and the sorugh cesed not. Than saide 185
Seint Petre: 'Cusse the bere and | saie: "I beleue in God Ihesu Crist that f. 186rb
this same bare in her wombe and abode virgine after her childinge."'
And whan he hadde so saide he was perfitely hole, and thanne saide
Seint Petre: 'Take the palme of the honde of oure brother Iohn and
touche the blynde peple therwithe, and who that beleuithe shalle mow 190
see ayenne, and tho that will not beleue shall neuer see.'

And thanne the aposteles beringe Marie leiden her in her
monument and sette hem downe besydes her as oure Lorde hadde
comaunded hem. And in the thridde day Ihesu Crist came withe gret
multitude of aungelles and grette hem and saide: 'Pees bc withe you.' 195
And they ansuered: 'God of ioye be withe the that doest only the gret
meruayles.' Than saide oure Lorde to the aposteles: 'What semithe
you now that I aught to do of worship and grace to my moder?' And
they ansuered: 'Lorde, it semithe to us thi servauntes that, right as
thou hast ouercome the dethe and regnist worlde witheoute ende, 200
that thou also areyse the body of thi moder and sette her on the right
syde of hym that is euerlastinge.' And he graunted [it] and Seint
Michaell the archaungell presented the soule of Marie to oure Lorde.
And thanne oure saueoure spake and sayde: 'Arise vp, haste the, my
dovue, tabernacle of glorie, vessell of lyff, heuenly temple, and right 205
as thou [felt]est neuer felth by no touchinge, thou shalt not suffre in
thi sepulcre corrupcion of the body.' And anone the soule of Marie
came ayenne to the body, and in suche wise went oute glorious of the
toumbe and tourned up [to] the chaumbre of the eyre withe grete
felawship withe her. And so it fell that Seint Thom`a's | was not f. 186va
there, and so it fell [anone] that the [girdell] wherwithe [the body] 211
was gert came to hym from the eyre, wherby he vnderstode that she
was stied up into heuene bothe body and soule.

And al that is saide here before is apocrifom, wherof Seint Ierom
saithe in a sermon to Paule and Eustachien: 'This boke is sayde to be 215

187 same] *add* womman D   191 ayenne] aye ayene T2   not] neuere D   192 in
her] *twice* T2   193 monument] *so with* t.. *del. after* u H1, mountment T2   sette] sat
H1T2   194 gret] *om.* D   195 withe] amonge D   201 the²] here *del.* `the H1,
hire T2   202 it] *om.* EH1T2   203 archaungell] *add* come and D   of] *add* the
blessid D   205 dovue] divine D   temple] tererilem T2   206 feltest] L, sufferedest
EH1T2, suffrist D   thou . . . not] *twice* T2   209 to] *om.* E   211 anone] *om.* E
girdell] body E   the body] she E, *add* of þe blessid ladi D   215 Eustachien] *add* seith D
sayde to be] *om.* D   to be] *twice* T2

apocrif saue only to sum wordes that be worthi of faithe and bene
aproued of seintes, that is [as to] .ix. thinges, that is to wete that þe
comfort of the aposteles was behight and youen to the Virgine, and
that thei were assembeled there, and that she passed witheoute
220 sorugh, and that her sepulcre was in the vale of Iosephat, and
there were ordeyned her obsequies, and the deuocion of Ihesu Crist,
and the cominge of alle [the] heuenly felawship, and the persecucion
of Iewes, and the cleringe of myracles, and that she was rauisshed
into heuen in body and soule.' But many other thinggez be sette
225 more there, more of feyning thanne of trouthe as of that Thomas was
not there and that he dredde, and other suche lycly that be rather to
be refused thanne to be beleued.

The clothinge of her as it is wretin were lefte in the comfort of
gode cristen peple, and of one partie of her clothinge sayen men that
230 ther fell a myracle. As the duke of Romaynes had beseged the citee of
Chartres, the bisshop of the citee toke the cote of oure Lady that was
there in kepinge and sette it vpon a spere and went [oute] suerly
ayenst her enemyes and folowed hem, and anone the oste of enemyes
f. 186ᵛᵇ turned into wodenesse and were made blinde and | trembeled and
235 were alle abasshed in her corage. And whanne tho of the towne sawe
this thinge, aboue the devine shewynge thei went fersely and slowe
her enemyes, the whiche thing displesed gretly to the blessed Virgine
Marie so as it was proued by that the cote vnapered anone, and the
duke her enemy felt it in his bosom.

240   It is redde in the Reuelaciones of Seint Elizabethe that, in a tyme
as she was rauisshed in sperit, she sawe in a place fer from the peple
a toumbe or a sepulcre alle environid withe gret lyght, and there was
witheinne the fourme of a woman, and hadde aboute her a gret
multitude of aungeles, and a litell after she was hadde oute of the
245 sepulcre and lefte up an high with that multitude. And thanne came
ayeinst her a man beringe in his right side the signe of the crosse and
hadde withe hym aungelles witheoute noumbre, that receiued her
withe gret ioye and brought her withe gret songe into heuen. And a
lytell while after Elizabethe asked an aungell, that used moche to
250 speke with her, of this vision, the whiche said to her: 'It is shewed to

217 as to] to saye E   218 the²] add blessid D   222 the²] om. EH1T2
225 there] ther 'ere' H1, and T2   more²] om. D   that] ins. T2   232 oute] om. E
233 oste] coste T2   of] add 'þe' H1, so T2   enemyes] enemye H1   236 fersely]
fresshely H1D   239 enemy] enymyes T2   240 redde in the] om. T2   Elizabethe]
add 'þat was þe kynges doȝhter of honglerie' H1   241 she sawe] twice T2   in²] om. T2
244 and] add withynne D   litell] add while D

the in this vision that the Virgine oure Lady is stied up into heuene
as well in flesshe as in sperit.' And so he saieth in this Reuelacion
that it was shewed to her that .xl.^{ti} dayes after her passinge hennes
she was lefte up into heuene in body and soule, and that whanne the
blessed Virgine Marie spake to her, she hadde saide to her that in the 255
yere hole after the ascencion of oure Lorde that she hadde ouerleued
as many dayes as there bene from the day of [the] assencion vnto the
assumption day, and saide her þat | alle the apposteles were withe her f. 187ra
at her passinge hennes and beried her body worshipfully and .xl.
dayes she rose ayenne. And whanne Elizabeth asked her wheder she 260
shulde hide þis misterie or open it, she was ansuered it was not to
shewe it to flesshely peple and misbeleued, nor it is not to hyde
[from] deuoute and cristen peple.

It is [to] knowe that the glorious Uirgine Marie was receyued and
so hadde into heuene worshipfully and excellently. She was receiued 265
holy so as the Chirche beleuithe debonairly, and that [affermen] mani
seintes and shewen it by many resones. And Seint Bernardes reson is
this: sethe God hathe made the bodies of his souerayne seintes as of
Seint Peter, Seint Iames, so gloriously worshipful that he hathe lefte
hem up bi so meruaylous worship that he hathe yeuen hem a 270
couenable place to be worshipped in and that alle the world gothe
to hem. And thanne yef men sayen that the body of Marie is in erthe
and is not haunted by deuout visitacion of good cristen men, it
shulde be meruaile to here that God wold haue done no worship to
the body of his moder and that he hathe not ordeyned her a place to 275
be worshiped inne sethe he worshipithe the bodies of other seintes
here in erthe.

Seint Ierome saiethe that the Virgine Marie stied into heuene the
.[x]viij. kalendes of Auguste, and that saiethe he of the bodely
assumpcion of oure Lady, but the Chirche wol rather mekely 280
drede thanne to de[f]ine any devout cause. And he preuithe that
this thinge is to be byleued: 'Sethe tho that arisen withe oure Lorde

251 Lady] *add* Marie D   257 the day of] *om.* D   the²] *om.* E, *ins.* T2
257–8 vnto . . . day] *ins.* H1, day T2   258 day] *om.* D   and] *add* also she D
259 and²] *add* at the D   260 dayes] *add* ende D   asked . . . wheder] where D   wheder]
'wheþer' H1, *om.* T2   261 it²] *add* þat hit D   262 is] was D   263 from] L, to
EH1DT2   264 to] *om.* ET2   glorious] blessid D   266 holy] ho'o'ly H1   affermen]
after E, affermed T2   269 so] *om.* T2   gloriously] *add* so E, *add* and D   worshipful]
worshipfully ED   271 world] worde T2   272 is] *add* here D   273 is] hit is D, hit
T2   good] *om.* T2   men] peple D   275 his] *add* blessid D   278 the¹] *add* blessid D
279 .xviij.] L, .viij. EH1D   bodely] holy T2   281 define] devine E, defend T2   any]
om. T2   devout] debent D, violent T2   282 withe] withoute D

f. 187rb sayen that the | euerlastinge resureccion is not fulfelled in hem, and
mani leuen that Seint Iohn the Euuangelist reioysethe now in flesshe
285 gloriously withe Ihesu Crist, and whi shulde we not thanne
denouncen that it is in like wise of the blessed Uirgine Marie?'
    Seint Austine [ne] affermithe not this thinge only but prouithe it
withe thre resones. And the furst reson is of the assembelinge of
Ihesu Crist and of the Virgine and saiethe in this wyse: 'Rotones of
290 wormes and reproef of mankinde touchid neuer to Ihesu Crist, and
sethe Ihesu Crist is al oute of that reproef, the nature of Marie is
clene oute for it is preued that Ihesu Crist toke it of her.' The
secounde reson is the dignite of her bodie, wherof he saiethe
hymselff: 'That is the sege of God, the chaumbre of oure Lorde
295 and the tabernacle of heuene, and sethe it is so precious a tresour it is
more able to be kepte in heuene thanne in erth.' The thridde reson is
perfyte holnesse of virginel flesshe, and saiethe in this wise: 'Reioyse
the, Marie, of worshipfull gladnesse in body and in soule, in thin
only sone, [with thin only sone and bi thin only sone], for thou
300 shuldest in no wyse fele the euell of corrupcion that haddest neuer
corrupcion in virginite in childinge so grete a sone, so that thiselff,
that he dowid withe so gret a glorie, be alwey witheoute corrupcion
and leue pure that barest the pure and perfite lyff of alle. She be
withe hym that she bare in her wombe and be in hym, she that bare
305 hym and fedde hym and norisshed hym, Marie moder of Ihesu Crist,
aministresse and seruaunt. And for that I fele none other thinge of
f. 187va her I dare | none other thinge saie.' [And] of her saiethe a noble
versifioure:

310 *Transit ad ethera virgo puerpera uirgula Iesse.*
      Non sine corpore sed sine tempore tendit adesse.

    Secoundely she was lefte up gladly. And of that saiethe Seint
Gerarde bisshop and marter in an omely: 'The heuene receyued this
day the blessed Uirgine, the aungeles were gladd, [the] archaungeles
made ioye, the trones sungen, the dominacions worshipeden, the

283 sayen] seyinge T2   287 Austine] 'Ierom' H1, *so* D, *om.* T2   ne] *om.* E
289 the] *om.* T2   saiethe] sith H1DT2   Rotones] Raciones D   291 sethe] *add* that
T2   293 wherof] where D   297 holnesse] holynesse EH1DT2 (*entierete* P2)
298-9 in thin . . . sone²] *om.* DT2   299 with . . . sone²] *om.* H1   with . . . sone³] L,
om. E   300 of] *ins.* H1, *om.* T2   of . . . neuer] *om.* D   301 in] *add* thi E
virginite] *add* ne D   303 that barest . . . pure] *om.* T2   306 aministresse] a
ministresse E, a minister D, and my fresshe T2   and] *om.* T2   fele] felde T2   none] no
H1, not T2   307 thinge] *om.* H1T2   And] *om.* E   309-10 *space left for Latin* T2
313 the³] *om.* EH1T2

princes made minstralsye, the mightes harpeden, cherubin and 315
seraphin sungen in ledynge her into the sege of the diuine mageste.'

Thirdely she was lefte up worshipfully, for Ihesu Crist hymselff
withe the strengthe of [the] alle heuenly felawshippe came [a]yens
her. Wherof Seint Ierom saiethe: 'What is he that is sufficiaunt to
thenke how the glorious quene of the worlde went in this day, and 320
how alle the multitude of heuenly legiones came ayeinst her withe
gret ioye and deuocion, and with what songe she was brought to her
sege, and how she was receiued of her sone and clipped withe pesible
chere and clere visage, and how she was so haunsed aboue alle
creatoures.' And he saiethe more: '[It] is to leue that in this day the 325
knighthode of heuene cam ayens her with gret haste and environed
the moder of God withe right grete lyght and ledde her euene to her
sege withe praisingges and spirituel songe, and thanne alle the
heuenly Ierusalem gladed hem withe so gret gladnesse that none
herte might thenke it ne tunge tell it, and thei made [ioy and songe] 330
in alle the reioysinge of charite. For this feste whiche is eucry yere
atte this tyme halwed of us, to hem alle there is euer continuel, and it
is to beleue þat | oure saueoure hymselff came in gret haste ayens her f. 187ᵛᵇ
and ledde her withe gret ioye into his sege. And how shulde he haue
fulfelled otherwise that which he hathe comaunded in the lawe: 335
"Worship thi fader and thi moder."'

Ferthely she was lefte up excellently. Seint Ierom saiethe: 'This is
the day in whiche the Uirgine Marie vncorrupte went into the
hynesse of the trone, and she so haunsed in the kingdom of heuene
sittithe glorious in the sege nexst Ihesu Crist.' And the blessed 340
Gerarde in his Omelyes shewithe how she was so haunsed in the
heuenly kingdom and worshipped, and saithe: 'Oure Lorde only may
preise as he dede, so that by continuel praysinge of that mageste
[she] be worship[ed] and environed with alle the compani of
aungeles, enclosed withe the tourbes of archaungeles, posseded 345

315 mightes] potestates D   316 sungen in ledynge] singin del. 'in ledynge' H1,
singes T2   the²] om. T2   318 the²] L, om. EH1DT2   ayens] to yens EH1
322 what] that T2   323 sege] om. T2   324 clere] clerer H1T2   so haunsed]
enhaunsed D   alle] a T2   325 he] om. T2   It is] that is E, that it is H1D (cest P2)
326 ayens] to yens H1   330 ioy and songe] reioysinge E, songe and ioye D   331 in]
with D, om. T2   euery] euyn T2   332 continuel] contynued in hevene D   333 is]
om. T2   haste] hate T2   ayens] add hens del. H1   334 ioye] honoure T2
338 whiche] add was T2   into] in'to' H1   339 she so] trs. D   haunsed] enhaunsid D
341 haunsed] enhauncid D   342 saithe] sith H1D   343 by] om. T2   continuel]
continuelly H1   344 she] L, and EH1T2, om. D   worshiped] worship E   the] om. T2
compani] companyes D

withe trones on eueri syde, gert rounde aboute with songges of
dominaciones, enuironed withe the seruice[s] of mightes, beclipped
withe the embrasinge of princes, turnid aboute withe the worship of
vertues, and obeyed withe the praisinges of cherubin, and posseded
350 alle tyme with the vnspekeable songges of seraphin. And the right
vnspekeable Trinite reioysethe her withe euerlastinge gladnesse, and
his endeles grace reboundethe alle in her and makithe alle other
entende vnto her. The right shyninge ordre of aposteles worshipithe
her, the multitude of marteres besechen her in alle wayes as to her
355 souerayne Lady, the strengthe withoute noumbre of confessours
contynuen her songe before her, the right noble companie of virgines
maken her caroles to the ioye of her, helle full of envy criethe to her
and the wicked fendes dreden her.' |

f. 188ra   A deuout clerke to oure Lady Seint Marie stodied eueri day how
360 he might comfort her ayeinst the .v. woundes of Ihesu Crist,
saienge: 'Reioise the, Uirgine moder of God, reioise the, vncorrupte
that receiued ioye bi the aungell, reioyse the, that bare the lyght of
his euerlastinge lyght, reioise the, moder that were neuer entamid.
Alle feture and alle creature preisin the, holy moder, the Uirgine
365 that bare God, praie for us we beseche the.' And as he hadde be
vexed withe a gret siknesse and drowe to his ende he beganne to
drede and was sore itroubeled. And anone the blessed Virgine
appered to hym and saide: 'Sone, whi art thou troubeled with so
grete fere that so many tymes hast anounced ioye to me? Wherfore
370 reioyse the now thiselff, and for that thou shalt [haue] endeles ioye,
come forthe with me.'

Ther was a wylde monke but yet he was devoute to oure Lady.
And as he went in a night to his leude custume but yet as he went by
the auuter of oure Lady he salowed the Virgine and so he went forth,
375 and as he passed a flode he fille into the water and was drowned. And
anone the fendes rauisshed the soule, but anone there come aungeles
to deliuer her. And the fendes saide to hem: 'What do ye here? Whi
come ye hedir? Ye haue no part in this soule.' And anone the blessed
Virgine Marie came and blamed hem for thei hadde take the soule
380 that was hers. And thei saide that he was take in his wicked dedes

347 seruices] L, seruice EH1DT2   353 ordre] virgyn othir D   354 besechen]
besechinge T2   356 contynuen] continuent T2   357 maken] makynge T2   helle]
hele H1T2   full] foull T2   envy] erased H1   361 Reioise] reioisinge T2   365 he]
this clerke D   370 haue] om. E, ins. H1, to T2   372 wylde] wicked H2T2
375 flode] folde T2   the] a T2   377 her] add of the fendes T2

and there they founde hym. And she saide: 'That is fals that ye saye, for I wote well that whanne he went into any place he wolde salowe me atte his goinge and atte his comynge. And | yef ye saie that I do you wronge, late us putte it in the iugement of the souerayne kinge.' And whanne they strouen before oure Lorde of this thyng, yt lyked hym that the soule shuld turne ayenne to the body and repent hym of his misdedes. And than the bretheren sawe that Matenes taried to longe and went and sought her sextayne, till atte the laste thei come to the water and there they fonde hym drowned, and whanne thei hadde drawen oute the bodye of the water and meruailed who had do that, he turned sodenly to lyff and tolde alle the manere, and so by helpe of oure Lady he ended his lyff in good werke[s].

Ther was a knight that was mighti and riche, the whiche hadde spended so vnwisely his goodez that he was come to so gret pouert that he that was wont to grete thingges was now full gladde to aske smal thingges. And he hadde a full chaste lady to his wyff and a full devoute to the blessed Virgine Marie. And so it fell that a gret sollempnite neighed, in which this knight was wont to yeue gret yeftes and now he hadde nothinge to yeue, wherfor he was full of sorugh and shame and went into a desert place full of sorugh and of wepinge into the tyme that the feste were passed, there for to wepe his wicked fortune and eschewe shame. And anone ther come to hym a man right foule and horrible sittinge vpon a foule blacke hors, that aresoned this knight and asked hym the cause of his sorugh and hevinesse. And he tolde al by ordre, and thanne he saide: 'Yef thou wilt a litell obeye me, thou shalt habound | in more ioye and richesse thanne euer thou dede.' And he anone made promesse to the prince of derkenesse þat yef he wolde fulfell that, that he wolde do what he wolde. And thanne he saide hym: 'Go home into thine hous and seke in suche a place, and thou shalt finde there so moche golde [and] so moche siluer and so moche of precious stones, and thanne do so moche for me that thou bringe me thi wiff atte suche a day.' This knight retorned to his hous by the promys and sought in the place

f. 188rb

385

390

395

400

405
f. 188va

410

381 That] it H1H2T2   is] was H2   fals] falsi *on* falti H1   ye saye] thei seide T2
383 atte²] as T2   384 the¹] *om.* H1T2   387 to] *om.* H2   388 her] the T2
390 who] he *del.* 'who' H1, how he H2   391 sodenly] ayen H2   392 werkes]
werke E   399 and now] anow T2   400 a] *om.* H2   401 the²] *om.* H1
403 right] *om.* H2   foule] full H1T2   405 he¹] the knyȝte H2   al] him T2   ordre]
oþe T2   he²] the feende H2   409 he] the feende H2   410 and²] *om.* E
413 retorned] *add* ayene H1H2T2   hous] place H2   by the] and made H2   promys] *add*
to the feende that he shold bringe him his wyfe. And whan he come home H2

wher he hadd saide and he fonde alle that was behight hym. And
415 anone he bought hym places and gaue gret yeftes and bought ayenne
his heritage and toke mani seruauntes to hym.

And so it fell that the day neyghed fast that he hadde behight to
lede his wyff to hym, and called his wyff and saide: 'Take youre hors,
for ye most ride withe me into a sertaine place.' And she trembeled
420 and hadde gret drede, and she durst not withesaye the comaundement of her lorde, but recomaunded her deuoutely to the kepinge of
the blessed Uirgine Marie and went with her lorde. And whanne
they were go a litell ferre, they sawe in the way a chirche, and she
lyght downe and entred into the chirche and her husbonde abode
425 witheoute. And she recomaunded her deuoutely to the blessed
Virgine Marie, and sodenly she fell aslepe, and the glorious Virgine
clothed her in the clothinge of that lady and parted from the auuter
and went oute and toke the hors and lefte the bodi lyenge aslepe, and
he wende that it had be his wyff and rode forthe hys waye.

f. 188vb   And whanne he was come | into the place ordeyned, the prince of
431 derkenesse cam withe gret afraye to the place, and whanne he
neyghed he beganne to tremble and quake and durst go no nere,
but saide to the knight: 'Thou most traitour of alle men, whi hast
thou scorned me thus and hast yolde me euell for right gret good that
435 I haue done to the? I bade the that thou shuldest haue brought me
thi wiff, and thou hast brought me the moder of God. I wold haue thi
wiff, and thou hast brought me Marie. For thi wyff hathe done to me
many gret iniuries and I wold haue take veniaunce of her, and thou
hast brought me suche one for to turment me and sende me to helle.'
440 And whanne the knight herde this he was gretly abasshed and might
not speke for drede and for meruayle, and thanne the blessed Marie
saide: 'Thou felon sperit, by what folye durst thou wilne for to anoye
my devout seruaunt? It shall not be lefte in the vnponisshed, wherfor
I iuge the in this sentence that thou descende into helle and that thou
445 fro hennes forwarde haue none presumpcion to anoye none that
requirethe myn helpe.' And thanne he strongely crienge and roring
[fledde awaye], and this knight lyght downe of his hors and fell on

414 he] the feende H2   418 hym] the feende H2   423 ferre] wey T2
425 she] s`h'e H1   428 oute] *add* of the chirche H2   bodi] ladi H2   429 he] the
knyght H2   that] *om.* H1   it] she H2   430 was] *add* nyghe H2   into] ny to H1H2T2
434 thou] *om.* T2   435 the^1] *add* And H1T2   437 and . . . Marie] *om.* H2
439 brought] *om.* H2   sende] sene T2   441 blessed] *add* virgyn H2   442 by what]
twice T2   wilne] wille H2   446 crienge] cried H2, criden T2   roring] rorid H2
447 fledde awaye] L, *om.* EH1H2T2   fell] *add* adoun H2

his knees and asked mercy of that blessed Lady, and she blamed hym
and comaunded hym to retorne to his wyff that slepte yet in the
chirche, and bade hym that he shulde putte oute alle the richesse of 450
the fende and abide alway in the praysinge of oure Lady. And sethe
they receyued gret richesse bothe bodely and gostely that oure
blessed Lady sent hem, to whos goodnesse be endeles worship and
ioye. Amen.

Ther was a man that was ra|uisshed in iugement before God for he f. 189ra
hadde done gret synnes, and the fend was there redy and sayde: 'Ye 456
haue nothinge in this soule but she aught to be myn for I haue
[thereof an] instrument publike.' 'Wher is thine instrument?' saide
oure Lorde. 'I haue,' he saide, 'instrument that thou saydest with
thine owne mouthe and ordeyne[de]st it to endure perpetuelly, for ye 460
saide: "What oure that ye ete of that fruit ye shull deye." And this
here is of the kynrede of hem that ete of the mete that was forboden
hem, and therfor bi right of this instrument publike he shulde duell
withe me by iugement.' And thanne saide oure Lorde: 'Lete the man
speke for hymselff.' And he helde his pees. Thanne the fende spake 465
ayenne and saide: 'She is myn by prescripcion of tyme, for I haue
hadde possession of her this .xxx.ti wynter and hathe obeyed me as
my propre seruaunt.' And yet the man held hys pees. And yet saide
the fende: 'She is myn, for though she haue done any good dede the
euil that she hathe do passithe it witheoute any comparison.' And 470
thanne oure Lorde wold not geue anone sentence ayeinst hym, but
gaue hym respite of .viij. dayes so that atte the .viij. dayes he shulde
apere before hym and yeue reson to alle these thingges.

And as he went [fro] before oure Lorde trembelinge, he mette a
man that asked hym the cause of so grete sorugh. And he tolde hym 475
alle by ordre, and thanne he saide hym: 'Drede the not and haue no
fere, for I shall helpe the mightely of the furste.' And he asked hym
what he hight, and he saide: 'My name is Veritee.' And after that he
mette withe another and he behight hym to helpe hym of the 479
secounde, and whanne he as|ked hym his name he saide: 'I am f. 189rb

450 bade] om. H2   the richesse] thoo richesses H2   451 fende] feendis H2
454 Amen] om. H2   457 she] om. T2   for] om. H2   458 thereof an] L, om.
EH1H2T2 460 thine owne mouthe] oon moneth with e subp. H1, so T2   ordeynedest] L,
ordeynest EH1H2T2   ye] yet changed to ye H1, he H2   461 oure] euer T2   463 bi]
om. T2   467 me] followed by erasure H1   469 though] trouthe T2   470 euil] wil
H1T2H2   471 ayeinst] vppon H2   472 that] om. H2   atte] om. H1   dayes²] add
ende T2   474 as] om. H1T2   fro before] fro L, before EH1H2T2 (de deuant P2)
trembelinge] add and H2   477 mightely] myghti T2   of the furste] om. H2
479 another] add man H2   hym²] add also H2   480 whanne he] than the soule H2

called Rightwisnesse.' And thanne whan he come before the iuge and
the fend apposed hym of the furst cause and Trouthe ansuered: '[W]e
kn[o]we welle that there is double dethe, that is bodely and gostely,
and that instrument that the fende alegithe ayens the spekithe not of
485 the dethe of helle but of the dethe of the body. And of that he is alle
clere, that sethe alle be enclosed in that sentence that they shull deye
in her bodyes, yet shull they not deye alle in dethe of helle. For as to
the dethe of the body, the sentence is to endure alwaye, but as to the
dethe of the soule, that is repeled bi the dethe of Ihesu Crist.' And
490 [than] the fende sawe that he was caste of the furst, and purposed the
secounde, but Rightwisnesse came and ansuered for that in this wyse:
'Though it be so that he hathe be thi seruaunt many yeres, yet alweye
reson withesaide hym euer, and groched euer that he saide hym so
wicked a seruaunt.' But to the thridde obiecte he hadde no helpe, and
495 than oure Lorde sayde: 'Do bringe forthe the balaunce and alle shalle
be wayed, good and euill.' And thanne Trouthe and Rightwisnesse
saide to the sinfull: 'Renne withe alle thi mynde to the Lady of mercy
that sittithe besydes the iuge and studye in what wise thou maist beste
calle her vnto thine helpe.' And whanne he hadde so done, that
500 blessed Lady come vnto his help and leyde her hande vpon the
balaunce in that partye wher that ther was but litell goodes, and the
fende enforsed hym to drawe in his partie, but the moder [of mercy]
ouercome hym and delyuered the synfull. And thanne he came to
f. 189ᵛᵃ hymselff and chaunged | his lyff into beter.
505   Hit befell in the citee of Burgis aboute the yere of oure Lorde fiue
hundred .xxvij. that as cristen men were hoseled on a Esterne Day, a
childe of a Iewe went to the auuter withe other children of cristen
men and receiued the body of oure Lorde as other dede. And
whanne he come home [his fader] asked hym whennes he come, and
510 he saide he come from the chirche withe cristen children that he
hadde goo to scole with and hadde be hoseled withe hem at the
masse. And thanne the fader full of wodenesse toke the childe and
cast hym in a brenninge furneys that was there. And thanne the

481 and] *om.* H2   482 of] *om.* H1T2   482–3 We knowe] L, he knewe EH1T2,
ye knowe H2   485 helle . . . of³] *om.* T2   486 sethe] seithe H2   487 to] *om.*
H1T2   489 the²] *om.* H1T2   490 than] *om.* E   491 and] *om.* T2   492 that]
add þat T2   alweye] *twice once del.* H1   493 groched] gorched T2   494 he hadde]
twice T2   no] none to his H2   495 alle] *om.* T2   499 her] *om.* H2   501 goodes]
godesse T2   502 of mercy] L, *om.* EH1T2, of God D   503 came] *add* aȝen D
504 beter] *add* Amen D   505 Burgis] Brugis D, Bruges T2   509 he¹] the childe D
his fader] L, he EH1T2, the fader D   510 he come] *om.* D   511 be] *ins.* H1
513 brenninge] *om.* T2   thanne] *om.* T2

moder of God cam in the same lyknesse that the childe hadde sayen
the image vpon the auuter, and kepte hym fro the fire that he hadde 515
none harme. And the fader bi his crienge hadde assembeled togedre
bothe cristen men and Iues a gret noumbre whiche sawe the childe in
the furneis and hadde none disese, and toke hym out and asked hym
how he scaped that harme. And he saide that a worshipfull lady that
was vpon the auuter halpe hym and dede awaye the brenninge of the 520
fire from hym. And [than] the cristen vnderstode that it was the
image of the blessed Uirgine Marie and toke the fader of the childe
and caste hym in the furneis and he was anone brent and wasted.

In a tyme there were monkes that before [the] day walked on a
watersyde and iangeled fast many fabeles and ydel tales. And thanne 525
thei herde grete rowynge withe ores in the water and cominge faste
to hem warde, and the monkes asked what thei were | and thei saide: f. 189ᵛᵇ
'We be deueles that bere the soule of Eubronen into helle, þat was
stuarde of the kingges hous of Fraunce, and was apostata of the
chirche [of] Seint Gal.' And [whan] the monkes herd that thei 530
dradde hem gretly and crieden strongly: 'Seint Marie, praie for us.'
And thanne the fendes sayde: 'In a good tyme ye haue called Marie,
for we wolde haue deuoured you and drowned you for that we
founde you so dissolutly iangle ouer youre houre.' And thanne the
monkes turned to her couent and the fendes into helle and the helpe 535
of oure Lady [is] euer redy to alle, blessed mot she be. Amen.

Ther was a woman that susteyned gret iniurie[s] withe a fende the
whiche appered to her visebely in fourme of a man, and many
remedies were taught her, sumtyme holy water, sumtyme other
thingges, but his malyce sesed not. And thanne an holy man 540
counsailed her that whan he come to her that she shulde lefte up
her hondes and saye withe alle her herte: 'Seint Marie helpe me.'
And whanne she dede so, the fende helde hym stille and fulle of
drede as thou he hadde be smeten withe a stone and saide: 'A wicked
fende entre into the mouthe [of hym] that taught the that.' And 545
anone he vanisshed awaye and came neuer after to her more.

514 hadde] om. T2   518 disese] disseease with ease del. and ese ins. H1
519 that²] suche D, om. T2   521 than] om. EH1T2   524 the] a E, om. D
525 fast] add of T2   526 grete] om. D   rowynge] rounynge changed to rowynge H1,
rownynge T2   530 of] and E   Gal] Gill T2   whan] om. EH1T2   that] add and
EH1T2   531 strongly] stoutly T2   532 fendes] feende D   535 turned] add
aȝen D   536 is] om. EH1T2   537 iniuries] iniurie EH1T2   541–2 that² . . . her¹]
om. DT2   542 and] þat she shold D   withe . . . herte/Seint . . . me] trs. D
543 stille] fall T2   545 of hym] om. E   that²] ins. H1, om. DT2

The manere of the assumpcion of the right holy Virgine Marie is
take in a sermon made and ordeyned of diuerse sayengges of seintes,
the whiche is solempnely redde in many chirches, and therein is
550 conteyned: 'Alle that euer I might [fynde] in alle the worlde in
narraciones of faders of the passinge hennes of the right holy Virgine
moder of God, the whiche I haue sette here to her praysinge endeles.'
f. 190ra   Seint Cosme that | was named [V]esture saide that by sertaine
reuelaciones he lerned of his beforegoers whiche is not to be foryete
555 and saiethe: 'Whanne Crist disposed to lede to hym the lyff of his
moder, he sent to her the custumed aungell for to shewe her the tyme
of her partynge, that dethe shulde not come sodenly to her, to yeue
her ani tribulacion. For she had praied hym face to face in erthe that
she shulde see no wicked sperites. Wherfor he sent [the] aungell
560 before to her withe suche wordes: "It is tyme to take my moder to me
and withe me. And right as thou hast fulfelled the erthe with ioye,
now make heuene [to] reioyse; thou shalt yelde ioyfully alle the
duellynge places of my fader, thou mayst comfort the sperites of my
seintes; be not lothe to leue the world withe his coueytise, but take the
565 heuenly palays. Moder, be not aferde to be take oute of the flesshe,
thou þat art called [to] euerlastinge lyff, to ioye withoute faylinge, to
rest of pees, to a sure conuersacion, to a refeccion vnnumerable, to
lyght that may not be quenched, to the day that hathe none euetyde,
to the ioy that may not be tolde, to myselff thine owne sone þat am
570 maker of alle thinge. For I am lyff euerlastinge, a love withoute
comparison, a duellynge place vnspekable, a lyght that hathe no
derkenesse, a goodnesse that may not be ymagened. Yeue witheoute
trembelynge to the erthe that is his. For none may rauisshe the oute of
myn hondes, for in myn hondes be alle the endes of erthes. Take me
575 thi body, for I putte in thi wombe my godhede. The dethe shalle
neuer haue ioye in the, for thou bare the lyff; the shadue of derkenesse
f. 190rb may neuer derken the, for thou broughtest the lyght; | contricion of
peyne may not environe the, for thou deseruedest to be my vessell.
'"Come now anone to hym that is born of the, for to receiue the
580 guerdon of the wombe of the moder and the mede of the melke and

549 many] om. D   550 fynde] om. ET2, ins. H1   552 here to] to D, om. T2   to
her] ins. H1   endeles] enelles T2   553 Vesture] Besture ED, so with initial b or v H1
555 saiethe] sith H1DT2   lede] be ledde H1T2   the] add last D   557 partynge] add
hens D   559 she] om. D   the] L, an EH1DT2   560 before] om. D   562 to]
om. E   ioyfully] ioyful thingis to D   566 to¹] om. E   567 a sure] assure D
572 ymagened] add I D   withoute] with T2   573 is] add of E   574 for . . . hondes]
om. T2   577 of] nor D   578 not] neuer D

of þe mete thou gauest hym, come on faste and haste the to be
ioyned to thine only sone. I wote well thou shalt not be constreined
by none other sone, but by me only that shewed the Virgine and
moder. I haue shewed the a walle to alle the worlde, an arche of
sauacion, a brigge to hem that be fletynge, a staffe to the feble, a 585
ladder for stiers to heuene, a meke besecher for the synfull. I shall
bringe alle my apposteles to the, of whiche thou shalt be beryed right
as of myn owne hondes. For it longithe to my spirituel children of
my lyght, to whom I haue take the holy goste, to byrie thi body and
that they fulfelle in thi persone the seruise of thi meruaylous 590
passinge hennes." And after that the aungell hadde tolde this to
the Virgine he gaue her a bowe of palme sent fro the p[lant]e of
paradys in certeinte of victorie ayeinst the corrupcion of dethe and
clothinge of dedlynesse, and whanne he hadde alle this saide and
done he went to heuene whennes he come. 595

'And thanne the blessed Virgine assembeled her neygheboures and
frendes togeder withe her cosenes and saide hem: "I do you to wete
that I am at the departinge of this bodely lyff, wherfor it behouithe to
wake, for to eueriche that passithe oute of this worlde the devine
aungeles and wicked sperites comyn gladly." And whanne thei hadde 600
herde that, they beganne alle to wepe and to saye: "A, whi dredest
thou the faces of sperites, | that hast deserued to be moder of the f. 190va
maker of alle thinge, that bare hym that robbed helle, that hast
deserued to haue the sege aboue cherubin and seraphin? What shull
we thanne do and wheder shull we flee?" And there were gret 605
multitude of women wepinge and sayenge that she lefte hem not
orphanins. And the blessed Virgine saide in comfortinge hem: "Ye
that be moders of corruptible sones kunne not suffre a while to be
departed from hem; how shulde I than [not] desire to go to my sunne
that am moder and Virgine, and he only the sone of God the father?" 610
And in the mene tyme that they spake these wordes, blessed Seint
Iohn cam and enquered how that thinge went. And whanne the
Virgine hadde told hym her hasty passinge hennes, he felle hym

581 on] oute D   582 ioyned] ioyed *del.* ioyned T2   thine] him *del.* `þyne´ H1, him
thyne D, him T2   well] *om.* D   588 of¹] *om.* DT2   589 to²] *om.* H1DT2
592 the¹] *add* blessid D   plante] palme E   593 certeinte] certeyn T2
594 dedlynesse] delynesse T2   alle this saide] *twice* T2   598 the] *om.* T2
bodely] dedeli H1DT2   600 comyn] commyng H1T2   601 A] *om.* T2   dredest]
deddest T2   603 hym] *add* And D   604 cherubin] þe rubin T2   seraphin] *add* in E
609 how] whi D   not] *om.* E   go] to *changed to* go H1   610 and¹] a T2
613 hasty] hastely H1

downe to the erthe and cried withe teeres sayenge: "Lord, what be
615 we? Whi sendest thou us so moche tribulacion? Whi hast thou not
rather take aweye my soule fro [the] body so that I were rather visited
of the moder of my Lorde and þat I were not atte her passing
hennes?" And thanne the blessed Virgine ledd hym wepinge into her
chaumbre and shewed hym the palme and her clothinge, and sethe
620 she leyde her on her bedde for to be there vnto her passinge.

'And anone a right grete thunderclappe cam, and sodenly all the
aposteles were brought in a white cloude as thou thei hadde reyned.
And as they meruailed of this thinge Seint Iohn came to hem and
tolde hem that was anounced to the blessed Virgine Marie. And as
625 thei sore wepten alle, Seint Iohn comforted hem. And thanne thei
f. 190vb wyped her eyen and went to | the blessed Virgine and salwed her
worshipfulli. And she saide to hem: "My dere children, God my
sone kepe you." And whanne thei hadde tolde her thaire coming, she
tolde hem al her estate. And thanne the aposteles said: "Right
630 worshipfull Virgine, we behold the and be comforted right as in
hymselff oure Lorde and oure maister, and we haue that only
comfort in you that we hope that ye will be a mene to God for
us." And whanne she hadde salowed Paule by name he saide to her:
"God saue the, expositour of myn comfort, though it be so that I
635 haue not seyn Ihesu Crist in flesshe, yet alway I haue sein the in
flesshe, and I am comforted as though I sawe hym. And into this day
I haue preched vnto the peple that thou hast born Ihesu Crist, and
now I shall preche that thou art born to hym."

'And after that the Uirgine shewed hem that the aungell hadde
640 brought to her, and charged hem that the lightes were in no wise
quenched till her passing hennes. And ther were six score uirgines
to serue her and than she clothed the clothinge of mortalite and
salowed hem alle and ordeyned her body into her bedde to abide her
tyme, and Se[i]nt Peter sette hym atte her hede and Seint Iohn atte
645 her fete, and the other aposteles were aboute the bedde and praised
the Virgine moder of God. And thanne Seint Petre beganne to
syngge and saide: "Reioyse the, spouce of God, in the heuenly

614 cried] L, *add* hym EH1DT2   615 thou not] *trs.* H1   616 the] my E
617 of¹] than D   621 a right] *trs.* H1   all] *om.* T2   622 white] *om.* D
623 meruailed] L, *add* all EH1DT2   625 Seint Iohn] *om.* D   hem] *add* alle T2
628 tolde] *add and del.* yeue T2   629 thanne] thus T2   632 in] in//in T2
a mene] amen T2   638 I] *om.* T2   642 clothed] *add* her in H2T2
mortalite] moralite T2   644 and¹] *twice* T2   Seint] sent E   647 the¹] *twice*
EH1

chaumbres, thou chaundeler of light witheoute derkenesse, bi the only ys shewed the euerlastinge light."'

The blessyd Archebisshopp of Constantynople witnessithe that 650 alle the aposteles were assembled atte the passinge hennes of the holy Uirgine and the | right suete moder of God, and saiethe in this wise: f. 191ra 'Though it be so, thou Goddes moder, that thou hast receyued of mankinde the dethe that may not be eschewed, yet the yee that beholdith there shall neuer slepe ne slombre. Thi passinge and thi 655 slepinge shal not be witheoute witnesse, the heuene shall tell the ioy of hem that singe ouer the, and the erthe shall shewe the trouthe of hem, the cloudes shull crye worship to the and to hem that amynistre the fro hem, the aungelles shull preche the seruise of lyff done to the by the aposteles that were assembled in Ierusalem to the.' 660

The grete Denice Aropagite witnessithe this thinge in this same wise sayenge: 'We, as I knowe wel, and they and many other of oure bretheren were assembeled to see the body of her that bare God. And Seint Iame, brother of God, and Seint Petre, noble doctour and right grete souueraigne of the noble theolegens were present, and it liked 665 hem all after the vision, alle tho souerayne prestes to syng praisingges after that eueriche hadde conceiued the bounte of her in his thought.'

And Seint Cosme foluyng his narracion saiethe: 'After [that], the grete thunderclap smote atte the hous and a suete sperit fulfelled the hous withe so grete suetnesse of suete saueoure þat alle tho that were 670 there save the aposteles and .iij. uirgines that helde the lyghtes slepte strongely. And than came oure Lorde withe grete multitude of aungelles and toke the soule of his moder. And the soule of her shyned bi so gret clerenesse that none of the aposteles myght beholde it. And thanne oure Lorde saide to Petre: "Berye the body of my 675 moder withe gret reuerence and kepe her | .iij. dayes, and thanne f. 191rb shall I come and bere her to a place witheoute corrupcion and I shall clothe her with likly light of myselff, so that [that] I haue take of her [and] that she hathe take of me be togederes assembled and accorded."' 680

That same Seint Cosme tellithe a dredfull and a meruailous misterie, and that hathe no nede of naturell discussion ne of corious inquisicion, for alle tho thingges that be saide of the Uirgine Marie

650 Archebisshopp] archibisshuppis T2   651 holy] blessid H2   653 Goddes] good H2   654 the²] *om.* T2   657 shewe] tell T2   658–9 amynistre the fro] haue ministred to the for H2   668 saiethe] *add* that T2   that] L, *om.* EH1H2T2 669 and] *om.* H2   671 save] sawe H1H2T2   674 gret] *add* light and H2 678 likly] lightly H1T2   that²] L, *om.* EH1H2T2   679 and¹] L, *om.* EH1H2T2

moder of God be meruailous and aboue kinde, and be more to drede
685 thanne to enquere. 'For whanne the soule went oute of the body, the
body saide these wordes: "Lorde, I yelde the thankingges that am
worthi of thi grace, remembre the of me for I am but a thinge feint
and haue kept that thou tokest me." And thanne they awoke and
sawe the body witheoute soule and beganne to wepe and make moche
690 sorugh. And thanne the apposteles toke the body of the Uirgine and
bare it to the monument, and Seint Peter beganne the [ps]alme of *In
exitu Israel de Egipto etc.* And the companies of aungelles preised the
Virgine in suche wise that alle Ierusalem was meued withe gret ioye
so that the souerayne prestes sent gret multitude of peple with
695 suerdes and staues. And one of hem maddyng come to the bere withe
gret bruit and wolde haue drawe it doune to the erthe with the body
of the Uirgine moder of God. And for that he enforced hym
wickedly for to drawe [doune] the body, he loste hys hondes by
desert, for bothe hondes were cutte of by the wrestys and hangged bi
700 the bere and was turmented withe horrible sorugh. And thanne
anone he asked foryeuenesse and behight amendement, and than |
f. 191ᵛᵃ Seint Peter saide to hym: "Thou maist in no wise haue foryeuenesse
but yef thou kesse the bere of the blessed Virgine, and also but yef
thou knowlache Ihesu Crist to be the verray sone of God formed
705 witheinne her." And whan he hadde so done his hondes were ioyned
to his wrestes ayenne and were al hole, and Seint Peter toke after that
a leeff of [the] palme and saide: "Go into the citee and laye this vpon
the sike, and tho that wol beleue shull resseiue hele."

   'And thanne whanne the apposteles come to the place of Ghersa-
710 mye, thei founde a sepulcre like to the sepulcre of Ihesu Crist, and
therinne thei putte the body with gret reuerence, and durst not
touche the right holy vessell of God, but toke the sydoyne wherinne
she was wrapped and leyde her witheinne the sepulcre. And as the
apposteles were aboute the sepulcre after the comaundement of oure
715 Lorde, the thridde day a cloude right shyninge environed the
sepulcre, and the voys of aungelles sowned, meruailous suetnesse
was felt, and whanne oure Lorde was sayen descende there alle were
meruaylously abasshed, and he toke withe hym the body of the

687 feint] sent T2   690 the³] *add* blessid H2   691 psalme] spalme E
696 bruit] briut῾ht′ H1   697 the] *add* blessid H2   698 doune] *om.* EH1T2
699 by] *om.* T2   704 the] *om.* T2   705 ioyned] *add* here *del.* ῾to hys′ H1
707 the¹] L, *om.* EH1T2   710 like to the] þe *del.* ῾like to þe′ H1   like . . . sepulcre] *om.*
H2T2   717 sayen] slayn T2   descende] descendid H2T2   718 the²] *add* blessid
H2

Virgine withe right gret ioye. And thanne the aposteles kessed the
sepulcre with right gret reuerence and retorned into the hous of 720
Seint Iohn the Euuangelyst in praysinge that he was keper of so
noble a Uirgine. And notwithestondinge one of the aposteles fayled
at so grete a solempnitee, and whan he herde the gret miracles he
required withe gret desyre that they wolde open the sepulcre that he
mighte knowe the trouthe of all these thingges. And whanne the 725
aposteles refused it and sayde that it ought suffise | the witnesse of so f. 191vb
gret persones, leste perauenture [that] misbeleued folke wold saie that
the body were stole away, and thanne was he wrothe and said: "Whi
defrauude ye me that am lyke to you in youre comune tresoures?"
And so atte the laste thei opened the sepulcre and fonde not the body, 730
but thei founde alonly the vestement and the sidoine.
    'Seint Germain, archebisshop of Constantinenople, saiethe that he
fonde wrete in a Storie Euthimathien in the thridde boke in the .xl.^ti
chapitre, and that same witnessithe the gret Damecien, that as the
right noble emperice in mynde of holy Chirche and made many 735
chirches in Constantinople, and among other she edefyed in the tyme
of Mercien emperour, of Balthenis a meruailous faire chirche in the
worship of the Virgine Marie, and called to her Iuuenall the
ershebisshop of Ierusalem and other bysshopes of Palestine that
duelled [than] in that citee riall, for the same that hadde be done in 740
Calcedonie, and saide to hem: "We haue herde that the body of the
right holy Virgine is in a tombe in the gardyne of Getsemany,
wherfor we desyre for kepinge of this citee that the blessed body of
that holy Virgine be brought hedir withe dewe worship." And
Iuuenal ansuered her as he hadde founde in olde stories, how that 745
the body had be bore into ioye withe her sone and that ther was
nothing lefte in her sepulcre but only her clothinge and her sidoigne,
and that same Iuuenal sent tho vestementes into Constantinople and
there thei were ordeyned full worschipfully. And lete none suppose
that of my propre witte I haue saide and feyned these thingges, but I 750
haue sette here suche thingges as by | doctrine and studie I hadde f. 192ra
lerned of hem that by verray tradicion haue receiued hem of the furst
of her forgoers.' And vnto this tyme bene the wordes of the forsaide
sermon.

722 a] om. H1   723 gret] add mervailes of þe H1H2T2   726 refused] add for to do
H2   suffise] suffice with s on erased þe H1, add him H2   727 that¹] L, her EH1H2T2
729 that] and H2T2   730 thei] their E   733 the²] `þe´ H1   734 as] is T2   738 to
her] om. H2   740 than] L, om. EH1H2T2   742 right holy] blessid H2   744 that holy]
the H2   748 tho] two H1H2T2   752 by] om. H1T2   753 her forgoers] the forgers H2

755   Verrely Iohn Damacyen, that for that tyme was a Greke, saieth
mani meruailous thingges of the assumpcion of the right holy
Virgine Marie, the whiche he preised in his sermones and saide:
'On this day was the right holy Virgine borun into heuene; on this
day the holy [an]nuel arche that bare withinne her hir maker is sette
760 in the temple that is not made withe honde; on this day the right
holy innocent dowue flie from the arke, that is to say her body, the
whiche God receyued and she fonde reste atte his fete; on this day
the Virgine witheoute any spotte, vnknowen of erthely passiones but
taught withe heuenly vnderstondyngges, shall not faile but shall be
765 called verrai [an]nuel heuene, duellinge in heuenly tabernacles. And
thow it be so that the right holy and blessed soule be deseuered fro
the right holy body and that the blessed body be laide in the
sepulcre, sothely he shall not duell in dethe ne it shall neuer be
dissolued by corrupcion. That is to saye, the body of whos birthe the
770 virginite abideth witheoute corrupcion, and of this uirginite abidethe
the body witheoute any dissolucion and is bore to a beter and a more
holy lyff, neuer for to be corrupte withe dethe but for to abide in the
euerlastinge tabernacles. And right as this shining sonne is lefte up,
the body seminge for a whiles defaylinge, notwithestondinge that she
775 hath nothinge loste of her lyght but hathe in herselff a welle of
euerlastinge lyght, and thou art verray welle of light withoute
wastinge and perfit tresour of lyff, thou it be so that by a shorte
f. 192rb inter|ualle of tyme thou be bodely ledde to the dethe, yet alway thou
yeuest us abundaunce of clerenesse of light with[oute] defaylinge.
780 And thin holy slepinge is not called dethe, but a passinge or a
departinge, or more properly a comynge. And thou departinge from
the body cam to heuene, and Ihesu Crist and aungelles and
archaungeles came ayeinst the, and the foul wycked sperites dreddin

755 that[1] . . . tyme] tellith that to fore the tyme there H2   757 Marie] *add* `borne in
to heuen on this day' H1   sermones] sermon H2   saide] *add and del.* on this day was the
right holy virgine marie the which he praysed in his sermones and seid H1
758 Virgine] *add* Marie þe whiche he preysed in his sermones and seid on this day was
þe riȝte holy virgine T2   borun] *ins.* T2   759 day] *ins.* H1, *om.* T2   annuel] L,
amanuel E, Emanuel H1, Emanues H2T2   761 holy] *om.* H2   dowue] doun H2
762 reste] nerest H2   763 the] *add* blessid H2   vnknowen] vnknowinge T2
764 taught] thought H1T2H2   765 annuel] L, emanuel E, Emanuell H1H2T2
766 deseuered] deseruyd T2   768 shall[2]] *add* not H1T2   769–70 of . . . virginite] was
brighte the virgin H2, and whos bright the virginite T2; H2T2 *punct. after* brighte
769 of] *ins.* H1   birthe] brith *del.* `berthe' H1   773 tabernacles] tabernacule T2
774 seminge] seiming *with first* i *ins. and subp.* H1, seyinge T2   defaylinge] failinge H2
778–9 thou yeuest] thei ȝevith T2   779 light] syȝt D   withoute] with E   781 or
more . . . departinge] *om.* H1T2   thou] a D

thi comynge, and, blessed Virgine, thou wentest not to heuene as Ely
or as Paule, ne thou stiedest not up [to] the thridde heuene only, but 785
thou came and touchedest the sege riall of thi sone.

'The dethe of other seintes is well called dethe, for that dethe
makithe hem blessed, but she hathe no place in the, for thi dethe ne
thi transmigracion or thi departinge ne makith the ne yeuithe the eny
point of suerte to be blessed, for thou thiselff art begynninge middel 790
and ende of alle welthes that excede mannes thought. Thi suerte and
thi verray perfeccion, and thi concepcion witheoute sede, and thine
devine habitacion haue made the blessed. Wherof thou saidest
thiselff that thou were not only made blessed by thi dethe bi
thi concepcion in alle generaciones. And dethe made the not blessed 795
but thou worshippedest the dethe in takinge fro her sorughe and
payne and conuertyng her in ioy. For God saide: "Lest perauenture
the furst fourme of man streche forthe his hond and take of the tree
of lyff and lyue endelesly", how thanne shal not she lyue endelesly
that bare that lyff that is euerlastinge and witheoute ende? Sumtyme 800
God putte oute the furst faders of paradys that slepte in the dethe of
synne beried fro the begynning in the synne of inobedience and of
glotenye. And now she that hathe brought | lyf to alle mankinde, and f. 192ᵛᵃ
dede obedience to God the fader, and putte oute alle the filthe of
synne, whi shulde she not be in paradys and why shuld she not 805
opene ioifully the gates of heuene? Eue streched oute her ere to the
serpent of whom she toke the mortal venym, and for she dede it by
delite she was ordeined to bringe her children forthe withe sorugh
and was condempned withe Adam. But this blessed Virgine that
enclined her ere to the worde of God, the whiche the holy goste 810
hadde fulfelled, that bare in her wombe the merci of the fader, that
conceiued witheoute knowlage of man and bare witheoute sorughe,
hou durst dethe sualw her, how might anythinge haue corrupcion in
her, that bare all lyff?'

And yet saithe the same Damacyen in his owne sermones: 815
'Verrely, the apposteles departed thorugh alle the worlde and

785 to] om. EDT2, ins. H1   787 is well] may wel be D   789 thi²] þe T2
departinge] twice T2   791 welthes] wel þis D   792 thi²] om. T2   793 Wherof]
wherefore DT2   794, 795 thi, thi] þe, þe H1T2   796 sorughe] sorwes DT2
798 streche] strecchid DT2   take] toke D   799 and lyue] and lyved D, om. T2   how]
ho'w' H1, whi D   800 and] om. T2   806 ere] here ET2, so with h erased H1, eeres D
808 sorugh] add and peyne D   810 ere] eere L, here ET2, so with h subp. H1   the holy
goste] she D   811 the¹] the//the T2   813 anythinge haue corrupcion] eny
corrupcion be had D   815 saithe] om. T2   Damacyen] Dacyen T2

entended only to preche to the peple and drowen men oute of
derkenesse withe one holy worde and brought hem to heuenly table
and to the sollempne weddingges of God, and thanne the devine
820 comaundement that is right as a nette or a clowde bare hem fro alle
the parties of the worlde into Ierusalem, in assembelynge hem
betwene his wynges. And thanne Adam and Eue the furst faders
cried and saide: "Come to us, right holy and most holsom seler that
fulfell[ed]ist oure desires." And the felawship of seintes saide:
825 "Abide withe us, oure comfort, and le[u]e us not orphanions, for
thou art comfort of oure trauailes, refressinge of oure swotes, that yef
thou lyue it is to us glorious to lyue withe the, and yef thou deye it is
to us most comfort to deye withe the. How shulde we lyue in this
f. 192ᵛᵇ worlde and be vnordeyned fro | the presence of thi liff?" And, as I
830 wene, suche thingges and lyckly saide the apposteles withe gret plente
of teres and withe gret plente of hem of the Chirche in compleyninge
hem of that hard and heui departinge.

'And thanne she turned towarde her sone and saide: "Good
Lorde, be ye a verray comfortour to my sones whiche thou hast
835 lyked to calle thi bretheren, that be full heui of my partinge hennes,
and blessed Lorde, withe that I shalle blesse hem withe my honde,
yeue hem thi blessing vpon my blessinge." And thanne she putte
forthe her honde and blessed all the collage of cristen men, and than
after that she saide: "Lorde, into thin hondes I betake my sperit.
840 Resseiue my soule that is thi loue, the whiche thou hast kepte
witheoute blame fro synne vnto thiselff, and I comaunde my body to
the erthe, kepe her hole in whiche thou hast liked to duelle. And
bringe me to the, that wher thou art, the fruit of my wombe, that I
may be withe the." And suche thingges herde the apposteles, and
845 thanne oure Lorde saide: "Arise up, my beloued and come, O thou
faire aboue alle women, my loue thou art so faire that no spotte of
filthe is in the." And whanne the right blessed Virgine herde that,
she recomaunded her sperit into the hondes of her sone. And thanne
the apposteles bewette hemselff withe teres and cussed the tabernacles,
850 and by the blessynge and the holynesse of that holy body, what syke

818 one holy] onli D   820 comaundement] add of God D   823 most] om. T2
824 fulfelledist] L, fulfellist EH1DT2   825 leue] lede E, so corr. to lefe H1, lede T2
826 swotes] sebotes changed to swotes H1, swetnesse D, sebotes T2   828 to us/most
comfort] trs. H1   829 fro] for T2   831 teres . . . of ¹] om. T2   837 vpon my
blessinge] om. H1T2   842 kepe her hole] for to kepe and holde D   her hole] 'hir' hele
changed to hole H1, hele T2   843 wher] w`h´ere H1   art] add þou were D   the²] þu T2
848 recomaunded] commanded T2   849 bewette] bewepte H1DT2

body that touched to the bere were heled of what maner syknesse they hadde. Fendes were chased awaye, the eyre and the heuene were halowed bi the assencion, and the erthe bi the deposicion of the body, for the holy body was wasshe withe most clene and holy water. And the water was halowed | bi the wasshinge of the right holy bodi, for the holy body was not clensed bi the wasshinge of the water but þe water was clensed bi her. And after that the holy bodi was wrapped in a clene sidoyne and leyde upon her bere, and lampes brenned bright, and oynementes smellinge sote, and praising of aungelles made gret melodye. And the apostelles and other that were there songen diuine songges, and the arche of oure Lorde was born fro the hille of Syon into Gethsamanye vpon the hedes of [the] aposteles. And other went before and sum folowed the holy bodi, and sum ronnen, and so she was felawshipped withe alle the plente of the Chirche.

'And sum of the Iwes that were harded in her olde malyce, as the felawship discended fro the mount of Syon beringe the holy body of the moder of God, came theder, and one that was a membre of the fende in foluing his steringe ran to the holy body and assailed it wodely, and toke the bere withe bothe hondes to haue drawe it doune to the erthe. And anone his two hondes were as drie as any stocke and was there as a drie stocke till faith had chaunged his thought and that he waylinge and sorwinge repented hym. And thei that bare the bere abode and made that cursed touche the hondes to that holy body, and thei come ayenne into her furste astate. And thanne it was born into Gethsemany, and ther it was clipped and kissed, and sunge withe holy preisingges, bywette withe many a piteous tere that ronnen downe in all parties, and so this holy body was leyd in the toumbe worshipfully, but thi soule was not lefte in helle, ne thi flesshe felt neuer corrupcion. And thei | saide: "Lo, here the welle that was neuer digged, the felde that was neuer ered, the vyne that was neuer cutte, the olyue beringe fruit shall not be holde in the bosum of the erthe. For it apertenithe that the moder be so haunsed withe the sone and that she stie up to hym right as he dissended downe to her, and that she whiche hadde kepte virginite in childing shulde fele neuer no corrupcion in body, and she that hadde bore the

f. 193ʳᵃ

856

860

865

870

875

f. 193ʳᵇ

881

885

853 assencion] Assumpcion D   and] of T2   856 body] ins. H1   862 the³] om. EH1T2   866 that] þei T2   871 anone] om. H1DT2   872 as] om. D chaunged] touchid D   874 the] his D   877 bywette] biwetpe with p on erased t H1, biwepte DT2   881 ered] trodde T2   882 be holde] beholde E   883 erthe] ins. H1, om. T2   886 no] om. H1DT2

creatour in her bosum shulde haue her duellinge in the heuenly
tabernacles, and that she that the fader hadde take to his spouse were
kepte in heuenly chaumbres, and that the thingges that be of the
890 sonne be posseded of the moder."' And thus saiethe Damacyen.

Seint Austin saiethe multeplienge resones in a sermon of the holy
assumpcion, sayeng thus: 'We that haue take upon us to speke of the
body of the euerlastinge Virgine and of the assumpcion of her right
holy sone seyen this atte the begynninge, that we finde nothinge
895 wrete of her sethe that oure Lorde hanging on the crosse recomaunded her to his disciple, but only that Seint Luke recordithe in
his writynge and saieth: "Alle tho weren by one corage receyued and
perseueraunt in orison with Marie the moder of Ihesu." What is
there thanne to saye of her dethe and of her assumpcion? Sethe the
900 scripture recordithe nothinge therof, thanne me thinkithe it is to seke
by reson thing that acordithe to trouthe. Now thanne b[e] this
auctorite made trouthe witheoute whiche auctorite is nothinge worth.
We that recorden the condiciones of mankinde drede not to saye but
f. 193ᵛᵃ þat she vnderwent temp[oral] dethe, but yef | we saie that she be
905 resolued in comune rotunnesse of wormes and asshin, it behouithe us
to serche and to thenke suche thinge as apertenithe to so grete
holynesse and to the lordshippe of such a chaumbre of God. We
knowe well that it was saide to the furst fader: "For that thou art
pouuder, thou shalt turne to pouuder." But the flesshe of Ihesu Crist
910 ascaped this condicion, for she susteined nothinge of corrupcion.
And thanne is excepte of this general sentence the nature taken of the
Uirgine. And thanne he saide to the woman: "I shall multeplie thi
disseses, for thou shalt bringe forthe thi children [in] sorugh." And
Marie susteyned neuer suche sorugh of whom the suerde of sorugh
915 perisshed the soule, but Marie bare her childe withoute sorugh, and
therfor thou Marie commune in sum thingges withe sorwes of Eue,
she communithe not in beringe her childe withe sorugh. But she is
excepte of many generalitees, for that her dignite yeuithe her suche

893 Virgine] virginite H₁T₂   894 seyen this] seynge this T₂, seithe þus D
895 that] at D   hanging] hongid DT₂   896 disciple] disciples T₂   896–7 recordithe
. . . writynge] writith D   898 orison] orisones T₂   Ihesu] god D   900 it is] his D
901 be] L, bi EH₁DT₂ (soit P₂)   902 worth] wrothe T₂   903 saye] assaie DT₂
903–4 but þat] that but H₁   904 she¹] he T₂   temporal] tempere EH₁T₂
905 comune] continue H₁T₂   907 lordshippe] worship DT₂   chaumbre]
chamberer D   909 to] ins. D   911 the²] add blessid D   912 multeplie] add
alle D   913 in] with EH₁T₂   914 of whom . . . sorugh] ins. H₁, om. T₂
915 the] her D   916 commune] commaunde D   withe] add 'þe' H₁
917 communithe] commaundeth D   not] ins. H₁, om. DT₂

lordeship. And therfor though we saye that she susteine[d] dethe, we
mowe not saie that she is withhold withe the bondes of dethe. Yef 920
oure Lorde wolde kepe his moder hool and the chastite of her
uirginite, whi might he not kepe her thanne witheoute corrupcion of
stinke and of rotonnesse? Aperteinithe it not to the debonairte of
oure Lorde to kepe the worship of his moder that was not come to
breke the lawe but to fulfelle it, and that in his lyff hadde worshipped 925
her before alle other bi the grace of his conceiuing? And therfor we
ought goodly beleue that he worshiped her in hcr dethe withe a
singuler salutacion and a special grace.

'Rotones and wormes is the repreef of | mankinde, and sethe Ihesu f. 193vb
Crist is oute of that repreef, the nature of Marie is except, [the 930
whiche is the nature] that he toke of her. For the flesshe of Ihesu
Crist is the flesshe of Marie, the whiche he bare aboue the sterres in
worshippinge man in mankinde and must spesially his moder. Yef
verrily the nature of the moder be the sones, hit is conuenient that
the sones b[e] the moders, not as to vnite of persone but as to vnite of 935
corporall nature. Yef vnite may make grace witheoute properte of
spirituel nature, how moche more may it make vnite of grace by
bodely and spirituel natiuite? The vnite of grace is as of the disciples
in Crist, of whiche hymselff saiethe "that they be one as us", and
after he saiethe: "Fader, I will that ther I am thei be with me." And 940
thanne yef he will haue hem withe hym that ioyned hem here in the
faithe withe hym and that thei be iuges withe hym, what shulde men
deme thanne of his moder, wheder she is worthi to bc in the presens
of her sone?

'And therfor as fer as I vnderstonde and beleue that the soule of 945
Marie be worshipped of her sone by a right excellent prerogatif,
possedinge in Crist [his] body glorified that she conseiued and bare.
And whi shulde she not possede hym by whom she conceyued, for so
gret an halowynge is more worthier heuene thanne erthe? The sege
of God, the chaumbre of oure Lorde and the worthi tabernacle of 950
Ihesu Crist aperteinithe to be ther as he is, and so precious a tresour
is more worthi to be kepte in heuene thanne in erthe. For be right,
no resolucion of rotonnes might not folowe so gret purete of thinge

919 susteined] susteinethe EH1T2   930 except] *on erasure and add* of T2
930–1 the which is the nature] *om.* EH1T2   934 be . . . that] but T2   935 be] by
EH1T2   as¹ . . . of¹] but as a T2   to¹] *ins.* H1   937 more] *add* encrece D   941 he]
ye H1DT2   that] *add* thei EH1DT2   ioyned] ioyne D   944 sone] *add* or no D
945 of] *add* the blessid D   947 Crist his] L, Cristes EH1DT2   she] *om.* D   952 is]
twice H1   953 purete of] pure D

vncorrupte, and for I fele not that this right holy body be take into
955 wormes mete, I drede to saie it. And for that that the yefte of grace
f. 194ra vncompar|able surmountithe gretly this estimacion that I fele that the
consideracion of many scriptures haue taught me to saie. Verite seith
ofte tyme to his ministres: "Ther as I am, there shalle be my
ministres." Yef this sentence is generall to alle tho that aministri[the]
960 Ihesu Crist bi faithe and bi werke, how is it thanne moche more
especial of Marie. For whi witheoute doute she was aministresse in
alle werkes, for she bare hym in her wombe and brought hym forthe
and norisshed hym and leide hym in his crache and hidde hym withe
fleinge withe hym into Egipte and kepte hym al her lyff vnto the
965 dethe of the crosse, and parted neuer fro hym but folowed hym. His
dyuinite may not be increduble, for she knewe wel that she hadde
not conseyued hym by the sede of man but by deuyne enspiringe.
Wherfor she, trustinge her in the might of her sone as of the vertu of
God vnmeuable, saide whanne the wyne failed: "Sone, thei haue no
970 wyne." And she wost well þat he might do that, and he fulfelled
anone that miracle.

'And thanne seeste thou that Marie was aministresse to Ihesu
Crist by faithe and by werke. And thanne, and she were not there as
Ihesu Crist wole that his ministris be, wher shulde she be? [And yef
975 she be] there, [is it] not by grace pareill? And yef it be by grace
pareill, wher is this egall mesure of God that yeldithe to eueri after
his desert? For sethe so moche grace is youe to Marie here levinge by
her desert, shulde than that grace be lessed to her after her dethe?
Nay, God defende, for the dethe of alle seintes is precious, certainly
980 we must deme the dethe of Marie to be right precious, that is
receiued to [the] euerlastinge ioyes bi the debonairtee of her sone
Ihesu Crist more worshipfully than any other, the whiche he hadde
f. 194rb wor|shippe bi grace before alle other, and I saye that she is not ledde
to the comune humanite after the dethe, that is to wete of wormes, of
985 poudre, yef [that sche] bare in her wombe the sauioure of alle. Yef
the devine wyll deyned to kepe the clothes of the children witheoute

959 alle] *om.* D   aministrithe] L, aministrid EH1DT2   961 aministresse] a
ministresse EH1T2, ministresse D (*amenistresse* S)   963 hidde hym] hid *ins.* hym H1,
him T2, wente D   963–4 withe fleinge] *om.* D   964 withe hym/into Egipte] *trs.* H1T2
hym¹] *add* fleynge D   967 by²] *om.* H1   969 wyne] wynde *with* d *subp.* H1
972 aministresse] a/ministresse H1, a ministresse EDT2 (*aministreresse* S)   974 wole]
wolde D   ministris] ministresse D   974–5 And yef she be] *om.* EH1T2   975 is it]
trs. EH1L   977 sethe] *om.* D   978 lessed] blessid DT2L   981 the¹] *om.*
EH1DT2   982 he] *om.* E   984 the¹] *om.* H1   985 that sche] *trs.* EH1DT2
986 witheoute] fro D

brennynge amonge the flawmes of the fyre, whi shulde he not kepe in
his propre moder that he kepte in a straunge clothinge? Hit liked
hym to kepe Ionas in the wombe of baleyne witheoute corrupcion,
and by his only grace shulde he not kepe his moder vncorrupte? He 990
kepte Daniell alyue in a pitte of lyons fro her disatempre hunger, is it
not thanne to kepe Marie by so many yeftes of merites and of
dignites? For we knowe well that alle these thingges that we haue
sayde haue not kepte nature, for we drede not but that grace hathe
kepte more the purete of Marie thanne nature. And thanne this Ihesu 995
Crist maye make reioise Marie in soule and in body in her propre
sone, as she that neuer hadde spotte of corrupcion, the which hadde
none in berynge so grete a sone, for she was alway incorrupte that
was made alle full of so moche grace; she is lyving enterly, she that
enter bare the lyff of all. And thanne yef I haue saide as I aught, 1000
Ihesu Criste approue [it] thou and thine, and yef I haue not saide as I
shulde, I praie the foryeue it me, thou and thine.'

Here endithe the Assumpcion of Oure Lady, and nexst
beginnithe the liff of Seint Bernard, Cap. .C.xiij.

Seint Bernard was born in Burgoyne in the castell of Founteines of
noble kinrede and right noble religious. And his fader hight Celestin,
a noble knight of the worlde and was | not [less] religious to God, and f. 194ᵛᵃ
his moder was called Aleth. And she hadde .vij. children, .vj. sones
and a doughter, the sones she norisshed for to be monkes and the 5
doghter to be a nonne. And euer as sone as she hadde a childe she
wolde offre it to God with her propre hondes. She had no cure that
thei were norisshed with straunge brestes, but right as she wolde
shede with the melke of the moder within hem sum nature of
goodnesse. And as long as thei were vnder her honde she norisshed 10
hem more for the desert thanne for delite, for she fedde hem with
the moste comune metes and most harde, as thow she wolde haue
sent hem anone into desert.

And in a tyme as she was withe childe with the thridde childe in
her wombe, whiche was Bernard, she saw a dreme whiche was 15

988 straunge] strong H1T2   989 baleyne] the whaale D   991 is it] *trs.* L   it]
om. H1T2   992 yeftes] *add* and EH1   994 for] *on erasure and repeated above* H1
995 of] *add* blessid D   997 as] and T2   that] *om.* DT2   neuer hadde] *trs.* D   hadde]
ins. before neuer H1   999 lyving] lovinge D   that] *add* is D   1001 approue it] L,
approued E, approued 'it' H1, approueth T2

EH1DH2A1A2L   3 less] *om.* E   6 euer] *om.* H1D   11 for²] *add* the H1D

shewyng of thinges to come, that she hadde in her wombe a whelpe
all white and rede upon the backe berkinge in her bely. And whan
she had tolde her dreme to an holi man, he answered her bi voys of
prophecie and saide: 'Thou art moder of right a noble whelpe, that
20 shal be a keper of the hous of God and gretly berke ayenst the
enemyes. For he shal be a noble prechour and shal hele mani folke bi
grace of medicine of his tunge.'

And as Seint Bernard was yet a litell childe he was sik of a greuous
siknesse in his hede, and there come to hym a woman for to aswage
25 that disese bi her charmes, but he putte her from hym with gret
indignacion. And the merci of God failed not to his childhode in
good loue, but he arose anone and felt hymself perfitly hole.

In the right holy night of the Natiuite of Oure Lorde that the
childe Bernarde abode in the chirche the office of Mateins, and
30 coueited to knowe atte what oure Ihesu Crist had be born, the childe
f. 194vb Ihesus appered to hym right | as bering before his eyen of the wombe
of his moder. Wher thorugh, as long as he leuid, he went that hour
hadde be the hour of the natiuite of our Lorde. And fro that hour
there was yeue hym more perfit witte and worde more abundaunt in
35 tho thinges that aperteine to the sacrement. And after that he made a
noble werke among the beginningges of his other tretys in the
preising of the moder and of the sone, in whiche werke he expounid
that lesson of the gospell how aungell Gabriel was sent to the Uirgine
Marie.

40 And whanne the auncien enemy sawe the purpos of the childe full
of grace, he had enuye of his chastite and sette ayenst hym mani snares
of temptaciones. And as he had in a tyme a litell while set his eyen to
beholde a woman he was anone ashamed of hymselff and was right a
cruel venger of hymself, for he lepte into a pole full of frore water and
45 there he stode so long tille he was nighe al frore, and so bi the grace of
oure Lorde God he akeled al the hete of flesshely couetise.

Abought that tyme bi the teching of the fende a mayden laide her
in his bedde al naked as he slepte, and whanne he felt her he lefte her
al in pees the parte of the bedde that she had take and turned hym
50 into that other side and slepte, and she helde her there a litell tyme

19 noble] *add* and holi D   23 of] in D   32 leuid] *add* aftir D   34 and] in D
worde] *add* and D   35 tho] thos *with* s *erased* H1   aperteine to] perteyneth toward H1
36 beginningges] begynnyng H1D   37 werke] *om.* D   42–3 to beholde] vppon D
43 anone] anoine E   and was right] for he was D   43–4 and was ... hymself] *ins.* H1
44 lepte] *add* anone D   into] in H1   frore] *om.* D   45 nighe al] *om.* D   al] *om.* H1
48 al naked] *om.* H1D   whanne] *add* he awoke and D   50 she] he H1

and abode and the fende daunsed and tripped and moued hem to
synne, and at the laste she was ouercome with shame and meruaile
and fledde away.

Another tyme he was herborued in the hous of a lady and she
consi[de]red his youthe and his beauute and beganne to coueite hym 55
vnordinatly, and thanne she lete ordeine his bed fer from other, and
in the night she aros wrechidly and cam to hym. And whanne he felt
her he cried anone: 'Theues, theues!' And she fled, and her meyne
arose and light a candell | and sought the theef but he was not found, f. 195ʳᵃ
and thanne thei went to her beddes for to reste hem, but that leude 60
wreche rest not but aras ayen priueli and come to Bernardes bedde,
and he cried ayen: 'Theues, theues!' And the theef was sought, but
she was not publisshed of hym that knewe her wel, and so that
wicked woman was chased away thre tymes and sesed of her malis
for drede and dispeir. And in the morw whanne he went his way, his 65
felawship undertoke hym in pley of that he hadde so besely the night
before dremed of theues and asked hym what hym ayled that he was
so afraied. And he ansuered: 'Truly y haue suffered this night the
assailingges of a theef, for myn ostesse enforced her to take from me
tresour that may not be recouered.' 70

And he bethought hymself that it was no sure thinge to duelle
with the serpent, and thought for to fle her and ordeined hymself to
entre into the ordre of Cisteux. And whanne his bretheren wost it,
thei lette hym in al that thei couthe of that purpos, but oure Lorde
gaue hym so gret grace that thei might not turne hym of his holy 75
purpos in no wise, but he demenid hym so that he conuerted alle hys
bretheren and mani other to religion, notwithstonding that Sire
Gerard his brother went alwey that it had be but veyne wordes and
refusid his techinges. And thanne Bernarde hette in faithe and in
meruailous loue of charite spake withe a gret sperit and saide: 'My 80
brother, y know wel that on sharpe trauaile shall yeue understondinge to thin eeres.' And thanne he sette his finger upon his
side and saide hym: 'One day shal come and that hastely that a spere
shal perse thi side and make a wey to thin hert for to take that
counsaile that thou refusest now.' And so it fell that within a while 85
after Sire Gerarde was take with his enemyes and sore wounded | in f. 195ʳᵇ

54 a] *on erasure* H1   55 considered] consired E   56 bed] *add* not D   57 he]
ins. H1   59 and¹] a H1   and² ... theef] *om.* D   60 leude] leude *changed to* lewde
H1   61 come] *add* ayen H1D   63 wel] *add* ynow3e D   69 me] *add* the H1D
76 demenid hym] denyed *del.* 'demenyd hym' H1   that] *twice once del.* H1   79 hette]
hote H1, sette D

the side in the same place wher his brother had set his finger and was
cast in preson and sore bounden. And thanne come Bernarde for to
haue sene hym, but thei wolde not lete hym speke with hym, and
90 thanne Bernard with a gret voys cried to hym and saide: 'Gerard,
brother, wete wele that we shulle in shorte tyme entre into a
monestarie.' And that same night the yrnes brast and fel from
hym and the dore openid bi hymselff and he fledde and said to his
brother that he had chaunged his purpos and wolde be made a
95 monke.

In the yere of the incarnacion of oure Lorde .M^l.C.xij. in the yere
.xv. of the ordre of Sisteux, the servaunt of God Bernard of the age
of .xxij. wynter entred into the ordre of Sisteux with mo thanne .xxx.
felawes. And as Bernard went oute of his faderes hous with his
100 brother Gerard (he was the eldest) sa[w]e Niuard his brother that
was a litell childe and pleied in the place with other children [and]
said to hym: 'A Niuard, brother, now al the possession of oure
lyvelode shal longe to the.' And the childe ansuered hym not as a
childe but saide: 'Shul ye thanne only haue heuen and leue me a litell
105 plot of erthe? This parte is not well deuided for me ne euenly.'
Wherfor this childe was a litell while wrothe and was with his fader,
and after folued his bretherin.

Whanne the seruaunt of God Bernard was entered into that ordre
he was so sharpe to hymself and his mynde so ocupied in God that
110 he vsed none of his bodely wittes. He hadde duelled a yere in the
hous of novices and yet he wost not wher there were ani wyndowes
thereinne. And yet he had gone in and oute mani a tyme, and at the
ende of the yere wher there were thre wyndowes he went there
hadde bene but one.

115 And the abbot of the Sisteux sent bretheren for to edifie Clereuany
f. 195va and made Bernard abbot, | that was there longe tyme in gret pouerte
and made ofte tymes his mete with leues of holme. And the seruaunt
of God wolde ouer mannes power and saide that he lost no tyme so
moche as whan he slepte, and saide that the comparison of slepe and
120 of dethe was right resonable, for right as tho that slepen be dede to
men, so tho that be dede slepen to God.

87 had] *om.* H1D   91 a] þe H1D   93 to] *add* Bernard D   96–7 D *puts* In . . .
M^l.C.xij. *in previous sentence and begins paragraph at* in the yere .xv.; H1 *similarly but with
paraph after* God   100 sawe] L, saue EH1D   101 and^1] that D   and^2] L, *om.*
EH1D   102 now] *om.* H1D   104 saide] *add* What H1D   105 euenly] heuenli D
111 of novices] of no vices EH1   were] *ins.* H1   120 to] *add* the syȝte of D

He was unnethe drawen to ani mete bi ani delite of appetite, but
onli for drede of failinge and he went to take his mete right as a man
shulde go to his turnement. And he had alway in custume whanne he
had ete to wete wher he had take more of mete thanne he had 125
acustumed, and yef at any tyme he fonde that he had, he wolde so
ponisshe hymself and refreine his mowthe in suche wise that he had
lost for the most parte the feling of sauoure of ani mete, for sumtyme
he drank oyle in stede of botre that was take hym bi errour, and he
perceiued not that he hadde drunke oyle till other perceiued his 130
lippes anointed. And in suche wise also he ete sumtyme grasse al raw
that was yeue hym bi errour in stede of botour.

He said that al that he had lerned of holi scripture that he had
lerned it in the wode and in the feldes in thenkinge and in praienge,
and that he had none other maistres but the oke and the holme, and 135
that wolde he saie amonge his frendes. And at the ende he confessed
that whanne he praied or thought sumtyme holi orison and holy
scripture appered to hym right as fully expouned. And as he tellithe
amonge his Canticles that he putte amonge his wordes mellyngly of
tho that the holy goste counsailed hym that whanne he made a trete 140
he wolde bethinke hym what he wolde do after that, and thanne a
voys cam that said to hym: 'Before that thou haste fulfelled this, thou
shalt haue none other.'

Pouerte plesid hym euer in clothinge, for | he said that outrageous f. 195vb
clothinge was shewyng of a necligent corage, either folily to glorifie 145
hem in hemself or coueityng outwarde man[nes] preisinge. He had in
his hert alway this prouerbe and ofte tyme said it: '[Who] dothe that
none other dothe, makith men to meruaile or wondre on hym.' He
bare mani yeres the haire, and as longe as he might hide it, but
whanne he sawe that it was knowen he toke it of anone and vsed 150
comune clothinge. He loughe neuer but that it was more peine to
hym to laughe thanne to refreine hym. He wolde say that the manere
of pacience was in thre thingges, [that is to saie, in wronge of wordes,
in harme of thingges,] and in misdoing of the bodi, and he proued by
ensaumple to haue this paciens.   155

There was an abbot that sent hym .vj. hundred mark of siluer for

124 to] add take H₁D   125 to wete] ins. H₁   take] ins. H₁   126 at] om. H₁D
131 also] om. H₁D   133 said] add also D   of] by H₁D   138 scripture] add hit D
140–1 that² . . . hym] om. L   144 Pouerte . . . clothinge] Also poure clothinge plesid
him euere D   145 shewyng] shewed H₁D   146 mannes] mani E   147 Who]
He E   149 hide] hidde H₁   153–4 that . . . thingges] om. E   154 and²] om. D

to make a couent, but al the money was take away bi the waye with
theuis. And whanne he herde it he saide no more therto but 'Blessed
be God that hathe spared me of this charge.'

160 In a tyme a chanon reguler come to hym and praied hym hertely
that he might be receiued a monke, but he counsailed hym to turne
ayen to his hous. And thanne the chanon saide: 'Whi hast thou
preised so moche in thi writinge perfeccion so longe tyme but yef
thou shewe it and yeue it to hym that coueite it? Y wolde y had al thi
165 bokes and y wolde al torende hem.' And Seint Bernard ansuered:
'Thou hast not redde in ani of hem but that thou maist be perfite in
thine owne cloistre, for y haue preised in al my bokes the correccion
of maneres and not the chaunging of places.' And that wode man
ranne to hym and smote hym on the cheke that it was al rede and
170 swollen. And tho that were there arose up ayenst that cursed man for
to haue smete hym, but Seint Bernarde come betwene hem crienge
and coniuringe hem bi the name of Ihesu Crist that the[i] shulde not
touche hym ne do hym none harme. |

f. 196ra   His custume was to saie to nouices whan thei entred into religion:
175 'Leuithe witheoute there the bodies that ye haue used in the worlde
and fastin you to hem that ben here within. Lete the sperites entre
only, for the flesshe profitethe not.'

The fader of Seint Bernard that was lefte alone in his hous went to
the monasterie and there he duelled a while, and sethe he deied in
180 good age. The suster was maried to the worlde and as she perissed in
riches and in delites of the worlde, she went in a tyme to the
monasterie for to visite her brother and she come in proude astate
and riche array, and her bretheren dreddin [her] right as [the net of]
the fende to take [awey] the soules, ne there wold none of hem
185 acorde to go oute to her ne see her. And whanne she sawe that none
of her bretheren come oute to her to speke with her, but one of her
bretheren that was thanne portoure said to her that she was al
bewrapped in stinkinge felthe, and thanne she melt all in teres and
saide: 'And yef y am suche a synner, God deied for the sinfull; and
190 for y am [a synner] y come to haue the counsaile of hem that be

158 he¹] Bernar`d´ D        163 writinge] wr`ï´ting H1   171 hym] add aȝen D
172 thei] the E   180 perissed] perisshed changed to `flor´isshed H1   182 brother]
add Bernard D   183 her²] om. EH1   the net of] thei had met with EH1D (la roys au
P2)   184 awey] L, with EH1D   the²] him D   of hem] om. D   185 see her] add
And whan she sawe that none of hem accorde to go oute to hire ne to se hire H1
188 in²] to H1D   189 saide] ins. H1   And] om. H1   190 a synner] synfull E,
synner H1   haue] here changed to haue H1

good. And thow my brother dispise my flesshe, lete not the seruaunt
of God dispise my soule. Lete my brother come, and that he
comaundithe y will do.' And she helde her promesse, and thanne he
come to her with his bretheren, and for that it was not lefull to departe
her from her husbonde, he made her putte abacke al wordly vanite and 195
folu the stappes of her moder. And thanne whan she was parted fro
hym she was so strangly chaunged that in the middes of the worlde she
liued lyche an ermite and was al straunge to the worlde. And atte the
last she ouercam and entred into religion and ouercame her husbonde
bi praieres and was assoiled of the vowe of mariage. 200

This holi man was on a tyme so sike þat hym thought that he
yelde up the sperit | and was al passed th[is] worlde, and hym f. 196rb
thought that he was brought before God in iugement, and there was
the fende in that other parte and putte upon hym mani accusaciones
of reproues. And whan he had al saide, the seruaunt of God Bernard 205
saide and ansuered withoute ani wratthe or drede: 'I knoulege that y
am noght worthi for to haue the kingdom of God bi my merites. But
oure Lorde that holdithe it bi double right, that is as his eritage and
bi the merites of his passion that he suffered, so that it suffisith to
hym that one, and of his merci he shal geue me that other, and so y 210
shal not be confounded for it shal be myn be right.' And thanne the
fende was ouercome and the uision passed away and this holi man
come to hymself. And he distreined his bodi bi so gret trauaile of
fastingges and wakingges that he languisshed of the continuel
siknesse so ferforthely that almost he might not folw the couent. 215
Another tyme he was greuously syke, and his bretheren praied for
hym so that he felt hymself a litell esed of his siknesse, and thanne he
made al his bretherin come before hym and saide to hem: 'Whi holde
ye me here thus bi strengthe of youre praieres? Y praie you sa[u]e me
and lete me go.' 220

The seruaunt of God was chose to be bisshop ouer mani citees,
and namely of Iene and of Melan, and that not refusinge lewdely ne
grauntinge saide to hem that required hym that he hadde no power

191 brother] bretheren D   seruaunt] servauntis D   192 brother] *add* Bernard D
come] *add* to me D   194 come] *ins.* H1   195 her] *om.* D   196 her] his H1
197 worlde] wo'r'lde H1   199 ouercam] *add* hit D   201 man] *add* Bernard D   on
a tyme] *om.* D   thought] *ins.* H1   202 this] the E   203 before God] *ins.* H1
205 he] þe feende D   209 so that] *om.* D   213 he] *om.* H1D   so gret] *om.* D
215 almost] vnnethe D   not] *ins.* H1, *om.* D   219 saue] saie E, sey *del.* 'suffer' H1, seie
for D (*espargnez* P2)   221 God] *add* Bernard D   to be] *om.* H1D   222 lewdely]
lowidli D

of hymself, but he was ordeined to the seruice of other. And bi the
225 counsaile of this holy man his bretheren were so purueied and
ordeined for bi the auctorite of the pope that nobodi might parte
hym from hem, for he was al her ioye and comfort.

In that tyme whanne he visited the ordre of Charterhous and
f. 196ᵛᵃ whanne the freres were wel edefied by hym, ther | was one thinge that
230 meued the prioure of the place, and that was [that] the sadille that
Seint Bernarde rode in was to gay and shewed litell the pouerte of the
bretheren. And whanne it was spoke to hym therof, he meruailed
moche what sadell it was [and knewe not the sadell], and yet he hadde
ride ther[o]n from Clerevaus to Charterhous. And in a day as he went
235 beside the lake of Lozein and sawe neuer the lake. And atte euen
whanne his felawship spake of the lake he asked hem wher that lake
was. And whanne thei herde that thei had gret meruaile.

For certeinly the humilite of herte ouercame in hym the highnesse
of name, for the worlde coude neuer enhaunce hym so high but that
240 he made hymself the lower. He was holde soueraine of alle, and he
helde hymself soget to alle. And atte the last as he confessed of
hymself that amonge alle the worshipes and fauoures that he hadde
of the peple, hym thought it as it semed as [he] had ben another man
chaunged or as he hadde be in a dreme. And whanne he was amonge
245 the most simple freres and bretheren and vsed an amiable mekenesse
there, he reioised hym and cowde finde hymself in his propre
persone. He was alway founde bifore the Houres other reding or
writing or thenking or edefieng his bretheren by wordes.

In a tyme as he preched to the peple and that al entendid to his
250 sermon deuoutely, suche a temptacion arose within his herte that
said: 'A, lorde, thou prechest wel and how this peple here the gladly!
How thou art holde wys of alle that here the!' And whanne the
seruaunt of God [felte] this steringe within hymself of temptacion he
abode a whiles and bethought hym whedir he wolde make an ende of
255 his sermon or leue evyn there. And anone he, comforted bi the
f. 196ᵛᵇ mighti helpe of God, an|suered pesibly [to hym that tempted hym]
and saide: 'Y beganne not bi the ne y will not ende bi the.' And so he
performed oute al his sermon suerly.

224 the²] om. H₁   226 for] 'fore' H₁   the¹] ins. H₁   230 that²] om. E   233 and
... sadell] om. E   yet he] yet on erasure H₁   234 theron] therin E   235 of Lozein and ...
lake] ins. H₁   neuer] not D   238 of] add his D   highnesse] liʒtnesse D   241 to] of H₁
242 that he hadde] om. H₁   243 it²] him H₁D   he] it E   245 and vsed] om. D
251 this] þe H₁   252 How] and D   253 God] add Bernard D   felte] herde E
hymself] him H₁D   256 to ... tempted hym] om. E   257 bi¹] with D

Ther was a monke that had be a ribauude al his lyf and a iaper, and was tempted with a wicked sperit for to turne ayen to the worlde. And as blessed Seint Bernard might not withholde hym, he asked hym wherwith he wolde lyue. And he ansuered hym that he coude wel pleie atte the dys and that was lyving good ynow for hym. And thanne Bernarde saide to hym: 'Yef y take the any cheuisaunce, wilt thou come euery yere to me and part with me of thi wynnynge?' And he was glad and behight hym truly that he wolde. And thanne Seint Bernard toke hym .xx. *solidi* and he went his way. The holi man dede this in hope that he might withdrawe hym, and as it happed afterwarde. Thanne he went his way and loste alle, and whanne he had al loste he come ayen al confused before the yate. And whanne Seint Bernard wost it he come to hym gladly and helde furthe his lappe for to haue parte of the wynnyng. And thanne he saide to hym: 'Fader, y hauc nothinge wonne, but y haue loste youre good, wherfor y beseche you to receiue me for youre good and catell.' And Bernard ansuer[ed] mekely: 'Sethe it is so, it is beter that y receiue [the] thanne lese bothe', and so he receiued hym and was after a vertuous man.

In a tyme as Seint Bernard rode in hys waye he met with an vplondisshe man, and he made his compleint to this man that he hadde not hys herte stable in praier. And whanne this man herde this, he dispised Seint Bernarde and saide that he had a stable and a sadde herte in his praiers. And Bernard that wolde ouercome hym in his foly saide to hym: 'Part a litell from me and begynne thi *Pater* | *noster* in the saddest entent that thou canst, and yef thou maist ende withoute thought of ani other thinge, withoute faile thou shalt haue the hors that y sitte on. And thou shalt behight me to tell me trouthe.' And he was gladde and behight hym truly to telle hym the trouth, for he thought fully the hors hadde be hys. And thanne he went a litell awey thennes and beganne his *Pater noster*, and unnethe he hadde saide half but he thought wher he shulde haue the sadell also. And whanne he hadde avised hym he went to Bernard and tolde hym what he hadde thought in his praiere, and sethe he hadde no wille to avaun[t]e hym more.

260
265
270
275
f. 197ra
285
290

259 had] *ins.* H1   261 hym] *om.* D   266 glad] *add* þerof D   wolde] *add* do hit D
269 alle] *add* his moneye D   270 yate] *add* of the monasterie D   272 haue] *add* had E
272 he] þe monke D   275 And] *add* than D   ansuered] ansuering EH1   275–6 it is² . . .
and so] *ins.* H1   276 the] *om.* EH1   282 hym] þis man D   284 ende] *add* it H1
287 he] than þis man D   and] *add* he H1   289 a] *ins.* H1   thennes] *om.* D   290 saide]
add the H1   291 avised] *so with* a *and* ed *on erasure* H1   293 avaunte] avaunce ED

Frere Robert, a monke of hys and ny hym as to the worlde, hadde
295 be deceiued in his youthe bi the teching of some and was sette at
Clyni. And the worshipfull fader lete hym be there a while, and after
he wolde calle hym home by letteres. And as he endited this lettre
withoute in the clere day and another monke wrote it, there come
sodenli a gret reyne. And [thanne he that wrote the lettre wolde haue
300 folde it vppe fro the reyne, and] Bernard saide: 'This is a werke of
God, and therfor write and handle and drede the not. And thanne he
wrote this lettre in middes of the reyne withoute any wetynge of the
lettre. And yet it reynid largely rounde aboute, and the vertu of his
chartre toke awey the moisture of the reyne.

305 A gret multitude of flyes had al besette a chirche that he had do
make, so that they dede gret harme to all, and he saide: 'Y curse
hem.' And on the morw they were al founde dede.

He was sent fro the pope to Melan for to reconsile hem to the
Chirche, and whanne he had done and was returned fro Melan, a
310 man brought hym his wyf that was uexed with a fende, and anone
the fende beganne to chide thorugh the mouthe of the wreche and
f. 197rb saide: 'Thou eter of lekys, wenist thou to | putte me oute of my
hous?' And this holy man sent her to Seint Sire into hys chirche.
And Seint Sire bare worship to hys oste and wolde not hele [her] that
315 night, and so she was brought ayen to Seint Bernarde. And thanne
the fende began to chide and to saie: 'Neither Sire ne Bernard shull
not putte me oute.' And Bernard ansuered: 'Neither Sire ne Bernard,
but oure Lorde Ihesu Crist.' And as sone as he had made his praiere
the wicked sperit saide: 'A, how y wolde fayn go oute of this place,
320 for y am greuously turmented, but y may not, for the gret Lorde will
not.' And the holy man saide: 'Ho is that gret Lorde?' And he saide:
'Ihesus of Nazareth.' And he asked hym: 'Sawest thou hym euer?'
And he sayde: 'Ye.' And he asked hym: 'Where sawe thou hym?'
And he sayde: 'In his glorie.' And he asked hym: 'How cam thou
325 thennes?' And he saide he fell oute with Lucifer. And he saide all tho

295 sette at] sente to D   at] *ins.* H1   296 fader] *add* Bernard D   297 home] *add*
a3en D   299–300 thanne . . . and] *om.* E   300 vppe] *add* and hid it H1   301 and
handle] on D   he] þe monke D   304 chartre] letter D   306 all] *add* the werk H1D
307 hem] *add* alle D   308 was] *add* also D   312 eter] art H1   313 man] *add*
seinte Bernard D   into] 'in'to H1   314 bare] put the D   her] hym EH1
316 Bernard] *add* ne H1D   317 ansuered] *add* þat H1, *add* and seide D   318 Crist]
add shal D   319 the wicked] *twice once del.* H1   319 how] thu H1   321 man]
add seynte Bernard D   he] the feende D   322 asked] *add* of H1D   Sawest] where
sau3e D   323 he²] than Bernard D   324 he¹] the feende D   he²] than Bernard D
hym] *om.* H1   325 thennes] *preceded by del. letter* H1   he¹, he³] the feende D

thinges bi the mouthe of the olde wreche with an orrible voys before
all. And the holy man asked hym: 'Woldest thou not gladly turne
ayen to that ioye?' And he saide, mowing meruelously: 'Hit is to
late.' And thanne the holy man made hys praiers and he went oute of
the woman, but whanne that holy man was gone the enemy assailed 330
her ayen, and her husbonde cam after the holy man and tolde hym
how it was falle. And he lete hange a writte about her necke withe
these wordes conteined therin: 'I comaunde the in the name of Ihesu
Crist that thou ncigh no more this woman.' And after that he durst
neuer touche her. 335

There was a pitous woman in Aquitaigne that was laboured with a
fende .vij. yere in doyng with her his luxurie. And as God wolde,
that holy man cam into tho parties, and the fende manaced strongly
that thow she went to hym that he might not profite her, and that
whanne the seint were gone | he that was her loue shulde be her most f. 197ᵛᵃ
enemy. But she went suerly to this holy man and full sore weping 341
tolde hym what she suffered. And he saide to her: 'Take my staffe
here and laie it in thi bedde, and yef he may do anithinge to the, lete
hym do.' And she dede so and went to her bedde, and he came
anone, but he durst neuer come nigh her as he was wont, ne touche 345
the bedde, but stode afer and manaced her cruelly that whanne the
holi man were gone that he wolde reuenge hym on her. And whanne
she had tolde that [to] Seint Bernard, he assembled alle the peple and
comaunded that eueriche shulde holde a candell brenning in her
honde, and he cursed thanne that fende with assent of alle the 350
felawship and entredited hym that he shulde neuer haue to do with
her ne with none other, and so she was deliuered of that illusion.

So as this holy man in a tyme was sent as a leget into the prouince
for to reconsile the duke of Aquitaign into the Chirche and he
refused to be reconsiled in alle wises, this holy man went to the 355
auuter to saie his masse and this duke abode withoute as a cursed
man. And as he had said: '*Pax Domini*' he putte the holi sacrement
upon the patene and bare it with hym and went oute al sette afere
with charite and assailed the duke with dredfull wordes and saide

326 the¹] *om.* H₁   olde] *om.* H₁D   329 he] the feende D   331 man] *add* seinte
Bernard D   337 luxurie] lecheri H₁D   God] *ins.* H₁   338 man] *add* Bernard D
into] in H₁   339 not] *ins.* H₁   340 seint] holi man D   341 But] *add* for al this D
man] *add* Bernard D   343 it] *om.* D   345 he²] she *with* s *erased* H₁   ne] to H₁D
346 cruelly] gretli D   348 to] *om.* E   351 to do] ado H₁   353 So] Also D
man] *add* Bernard D   355 man] *add* Bernard D   357 he¹] þis holi man D
358 oute] withoute H₁D   afere] a ferre H₁

360 hym in this wise: 'We haue praied the and thou hast dispised us. Lo, here the sone of the Uirgine that is come to the, whiche is Lorde of the Chirche whiche thou pursuest. This is thi iuge, in whos name alle knees bowen, in whos hondes thi soule shal come, dispise hym not as thou hast done hys seruauntes. Be contrarie to hym if thou
365 maist.' And anone the duke waxe al stif and was sodenly impotent in al hys membres and fill adowne to his fete. And this holi man putte
f. 197vb hym with his fote | and comaunded hym to rise [and here the sentence of God]. And thanne he arose al tremblyng and fulfelled anone that the holi man had comaunded hym.

370   In a tyme as this holi man entered into Almayne the Gret for to apese gret discorde, an ershebisshop sent a worshipfull clerke ayenst hym. And whanne the clerke tolde hym that his lorde had sent hym ayenst hym, the seruaunt of God ansuered and said: 'Another lorde hathe sent the.' And he, meruailing gretly, saide that he was sent of
375 none other but of his lorde the ershebisshop. And thanne the holy man saide: 'Sone, thou art deceiued, for Ihesu Crist that hath sent the is gretter lorde thanne he.' And whan the clerke understode hym he saide: 'Syr, wene ye that y will be a monke? Nay, thenke it fully that y thought it neuer, ne it entred neuer into my [herte].' And
380 notwithstonding al that, in that same iorney he toke his leue of the worlde and toke the abite of that holy man.

    Another tyme as he had take into his ordre a noble knight and whanne he had folued this holy man a while, he beganne gretly to be tempted. And as a brother of his perceiued his heuinesse and asked
385 hym what hym ayled, he ansuered and saide: 'Y wote wel y shal neuer be glad.' And thanne that brother tolde it to that holy man, and he anone preide [ententifly] for hym and sodenly that brother that was so pensif and so heui appered more glad thanne ani of that other. And thanne the brother forsaid blamid hym of the worde that
390 he saide of heuinesse, and he ansuered and saide: 'Y wote well that y saide that y shulde neuer be gladde, but y saie now that y shal neuer be sori.'

361 here] *add* is D   sone] *add* of god *subp.* H1   is²] *add* the H1D   363 bowen] bowes H1   364 Be] ben *with* n *erased* 'not' H1, Do the D   364–5 if thou maist] *del.* H1   366 man] *add* seinte Bernard D   367–8 and² ... God] L, *om.* ED, *ins.* H1   368 he] þe Duke D   369 had] *om.* H1   370 man] *add* Bernard D   372 had] *om.* H1   374 gretly] *om.* D   that] *om.* H1   375 his lorde the] the lord D   375–6 the holy man] seinte Bernard D   379 into] withynne D   herte] L, thought EH1D   381 man] *add* seinte Bernard D   382 take] *ins.* H1   386 man] *add* seinte Bernard D   387 ententifly] entifly E, tentifly H1   388 glad] gladly EH1   391 shulde] shulddest *with* dest *subp.* H1

As Seint Malachiel a bisshop of Irlond, of whom he wrote the lyff
full of vertues, passed in his chirche blessidly to Ihesu Crist and this
holi man offered to God for hym solempne sacrifices of helthe, he 395
sawe the ioye of hym bi the reuelacion of oure Lorde, and bi the
inspiracion of God he chaunged the forme | of his orison after the f. 198ra
communion in saienge: 'Lorde, that hast Seint Malachiel bi his
merites felawshiped with thi seintes, we praie the yeue us that we
that do the fest of his precious dethe mow folw the ensaumple[s] of 400
his blessed lif.' And whanne the chauntour herde hym, he shewed
hym and saide that he erred, and he saide ayen that he erred noght,
'bote y wote wel what y saye.' And thanne he went to the bodi and
kessed his fete.

In the dayes that Lentin neighed, whiche is called amonge us 405
Shroftide, he was uisited with diuerse knighte[s], and he praied hem
that thei wolde absteine them in tho holi dayes from her leudenes
and fro her uanitees. But thei wolde in no wise accorde to hym, and
thanne he asked wyne and saide to hem: 'Now drinkithe the hele of
soules.' And whanne thei hadde dronke thei were sodenly chaunged 410
and went her way, and within a while after thei gaue to God all the
remenaunt of thaire lyf.

And at the last, the blessed Seint Bernard neighed to his ende, and
thanne he saide blessidly to his bretheren: 'Y recomaunde to you thre
thinges principali to kepe, the whiche y haue truly kept to my pouer 415
as longe as y haue be in this present lyf. And that y wold neuer
sklaundre to none, and yef ani thing haue falle, y haue kepte it as
longe as y might. I haue alway leued lasse myn owne witte thanne
any other. Yef y haue be smite y desired neuer uengeaunce to the
smiter, and therfor y leue to you charite and humilite with pacience. 420

And so after that he hadde do mani miracles and had do made an
.C.lxxj. chirches and ordeined mani bokes and tretis, he hathe
fulfelled the dayes of his lyf in the .lxiij. yere and in the yere of
oure Lorde a .M.C.lvj. he slepte in oure Lorde betwene the hondes
of hys sones. And his glorie sheued his passing hennes to miche 425
peple. He appered to an abbot in a chirche and bade hym to folu

394 in] into H1   395 man] add seinte Bernard D   solempne] solempnely H1D
398 Seint] sente D   399 felawshiped] for to felauship D   thi] his changed to 't'hi H1,
his D   399–400 we that] om. H1, shal D   400 the¹] add service and the D
ensaumples] L, ensaumple EH1D   406 Shroftide] Shroft tyde H1   knightes] knighte E
409 he] þe holi man Bernard D   drinkithe the] add wyne of H1   409–10 hele of soules]
saules hele H1   415 thinges] ins. H1   417 as] Also as D   418 leued] lyued
changed to leued H1, lovid D   423 in¹] ins. H1   424 a] om. H1

f. 198rb hym. And [so] he dede, and Bernard saide: 'We | be come to the
mount of Lyban. Thou shalt abide here and y will stie up an hye.'
And he saide: 'Whi will ye stie up?' 'For y will', he saide. And he
430 meruailed gretly and said: 'What menithe this, fader? There is none
this day holde so wys in kuninge as ye be.' And he saide: 'This
kunninge is none, but there aboue is verrey kuninge and plente of
science, there aboue is verraye knowleche of trouthe.' And with that
worde he unapered. And thanne he marked the day and fonde that
435 Seint Bernard was passed the same day and the same hour. And
Ihesu Crist dede mani miracles for his seruaunt.

Here endith the lif of Seint Bernard, and nexst beginnithe
the lyf of Seint Timothe, Cap.^m .C.xiiij.

Timothe was taken under Neroun that was prouost of Rome, and
was greuousli bete and hadde hote lyme caste in his throte and upon
his woundes, and he gaue thankingges to God with al his herte. And
thanne .ij. aungelles come to hym saieng: 'Lefte up thin hede to
5 heuen and beholde.' And thanne he loked and sawe the heuen open
and Ihesu Crist that helde a crowne doublid and saide to hym: 'Thou
shalt receiue this of myn honde.' And a man that hight Apolinare
sawe this thing and made hym to be baptised anone. And therfor the
prouost comaunded that thei two togederes perseuering in the
10 confession of oure Lorde werin beheded about the yere of oure
Lorde .lviij.

Here endithe the lif of Timothe, and nexst beginnithe the
lyf of Simphorian, C. .C.xv.

Simphorian was born in the cite of Daugustinence, and as he was yet
but yong he shinid bi so gret abundaunce of good werkis that he
surmounted the lyf of hem that were aunsient. And thanne as the |
f. 198va painymes halued the fest of Venus, Symphorian was there and wolde
5 in no wise worship the ymage that was bore before Eradien, and
thanne he was long beten and after putte in prison. And whanne he

427 so] om. EH1   Bernard] he H1D   come] 'comen' H1, om. D   429 he] than the
Abbot D   431 saide] add aȝen D   433 knowleche of] plente of grace and H1D
trouthe] throught H1   434 he] þe Abbot D   436 mani] om. H1

EH1DH2A1A2   3 he] om. H1   8 thing] add also D   9 prouost] add anone
H1   comaunded] add anone D   10 werin] add bothe D

EH1DH2A1A2   6 long] strong H1, strongli D

was take oute of prison and thei wolde haue constreined hym for to do sacrifise and behight hym mani gret yeftes, he saide: 'Oure Lorde canne wel guerdon the merites, and also he canne well ponisshe the synnes, and therfor late us paie to hym oure lyff that we owe hym of right. Youre yeftes be blake and annointed with the suetnesse of an hony that engenderithe venym in the hertis of fals beleuers. Youre couetise in havinge al thing hath right noght, for she is obliged in the artis of the fende and shall be withholde in the [b]ondes of his wicked wynnynge, and youre ioyes whanne ye begynne to shine shul be broke as glas.'

And thanne the iuge fulfelled with wrathe gaue sentense that Symphorian shulde be slayn. And as thei ledde hym to the place of his marterdom, his moder cried fro the [wall] of her hous and saide: 'Sone, bethenke the of euerlastinge lyf; beholde an high and se hym that regnithe in heuene, thi lyf shal not be take awey but it shal be chaunged into beter.' And he was beheded anone and his body was take of cristen men and beried worshipfully.

And so mani miracles were do atte his sepulcre that it was holde in gret worship amonge the payneims. Gregorie of Toures tellithe that fro the place wher his blode was shed, a cristen man bare thre stones that were wette with his blode and putte hem in a shrine of siluer closed aboute with tre and bare it into a castell, the whiche castell was al brent. And that shrine was founde in the middes of the fire al hole and sounde. And he suffered dethe aboute the yere of oure Lorde .CC.lxx.

Here endithe the lyf of Seint Symphori|an, and nexst beginnithe the lyf of Seint Bartilmew, Capitulum .C.xvj. f. 198vb

Seint Bartilmew the apostell went into Ynde that is in the ende of the worlde, and entred into a temple wher as was an ydole that hight Astrot and abode there as a pilgrime. And in that ydole duelled a fende that saide he coude hele al maner siknesses, but he lyed, for he coude yeue hem [no maner of] hele but he cesed to make hem sike.

7 constreined] confermed H1 to] *add* haue EH1 10 paie] praie D paie . . . lyff] *ins.* H1 hym oure] oure lord of D 11 the . . . an] *om.* D 12 in] and D 14 bondes] hondes EH1D (*lyans* P2) 19 wall] *om.* E 20 the] *om.* D of] *add* þe H1 23 take] *add* anone D 24 in] *om.* H1 25 payneims] payens H1 26 wher] *om.* H1

EH1DH2A1A2L 2 into] in H1 3 ydole] *add* there E 4 hele] *om.* D maner] *add* of D siknesses] sikenes H1 for] þat *subp.* 'for' H1 5 no maner of] none E, no maner H1 cesed] *add* not D

And that temple was full of sike folkes and thei coude haue none
ansuere of that ydole, so that thei went to another cite wher ther was
another ydole that hight Beriche and asked hym whi that Astrot
wolde geue hem none ansuere. And Beriche saide: 'Youre god is
10 harde strened and bounde with cheines of [fyre] that he dare not
ones brethe ne speke sethe that Bartilmew the apostell of almighti
God entred into the temple. And thei asked: 'What is that Bartilmew?' And the fende saide: 'He is an nigh frende of almighti God and
therfor he is come into this prouince for to uoide out al the goddes of
15 Ynde.' And thei saide: 'Telle us tokenes that we mowe knowe hym
[so] that we may finde hym.' The fende saide: 'He hathe blak here and
crispe, fayre skyn and glad eyen, his nose streite and even, a longe
berde and a litell hore, of right comly stature. He is clothed with [a]
white cote and with a white mantell, and his cote is wrought with
20 purpill, and in eueri corner of hys mantell there is a precious stone of
rede. And this .xxvj. yere his clothes wer neuer empaired ne wexse
foule. He worshipeth God eueri day and knelithe an .C. tymes in the
day [and an .C. tymes in the nyght]. The aungeles gone with hym that
suffre hym neuer to be weri ne to fele hunger. He is alway of one
25 semblaunt, glad and meri. He seithe alle thinges before and knowithe
f. 199ra al. He spekithe al ma|nere of langages, and he knowithe what y saie to
you now. And whanne ye seke hym, yef hym luste ye shull finde hym,
and yef hym luste he wil noght be found of you. And y praie you, yef
ye finde hym, that ye saie to hym that he come noght here, that his
30 aungeles do not to me as [they haue] do to my felawe.'

And thanne thei came, and whanne they had sought hym .ij. dayes
besily and coude not finde hym, in a day there was a demoniak, that
is a man vexid with a fende, that cried and saide: 'Apostell of God,
Bartilmewe, thine orisones brennen me.' And the apostell saide:
35 'Holde thi pees and go oute thennes.' And anone he was deliuered.
And whanne Polimien, kinge of the rewme, herde this thinge, whiche
had a doghter lunatike, he sent to the apostell praieng hym that he
wolde come and hele his doughter. And whanne the apostell was
come to hym and he sawe that she was bounde with cheynes and al

6 And . . . sike] *ins.* H1   was] *add* alweie D   9 god] *add* Astaroth D   10 harde
strened] sore constreyned D   fyre] yren E   16 so] L, and EH1D   17 crispe] *add*
'&' H1   18 a] *om.* E   21 .xxvj.] .xxxvj. E   yere] wynter D   wexse] werid D
22 knelithe] kneled H1   23 and an . . . nyght] *om.* E, *ins.* H1   27 hym²] 3e D
29 that ye] *om.* D   30 they haue] he hathe EH1   33 vexid] envexed H1   a²] þe H1
36 Polimien] Polumen *with* ol *on erasure* H1   37 lunatike] lymatik *with first minim of* m
subp. H1

torent with her tethe al thinge that cam nighe her, he comaunded 40
that she shulde be unbounde, and the seruauntes saide thei durst not
go to her. And he saide: 'Y haue hym here bounde, the fende that
was bounde in her, and ye drede you?' And anone she was vnbounde.
And thanne the kinge wolde haue presented the apostell with
cameles charged withe golde and with precious stones, but thei 45
might in no wise finde hym. And in the morwtide after foluinge he
apered to the kinge in his chaumbre alone and saide to hym: 'Wherto
soutest thou me yesterday with golde and precious stones? Tho
yeftes be necessarie to hem that coveyten erthely thinges, but y
desire none erthely thinge.' 50

And thanne Seint Bartilmew beganne to teche the kynge of the
manere of redempcion of lyff, shewinge amonge other thinges how
Ihesu Crist had ouercome the fende by | merueilous and couenable f. 199rb
might and right and wisdom. For it was a sittyng thinge that he that
had ouercome the sone of the uirgine, whiche was Adam that was 55
fourmed of the erthe that was virgine atte that tyme, were ouercome
of the sone of a Uirgine. And he ouercome hym mightely whanne he
cast hym mightly oute of his lordship, the whiche he hadde take
awey bi castinge oute with strength the furst man. And right as he
that hath ouercome a tyraunt sent his felawes to sette his signe ouer 60
al and for to caste oute the other tyrauntes, right so Ihesu Crist
sendithe ouer al his messengeres for to fordo the worship of fendes.
Rightwysely, for it was right that he that had ouercome man by eting
and helde hym yet, that he were ouercome bi a man fastinge, and
that he shulde holde hym no more. Wisly, whanne the art of the 65
fende was ouercome bi the art of Ihesu Crist. The art of þe fende was
for, right as the faucon takith the bridde, right so toke he Ihesu Crist
in þe desert. For that he fasted he assaied whedir he hadde hungir,
and yef he hadde had hunger for to haue deceiued hym by mete, and
yef he hadde not hungir he wist wel withoute faile that he was God. 70
But he might in no wise deceiue hym, for he had hunger and yet he
consentid nothing to hym in his temptacion.

And whanne he had longe preched to hym þe sacrementis of the

41 that] *om.* H1   43 was bounde in] bounde H1   and] wherfore D   vnbounde]
add and delyuered D   44 haue] *add* be *erased* H1   50 thinge] þinges H1D
52 of lyff] *om.* D   59 awey] *add* bi casting oute of his lordeshipp þe which he hadde cast
awey *del.* H1   62 worship] worshipinge D   64–6 bi . . . ouercome] *ins.* H1
66 The art of þe fende was] *om.* D   67 as] *ins.* H1   68 in] *ins.* H1   hadde] *add*
eny D   69 mete] *add* And if he hadde not hungour//fore to haue deceyued him by mete
del. H1   70 withoute] *add* eny D   73 he] Bartilmew D

faithe, he saide to the kinge that yef he wolde resseiue baptyme he
75 wolde shewe hym his god bounden withe cheines. And so the day
foluyng whanne the bisshopes of ydoles did sacrifice bysides the
paleys of the kinge, the fendes begunne to crie and saye: 'Sese, ye
cursed wrechis, to sacrifie to us, lest ye suffre wors thanne y that lye
here harde bounde in cheynes of fire with the aungell[es] of Ihesu
f. 199ᵛᵃ Crist that the Iwes crusified and wende to haue brought | hym to
81 dethe. And that dethe hathe enc[hey]ned us and oure kingdom and
bounden with bondes of fire oure prince [and] anone cast hym in the
bondes of dethe.' And thanne anone thei cast cordes abought the
ydole for to throwe hym downe, but thei might noght. And thanne
85 the apostell comaunded to the fende that he shulde go oute and breke
the ydole, and anone he went oute and destroied al the ydoles of the
temple. And thanne the apostell made his orisones, and alle the sike
men were heled. And thanne the apostell halowed the temple of
God, and comaunded to the fende that he shulde go into desert there
90 he shulde noye no man.

And thanne the aungell of God appered there and flye al aboute
the temple, and marked the signe of the crosse with his fyngre in the
.iiij. corners of the temple, saieng: 'Oure Lord saithe that right as ye
be clensed of alle youre siknesse, this temple be clensed of alle filthe.
95 But now y shal shewe you hym that duelled here before this tyme, to
whom the apostell comaunded to go into desert, and drede you noght
of the sight of hym, but makithe yn youre forehedes the signe that y
haue titled in these stones.' And thanne he shewed hem an Ethiope
blacker thanne any tempest, þe visage sharpe, the berde longe, his
100 [h]eres strechinge to his fete, his eyen flamyng as brenninge yren,
castinge oute sparkeles of fire by his mouthe medeled with brim-
stone, his hondes bounden withe brenninge cheynes behynde his
backe. And thanne the aungell saide: 'For that thou hast herde the
comaundement of the apostell and hast tobroke alle the ydoles of the
105 temple, y shalle unbinde the, and go thi way in suche place wher
thou noye no creatoure, and be there into the day of iugement.' And

74 yef . . . baptyme] *om.* D   74–5 resseiue . . . wolde] *ins.* H₁   75 god] goddis D
76 sacrifice] sacrafices H₁D   78 lest] lesse H₁   y] we D   79 harde] fast D
aungelles] aungell E   81 encheyned] enclined E   82 and] *om.* EL, *ins.* H₁   anone/
cast hym] *trs.* H₁   84 ydole] Idollis D   85 fende] feendis D   he] þei D
86 ydole] Idollis D   he] þei D   88 temple] *add* in the worship D   89 to the fende
that] that the feendis D   91 aungell] aungellis D   92 his fyngre] her fyngris D
96 go] *add* oute D   98 these] 't'his H₁   100 heres] eres EH₁D (*cheueulx* P2)
strechinge] streggyng H₁   101 of] *add* brennynge D

whanne he had so saide, the fende went his waye with a gret thunder
and lighteninge, | yollinge and crienge, and the aungell of oure Lorde f. 199ᵛᵇ
stied up into heuene before alle the peple.

And thanne was the kinge cristened with his wif and alle the peple, 110
and lefte his kingdom and becam disciple of the apostell. And thanne
alle the bisshoppes of ydoles gadered hem togederes and went to
Astriardes king, the brother of Polomen, and compleined hem of the
losse of her goddes, and of the distruccion of her temple, and of the
conuersion of his brother that was conuerted by wichecrafte. Than 115
the kinge Astriardes was wonder wroth, and anone he sent a .Mˡ.
armed men to take the apostell. And whanne he was brought before
the kinge, he saide: 'Art thou he that hast peruerted my brother?'
The apostell ansuered and saide: 'Y haue noght peruerted hym, but y
haue conuerted hym.' And the kinge saide: 'Right as thou haste made 120
my brother to forsake his god and leue in thine, right so will y make
the to forsake thi god and beleue in myne.' And þe apostill saide: 'Y
bonde the god that thi brother worshipped and shewed hym to the
peple fast bounde, and constreined hym to breke his fals ymages, and
yef thou might do that to my God thou mightest lyghtly bringe me 125
to thine entent, and yef not y shall tobreke alle thine goddes and leue
thanne in [my God].' And as he saide these thinges, it was saide to
the king that his god Baldak was al tobrokin and throuen downe to
the erthe. And whanne the kinge herde that, he al torent his purple
that he was clothed in and comaunded that the apostell were bete 130
withe staues and that he were flaine al quik. And so he made his
blessed ende. And cristen men toke the bodi and beried it worshipfully. And thanne the kinge Astrages with the bisshopes of the
temple were rauisshed of the fende and deiden sodenly. And the
kinge Polymen was ordeined into a bysshop and fulfelled the office of 135
bisshop | .xx. yere, and after that he rested in pees full of uertues. f. 200ʳᵃ

There is diuerse opiniones of the manere of his passion, for the
blessed Dorothe saithe that he was crusified. And he saithe in this
wise: 'Bartilmew prechid to hem of Ynde, and gaue hem the gospell
after Matheu in [her] propre tunge. And he was crucified in the Gret 140
Ermenye, the hede dunwarde, and beried in the cite of Dalbane.'

112 alle] *om.* D   114 goddes] goodes *changed to* goddes H1   116 Astriardes]
Astri`a´ges D   a] *on erasure* H1, .ij. D   117 apostell] apostels *with final* s *erased* H1
119 hym] *om.* H1   121 god] goddis D   thine] thi god D   126 yef] *add* þou doo
hit D   127 my God] L, myn EH1D   128 throuen] þe owen *changed to* þrowen H1
131 he²] Bartilmewe D   138 Dorothe] Theodore *on erasure* H1, *so* D   140 her]
his E

And the same Theodore saithe that he was hilt, and in sum bokes it
is saide that he was only beheded. And these contrarie thingges mow
be assoiled in this wise: as men sayne, he was furst crucified and
145 before he deied he was take doune of the crosse, and for to haue
gretter turnement he was hilt, and at the laste he was beheded.

In the yere of oure Lorde .CCC.xxxiij. the Sarisenes assailed
Sisile, and wasted al that yle wher the body of Seint Bartilmew
rested, and brostin hys sepulcre, and castin his bones here and there.
150 And it is redde that his body cam oute of Ynde in this wise: whanne
the paynimes sawe that [the] sepulcre [of hym] was gretly worshipped for the miracles that felle there, thei had gret dispite, and
putte hym into a tumbe of lede, and caste hym into the see, and so bi
the will of God he cam into that yle. And whanne the Sarisenes
155 hadde departed his bonis here and there and [th]rewe hem abrode,
the apostle apperid to a monke and saide to hym: 'Go gadre my bonis
that be departed here and there.' And he ansuered and saide: 'Bi
what reson shulde y gadre thi bones or what worship shulde y do
hem, sethe thou hast lete us to be destroied?' And the apostell saide:
160 'Oure Lorde hathe spared this peple here a longe tyme thurgh my
merites, but for her synnes that be so grete and crien to the heuene y
may aske ne gete no foryeuenesse for hem.' And thanne the monke
f. 200rb saide hym: 'How shulde y finde youre bones | amonge so mani other
as be ther?' And þe apostill saide: 'Thou shalt gadre hem by night,
165 and tho that thou findest shininge as fire, take hem up anone.' And
thanne the monke fonde hem euene as he saide, and toke hem up and
went into a shippe and come to Bonifaunt that is the maister cite of
Poile, and thedir he bare hem. And men saye that thei be now atte
Rome, but thei of Bonifaunt saie that they haue the body.

170   A woman brought a vessell full of oyle for to putte into the lampe
of Seint Bartilmewe, and as she enclined the vessell for to haue
poured it into the lampe, there wolde no licoure come oute in no
wise, and yet it was even atte the mouthe of the vessell. And t[h]anne
one of hem saide: 'I trowe it be not agreable to the seint that this oyle
175 be putte in his lampe.' For whiche cause thei putte it in another
lampe, and the oyle cam oute anone.

145 haue] *add* more and D   147 .xxxiij.] and .xxiij. Than D   Sarisenes] *add* come
and D   149 brostin] brake D   150 body] bones D   151 paynimes] L, *add* of hym
EH1D   the²] his EH1   of hym] *om.* EH1   152 felle] were do D   155 threwe] drewe E
157 he] the monke D   159 the] *om.* H1   161 crien] criden H1   162 saide] *add* to H1
163 youre] þi D   165 shininge] shyne D   168 And] *add* som D   169 that] *om.* H1
170 the] a H1   172 poured] p`o´ured H1   into] in H1   173 thanne] tanne E

So as the emperour Peduyk distroied Bonifaunt, and hadde
comaunded that all the chirches that were there [were] destroied,
and did al his powere to bringe that citee into another place and that
a man fonde and sawe men al in white and shininge, and hym thoght   180
that thei were in a gret counsaile togeder. And as he had gret
meruaile what thei were, he asked one of hem, and he ansuered:
'This is Seint Bartilmewe the apostill with other seintez that hadden
chirches in this citee, that spekin and ordeine togederes to what
peyne thei may be demed that haue take hem from her tabernacles.   185
And thei haue confermed among hem by sentence that withoute ani
delaie thei shul go to the iugement of God for to ansuere upon that.'
And anone that emperour deied cursidly.

Seint Ambrose saithe in this wise in his Preface that he made of
this apostell in abregging his legent: 'Ihesu Crist, thou hast dey|nid   f. 200ᵛᵃ
to shewe to thi disciples preching mani thingges of [thi] diuinite and   191
of thi Trinite in meruailous manere and of thi mageste, amonge the
whiche thou sentest the blessed Seint Bartilmew, worshiped bi right
gret prerogatif, to peple of ferre cuntre. And tho it were so that he
were vtterli ferre from mannes conuersacion, alwey he deseruid bi his   195
predicaciones to marke with thi signe the begynninge of that peple.
A, with how gret preisinges is to be worshipped this meruailous
apostell, whanne it suffisithe hym noght to sowe the faithe amonge
the hertes of the peple, but he persid as in fleing the ferrest contrees
of the londes of Inde, and entred into the temple wher there were a   200
gret cumpanie of sike folke withoute nombre, and made the fende so
dume that he gaue none ansuere to none of tho that worshipped
hym. And the quene that was lunatik bi the malice of the fende he
made vnbinde and gaue her to her fader al hole. A, how is he worthi
to be nombred amonge [the] heuenly felawship, to whom the aungell   205
appered to preise the faithe of hym bi his miracles, and cam fro the
soueraigne and shewed to all the peple the fende bounde in cheynes,
and had entailed in the stone the signe of the crosse of ourc Lorde
bering hele. And the kinge and the quene were baptised with the
peple of her citees. And atte the laste the tiraunt brother of the king   210
Polymen, newe in the faith, bi the relacion of the bisshop[es] of the

178 were²] to be E, shold be D   179 into] to H₁D   180 shininge] *add*
clothinge D   189 saithe] *om.* H₁   190 deynid] deuydid *or* denydid D   191 thi²]
om. E   193 sentest] sendest H₁D   194 gret] *om.* H₁   196 thi] þe D
198 sowe] shewe D   200 the londes of] *om.* D   203 lunatik] lymatyk *with first* y *del.*
and first minim of m *subp.* H₁   204 her²] he`r´ D   205 the¹] *om.* E
211 Polymen] *om.* D   relacion] clamacion D, reclamacion H₁   bisshopes] bisshop EH₁

temples made the blessed apostell to be bete, to be flayne, and to
receyue right piteous dethe. And as he denounced the mischef of
dethe, he had and bare with hym into heuenly ioye victorie of his
215 glorious strif.'

And the blessed Theodore, abbot and noble doctour, seithe of this
f. 200ᵛᵇ apostell in this manere | amonge the other thinges: 'Seint Bartilmew
preched furst in Lycony and after in Inde, and atte the last in the
citee of Alban in the Grettest Ermony, and there he was hilt and
220 sethe his hede smete of, and ther he was beried. And whanne he was
sent to preche of oure Lorde, as y rede, he herde that God saide to
hym: "Go preche, go oute and fight, and take upon the þe gret
periles. I haue furst fulfelled the werke of my fader and am the furst
witnesse. Fille the vessell that is necessarie, folu thi maister, loue thi
225 Lorde, putte thi blode for his and thi flesshe for his flesshe, and
suffre that he hathe suffered. Thyn armures ben debonairte in thi
suetingges, mildenesse amonge wicked men, pacience." And the
apostell refusid not, but as true seruaunt obeied to his maister and
went reioysinge, and as the lyght of God he enlumined the
230 derkenesse, so as Seint Austin witnessithe in his boke, and right as
a teler of Ihesu Crist he profited in spirituel tilthe. Seint Petre the
apostell tellithe the nacions, and Bartilmewe, foluinge, dede thinges
like. Seint Petre dede mani gret wonders, and Bartilmewe did worthi
miracles. Seint Petre was crucified the hede dunwarde, and Bartil-
235 mewe was hilt al quik and had his hede smete of atte the last. And
they encresed the Chirche semblably by the yefte of the holi gost.
And right as an harpe yeuithe a swete sowne with mani strengges,
right so alle the aposteles gaue suete melodie of diuine vnite. And
thei were ordeined for to be crioures of the kinge of kingges, and thei
240 departed amonge hem alle the worlde. And the place of Ermeny was
the place of Seint Bartilmew, that is fro Euylach into Gabaon. And
there he ered the unresonable feldes with the plowe of the tunge, in
hyding within the depnesse of hertis the wordis of feith, and in
plantinge the vyne of oure Lorde and trees of paradys, in ympinge in

212 made] *add* tho E   213–4 And . . . dethe] *ins. omitting* as H1   214 had] made D
into] int`o' *with* `o' *on erasure and add* þe H1   220 hede] *add* was E   225 his¹] *add*
`blode' H1   and¹] *add and del.* his flessh for þi flessh *with* þi *marked for trs.* H1   thi², his²]
trs. D   thi flesshe . . . flesshe] *ins.* H1   226 debonairte] devoured *with* v *and final* d *on
erasures* H1, devoured D   227 mildenesse] meldewes H1   228 as] *add* a H1   as . . .
seruaunt] mekeli D   229 he enlumined] enlumyneth D   230 right] *om.* D
233 dede] *ins.* H1   did] *add* many H1D   236 semblably] semblauntli D
237 mani] meri H1D   238 alle] *om.* H1   243 hyding] hi`l'dyng H1

euerich | the remedies medicinables of passiones, and raced up the f. 201ra
thornes not vnderstonding, and cutte downe the wodes of felonie, 246
and closid it aboute withe thornes of techinge.

'But what worship yalde these tyrauntes to the creatoure? Forsothe
unworship for worship, cursinge for blessinge, paynes for guerdones
and tribulacion for rest, and right bitter dethe for lyf. And sethe that 250
this holi seint had suffered mani turmentes, he was atte the last hilt of
hem. He deied noght, and therfor he dispised not hem that slow hym,
but taught hem by miracles. But ther was nothing that might
withdrawe her bestiall thoughtes ne that might withdrawe hem
from euell. What dede thei after? Thei arose in wodenesse ayenst 255
the holy bodi, the seke refused her medicine, the citee forsoke his
keper, the blynde hym that gaue hem sight, tho that perisshed her
gouernour, and the dede hym that gaue lyf. And how trowe ye thei
caste hym oute? Forsothe thei caste the holy bodi into the sec in a
cofre of lede, and the cheste remeued from that region of Armoni 260
with the chestis of .iiij. other marteres that were caste with hym in the
see. And these .iiij. went before in that large space of the see and
dedin seruice to the apostell right as his seruauntes in a manere til
that thei come into the parties of Sesile, into an yle that is cleped
Lyparis, as it was sheuid to the bisshopp of Ostione that thanne was 265
present. And this right riche tresour cam to right a pore woman, and
these right precious margarites cam to a right simple creatoure. And
thanne the other .iiij. went into other cuntrees and lefte þe holy
apostell in that yle. And one of hem that hight Papyen went into the
citee of Sesile, and he sent that other that hight Lucien into the citee 270
of Massien, and he sent that other two into the londe of Calabre. And
thanne was the apostell resseiued worshipfulli with gret preisingges, |
and there was ordeined a chirche in the worship of hym. And the hille f. 201rb
of Vulcan was nye to that yle, and was to hym full disesi for that she
receiued fire, the whiche hille by the merites of Seint Bartilmew 275
withdrow hym from that yle .vij. myle withoute sight of ani man and
sette herself towardes the see, and yet she aperithe there into this
same day. I sa[lu]e Bartilmewe, blessed of blessed, clerenesse of the

245 up] upon E   247 withe] add the E   252 hem¹] add and H1
253 hem] him changed to hem H1   256 his] this changed to his H1   257 the
blynde] þe`ï´ `blyndid´ H1, so D   hem] om. H1   perisshed] preysed H1, prechid D
258 gouernour] gouernaunce D   dede] add `to´ H1   the dede hym] dide him to þe
dethe D   259 holy] hole H1   260 the cheste] that cofre D   266 woman]
man D   274 to¹] vnto H1   disesi] vnesy D   277 towardes] to`o´wardes H1
278 salue] sawe EH1D (salue P2)

devyne light of holy Chirche, fisher of resonable fisshes, wounder of
280 the fende that hadde wounded the world by his thefte. Thou
reioycest, the sonne of the worlde, enluminynge all erthely thyngges,
the mouthe of God, the tunge enbrasid puttinge oute wisdom, a welle
goodly renninge full of holynesse, that haludest the see by thi
goingges vnremuables, that madest the erthe rede bi thi blode, that
285 repairest shininge in heuene in the middell of the devine cumpanie
clere in the shininge of glorie, and reioisest the in [the] gladnesse of
ioy withoute ende.' And this is that Theodore saithe.

Here endithe the lif of Seint Bartilmew, and nexst
beginnithe the lif of Seint Austin, Capitulum .C.xvij.

Seint Austin the noble doctour was born in Aufrike in the citee of
Cartage [and was] of full honest kinrede, and his fader hight Patrice
and his moder Demomark. He was sufficiauntly taught in all the
liberall artes so that he was holde for a soueraigne philosophre and a
5 right noble rethour. He lerned by hymself withoute maister alle the
bokes of Aristotle and alle other that he might finde of liberall artes
and understode hem, so as he saithe and witnessithe in his boke of
Confessiones that he made, saieng: 'alle the boke[s] that thei calle now
of the liberall artis, I right felon seruaunt of couetise red by myself
f. 201ᵛᵃ and understode | al tho that y might rede, and alle tho of the crafte of
11 spekinge and deuisinge, alle tho of diuisiones and of figures of musik
and of noumbres; y redde hem and understode hem withoute gret
strengthe and withoute that anibodi taught me. That knowest thou,
my Lorde and my God, for þe hastinesse of myn understondinge and
15 the largesse of my lerninge come of the, but y sacrified noght to the.'
And therfor science withoute charite edifiethe noght but bolnithe up
in the errour of Mani[c]hiens, þat affermyn that Ihesu Crist was
fantastik and denie the resureccion of the flesshe, in whiche errour
Austin felle and was therin .ix. yere. And whanne he was a childe he
20 beleued suche trifeles that he said that the figge tre wepte whanne
men toke away either the figge or the leef.

279 fisher] fisshe *changed to* fisshere H1   wounder] wonderer D   280 his] *ins.* H1,
om. D   281 worlde] worlis D   283 thi] þe H1   284 thi] þe H1   286 the³]
om. E, þi D

EH1DH2A1A2L   D breaks off after 163 *gaue me* and resumes at 429 *to Pavie*
2 and was] and D, *om.* E   3 moder] *add* hiȝt D   taught] *so with* a *on erasure* H1
8 bokes] boke E   8–9 now of the] *om.* D   11 and²] *om.* H1D   13 withoute]
with'oute' H1   15 come] *add* onli D   but . . . the] *om.* H1   sacrified] sacrifice D
17 Manichiens] L, Manithiens EH1D   19 a childe] *ins.* H1

And whanne he come to the age of .xix. yere he beganne to rede
upon a boke of philosophe, in the whiche he taught to dispise the
uanite of the worlde and to lerne philisophie, and this boke lyked
hym wonder well, but he was sori that the name of Ihesu Crist, 25
whiche he hadde lerned of his moder, was not in that book. And his
moder wepte continuelly for hym and enforced her with al her
powere to bringe hym to the trouthe of the faithe. And as it is wretin
in his Confessiones, as she stode in a place al sorufully her semed
that she sawe a yonge man stonde besydes her þat asked her the 30
cause of her heuinesse. And she saide: 'Y wepe the losse of my sone
Austin.' And he ansuered her: 'Be sure, for as thou art, he is.' And
anone she sawe her sone bysides her. And whanne she hadde tolde
this to Austin he saide to her: 'Moder, thou art deceiued, for it was
not saide so but "there y am thou art".' And she the contrarie: 'Sone, 35
it was not so saide to me but "there y am thou art."' And the moder
ententifly praied with al her herte to a bisshopp, so as Austin
witncssith | in his boke, that he wolde vouchesauf to praie to God f. 201vb
for her sone. And he was in maner anoyed of her continuel praier
and ansuered her by voys of prophecie and saide: 'Go thi waye, 40
woman, and be sure, for it were impossible that a sone of so many
tiers might perisshe.' And whanne he had mani yeres taught retorik
in Cartage, he come to Rome priuely withoute wetinge of his moder
and ther he assembled mani disciples. And his moder had folued
hym to the yate to that ende she might haue withholde hym or elles 45
to haue go with hym, but he abode that night and parted away
priuely. And in the morw whanne she perseiued it she filled the eeres
of God with clamours and went night and day to the chirche and
praied for her sone.

In that tyme tho of Mylan required a doctour of Symach the 50
provost of Rome that redde retorik. And Seint Ambrose was that
same tyme bisshopp of the same citee, and Seint Austin was sent
thedir atte the praier of hem of Melan. And his moder might haue no
rest but she sette gret laboure to come to hym, and whanne she come
she fonde that he was neither verrey Many[c]hien ne verrey catholyk. 55

    23 philosophe] philosophre H1   taught] *so with* a *on erasure* H1   25 wonder] *om.*
H1D   29 Confessiones] Confession H1D   33 sone] *add* Augustyn D
34 Austin] *add* her sone D   her] his D   35 so] *om.* H1   there . . . art] *on erasure* H1
she] *add* seide aȝen to him D   36 there] as *on erasure* H1   y am] I am *subp.* H1   thou
art] *add* 'he is' H1   40 by] b'i' *on erasure* H1   41 so] *om.* H1D   42 yeres] *add* he
H1, *add* be D   48 clamours] clamoure H1D   55 that . . . was] him D   Manychien]
L, Manythien EH1D

And thanne Austin began to drawe to Seint Ambrose and herde
often tymes his predicacions. And he was full ententif in heringe of
sermones that there were nothinge saide ayenst the Manythiens nor
other eresye. In a tyme it fell that Seint Ambrose disputed ayenst
60 tho errours longe and comaunded hem by opin resones and by
auctoritees, so that the errour was all putte oute of the herte of Seint
Austin. And what that fell after, he tellithe in his boke of Confessiones and saith: 'Whan y knewe the furst, thou chasedist away
from me the infirmite of my sight with a mighty beme of shinynge,
f. 202ʳᵃ and y trembeled for the drede of thi loue, and y | fonde me to
66 be ferre from the, in a region of unliklyhede, as though y herde thi
uoise fro an hye that saide: "Y am mete of gretnesse encresed, and
thou shalt ete me, but thou shalt not chaunge me into the as mete of
flesshe, but thou shalt be chaunged into me."'

70   And as he tellithe there, hit liked hym well, but yet he dradde
hym to go by þat streite way, but anone oure Lorde putte in his
thought that he shulde go to Symplicien, in whom alle devine grace
shyn[ed], that he might putte oute to hym his desires, and in
talkinge togederes þat he might haue knoulache in what manere he
75 might most couenably liue for to go in the waye of God, as he dede,
for as moche as he dede displese witheoute the suetnesse of God and
withoute the beauute of the hous of God, the whiche he loued. And
Symplicien taught hym in his best wise, and he hymself monestid
hymself and saide: 'A, how mani children and how mani maydenes
80 seruin in the Chirche of God to oure Lorde, and whedir thou maist
[not] do as thei done. What abidest thou? Cast al in hym and he
will resseiue the and hele the.' And amonge these talkingges betwene
hem cam to mynde a good man that hight Victor. Wherof
Symplicien was gladde and tolde how that the same Victor, that
85 tyme a paynim, by hys souerayne wisdom deserued that there was
made in Rome an ymage to hys lyknesse in the market place and not
for that he saide he wolde be cristen. And as Symplicien saide that
'Y shulde neuer leve that til y sawe hym in the chirche,' he ansuered
in pley and saide: 'The walles make not the cristen man.' And atte

57 in heringe of] to hure D   60 tho] þe H1D   66 be] *ins.* H1   67 hye] *ins.*
H1   68 ete] *ins.* H1   not] *ins.* H1, *om.* D   69 me] mete D   73 shyned]
shynithe E   desires] *add and del.* And in takyng togiders þat he might put out to him his
desires H1   74 talkinge] ta`l´king H1   76 displese] despised H1   the] *om.* H1D
79 how mani²] how `many´ H1, *om.* D   80 whedir] whi D   81 not] *om.* E
81–2 and he will] þat he D   82 betwene] *om.* D   84 Victor] *add* beynge D
87 as] L, *add* y EH1D

the laste whanne he come to the chirche, the boke wherin the 90
Cr[e]de of the masse was yn was take hym to rede as the custume
was, and he went up an hye and with an hye uoys beganne to rede it
and to pronounce opinly, and tho of Rome mer|uailed and the f. 202ʳᵇ
chirche reioised and alle the peple crieden sodenly: 'Victor, Victor',
and thanne thei helde her pees for gladnesse. 95

And after that there come from Aufrike a frende of Seint Austines
that hight Ponsiane and tolde the lyf and the myracles of that gret
Antony that was but late dede before under Constance the emperoure. And thanne by her ensaumples Austin enchaufid hym strongly,
and saide to a felow of hys that hight Lypin with gret corage: 'Alas, 100
what suffre we, what abide we? Arise we up, f[or] the foles taken
hcuene and we be plunged into helle with oure doctrines, and for
thei be go tofore us we haue shame to folw hem.'

And thanne he ranne hym into a gardin and, as hc saithe hymself,
cast hym under a figge tree and [w]lepte right bitterly and gaue 105
wepinge voise for that he hadde abidde so longe fro day to day and
fro litell to litell. And he was hougely turmented with his taryenge as
he writithe after that same boke, and saide: 'Alas, Lorde, how thou
art high in hyghe thinges and depe in depe thingges and thou gost
neuer oute of the waye and vnnethe we come to the. A, Lorde,' saide 110
he, 'calle me and chaunge me and rauisshe me and enlumine me and
make softe alle myn enponchementis, for y drede hem sore as y haue
cause. Alas, y haue loued the to late, beaute right auncien and so
newe. Y haue to late loued the. Thou were withinne and y was
withoute and there y sought the, and in these faire thingges that thou 115
hast made y fille alle defourmed. Thou were with me and y was not
with the, thou calledist and criedist and hast broke my defenes, that
hast enlumynid and clered my blyndenesse, and thou hast fulfelled
me with suete sauours and y haste me to the. Y haue tastid the and y
haue hunger and coueite the, thou hast touched | me and y am f. 202ᵛᵃ
enchaufed in thi pees.' And as he wepte bitterly he herde a uoys þat 121
saide: 'Take and rede, take and rede.' And anone he openid a boke
and cast his eyen upon the furst chapitre and redde: 'Clothe us in

91 Crede] crde E   was yn] ins. H₁, om. D   98 under] add to E   99 enchaufid]
enhaunsed H₁D   101 for] fro E, for on erasure H₁   102 be] om. H₁D   oure] om. D
105 wepte] slepte E, slept changed to wept H₁   109 and²] add lord D   112 make]
add me H₁   113 late] add and þi D   beaute] add is D   114 newe ... haue] I have
nowe D   119 and¹] wherfore D   120 hunger and coueite] coueitid D
121 enchaufed] enhaunsed H₁D   thi] þe H₁   122 take and rede] om. H₁D   And] ins.
H₁

oure Lorde,' and anone alle the doutes of derkenesse weren
125 quenched.

And in the mene tyme he began to be so gretly turmented with the
toth eake that he was nigh brought into the opynion of Cornelyen the
philysophre that helde that the souerayne helthe of the soule was in
wisdom, and that the souerayne welthe of the body was not to fele
130 none euell in no place. And that peine was so strong that he lost his
speche, and therfor he wrote in tables of wexe that alle men shulde
praie for hym that oure Lorde wolde lisse his payne. And he kneled
downe with other and fonde hymself al sodenly hole.

And thanne he sent lettres to the holi man Seint Ambrose praieng
135 hym that he wolde sende hym worde whiche of the bokes of holy
writte were most expedient for to rede for to make a man more
couenable to cristen faithe. And he sent hym worde ayen that Ysaie
the prophete, for that he ys sayne to be the moste couenable
pronouncer of the gospell and of the callinge of men. And as
140 Austin understode not all the begynnynges, but went that sum
thingges had be otherwise thanne thei were, he abode to rede hem
til he was more cunnyng in holy writte.

And whanne Ester Day come and Austin was .xxx. wynter, he and
his sone that hight Deodat[o], a childe of noble witte, the whiche he
145 had gote in his youthe whanne he was paynim, and his felaw Apyen,
thorugh the merites and exortaciones of his moder resseiued bapteme
f. 202ᵛᵇ of Seint Ambrose. And thanne as it is redde | Seint Ambrose saide:
'Te Deum laudamus,' and Austin ansuered: 'Te Dominum confitemur,'
and so these two ordeined and made fro that one to that other this
150 ympne and songe it to the ende, and Honerien witnessithe this same
in his boke that is clepte [The] Mirrour of the Chirche. And in sum
other bokes is sette this title: The Canticle of Ambrose and of
Austine. And anone he was merueilously confermid in the faithe of
holy Chirche, and anone he forsoke al the hope that he hadde in the
155 worlde and he renounced his scoles that he gouernid.

And he tellithe in the boke beforesaide how he was fro thennes
forwarde enchaufed in the loue of God, and saithe: 'Lorde, thou
haste persed myn herte with thi charite and y bare thi wordes ficched

125 quenched] *add* in him D   126 gretly] grevousli D   129 was] *add* is E
130 no] *on erasure* H1   133 al] *om*. D   al sodenly] *trs*. H1   134 Seint] *om*. H1D
136 writte] *add* whiche D   138 moste] maister and D, mestre H1   141 thingges]
thing H1   143 wynter] 3ere D   144 Deodato] Deodata E   145 whanne] was
changed to w'h'an H1   150 Honerien] Evrien D   151 The] *om*. E   in] *om*. H1
152 The] is H1, *om*. D   156 boke] *om*. H1   157 enchaufed] enhaunsed H1D

in my mynde, and th[e] ensaumples of thi meruailous maners, how
thou makest of blacke bright shininge and of dede thou makest quik, 160
the assembles of thoughtes brenne[d] me [and toke awey my grevous
slothe]. I stied up into the hille of wepinge, and synginge the songe
of degrees thou gaue me sharpe arowes and wastinge coles, ne y was
not in tho dayes salowed of thi merueylous swetnesse for to considre
the besinesse of the diuine counsaile upon the hele of mankinde. 165
How ofte haue y wepte in thi ympnes and in thi canticles suete
sowning; the voys of th[e] Chirche y haue meuid sharpely. Thi voys
ranne in my eeres and thi trouthe ranne doune evin into myn herte
and teres ranne downe and y was wel in ease with hem.

'And thanne [tho] thingges were ordeyned to be songe in the 170
chirche of Melan. And y song and cried with an hye crie of myn
herte: "*O in pace, O in id ipsum:* O thou that saiest: 'Y shal slepe in
that same and take my reste.' Thou art that self, for thou art not
chaunged, and in the is rest, foryeting al laboures." I redde | al that f. 203ra
psalme and brende, I that had be a biter berker and blinde ayenst þe 175
letteres medlid with the hony of heuen and now enlumyned with
[thi] light of grace. Ihesu Crist myn helper, how suete hast thou
made to me sodenly to forsake the swetnesse of my trifeles, and that
whiche was fere for me to leve, now y forsake withe gret ioye. Thou
hast putte hem oute fro me, and hast made thi soueraigne suetnesse 180
entre into me that is swete aboue alle suetnesse and aboue alle delites,
more clere thanne ani lyght and more secrete thanne alle counsailes,
more hye than alle worship and none so high as he.'

And after this he toke Nebroyen and Euodyen and his moder and
returned ayen into Aufryke, but whanne they come to Tyberin his 185
debonayr moder deide. And after her dethe he returnid to his propre
heritage, and ther he gaue hymself to the seruise of God and lyued in
fastingges and in orisones with hem that were ioyned to hym. He
wrote bokes and taught the vnwise, and the renoun of hym spred al
abrode, and in al his bokes and in al his dedes he was holde 190
meruailous. And he escheued to go to ani citee that had no bisshop
lest he were lette bi that office.

159 the] tho E   161 brenned] L, brennen EH1D   161–2 and . . . slothe] L, *om.*
EH1D   163 ne] For H2   164 tho] the H2   salowed of thi] halowed in the H2
167 the voys . . . sharpely] *om.* H1   the²] thi E   Thi voys] the voice that H2
168 doune] *om.* H1H2   into] to H1   170 tho] *om.* EH1H2L (*ces* P2)   171 and
cried] *om.* H1H2   172 O¹ . . . *ipsum* O] Lo H1   173 my] *om.* H1H2   175 biter]
better H2   176 the] `þe´ H1   177 thi] his EH1L, the H2 (*ta* P2)   179 for] fro
H1H2   181 into] in H1   186 her] *om.* H1   187 seruise] heritage H2

And in that tyme there was in Iponence a man full of gret ricches,
that sent to Seint Austin to saie that, yef he wolde come to hym and
195 that he might here of hym the worde of God, he wolde forsake the
worlde. And whanne Austin herde that, he went to hym in haste, and
whanne Valerian bisshop of Iponence herde of his renomee, he
ordeined hym to be preste in his chirche, notwithstonding he refusid
it gretly and wepte sore. And sum demed his weping made of pride
200 and saide to hym that it was tyme for hym for to be made preste that
f. 203ʳᵇ it were so that he were worthi gret|ter dignite, but thus he neighed to
the bisshopriche. And anone he ordeined a chirche of clerkes and
beganne to leue after the rule of the aposteles, of whiche chirche
there were .x. chosen bisshopes. And for as moche as the said
205 bisshop was a Greke and lesse taught in that tonge, he gaue power to
Austin for to preche, ayen the maner of the Chirche of the Orient.
And therfor mani bisshoppes dispised hym, but he raught neuer
whiles he might make done by hym that he coude not do bi hymself.

In that tyme he ouercome Fortunat the preste, and Manachien
210 that was heretik, and other heretikes he ouercome hem [and
confounded hem]. And thanne the blessed Valerian beganne to
drede lest Austin were take awey fro hym for to be made bisshop
of ani other citee. And he wolde full gladly haue profered hym his
cure yef he dredde not that he wolde haue gone awey to sum secrete
215 place that he might not be founde. And thanne he praied to the
ershebisshop of Cartage that he might cese and that Austin might be
promoted in his stede into the chirche of Iponence. But Austin
refused it in all wises, but he was constreined so ferforthely that he
resseyued it atte the laste and toke upon hym the cure of the
220 bisshoppriche. And it is redde how that he saide oftin of hymself
in this wise: 'I fele not oure Lorde so wrothe with me in nothinge as
in that y was not worthi for to be sette in the hynesse of the
gouernaunce of the Chirche.'

His clothing and al his other aray were not to vile nother to good,
225 but weren homly withoute preciouste. And therfor he said of
hymself: 'I am of precious clothinge, and therfor whanne ani ys
geue me y selle it, and for the vestement may not be comune y make

194 sent] seint E   to saie] word H2   that yef] trs. H1   196 whanne] add seinte H2
200 for¹] to H1H2   201 he¹] it H1H2   202 bisshopriche] bisshopp H1
203 chirche] chirchis H2   204 .x. chosen] trs. H1H2   208 make] add to be H2
210 and¹] add meny H2   210–11 and confounded hem om. E   211 beganne to] om.
H2   217 promoted] promittid H2   But] add seinte H2   219–20 the bisshoppriche]
a bisshop H2   222 not] om. H1H2   the¹] om. H1   225 of] to H2

the prise comune.' He vsed alway plente at his borde, but scarsly to hymselff. And betwene his wortes and other potages | he hadde f. 203ᵛᵃ flesshe for other gestes and for other sike folke, and he loued more 230 atte his borde lesson or dispituson thanne the mete. And this vers was wreten in his borde ayens hem that loued detraccion:

> *Quisquis amat dictis absentum rodere uitam,*
> *Hanc mensam vetitam noueris esse sibi.*

This is to saie, whosoeuer loue for to missaie of ani creature that is 235 not here present atte this borde, he may wel saye it ys deuied hym atte alle. For in a tyme as a man had losid his tunge to saie evell of a bisshopp that was familier withe hym, anone he reproued hym sharpely and saide that but [yef he] wolde go fro that table he wolde afface that vers fro the table. 240

In a tyme he had bodin to diner sum of his familier frendes, and one of hem that [was more familier] than another went into the kichin and fonde al colde that ther was. And thanne he come to Seint Austine and asked hym what he had ordeined for her diner, and he ansuered he coude no skille in suche metes. And he saide: 'Y will ete 245 with you.'

And than saide Seint Austine that he had lerned thre thingges of Seint Ambrose: the furst was that he shulde make no mariage, the secund that he shulde neuer counsaile man to ride but yef he wolde hymself, the .iij.ᵉ that he shulde go to no festis. The cause of the 250 furst, that yef thei be not of one acorde thei shul curse the maker; the secounde, yef the rider toke ani harme in rydinge he shulde ch[ide] the councellour; the cause of the thridde [is] that perauenture he shalle lese the manere of his attemperaunce.

He was of so gret attemperaunce of purete and of humilite that the 255 right lytell synnes that he dede whiche we sette litell by, he acounted hem grete and confessid hym to God in the boke of his Confession[s] and acusid hym full humbly before God. For he acusid hym there that, whan he was a childe, how he pleyed atte the | balle whanne he f. 203ᵛᵇ shulde haue go to scole. And of that he wolde not haue lerned but yef 260

228 pris] prince *with n subp.* H1   but] *add* right H2   230 for other] for oþer *on erasure* H1   238 hym¹] *add* and EH1   239 yef he] we E, he *on erasure* H1 240 that vers] these versis H2   241 diner] dyuerse H2   familier] *om.* H2 242 was/more familier] *trs.* EH1   245 And] *add* also H2   252 chide] chese E, 'chide' H1, curse H2   253 is] *om.* E   255 attemperaunce] *add* for H2   of¹] *ins.* H1 purete] pouerte H1H2   256 we] he *del.* 'we' H1   257 hym] hem H2   Confessions] confession E   258 full . . . hym²] *om.* H1

he had be constreined bi his maister and bi his kynne. And of that [þat] whanne he was a child he vsed to rede gladly the fables of Enee, and wepte Dydo that was dede for loue. And of that he hadde stole ani thinge out of the seler and fro the table of his fader and moder for
265 to yeue children that pleied with hym. And also of that [þat] whanne he pleied with children how he had the victori by frauude. And also of that þat whanne he was .xvj. yere olde how he had stole peres oute of a gardin that was nye a vynge of his.

And also he accused hymself of that litell delectacion that he felt
270 sumtyme in etinge, and he saide: 'Thou hast taught me that y shall go right in suche wise to take my norisshing of mete as of medicine. But whanne y go to reste of fillinge bi heuinesse of nede, in that wey the snare of couetise aspiethe me; for this goinge is delite and is none other thinge to whiche necessite constreinithe the. And how it be
275 that cause of etinge and of drinkynge [be] hele, [yet it] ioynithe with her a perilous chaumbrere that is ioyouste, the whiche aforcith her oft tymes to perisshe. A, Lorde, ho is he that is not sumtyme a passed his metes? What that euer he be, forsothe he is gret, preised his name, for it [am] not y, for I am a sinful man. Ther is no man
280 sure in this lyf, the whiche is alle temptacion.'

And also he acusid hym of the apetit of preisinge and of the mevinge of veyne glorie, saieng: 'Ho that will be preised of man and thou blame hym, shal not be defended of men whan thou shalt iuge hym, ne be withdrawe whan thou shalt dampne hym. For man is
285 pre[i]sed for sum yefte that thou hast geue hym, and alway he reioysith more to be preised than he dothe of the yefte.'

This holy man confounded right worthely the heretikes so ferforthly that thei preched .iij. tymes opinly that it shulde be no synne to sle Austin, and mani tymes thei leide aspies for hym. But
f. 204ra he | askaped alwaies that thei might not finde hym.
291 His mynde was alway upon the pore, and socoured hem frely of suche as he had, and sumtyme he comaunded to breke the vessell of the chirche for the pore and the nedi and prisoners. He wolde neuer

261 bi¹] of H2L   262 þat] *om.* E   263 that¹] *om.* H1   265 yeue] *add* þe H1, *add* to the H2   þat] *om.* EH2   267 þat] *om.* H2   268 a vynge of his] beynge to him H2   274 how] though H2   be] *add* so H2   275 be] by EH1   yet it] *om.* EH1
276 ioyouste] ioyes to H2   aforcith] afor`si´th H1, enforsith H2      277 sumtyme] som`tyme´ H1   278 forsothe] fore suth H1   gret preised] gretly to be praised H1, gretli to be perisshid H2   279 am] an E   280 is] *add* withoute H1H2   alle] *om.* H2
282 Ho] he H1H2   that] *add* hath H1H2   will] *add* to H1H2   285 preised] presed E
287 man] add Austyn H2   288 ferforthly] ferforthe shortly H1H2   289 for] to slee H2   291 hem] him H1

beye hous ne londe, but refused many heritages that were lefte hym, and was content with that he posseded of the chirches, and night and 295 day his mynde and thought was in divine scripture[s]. He sette neuer his studie to newe bildinge[s], but eschewed to sette his corage therin, the whiche he wolde alwaies haue fre fro all bodely ocupacion that he might the more frely and the more continuelly entende to the lesson. But he deuied not to hem that wolde edefien but yef he sawe 300 hem do it to moche oute of rule.

He preised gretly hem that had desire to deye, and recorden upon that many tymes the ensaumples of .iij. bisshoppes. For whanne Seint Ambrose was atte his ende and that they praied hym that he wolde gete hym lengthinge of his lyf bi his praiers he ansuered: 'I 305 haue not so lyued that y haue shame to leue among you, and y drede not to deye for y haue a good Lorde.' The whiche ansuere Seint Austin preised meruailously.

He wolde no tyme speke alone with no [wo]man but yef it were bi necessite of gret counsaile. He dede neuer good to hys kynne so 310 ferforthely that he habounded in richesse so thei were kepte fro [to] gret pouerte. He roght neuer he wolde neuer praie for ani cause, other bi lettres or by worde, withoute gret cause, and whan he dede, he attempred so the manere of his enditinge that it was not chargeable, but the curtesye of his enditinge deseruid to be herde. 315 He wolde rather here causes betwene unknowen men thanne betwene his frendes, sayenge betwene hem he might lyghtly knowe one yvell and of hym he might make a frende for whiche he gaue the sentence rightfully, but yef they were his frendes he shulde lese that one, hym | whiche that he had geue sentence to ayenst hym. f. 204rb

Whanne he preched he had in custume sum tyme to departe hym 321 fro his purpos, and thanne he wolde saie that it was so ordeined of God for the profit of sum creature, as it aperid in one of the secte of Manithenes that in a sermon that Seint Austine preched wherin he made a departinge and preched furthe ayenst that errour and he was 325 conuerted to the faithe.

295 chirches] Chirche H2   296 scriptures] scripture E   297 bildinges] bildinge EHɪ   301 it] *om.* Hɪ   of] *add* reson and HɪH2   302–3 upon that] openli þat Hɪ, openli H2   303 the] yevyng HɪH2   ensaumples] samples Hɪ   305 ansuered] *add* and seide H2   307 ansuere] seide H2   308 Austin] *add* is H2   309 alone] of loue *changed to* `a'loue Hɪ, *om.* H2   woman] man E   311 were] wer *changed to* ner H2 kepte] *ins.* Hɪ   fro to] L, fro the Hɪ, to H2   313 dede] *add* so H2   314 attempred] attemptid H2   his] *om.* Hɪ   it] he H2   not] *om.* H2   318 he²] *ins.* Hɪ   the] *om.* H2 sentence] seintes *changed to* sentens Hɪ   319 that] *om.* HɪH2   320 hym] of hem HɪH2   geue] *add* the Hɪ   322 so] *om.* H2   323 aperid] appereth HɪH2

In that tyme that the Gothes had take Rome, and that the idolatris
and the fals cristen reioysed hem gretly, Seint Austin made for that
cause the boke of þe Citee of God, in whiche he shewed furst that
330 the rightwys men were destroied in this lyf and the wicked men
flouredin, and he likened hem to two citees, that is Ierusalem and
Babiloine and of the kinges of hem, for the king of ʒerusalem is Ihesu
Crist and he of Babiloyne is the fende. The whiche .ij. citees maken
.ij. loues to hemself, for the erthely citee ordeinithe a loue to herself
335 encresinge to the dispite of God, the heuenly citee a loue to God
encresing to the dispising of hymself.

In his tyme the Wandelyens about the yere of oure Lorde .CCCC.lx.
tokin alle the prouince of Aufrike an wasted alle the cuntre, and spared
nother man ne woman of ordre ne of age. And after that thei come to
340 the citee of Iponence and beseged it with gret powere. And vnder this
tribulacion Seint Austin before alle other ledde right a bitter lyf in his
age, for his teres were his brede night and day whanne he sawe that one
slayne, that other chasyd, and the chirches wedowes of her prestes, and
the citees wasted with her dwellers. And amonge alle these sorwes he
345 comforted hym in the sentence of a wise man that saide: 'Be thou not
gret in deminge gret thinges, for stones and trees falle downe and dedly
f. 204ᵛᵃ men deyen.' Thanne he called his | bretheren and saide to hem: 'I haue
praied oure Lorde that he take us oute of these periles or elles he geue
us pacience or take me oute of this lif, that y be not constreined to so
350 moche cursidnesse.' And than oure Lorde graunted hym the thridde
request, and in the thridde monthe of the sege he was laboured with the
feuer and laye downe in his bedde. And whanne he understode the
departing of his body, he made write the sevene psalmes before hym,
and sette hem upon the walle at his beddis fete and redde hem lyeng in
355 his bedde and wepte habundauntly. And for that he wolde tende to
God more frely, and that his entencion shuld not be lette with nothing,
.x. dayes before his partinge he wolde suffre none to entre unto hym
but yef it were whanne the fisicien come or whanne his refeccion was
brought to hym.

360   In this mene tyme a sike man come to hym and praied hym gretly
that he wold leye his honde upon hym and hele hym of his siknesse.
And Seint Austin ansuered: 'Sone, what is that [that] thou requirest

333 he] the kynge H2   335 citee] add ordeyneth H2   336 hymself] hemselfe
H2   337 his] this H2   Wandelyens] Wandekens H2   342 day] add wha E, add And
H2   343 slayne . . . other] slee that othir or H2   of her] and H2   344 the citees]
þe cite H1H2   355 tende] tent H1, entende H2   356 nothing] add in H1
357 partinge] add hens H2   suffre] ins. H1   362 that²] om. EH1

me? Wenist thou, and y coude do suche thingges, that y wolde not do
it to myself?' And that other alwaye required hym, affermyng that he
had be comaunded so by a vision that he shulde come to hym. And 365
thanne Seint Austine seing the faithe of hym praied for hym and he
receiued hele. He heled many sike folkes and dede mani other
miracles.

And whanne his departing neighed, he taught his bretheren that
thei shulde kepe in mynde that no man of what degre that he were 370
shulde not passe oute of this worlde withoute confession and
resseiuyng his saueoure. And whanne he come to his last houre he
felt hymself al hole of alle hys membris, of good understondinge and |
clere seinge and heringe, in the yere of his age .lxxvj., and .xl. of his f. 204ᵛᵇ
bisshoprich, and leyde hymself in praiers with al his bretheren that 375
praied. He made no testament, for he was pore in Ihesu Crist and had
not wherwith. And he floured about the yere of oure Lorde .CCCC.

And this Seint Austin, right clere by light of wisdom, fyting in
defence of trouthe and of feithe and garnison of the Chirche,
surmounted alle the other doctours of the Chirche as wel by 380
engyne as be cunninge, flouring withoute comparison as well bi
ensaumples of vertues as bi habundaunce of doctrine. Of whom the
blessed Remy in recording Seint Ierom and sum other doctours saien
in this wise: 'Seint Austin concludid alle the other be engyn and be
cunning, for though it be so that Seint Ierome saithe that he had red 385
.vjMˡ. volumes of Origenes, this same alway wrote so many that none
ne might by day ne be night not only write his volumes but also not
mowe rede hem.' Uolusien, of whom Seint Austin writithe the
episteles, saithe in suiche wise of hym: '[It] failethe in the lawe of
God al that Austin vnknewe.' 390

And Seint Ierome saithe in a pistell that he writith to Seint Austin:
'I hadde not mowe ansuere to thi .ij. grete bokes shining thorugh alle
of faire speche, and suerly [that] y haue saide and lerned by engyne
[or] by kunynge and drawen out of the wellys of scriptures, is putte
away and as a desert to the, but y praie thi reuerens suffre me a litell 395
while to preise thin engine and kunning.'

Seint Gregori saithe also of his bokes in a pistell that he wrote to
Innocent provost of Aufrike: 'For that it hathe liked the to sende to

363 coude do] couth H1H2   367 other] om. H1   370 man] maner *with* er *erased*
H1   372 resseiuyng] *add* of H1H2   375 bisshoprich] bisshopps H1   376 was]
ins. H1   382 ensaumples] ensample H1H2   387 but] ne H2   also] *add* myght H2
389 It] That E   393 that] om. E   394 or] *om.* E   wellys] welle H2

us for the exposicion of Seint Iob, we reioyse us in the studie, but yef
f. 205ra   thou wilt be made fatte in kunning, | rede the suete and delicious
401   pisteles of thi patron Seint Austin, but thenke not that oure whete
may be lykened to his rye.'

And the blessed Prosper saithe of hym: 'Seint Austin the bisshop
was softe in kunninge thinges in faire speche, wise of letterure, a
405   noble werker in werkes of the Chirche, clere in disputison eueri day,
sharpe in assoylinge questiones, right opin in confoundinge the
eresies, and right cristen in expouninge oure faithe and sotill in
the exposicion of scriptures of the canon.'

And so after this, straunge peple had occupied that londe and had
410   corrupted the holi places, the good cristen token the bodi of Seint
Austin and bare it into Sardonie. And after that .CC. wynter and
.iiij^xx. passed, Lyprand, a devout kinge of Lumbardie, sent his noble
messengers for to bringe to Pavie the holy reliques of the holy
doctoure, and so thei brought this holy body to Ienys. And whanne
415   this holy king herde that he came, [he] went ayenst h[y]m with gret
ioye and resseived hym worshipfully. And in the morwtyde whanne
thei wolde bere furthe the body, thei might not remeue it in no wise,
into the tyme that the kinge made a solempne avowe to make there a
chirche in the worship of that glorious corseint. And as sone as he
420   hadde done, thei lefte hym up withouten ani strengthe. And the day
folwing there fille a miracle in a towne of the bisshopriche of Tridone
that hight Cassell, and there the kinge made another chirche in
worship of the seint, and gaue that towne with alle the aportenaunces
to hem that serued in the chirche of Seint Austin in pleine possession
425   for euermore. For the kinge desired to plese that holi seint, and that
his chirche were made after his desire, and he dred sore lest the seint
wolde chese sum other place thanne he desired, and the kinge
f. 205rb   herborued hym in eueri place | with the body. And thus he was
ledde to Pavie with gret ioye and there he was sette worshipfully in
430   the chirche of Seint Petre that is called *Ciel Dore*.

Seint Bernarde in a night as he was atte Mateins he slombered a

400 rede] and H1   403 And] *add* as H1H2   Prosper] prophet H1   404 in²] of
H1   letterure] letture H2   406 confoundinge] confounddy`ng´ H1   409 had¹] *om.*
H2   that] þe H1   410 the¹] *add* goode H2   411 Sardonie] Sardoyne H1
411–12 wynter/and .iiij^xx.] *trs. with* wynters H1   415 he²] and E   hym] hem E
417 not] *ins.* H1   418 avowe] a *with* vowe *on erasure* H1   421 folwing] folowyng
with yng *above three del. letters* H1   423 aportenaunces] apportenaunce H1
425 holi] *om.* H1   426 he] the kynge H2   429 ledde] brought H1H2
430 *Ciel*] tiel H1

litell, and thei redde the lessones of a trete of Seint Austin. And thanne he sawe right a faire yonge man stondinge before hym, and so gret habundaunce of watres cominge oute of his mouthe that hym semed alle the chirche was full therwith. And thanne he wost wel 435 that it was Seint Austine, that had fulfelled alle the Chirche with his doctrine.

A man that hadde gret deuocion to Seint Austin gaue gret good to a monke that kepte the body of Seint Austin so that he might haue a finger of hys, and toke the money and gaue hym a finger of a dede 440 bodi wrapped in silke, and feyned that it was the finger of Seint Austin. And he receiued it worshipfully and kepte it in gret cherete and mani a tyme leide it to his mouthe and to hys eyen and strengid it reuerently to his brest. And oure Lorde behelde the faithe of hym and gaue hym for that finger the proper finger of Seint Austin and 445 dede awey that other bi pite and meruaile. And whanne he come into hys cuntre and mani miracles were there done, the renome of that finger come to Pavie. And the monke beforesayd afermed alway that it was the finger of a dede bodi, and thanne thei openid the sepulcre and fonde that he fayled a fynger. And whanne the abbot had 450 knoulache hereof he putte the monke oute of his office and chastised hym sore.

Mani a noble and glorious miracle this holy seint dede bi the goodnes of oure Lorde in his lyf and after his dethe, whiche were to longe to be wretin in this litell volume for it conteynith | more thanne alle this f. 205ᵛᵃ boke, wherfor y leue atte this tyme and recomaunde us to his praiers 456 that for the loue of God was of so gret perfeccion that he dispised al richesse [and] lordshipes and refused al worshippes. He dredde delites and that shul they clerely finde that lust to rede his devout writinges.

Here endithe the lyf of Seint Austin and nexst beginnithe the lyf of Seint Felix, Capitulum .C.xviij.

Felix prest and his brother also that hight Felix [and was] a prest, were presented to Maximan and Dioclician emperoures so that the

432 of¹] *erased* H₁   435 semed] *add* þat H₁   full] filled H₁, fulfillid D
436 Chirche] chirchis D   438 hadde] *add* a H₁   440 and¹] *add* so þe monke D   of
a] and anothir D   442 he] þis man D   443 strengid] strecchid D   446 he] þis
man D   447 and] *om.* H₁D   448 beforesayd] aforseid H₁, *om.* D   449 a]
anothir D   452 hym] *ins.* H₁   453 and] *add* many a H₁   454 and] *om.* H₁
dethe] dede H₁   458 and¹] *om.* EH₁   459 shul] shuld H₁

EH₁DH2A1A2   1 and was] *om.* E   prest²] *add* also D   2 the] *om.* H₁D

eldest of hem two was ledde to the temple of Sarapis for to do
sacrifice, and there he blewe in the face of the ydole and anone she fel
5 downe and al tobrast. And thanne he was led to the ydole of
Mercurie and he blew upon her also and [she] fille doune. And
than the thridde tyme he was ledde to the ymage of Dyane and he
did the same. And thanne he was turmented in the turnement that is
called eculee, that is a turnement that is made like a sawtier which
10 hathe .ij. endes upward [and .ij. endes downward] and therein thei be
hangged. And thanne he was brought to the tree of sacrilege for to do
sacrifice, and thanne he praied upon his knees and blew ayenst that
tre and anone she turnid upsodoune, þe rote upwarde, and fille, and
in the falling he brake doune the temple and the auuter. And whanne
15 the prouost herde this thinge, he comaunded that he were beheded
there and that the bodi were lefte to wolves and to houndes. And
than there was a man that cam sodenly rennyng in amonge hem and
saide sikerly that he was frely a cristen man. And than thei kisten
togederes and were beheded togederes, and the cristen men that
f. 205vb knew not the name of hym named hym Hardy, | for that he went
21 hardely with Seint Felix to the crowne of marterdom. And whan
[the] cristen men hadde beried hem in the pit that the tree had made
the paynimes wolde haue digged hem up ayen anone, but thei were
uexid with the fende. He suffred dethe about the yere of oure Lorde
25 .CC.iiij^xx.vij.

Here end⟨ithe the lyf of⟩ Seint Felix, and nexst begin⟨nithe
the lyf of⟩ Seint Sauinien, ⟨Capitulum .C.xix.⟩

Seint Sauinien and Savine were children of Savin a right noble
paynim, and he had Sauinien bi his furst wif, and by the secounde he
had Savine his doughter and gave hem bothe that name. In a tyme as
Sauinien redde this vers: [Asperges] me Domine, and asked what it was
5 to saie, but he could in no wise understonde it. And thanne he went

4 the ydole] Idollis D   she] hit D   5 ydole] Idollis D   6 her] hem D   she] om.
EH1D (elle P2)   8 same] add to him and fel doun D   9 sawtier] sautrer D   10 .ij.
. . . upward] .iiij. endis one vpward and two donward D   and .ij. endes downward om. E
therein] þereon D   be] om. H1D   11 hangged] add him D   11–12 do sacrifice]
sacrafie H1   13 she] hit D   upsodoune] add and D   fille] add a doun D   16 that]
om. H1D   were] om. D   17 than] om. H1D   21 with] to D   22 the^1] om. EH1
made] add and E   24 fende] add and D

EH1DH2A1A2; D has Navien in rubric, otherwise Navinien   1 Savin] add and D
4 Asperges] Absterge E   Domine] om. H1

into his chaumbre and dede on the heyre and kneled in asshin, and
saide that he had leuer to deye there thanne he shulde not understonde the sen[se] of that vers. And thanne the aungell of God
apered to hym that saide to hym: 'Turment thiself no lenger, for
thou hast founde grace before oure Lorde. Whan thou shalt be 10
baptised thou shalt be whitter thanne snawe, and thanne thou shalt
understonde that thou sekist now.' Thanne was he glad bi the
comfort of the aungell and dispised alle the ydoles and wolde no
more worship hem, wherfor he was reproued and ofte tymes chyd of
his fader. And the fader wolde ofte tymes saie to hym: 'Whi 15
worshippist thou not oure goddes? Hit is beter that thou deye
alone than that we be al wrapped with the in the dethe.'

And thanne Sauinien fledde awey priuely and come to the cite of
Troyes. And whanne he passed the water he praied oure Lorde that
he might be baptised there, and so he was, and thanne oure Lorde 20
saide to hym: | 'Now [hast thou] founde that thou hast long sought f. 206ʳᵃ
with gret laboure,' and thanne he sette his staffe in the erthe, and
anone as he had made his praier his staffe waxe fulle of leuis and
floured before alle the peple, so that a .Mˡ.C.viij. leuedin in God.

And whan Aurelyen the emperour herde this thinge he sent mani 25
knightes for to take hym, and thei fonde hym praieng and dradden
for to go to hym. And thanne the emperour sent as mani mo as the
furst, and whanne thei come to him thei founde hym praienge and
thei praied togederes with hym, and whan he was risen from prayer
thei saide to hym: 'The emperour wolde see the.' And thanne he 30
went thedir, and [for] he wolde not do sacrifice he made hym be
bounde fote and honde and to be bete with cheines of yrne. And
Sauinien saide to hym: 'Encrece these turnementes yef thou maist.'
And he comaunded that he were bounde in the middell of the citee
upon a forme, and that thei shulde sette aboute hym wode, fyre and 35
oyle anone that he were brent up. And thanne the emperour behelde
hym and sawe hym stonding within the flawme praienge. And he was
abaisshed and saide to hym: 'A, wicked beest, suffisithe not to the the
soules that thou hast deceiued but yef thou assaie to deceiue us bi

8 sense] sentence ED   12–13 the comfort of] om. D   14 and] om. D   chyd]
om. D   17 with] within E   21 hast thou] trs. E   24 a] om. H1   27 the²] he
dide D   28 and²] add so D   29 from] add his D   31 for] om. EH1   hym] add to
H1   32 fote] bote changed to fote H1   33 these] þi D   34 he¹] than þe
emperoure D   38 A] add thou EH1   suffisithe] add it E   the²] ins. H1   39 thou²]
add do E   to] add do

40 thin art magike?' To whom Sauinien saide: 'Yet be ther many soules,
and thou art one of hem that shal beleue in oure Lorde by me.'
   And than the emperoure blamed the name of oure Lorde therfor,
and comaunded that in the morw he were bounde to a piler and
shette therto with arwes, and whan men shette to hym the arwes thei
45 hinge in the eyre on eueri syde of hym and none touched hym. And
the nexst day the emperoure come to hym and saide: 'Where is thi
God nouthe? Whi comithe he not and deliuerithe the fro these
arwes?' And anone one of the arwes lept and smote the kinge in the
f. 206ʳᵇ eye that he was blynde. And thanne | he was right wrothe and
50 comaundid hym to be putte in prison and in the morw to be biheded.
And thanne Sauinian praied to oure Lorde that it might be in the
same place where he was baptised, and thanne his cheynes tobraste
and the dores were openid and he went thurgh the knightes right to
the same place. And whanne the emperour herde that, he comaunded
55 that he were folued in that place and that he were beheded evene
there. And whanne Sauinien sawe the knightes that folued hym he
went upon the watir til he come to þe place of hys bapteme. And
whanne the knightez had passed the water and thei come to hym,
thei dredde for to smite hym, and he saide to hem: 'Smite me suerly
60 and bere of my blode to youre emperour and he shall resseyue his
sight and knowleche the vertu of God.' And whanne his hede was
smiten of he toke his hede and bare it .xlix. pac[e]s. And whan the
emperour had touched the blode and leide it to his eye, he was hole
anone, and thanne he saide: 'Now verily the god of cristen men is
65 gret and full of goodnesse.' And thanne a woman that had lost her
sight .xl. wynter made her to be bore thedir and made her praier and
receiued her sight anone. And he suffered dethe aboute the yere of
oure Lorde .CC.lxx. in the .ix. kalendes of Feferere. And the stori of
[his] suster is ioyned hereto, for that the feste is the same day.
70   And as Savine his suster wepte eueri day her brother, [and]
sacrified for hym to the ydoles, at the last the aungel appered to
her in slepe and saide: 'Savine, wepe not, but leue as moche as thou

41 beleue] *ins.* Hı   by me] Ihesu Crist D   42 oure Lorde] Ihesu Crist D
44 arwes¹] *add* hanginge in the eyre EHı   men] þei D   to hym] *om.* D   thei] *om.* D
45 hinge] *add* fulle D   51 it] he HıD   52 his] þe Hı   53 right to] into D
54 whanne] *ins.* Hı   55 in] into HıD   56 whanne] þan *with* þ *subp.* 'w' *and add*
seint Hı, *add* seinte D   57 hys] here Hı   58 and] *om.* D   hym] *add* but D
60 youre] þe HıD   61 sight] *add* aȝen D   62 hede] *add* himselfe D   paces] pacs E
64 men] *om.* D   66 be] *om.* D   69 his] *om.* E   day] *ins.* Hı   70 her brother]
om. D   and] *om.* E, *ins.* Hı   71 for hym] *om.* D   to the] to *ins.* Hı   aungel] *add* of
God D

hast and thou shalt finde thi brother that is in gret worship.' And
thanne she awoke and saide to her woman: 'My frende, haue ye
anithing herde?' And she saide: 'Ye, madame.' And thanne she saide: 75
'I suppose thou wilt not accuse me.' And she saide: 'No, forsothe,
madame, and therfor dothe right as you luste.' And so thei went
forthe in the morwtyde togeder. | And whanne the fader had do seke f. 206ᵛᵃ
her mani longe tyme, he lefte up his eyen towarde heuen and saide:
'Yef thou be almighti God in heuene, distroie my ydoles that might 80
not haue saued mc my children.' And thanne oure Lorde withe a
thunder tobrast al his ydoles, and many men sawe it that leued in
God.

And thanne the blessed Savine come to Rome and was baptised of
blessed Euseby the pope and duelled there .v. yere and heled .ij. lame 85
and .ij. blinde. And thanne the aungell appered to her in her slepe
and saide: 'What is this that thou doest, Savinc? Hast thou not lefte
al thi richesses and now thou duellest here in delites? Arise up and
dyne and go into the citee of Troyes and ther thou shalt finde thi
brother.' And thanne she saide to her chaumbrere: 'We will no 90
lengger duelle here.' And she saide: 'Madame, whedir will ye goo so
as folkes louen you gretly here and ye will go deye.' And she saide:
'God shalle purueie for us.'

And thanne thei toke a barly lofe and went to the citee of Ravenne
to the hous of a sike man of whiche men wept the doughter that was 95
dede, and there she praied the maide of the hous that she might be
herbured there. And shc saide to her: 'Madame, how might ye be
herborwed hcre sethe the doughter of this hous is dede and al ben
full of hevinesse.' And she saide: 'She shal not dcye for me.' And
thanne she entred inne and toke the honde of the mayde and lefte her 100
up all hole. And than thei wolde haue withholde her, but she wolde
in no wise acorde to hem.

And whanne she cam a mile from Troies, she saide to her
chaumbrere that she wolde rest a while. And thanne there come a
noble man oute of the towne, that hight Lycherien, and asked 105
whennes thei were. And Savyne said: 'Of this towne.' And he
saide: 'Whi make ye a lesinge, sethe your | tunge shewithe that ye f. 206ᵛᵇ

73 that . . . gret] in moche D   75 And thanne she saide] *om.* D   75–6 Ye . . . saide]
ins. H₁   76 forsothe] *add* y EH₁   77 dothe] do ȝe D   you] þ'o'u H₁, ȝe D
82 men] that D   that leued] bileevid D   86 aungell] *add* of God D   87 thou¹] *ins.*
H₁   lefte] lost H₁D   91–2 so as] al H₁   92 gretly] *add* for *subp.* H₁   she] than
Savyne D   99 she] than Savyne D   101 haue] *ins.* H₁   wolde] *add* not D
103 Troies] Troiles *with* l *subp.* H₁   107 tunge] *add* sheweth youre tonge *del.* H₁

be a straunger.' And she saide: 'Y am a straungcr sothcly and seke
Sauinien my brother.' And he saide to her: 'That man that ye seke
110 was slaine but a whiles gone for the name of Ihesu Crist and is beried
in suche a place.' And thanne she sette her in praier and saide:
'Lorde, thou hast kepte me alway in chastite, lete me now no lenger
be trauailed bi this harde weyes ne my bodi be remeued fro this
place. Lorde, y recomaunde to the my chambrere, that hathe
115 susteined so gret peine for my sake, and my brother, that y ne
haue ne may see in this worlde. Make me worthi to see hym in thi
kingdom.' And whanne her praier was ended she passed to oure
Lorde.

And whanne her chambrere sawe and herde this thinge, she
120 beganne to wepe for she had nothinge to berie her with. And
thanne that man sent a crioure thorugh the citee that alle shulde
come to berie the straunge woman. And thanne the peple come and
buried her worshipfully.

And in this same day is þe feste of Seint Savine that was wif of
125 Seint Valentine knight that was beheded vnder Adrean emperour for
that he wolde not do sacrifise to the ydoles.

⟨Here⟩ endithe the lif of Seint Sauine, and nexst beginnithe the lif of Seint Lowe, Cap^m .C.xx.

Seint Lowe was born atte Orliaunce and was of the rial lynage, and as
he shined bi gret miracles and vertues he was made Ershebisshop of
Seyns. And he gaue as moche as he had to the pore. In a day whanne
he had all yeuen, it fell that he had mani men to diner and his
5 servauntes tolde hym that he hadde not half wyne ynow. He
ansuered hem þat he that fedde the briddes of heuene wold performe
his charite with wyne, and anone there cam a messenger that saide |
f. 207ra that there was come before the gate an .C. cuys of wyne.

And as alle tho of the court saide euell of hym, for he loued and
10 cherisshed a uirgine that was doughter of his predecessour, for thei
saide that he loued her to unordinatly, and thanne he toke this

108 a straunger'] straungers D   a²] ins. D   109 to her] om. D   111 her] add
doun D   praier] her praiers D   112 me now no lenger] no lenger me H1
114 hathe] þou H1   121 thorugh] aboute D   alle] add men E   122 the'] a D
124 Seint] ins. H1

EH1DH2A1A2   2 gret/miracles and] trs. D   4 all] om. H1   5 hym] om. D
half] om. D   7 cam] to þe ȝate D   8 was] om. H1, were D   an] om. H1
9 court] cuntre D   11 her to] om. D

virgine and cussed her before all the meyne and saide: 'It noiethe
nothinge to man straunge and vnsittinge wordes, [y]f his owne
conscience be noght blemisshed.' And for he knew wel that she
loued Ihesu Crist purely, he loued her with pure thought.   15

So a[s] Clotarie kinge of Fraunce entrid into Burgoyne he sent his
stuarde ayenst hem of Seyns for to sege the citee, and thanne Seint
Lowe entred into the chirche of Seint Stephen and beganne to ringe
the belle. And whan the enemyes herde that, they toke so gret drede
to hem that thei went neuer to haue ascaped the dethe but yef thei 20
fled, and atte the laste was the duchie of Burgoine take. And whanne
it was take he sent another stuarde into Burgoine, and he come to
Seyns, and for that Seint Lowe had geue hym no yeftes he had so gret
despite that he defamed hym to the king, so that the kinge sent hym
into exile, and there he shynıd bı gret doctrine. In this mene tyme tho 25
of Seyns slow her bisshop that had take the place of Seint Lowe, and
thanne thei praied to haue Seint Lowe ayen fro his exile. And whan
the kinge sawe that dede [he] was so chaunged bi the will of God
tha[t] he kneled doune before that holi man and required hym
foryeuenese and restablissed hym to his chirche with mani yeftes.   30

In a tyme whanne he come from Parys, a gret cumpanie of
prisoners came ayens hym her cheynes tobroken and alle her dores
opin. In a Sonday as he songe his masse, a precious stone fell from
heuene into his chalys, and the kinge sette it amonge his reliques.

The kinge Clo|tarie herde saie that the bellis of Seyns had f. 207rb
meruailous swetnesse in her sowne and sent for hem that thei 36
shulde be brought to Paris, for that he wold here hem ofter. And
that mislyked to Seint Lowe, and as sone as thei were out of the
towne thei lost her sowne. And whanne the kinge herde it he
comaunded that thei were sent home anone, and as sone as thei 40
come .viij. myle nighe the towne thei souned her sowne ayen. And
Seint Lowe went ayenst hem and receiued hem with gret ioye that he
had lost with sorw.

On a night as he was in his praier, he had gret thruste bi steringe
of the enemye, and he asked colde water to drinke and knewe wel the 45
trecherie of the fende. And whanne he had the vessell he leide his

13 yf] of EH1   15 loued¹] add wel H1D   purely] and puridly D   her] add
þerfore D   16 as] a E, a`s' H1          17 stuarde] stu`w'ard H1   20 yef] om. D
21 duchie] Duke D   22 it] he D   23 Lowe] add he D   28 he] om. E
29 that¹] thanne E   hym] add aȝen D   32 her²] þe prison D   36 swetnesse]
swetnesses H1   her] þe H1   37 ofter] om. D   39 it] them D   41 nighe] add to
H1D   43 with²] add gret D   44 thruste] trist H1   45 enemye] add þe feende D

pelowe theron and closed therin the fende, and al the night he brayd
and cried. And in the moru he that was come in the night to tempte
hym priuily he went in the day confused opinly.

50 In a tyme as he visited as his custume was the chirches of the citee,
and whanne he come home he herde his clerkes striuynge and
chydinge for that thei wolde haue done fornicacion with women.
And thanne he entered into the chirche and prayed for hem, and
anone al that temptacion vanisshed away and thei come before hym
55 and asked foryeuenesse. And atte the last he, worschiped with mani
vertues, rested in pees in the yere of oure Lorde .CCC. and .x.

Here endith the lif of Seint Lowe, and nexst beginnith the
lif of Seint Mamertin, Cap.^m .C.xxj.

Mamertin was furst paynim, and in a tyme as he worshipped his
ydoles he lost an eye and his one honde dried up. And he went that
f. 207va he hadde wrat|hed his goddes and went to another temple to worship
the ydoles, and as he went he mette with a religious man that asked
5 hym how tho mishappes were fallen hym. And he saide: 'Y haue
wratthed my goddes and therfor y go to worship hem to haue
remedye of my disese.' And he saide to hym: 'Thou errest, thou
errest, brother, that wenist that the fals ydoles be goddes, but go to
Seint German bisshop of Auserie, and yef thou wilt leue his
10 counsaile thou shalt be hole anone.'

And thanne anone he toke the waye [and went] to the sepulcre of
Seint Amadour bisshop and of mani other seintes, and the night fel
on hym and so gret a reine that bi fors he must abide in a sell wherin
was the sepulcre of Seint Concorde. And as he slepte that night he
15 sawe a mervailous uision, for hym thought that there come one to the
dore of the selle and called Seint Concordian and saide that he must
come to the feste that Seint Amador and Seint Peregrin and other
bisshoppes maden. And she that was in the to[mb]e ansuered that
she might not now, for a gest that she had that she must kepe from

49 day] *add* al D   54 temptacion] temptacions H1   55 asked] *add* him H1
56 .CCC. and .x.] .iiij^C.x. H1

EH1DH2A1A2; D 40–50 has minor losses caused by a tear   2 eye] hy3e D   honde]
om. D   7 he] than þe religious man D   7–8 thou errest²] *om.* H1D   9 leue] *so
changed to* loue H1   10 anone] *om.* H1D   11 and went] *om.* E   13 a sell] assell E
16 he] she E   17 feste that] forthe of D   Seint¹] *om.* H1   and²] *add* to D
18 maden] *om.* D   tombe] towne E, towne be *changed to* townb H1   19 not] *add*
come D

the serpentes that haunted her lest thei wolde sle hym. And thanne 20
he went his waye and tolde to that other what he hadde herde. And
than he was made come ayen and saide: 'Seint Concordian, arise and
come anone and bringe with the Viuiane dekene and Viuiane
subdekene for to do her offices, and Alisaundre shal kepe thi gest.'
And thanne it semid to Mamertin þat Seint Concordian toke hym bi 25
the honde and ledde hym with her, and whanne Seint Amadour sawe
hym he saide to her: 'Ho is this that is come with the?' And she
saide: 'This is my geste.' And than he saide: 'Putte hym oute, for he
maye not be with us, he is so foule.' And whan | thei putte hym oute   f. 207vb
he kneled pitously before hem and asked grace of Seint Amadour, 30
and he comaunded hym anone that he shulde go to Seint Germain.
And than he awoke and cam to Seint Germaine and kneled before
hym and asked hym foryeuenesse and tolde hym al that was befalle
hym. And thanne thei wente togederes to the tombe of Seint
Concordian and lefte up the stone and there thei fonde mani 35
serpentes that hadde .x. fote of lengthe and wolde haue fledde, and
Seint Germain comaunded hem to go ther as thei shulde neigh no
creature fro thennes forwarde.

   And thanne was Mamertin baptised and heled perfitly and was
made a monke of the monasterie of Seint Germain and was abbot 40
after Eulodien. And in the tyme of this was Seint Marin, and Seint
Mamertyn wolde preue the obedience of hym and committed hym to
the foulest office of the chirche and made hym sheparde of bestes.
And whanne he kepte his oxen and his kyne in an yle he was so full
of gret holynesse that the wilde swyne wolde come to hym and he 45
norisshed hem with his hondes. And he toke a wilde bore from the
houndes that was come to his selle for refute and deliuered hym.

   In a tyme theues had robbed hym, and as thei bare awey his
clothes and had not lefte hym but his mantell, he called hem ayen
and saide: 'Turnithe ayen, my lordes, lo, here yet a peny bounden in 50
this mantell [that perauenture ye had nede of].' And thei turned ayen
and toke the peny and the mantell and lefte hym al naked. And as
thei went hastely to her receyt thei erredyn all þe night and in the

21 what] *add* þat H1D   22 come] to go D   Seint] to D   Concordian]
'cun'Cordian H1   23 the] 'þe' H1   25 to] *ins.* D   27 she] Concorde D
32 And . . . Germaine] *om.* H1   kneled] knele H1   33 asked] aske H1   34 to] into
EH1   36 hadde] 'had' H1   37 ther as] þider that D   39 heled] he lyved D
41 was²] *om.* D   Marin] Martin H1   42 committed] comaundid D   43 of] in H1
hym²] *om.* D   44 so] *om.* H1   47 was] were D   48 theues] Theses H1
50 here yet] yet here is H1D   51 that . . . of] *om.* E   ye] he H1

morwtyde thei fonde hemself atte his selle. And he grette hem and
55 receiued hem debonairly and wisshe her fete and serued hem in the
best wise that he couthe. And than they were abasshed and sorueden
f. 208ra for that thei had | done and weren conuerted to the faithe.

In a tyme it felle that sum of the monkes that were with Seint
Mamertin hadde leyde snares for a bere that vsed to ete her shepe.
60 And whanne he woste it he rose oute of his bedde or ani wist it ande
went thedir and losed the bere and saide: 'Fle hennis, [thou shrewe],
or elles thou wilt be take.'

And whanne he was dede and men bere his body to Angers, as he
come by a towne, men might not remeue the body in no wise into the
65 tyme that a man whiche was in prison went oute sodenli, his cheines
brokin and come al quite to the bodi and halpe to bere hym to the
citee, where he was beried worshipfulli in the chirche of Seint
Germain.

Here endithe the lyf of Seint Mamertin, and nexst
beginnithe the lif of Seint Gile, Capitulum .C.xxij.

Seint Gile was born in Athenes and comin of riall kinrede, and of his
childhede he was taught in holi scripture. And in a day as he went to
the chirche he fonde a sike man that laie in the way and asked almes,
to whom he gaue his cote, and whanne he hadde done it on he
5 resseiued fulle hele. And sone after that his fader and moder deied
and rested in oure Lorde, and he made Ihesu Crist heyre of his
heritage. In a tyme as he come from the chirche a man was smite
with a serpent and deyde, and Seint Gile came to hym and made his
praier for hym and chased awey the venym. A mad man was in the
10 chirche with other and troubled the peple gretly with his crienge and
Seint Giles chased awey the fende fro hym and heled hym.

And thanne Seint Gile dred gretly the perell of the worlde and
went hym priuely upon the see syde and sawe shipmen in the see in
f. 208rb point to perisshe | and made his praier for hem and apesed al the
15 tempest of the see. And than the shipmen come to londe and thanked
hym and seide hym that thei went to Rome and that thei wolde lede

57 and] *add* so D   61 thou shrewe] *om.* E   63 he¹] seinte mamertyn D
66 quite] quik H1

EH1DH2A1A2L; D has minor losses from 68–76 caused by a tear and breaks off after 76
And   4 he²] the sike man D   5 and] *add* his H1   6 he] than seinte Gile D
13 hym] *om.* H1D

hym thedir for not and he wolde. And than he come to Arle and
duelt there two yere with Seint Serasien that was bisshop of that
citee and there he heled a man that had hadde the feuer thre yere.
Than he coueited to go into desert and parted hym priuely and 20
duelled with an ermite that was a noble man by gret holinesse, and
there by his holinesse he chased awey the gret derthe that was in that
londe. And whanne he had do this miracle he dredde the peine of
veyne glorie of this worlde and that hermite, and he entred further
into desert, and there he fonde a pitte and a litell welle and an hynde 25
that withoute faile was purueied hym of God for to be his norice and
for to geue hym melke atte sertaine tymes.

And as the kingges children went on huntinge thei sawe that
hynde and lefte alle other game and folowed her with her houndes,
and whan she was sore chased with hem she fledde to the fete of hym 30
that she norisshed. And thanne he meruailed gretly whi she hiddc
her more thanne she was wont, and went oute and herde the hunters,
and thanne he praied oure Lorde that as he had sent her hym for his
norice that he wolde saue her. And thanne none of the houndes durst
not come ny bi a stones cast, but howledin and turned ayen to the 35
hunters. And thanne the night came and thei turned ayen home. And
the day foluinge thei went thedir ayen and dede nothinge and went
home ayen.

And thanne whan the kinge herde this thinge how it went, he
hadde suspecion and toke the bisshop with hym and went thedir with 40
grete | multitude of hunters, and whannc the houndes durst not go f. 208va
nye as thei were wont but turned ayen howling and crieng, thei
besette the busshe that was so thicke and so stronge of breres that
ther might no man entre. And one of hem shotte an arw lewdely for
to haue drevin oute the hynde, and made a gret wounde in the holy 45
man that praied for the hinde. And thanne the knightes made a wey
with her swerdes and camin to the pitte, and thanne thei sawe this
holy man clothed in the abite of a monke whiche semed worshipfull
bi age, and the hinde lyenge bi hym. And thanne the kinge and the
bisshop wentin alone to hym and asked hym what he was and whi he 50
had take so gret a thiknesse in desert and who had wounded hym so
greuously. And whan he hadde ansuered to euerithinge, thei asked

17 not] not *del.* `nouȝt' Hɪ   19 hadde] *om.* HɪD   20 parted] *add* fro Hɪ
22 was] *add* that tyme D   28 went] ryden D   31 he] seinte Gile D   whi] with
þat D   37 went¹] come D   43 besette the] be`t þe' Hɪ   so²] *om.* D   44 entre]
add withynne D   46 man] *add* seinte Gile D   47 camin] came yn Hɪ

hym foryeuenesse full humbly, and sent hym leches to hele his
wounde and profered hym gret yeftes, but he wolde in no wise put
55 medicine to his wounde and refused al the yeftes and praied oure
Lorde that he shulde neuer be heled in his lyf, for he knewe well that
vertu is perfit [in] infirmite.

And the king visited hym ofte and receiued of hym [the] pasture of
hele. The kinge offered hym mani richesses but he refused hem alle,
60 but he stered the kinge that he shulde make a monesteri wher the
discipline of the order of monkes might bene. And whanne the kinge
had made hit, Seint Gile refused mani tyme to take the cure, but atte
the laste he was ouercome atte the praiers of the kinge and toke it.

And thanne the kinge Charles herde the renoun of hym and
65 desired gretly that he wolde come to hym, and he cam and was
receiued worshipfulli. And the kinge praied hym that he wold hertely
f. 208vb praie for hym amonge all other | thinge for his gostely hele, for he
had do a shamfull synne that he durst neuer be confessed of [to] no
creature. And the Sonday after, so as Seint Gile songe his masse and
70 praied hertly for the kinge, the aungell of oure Lorde appered to hym
and leide a scrowe upon the auuter wherein the synnes of the kinge
were wretin by ordre, and that thei were foryeue hym bi the praier of
Seint Gile yef he wolde be repentaunt and shriue hym and do no
more so. And it was wretin in the ende that whosoeuer askid helpe of
75 Seint Gile for ani synne that he had done, that yef he wolde leue it
he shulde be foryeue. And thanne he toke the scrowe to the kinge
and the kinge confessed his synne and asked foryeuenesse mekely.

And thanne Seint Gile returned ayen, and whanne he come to the
citee of Verence he refused the sone of a prince that was dede. And
80 withinne a [litell] while after he denounced that his chirche shulde be
destroied with enemyes of the faithe. And thanne he went to Rome
and gate priuileges of the pope to his chirche, and two dores of
cipresse in whiche the images of Seint Petre and Seint Paule were
corven yn, [and] threwe hem into the riuer that hight Tybre and
85 recomaunded hem to the kepinge of God, and whanne he came to his
chirche ayen he gaue to a la⟨me⟩ man his goinge, the whiche he fonde
at Childerne. And whanne he cam to his chirche he fonde the yates

53 hym¹] *om.* H₁   full] *om.* H₁D   57 is] *add* so D   in] L, *om.* EH₁D   58 ofte]
om. H₁   the²] *om.* E   62 take] *add* vppon him D   63 it] *add* vppon him D
66 hertely] parfi3tli D   68 to] *om.* E   69 after] *om.* D   75 had done] do D
79 he] þe'ï' H₁   80 litell] L, *om.* EH₁H₂   83 Petre] *ins.* H₁   84 and¹] L, he
EH₁H₂   86 ayen] *om.* H₂   86–7 ayen . . . chirche] *om.* H₁   87 at Childerne]
Children H₂   yates] *add* of cipres H₂

in the porche of the chirche, and gaue gret thankinges to God that
had so graciously kepte hem in so mani gret periles. And thanne he
sette hem in the chirche for the beauute of hem, and in tokin of the 90
grace that the Chirche of Rome had do to hem.

In the ende oure Lorde shewid [to hym] his passinge hennes and
he tolde it to his bretheren and praied hem to praie for hym, and so
he slepte graciously in oure Lorde. And | mani haue borun witnesse f. 209ra
that thei haue herde the felawship of aungeles bere the soule of hym 95
to heuene. And he was clere to God about the yere of oure Lorde
.vijC.

Here endithe the lif of Seint Gile, and nexst beginnithe the
blessed Natiuite of oure Ladi, Capitulum .C.xxiij.

The natiuite of oure most glorious Uirgine Marie of the kinrede of
Iuda and of the rial kinred of Dauid, of whiche Seint Mathew and
Luke ne discreue not the right generacion, [but] discreuin that of
Ioseph, that was in all a strauniour of the concepcion of oure Lorde,
but the custume of scripture was suche that the ordinaunce of the 5
generacion of women was not recorded, but tho of men.

But right verili that blessed Uirgine descended of the kinrede of
Dauid, for as the holy scripture witnessithe Ihesu Crist toke his
byrthe of the kinrede of Dauid. And whan it is certaine that she was
born of Dauid and of the kinrede of Nathan, for Dauid had .ij. sones 10
Nathan and Salamon amonge other. And Iohn Damacien tellithe and
witnessithe of the kinrede of Nathan sone of Dauid, Leui engendered
Melchi and Panthem, and Panthem engenderid Melchi bar Pantham,
Barpantan engendered Ioachim, and Ioachim engendered the Uirgine
Marie. Of the kinrede of Salamon Nathan had a wiff, bi whom he 15
gate Iacob, and whanne Nathan was dede, Melchi the sone of
Nathan, that was sone of Leui, brother of Panthem, wedded the
wif of Natha[n], moder of Iacob, and engendered Heli. And than was
Iacob and Ely bretheren of [one] wombe, and Iacob was of the

90 hem¹] om. H1   the³] om. H1; H1 punctuates after end   92 to hym] om. EH1 (luy
P2)   93 it to] om. H2   95 the²] add blessid H2

EH1H2A1A2L; D resumes at 98 whiche   1 most] add blessid and H2   Marie] add
was H2   3 but discreuin] vndiscreuin E, but discrien H2   7 Uirgine] add marie H2
9 whan] thanne H2   10 of¹] add the kynrede of H2   13 and Panthem and
Panthem] an Panthomstet H2   15 H1H2L end sentence after Salamon, E is ambiguous.
17 Leui] add and H2   18 Nathan] Natham E   of²] to H1   and] om. H2   19 one]
om. E, `oo' H1    and²] overwritten by of del. `and' H1

20 kinrede of Salamon, and Ely of the kinrede of Nathan. [And than Ely
of the kinrede of Nathan] deyed, and Iacob toke his wif and
recouered the lyne of his brother and engendered Ioseph the
f. 209rb husbonde of Marie. And | thanne was he his sone bi nature of
discent of Salamon, that is to wete Ioseph is sone of Iacob, and after
25 the lawe he was sone of Ely that descended of Natha[n]. For the sone
that was born as bi nature was hys that engendered hym, and he was
also sone of hym as bi the lawe.

As it is saide in the Maister of Stories, and Bede witnessithe it in
cronicles, so as alle the generaciones of Ebrewes and of other
30 straungers were kepte in the most secrete cofers of the temple,
Eroudes comaunded to brenne hem and wende for to haue made
hymself noble and worthi amonge other yef the preuis of kinrede[s]
were failed, and he wolde haue made beleue that his kinrede
aperteined to hem of Israel. And there were sum that were called
35 Domenikes for that thei were so nighe to Ihesu Crist and weren of
Nazarethe, and tho hadde lerned the ordre of generaciones of oure
Lorde, in partie of thaire grauntsyres and in partie by other bokes
that thei had in her houses, and taught hem as moche as thei couthe.

For Ioachim toke Anne to his wif, that had a suster that hight
40 Hymarie. And this Hymarie had a doughter that hight Elizabeth and
Elyude was her sone. Elizabeth bare Seint Iohn Baptist and Elyude
engendered Seint Neemynen, and Seint Seruacien of whiche the
bodi ys in the castell of Troussiet vpon the flode of Meuse in the
bisshopriche of Lige. Seint Anne hadde .iij. husbondes, Ioachim,
45 Cleophas and Salame. And of the furst she had a doughter whiche
was Marie the moder of Ihesu that was geue [to Ioseph] to wif and
bare oure Lorde Ihesu Crist. And whan Ioachim was dede she toke
Cleophas, the brother of Ioseph, and had by hym another doughter
that she called Marie also, and wedded the same doughter after to
50 Alphee. And this Marie had by Alphee her husbonde .iiij. sones,
f. 209va whiche | were Iame the Lesse, Ioseph the Rightwis, Simon and Iude.
And thanne the seconde husbonde of Anne deied, [and] she toke the
thridde that hight Salome and had a doughter by hym also that she
called Marie and gaue her to wif to Zebede. And this Marie had by

20–1 And than . . . Nathan] om. E   21 of the²] that was H2   lyne] line on erasure
H1   25 Nathan] Natham E   27 as] þat was H1H2   29 Ebrewes] Euebrewes
with Eu erased H1   32 kinredes] kinrede E   34 aperteined] apperteyneth H1
35 for that] trs. H1   to] om. H1   37 grauntsyres] graunte desires H1   other] thaire
H2   43 bodi ys] bodies bene H2   Troussiet] Concient H2   46 to Ioseph] om. EH1
51 Rightwis] right wis H1   52 and] om. EH1   54 wif] add also H2

Zebede .ij. sones, and tho were Seint Iame the Grete and Seint Iohn 55
Euangelist.

But this is a wonder thinge to see how that the blessid Virgine
Marie might be cosin to Elizabeth so as it is saide aboue. Hit is
certaine that Elizabeth was wif to Zakarie, that was born of the
kinrede of Levi, and after the lawe eueriche shulde wedde a wif of his 60
owne kinrede and of his meyne, and she was of the doughters of
Aaron so as Seint Luke witnessith it. And Anne was of Bedlem so as
Seint Ierom saithe, and of the kinrede of Iuda, but it is to understonde that the kinrede and that of prestes were alwey ioyned togedre
by cosinage. So that as Bede saithe that this kinrede might be made 65
fro the furst tyme and so be norisshed furthe fro kinrede to kinrede,
and it shal be verrey certaine that the blessed Virgine Marie, whiche
descendid fro the riall kinrede and had cosinage with the kinrede of
prestes. And so that most blessed Virgine was of bothe kinredes, and
so oure Lorde wolde that for gret misterie these two kinredes most 70
priuileged shulde be medled togederes, for it aperteynid to hym to be
born of hem that shuld be offered for us verrey God, verrey prest,
verrey kinge, and that he shulde defende his good championes in the
knighthode of this worlde and croune hem after her victori. The
whiche thinge shewithe of the name of Crist, for Crist is as moche to 75
saie as anoynte, for in the olde lawe there was none anoynted but
kinges and prestes, and we be callyd cristen of Crist and be chosin
for the chosin kinrede | of the reall presthode. f. 209vb

Thanne to oure purpos of the most blessed natiuite of oure Ladi as
Seint Ierome tellithe in his Prologe, that whanne he was a childe he 80
redde in a boke the stori of the natiuite of oure blessed Ladi, but as
he recordithe that longe tyme after he drow it oute atte the praier of
a deuout frende of his, and fonde therin that Ioachim that was of
Galile weddid Seint Anne of Bedlem, and thei were bothe rightwys,
and withoute any reproef. In the comaundementes of oure Lorde thei 85
kept hem. And thei deuided all her substaunce in thre parties, that
one partie was for the temple, that other thei gaue to pore [men and
to pilgrimes], and the thridde thei kepte for hemself and for her

55 Zebede] `Ze'bede *with* b *on* l H1   the Grete] *om.* H1   Iohn] *add* þe H1   62 it]
om. H1H2   63 and] *om.* H1   64 that²] tho H2   65 that¹] *om.* H1H2
70 misterie] misteries be of H2   71 aperteynid] apperteineth H1H2   73 the] þeire
H1   76 as] *add* for the H2   80 childe] chide H2   81 in] *om.* H1   blessed] *om.*
H1H2   82 after] afore *erased* `after' H1   83 that was] *om.* H2   87 partie] *om.*
H1   other] *add* partie H2   87 to] *add* the E   87–8 men and . . . pilgrimes] *om.* E
88 thridde] *add* part H2

meyne. And thus thei lyued .xx. wynter withoute childe, and than
90 thei avowed to oure Lorde that yef he wold graunte hem a childe thei
wolde offre it fully to his seruice. For whiche thinge thei went eueri
yere to Ierusalem in the .iij. principall festis, and so in the feste day
of the yere Ioachim went into Ierusalem with his kinredes, and come
to the auuter with other and wolde haue offerred his offering. And
95 whanne the preste sawe hym he putte hym abacke bi gret dispite and
blamed hym gretly that he presumed to come to the auuter of God,
and saide hym that it was not sittinge ne couenable that any man
whiche was cursed in the lawe shuld make any offeringe to oure
Lorde, neither he that was barein be amonge hem that had fruit,
100 sethe he had not encresed the peple of God.

And thanne Ioachim, [thus] confused, whanne he herde this he
durst not go to his owne hous for shame, lest tho of his kynne and of
his neigheboures whiche had herde this wolde reproue hym after.
And thanne he went to his shepardes and there he was longe tyme,
105 and so in a day the aungell of God apered to hym alone and
f. 210ʳᵃ comforted hym with gret light and saide hym that he | shulde not
drede of that vision and saide: 'Y am the aungell of oure Lorde, sent
to the for to anounce to the that thi praiers be herde and thin
almesses be stied up before God. Y haue sayne thi shame and haue
110 herde the reproef that thou hast be reproued with wronge, for God is
reuenger of synne and not of nature, and whanne he closith the
wombes he openithe hem after more meruailously, for that the fruit
that is born of hem shulde not be saine to be brought furthe bi
luxurie, but it shulde be sayne and knowen only the yefte of God.
115 The furst moder of youre peple was Sarra and she was barein into
.iiijˣˣ. yere and yet she brought furthe Isaak to whom the blessing of
alle peple is behight. Was not Rachel longe barein and yet [s]he
brought forthe Ioseph that helde all the lordeship of Egipte? Who
was strengger thanne Sampson ne more holier thanne Samuel? And
120 yet hadde they moderes that were barein. So that thou may wel
beleue bi reson and by ensaumple that th[o] children long abide be
more wont to be meruaylous, and therfor Anne thi wyf shall haue a
doughter whiche thou shalt calle Marie. And that same shall be full

89 wynter] yere H2   93 into] to H1H2   94 the auuter] ther H2   99 be]
om. D   101 thus] that was E   106 that] *om.* H1   107 Lorde] *add* þat H1D
sent] *add* me D   109 thi] þin *with* n *erased* H1   110 the] þi H1D   is] *om.* D
111 closith] closed H1   114 luxurie] lecherie H1D   but] *add* þat H1   only] *add* of
H1, opinly for D   yefte] feste *del.* 'ȝift' H1   115 youre] tho D   117 longe] of long
tyme D   she] he E   121 tho] the E

of the holy goste fro the wombe of her moder, and she shal duelle in
the temple of oure Lorde and withoute amonge the comune peple,   125
bicause that none euell suspesion shall be had of her. And right as
she is born of barein moder, right so ther shalle be bore of her
merveilously the sone of the right [high] Lorde, of whom the name
shall be Ihesus, and by hym shal be hele yeue to all the peple. And
this y yeue the in token: that whanne thou shalt come to the Gildin   130
Gate in Ierusalem, thou shalt mete with Anne thi wyf that is full hevi
of thi longe abidinge and she shal haue gret ioye of thi comyng.' And
thanne the aungell, whanne he hadde saide this, he parted fro hym.

And | as Anne wepte bitterly and wist not wher her husbonde was   f. 210rb
become, the same aungell apered to her and saide to her alle that he   135
had saide to her husbonde, and gaue her in token that she shulde go
to the Gildin Yate in Ierusalem and there she shulde mete with her
husbonde that came to her warde. And so bi the comaundement of
the aungell thei mette togederes and haddyn gret ioye eche of other
and worshipeden oure Lorde and retourned to her hous [and abiden]   140
with gret gladnesse the divine promesse. And thanne Anne conceiued and brought furthe a doughter and called her Marie. And
whanne she was .iij. yere olde that she hadde lefte the breste thei
ledde þe Virgine to the Temple with her offeringges. And there were
.xv. degrees to stie up to the Temple, for that the Temple is high   145
sette, and the Virgine Marie was sette in the furst degree binethe and
she went hem up withouten ani helpe as thow she hadde be of perfite
age. And whanne thei hadde perfourmed her offeringes, thei lefte her
doughter in the Temple with other virgines and went ayen to her
propre place, and that holy Virgine profited eueri day in al holynesse   150
and was eueri day visited with aungeles.

Seint Ierome saithe in a pistle that he wrote to Cromacyen and to
Elyadore, that the blessed Uirgine hadde ordeined this custume to
herself, that fro the morwtide into Tierce she was in praier, and fro
Tierce into None she entendid to werke, and fro None she stint not   155
to praie til the aungell cam that gaue her mete.

And in the .xiiij. yere of her age the bisshop comaunded in
comune that the virgines that were taught in the Temple and had

127 of'] add a H1   128 high] om. EH1   129 be hele yeue] hele bi you D
130 y] is D   132 she] om. H1D   133 saide] add all EH1   134 as] om. D
136] token] tokening D   137 the] om. H1   138 so] she D   139 aungell] add
went thedir and thanne D   140 and abiden] om. E   145 .xv.] .xiij. H1   is] was D
146 degree] degrees D   154–5 and fro Tierce] om. D   155 entendid . . . she] om.
H1

fulfelled the tyme of her age shulde retorne ayen to her houses. And
f. 210va alle obeyeden to his | comaundement, saue Marie ansuered that she
161 might not do it in as moche as her fader and moder had geuen her
alle to the seruice of God, and also for she had solempn[el]i avowed
her virginite to oure Lorde. And thanne the bisshop was full of
sorugh, for he durste not make her to breke her avowe ayenst the
165 scripture that saithe: 'Vowithe and yeldithe youre avowe', and in that
other syde he durst not breke the custume of the peple. And than
atte the fest of Iewes he called the aunciens of Iewes to counceill, and
the sentence of alle was suche that in ani so doutable a matere men
shulde aske the counsaile of God. And than they went al to praiers
170 and the bisshop went for to counceile with oure Lorde, and anone a
vois cam from the oratorie that saide that alle tho of þe meyni of
Dauid that were couenable to be maried and withoute wives shulde
bringe eueri of hem a yerde to the auuter, and the yerde that floured
after the se[y]inge of Isaye and that the holy gost apered on in
175 lyknesse of a doue shulde be maried to the Virgine.

And so it fell amonge other, Ioseph of the meyne of Dauid come
thedir amonge other, and for as moche as hym semed that it was an
vncouenable thinge that so olde a man as he was shulde wedde a
virgine, he hidde his yerde and alle other brought furthe her yerdes.
180 And so as nothinge apered that acorded to the heuenly voys, the
bisshop went that thei shulde axse counsaile ayen of oure Lorde, and
it was ansuered that he only that shulde wedde the Virgine had not
brought forthe his yerde. And than Ioseph brought forthe his yerde
f. 210vb by the comaundement of the bisshop, | and anone she floured and the
185 holy goste in lyknesse of a dove descended from heuene and was
sayne upon þe yerde, so that it was clerely shewed to alle that he
shulde haue the Uirgine.

And thanne he weddid the Virgine and retorned into the citee of
Bedlem for to ordeyne his meyne and his hous and to gete thinges that
190 were necessarie to housholde, and the blessed Virgine Marie retornid
to the hous of her fader with .vij. other virgines her felawes, that were
of her age and had sayne the shewinge of that miracle. And in tho dayes
the aungell of God apered to the Virgine as she was in her praiers and
denounced her that the sone of God shulde be bore of her.

161 it] *add* in no wise D   162 solempneli] solempni E   164 avowe] *add* and it
was D   165 avowe] own H1   167 the¹] a D   the²] to H1   170 oure Lorde]
God D   173 eueri] erly H1   174 seyinge] seinge E   176 other] *add* that D
180 as] was EH1, there was D (*comme* P2)   nothinge] *add* that EH1D (*nulle chose* P2)
181 that thei shulde] to D   182 ansuered] *add* ayen to hym D

The day of the natiuite of oure Lady was not knowe longe tyme 195
amonge cristen peple. And as Iohn Belet saithe that it fell that an
holy man of hi[gh] contemplacion herde eueri yere in the .vij.
ide of Septembre whanne he was in his praiers a felawship of aungels that
made gret solempnite, and thanne he required deuoutely that the
cause might be shewed hym whi eueri yere atte that tyme only he 200
herde that solempnite. And thanne he hadde an ansuere fro heuene
that in that day the holy Virgine Marie moder of God was bore to the
worlde, and he shulde make it to be knowe to the sones of holy
Chirch, so that in that solempnite thei were made acordinge to the
heuenli court. And whanne he had tolde this to the pope and to other 205
and that thei had be in praiers and in orisones, and had enquered the
trouthe bi witnesse of auncien scriptures, thei ordeined this day of
the natiuite of oure Lady to be halowed generally of alle the Chirche.

But in the olde tyme the vtauuce | of the natiuite were not f. 211ʳᵃ
halowed, but Pope Innocent the .iiij. lete ordeine hem to be halowed, 210
and for this cause. Whan the pope Gregori was newly dede alle the
cardinales of Rome were enclosed bi the men of Rome for that thei
shulde purueie the sonner an hede to the Chirche. But thei might not
acorde in mani dayes but sustenid gret sorwe[s] of the Romaynes,
and thanne thei avowed to the quene of heuene that, yef thei might 215
acorde bi her merites and that thei might go quite fro thennes, thei
wolde ordeine to halw the vtas of her natiuite that had longe tyme be
sette litell by. And thanne thei chase alle Celestine, and so thei were
deliuered and fulfelled her avowe by Innocent. For Celestine liued
but a litell tyme and therfor thei might not fulfell it by hym. 220

And hit is to knowe that the Chirche halowe[th] .iij. natiuitees that
ben these: the natiuite of Ihesu Crist, the natiuite of oure Lady and
the natiuite of Seint Iohan Baptist, and these .iij. betokene .iij.
spirituel natiuitees, for we be born ayen with Iohn in water of
bapteme, and with Marie in penaunce, and with Ihesu Crist in ioye. 225
And hit behouithe that the natiuite of bapteme go before the
circumcision and that of ioye also, for these two by reson haue
Vigile, but for as moche as penance is committed for Vigile that
Marie hathe no Uigile. But thei haue alle vtas, for all thei hast to the
.viij. resurreccion. 230

197 high] his E   ide] changed to day H1   200 be shewed] shew H1   202 holy]
blessid D   to the] into this D   205 other] add clerkis D   209 vtauuce] vtauce with
uc subp. H1, utas D   214 sorwes] sorwe EH1   217 vtas] oeptas changed to vtas H1
218 sette litell by] litell sette by D   alle] om. D   221 haloweth] halowed E
224 Iohn] Ihesu Crist D   228 but] om. D   229 alle] om. H1   230 resurreccion]
resurreccionce et c. D

A noble knight and a devouut to the blessed Uirginc Marie in a
tyme as he went to a turnement he fonde a chirche bi the way that
was halowed of oure Lady and he went in to here masse. And so
thanne were mani masses to done and he wolde leue none, but herde
235 hem alle in the worship of that blessed Uirgine. And whanne thei
f. 211rb were | alle done he hied hym fast to go in his iorney. And as he went
he mette with hem that cam from thennes, and anone as they sawe
hym thei saide to hym that he had nobly and worthely turne[i]d. And
tho that hated hym saide that he hadde the pris of the felde that day,
240 and sum came to hym and offered hem to hym and saide that he toke
hem prisoners that day. And thanne he that [was] wys avised hym
how that curteys Uirgine quene of heuene had so worthely wrought
for hym, and tolde to hem alle how it was falle hym and returned
ayen to the chirche and rode alweyes after to oure Lorde.
245   A bisshop that had that blessed Virgine in soueraigne deuocion
and in worship, went at midnight by deuocion to the chirche of the
blessid Virgine with souerayne deuocion, and there he sawe the
Virgine of virgines felawshipped with all the cumpany of virgines
that camen ayens hym and beganne to lede hym to the chirche with
250 gret worship. And .ij. of the virgines of the same felawship went
before synginge and sayeng these vers:

Cantemus Domino, socie, cantemus honorem.
Dulcis amo[r] Cristi personet ore pio.

That is to saie: Singe we to oure Lorde, felawship, singe we hym
255 worship, singe we with debonair voys that suete loue that oght like
hym. And that other felawship of virgines ansuered that same vers,
and thanne two the furst singgers beganne this vers that foluith:

Primus ad yma ruit magna de luce superbus,
Sic homo cum tumit primus ad yma ruit.

260 And so thei ledde the seruaunt of God with suche procession to the
f. 211va chirche, and the .ij. furst begunne alway and that other folw|ed hem.
Ther was a wedu whiche hadde a sone that she loued tenderly.
And that sone was take of his enemies and leide in prison and sore
bounden. And whanne she herde this thinge she wept withoute

---

234 thanne] þere H₁D   237 as] *ins.* H₁   238 turneid] turned EH₁
241 was] *om.* ED   244 rode] yede *on erasure* H₁   after] *om.* D   to²] *del.* H₁
247 deuocion] *add* and worship EH₁   253 *amor*] amo E   259 *yma*] arma H₁
262 wedu whiche] wicked *subp.* wiche *erased* 'widowe' H₁

comfort and besought that blessed Virgine with right gret preiours, 265
to whom she was right deuout, to that ende that she wolde deliuer
her sone. And atte the last she sawe that her praiers profited her
noght, and she went in priueli to the chirche wher the ymage of oure
Ladi was corue and peinted, and she kneled her adoune before the
ymage and aresonid the ymage in this wise, saieng: 'Blessed Virgine, 270
y haue ofte tyme praied to the for the deliueraunce of my sone and
thou hast in no wise take hede to my wrechid praiers, and yet y
beseche the of thin helpe for the deliueraunce of my sone, but y fele
no profit of my praier. And therfor, right as my sone is take awey
from me, right so shall y take thine and putte hym in prison in 275
hostage for myn.' And whan she hadde saide these wordes she
neyghed the ymage and toke the childe that the ymage of oure Ladi
helde in her lappe, and wrapped it in right a clene clothe and bare it
with her and leide it in her cofre and shet it right faste. And thanne
the night foluing the blessid Uirgine appered to the sone of that 280
woman and openid the dore of the prison and comaunded hym that
he shulde go thennes, and she saide hym: 'Sone, saie to thi moder
that she yelde me ayen my sone, sethe y haue yelde her heres.' And
he went oute and came to his moder, and saide her how that the
blessed Uirgine had deliuered hym. And she reioised her gretly and 285
toke the ymage of the childe and came to the chirche and gaue ayen the
blessed Uirgine Marie her sone, seieng: 'Blessed Ladi, y yelde you
thankingges with | al myn herte for the goodnesse that ye haue do to f. 211ᵛᵇ
me in yeldinge me myn owne sone, and, good Ladi, here y yelde you
youres ayen, for y knolage that y haue myn by youre merci and pitee.' 290

There was a theef that dede ofte tymes thefte, but yet he had
alwey gret deuocion to that blessed Uirgine oure most blessed Ladi.
And so in a tyme he was take and hanged. And whanne he was
hangged that blessed Virgine Marie come thedir and as hym semed
she susteined hym thre dayes that he felt no disese. And þo that 295
made hym to be hangged passed therby be auenture and fonde hym
lyvinge and of glad chere, and supposed that the corde had not be
wel streined about his necke, and wolde haue slaine hym with her
suerdes and cutte his throte, but oure blessed Ladi putte her honde
euer ayenst the strokes so that thei might in no wyse noy him. And 300

265 right] om. H₁D   275 thine] aweye thi sone from the D   282 she] the blessid virgine D   284 oute] add of prison D   the] om. H₁   285 hym] add oute of prison D she] the moder D   286 ymage, childe] trs. D   gaue] add it D   ayen] add to H₁D 287 her sone] om. D   289 me²] add ayen D   290 for] om. D   291 was] add also D   292 alwey] euer D   299 putte] helde D   300 so] om. D   noy] neigh D

thanne thei knew bi that he tolde hem that the most blessed Uirgine moder of God halpe hym, and than thei toke hym downe and lete hym go in the worship of oure Ladi. And [thanne] he entrid into an hous of religion and serued oure Ladi all his lyf after.

305 Ther was a clerke that hadde a soueraine deuocion to oure Ladi and saide eueri day the Mateins of her ententifly. And whanne his fader was dede he had none other heire and so he hadde alle the heritage. And thanne he was constreined of his frendes to take a wif. And so in a day as he was besi to ordeine for his mariage, he came by

310 a chirch, and thanne he remembred hym of the seruice that he vsed to do to oure Ladi and went in and beganne to saie his Mateins and his Houres of that blessed Uirgine. And thanne that blessed Ladi appered to hym and saide to hym in sharpe wise: 'O thou fole

f. 212ra unhappi, whi hast thou lefte me that am thi wif and thi loue | and

315 hast putte annother now before me?' And thanne he sodenly chaunged and all set afire with her loue saide: 'Ladi, y crie the merci with al my herte, for y shal neuer forsake the more bi thi grace.' And thanne he returned to his felawship and feined hym to kepe furthe his mariage, and whanne midnight cam he fledde awaye

320 priuili and went into an hous of religion, and ther with al the deuocion of his herte he serued that blessed moder of God as longe as he leued and after his passing hens was full glorious[ly] resseiued of her to endeles blysse.

Ther was a symple preest of a parisshe, a man of honest lyff and

325 coude sing no masse but only of oure Lady, the whiche he songe full deuoutly in þe worship of her. And so he was accused before the bisshop and called furthe anone before hym. And he knowleched well that he coude saie none other masse, and the bisshop reproued hym gretly and putte hym oute of the office [of presthode] that he

330 shulde singe no more fro thennes forwarde. And thanne the night foluing the holy Uirgine appered to the bisshop and blamed hym gretly for he hadde treted so wickedly her seruaunt and her chapelein, and saide to hym he shulde deye within .xxx. dayes but yef he ordeined hym into his office ayen of presthode. And [thanne]

301 knew] *add* wel D   303 thanne] *om.* EH1   305 a²] *om.* H1   306 her] oure ladi D   311 do to] *om.* H1   Ladi] dady *changed to* lady H1   in] *om.* H1D   to saie] *om.* D   312 Ladi] virgine D   313 thou] *om.* D   316 all . . . her] also with al his D   loue] loved *with* d *erased* H1   317 with . . . herte for] *om.* D   thi] þe H1 318 returned] *add* ayen D   322 gloriously] glorious E   325 songe] saide D 329 of presthode] *om.* E   330 no] *add* masse no D   331 holy] blessid D 334 hym] *ins.* H1   his office] *ins.* H1   thanne] *om.* EH1

the bisshop was aferde and sent to the prest and asked hym 335
foryeuenesse, and charged hym to singe the masses of oure Ladi
that he was wont to singe.

Ther was a clerke that was right vayn and wilde, and notwithstondinge he loued well the moder of God and saide eueri day the
Matenes and Oures of her. And in a night he sawe a uision that he 340
was brought before the iugement of God and that oure Lorde saide
to hem that were aboute hym: 'What shull we do with this wreche
here? Deuise ye, for y longe suf|frid hym and y see no token of f. 212ʳᵇ
amendement.' And thanne oure Lorde gaue sentence of dampnacion,
and alle aproued hym. And thanne oure blessed Ladi turned her to 345
her blessed sone and saide: 'My blessed sone, y praie the of thi gret
mercie for this here that thou aswage upon hym the sentence of
dampnacion, and that he may leue yet bi the grace of me whiche is
condempned to endeles dethe by his propre merites.' And ourc
Lorde saide to his moder: 'I deliuer hym atte thi request.' And 350
thanne the Uirgine turned her to hym and saide to hym: 'Goo and
synne no more lest wors falle to the.' And thanne he awoke and
chaunged his lyf and entred into religion and ended his lyff in the
werkes of oure Lorde the yere of oure Lorde .iiijC.xxxvij., and this
was done in Sesile.   355

Ther was a man that hight Theophile that [was] a vikery with a
bisshop, so as Fulbert the bisshop of Chartris tellithe, and he
dispended ful wisely the thinges vnder the bisshop, so that
whanne the bisshop was dede alle the peple saide þat he was
worthi to be bisshop. But his office of vikership suffised hym and 360
he wolde not receiue the state of bisshop. And at the laste he was take
fro that office bi the bisshop, and thanne he fell in so gret dispeire
that he counsailed withe a Iewe that was an enchauntour to wete how
he might be restored ayen to his office. And than he called the fende
and he came anone. And thanne Theophile by the comaundement of 365
the fende reneyed Ihesu Crist and his moder and his cristendome
and wrote a chartre of his owne blode and enseled hit with his seale,
and so bi the fendeys crafte he was brought ayen to his seruice. And
in the morw foluinge he was resseiued into the grace of the bisshop

336 to] that he shulde D   338 and²] om. D   341 before . . . of] vnto his
iugement before D   343 suffrid] suffre H1   no] twice D   345 aproued] prouide
H1, depreuid D   347 this] add clerke D   350 his moder] her Moder H1D   thi]
youre D   351 the] add blessid D   352 he] this clerke D   353 and entred . . .
lyff] om. H1   and²] add so D   354 .iiijC.] iiijˣˣ D   356 a man] one D   was²] om. E
365 of] wᵗ del. ` of' H1   367 of] with on erasure H1

370 by the procuracion of the fende and was restabled to the dignite of
his office. And atte the laste whan he cam to hymself he sorwed
f. 212ᵛᵃ aboue alle | mesure and turned hym fully to the glorious Uirgine
with alle the deuocion of his herte and besought her of grace and of
helpe. And thanne in a tyme that blessed Ladi apered to hym and
375 reproued hym of his feloni and comaunded hym that he shulde
renounce the fende and knowlage Ihesu Crist the sone of God and
alle the verrey ordre of cristen faithe. And so he recouered the grace
of her and of her sone, and in tokene that he was verily foryeue, oure
Lady toke hym ayen the chartre that he hadde wrete to the fende and
380 leide it upon his breste, so that he shulde neuer drede for to be
seruaunt more to the fende. But who was than full of ioye but
Theophile that was thus deliuered bi that blessed Uirgine. And
thanne Theophile tolde this before the bisshop and before alle the
peple how that it was befalle hym, and alle the peple thanked and
385 preised that glorious Uirgine moder of God, and thre dayes after he
rest in pees. Amen.

Here endithe the blessed Natyuite of oure Ladi, and nexst
beginnithe the liff of Seint Cecile, Capᵐ. .C.xxiv.

Seint Cecile the glorious virgine was of the noble kinrede of Rome,
and fro her cradell she was norisshed in the faithe of Ihesu Crist, and
she bare alwey the gospell of oure Lorde hid within her herte, ne she
sesed neuer night ne day for to worship ne for to praie to oure Lorde,
5 and her praier w[as] specially that oure Lorde wolde kepe her
virginite.

But atte the laste her frendes wolde nedes wedde her to a noble
yong man that hight Valerian. And whanne the day of wedding
come, Seint Cecile clothed her with þe heyre nexst her tendre
10 flesshe, and aboue that she arraied her with precious clothes of
f. 212ᵛᵇ golde. And whanne | the instrumentes songe she songe to oure Lorde
and saide: 'Mi blessed Lorde God, y beseche the that my herte and
[my] bodi be thi grace may be kepte vndefouled and that y be not

370 by the] with H₁D   372 the] þat H₁D   374 Ladi] uirgine D   378 and
of her] om. H₁   380 it] om. D   380–81 drede for to be seruant] om. D   381 to]
be the seruaunt of D   382 Uirgine] add marie D   385 and] add at the D

EH₁DH₂A₁A₂L   5 and . . . Lorde] om. D   praier was] praiers were E
9 come] was H₁D   9–10 with . . . heyre/nexst . . . flesshe] trs. H₁D
11 instrumentes] mynstrelis D   12 the] add bi thi might D   my herte and] om. D
13 my] thi E   be thi grace] om. D

deceiued.' And she fasted thre dayes in the recomaunding her to
oure Lorde.   15

And thanne come the night that she shulde entre into the
chaumbre with her spouse, and whanne thei were togederes allone
she aresoned hym in this wise: 'Lo, right suete and louely yong man,
y knowe a counsell that y shulde telle you yef ye wolde suere to me
not for to discouer me, but kepe it counsaile with al youre powere.'   20
And thanne Valerian suore her that he wold not discouer her for
nothinge. Thanne she saide to hym: 'I haue an aungell of Goddes to
my loue, and he kepithe my bodi with so grete loue and tendirnesse
that yef he might fele that ye wolde touche me bi ani vnordinat loue
he wolde smite you in suche a wise that ye shulde lese the floure of   25
youre age, and yef he knowe ye loue me with pure loue he will loue
you as well as me [and shewe you his loue].'

And thanne Valerian, t[au]ght bi the wille of oure Lorde, seide:
'Yef ye will that y l[e]ue you, shewe me that aungell, and yef y may
truly knowe that he an aungell y will do that ye require me.' To   30
whom Cecile ansuered and saide: 'Yef ye leued in the verrey God
and were baptised ye might [well] see hym, but while ye stonde in
this blyndenesse ye may not, wherfor y shall sende you into the way
that is called Apien, whiche is a mile from Rome, and ye shulle saie
to the pore man that ye shull finde there: "Cecile hathe sent me to   35
you that ye shull shewe me Vrban the holy man, for y haue a secrete
counsell to telle hym [fro] her." And whanne ye see hym, telle hym
al that y haue tolde you, and doute you not but whanne ye shall [be
baptised of hym ye shall] | se the aungell that y haue tolde you of.'   f. 213ra

And thanne went Valerian to the bisshop Vrban that was hidde   40
withinne the sepulcres of dede men for drede of gret persecucion
that was ayenst the cristen religion, and tolde hym alle the wordes of
Cecile. And whanne Vrban herde hym he helde vp his hondez to
heuene and saide: 'O thou Lorde Ihesu Crist, the sower of rightwys
counsaile, resseiue the sede that thou hast sowed in thi yonge   45
servaunt Cecile. [For, blessid Lorde Ihesu Crist, Cecile] thi yong
mayden seruithe the as a bee to the honi euer in encresing, for her
husbonde that she toke as a lyon she hathe sent hym to me as a

18 aresoned] resound H1   20 it] my D   23 kepithe] kept H1   24 that²] add
yef E   25 wise] add so E   27 and shewe . . . loue] om. E   28 taught] L, thought
EH1D   Lorde] add and H1D   29 leue] loue EH1D (croye P2)   30 me] om. D
32 well] om. EH1   33 into] in H1   34 is¹] ins. H1   37 fro] for E   38–9 be
baptised . . . ye shall] om. E   42 was] add that tyme D   44 rightwys] two words ED
46 For blessid . . . Cecile] om. E   48 lyon] add and now D

debonair lambe.' And anone there apered betwene hem an auncien
50 man clothed in white clothinge that helde a boke in his honde wretin
with letteres of golde. Ande whanne Valerian sawe hym he fel down
for drede as dede, and anone this auncien man lefte hym up and
redde hym that was wrete in the boke aforesaid, whiche sentence was
this: 'On God, on beleue, one bapteme. One is God and fader of alle
55 and is aboue alle and in vs alle.' And whanne he had red thus he
saide to Valerian: 'Levist thou that this is trewe, or doutest thou yet?'
And Valerian answered: 'There is nothinge under heuene so wel to
[be] beleued.' And anone he vanisshed awaye and Valerian resseiued
bapteme of Seint Vrban.
60　　And whanne he had done he turned ayen and fonde Seint Cecile
in her chaumbre spekinge with the aungell, and the aungell helde in
his hondes .ij. crownes of roses and of lelyes. And whanne Valerian
sawe the aungell he fell ayen downe for drede, and the aungell
benigly toke hym up and saide: 'Ualerian, for thou hast goodly leued
65 the profitable counsaile of thi wiff, oure Lorde hathe sent the here
one of these .ij. crownes for to be of the sewte of thi wiff. Wherfor
f. 213ʳᵇ loke | ye kepe these crownes with herte and body withoute
defoulynge, for y haue brought hem from paradys to you by the
comaundement of almighti God, ne thei shull neuer fade ne neuer
70 lese her odour, ne thei mowe not be sein of none but yef thei haue
charite. And Valerian, for thi mekenesse oure Lorde hathe
comaunded me to saie to the that loke what thou desirest of hym
he will graunte the.' And thanne Valerian with soueraine gladnesse
saide: 'Worship and ioye be to oure soueraigne Lorde of his gret
75 merci done to me, wherfor yef it like his high goodnesse to do me
suche grace, y wolde besече hym to shewe his gret merci to a
brother of myn that he might come oute of his blyndenesse and se
the clere waye of trouthe.' The aungell ansuered and saide: 'Hit
likithe to oure Lorde that ye haue required, wherfor ye shull bothe
80 come to hym by the peine of marterdom.'
　　After this Tiburcien, brother of Valerian, entred into the chambre
of his brother, and as he entred he felt so gret a sauour of swetnesse
of roses that he was all astonied and saide: 'I meruaile gretly that y
fele in this tyme suche sauour of roses and of lelyes, for thou myn

55 thus] *add* this boke D　　56 yet] it D　　58 be] *om.* E　　he] this auncient man D
and] *add* thanne E　　67 these] *add* .ij. H1D　　73 will] *om.* D　　graunte] *add* it D
74 to] *add* the EH1　　75 merci] *add* hathe D　　like] *add* to H1, *add* vnto D　　76 to¹]
that he wolde D　　80 peine] crowne D　　82 entred he] *om.* H1　　84 of²] *om.* H1

hondes were full y might not fele so gret a sauour of swetnesse as y 85
do. Truly, my dere brother and suster, y knowlache to you that y fele
me so refresshed with this suetnesse that y am a[l]tered and
chaunged.' To whom Valerian saide: 'Dere brother, we haue crownes
that thin eyen mow not se of coloures of roses and of lelies, and right
as thou felest the sauour, thou maist see hem yef thou wilt beleue in 90
God.' Thanne Tiburcien saide: 'Is this a dreme that y do here or is
this trwe that thou | saiest, Valerian?' And Valerian saide: 'We haue f. 213va
be vnto this tyme in a dreme, but we be now in the verray trouthe.'
And thanne Tiburcien saide: 'Where hast thou lernid this, brother?'
And Valerian saide: 'The aungell of God hathe taught me, the 95
whiche thou mightest see with thin eyen yef thou were purified and
haddest clene forsake alle the ydoles.'

This same miracle of crownes of roses witnessithe Seint Ambrose
in his Preface and saithe: 'Seint Cecile was so utterly fulfelled with
the yefte of the holy gost that she dispised the worlde and toke upon 100
her the paine of marterdom, and of that is witnesse the confession of
Valerian her husbonde and of Tiburcien his brother, the whiche oure
Lorde crouned bi the honde of the aungell with smellinge floures.
And the uirgine ledde these men to ioye, and the worlde might
clerely perceiue how moche deuocion of chastite is worthe.' These be 105
the wordes of Seint Ambrose.

Thanne Seint Cecile shewed hem clerely that alle the ydoles were
but deef and dowme [and] withoute ani witte. Thanne ansuered
Tiburcien: 'Trewly whoso leuithe not that ye saie is worse thanne an
vnresonable beste.' Cecile heringe hym with gret ioy she kist his 110
breste and saide: 'This day y knoulache the to be my brother, for
right as the loue of God hathe ioyned to me thi brother, right so the
forsaking of ydoles hathe made me thi cosin. Goo now, my dere
brother, with thi brother, for to resseiue purificacion so that thou
maist see the uisages of aungels. And thanne saide Tiburcien to his 115
brother: 'Y wolde praie you, telle me to whom ye wolde lede me.'
And Valerian saide: 'To the bisshop Urban.' And Tiburcien saide:
'Is that Vrban that so mani tymes hathe be condempned, the whiche
is hidde in priue places and yef he might | be founde he shulde be f. 213vb

86 knowlache] add me H1   87 altered] alle attered E   91–4 saide . . . Tiburcien]
ins. H1   94 lernid] ins. H1, om. D   97 the] om. H1D   101 that is witnesse] þis
witnesseth H1   102 his] her D   103 Lorde] ins. H1   104 uirgine] add Cecile D
ledde] 'ladde' H1   might] may D   107 hem] Tiburcien D   108 but] om. D   and²]
om. EH1   110 she] om. D   112 to me] trs. D   116 wolde] will H1   117 the]
add holy EH1

120 brent, and we with hym yef it were knowe that we went to hym? And
thus whanne we shulde seke the diuinite that is [hidde] in heuene we
shulle renne in the brenninge woodnesse of tirauntes here in erthe.'
Thanne saide Seint Cecile: 'Yef there were no mo lyues but this one,
bi reson we shulde drede to lese it, but there is a beter lyf that may
125 not be loste, the whiche the sone of God hathe tolde us of. For they
that be made the sone engendered of the fader made, and alle
thingges made the holi goste cominge from the fader. And this same
sone of God techithe us that there is annother lif.'
    Than saide Tiburcien: 'Truli this is a gret meruaile to me that ye
130 afferme o God to be, and now ye sheue us to be .iij. goddes.' Cesily
ansuered and saide: 'Right as in the wysdom of on man be thre
thingges, that is cunninge, mynde and understondinge, right so in
one beinge of diuinite be thre persones.' And thanne she beganne to
preche of the cominge of the sone of God into this worlde, of his
135 most [bl]essed lyvinge, and of his peinfull passion. For she saide that
Goddes sone suffered for to be take and bounde that mannes soule,
whiche was holde and bounde in synne, might goo at large; he that
was most blessed suffered to be cursed, for that cursed man shulde
resseyue blessinge; he suffered for to be dispised for to bringe man
140 oute of despit of the fende; he suffered his precious hede to be
crowned with sharpe thornes for to deliuer man from the capitall
sentence of dampnacion; he resseiued bitter galle for he wolde restore
man to his suete taste; he was dispoiled for he wolde couer oure
nakidesse of oure furst fader; he was hangged on a crosse for that he
145 wolde take awey the trespas and the outrage of the tree of lif.'
Whanne Tiburcien had herde alle this he saide to his brother: 'A, my
f. 214ʳᵃ dere brother, haue pite on me and bringe me to that | blessid man so
that y may resseiue purificacion.' And thanne Valerian ledde hym to
Vrban, and whanne he was baptised he sawe often tymes the aungell
150 of God and had of hym anone what he desired.
    And thanne Tyburcien and Valerian departed for the loue of God
her goodes to pore men largely, and beried the holy bodies that
Almachien the provost slow for cristen faithe. And whanne this
tiraunt perceiued that, he lete calle hem before hym and asked hem

120 it] we H1   121 we¹] he H1   hidde] *om.* E   122 tirauntes] Tiranny H1D
125 they] tho H1, ye D   126 engendered] engendireth H1   130 be¹] me D
133 one beinge] obeynge D   diuinite] derinite D   134 cominge] kunnyng H1
135 blessed] pressed E, *so changed to* blessed H1, precious D   138 that] *add* þat H1
142 he wolde] to H1D   143 couer oure] ouercome H1   144 fader] *add* Adam D
146 had herde alle] herde of D   154 he] *ins.* H1   hem¹] hym D

ho made hem so hardi to berie tho bodies that be dampned to the 155
dethe for her felonies. And Tiburcien answered: 'Mi will were that
we were seruauntes to hem that thou settist so litell by, for thei haue
dispised that that semithe to be and is not, and haue founde that that
is not sayn to be and is.' The provost saide: 'What thinge is that?'
And Tyburcien saide: 'That that is saine to be and is not, is all that is 160
in this worlde that bringithe men to not. And that that is not seine to
be and ys, is the lyf of rightwis men, whiche is euerlasting ioye.'
Than saide the prouost to Tiburcien: 'I trowe thou saiest not this in
ernest or ellys thou art not well with thiself.'

And thanne he comaunded Valerian to come before hym and saide 165
to hym: 'Valerian, I suppose that thi brother is not wel with hymself,
and therfor thou must ansuere more wisely.' Thanne saide Valerian:
'It semithe to me that ye be to gret folcs that refusen the ioyes and
coueiten peyncs. For y haue sayen in tyme of gret frostes children
and ydel folke renne and plaie upon the yse and scorned werkemen 170
and laboreres, but whanne somer came that the glorious fruytes were
ripe, thanne the laboreres reioised hem and tho that scorned hem
wepte, and so fare ye now. Ye laghe and scorne us for we suffre
tribulacions and laboures, but in tyme to come whan ye shul waile
and sorw we shull haue for oure mede euerlastinge ioye.' Thanne | 175
saide the prouost: 'What, wenist thou that we noble princes shull f. 214rb
haue euerlastinge wepinge and [y]e vile persones euerlastinge ioye?'
Thanne Valerian saide: 'Ye be men and not princes, born in oure
tyme for to deye hastely and shul yelde acountes to God more thanne
any other of lower degree.'   180

Thanne saide the prouost: 'Wherto tarie we so longe in wordes?
Offrithe sacrifices to [oure goddes] and gothe quite.' And the seintes
ansuered: 'We yeue eueri day sacrifice to almighti God.' And the
prouost saide: 'What is his name?' And Valerian saide: 'Thou might
not finde his name, thow thou might fle with wynges.' And the 185
prouost saide: 'Is not Iubiter the name of a god?' And Valerian saide:
'That is the name of a mansleer and of a vouterere.' Thanne saide the
tiraunt: 'And this were true thanne were al the worlde blynde, and

159–60 not . . . is'] om. D   160 not] del. 'nou3t' H1   163 I trowe] om. D
167 and therfor] for H1   168 to'] om. H1D   172 hem²] om. H1D
176 noble] om. D   177 ye] L, the EH1D   179 yelde] yeue D   180 any]
om. D   of] om. H1D   182 sacrifices] sacrifice D   oure goddes] god EH1
183 sacrifice] sacrifices EH1   186 Iubiter] Impiter with third minim of m subp. H1
a] om. D   187 a vouterere] one word E   188 true] tru'we' H1   were/al . . .
worlde] trs. H1

thou and thi brother knowynge only the trouthe.' To whom Valerian
190 saide: 'We be not alone, for gret multitude of men withoute nombre
haue receiued this holynesse.'

And thanne were these seintes putte in prison in the keping of
Maxymien, to whiche he saide: 'O beauute of youthe, whi haste ye so
fast to youre dethe and that with as good a will as thou ye were bode
195 to a feste?' To whom Valerian saide: 'Yef thou wilt behote us that
thou wilt beleue in God, thou shalt see us after oure dethe.' And
Maxymien saide hem: 'Yef it be true that ye sayne, y shal confesse
hym only God that is of suche power.' And thanne Maxymien and
alle his housholde leuedyn in God and weren baptised of Seint
200 Urban that cam thedir priuely.

And whanne the dawninge of the day apered, Seint Cecile cam to
the prison to comfort hem and cried with a lowde vois to hem and
saide: 'O ye knightes of Ihesu Crist, partithe awey the werkis of
f. 214ᵛᵃ derkenesse and clothe you with | the armes [of light].' And thanne
205 the seintez were ledde .iiij. myle fro the citee to the ydole of Iubiter,
and whanne thei wolde in no wise do sacrifice thei were beheded in
the same place. And Maximian swore truly that whanne the holy
seintes were martired he sawe a gret multitude of aungels aboute
hem and her soules go oute of her bodies as faire virgines oute of her
210 chaumbres, and the aungeles bring hem up to heuene. And whanne
Almachien herde that Maxymian was cristen, he made hym to be
bete with scourges knotted with lede so long til he yelde up the
sperit.

And [thanne] Almachien toke al her goodes and sent for Cecile as
215 for the wif of Valerian, þat she shulde come and do sacrifice or elles
resseiue sentence of dethe. And whanne she herde this message she
armed her gladly with the signe of the crosse and recomaunded her
holy to her souerayne Lord Ihesu. And whanne the peple and her
servauntes sawe that so noble and so faire a mayde putte herself frely
220 to the dethe, thei wepte and cried that it was pitee to here. To whom
Cecile said: 'O ye yonge peple, bethe of good comfort, for y lese not
my youthe but y chaunge it into betir; y yeue my[r]e or fenne and
receyue golde; I leue a foule abite and receyue a precious clothing; I
yeue a litell corner and resseiue a large and a right gret place. O good

189 and²] þat del. '&' H1   194 thou] om. H1D   were] add bothe E   198 hym
only] me oonly to H1D   201 Seint] om. H1D   204 armes] werkes H1D   of light]
om. E   205 myle] add thennis D   to] of D   207 that] to hem for D   the²] þies
H1D   210 bring] bringing H1   214 thanne] om. EH1   218 her souerayne]
oure D   Ihesu] add Crist H1D   219 frely] om. D   222 myre] myte E   or] and H1

lorde, yef any man wolde geue shelinges for a peny, how ye wolde 225
high you fast thedirward. Whi take ye none hede, thanne, how our
blessed Lorde takithe a symple thinge and yeuithe an .C. folde? Leue
ye not this that y saie?' And thei ansuered: 'We beleue it, and also we
beleue verily that Ihesu Crist is verrey God that hathe suche a
seruaunt.' And thanne Cecilie sent priuely for Vrban, and there were 230
baptised atte that tyme .iiijC. and mo.

And thanne the tyraunt Almachien called Seint Cecilie to hym
and | saide to her: 'Of what condicion art thou?' And she ansuered f. 214ᵛᵇ
and saide: 'I am of a noble kinrede.' And Almachien saide: 'Y aske
the of what relygion?' And Cecile saide: 'Thi demaunde hathe a 235
leude begynninge. What wenist thou that y conclude .ij. answeres
vnder one demaunde?' And Almachien saide: 'Fro whennes comithe
to the this gret presumpcion to ansuere me in suche wise?' And she
saide: 'Of verrei conscience and of stedfast faithe.' Thanne Almachien saide: 'Wost thou not of what might y am?' And Cecilie saide: 240
'Yes, ful wel, for youre might is in youre bely that is full of wynde,
for yef it were pricked a litell with a nedill or a pynne, alle youre
might wolde sone fade.' 'What,' saide Almachien, 'Thou began with
iniuries and so thou perseuerist.' Cecilie saide: 'Iniurie is not saide
[but] bi deceyuable wordes. Shewe me the iniurie [yef] y haue spoke 245
vtterly, or elles amende thiself seying malice. For we that knowe the
holy name of God mow not denie hym, for it is moche beter to deye
goodly thanne for to leue wickedly.' And Almachien saide: 'Whi
spekest thou with so gret pride?' She ansuered: 'As y tolde the ere, it
is no pride but sadnesse of feithe.' Thanne Almachien saide: 'A, thou 250
wreche, wost thou not wel that it is in my might for to yeue the lyf or
dethe?' Cecilie ansuered and saide: 'Y shal preue anone that thou
hast made a gret lesinge ayenst the comune trouthe, for thou maist
take awey the lyf of hem that be quicke, but thou maist not yeue no
lyf to hem that be dede, and than art thou a ministre of dethe and not 255
of lyf.' To whom Almachien saide: 'Holde thi tunge and do awey thi
madnesse and sacrifice to oure goddes.' And Cecilie saide: 'I trow
thou hast loste thi sight, for tho that thou saiest be goddes we see alle
that thei be stones. Putte forthe thin honde and fele but yef thou may
see.'   260

226 how] *om.* H₁   228–9 it . . . beleue²] *om.* D   234 a] *om.* H₁D   238 gret]
om. D   me] *om.* D   245 but] *om.* E   yef] that E, þat if H₁D   246 that] *om.* D
250 is] was D   sadnesse] gladnesse D   251 wel] *om.* D   yeue] yeld H₁   254 no]
om. H₁   255 to hem] *ins.* H₁   256 thi²] *ins.* H₁   258 sight] light D

f. 215ʳᵃ   Than Almachien, fulfilled with wodenesse, co|maunded that she
shulde be ladde to hys hous, and there al a night and al a day he
made her to stonde in a bathe contynuelly boylynge. And she felt
neuer disese of hete but satte freshely as she had sete in a medw of
265 sote floures. And [whanne] Almachien herde it he comaunded that
she shulde be biheded in the bathe. And the bocher smote .iij.
strokes and might in no wise smite of her hede, and for it was the
custume that tho that shuld be biheded shulde not haue the ferthe
stroke, he left her half dede al blodi. And she ouer that lyued .iij.
270 daies and gaue alle that she had to pore men, and alle tho that she
had conuerted to the faithe she recomaunded to Seint Vrban, saieng:
'Y haue required the space of .iij. dayes for to recomaunde hem here
to thi blessidnesse, and for that also that thou shalt sacre myn hous
into a chirche.' And atte the ende of thre daies she offered up her
275 blessed soule to the high blesse of heuene, where it was receiued with
souerayne worship and ioye of alle that blessed court. And Seint
Vrban beried her body amonge the bisshoppes and dedied her hous
into a chirche as she had praied hym. And she suffered dethe and
fonde euerlastinge lyf about the yere of oure Lorde .CC. and .xxiij.
280 in the tyme of the emperour Alisaundre.

Here endithe the lif of Seint Cecilie, and nexst beginnithe
the lyf of Seint Adrian, Cap. .C.xxv.ᵐ

Adrian suffered dethe vnder Maxymian the emperour. For as the
said emperour was in the citee of Nichomede wher he sacrified to
ydoles, and by hys comaundement al cristen men were sought, and
sum sought hem for loue, and sum for drede, and sum for bihest of
5 money, so that one neighbore led his neighbore to martirdome,
amonge whiche .xxxiij. were take of tho that sought hem and were
broght before the kinge. And the kinge saide to hem: 'Haue ye not
f. 215ʳᵇ herde what peyne is ordeined a|yenst [the] cristen?' And thei
ansuered: 'We haue herde the comaundement of thi foly.' And
10 thanne the kinge was wrothe ande comaunded that thei shulde be

263 to] *om.* HₚD   264 satte] *add* as HₚD   265 whanne] *om.* EHₚ   271 had]
om. Hₚ   275 blessed] *om.* DL   high] *om.* HₚD   277 dedied] edified HₚD
279 .xxiij.] .xxij. D

EHₚDH2AₚA2; Aₚ breaks off after 118 *noumbre*   2 Nichomede] Nichodeme Hₚ
to] *add* his HₚD   3 by] *om.* D   comaundement] comaundmentes HₚD   5 led his
neighbore] *ins.* Hₚ   7 kinge . . . kinge] Emperoure D   8 the] *om.* E   9 herde]
ins. Hₚ   10 kinge] Emperoure D

bete with rawe synwes, and that her mouthes were bete with stones,
and that eueriche of hem shulde haue her tunge persed with an hote
yren and that thei weren bound and closed in prison. And thanne
Adrean that was the furst in the office of knighthode saide to hem: 'I
coniure you bi the vertu of youre goddes, that ye telle me what vertu 15
and guerdon that ye abide to haue for these turmentis that ye suffre
thus.' And thanne the seintis saide to hym that there nas neuer eye
that might see, ne eere that might here, ne hert that might [th]inke
the ioyes that oure Lorde hathe araied to hem that drede hym
perfitely. And thanne Adrean lepte amonge hem and saide: 'Acounte 20
me for one of you, for y am cristen.' And whanne the emperour
herde it, and that he wolde not sacrifice, he made binde hym and laie
hym in prison.

And whanne Natalye his wif herd that her husbonde was in
prison, she al torent her clothes and wepte strongely. But whanne it 25
was tolde her that he was in prison for the faithe of Ihesu Crist, she
was gretly rcioysed and ranne to the prison and cussed the bondes of
her husbondes and of other. For she was secretly a cristen woman,
but she durst not opinly shewe it for the gret persecucion that was
done upon the cristen. And thanne she saide to her husbonde: 'A, my 30
lorde and my Adrean, how thou art blessed, for thou hast founde the
richesse that was neuer lefte to the bi thi kinrede, wherof they haue
now right gret nede, for tho that possedid here many thingges shul
haue gret nede whanne there shal be no tyme of boruinge ne of
lenynge, whan that one shal not deliuer that other fro pcinc, ne the 35
fader the sone, ne the moder the doughter, ne the seruaunt the
maister, | ne the frende his frende, ne richesse hem þat owen hem.' f. 215va
And whanne she hadde diligently taught hym that he shulde despise
alle erthely ioye, kinrede and frendes, and that he shulde alwey haue
his hert to heuenly thinges, Adrian said to her: 'Go now, my suster, 40
and haste the tyme of oure passion so that thou maist see oure ende.'
And thanne she recomaunded her husbond to the thother seintes and
praied hem to comfort her husbonde in oure Lorde, and so she
returnid to her owne hous.

And thanne Adrean herde that the day was come of his passion, 45

12 her] his D   persed] partid D   13 closed] add and put H1   14 office] ordre D
18 thinke] drinke E   19 araied] `a´/raied with a on erasure H1   21 whanne] om. D
23 in prison] om. D   29 opinly] om. D   32 neuer] ins. H1   lefte] loste D
33 right] om. D   possedid here] possedeth now with now del. `here´ H1, passeden now D
37 his frende] om. H1D   39 ioye] add be D   42 her husbond] om. H1   45 day
was] dayes were D

and gaue yeftes to the kepers that thei wolde geue hym leue to go to
his hous and calle Natalie his wyf, for he hadde behight her bi his
trouthe that she shulde be present atte his passion. And one that
sawe hym renne before hym [and] seide to Nataly: 'Adrean is
50 deliuered, lo, where he comithe.' And whanne she herde that she
leuid it not, but saide: 'Who might deliuer hym from the bondes of
charite, and þat he were departed from these seintes of God, God
defende it.' And as she saide that, a childe of her meyne came that
saide: 'Sekerly my lord is lete go.'
55   And she went that he hadd fled marterdom, and beganne to wepe
bitterly, and whanne she sawe hym she shette her dores ayenst hym
and saide: 'Go here ferre fro me, that is take awey fro God, ne falle it
neuer to me that y speke with that mouthe that hathe renied his God
and his Lorde. O thou cursed withoute God, who constreined the to
60 vndertake that thou might not performe? Who hathe take the from
the seintes? Alas, who hathe deseiued the for to departe the from
hem? Tell me, cowarde, whi art thou fledde before the bataile
beg[anne] and or thou sawe the fighters fight? Wherwith art thou
wounded?. Hit is with none arwe that was shotte to the. Sykerly y
65 shulde haue meruailed me yef any of the men withoute God and of
the k[ynde] of wickidnesse had be offered to God. But alas to me, |
f. 215ᵛᵇ wrechid and caitiff, what shal y do, that am ioyned to this that is of
the kinrede of felones? He is not geue me by only space of tyme.
Alas, my hope and ioye that y shulde haue be called the wif of a
70 marter, but now alas, for y shall be called the wyf of a renogate. Alas,
my ioye hathe litell dured and this shalle be to me a repreef for euer.'
    And Adrean, hering this, reioised it gretly and meruailed hym of
the gret sadnesse of his wif that was yonge and right faire and noble
and thei had be maried but .xiiij. monthes, how she might saie alle
75 this. And therfor he was made more brennynge to martirdom and
herde gladly her wordes, but atte the laste whanne he sawe her gretly
turmented, he saide to her: 'Openithe the dore, Nataly my wif, for y
haue not fledde martirdom so as thou wenist, but y am come to calle
the so as y behight the.' And she leued hym noght but saide to hym:
80 'Lo, how this traitour renegat deceiuithe me. Whi liest thou, thou

46 hym] hem H1   49 and] om. EH1D (et P2)   50 she'] 's'he H1   57 here]
her changed to hens H1, he D   falle it] falleth H1   58 God] ins. H1   60 performe]
add the wil of God H1D   61 the'] these EH1   63 beganne] be gone E, begone H1
fighters] add to E   64 y] it H1D   66 kynde] king EH1D (gent P2)   67 and] om.
H1   68 not] om. H1D   71 be] do D   72 hering] add al D   75 therfor] þere
H1D   78 wenist] add and del. but I am come to call þe so as thou wenest H1

secounde Iudas? Fle from me, thou cursed. Y shal slee myself so that
thou be fulfelled.' And as she taried to open the dore, he saide:
'Open anone, for y go my way and thou shalt see me no more, and
thanne thou wilt wepe that thou hast not saie me before my dethe. Y
haue geue pleges the holy martires, and yef the ministres seke me 85
and finde me not, the seintes shull suffre her martirdom and myn
shall be lefte.' And whanne Natalie herde that, she openid the dore
to hym and thei went togederis to the prison, and Natalye wiped the
woundes of the seintes with precious clothes .viij. daies togederes.

And thanne the emperour made hem to be brought before hym, 90
and thei were so tobrostin with peynes that thei might not go, but
were born as bestes. And Adrean was bound, his hondes behinde
hym, and was born upon the turment that is called ecule [and]
presentid to Cesar. And Natalie ioyned her to hym and saide: 'Mi
lorde, loke that thou tremble not in no wise whanne thou seest the | 95
turmentes, for thou shalt suffre here but a litell, and after that thou f. 216ʳᵃ
shalt be lefte up into heuene with glorious aungels.' And whanne
Adrean wolde in no wise do sacrifise he was greuously beten, and
thanne Natalye ranne to the seintes that were in the prison and saide:
'My husbonde hathe begunne his marterdom.' And thanne the 100
emperoure bade hym that he shulde no more blame her goddes,
and Adrean saide: 'Yef y am thus turmentid that be noght, how shalt
thou be turmentid for blamyng of hem that disp[i]sist the verrey
God?' And thanne the king saide: 'These other traitours haue taught
the these wordes.' And Adrian saide: 'Whi callest thou hem traitours 105
that be doctours and techers of euerlastinge lyf?' And whanne Natalie
herde her husbonde speke so well, anone she ranne with gret ioye and
tolde to the seintes that were in prison how wel he had said.

And thanne the king made hym greuously to be bete with .iiij.
men that were of gret strengthe, and anone Natalie reported to the 110
martires that were in prison alle the martirdomes and all the ansueres
of her husbonde. And thanne was Adrean so cruelly bete that alle his
bowels appered. And thanne he was fast bounde with cheines and
enclosed with the other in prison. And Adrean was a yonge delicate
man, ful faire, of the age of .xxviij. winter, and whanne Nataly sawe 115

83 Open] *add* it D   84 wepe] wipe H1   85 pleges] *add* to H1   87 lefte]
loste D   88 wiped] wept H1   93 and²] *om.* EH1   96 that] *add* s *del.* H1
102 turmentid] *add* for blamyng of hem E   103 dispisist] displesist E   104 king]
Emperoure D   106 and techours] *om.* D   109 king] Emperoure D   110 gret]
om. H1   111 martires] seintes D   113 he was] was Adrian so cruelli bete and H1
114 other in] *ins.* H1

her husbonde lye groueling on the erthe al tobrostin, she laide her honde vpon his hede in comforting of hym and saide: 'Thou art blessed, my lorde, that art made worthi to be in the noumbre of seintes, thou art blessed, my dere husbonde, that sufferest for hym

120 whiche suffered dethe for the. Go forthe anone, my suete man, so that thou may see the ioye of hym for whom thou sufferist.'

And whanne the emperoure herde that meny ladies come and

f. 216rb seruid the holy sein|tes in prison, he comaunded that men shulde not suffre hem to come to hem no more. And whanne Natalye herde þat,

125 she cutte of her here and dede on mannes clothinge and seruid forthe the seintes in prison and made other ladies to do the same by her ensaumple. And she praied her husbonde that whanne he were in ioye that he wolde make this praier for her, that she might be kepte chaste and sone take oute of this worlde. And whanne the kinge

130 herde how these ladies hadde done, he ordeined an orrible turment, so that the holy martires shulde be al tobroste vnder the peyse of the turment and so to deie the rather. And thanne Natalie dredde her lest her husbonde wolde be aferde by the turmentis of other, and praied the ministres that thei wolde beginne [at hym]. And thanne

135 his thies and his fete were kutte of, and Natalie praied hym that he wolde suffre his hondes to be cutte of. And Natalye praied hym to that ende that he might be even felowe with the other seintes that had suffered more thanne he. And whanne his hondes were cutte of he yelde up the sperit to God. The other seintes helde forthe her fete

140 of her owne fre wille and passedin to oure Lorde.

And the kinge comaunded that her bodies were brent, and Nataly hidd in her bosum an honde of her husbondes. And the bodies of the seintes were caste in the fire, and Natalie wolde haue ronne into the fire with hem, and anone sodenly a gret reyne come that quenched al

145 the fire so that the bodies of the seintes had no harme. And than the cristen toke her counsaile togedre and bare the bodies of the seintes into Constantinople, vnto the tyme that pees was yolde vnto the Chirche and that thei might be brought ayen worshipfully. And thei

f. 216va suffered marterdom about | the yere of oure Lorde .CC.iiij^xx.

150 Nataly thanne duelled in her hous, kepinge the honde of her

118 to be] om. H1   120 dethe/for the] trs. D   121 sufferist] add al this D
122 herde] sey H1   124 þat] add þat del. H1   125 on] upon her D   129 kinge]
Emperoure D   134 at hym] om. EH1   135 hym] hem H1   135–6 hym . . .
praied] om. D   136 hym] hem D   140 and] add so D   Lorde] add god D
141 kinge] Emperoure D   142 the] om. H1   143 ronne] ins. H1   145 than] om.
H1   149 marterdom] dethe D   150 duelled] dwelling H1D   kepinge] kept H1D

husbonde, and for to haue comfort in her lyf she leide it alway atte
her beddes hede. And after this the iuge saw Nataly so right faire, so
yonge and so noble so that bi the will of the emperour he sent ladies
to her for that cause that she shulde consent to hym by mariage. To
whom Nataly ansuered: 'What is he that be ani yefte might ioyne me   155
to ani suche man bi mariage? But y praie you that y may haue respite
of .iij. dayes so that y may araye me.' And that she said for she wolde
fle thennes fro hem. And thanne she praied oure Lorde that he wolde
kepe her body undefouled, and than she fel aslepe sodenly and one of
the marteres apered to her and comforted her full suetly and   160
comaunded her to go to that place where the bodies of the martires
were.

And whanne she awoke she toke the honde of Adrean alonly and
entred into [a] shippe with mani other cristen. And whanne the iuge
herde it he folowed her in shippes with many knightes, and thanne   165
the wynde come so stronge ayenst hem and drowned many of hem
and constreincd the remenaunt to retorne home ayen. And thanne
atte midnight the fende apered to hem in a shippe in liknesse of a
shipman and said to hem: 'Whennes come ye or wheder will ye?'
And the cristen saide: 'We come fro Nichomede and go towarde   170
Constantinenople.' And he saide [to hem]: 'Ye erren, turnithe in the
lefte honde and ye shull finde and saile more right.' And he saide
that for to haue drowned hem in the see. And as thei turned her
saile, anone sodenly Adrean apered vnto hem and went before hem
and taught hem the waye, and whan Natalie sawe hym she was   175
fulfelled with right grete ioye.

And so or it were day thei come into Constantinenople. And |
whanne Natalye entred into the hous of the martires she toke the   f. 216vb
honde of Adrean and sette it to the bodi and made her praier and fill
aslepe, and Adrean apered to her and grette her and bade her come   180
with hym into euerlastinge pees. And whanne she was wakyn she
tolde to hem about her of her vision, and grette hem, and anone she
yelde her blessed spirit to oure Lorde, and the good cristen men toke
the bodi and beried it amonge holy martires.

151 lyf] self D   152 so¹] *om.* D   154 she] `s´he H1   156 ani] *om.* D
158 hem] hym D   159 kepe] help H1   160 marteres] seintes D   164 a] the
EH1   165 her in shippes] after D   170 Nichomede] Nichodeme H1D   171 he]
the fende D   to hem] *om.* EH1   erren turnithe in] aren turned on D   in] on H1
172 finde] *add* it H1D   174 anone] *om.* D   180 and bade her] `& baþe her´ H1
182 tolde] *ins.* H1

Here endithe the lif of Seint Adrean, and nexst beginnithe
the lyf of Seint Gorgonien, Cap^m. .C.xxvj.^m

Seint Gorgon[ien] and Seint Dorothe were in Nichomede the furst
in the paleis of the emperour Dioclisian, and thei renounsed her olde
knighthode for to folw more frely her kinge, and thei confessed with
high vois that thei were cristen. And whanne the emperour herde
5 that he was gretly displesed, and greued right sore to lese suche .ij.
men that hadde be norisshed in his paleis and were noble of kinrede
and of condiciones. And whanne he sawe that thei might not be
turned by manaces ne bi wordes, he made hem to be streched oute
upon the turnement that is called ecule and made her bodies to be al
10 tobroste with flailes and with hokes of yren, and sethe he made hem
to be froted with salt and vinegre, the whiche entred nigh into her
boweles, and they suffered al this right gladly. And thanne he made
hem to be rosted upon gredyrnes, and thei laie theron as thei hadde
leie on a softe bedde of floures and it apered that thei felt none
15 harme. And thanne the emperoure made hem to be hanged with
cordes, and so thei yelde up her holy spirites to God. And thanne her
bodies were thrauen to houndes, but thei touched hem neuer but
f. 217ra were gadered and beried of good cristen men. And they suf|fered
dethe in the yere of oure Lorde .CC.iiij^xx.
20   And thanne bi mani yeres after, the body of Seint Gorgonien was
translated into Rome the yere of oure Lorde .CCC.xxxiij. and than
the bisshopp of Meuse, nevew of Pepyn, translated that bodi into
Fraunse and putte it in the chirche of Gorgonien worshipfully.

Here endithe the lyf of Seint Gorgonien, and nexst
beginnithe the lyues of Prothe and Iacincty, Cap^m.
.C.xxvij.^m

Prothe and Iacincte were yonge men of noble kinrede, and were
felowes in the studie of philosophie with Eugeni that was doughter of
Philip of the right noble kinrede of Romaynes. And this Phelip had
take of the senatours of Rome the prouoste of Alisaundre, and thedir
5 he went and ledde with hym his wif that hight Claudien and his .ij.
sones Auit and Sergius and Eugenie his doughter. And that Eugenie

EDH2A2   1 Gorgonien] Gorgone E   Nichomede] Nichodeme D   9 al] om. D
12 he made] twice D

EH1DH2A2; A1 resumes at 62 cussed   2 doughter] on erasure H1, doctoure D
6 Auit] Amit D

was perfit in all the artes liberall, and Prothus and Iacincte hadde
studied with her and were come to the perfeccion of her sciences.

And Eugenie in the .xv. yere of her age was required of mariage
for the sone of the consult that hight Aquile. And she ansuered that 10
it apertein[ed] to her for to chese an husbond ful of good maneres
and not only of highnesse of kinrede. And thanne there come to her
honde the doctrine of Seint Paule, and with that she beganne in her
hert to be cristen by all good condicions. And in that tyme the
cristen were suffered to duelle bisides the citee of Alisaundre, and as 15
Eugenie went in disportinge her by the citee she herde the cristen
men singe a vers of the Sawter whiche saithe that 'Alle the goddes of
misbeleued men be fendes, oure Lorde God only made heuene.'
Thanne saide she to Prothe and to Iacincte that hadde studied with
her: 'We haue ouerpassed the sillogismes of philosofers, the argu- 20
mentes of Aristotle and the yddes of Plato and | the techinges of f. 217^{rh}
Socrates, and shortely as moche as the philosofers synggen and as
moche errour as he thenkithe is al forclosid bi this sentence. And
therfor be we bretheren and lete us folw Ihesu Crist.' And þat
councell liked hem wonder wele. 25

And thanne she toke the abite of a man and came to the chirche
where Eleyne was abbot, the whiche ne suffered no woman to come
to hym. And that same Eleyne had in a tyme disputed with heretikes,
and whan he sawe that he might not sustene the strengthe of her
argumentes, he made do light a gret fire for to proue that he that 30
shulde not be brent for to entre into the fire shuld haue verrey true
faithe. And whanne the fire was made, he entred furst withynne and
went oute withoute ani hurtinge, and that other wolde not entre that
was an eretik, and therfor he was chased confused and putte [oute]
from all other. And whanne Eugeni was comen to this holy man and 35
tolde hym that she was a man, he ansuered and saide: 'Thou seist
verrely well that thou art a man for thou werkest vertuously', for the
condicions of her were sheued hym by God. And than she receiued
the abite of hym with Prothus and Iacinct and she was called of alle
Frere Eugenie. 40

And whanne her fader and her moder sawe her chare come voide,

8 the] *om.* H1D   11 aperteined] aperteinithe E   13 doctrine] doctoure H1
15 suffered] *om.* H1   17 the¹] þe *on erasure* H1   20 of] and the D   23 as he] as
on erasure 'me' H1   26 and] *add* of no woman and D   27 no woman] *ins.* H1
30 that²] *om.* D   31 fire] *add* he D   32 whanne] *om.* H1   he] she H1   33 went]
add ayen D   hurtinge] harme D   34 chased] shasid H1   oute] *om.* E   39 with]
ins. H1

thei made seke her doughter thorugh all the londe, but she might not
be founde. And thanne thei went to the devinours and asked hem
wher her doughter was become, and thei tolde hem that she was
45 rauisshed with her goddes and sette up amonge the sterres. And for
that cause her fader made an ymage of his doughter and comaunded
that she shulde be worshipped of alle. And she duelled with her
felawshipp in the drede of God, and whan the prouost of that chirche
deied she was made prouost.

50   And thanne was there in Alisaundre a riche lady and a noble | that
f. 217ᵛᵃ hight Melancie, the whiche Seint Eugenie had anointed with an
oynement and heled her of the quarteine in the name of Ihesu Crist,
and she sent her mani yeftes but she resseiued none. And this same
lady went that Frere Eugenie had be a man and visited hym ofte, and
55 behelde the semelihede and the beauute of his bodi so that she was
right feruently take with his loue, and was full of anguisshe for to
bethenke her how she might bringe this frere to her wreched
consent. And thanne she feined herself sike, and sent to seke that
frere for to come and to haue pitee of her. And whanne he was come,
60 she tolde hym how she was sike for hym and how she brent in the
couetise of his loue, and praied hym to fulfell her wreched desire,
and with that she clipped hym and wolde haue cussed hym. But
Eugeni hadde utterly abhominacion of her and saide: 'Thou maist
well be called Melancie, whiche is a name of blaknesse fulfelled with
65 treson. Thou art called blacke and derke doughter of derkeness,
frende of the fende, norissher of cruell pollucion, suster of lecherie,
the wofull doughter of euerlastinge dethe.'

And whanne she sawe her so deceiued she dredde lest he wolde
haue [vt]tred her felonie, and beganne furst to crie, and said that
70 Eugenie wolde haue enforced her. And thanne she went to the
prouost Phelip and compleined her, saienge that 'a yonge fals cristen
man come to me bi cause of medicine and wolde haue enforced me
but yef y hadde be deliuered bi the strengthe of one of my
chaumbreres that was in my chaumbre.' And whanne the prouost
75 herde that, he was gretly meued with anger and sent a grete hepe of
officers as baylies and constables after Eugenie and after other
servauntes of Ihesu Crist, whiche were faste bounden in irnes and

44 hem] him *changed to* hem H₁   47 be worshipped] *ins.* H₁   55 his] *twice* E
58 herself] her D   60 she²] 's'he E   62 and wolde ... hym] *om.* D   65 derke]
add and D   67 dethe] *ins.* H₁   69 haue] *ins.* H₁ vttred] entred E   73 hadde]
add not E   the] *om.* H₁D   76 after²] *add* that EH₁

brought before hym. And whanne they were comyn to the provost, the provost | saide to Eugenie: 'Telle me, thou cursed wreche, yef f. 217vb youre Ihesu Crist teche you to corrupte women and for to wodely 80 enforce women.' And thanne saide Eugenie with hede enclined for she wolde not be knowe: 'Oure Lorde techithe us chastite and puerte and behotithe to hem that kepe it euerlastinge lyf. And we mow wel shewe that this Melancie is fals and lyethe, but it ys beter that we suffre tha[nne] she be ouercome and ponissed, and that the fruit of 85 oure pacience perisshe not. But for alle that, lete bringe forthe the chaumbrere that she saithe shulde bere witnesse of oure wrechid-nesse, so that the lesyngges of hem may be reproued.'

And whanne she was come, she that was taught of her ladi bare hym an honde strongely that he wolde haue enforced her, and also 90 alle that other of that mcyni corruptc bi the ladi bare witnesse that it was so. Thanne saide Eugenie: 'The tymc of silcnce is passed and now it ys tyme to speke. Y will no lenger suffre this shameles creatoure to putte suche blame in the seruaunt of Ihesu Crist, ne that she glorifie her in her falsnesse. And for that trouthe surmount her 95 lesing and that wisdom ouercome her malice, y shalle shewe the trouthe, not in the way of avauntinge but for to shewe the worship of God.' And thanne she toke her cote and rent it bynethe her breste and saide: 'Now may ye se that y am a woman as it apperithe be my brestes.' And thanne she saide to the prouost: 'Thou art my fader 100 and Claudien is my moder, and these .ij. that [be] with the be my bretheren, and y am Eugenie thi doughter, and these .ij. here with me be Prothe and Iacincte.'

And whanne the prouost herde it he knewe his doughter. And thanne he and the moder ranne to her and clipped her and kissed her 105 and wepten for ioye. And thanne was Eugenie clothed richely in clothes of golde and was lefte up gretly, and than | sodenly there f. 218ra come a fire fro heuene and brent Mela[n]cy and alle heres. And thanne Eugeni conuerted to the faithe of God fader and moder and

78 to the prouost] *om.* H1D   80 youre] *add* lorde H1D   80–81 and for . . . women] *om.* H1   81 women] hem D   81–2 for she wolde not] *twice* D   82 puerte] pouerte H1D   84 that'] bi D   85 thanne] that E   86 that] *add* þat he *del.* H1   lete] *add* 'lete hir' H1   lete] *add* her EH1   87 saithe] seid H1D   of] to H1D   90 an] on H1   91 of that] *om.* D   95 surmount] surmounted H1   97 the way of] *om.* D   way] *ins.* H1   avauntinge] a vauntinge H1   99 and saide] *om.* H1   100 she] Eugeni D   101 be'] sittin E, *so ins.* H1   102 here] *add* that bene D   105 clipped her and] *om.* D   107 than] *ins.* H1   there] *om.* H1   108 Melancy] Melacy E, Melancien D   109 Eugeni] Eugeny *on erasure* H1   conuerted] coueyted *with* y *on erasure* H1

110 bretheren and alle the meyne, and thanne her fader lefte provostie
and was made bisshop of the cristen, and as he was in his praiers he
was slayne of the paynemes.

And thanne Claudyan with her sones and Eugenie went to Rome
and there thei conuerted moche peple to Ihesu Crist. And thanne
115 Eugenie had bi the comaundement of the emperour a gret stone
bounde aboute her necke and was caste into Tybre, and the stone
brake from her and she went upon the water hole and sounde. And
thanne was she caste into a furneys brenninge, but the furneis wax al
colde. And thanne was she putte in a derke prison, but right clere
120 light apered to her, and whanne she hadde be .x. dayes withoute
mete, oure Lord Ihesu Crist appered to her and brought her right a
faire white loef and saide to her: 'Take this mete of myn honde that
am thi saueoure that thou hast loued with al thi herte. And in that
same day that y descende[d] doune to the erthe y shal resseiue the.'
125 And thanne in the Day of the Natiuite of oure Lord the turmentours
were sent to her to smite of her hede. And after that she apered to
her moder and saide to her that she shuld folowe her the secound day
after. And whan that Sonday come, Claudyan sittinge in her praiers
yelded up the sperit to oure Lorde. And Prothe and Iacinct were
130 drawen to the temple to do sacrifice, and they al tobrake the ydole by
her orison, and whanne they wolde not do sacrifice thei fulfelled her
martirdom in havinge her hedes smiten of. And thei suffered dethe
vnder Valerian and Gallie about the yere of oure Lorde .CC.l vij.

Here endithe the liues of Prothe and Iacinct, and nexst
beginnith the Exaltacion of the Holy Crosse, Capitulum
.C.xxviij.ᵐ

f. 218ʳᵇ   The Exaltacion of the Holy | Crosse is saide for that cause for in
that day the holy crosse and the faithe was gretly enhaunsed. And it
is to knowe that bifore the passion of Ihesu Crist the tree of the
crosse was a tre of gret filthe, for the crosse was made of vile trees
5 that bare no fruit, for as moche as [it] was planted in the Mount of

110 lefte] add þe H1   113 Eugenie] add her doughter D   116 bounde] add al E
117 upon] up on E   118 into] in H1   furneys] add al D   119 a] om. H1
120 her] add anoone D   121 right] om. D   124 descended] descende E
127 shuld] wold subp. `shulde' H1   130 to the temple] om. D   ydole] ydollis D   by]
with H1D

EH1DH2A1A2L   1 Holy] om. D   4 crosse²] add þat time D   5 it] om. EH1

Caluary ne bare no fruit. It was vile for it was the turment of theues; hit was derke for it was a tree of dethe, for men were sette there[o]n to deye; hit was a tre of [stenche] for it was planted amonge the careynes.

And after the passion the crosse was gretly enhaunsed, for his filthe was turned into preciouste, wherof Seint Andrew saithe: 'Holy crosse, God the saue.' His bareinesse was sette into fruit, so as it is saide in the Canticles: 'I shal stie up on the palmer.' His vnworship was turned into hinesse, wherof Seint Austin saithe: 'The crosse that was turment of theues is now bore bi[fore] emperoures.' His derkenesse is conuerted into light, wherof Crisostom saithe: 'The crosse and the woundes shul be more shininge atte the day of iugement thanne the bemes of the sonne.' His dethe is conuerted into perdurablete of lyf, wherof it is songe that 'Where [that] dethe was brought forthe, lif shal arise.' And his stink is turned into suetnesse, wherof the Canticle saithe: 'Whanne the kinge was in hys couche, narde gaue his suete sauour.' That is to saie that the crosse of Crist yeuithe suete sauour in erthe.

This Exaltacion of the Holy Crosse is halowed solemply of the Chirche, for the faithe hathe gretly be enhaunced therby. For it felle that in the yere of oure Lorde .vjC.xv. oure Lorde suffered his peple to be cruelly turmented with paynimes, and Cosdre kinge of Perse putte under his power all the kingdomes of the worlde. And whanne he come into Ierusalem he was adradde of the sepulcre of oure Lorde and returned [hym] ayen; but not for that he bare with hym a partie of the holy crosse that Eleine hadd lefte there. And thanne | he coueited to be worshipped of alle as God. And thanne he made hym a toure of golde and of siluer and of precious stones whiche shined bright, and made the ymage of the sonne and of the mone and of the sterres, and thei casted bi sotel condites that were hydde water like in manere of rayne; and in the laste stage horses ledden horses rounde aboute, as thow thei hadd meued the tour. And he deliuered his kingdom to his sone so that the cursed wreche might duelle in his

f. 218va

6 It] this D   theues] *add* Also D   7 a] þe HɪD   were] was *changed to* were Hɪ thereon] therein E   8 deye] *add and del.* It was a tre of dethe for men was set þeron to die Hɪ   was¹] *add* also D   stenche] L, strengthe EHɪD   11 into] *add* a HɪD 12 the saue] *trs.* Hɪ   into] in Hɪ   14 was] is D   15 of] *add* þe Hɪ   bifore] bi E 18 iugement] dome HɪD   19 wherof] where Hɪ   Where that] whereas E 22 couche narde] chaucheuarde D   his suete sauour] *twice* D   24 Holy] *om.* D 27 Cosdre] Cassedre D   Perse] Pruce L   29 into] to Hɪ   30 hym¹] home E 31 Eleine] Heleyne *with* H *erased* Hɪ   35-6 like ... of] in maner like D   in ... of] and manere of a Hɪ

temple, and he made the crosse of oure Lorde to be sette besides
40 hym, and comaunded that alle shulde calle hym God. And, as it is
redde in the office of [. . . . .], this Cosdree duellinge in his throne
sette on his right side the tree of the crosse and in his lefte side he
sette a [cokke] in stede of the holy goste, and comaunded that
hymself were called 'Fader'.

45 And thanne the emperour Eracle assembled a gret oste and come
for to fight with the sone of Cosdras bisides the flode of Danib. And
thanne it liked to bothe princes that thei shulde fight alonly togederes
upon the brigge, and he that had the beter shulde haue the empire
withoute harminge of either oste. And thus it was ordeined and
50 suorn that hosoeuer halpe his prince shulde be dismembred and caste
in the flode.

And thanne Eracle gaue hym alle to oure Lorde and to the holi
crosse with all the deuocion that he couthe. And thanne thei faught
longe togedre til that oure Lorde gaue to Eracle the victorie and
55 putte under his empire the oste of his aduersarie, in suche manere
that alle the peple of Cosdro shulde submitte hem to the faithe of
cristen and resseiue bapteme. And Cosdre wost nothing of this
bataile, for he satte in his toure and was worshipped of alle as a god
and none durst telle hym these tydingges.

60 And thanne Eracle came euene to hym ande fonde hym sittynge in
f. 218ᵛᵇ his sege of golde | and thanne he saide hym in this wise: 'For as
moche as thou hast worshipped the tree of the crosse, yef thou wilt
resseiue bapteme and the faithe of Ihesu Crist y shalle yeld the thi
rewme and thou shalt holde it a while, and yef thou wilt not y shall
65 sle the with my suerde and smite of thi hede.' And whanne he wolde
not acorde, he beheded hym anone and comaunded that he shulde be
beried bicause he was a kinge. And there he fonde a yonge sone of his
of the age of .x. yere olde, the whiche he made to be baptised and
lefte hym up atte the funte and lefte hym the rewme of his fader.
70 And thanne he made the toure to be broke and gaue the siluer to hem
of his oste, and the golde and the stones he yaf to make ayen the

41 Libro . . . officio] space EH1D   42 his¹] þe D   side¹] add of D   his²] the D
43 cokke] gallum E, koc ins. in space H1   43–4 that hymself] trs. and add he D
44 were] shuld be H1   47 bothe] add þe H1   52 oure Lorde] þe worlde D
55 under] om. D   empire] add and D   57 And] add the Fadir of D   of this] om. D
58 alle] L, add his EH1D   60 ande . . . sittynge] where he sate D   61 sege]
seete D   63 and] of H1   64 rewme] add ayenne D   66 beheded hym] smote
of his heede D   68 of the] om. D   olde] om. D   69 up] om. D   lefte²] bitoke D
71 ayen] om. D

chirche[s] that the tyraunt hadde destroied, and toke the crosse and bare it with hym into Ierusalem.

And as he decended from the Mount of Oliuete and wolde haue entred bi the gate bi the whiche oure Lorde went to his passion on 75 horsbacke araied like a kinge, sodenly the stones of that yate descended and ioined hem togedre as a walle. And alle that sawe this weren gretly abaisshed, and thanne the aungell of oure Lorde apered aboue the gate, holdinge in his honde the signe of the holy crosse and saide: 'Whanne the kinge of heuene went to his passion 80 thurgh this yate, he went with no riall apparaill ne on horsbak, but came upon an asse mekely in shewinge ensaumple of humilite, the whiche he lefte to hem that wolde worship hym.' And that saide, he vanisshed awey.

And thanne the emperoure anonc dede hymself of his hosin and 85 his shone in sore wepinge, and dede of alle his clothes into his sherte, and toke the crosse of oure Lorde and bare it full humbely unto the gate. And anone the harde stones felt the comaundement of God and withdrowe hem ayen and opened the entre of hem that come yn. And thanne the right suete sauour that was felt whanne that holy crosse 90 was take | from the toure of Cosdre was flowed abrode in alle f. 219ra Ierusalem and fulfelled alle the cuntrees with the suetnesse of his sauour. And thanne the right deuout emperour beganne to crie and saie this praisinge of the crosse: 'O holy crosse, more bright shyning thanne alle the sterres, worship of the worlde, right holy and amiable 95 to all men, the whiche only were worthi for to bere the raunson of the worlde, suete tree, suete nailes, suete yrne, suete spere, that bare God, make thou sauf this present felashippe that be this day here to do presing of the.'

And thus was the precious crosse restabled to his place ayen. And 100 the aunciene miracles were renoueled, for .iiij. men that had the palsei were heled, and .x. lepres cured and made clene, .xv. blinde had her sight, the fendes weren chased oute, and mani other were deliuered of diuerse syknesses. And thanne the emperoure made to reparaile the chirche[s] and gaue hem gret geftes, and sethe he 105 returned to [his] propre places.

72 chirches] chirche EH1   75 to] touard H1   79 holy] om. D   82 the] om.
H1   83 that²] whan it was D   85 anone] om. D   his] þe H1, om. D   86 his¹]
om. H1D   89 hem²] add ayene H1   98 here] to hire D   101 renoueled]
reuolued D   104 diuerse] othir D   105 reparaile] repaire D   chirches] chirche
EH1   106 his] her EH1, add owne D   places] place D

And it is saide in a cronicle that it was done otherwise. For he
saithe that whanne Cosdre had take mani rewmes, he toke Ierusalem
and Zakarie the patriarke and toke with hym the tree of the crosse,
110 and as Eracle desired pees of hym Cosdre swore that he wolde haue
no pees with the Romaynes but thei wolde renie hym that was
crusified and worship the sonne. And thanne Eracle, armed in faith,
brought his strengthe ayenst hym and destroied hem of Perse by mani
batailes and constreined Cosdre to flee to Celiforne. And atte the laste
115 Cosdre had the flux and wolde crowne his sone kinge. And Siriace his
eldest sone herde that; he made aliaunce with Eracle for to pursue his
fader with alle the nobles of the londe and toke hym and putte hym in
stronge bondes of yren. And there he susteined hym with brede of
tribulacion and in water of anguisshe, and atte the laste he made hym |
f. 219ʳᵇ to be shotte thorugh with arwes and so slow hym. And after [that], he
121 sent to Eracle the patriarke with the crosse and with alle the prisoners
that there were, and Eracle bare into Ierusalem the precious tree of
the crosse. And thus it is wretin in mani cronicles.

Sibille saithe of that tree of the crosse that that blessed tree on
125 whiche oure Lorde hangged on was .iij. tymes amonge the paynime.

In Constantinenople a Iwe entred into the chirche of Seint Sophie
and considered that he was there allone, and sawe an ymage of Ihesu
Crist and toke a swerde and smote the ymage of Ihesu Crist in the
necke, and anone blode ranne oute a gret quantite and al bewette the
130 hede of the Iewe and the visage. And he was sore aferde and toke the
ymage and throw it in a pitte and fledde thennes anone. And thanne
he mette with a cristen man that saide to hym: 'Whennes comist
thou, thou Iewe, thou hast slaine sum man.' And he saide: 'That is
vntrue.' Thanne saide the cristen man: 'Truly thou hast do sum
135 cursed dede, for thou art alle blodi therof.' And thanne saide the
Iewe: 'Verrily is the God of cristen men grete and the faithe of hem
is aproued stable in al wises. I haue smete no man, but y haue smete
the ymage of Ihesu Crist and thus moche is the blode go oute of his
throte.' And thanne the Iewe ledde the cristen man to the pitte and
140 drow oute the holy ymage. And yet atte this day the wounde is saie
in the throte of the ymage, and the Iewe was anone made cristen.

110 that] `þat´ H₁   111 hym] hem *changed to* hym H₁   112 thanne] *om.* H₁
116 herde] sawe D   120 slow hym] *add* And after þat *del.* H₁   that] *om.*
122 and] *om.* H₁   124 the] þat *changed to* þe H₁   that³] *om.* H₁   131 ymage]
add of *subp.* H₁   133 saide] *add* ayenne D   That] *add* it H₁   136 Verrily is]
om. D   men] *add* is D   and] & / and E   of hem] *om.* D   137 wises] *add* for D
140 wounde] woundes E

In Surre in the citee of Beruth there was a cristen man that had an hous whiche he hired eueri yere, and he had sette atte hys beddes hede an ymage of the crucifixe and therto he made his praiers continuelly. And thanne that yere passed, he hered another hous 145 and forgate there his ymage, and thanne a Iwe hered that hous and bade to dinere on a day one of his cosynes. And as thei satte atte the mete | he that was bodin by happe he behelde þat ymage that was f. 219ᵛᵃ fastenid in the walle, and he beganne to groche ayenst hym that had bode hym to diner and to manace hym, askinge hym ho made [hym] 150 so hardy to haue in his hous the ymage of Ihesu of Nazareth. And that other suore as moch as he might that he neuer sawe hym before that tyme ne wost of hym. And than he feined as thou he hadde leued hym and went to the prince of Iewes and accused hym of that he had seine. And thanne the Iewes assembled togederes and come to the hous of 155 hym [and sawe the image and rebuked hym] and dede hym al the sorugh that thei coude and caste hym half dede oute of her sinagoge, and thanne thei defouled the ymage with her fete and renued in hym alle the turnement of the passion of oure Lorde. And whanne they persid his side with a spere, blode and water come oute haboundantly 160 that it felled a vessell full that thei sete under. And [thanne] the Iewes were abaisshed and bare that blode into her sinagoge, and alle seke men that were anointed therwith were hole. And thanne the Iewes tolde all bi ordre to the bisshopp of the lande and receiueden alle with one will bapteme and the faithe of Ihesu Crist. 165

And the bisshopp put that blood in violes of cristall and of glas for to kepe it, and thanne he lete calle the cristen man and asked hym who [had] made hym that faire ymage. And he saide that Nichodeme had made it, 'and whanne he deied he lefte it to Gamaliel, and Gamaliel to Zachie, and Zachie to Iames, and Iames to Symon, and 170 so it hadde be kepte in Ierusalem into the distruccion of the citee, and fro thennes it was born into the rewme of Agrip of cristen men, and fro thennis it was brought into my cuntre and so it was lefte me bi kinrede as bi right of heritage.' And this was done the yere | of f. 219ᵛᵇ oure Lorde .vijC.l. And thanne alle the Iewes sacred her sinagoges 175 into the chirches, and fro thennes come the gise that the chirches

---

148 ymage] add and EH1   149 he] om. H1   150 askinge] as king changed to asking H1   hym⁴] om. E   151 Ihesu] add Crist H1   153 hym¹] add noo thinge D   156 and sawe . . . rebuked hym] om. E   161 thanne] om. EH1   166 violes] vessellis D   168 who . . . hym] 'of' H1   had] L, om. ED   169 had] om. D   170 Gamaliel] add lefft it D   Zachie²] add lefft it D   Iames²] add lefft it D   Symon] Symeon D   171 hadde] hath H1D   172–3 born . . . was¹] om. H1   176 the¹] om. H1D   gise] gises D

were sacred, for before that tyme the auutres were sacred only. And
for that miracle the Chirche ordeined only that in the kalendes of
Decembre men shulde make minde of the passion of oure Lord or
180 elles, as it is redde elleswhere, in the ide of Nouembre. And thanne
was sacred the chirche of Rome in the worship of the saueoure, wher
the viole is kept with that holy blood and men make thanne a
solempne feste. And there is proued the grete uertu of the crosse,
and namely to the misbeleuers in alle thinge.

185   Seint Gregorie tellithe in the .iij. boke of his Dialoges that as the
bisshop of Fondon whiche hight Andrew suffered a religious woman
to drawe meche to hym, the auncien enemy biganne to emprinte in
the herte of hym the beauute of her, so that he thought in his bedde
in cursed thingges. And so it happed that as a Iewe was cominge to
190 Rome warde, and the day failed hym and he might finde none
herburgh, he caste hym to duelle all that night in a temple of Apolyn.
And for he dredde the sacrilege of that place, thou it were so that he
had no feithe in the crosse, yet he blessed hym withe the tokin of the
crosse. And thanne atte midnight as he awoke he sawe a cumpanie of
195 wicked spirites entre in, amonge whiche there was one that semed of
more powere thanne another, and he was sette on [an] high benche,
and he beganne to enquere the causes and the dedes of eueri of these
spirites that obeied hym for to wete how myche eueriche of hem had
do of euill.

200   But Seint Gregore passithe the manere of this diuision for cause of
shortnesse, but we finde the like ensaumple in the lif of *Vitas Patrum*,
f. 220ra that as a man entred into a temple of ydoles the | fende come and alle
his cursed meyne about hym. And one of the wicked spirites come
and worshipped hym, and he asked [hym]: 'Whennes comest thou?'
205 And he saide: 'Y haue be in such a prouince and y haue meued mani
werres and made moche tribulacion and shed moche blood, and y am
come to telle you this.' And the maister fende saide: 'In how miche
tyme hast thou do this?' And he ansuered: 'In .xxx. dayes.' And
thanne the fende saide: 'Whi hast thou be so longe here aboute?' And
210 thanne he saide to hem that were aboute hym: 'Gothe and betithe
hym right sore.' Thanne come the secound and worshipped hym and

    177 for¹] onli 'for' H1   183 there] *add* it EH1   186 Fondon] London H1
187 enemy] *add* the Feende D   emprinte] prente D   196 an] L, *om.* EH1D   high]
his D   197 eueri] euer'y' H1   200 diuision] vision H1   202 as] *om.* H1   of]
add þe H1   204 hym²] *om.* EH1   208 he] *add* hadde E   209 the] *add* maister D
210 hym] *om.* D

saide: 'Lorde, y haue be in the see and y haue meued gret tempestes and turmentes and drowned mani shippes and slayne mani men.' And thanne said Sathanas: 'In how moche tyme haste thou do this?' And he sayde: 'In .xx. dayes.' And he comaunded that he shulde be 215 bete also and saide: 'Hast thou do so litell good in so longe tyme?' And thanne come the thridd and saide: 'Y haue be in a citee and y haue meued debate in mariage, and there y [haue] made moche blood to be shedde and y haue slaine the husbonde,' and Sathanas saide: 'In how longe tyme dedist thou this?' And he saide: 'In .xx. daies.' 'Hast 220 thou do no more,' quod Sathanas, 'in so longe tyme?' And comaunded that he were bete. And another come and saide: 'Y haue duelled in desert this .x. yere and laboured about a monke and unnethe y made hym falle into the synne of his flesshe.' And whanne Sathanas herde that he aros from his sege and cussed hym and toke 225 the crowne of his hede and sette it upon his hede and made hym sitte with hym and saide to hym: 'Thou hast done a gret thinge and hast more laboured thanne all that other meyne.' And this may be the manere of this vision, or like to this, whiche Seint Gregori levithe.

And whanne euery hadd saide what he wolde, one come in the 230 middes of hem alle and saide: | 'I haue meued the corage of the f. 220ʳᵇ bisshopp Andrew towarde a nonne sethe yesterday Euesonge tyme, and he is fulli consented that [the] synne shall be do.' And [thanne] the maister comaunded that he shulde go forthe and performe that he hadde begonne so that by that synne he might haue [singuler] 235 victorie amonge his felawes.

And than Sathanas behelde about [hym] and asked ho that was that laye there in the corner and bade that anone he shulde be brought to hym, and as he laye in grete sorugh and drede, the spirites that were sent for hym founde hym marke[d] with the [signe 240 of the] crosse, and thei cried with houge voys: 'Alas, alas, hit is a voide vessell but he [is strongly] signed and marked.' And with that alle that cursed cumpanie fled aweye. And thanne the Iewe come al

212 meued] *add* there D   214 moche] longe D   216 saide] *add* whi D
218 meued] *add* a grete D   haue²] *om.* EH1   220 .xx.] *changed to* .x. H1   daies] L, *add*
and he saide EH1, *add* And Sathanas seide to hym D   221 quod Sathanas] *om.* D
222 bete] *add* also D   223 .x.] .xl. H1D   a] þe H1   224 y] *add* haue H1   hym] *add*
to H1D   his] *om.* H1   225 sege] seete D   228 may] *add* welle D   232 towarde]
ins. H1   233 that the] to that E   thanne] *om.* EH1   234 maister] *add* feende D
235 singuler] a signe ther of EH1, a signe of D (*singuliere* P2)   237 hym] *om.* E   ho
that] hym what he D   238 the] a H1D   239 to] bifore D   he] þis Iewe D
240 marked] market E   240–1 signe of the] *om.* EH1   242 but he] þat D   is
strongly] *trs.* E   that] þe H1D

ameuid and astonied for drede and fere to the bisshoppe Andrew and
245 tolde hym al this tale by ordre. And whanne the bisshopp herde it he
wepte bitterly and made to voide alle [the] women out of his hous,
and thanne he baptised the Iewe.

Gregori tellithe also in his Dyaloges that a nonne entred into a
gardin and sawe letuse growinge and coueited for to ete therof and
250 foryate to make the signe of the crosse therouer and bote therof
sodenly, [and anone she felle doun sodenly] and was rauisshed with
the fende. And than ther come to her Seint Equicien, and whan the
fende perceiued hym he beganne to crie and saie: 'What haue y do to
the? Y haue sette upon the letuse and she come and bote me.' And
255 anone the fende went out of her by the comaundement of Goddes
seruaunt.

Here endithe the Exaltacion of the Holy Cros, and nexst
beginnit[he] the lif of Seint Iohn Crisostome, Cap^m.
.C.xxix.^m

Seint Iohn Crisostome was of Antioche and born of noble kinrede
and was the secounde sone of his fader, of whom the lyf, of the
f. 220va kinrede, the | conuersacion and the persecucion is more pleinly
conteined in the Stori Parted in Thre.
5   Whan he hadd be in [the] studie of philosophie he left it and gaue
hym to devine lessones and was ordeined to be preste, and for the loue
of chastite he was [holde olde]. And he entended more to the brenninge
of loue thanne to outwardes debonairte, and for the rightwisnesse of
his lyf he entend[ed] to thingges to come. He was demed proude of
10 hem that knewin hym not. He was noble in techinge, and wys in
expowninge, and right good in refreninge the [v]eyn maters.

Thanne reyn[ed] Archadyane and Honoreyne in the empire [and]
Damasco satte in the sege of Rome, and in this tyme was he made
bisshopp of Constantinople. He beganne anone hastely to correcte
15 the clerkes and stere[d] hem alle in hate ayenst hym, and alle they

246 the] om. EH1   249–50 and³ . . . therof] om. D   251 and anone . . . sodenly]
om. EH1   253 saie] sey`de´ H1   do] to changed to do H1   254 sette] ins. H1   the²]
`þe´ H1

EH1DH2A1A2L   Rubric beginnithe] beginnit E   5 the] om. E   7 holde olde]
olde holde E, holde bolde H1   8 of loue] loue of God D   9 entended] entendynge
EH1, ententid D   11 refreninge] receyuyng changed to ref'r´eynyng H1   veyn] deyn E
12 Thanne] þat time D   reyned] L, reyninge EH1; H1 punct. after reyninge   and²] of
EH1D (et P2)   13 he] Iohn Crisostome D   15 stered] stere E, stere`d´ H1

escheued hym as thei wolde haue do a mad man and an euell speker of
alle men. And for that he wolde bidde none to diner [n]e wolde not be
bode of none, thei saide that he did it for he ete his mete foule. And
sum saide [that] hit was for the excellence and the nobles of his metes,
and in trouthe it was for the febilnesse of his stomake whiche greued 20
hym contynuelly sore, wherfor he eschewed the gret dyners.

But the peple l[o]ued hym gretly for the sermones that he made,
and yaue litell of all that the enemyes saide. And thanne Iohn
beganne to reproue sum of the barones, and for that cause the enuye
was moche the gretter ayenst hym. And he dede other thingges þat 25
meued hem gretly alle. Eu[t]rope, prouost of the emperour, that
hadd the dignite of a counceillour, wolde be venged of some that fled
within the chirche, and studied that a lawe were ordeined bi the
emperour þat none shulde flee to the chirche and tho that were
fledde were drawe oute. And a litell while [after] Eutrope offended 30
the emperour and thanne he fledde to the chir|che, and whanne the f. 220ᵛᵇ
bisshopp herde that, he come anone to hym that was hidde vnder the
auuter and made an omelye ayenst hym, the whiche reproued hym
right sharpely. Wherfor mani were wrothe, for he wolde do no mercy
to that wycked man and yet he dede none other harme to hym but 35
chidde hym. And thanne the emperour rauisshed Eutrope from
thennes and smote of his hede. And he reproued right trustely mani
men for diuerse causes, and therfor he was hatefull to mani.

And Theophile bisshopp of Alisaundre wolde haue deposed Seint
Iohn and wolde haue sette in his place Isodre prest, wherfor he 40
sought diligently causes to depose hym, but the peple that was
meruailous[ly] fedde with his doctrine defended hym gretly. And
Seint Iohn constreined the prestes to liue after the holy ordenaunces,
and saide that thei shulde not vse the worship of presthode th[at]
despised the lyf of a preste and wolde not folue it. And Seint Iohn 45
gouerned not only the bisshopriche of Constantinople nobly, but also
he ordeined in other prouinces by auctorite of the emperour noble
lawes and profitable. And thanne whanne he woste that men did
sacrifice yet thereabout in other prouinces to the fendes, he sent

16 as] and *changed to* as H₁   a] *om.* D   17 ne] he ED, and H₁ (*ne* P2)   18 foule]
fouell H₁   19 that] for EH₁   22 loued] leued E   24 that] *ins.* H₁
25 gretter] more D   26 alle] ale *changed to* als (?) H₁   Eutrope] Europe EH₁D (*Eutrope*
P2)   28 within] to D   30 after] *om.* EH₁   Eutrope] Europe H₁D   36 Eutrope]
Europe H₁D   40 Iohn] *add* Crisostome D   42 meruailously] meruailous E
43 Seint Iohn] Iohn Crisostome D   Iohn] *ins.* H₁   44 presthode] *add* for D   that²] L,
thei EH₁, for thei D   46 nobly] *om.* H₁D   49 yet thereabout] about about D

50 theder monkes and clerkes and dede destroie alle the temples of
ydoles.

In that same tyme there was a man there that was made maister of
the knightes and hight Gannas and was of the kinrede of Cel[ique]
barbaryn, the whiche was strongly lefte up by study of tyrannie and
55 corrupte with the eresy of Arien. And than Gannas praied the
emperoure that he wolde graunte hym a chirche within the towne
that he and his might make her praiers therin. And whanne he had
behight hym, he praied Seint Iohn that he wolde fulfelle hys graunt
f. 221ʳᵃ that he by hys cruelte might be refreined. But Seint | Iohn that was
60 right stronge in vertu and al sette afire with the loue of God saide to
the emperoure: 'Syr emperoure, behotithe no suche thingges, ne
yeuithe not holy thingges to houndes, ne drede ye not this barbaryn,
but comaundithe that we be called before you and herithe pesibly
that shall be saide betwene vs. For y shal refraine so his tunge that he
65 shal not be hardy to aske no suche thinge more.'

And whanne the emperour herde that, he was right gladde, and
the nexst day after thei were called bothe of hem. And as Gannas
required auctorite for hym Seint Iohn sa[ide]: 'The devine hous [is]
open to the in eueri place where no man wernithe the to praie.' And
70 Gannas saide: 'Y am of another secte and require to haue a temple
for me, for y haue undertake mani a gret trauaile for the comune
profit of Rome, and therfor me thinkithe that y shulde not be werned
of my peticion.' And Seint Iohn ansuered: 'Thou hast resseiued
many guerdones that amountin more thanne thi paine and labour,
75 and thou hast be made maister of knightes and clothed with the
ornament of counsaile, and therfor thou must concidre what thou
were a whiles gone and what thou art now, and what clothing thou
vsedest before tyme and what thou vsest now. And therfor thilke
fewe laboures haue yeue the so grete guerdones, be not vnagreable to
80 hym that hathe so gretly worshipped the.' And by suche wordes he
stopped his mouthe and constreined hym to holde his pees.

And as this Seint Iohn gouerned nobly the citee of Constantyne-

---

52 same] *om.* D there²] *om.* D 53 the¹] *om.* H₁ Celique] L, Celagne EH₁D
(*celsique* P2) 55 the¹] *om.* H₁ 59 by] by *changed to* of H₁ 62 this barbaryn]
these barbariens D 64 saide] s`e´yde H₁ 67 of hem] bifore hym D 68 hym]
hem D saide] sawe E, seyde *on erasure* H₁ is] *om.* E, *ins.* H₁ 69–70 And Gannas saide]
ins. H₁ 71 undertake] vn`der´take H₁ 73 ansuered] *add* and seide D
74 many] *add* grete D 78 vsedest . . . thou] *om.* H₁ 79 guerdones] *add* wherefor D
80 gretly] grete`li´ H₁ 82 this] *om.* D Iohn] *add* Crisostome D gouerned] *add* welle
and D nobly] nombli H₁

nople, that Gannas coueited the empire, and for he might do
[no]thinge by day, he sent by night his barbereyns for to brenne
the paleis. And thanne was it well shewed how Seint Iohn kepte well 85
the citee. For a gret cumpany of | aungeles that had gret bodyes and f. 221rb
were armed apered to the barbarins and chased hem away anone.
And whanne they tolde this to her lorde he was gretly meruailed, for
he wist wel that the oste of knightes was disperplid thorugh the citee.
And thanne he sent hem thedir ayen the secounde tyme, and thei 90
were chased ayen by the vision of aungeles. And atte the laste he
went hymself oute with hem, and sawe the miracle and fledde anone,
and went that there hadde be knightes that were within by day and
wached anight. And than he went into Tr[a]ce with gret strengthe
and wasted al that cuntre so that the peple dradde the cruelte of the 95
barbarins. And thanne the emperoure betoke to Seint Iohn the
charge of his legacion, and he not remembringe of the enemyte
bytwene [hem] went ioyfully. And thanne Gannas that knewe the
trouthe of hym come ayenst hym in the waye, for he knewe that he
came for pitee and compassion, and toke th[is] holy manys honde 100
and cussed it with his eyen and with his mouthe, and comaunded to
his sones to kysse hys knees for he was holy. And of this vertu was
Seint Iohn that he constreined the most cruel to drede hym.

And whan these thingges were done and Seint Iohn floured in
Constantinenople by doctrine and was holde meruailous of alle, the 105
secte of Arienis encresed gretly. And thei hadde a chirche withoute
the citee, and in the Saterday and in the Sonday thei wolde singe
within the gates bi night ympnes and antemes thurgh the citee and
go oute by the yates and entre into her chirche, and secedin not to do
this for the dispite of the good cristen peple, ande thei songe ofte this 110
songe: 'Where be tho that saie one to be thre by his vertu?' And |
thanne Seint Iohn dredde that bi such songe the simple peple might f. 221va
be deceiued, and ordeined that the good cristen men shulde go be
night with torches and lanternes synginge glorious ympnes of the
Chirche, and he ordeined crosses to be bore before hem in 115

83 that] om. D   might] add not EH1   84 nothinge] thinge E, `no'þing H1
86 For] of H1   86–7 and . . . armed] there D   88 her] the D   89 disperplid]
disparklid D   91 chased] add aweie D   93 that¹] `þat' H1   94 anight] in the
nyghte D   he] Gannas D   Trace] Truce EH1   96 betoke] toke D   98 hem]
om. EH1   knewe] add welle D   99 knewe] add welle D   100 this] the E
102 this] suche D   102–3 was Seint Iohn] om. D   104 thingges] tidingis D
106 Arienis] add and D   107 Saterday] Satersday H1   110 ofte this] offten
tymes D

confirmacion of the faithe. And than the secte of Ariens sette afire with enuie rebelled anone to the vtterest, so that in a night Brison the chamberleyn of the emperoure was smite with a stone, which was ordeined by Seint Iohn for to go with hem that songen ympnes, and
120 moche of the peple were slayne on bothe parties.

And thus that holy Seint Iohn suffered mani a gret persecucion for rightwisnesse, the whiche was alway a stedfast stone withoute remouynge in the fundement of the Chirche, and so after mani a gret laboure he ended his blessed lyff beynge in exile the .xiiij. day of
125 Septembre. And whanne he was passed a stronge haile descended in Constantinenople vpon the citee and in alle the subarbes, and alle the peple saide that it was done for the wrathe of God for that Seint Iohn had be condempned with strengthe and withoute reason. And the dethe of the emperesse that was his enemye bare witnesse, for she
130 deyed the .iiij. day after the haile.

And whanne the doctour of men was passed oute of this worlde, the bisshoppes of the occident wolde in no wise comune with them of the orient before that the name of that right holy man were sette amonge the bisshoppes his predecessours. And Theodesien a right
135 cristen man, sone of the said emperoure, that helde the name and the partie of his graundsire, made bringe the holy reliques of that doctour into the ryall citee in the monthe of Ianiuere. And thanne Theodesien worshipped gretly the reliques and went ayenst hem
f. 221ᵛᵇ with al the trewe peple with multitude of torches and of lightes | and
140 besought humbly to that holy corseint that he wolde pardone Archadyane his fader and Eudoxe his moder that they had done bi h[er] ignoraunce.

This emperoure was of so gret debonairte that he wolde neuer iuge man to dethe that hadde offended hym, and he wolde saie that his
145 wille were to calle ayen to lyf tho that weren dede yef he might. Hit semid by his court that it was a devout chirche, for there was continuelly Mateins and Lawdis in due tyme, and redyng of devine scripture. His wif hight Eudochie, and he hadde a doughter that he called Eudoye, the whiche he gaue to Valentyniane that he made
150 sethe emperour. And alle these thinges more pleinly be wrete in the

116 Ariens] *add* were D   sette] *add* so H₁D   119 that] and D   120 bothe] *add* þe H₁   121 holy] *add* man D   Iohn] *add* Crisostome D   gret] *om.* L   122 whiche] *add* stone E   123 a] *om.* H₁   132 comune] comen H₁D   134 his] *om.* D   137 doctour] *add* seint Iohn crisostome D   139 of ²] *add* othir D   141 they] L, *add* might and EH₁, myght haue grace of that thei D   142 her] his EH₁

Stori Parted in Three. And he passed to oure Lorde about the yere
of oure Lorde .CCC.iiij.^{xx}.x.

Here endithe the lyf of Seint ⟨Iohn Crisostome⟩, and nexst
beginnithe the lyf of Seint Cornelien pope, Cap^m .C.xxx.

Seint Cornelyen the pope succeded to Fabian, and he was sent into
exile by Dacyen the emperour, bothe he and his clerkes, and there he
resseiued letteres of comfort from Ciprian bisshopp of Cartage. And
atte the laste he was brought oute of exile and presented to Dasyen
the emperour. And whanne Dacyen sawe hym stedfaste in the faithe, 5
he comaunded that he were bete with plummes of lede and that he
were ledde to the temple of Mars that he shulde do sacrifise there or
elles haue his hede smite of there. And as he was ledde thedir a
knight mette hym and praied hym that he wold turne to his hous and
praie for Saluste his wif that hadde laye .v. yere in the palesey. And 10
anone she was heled by hys orison, and .xxj. knightes with hym
leuedyn in God, and his wiff, and weren alle | ledde to the temple of f. 222ra
Mar[s] by the comaundement of Dasyen, and alle thei spetten ayenst
the ydoles and weren martired withe Cornelyen. And thei suffered
dethe the yere of oure Lorde .CC.liij.   15
     And Ciprian bisshop of Cartage was presented in that same citee
to one Patrin that was of the counsaile. And whan he might not turne
hym from the faithe in no wise, he sent hym into exile, and from
thennes he was called by Galeryen consult that come after Patrin,
and receiued martirdom of hede smityng of. And whanne the 20
sentence was youe he saide: 'Thanking be to God.' And whan he
come to the place of hys marterdom, he comaunded to hys men that
thei shulde yeue to hym that shulde smite of hys hede for hys reward
.xxv. d. of golde, and thanne he toke a clothe of lynnen and couered
his eyen with hys owne hondes, and so he receiued croune of 25
marterdom the yere of oure Lorde .CC.lvj.

151 about . . . yere] `in þe ʒere' H1, so D   152 .CCC.iiij^{xx}.x.] .iiijC.iiij^{xx}.x. H1D
   EH1DH2A1A2   Rubric, 1 and closing rubric Pope del. and bischop ins. E
5 emperour] add bothe he and his clerkes and there he resseiued letteres of comfort from
Cirian bisshop of Cartage EH1D with he . . . Cartage del. H1   stedfaste] stedfastely E
6 plummes] plomettis D   7–8 or elles . . . there] om. H1   13 Mars] da mart E
17 counsaile] add of the Emperoure D   19 Galeryen] Valerien D   20 of ^{1}] add his D
21 Thanking be to] þonked be H1, thankingis be it to D   23 reward] travaile H1
25 receiued] add þe H1

⟨Here⟩ endithe the lyff of Seint Cornelien pope, and nexst
begynnithe the lyff of Seint Eufemie, Capitulum .C.xxxj.

Seint Eufemye was doughter of an vsurere, and whan she sawe
cristen men suffre so gret turmentes in the tyme of Dyoclisian she
come to the iuge, and in knowleching Ihesu Crist she comforted the
corages of cristen men by her gret sadnesse. And as the iuge slow the
5　cristen one after another he made other stonde and beholde the
cruelte of the turmentis that thei shulde thereby be aferde and
sacrifice for drede. And whanne Eufemie sawe the seintes al
tomangeled with turmentes, she was more confermed by the
sadnesse of the martires, and thanne she come to the iuge and
10　saide that he dede her gret wrong. And thanne the iuge, wenyng that
she wolde haue do sacrifice, asked her what wronge he hadde done to
her, and she saide to hym: 'Sethe y am of noble kinrede, whi hast
thou putte before me straunge men and vnknowen to marterdom and
f. 222ʳᵇ　makest hem go before me to Ihesu | Crist?' Thanne the iuge saide
15　here: 'Y went that thou ha[dde]st turned thi thought, and therof y
reioysed me that thou recordest thi noblesse.'

And thanne she was closed in prison, and the day foluyng she was
brought forthe vnbounde. And thanne she compleined her right
greuously that she allone was spared ayenst the lawe of the
20　emperoures to be bounden. And thanne she was bete right sore
with paumes and putte ayen in prison. And the iuge folued her and
wolde haue enforced her, but she defended her mightly and the
devine vertu made the hondes of the iuge contract. And thanne the
iuge went that he hadde be enchaunted and sent to her the provost of
25　hys hous for to behight her many thingges for to make her consent to
hym. But he might neuer opin the prison dore nother with kaye ne
with axse, into the tyme that he was rauisshed of the fende and al
torent hymselff so that vnnethe he askaped.

And thanne she was drawe oute of the prison and sette upon a
30　whele alle full of brenninge coles, and the craftesman that was maister
of the turment had youen a token to hem that shulde turne the whele
that whanne he made a sowne thei shulde turne in alle haste, and

EH1DH2A1A2; D breaks off after 65 *virgine* (*Eufemye*)　　　1 Eufemye] *add* þat H1
3–4 the corages] *om.* H1　　　9 martires] maꞌrꞌters H1　　　11 she] he D　　　12 am] *add*
come E　　　15 haddest] hast E　　　and therof] þerefor H1　　　20 emperoures]
Emperoure D　　　bounden] vnbounde D　　bete] *ins.* H1　　　21 paumes] peynymis H1D
23 devine vertu] *trs.* H1　　　24 enchaunted] enhaunsed H1　　　25 behight] be hote H1
31 the] þat H1　　　32 turne] *add* the whele D　　alle] *om.* D

thanne the barres of yren that weren in the fire shulde al torende the
virgine. But by the will of God the yren that the maister helde in hys
honde fill to the erthe and made a sowne, and they herde the sowne 35
and turned in haste so that the whele brent the maister of the turment
and Eufemye was kept unhurte that satte upon the whele. And
thanne the kinrede of that man wepte and putte fere under the whele
for to haue brent Eufemye with the whele, but the whele was brent
and Eufemye was vnbounde with an aungel and was saie stonde in an 40
high place.

And thanne Apulien saide to the iuge: 'The vertu of the cristen is
ouercome by nothinge but by yrin, and therfor y | counsaile the that f. 222va
thou make her be biheded.' And thanne thei sette up laddres, and as
thei putte forthe her hondes to haue take her thei were smite with the 45
palesie and borun thennes half dede. And another that hight Sustenis
stied up, but he chaunged his wille anone and asked her foryeuenesse
and saide to the iuge pleinly that he hadde leuer sle hymselff [than
her], for he sawe the aungeles of God that defended her.

And atte the last whanne she was take downe, thanne the iuge 50
saide to his chaunceler that he shulde make alle the yonge men that
he might for to go to her and enforce her til she were dede. And
thanne he entered into her and there he sawe right faire uirgines
praieng with her, and she made hem alle cristen bi her teching. And
thanne the iuge made the virgines hange bi the here, but she was 55
stable withoute meuing. And thanne she was shette up in prison .vij.
dayes and in the .vij. day he lete presse her betwene .iiij. gret stones
as thou he wolde haue made oyle of her. And whanne she laye
betwene these harde stones she made her praieres and the stones
were conuerted into right gret softenesses. And she was fedde eueri 60
day with aungeles.

And than the emperour hadde gret shame that he was so ouercome
with a maide and he made her to be caste into a depe pitte, wherin
there were bestes of gret cruelte for to deuoure any creature. And
anone thei ronne to the virgine and as thei coude made gret ioye of 65

33 the¹] that holie D   34 virgine] add Eufemyen D   helde] had D   35 and they
. . . sowne] om. H1   the²] a D   36 turned] add the whele D   in] add alle the D
maister . . . turment] turmentours D   38 thanne] om. H1   39 with the whele] om. D
48 and] add he D   48–9 than her] here E, for her D   50 downe] add And H1
52 might] add gete H1   53 he¹] 'the'y' H1   56 shette] set H1   57 gret] om. D
stones] add that were grete D   59 harde] om. D   60 were] add anone D
softenesses] softenes H1D   63 and] om. H1   64 were] add grete multitude of D
65 virgine] add Eufemye DH2

hcr, and thei ioyned togedre her tailes and ordeined a maner of a chaier for her to sitte on. And whan the iuge sawe that, he was confused that he deied nigh for anguisshe, and the turmentour come for to reuenge the sorugh of hys lorde and smote the uirgine with his
70 suerde and made her the martir of Ihesu Crist. And the iuge for his
f. 222ᵛᵇ mede made clothe hym in clothes of selke and araied | hym with broches of golde, but as he wolde haue come oute of the pitte he was deuoured with bestis that there was nothinge lefte of hym but a fewe of his bones with the clothe of silke and the broches of golde. And
75 Priske the iuge ete hymself and was founde dede. Seint Eufemy was beried in Calcedonye and by her merites alle the Iwes and payneims of Calcidoyne were conuerted to the faithe of Ihesu Crist. And she suffered dethe the yere of oure Lorde .CC.iiij^{xx}.

Seint Ambrose saithe in this wise of this holy virgine: 'Victorious
80 withholdyng the mitre of virginite, [deserued to be clothed] with the crowne of the passion, by the praier of whom the enemy is ouercome, Priske her aduersarie is surmounted, and she went oute hole of the [furneys of the] fire, and the harde stones be conuerted into asshes, the wilde bestes were made priue and obeied hem to her praiers, and
85 atte the laste she, martered by suerde, lefte the cloistre of the flesshe and is ioyned to the heuenly felawship ful of ioye. Now holi virgine, y recomaunde to the thi Chirche, and we beseche the to praie for us synfull. And this holy uirgine florisshing withoute corrupcion graunte us oure desires by her holy merites. Amen.'

Here endithe the liff of Seint Eufemye, and nexst beginnithe the lyf of Seint Lambert, Capitulum .C.xxxij.

Seint Lambert was of noble kinrede but he was more noble bi holinesse, and he was well lettered from hys yonge age, so that for hys holinesse alle men loued hym, and atte the laste [he] was promoted to the bisshopriche of Trete after Theodart his maister, the whiche the

67 on] yn H1   was] *add* alle H2   68 turmentour] tormentours H2   69 hys] þe H1, hir H2   69–70 his suerde] her swerdis H2   70 his] her H2   71 hym¹] hem H2 72 he¹] thei H2   he was] thei were H2   73 hym] hem H2   74 of his] *om.* H2 clothe] clothis H2   80 mitre] merite H2   deserued to be clothed] *om.* E 81 enemy] enemyes H2   82 hole] *add* oute E   83 furneys of the] *om.* E   harde] *om.* H1   85 atte the laste] *add* 'houre' H1   she] *add* was H2   suerde] *add* and H2 86 heuenly] holie H2   87 to the thi] the to the H2   88 florisshing] florisshid H2 withoute] with'ou3t'; ou3t *is also written three times in margin* H1

EH1H2A1A2   2 yonge age] youg't'h H1   3 he] *om.* E   4 bisshopriche] bisshop H2   Trete] Terce H2

king Childeriche had gretly loued. But whanne the malice of Iewes 5
encresed, the felonis putte hym downe of hys worship withoute cause
and sette Feramount in the chaier. And Lambert entered into an
hous of religion and leued | there goodly .vij. yere.   f. 223ra

In a night as he rose from his praieres he lete passe wynde bynethe
by ignoraunce, and whanne the abbot herde it he saide: 'Hoeuer haue 10
do that, lete hym go oute to the crosse barefote and in his haire.' And
he went anone and stode there barefote in the snowe and in the
froste. And whanne the bretheren warmed hem by the fire after
Mateins and the abbot saw that he failed, and a brother tolde hym
that it was he that was go oute to the crosse by his comaundement, 15
thanne he lete calle hym in and he and his bretheren asked hym
foryeuenesse. And he not only foryaue hem but preched hem
moreouer the vertu of pacience.

And after the .vij. yere Ferament was putte oute and Seint
Lambert was brought ayen, bi the comaundement of the king 20
Pepin, to his furst sege. And there he shyned by worde and bi
ensaumple in alle vertues, and in that tyme .ij. wicked men arose
ayenst hym and blamed hym gretly, [whom the frendes of the
bisshop slowe as thei had deserued. And than Seint Lambert
blamed] king Pepin for a comune woman that he helde, and Did, 25
a cosin of one of the men that had be slaine and brother to that
comune woman, and priue in the kinges halle, assembled a gret
strengthe and beseged alle the bisshoppes place, and thought to
reuenge the dethe of his cosin in Seint Lambert that was in his
praiers. And whanne a childe had tolde this to Seint Lambert as he 30
was in his praiers he, trustinge in oure Lorde that he shulde wel
ouercome, toke a suerde, and whanne he come to hymself he kist his
suerde oute of his honde and iuged that it were beter that he
ouercome in sufferinge and in deyenge thanne to defoule his
sacred hondes with the blode of the felonis. And thanne the servaunt 35
of God comforted hys men and taught hem to confesse her synnes
and sustene the dethe goodly. And [thanne] the wicked men come
anone upon hem and slow Seint Lambert that was in hys praiers.
And whanne they were gone, some that ascaped toke the holy | bodi f. 223rb

---

7 Feramount] a feramounte H2   12 went] add oute H1   16 lete calle] called H1
17 he] ins. H1   21–2 bi ensaumple] om. H2   23–5 whom . . . blamed] A2, the EH1,
Than H2   25 Did] did and dede E, didde H1   27 priue] preue'ly' H1
28 place] places H2   32 suerde] add in his honde H2   34 defoule] diffende with H2
35 with] om. H2   36 men] meyne H2   37 dethe] add of the H2   thanne] om. EH1

40 and bare it bi water to the cathedrall chirche priuely and beried it
with gret sorugh of alle tho of the citee the yere of oure Lorde
.vi.C.iiij^{xx}.x.

> Here endithe the liff of Seint Lambert, and nexst begin-
> nithe the lyf of Seint Matheu the Euangelist, Cap^m.
> .C.xxxiij.

In the londe of Inde, where the peple be blake for the right grete
hete of the sonne, there were .ij. enchauntours of whiche that one
hight Zares and that other Arfaxat þat duelled in the citee that hight
Madabar. In that citee there duelled a kinge that hight Aglippus, and
5 these enchauntours deceiued so that kinge that he went thei hadde be
goddes, and so went alle the peple of that cuntre. And the renoun of
hem went thorugh al Ethiope so that the peple come from fer
cuntrees of Inde to see hem and to worship hem. These enchauntours made the peple to holde her pees whanne thei wolde, and also
10 they made hem deef and blynde, and that shulde laste as longe as thei
wolde, and men dredde hem for the gret euell that they dede as
custume is, for wicked men be more dredde for her euell dedes
thanne good men for her good dedes. And therfor, as y haue saide
before, God that hathe cure and mynde upon his peple sent Seint
15 Matheu his apostell ayens hem. And whanne the apostell come into
the citee he began to discouer her malys, for tho that thei made
blynde he made see, and tho that thei made defe he made here.

And as Seint Matheu was in that citee he was herborued with one
of the kepers of the quene of Candauce, the whiche Seint Phelip had
20 baptised before. And thanne he asked Seint Math[eu] how and in
what manere he vnderstode and spake so mani langages, and Seint
Matheu tolde hym that whanne the holy gost descended upon hem
they hadde lerned alle langages, for right as tho that had lerned by
f. 223va her pride to make a toure into heven, the | whiche seseden to make
25 hit for the confusion of tongges that chaunged, right so the apposteles

38 chirche] *ins.* H1   40 .vjC.iiij^{xx}.x.] vjC.iiij^{xx}.xj. H1

EH1H2A1A2L; D resumes at 55 anone   *Rubric* Euangelist] appostulle H2   2 of^2]
add þe H1   3 that hight] of H2   4 Madabar . . . hight] *ins.* H1   7 thorugh al
Ethiope] *om.* H2   10 deef] *add* and doumbe H2   11 hem] *add* gretelie H2
12 custume is] her custume was H2   13 thanne . . . dedes] *ins.* H1   17 he^1] the
Appostul H2   20 Matheu] Mathi E   21 vnderstode] vnderstonde *with second* n
subp. H1   22 descended] light H2   23 that] *om.* H1   24 seseden] seteden
changed to seceden H1   25 chaunged] chaunted *changed to* chaunged H1   apposteles]
`a´postell H1

made a toure bi the connyng of tongges, but not of stones but of
uertues, bi the whiche all tho that will leue in God mow stie into
heuene.

And thanne cam before hem .ij. men that saide the enchauntours
were come with .ij. dragones that casten fire and sulphre thorugh her 30
mouthe and thorugh her noses and slow the peple, and the apostell
blessed [hym with] the tokene of the crosse and went oute suerly to
hem. And as sone as these dragones sawe hym thei leide hem downe
atte his fete and slepten, and thanne saide Seint Matheu to the
enchauntours: 'Where is your powere? Awake hem yef ye may, and 35
yef y wolde praie oure Lorde y shulde returne in you the malice that
ye wolde do in me.' And whanne the peple was assembled he
comaunded to the dragones that thei shulde go her way and do
none harme to none creature, and anone thei went her waye.

And thanne the apostell made a glorious sermon of the ioyes of 40
paradys terestre, sayenge that it aperithe aboue alle the hilles and that
it is nigh heuene and that there were nother thornes ne breres, ne the
roses ne the lelies fade neuer there, ne there may none wexe olde
there, but the peple shulde euer be yonge and that the songe of
aungelles sounithe there, and thei come anone as thei be called. And 45
he shewed how man was cast fro that paradis, but he was called ayen
to the paradis of heuene bi the birthe of Ihesu Crist.

And as he saide these wordes to the peple a grete trouble and a
grete noyse arose amonge the peple for the kyngez sone that was
dede. And whanne these enchauntours might not releue hym, thei 50
made the kinge beleue that he was rauisshed in the felawship of
goddes and that he must make a temple and an ymage. And thanne
this forsaide keper of | the quene of Candace made kepe these f. 223ᵛᵇ
enchauntours and sent for the apostell, and whanne he was come he
made his praiers and releued hym anone. And thanne the kinge that 55
hight Eglippe sent thorugh alle his prouinces whanne he hadde sein
this and charged hem alle to come and se God in mannes liknesse.
And thanne ther come the peple with crownes of golde and diuers
maners of sacrifices and wolde haue do sacrifice to hym. And thanne
Seint Matheu behelde hem and saide: 'What do ye, men, y am not 60
God but y am seruaunt of Ihesu Crist oure Lorde.' And by the

26 connyng] commyng H1H2   29 saide] add þat H1   30 casten] caste in H2
32 hym with] om. EH1   33 thei] he del. 'they' H1   hem²] him changed to hem H1
36 oure Lorde] your wormes H2   40 apostell] add Mathewe H2   42 there] ins. H1
43 olde] colde H2   51 in] into H2   55 hym] the kingis sone H2   56 prouinces]
province H1D   59 sacrifice] sacrafices H1   60 men] mene D

comaundement of hym thci madc a grete chirche with that golde and
by that they hadde wrought and fulfelled it within .xxx. dayes, and
the .xxxiij. day the apostell sate within and preched and conuerted
65 alle the cuntre of Ynde. And [thanne] the king Eglippe and hys wiff
and alle the peple were baptised. And thanne he halowed to God
Euphegeny the kingges doughter and made her soueraine of .ij. noble
uirgines.

And after that Ciriake succeded and was kinge and coueited the
70 saide uirgine, and behight to the apostell half his rewme yef he wolde
make her consent to hym. And the apostell saide to hym that after
the custume of his predecessour he shulde come on Sonday to the
chirche and he shulde here, present Euphegeni and other uirgines,
how mariage is good and rightwisse. And than the kynge come thedir
75 with grete ioye and went that he wolde haue stered Euphegenie to
mariage. And thanne whan the kinge and alle the peple were
assembled he preched long of the uertu of mariage, and therfor
the kinge comendid gretly his prechinge, wening that he saide alle to
acorde the wille of the uirgine to hym bi mariage. And thanne he
80 comaunded that alle shulde be in pees and rehersed his wordes
f. 224ra saienge: | 'How it be that mariage be right good yef it be holde bi
good alliaunce, ye that be here knowen well that yef there were ani
seruaunt that wolde presume to take the kingges wif, he shulde not
onli renne in the kingges indignacion, but aboue that he deseruithe
85 dethe, not only for he wedded her but for he toke the kingges wif and
brake the mariage that was ioyned before. Wherfor y saie that thou,
kinge, that knowest that Euphegenie is wedded to the euerlastinge
kinge and is sacred with holy veille, how durst thou or might thou
take awey the wiff of thi Lorde that is a more mighti kinge thanne
90 thou art and couple her to the bi mariage?'

And whan the kinge had herde this he parted thennes as half mad
for anger, and thanne this holi uirgine felle doune prostrate before
the apostell and saide to hym in this wise before alle the peple: 'Holy
apostell of almighti God, in whom y perfitely beleue, y beseche you
95 that ye conferme in verrei faithe and pure chastite by youre holy
blessinge me and these uirgines that be with me that we may eschewe

65 thanne] *om.* EH1   66 the] here H1   he] seinte mathewe D   67 .ij.] two`C'
H1   69 was] *add* made D   73 here] *om.* H1   74 rightwisse] right wis H1
75 he] the appostulle D   78 he] *add* had D   79 And] *om.* H1   81 it¹] `it' might
it *with second* it *subp.* H1   82 ye] Yee alle *beginning sentence* D   here] *add* ye H1
83–4 he . . . kingges] *ins.* H1   84 deseruithe] deserued H1D   88 how] or D
95 conferme] *add* `me' H1

and be deliuered fro the manaces and the malice of this kinge.' Than
Seint Matheu, that hadde perfite truste in oure Lorde and dradde
nothinge the kinge, leide her veiles on her hedes with this blessinge:
'Blessed Lorde God, that madest of not bothe bodi and soule of alle   100
mankinde and that despisiste no creatoure, suffre us not to turne to
wickednesse, and that alle the worlde hast bought with [thi] precious
blode, thou vouchesauf to graunte to these uirgines that haue chose
the to her preste and gouernour, to kepe the crowne of her virginite
euerlastinge, grace and strengthe for to continue in her good werkes   105
that thei mowe by thi grace come to the soueraine ioyes of heuene.
Blessed Lorde | God that thou with the goodnesse of thin holy goost   f. 224rb
list to shadwe hem, that synne haue no power to encumbre hem ne
putte hem from the right waie of paradis, and that the heuenly
d[e]we maye touche her bodies and her soules dewe with perdurable   110
chastite so that the enemy finde none encheson in hem wherby he
might make hem forsake the right waye of helthe. In hem be holy
virginite armid with holi faithe and perfite hope of charite, and that
her reson and her wille haue so moche might and vertu be thi grace
that thei mowe ouercome mightly alle the wicked wiles of the fende,   115
and that thei mowe dispise this present vanitees and folowe the
goodes that be to come, and that thei alle flessheli metes sette abacke
by holy fasting and allwey be redy to holy praiers, and that thei be
enlumined and taught for to fulfelle the comaundementes of holy
Chirche. Blessed Lorde God, kinge of alle creatoures, y beseche the   120
that these virgines mow be kepte withinne and withoute with these
armes that y haue deuised so that thei mowe continue her virginite
unto the ende, as thou art kinge of alle kingges and truest
councellour and best gouernour to alle tho that calle thine holy
name in trewe faithe and perfit beleue.' And whanne he hadde alle   125
ended his orison alle the virgines ansuered: 'Amen.' And thanne the
holi apostell reuested hym ande went to masse and alle the peple
herd his masse with gret ioye and deuocion.

And whanne the masse was do he abode stille in his holy praiers
before the auuter, and the kinge Yrtakus that was fulle of cursed-   130
nesse sent a seruaunt to the chirche and comaunded hym that he

102 thi] his E   103 thou] than D   104 virginite] add and D   106 heuene]
punct. and add Good D   108 no] om. D   110 dewe] dowe E, so changed to dewe H1
113 of] and D   115 mightly] might`ily' H1   wiles] willes H1   116 this] these
wickid D   118 that] þat that D   123 the ende] th`e'ende H1   125 perfit] profite
changed to parfite H1   127 reuested] reuersid D   128–9 with gret . . . masse] ins. H1
130 Yrtakus] yrtakes changed to Syriake H1

shulde sle the apostell of Ihesu Crist, and he come behinde hym as
f. 224va he kneled afore the auuter and slow hym with | his swerde, and so he
was sacred marter. And thanne alle the peple wolde haue go to the
135 paleis of the kinge for to haue slaine hym, and vnnethes thei were
withehold of prestes and of dekenes, and thanne thei halowed with
gret solempnite the marterdom of the apostell.

And the king sent to Euphegenie ladies and enchauntours, and
whanne he sawe that he might not drawe her to his entent in no wise,
140 he environid alle the place aboute withe fire for to haue brent her and
all her nonnes. And thanne the apostell apered in the middes of the
fire and putte oute the fire alle about her place, and sodenly the fire
toke in the kingges paleis and brent up all that euer there was that
vnnethes the kinge and his sone ascaped. And anone the sone was
145 rauisshed with the fende and beganne to crie [the] synnes of his fader
and went to the sepulcre of the apostell. And the fader was made a
foule mesill, and whanne he sawe he might not be heled he slowe
hymself with his owne honde. And thanne the peple ordeined the
brother of Euphegenie to be kinge, the whiche the apostell had
150 baptised afore, and he regned .lxx. yere and ordeined his sone to be
kinge after hym, and he encresed gretly the worship of cristen peple
and he fulfelled all Ynde with chirches of Ihesu Crist. Zares an
Arphaxth fledden into Pers fro the day that the apostell rered the
kingges sone, but Seint Symond and Seint Iude ouercome hem
155 there.

And wetith well that .iiij. thingges be considered principaly in this
blessed Math[eu]: the furst is hastinesse of obedience, for as sone as
oure Lord called hym he lefte alle and dredde not his lordes and lefte
the acountes of his receites that were inperfit and ioyned hym perfitly
160 to Ihesu Crist. And for this hastinesse of obedience some tokin
f. 224vb occasion of errour in hym, so as Ierome recor|dithe in his Original
upon the said place: 'P[or]firie and Iulius Augustus repreuithe in that
place there as the folysshenesse of the stori lyinge, saienge that, like
as thei sodenly folued the sauiour, that thei wold as hastely haue
165 folued eche other man that hadde called hem. But that is verrey
untrewe, for there was sheued thanne bi his diuyne mageste so mani
vertues and tokenes that the apostell[es] leuid anone withoute doute.

132 the] *add* holie D   134 was] *add* a D   141 her] *ins.* H1   143 brent] *add* it
H1   145 the²] *om.* E   146 and . . . fader] *ins.* H1   148 peple] appostulle D
157 Matheu] Mathi E, *so changed to* Mathewe H1, martir D   160 this] his H1   tokin]
add of L   162 Porfirie] Profirie E   165 eche other] anoþer D   that²] *add* it H1
167 apostelles] apostell EH1   withoute] *add* any D

And certainly that shininge of his diuine mageste hit shined upon his face fro the begininge and upon alle tho that he wolde draue to hym by biholdinge and bi will. For yef suche vertu is in a stone that men 170 calle magnet that it will drawe stones to hym to and to, whi thanne moche rather may not oure [Lorde] draw to hym tho that he will.'

The secound is his largesse and his fredom, for anone he made oure Lorde in his hous a gret feste, the whiche was not most large by gret apparaill of metis but it was gret only bi reson of desire, for he 175 resseiued hym with a gret will and desire. And also it was grete bi reson of the seruice, for that was shewinge of a gret misterie. The whiche misterie the Glose expounithe upon Seint Luke, sayenge: 'He that receiuithe Ihesu Crist in his hous was fedde plenteuously within forthe with gret thingges, that is to knowe with delectaciones of good 180 delites.' And after, it was grete bi the reson of techinge, for oure Lorde taught there grete techingges, and that was of mercy, as whanne he saide: 'Y will merci and not sacrifice', and 'Tho that bene hole haue no nede of leches.' And it was also grete for tho that were bode to the feste were grete, that was Ihesu Crist and his disciples. 185

The thridde is humilite that apered in hym in .ij. thingges. Furst in that he knowlechid hymself a publican. The tother euuangelistes, as the Glose saithe, bicause of shame and for worship of the euangelist | putte not that name in comune, but as it is wreten f. 225ra 'The rightwis man is furst acusour of hymself,' and Seint Matheu 190 named hymself publican for that he wolde shew that none that is conuerted shulde haue mistruste of his sauacion, sethe he was made sodenly fro a publican apostell and euuangelist. Secoundely for he was pacient in his iniuries. For whanne the [Phariseis] murmured that Ihesu Crist was descendid to a publican and a sinfull man, Seint 195 Mathi might haue saide to h[e]m: 'Ye be more cursed and more sinfull that wenin that ye be rightwis and forsakithe the fisicien, for y may no more be called a sinfull man sethe y went to the fisicien of hele and shewed hym my woundes.'

The ferth is the gret solempnite of hym in the Chirch. For his 200

168 diuine] diuinite H1   hit] it del. 'had' H1, had D   171 to and to] om. H1D (deux et deux P2)   172 Lorde] om. E   174 not] om. D   177 was shewinge] sowing del. 'was schewynge' H1   182 as] And D   183 and²] for D   185 and . . . disciples] ins. H1   186 apered] appereth H1   187 knowlechid] knoweth H1   188 H1 begins sentence By cause   189 euangelist] Euangelistis D   193 publican] add to H1D 194 in his] ins. H1   Phariseis] Sarizenes E, so and add 'paynems' H1   murmured] murmuredid E   196 hem] hym EH1   197 wenin] venym changed to wenyn H1 forsakithe] fo'r'saketh H1

gospellis bene bifore the techer and the most haunted in the Chirche
right in the same wise as the Psalmes of Dauid and the Pisteles of
Paule byfore alle other scriptures be most recorded in the Chirche.
And this is the reson, that Iames witnessithe .iij. manere of synnes,
205 that is to wete, pride, lecherie and couetise. Saule sinned in the sinne
of pride, and therfor was he worthi [to] be called after the most
proude kinge S[a]ul, that is to saie right proude, for he pursued right
proudely the Chirche. Dauid synned in the synne of lecherie, for he
synned in avoutrie and in his avoutrie he slowe his right true knight
210 Vrie. And Math[eu] synned in the synne of couetise, for he medeled
hym with sinfull wynning. For he was upon a porte of the see wher
he receiued the tolle and other avauntages that longed to that crafte.
And thow that alle these thre were sinfull yet oure Lorde receiued
her penaunce mercifully, so that he forgaue hem not only her synnes,
215 but multeplied in hem his yeftes of grace. For he that was right a
cruel pursuer of the Chirche he made hym right a true prechour, he
f. 225ʳᵇ that was a vouterer and a mansleer he made hym an holi | profite, and
he that coueited so moche wrechidnesse and sinfull wynningges he
made hym apostell and euuangelist. And therfor these .iij. bene ofte
220 tymes rehersed to us for to shewe us that there nis none that will
conuerte hym to God but he shall haue foryeuenesse, considering
also how grete synnes thei were in and in how grete grace thei be in
now.

And also it is to knowe that sum thingges after Seint Ambrose be
225 to considre in the conuersyon of Seint Math[eu], that is to wete of
the partie of the fisicien, and some of th[e] partie of the sike pacient
heled, and also of the manere of helinge. As to the furst, there be .iij.
thingges in the fisicien: wisdom, bi whiche he knowithe the rote of
the sikenesse; bounte, by whiche he yaue hym medicine; might, by
230 whiche he chaunged hym sodenly and hastely. And of these thre
thinges Seint Ambrose in the persone of Seint Math[eu] saithe in
this wise: 'He that knouithe alle thingges that be hidde might best
take away the sorugh of myn herte and the wrechidnesse of my
soule', and this for the furst. The secounde he saide: 'Y haue founde

203 byfore] *repeat* 201–2 the techer . . . wise D   206 to] *om.* EH1   after] *om.* D
207 kinge] *subp.* H1   Saul] Soul E   pursued] pursueth H1   209 slowe] shewe *changed
to* slowe H1   right] *om.* D   210 Matheu] Mathi E, *so changed to* Mathew H1
218 wrechidnesse] and wrecchid D   225 Matheu] Mathi E, *so changed to* Mathe H1
226 the³] tho EH1   the partie of] *om.* D   228 he] yee D   229 yaue] yeueth D
230 chaunged] chaungith his medicine so D   231 Matheu] Mathy E, Mathew *with* ew
on erasure H1   233 of] in H1   myn] mynd *with* d *erased* H1   234 furst] *add* To D

a medicine that duellithe in heuene and shedithe into erthe his 235
medicine.' And for the thridde he saide: 'He may wel hele my
woundes that knewe none of his owne.'

In this blessed sike that was heled be considered thre thingges,
after Seint Ambrose. He putte perfitely awey his syknesse; he was
alway agreable to his fesicien; he was also clene euer after that he 240
hadde receiued hele where he saithe: 'Seint Matheu folued alway his
fisician al glad and reioised hym of his hele, sayenge: "Y am no
lengger a publican, ne y vse no more foule wynninge." And also he
saide: "Y hate my kinrede and fle my lyf and folowe the only, Ihesu
Crist, that haste heled my woundes. What is that [that] may departe 245
me from the charite of God that is in me, tribulacion [or] anguisshe
or hunger?" As ho saithe, no|thinge.'

His gospell that he wrote with his owne honde was founde with   f. 225ᵛᵃ
the bones of Seint Barnabe, the whiche gospell the blessed Barnabe
bare with hym and leide it upon sike men and thei were anone hole 250
bi the vertu of Ihesu Crist and the merites of blessed Seint Math[eu].
And thei were found the yere of oure Lorde .vC.

Here endithe the liff of Seint Math[eu], and nexst
beginnithe the lyf of Seint Moris, Capitulum .C.xxxiiij.ᵐ

Seint Moris was duke of the right holi region of Thebes, and thei
were called Thebayens after her citee that hight Thebes. And that
region is in the partie[s] of the orient towarde the ende of Arabie.
That londe is full of richesse, plenteuous of fruit, delectable of trees.
And the duellers of that region be semely men of bodies, noble in 5
armis, stronge in bataile, sotell in engyne, and right habundaunt in
wisdom. That citee hadde .vjC. yates of whiche men saien this vers:
Ecce uetus Thebe centum iacet obruta portis, that is to saie: the olde
Thebee of an hundred yates is now ouerthrawe. And Seint Iame the
brother of oure Lorde preched there the gospell of oure Lorde.   10

In that tyme Dioclucian and Maxymian that were emperours

235 medicine] medycine'r' H1   into] in 'to' þe H1, into the D   236 saide] seith H1
238 In] And D   sike] *add* man H1   be] he D   239 syknesse] *add* for D
242 reioised] receiued D   245 that³] *om.* EH1   246 or] and EH1   248 His]
'h'is H1   gospell] gospelles D   owne] *om.* H1   250 anone] *add* alle D   hole] *om.* H1
251 Matheu] Mathi EH1   252 Lorde] *om.* H1

EH1DH2A1A2; A1 breaks off after 29 *Cesar that lon(ge   Rubric* Matheu] Mathi EH1
1 holi] nobul D   2 Thebayens] Thebes D   3 parties] partie EH1   of²] *ins.* H1
7 .vjC.] .vjC. *with* v *erased* H1, twoo hundrid D   8 *portis] mortis* H1

wolde in alle thinge destroie the faithe of Ihesu Crist and sent suche
pisteles thorugh alle the parties where cristen men duelled: 'Yef it
were nedefull to determine or to knowe anithing and all the worlde
15 were assembled of that o parte and Rome alon that other parte, all
the worlde wolde flee as ouercome and Rome only abide in the
hynesse of cunninge. Wherfor thanne, ye that be but an handfull of
peple, contrarie to the comaundementes of her and refusin so folily
her ordenaunces? Wherfor ye shull receiue the faithe of vndedly
20 goddes, other vnchaungeable sentence of dampnacion shal be
pronounced upon you.'

f. 225vb   And than | the cristen receiued the letteres and sent the
messangers ayen al voide withoute ansuer. And thanne Dioclisian
and Maxymian were meued with grete wrathe and sent anone
25 thorugh alle the prouinces, and comaunded that thei shulde come
to Rome redi in armes for to fight and discomfite alle the rebelles of
the empire of Rome. And thanne were the letteres of the emperours
born to the Thebans, the whiche, after the comaundement of God,
thei yelden to God that longed to God, and to Cesar that longed to
30 Cesar. Thei assembled thanne that chosin legion of knightz, that is to
wete .vjMl.vjC.lxvj. and sent hem to the emperour for to helpe hym
in his rightwysse batailes, and not for to bere armes ayenst the cristen
but for to defende hem rather. And that noble man Moris was duke
of that right holi legion, and tho that gouerned the baners were Seint
35 Blane and Seint Innocent, Seint Sophie, Seint Victor and Seint
Constantine. Thanne Dioclysian sent Maxymian ayenst hem of
Fraunce, the whiche hadde gadered with hem all the felawship of
the empire and with hem grete strengthe withoute nombre, and he
ioyned with hym the legion of Thebes. And thei hadde be taught
40 before that thei shulde rather sle h[e]mself with her suerd[es] thanne
for to destroie the cristen faithe.

And whanne the grete oste withoute nombre hadde passed the
mountaynes, the emperoure comaunded that all tho that come with
hym shulde do sacrifice to the ydoles, and thanne thei ronne anone
45 upon the rebelles and specially upon the cristen. And whanne these

15 that o] the othir D   alon] on D   16 wolde] *om.* H1   wolde flee as] flee woolde
and D   17 that] *om.* D   but] *ins.* H1   19 Wherfor . . . the] of D   25 prouinces]
prouince D   comaunded] comaundeded E, comaund H1   26–7 redi . . . Rome] *om.* D
28 born] *om.* D   the¹] *ins.* H1   30 Thei . . . that¹] than thei assemblid and D   chosin]
add and D   32 to] *ins.* H1   34 right] *om.* H1   36 sent] seint E, *add* seint *subp.*
H1   37 hem] *om.* H1   38 and¹] *add* had D   39–40 thei . . . that] 'they seyd' H1
40 hemself] hymself EH1   suerdes] suerd E

holy knightes herde that, thei parted hem fer from the oste about
.viij. mile and toke her place upon goodly grounde faste by Rone that
hight Agonon. And whanne Maximyan wost it he sent to hem
knightes in haste, charging hem to come to do sacrifice to the
ydoles with other that were there. And thei sent hym worde ayen 50
thei might in no wise do it, for thei were cristen | and helden truly f. 226ʳᵃ
the faithe of Ihesu Crist. Than the emperoure sette afire in wrathe
saide: 'The heuenly iniurie is medeled with my despite and the
religion of Romaynes is despised with me. Now shull these foled
knightes knowe yef y may yeue veniaunce, not only by me, but by 55
my goddes.' And thanne he comaunded to his knightes that thei
shulde go and constreine hem to sacrifice to her goddes, or elles
anone that of eueri .x. of hem there were beheded one. And thanne
these holy knightes streight out her neckes with gret ioye, and hasted
eueriche afore other to receiue dethe for the louc of God.   60

And thanne Seint Moris arose up amonge hem and said to his
felawship: 'Reioise you with us, for we be all redi for to suffre dethe
for the faithe of Ihesu Crist. We haue suffered oure felawes to be
slaine and oure clothes be rede of her blode. Late us thanne folow
hem to martirdom, and yef it lyke you, late us sende this message to 65
the emperour: "We be knightes of thine empire and haue take armis
to the defens of the comune. There is nother treson ne drede founde
in us, but in no wise we will not leue the faithe of Ihesu Crist."' And
whanne the emperoure herde that, of eueri .x. there shulde be
biheded one. And [whanne] that was done, Seint Solpide that was 70
one of the banerers toke the baner in his honde and went amonge his
felawship that weren knightes and saide: 'Oure glorious duke Moris
hath spoke of the glorie of oure felawship of knightz, wherfor y lete
you wete that y Sulpice youre banerere toke none armes for to
withstonde to suche thingges, wherfor late us with oure right hondes 75
throw away the flesshely armes and arme us with vertues, and yef it
like you, late us send suche wordes to the emperour: "We be thi
knightes, Sire emperour, but we confesse us to be the verrai

47 upon] *add* a H1D   Rone] Rome D   50 other] alle thoo D   51 might] *om.*
H1   wise] *add* wold H1   52 sette] *add* alle D   53 The] *om.* H1   my] meche H1
54 religion] religiones EH1, region D (*religion* P2)   foled] fonned H1, folisshe D
55 by] *ins.* H1   57 to¹] *add* do H1D   58 that] *om.* H1   of eueri] *om.* D   there]
om. D   one] *om.* D   63 haue] *om.* D   64 clothes] *add* to H1D   65 to¹] *add* her
H1   this] þat H1   this message] þe messanger D   67 is] *ins.* H1   70 whanne] *om.*
EH1   73 of³] *om.* H1   75 wherfor] were 'for' H1   78 to be] *om.* D   the]
om. H1

seruauntes of Ihesu Crist. We owe to the knighthode and to hym
80 innocence, and of the we loke to haue mede for oure laboure and of
f. 226ʳᵇ hym we haue bygynninge of oure lyf, and we be redi | to receiue for
his loue alle the turmentis that thou canst deuise."' And thanne this
cursed tiraunt comaunded that his oste shulde environe alle that
blessed legion that none shulde scape alyue. And thanne were the
85 precious knightes of Ihesu Crist al besette with the deueles knightes,
and thei were all tohewin bi her cursed hondes and defouled with the
fete of her horses and thei were sacred precious marteres to oure
Lorde. And thei suffered dethe in the yere of oure Lorde .CC.iiijˣˣ.

But it is saide in diuerse places that mani of hem ascaped bi the
90 will of God and come into her regions for to preche the name of
Ihesu Crist and hadden in other places the victorie of marterdom.
And men saien that Solutor and Auentor and Ottauus went into
Tamnewse, and Alisaundre went to Bentone, and Secounde went to
Vitulien, and the blessed Victor and Constancien and Vrsin and mani
95 other weren of hem that ascaped.

And whanne these turmentours departed the praie betwene hem
and eten togederes, Victor an aunsien man passed of auenture bisides
hem and thei bade hym come dyne with hem. And he asked hem
how thei might ete with ioye amonge so mani dede bodies. And
100 whanne he herde for what cause thei were dede, he beganne to weile
sore and saide: 'Wolde God y hadde be so blessed that y hadde deied
with hem.' And whanne thei perceiued that he was cristen thei al
tohewe hym anone.

And after that Maxymian was atte Mileyn and Dyoclusian in
105 Nichomede, and thei ordeined vnder hem Constancien and Maxymien and Galerien. And as Maxymian bygan ayen his tyrannie, he
was pursued by Constancien his sone in lawe and ended his lyf upon
a gebet. And after that, the bodi of Seint Innocent of that legion that
had be caste in Rome was founde and beried with other in the
110 chirche of Genauence with Austin and Prothase that hadde be
f. 226ᵛᵃ bisshoppes of the Chirche. And there was | a paynim that was a
werkeman of that chirche with other, but he wolde in no wise werke
but in the Sondaies and other holy dayes, and specially whanne
folkes were atte the masse. And thanne there come a cumpani of

80 the] þat H1   86 tohewin] heuen *with* u *changed to* w H1   88 And thei . . .
oure Lorde] *om.* D   90 into] to H1   92 into] to H1   94 blessed] bisshop D
Constancien] Constantine D   97 an] and *with* d *erased* H1   100 were dede] died D
105 Nichomede] Nichodeme H1   106 ayen] ayens E, so *with* s *erased* H1   108 a] þe
H1   that¹] *twice* H1   Innocent] *add* oone D   111 of the Chirche] *om.* D

these seintes to hym and [blamed hym gretly and charged hym welle 115
and sharpely, and] asked hym who made hym hardi to do his werke
of masonri while he shulde here the devine seruice. And this
corrected, he come to the chirche and required to be cristen.

And Seint Ambrose saithe bi this blessed marteres in his Preface:
'The felawship of trouthe enlumined with the devine light comynge 120
from the ferrest parties of the worlde, the whiche armed hem with
spiritual armes and wenten gladly to marterdom by stable faithe, and
the tyraunt full of pestilence, for to withdrawe hem by fere and
drede, assailed hem .ij. tymes by slaughter of suerde. And after,
whanne he sawe that thei wolde not remeue but abode stabely in the 125
faithe, he comaunded that alle her hedes shulde be smite of. And
they, enchaufed bi so gret feruour of charitee, threwe of her armes
and sittinge on her knees resseiued sufferably with gladnesse of
hertes strokes of swerdes of hem that martered hem, amonge whiche
Seint Moris, the whiche was all sette afire in the loue of the faithe of 130
Ihesu Crist, receiued in fightinge the croune of marterdom.' And this
saithe Seint Ambrose.

A woman toke her sone for to lerne to the abbot of the chirche in
whiche these holy bodyes restedin, and in shorte tyme he deyed so
that she bywepte hym withoute ani remedie. And in a night Seint 135
Moris apered to her and asked her whi she wepte so heuily for her
sone, and she ansuered that as longe as she liued she wolde wepe for
hym. And thanne he saide to her: 'Wepe not for hym as thou wolde
wepe for a dede bodi, for wete it well he is alyue with us, and yef
thou wilt preue this, arise tomorw and eueri day after to Mateins and 140
thou shalt | here hys vois singynge amonge the monkes.' And she was f. 226vb
ther sethe alle her lyff and herde the vois of her sone alwaies and
knewe it amonge the vois of the monkes synginge.

Whanne the kinge Gutturam hadde yeue all his good to the pore
and hadde forsake the worlde, he sent a preste for to bringe hym of 145
the holy reliques of that cumpani. And as thei returned with the
reliques the tempest arose in the lake of Losan so that the shippe
was in point to perisshe, and thanne he putte the shrine with alle

115–16 blamed . . . sharpely and] *om.* EH1   116 hym²] *add* so H1
117 masonri] mesonri *with* e (?) *on erasure* H1   120 comynge] *add* doune D
123 hem] *ins.* H1   by fere and] bifore for D   138 hym¹] *add* as þou wold wepe for a
dede bodi for *del.* `and þan he seyde' H1   138–9 to her . . . for²] *om.* H1   140 preue]
add a proue D   141 amonge] a monke D   142 sethe] *om.* D   lyff] *add* time D
143 it] *add* welle D   144 kinge] *add* of D   147 Losan] bosan H1   shippe] shippes
EH1

the reliques ayenst the flodes of the water and anone alle was
150 apesed.

Hit fell in the yere of oure Lorde .ixC.lxiij. that certaine monkes
by the auys of Charles had asked the bodi of Seint Vrban and of
Seint Tiburci martir, and as they come ayen thei went to visite the
chirche of the holy martires knightes, and they desired of the abbot
155 and of the monkes that thei might bere with hem the bodi of Seint
Moris to Aucerie and laie hym in the chirche of Seint Germayne
hadde longe before [de]died in the name of these marteres. And thei
had graunt and bare hym with hem.

Pers Davyen tellithe that in Burgoyne there was a proude clerke
160 and a coueitous that hadde drawe to hym by wronge and strengthe a
chirche of Seint Moris fro a mighty knight that was contrarie to hym.
And as they songe in a day in the masse there was in the ende of the
gospell: 'All tho that lefte up hemselff shul be made meke, and ho
that mekithe hymself shul be enhaunsed.' This cursed clerke
165 beganne to laugh and saide: 'This is fals, for yef y had loued and
meked [my]self y hadde not hadde this day so moche richesse of the
chirche as y haue.' And as sone as he hadde saide that a
thundreclappe in liknesse of a suerde entred into his mouthe that
hadde saied so gret blasfeme and quenched hym anone sodenly.

Here endithe the lyf of Seint Moris, and nexst beginnithe
f. 227ʳᵃ   the liff of | Seint Iustine the Uirgine, Capitulum .C.xxxv.

Seint Iustine the Virgine was of the citee of Antioche, doughter of a
preste of ydoles, and eueri day she satte in a windowe ny a preste that
redde the gospell, and she herde it and was atte the laste conuerted bi
hym. And whanne her moder had told [it] to her fader in her bedde,
5 Ihesu Crist apered to hem with his aungleles saienge: 'Comithe to me
and y shalle geue you the kingdom of heuene.' And whanne thei
awoke thei made hem anone to be cristened with her doughter.

And this mayde Iustine was gretly vexed with Ciprien and atte the

149 flodes] floode D   151 of oure Lorde] ins. H1   .ixC.lxiij.] .ixC. iiij score and
iij D   152 of³] om. H1   156 Aucerie] Aucerre D   Germayne] add þat H1, add
and D   157 dedied] died EH1, edefied it D (dediee P2)   161 fro] for D   162 in
the¹] om. D   163 shul] shulde EH1   164 shul] shulde EH1   166 myself]
hymself E   this day] to dai H1   168 thundreclappe] add come D   suerde] add and D
169 hym] om. D

EH1DH2A2; A1 resumes at 8 with   4 it] om. EH1   bedde] add 'how' H1
8 vexed] envexed with en del. H1

laste she conuerted hym to the faithe. And this Ciprian fro his
youthe had be an enchauntour, for fro tyme that he was .vij. yere 10
olde he hadde be sacred to the fende bi his fader and moder and
serued the crafte of enchauntement and dede many wonder thingges.
And this Cipriane coueited gretly the loue of this uirgine and
beganne to werke his crafte upon her for to make her consent to
hym or elles to a felowe of his that hight Gladien whiche coueited 15
her gretly also. And thanne he called the fende to hym and he came
anone and askcd hym: 'Whi hast thou called me?' And Cipriane
saide: 'I haue a faire virgine. Maist thou do so moche that y may
haue her?' And the fende anone ansuered to hym: 'I that sumtyme
hadde might and power for to caste man oute of paradys, and 20
thorugh my procuringc and ordenaunce made and purueied that
thilke Kayme slowe his rightfull and iuste brother Abel, and afterwarde longe tyme made and procured the cursed Icwcs to sle Ihesu
Crist, and also thanne thorugh my malice and enuie troubled alle the
worlde, whi trowest thou now that y ne may | well helpe the to haue f. 227^{rh}
thi luste of a simple virgine and for to do alle thi lust with her and 26
plesaunce? Take this oynement and shede it all aboute her hous
withoute and y shall come myself ouer that and sette her afire in thi
loue and constreine her to obeie to the.'

And the night foluinge the fende went to her and enforced her and 30
meued her to vnordinate loue. And whanne she felt this she
recomaunded her deuoutely to God alle her body and also her
soule and blessed her with the holy signe of the crosse. And the
fende beinge all full of drede for the tokene and the signe of the
crosse fledde awaye and come to Ciprian and stode beforc hym. And 35
thanne Ciprian saide: 'Whi haste thou not brought me this uirgine?'
And the deuell saide: 'Y sawe [in her] a token that made me so feble
that it toke awaye alle my strengthe so that y fayled in myself.' And
thanne Ciprian lefte hym and called another more mightyer devill for
to fulfill his purpos. And the devell come anone and saide: 'Y herd 40
thi comaundement and am come and y haue saine the noun power of
my felaw, but y shall amende alle hardely and fulfell thi comaundement and thi will, and y shall go to her ande wounde her herte with
the loue of lecherie and thanne thou shalt mowe do alle thi will with

13, 15 coueited] conuerted *with* r *changed to* y H1   15 elles] *om.* D   19 anone
ansuered] *trs.* H1   22 thilke] *om.* D   rightfull] moost right D   25 y] 'I' H1
26 do] haue D   32 also] alle D   34 all] than D   and the] of þat D   37 deuell]
feende D   in her] her in E, 'in' her in *with second in del.* H1   39 another] a D
42 felaw] fellawis D

45 her.' And than the fende went to her and enforced hym al that euer
he might to stere and to meue her hert to lecherie and into wreched
loue and for to enflaume her corage into unlefull thingges. And
anone she recomaunded her to God deuoutly and putte away from
her all temptaciones bi vertu of the crosse and blewe ayenst the fende
50 and caste hym oute anone, and he fledde thennes al confused and
f. 227ᵛᵃ come before Cipriane. | And Cipriane sayd: 'Wher ys the uirgine to
whom y sent the?' And the fende sayd: 'I knowlage that y am
ouercome, and y drede to telle how, for y sawe her haue an orible
signe and y loste anone al my strengthe and vertu.'

55   And thanne Ciprien lefte hym and blamid hym and called the
prince of fendes. And whanne he was come he saide: 'Whi ys youre
powere and youre vertu so lytell that [it] ys ouercome with so yonge
a mayde?' And the prince saide: 'Y shal go and trauayle her with
diuers fires and enflaume her corage more brennyngly and make her
60 all frenetyk, and y shall offre before her diuers fantasies and brynge
the to her atte mydnight.' And thanne the fende transfigured hymself
in fourme of a virgine and come to that virgine and saide: 'I am come
to the for y desire to lyue with the in chastite, and y praie the telle
me what guerdon we shulle haue for oure laboure.' And the virgine
65 ansuered: 'The guerdon ys grete and the laboure ys litell.' 'And what
menith it thanne,' saide the fende, 'that God comaundithe for to
encrece and multiplie and fulfille the erthe? And therfor, good suster,
y drede yef we abide in virginite that we shulle not fulfille the worde
of God but make it vayne, and as dispisers and vnobediensers we
70 shull falle in full greuous iugement wher we shull no hope haue of
guerdon but greuous turmentis.' And than by the meving of the
fende the herte of the virgine was troubeled with greuous thoughtes
and was gretly enflaumyd with the synne of couetyse of the flesshe,
so that she was in point to go oute. And thanne the virgine come to
75 herself and considered ho it was that spake to her, and marked her
deuoutly with the [signe of the] crosse and blewe ayenst the fende,
and anone he fledde and meltyd as wexe.

And thanne after he transfigured hym in lyknesse of a faire yonge

45 hym] hir D   51 uirgine] virginite D   53 telle] helle D   55 called] add
vp D   56 of] add þe H1   57 it] om. E   58 trauayle] tˈraˈvail H1   62 in
fourme of] to D   andⁱ . . . virgine] om. H1   that] add holie D   virgine] add Iustine D
64 virgine] add Iustine D   65 guerdon] guerdonis E   66 thanne] is del. ˋthanˊ H1
72 virgine] add Iustine D   74 virgine] add Iustine D   75 her²] add anone D
76 signe of the] om. EH1   77 he] she with s erased H1   fledde] add aweie D
78 after] add þat ˋheˊ H1

man | and entred into her chaumbre [and found her in her bedde and   f. 227vb
went to bedde] to her and byclypped her and wolde haue hadde to do 80
with her. And whanne she sawe that and knew it was a wicked spirit,
she blessed her as she was wont and he vanisshed awaye as wexe.
And thanne by the sufferaunce of God she was turmentid with
feueres, and he slow many men and bestis and made to be saide to
hem that were vexed with fendes that ther shulde be gret mortalite 85
thoroughoute Antioche but yef Iustyne wolde consent to hym. For
whiche thinge all tho of the citee languisshed by syknesse and
cryeden to the kynrede of Iustine that thei shulde marye her and
delyver the citee fro the gret peryle that yt was inne. But Iustine
wolde in no wise consent therto, wherfor she was manased to dye of 90
many onc. In the .vj.^{e} yere of mor[t]alite she praied for hem and
chased oute all the pestilence.

And whan the fende sawe that he myght in no wise profit after hys
entent, he transfigured hym in the lyknesse of Iustine for to
sclaundre her name and to scorne Ciprien, and avaunted hym that 95
he hadde brought her to hym. And whanne Cipren sawe her and
went yt hadde be Iustine he was fulfelled with ioye and saide: 'Now
welcome Iustine the fairest of al women.' And anone as Cyprian had
namid Iustine, the fende myght in no wise suffre that name but
vanisshed awaye as wexe or smoke.   100

And whanne Cipriane saw hym deceyued, he was full of sorugh
and began to be more brennyng in the loue of Iustine thanne he was
before and woke longe at the dore of Iustine. And as hym semyd he
chaunged ofte into the liknesse of a woman and sumtyme into the
lyknesse of a bridde by hys enchauntyng, but as sone as he come to 105
the virgines dore he apered neither woman ne bridde but Cipriane.
And Cladyen was chaunged into a sparw bi the crafte of the fende,
but as sone | as he fley to the wyndowe of the virgine he apered   f. 228ra
Cladyen and not a sparw. And thanne he beganne to tremble and to
drede how he might come downe for brekyng of hys necke. And 110
thanne Iustine made hym to be take downe by a laddre, and exorted
hym that he shulde cese of his cursidnesse lest he were punisshed
after the lawes as full of wyckednesse.

And thanne the fende, ouercome and confused in all thingges,

79–80 and founde . . . bedde²]*om.* E   80 and byclypped her] *om.* H1   to do] do H1, a
doo D   81 and knew] *om.* D   82 wont] *add* for to doo D   83 she] she *with* s *erased*
H1   85 be] go H1   86 thoroughoute] *add* alle D   87 by] *add* grete D
91 mortalite] morialite E   101 hym] *add* so D   104–5 woman . . . of a] *ins.* H1,
om. D   105 enchauntyng] enchauntementis D   108 fley] sti3ed D

115 retourned to Ciprian and stode shamfully before hym. And thanne
Ciprian saide to hym: 'Thou wreche, art thou not ouercome? What
cursidnesse is youre vertu that ye mow not ouercome a symple
mayde nether haue no power ouer her, but in contrarie wise she
ouercomithe you and throwithe you downe in euery point shamfully.
120 Telle me wherin it ys that she hathe so myche power ouer you?' And
the fende saide: 'Y wyll not tell the but yef thou suere to me that
thou shalt neuer parte from me.' And Ciprian saide: 'By whom shall
y suere?' And the fende saide: 'Thou shalt [swere] by my gret
vertues.' Thanne saide Ciprian: 'I suere by thi gret vertues that y
125 shalle not parte from the.' And the fende saide to hym: 'As sone as
she makithe upon her the tokene of the crosse, anone we wexe so
feble that we lese alle oure vertues and we melt awaye right as wexe
before the fire.' And thanne said Ciprian: 'Hit semith herby that he
[that] was crucified is grette[r] than thou.' 'Ye, suerly,' said the
130 fende, 'he is gretter and mightier in all thingges, and he deliuerithe
all tho that we deceyve here for to turmente in the fire that may not
be quenched.' And thanne Ciprian saide: 'It ys good that y be made
seruaunt and frende to hym that was crucified lest y falle hereafter
into suche peynes.' And the fende saide to hym: 'Thou hast suore by
135 the vertues of my strengthes that none may forsuere that thou shalt
f. 228rb neuer departe from me.' To whom Cipriane saide: 'I dispise | the and
al thi vertues that bene as smokis, and I forsake the and alle the
fendes of hell, and y marke me with the [signe] of the crosse.' And
anone the fende parted fro hym all confused.
140   And thanne went Ciprian to the bisshopp. And whanne the
bisshopp sawe hym he went he hadde be come for to putte the
crysten in errour and saide: 'Suffice the, Ciprien, hem that be
withoute, for thou mayst not ayenst the Chirche of God, for the
vertu of Ihesu Crist may not be ouercome.' And Ciprian saide: 'I am
145 certayne that the vertu of God, Ihesu Crist, is vnuincyble.' And
thanne he tolde what had befalle hym and made hymself to be
baptised of the same bisshopp. And after that he profited gretly as
well in cunnynge as in lyff, so that whanne the bisshopp was dede he
was made bisshopp, and he putte the blessed virgine [Iustine] in a
150 monastarie and made her abbesse of many holy virgines.

118 mayde] 'virgyn' H1   she] but D   120 it] om. H1   123 saide] add that EH1
swere] om. E   129 that] om. E   gretter] grette E   129–30 gretter . . . he is] om. H1
131 to] ins. H1   may not] neuer mai D   136 dispise] forsake D   137 bene] add
but D   138 signe] token EH1   146 hym and made] om. H1   148–9 was . . .
bisshopp] ins. H1   149 Iustine] om. E

Seint Ciprian thanne sent pistles to martres and comforted hem in her batayle. And the erle of that region herde that gret renoun of Ciprian and of Iustine and made hem for to be presented before hym, and asked hem whedir thei wolde do sacrifice. And whanne he sawe that thei abode in the faithe of Ihesu Crist stabilly, he 155 comaunded that thei shulde bothe be putte in a caudron full of wexe and of piche and of grece and therin for to be boyled, and all that gaue hem a mervailous refresshing and dede hem no manere of harme. And thanne the prest of ydoles saide to the prouost: 'Comaundithe that y be sette before the caudron and y shalle 160 ouercome alle her vertu.' And than he was brought forthe and saide: 'Grete is the god of Ercules and Iupiter the fader of goddes.' And anone the fire went from under that caudron and brent that preste all euery dele. And thanne thei toke oute Cipriane and Iustine of the caudron and sentence was yeue vpon hem | and thei weren f. 228va beheded bothe togederes. And her bodies were caste to the houndes 166 and there thei were .vij. dayes, and after that thei were bore to Rome, and now as men sayen thei resten atte Plesaunce. Thei suffered dethe in the .vj. kl. of October about the yere of oure Lorde .CC.iiij^xx. vnder Dyoclisian. 170

Here endithe the lyf of Seint Iustyne, and nexst begynnithe the lyves of Cosme and Damyan, Capitulum
.C.xxxvj.^m

Cosme and Damyan were bretheren of the citee of Ege and born of a religious moder that hight Theodora. And thei were taught in the art of phisik and thei receiued so gret grace of God that thei putte awey all syknesse not only of men but also of bestis, and thei dede alle for the loue of God withoute anythinge taking. A lady that had wasted 5 all her good in medicines went to the seintes and she bare fro hem her hele perfitely. And than she offered a litell yefte to Seint Damy, and he wolde in no wise take it, and so she coniured hym bi so gret sueringges that atte the laste withe miche daungere he graunted for to take it, not for couetise of the yefte but for to obeye to her 10 deuocion, and that he were not seye for to dispise the name of

152 batayle] batailis D   161 her] the D   163 from] add hem þat was D   that¹]
þe H₁

EH₁DH₂A₁A₂   6 the] þies H₁D   9 daungere] angre H₁   9–10 withe . . .
take] he toke D

oure Lorde by whiche he hadd be so sore coniured. But whanne
Seint Cosme wiste it, he comaunded that his body shulde not be
putte with his brotheres. But the night foluyng oure Lord apered to
15 Seint Cosme and a[s]cusid hys brother.

And whanne Lysias herde saye what thei dede, he lete calle hem
afore hym for he was iuge, and asked of hem her names and her
cuntreys and what fortune thei hadde. And thanne the holy martires
answered and saiden: 'Oure names be Cosme and Damyane, and we
20 haue thre other bretheren that hight Amory, Leonce, and Eupyen,
f. 228ᵛᵇ oure cuntre ys | of Araby, but cristen men know not what fortune ys.'

And thanne the iuge comaunded that they shulde brynge her
bretheren and that they shulde do sacrifice togederes to the ydoles,
but they dispised hem in all wise to do sacrifice, and than he
25 comaunded thei shulde be sore manacled bothe fete and hondes.
And as thei dispised the turmentis he comaunded that they shulde be
bounde bothe honde and fote with a cheyne and throwen in the see,
but thei were anone deliuered bi an aungell and taken oute of the see
and come ayen afore the iuge. And whanne the iuge sawe hem he
30 said: 'Ye ouercome the gret goddes by youre wichcrafte and dispisen
oure turmentis and makyn the see pesible. Teche me youre
wychecraftes in the name of your lorde Adrian, and y shal folue
you.' And as sone as he hadd sayd that worde two fendes come and
bete hym about the mouthe and about the uisage greuously, and he
35 beganne to crye: 'O good men, y praie you to praie for me to [y]oure
lorde.' And they praied for hym and the fendes vanisshed awaye
anone.

And thanne the provost saide: 'Se ye not how thei werkyn
proudely ayens me? I hadde thought to haue lete hem goo, but y
40 wol not suffre hem to blame my god[des] in this wise.' And thanne
he comaunded that thei shulde be caste in a gret fire, but anone the
flawme flye fer fro hem and slow many of hem that stode aboute
hem. And thanne thei were comaunded to be sette upon the turment
that ys called eculee, but thei were kepte with [an] aungel, and the
45 turmentours turmented hem aboue all mesure, and yet they were

---

12 oure Lorde] god D   15 ascusid] acusid EH1   19 answered] answheren H1
24 hem] *del.*   sacrifice] *add* togiders in þe idoles but þei despised hem in all wise to do
sacrafice *with* but . . . sacrafice *del.* H1   27 honde and fote] hondes and fete H1D
30 wichcrafte] enchauntementis and wicchecrafftis D   31 makyn] making H1
32 folue] loue D   34 he] *om.* H1   35 crye] *add* and sey H1   O] *add* yee D   youre]
oure EH1   38 provost] *add* anone D   40 goddes] god EH1   42 flye fer] fled D
hem'] him H1   44 an aungel] aungeles E

take aweye witheoute any hurtyng and went alle hole byfore the iuge.
And he made her .iij. bretheren be putte in prison and made Cosme
and Damyane to be crusified and | for to be stonid upon the crosse f. 229ʳᵃ
with the peple, but the stones turned ayen to hem that caste hem and
hurte many of hem. And thanne the iuge fulfelled with wodenesse 50
made take oute the .iij. bretheren oute of the prison and sette hem
byside the crosse and made Cosme and Damyane to be take downe of
the crosse and that thei shulde be shotte with arowes as thicke as .iiij.
knightes might shete to hem, and the arrowes turned ayen and
wounded many of hem, and the iuge was very wode for thei might do 55
no harme to the seintes. And whan he sawe that he was ouercome in
alle thinge he was full of anguisshe even to the dethe and made alle
the .v. bretheren to be hedid togederes. And the cristen men recorded
the worde that Seint Cosme had sayd how that they shulde not be
buried togeders, and as thei thought what thei wolde do, there come a 60
voys that saide: 'Thei be all of one substaunce and therfor burye hem
in one place.' And thei suffered dethe under Dioclusian that beganne
the yere of oure Lorde .CC.iiijˣˣ.vij.

An vpplondisshe man slepte with opin mouthe as he hadd
laboured in hys felde of whete, and a serpent entred into hys 65
mouthe. And thanne he awoke and felt no harme, and went home
to hys hous, and whanne it drow to night he beganne to be sore
turmented and cried pitously and called to hys help Seint Cosme and
Seint Damyan, but as hys peyne encresed he went to the chirche of
the holy martires and there he fell sodenly aslepe, and there the 70
serpent went oute thorugh hys mouthe as he come inne, and so he
was deliuered by her holy merites.

Another man that shulde go a ferre viage recomaunded hys wyf to
the holy martires Cosme and | Damyane, and gaue her a tokene that f. 229ʳᵇ
yef so were that he sent for her that she shulde come to hym. And 75
after that the fende transfigured hym in fourme of a man and knew
wel the tokyn and come to the wiff and brought the tokin from her
husbonde and saide: 'Thi husbonde hathe sent me fro that citee for
to bryng the to hym.' And she dradde yet for to go thedir and sayde:
'Y know wel the tokene, but for as moche as he lefte me in the 80

47 .iij.] .iijᶜ. E   49 that caste hem] om. D   hem²] om. H1   51 .iij.] .iijᶜ. E
53 thicke] fast H1   54 arrowes] apostels subp. 'arwes' H1   ayen] add to hem D
58 .v.] .vᶜ. E   59 that¹] of H1   that²] om. H1D   not] om. D   70 the¹ . . .
martires] these holie seintis D   and there] that H1   71 thorugh] of H1
76 fourme] to the liknes D   77 brought] add hire H1   78 that] þe H1

kepyng of Seint Cosme and Seint Damyan the holy martires, suere
me upon her auuter that thou wilt lede me suerly, and thanne y shall
go with the.' And he swore to her as she desired. And than she
folowed hym, and as she come by a preue place the fende wolde haue
85 throw her downe under her hors for to haue slayne her. And whanne
she felt that she cryed: 'The God of Seint Cosme and Seint Damyan
helpe me, for y leuid you and folued hym.' And anone the seintes
were there with gret multitude clothed in white and deliuered her,
and the fende vanisshed aweye. And thanne thei saide to her: 'We be
90 Cosme and Damyane vnder whos suerte thou wentist, and therfor we
haue hasted to come to the and to helpe the.'

   Felix pope the .viij. after Seint Gregory made a noble chirche atte
Rome of Seint Cosme and Seint Damyane. And a man seruid the
holy martires in that chirche, whiche man a cancre hadde wasted
95 away alle hys thye. And this man sleping, the holy martires apered to
him and brought with hem oynementis and instrumentis, and that
one saide to that other: 'Where shull we take nwe flesshe for to sette
in the place where we take aweye the rotyn flesshe?' And that other
said: 'There is an Ethiope, a man of Inde, is buryed this day al
f. 229ᵛᵃ fresshe in the chircheyerde.' | And they brought the thigh of the dede
101 man, and than thei cutte of the thighe of the sike man and sette in
that place the thighe of the dede man, and anointed the wounde
diligently and bare to the dede man his thigh. And whanne he awoke
and felt hymself withoute peyne, he putte hys honde to hys thigh
105 and felt no manere sore nother hurte. And thanne he toke a candell,
and whan he sawe nothinge in hys thigh, he thought he was not
hymself but that he was sum other. And whanne he come to hymself
he lepte oute of hys bedde for ioye and tolde to alle the peple what he
hadde sayen in hys slepe and how that he was helyd. And thei sent
110 anone in haste to the tombe of the dede man, and thei fonde hys
thigh cutte of and the thigh of the syke man was leyde in the tombe
in stede of that other. And they suffered dethe in the yere of oure
Lorde .CC.iiijˣˣ.vij.

82 me²] add to hym D   85 her²] þe D   86 The] to þe H1, to D   of] and D
87 helpe me] of helpe D   88 clothed] add alle D   91 hasted to] om. D   92 .viij.]
add day EH1   95 And] add as D   sleping] slept D   99 Ethiope] add for to sette in
the place where we take aweie the rooten flesshe. And the toþer side there is an Ethiope D
101–3 and than . . . diligently and] set it in þat place of the quikke man and thei cut of the
thi3e of the quikke man D   103 bare] add it D   his thigh] om. D   he] þe man D
105 hurte] hurtyng H1   candell] add for to see D   106 he³] it H1   107 other] add
man D

Here endithe the lyff of Seint Cosme and Damyan, and
nexst begynnithe the lyff of Seint Fursyn that was a
bysshop, Cap^m. ⟨.C.xxxvij.^m⟩

Fursin was a bisshopp and Bede wrote the storie of hym, and as he
shined in al goodnesse and vertues he yelde up the spirit and as yt
semyd cam to hys last ende. And whan he was passed he sawe .ij.
aungeles comyng to hym that bare hys soule, and the thridde come to
hym armyd with a white shelde shyning and he went before, and 5
after that he herde the fendes cryeng, and he herde how thei saide:
'Go we before and lete us make a batayle ayenst hym.' And whanne
thei were go forthe, thei made a gret bataile and caste venym and
brennyng dartes ayenst hym, but the aungel that went before
reskewed hem with hys shelde. And thanne the fendes setten | 10
hem ayenst the aungeles and sayde: 'He spake allwaye ydell wordes f. 229vb
and therfore he shulde not withoute peyne vse the blessed lyff.' And
the aungell saide to hem: 'But yef ye purpose ayenst hym the
principall vices, he may not perisshe for the lytell.'

   Thanne sayde the fende: 'Yef God be rightfull, this man shall not 15
be saued, for it ys wretyn: "Yef ye be not conuerted and made as one
of my children lityl, ye shull not entre into the kingdom of heuene."'
And the aungell in excusyng hym saide: 'We shull be iuged before
oure Lorde.' Thanne saide the accuser: 'Yef ye foryeue not to men
her synnes, the fader of heuene shal not foryeue you youres.' The 20
holy aungel saide: 'Where dede he any vengeaunce, or to whom dede
he any vengeaunce or wronge?' The fende saide: 'It ys not wretin
"yef ye do ueniaunce" but "yef that ye foryeue not with herte."' To
whom the aungell excusing sayde: 'The foryeuenesse of hert he
hadd, but by the custume of man helde hys pees.' To whom the 25
fende saide: 'Right as he toke euell by custume, so lete hym resseyue
euell by the souerayne iuge.' The aungell saide: 'We shull be iuge[d]
before God.' And thanne the aungeles beganne to fight and the
fendes were discomfit.

   And thanne the fende saide: 'A seruaunt that knowithe hys lordes 30
wille and dothe it not ys worthi to be blamed in many wises.' And
the aungel saide: 'What thing hathe not this man fulfelled of the will

EH1DH2A1A1; in D an excised initial affects 14 the—20 youres, 49 abode—53 said, 78
thi—83 whanne, and 107 And—108 lyff   1 Fursin] Seinte Fursyn D   9 hym] hem
H1   10 hem] hym D   11 allwaye] om. D   22 he] ye H1   27 iuged] iuges
EH1   28 aungeles] aungelle D   30 lordes] seruantez del. 'lordes' H1

of hys lord?' The fende sayde: 'He hathe resseyued a yefte of a
wikked man.' The aungel sayde: 'He went that eueryche had do
35 penaunce.' And the fende sayde: 'He shuld haue proued the
perseueraunce of penaunce and thanne to take the fruyt.' And the
aungel saide: 'Lete this be iuged of oure Lorde', but the fende felle |
f. 230ʳᵃ downe. But he redressid hym up ayen and byganne to bataile faste
and said: 'Till now y went that God had be verrey trewe that said
40 that synne [that] was not ponisshed in erthe shulde be ponisshed in
euerlasting peine. This here hadde a gowne of an vsurere and was
neuer yet ponisshed therfor, where ys now the rightwisnesse of
God?' And the aungel saide: 'Holde thi pees, for thou knowist not
the secrete iugementes of God, for as longe as man hopithe and is in
45 will to do penaunce, the merci of God is with hym.' And the fende
saide: 'Here is no place of penaunce.' To whom the aungell saide:
'Thou knowist not the depnesse of the iugementes of God.'
And thanne the fende smote hym so greuously that after that he was
restored to lyff the trace of the stroke abode. And thanne the fende
50 toke one of tho that thei turmented in the fire and threwe hym ayenst
Fursin that it brend greuously hys shuldre, and thanne he knewe that
it was the man of whom he hadd resseiued the clothinge. And the
aungel said to hym: 'For thou tokist that clothe, therfor he hadde
power to brenne the. Yef thou haddest not take the yefte of hym that is
55 dede in synne, this peyne shulde not brenne the, and this peyne of
brennyng thou must suffre, for thou receyuedest that gowne of hym.'
And thanne another fende saide: 'Yet shal he passe a streit yate
and there w[e] shull ouercome hym.' And thanne he saide to the
aungel: 'God comaundid: "Loue thi neyghheboure as thiself."' The
60 aungel said: 'This man hathe do Goddes werkes to hys neyghhe-
boures.' And the aduersarie saide: 'That suffisithe not but yef he
haue loued hem as hymselff.' To whom the aungel saide: 'The fruyt
of loue stont in good werkes, for God shal yelde to euery after his
f. 230ʳᵇ werkes.' And thanne the | enemy saide: 'Yet he shall be dampned for
65 he hathe not fulfelled the werke of loue.' And thanne that cursed
felawship fightynge with the aungel were ouercome.

35 proued] prouide H1, prouised D   37 but] and H1, and than D   39 Till now]
om. D   that¹] *add* thilke D   40 that²] *om.* ED   was] *om.* D   41 here] hy⟨..⟩ D,
hyne *or* hyue *with* Her *in margin* H2   44 as²] *add* a H1D   hopithe] *add* welle D
48 hym] Fursynn D   49 lyff] *add* and D   50 thei] wer H2   52 hadd] *om.* H2
55 synne . . . and] *om.* H1   57 streit] streiter EH1   58 we] w E   59 comaundid]
commaundith D   62 haue] had H1   63 euery] *add* man D   65 that] þe H1D
66 aungel] angels H1D

And yet the fende saide: 'But yef God be a passer of his owne
worde, this man may not be withouten peyne, for he behight to
renounce the world, and in the contrarie he hathe loued the world,
ayenst that he saide: "Louithe not the world, ne that therein ys."' 70
And thanne the aungel ansuered: 'He hathe not loued tho thingges
that be in the world, but he hathe louid wel to dispende the goodes
that bene of the world to hem that were nedi.' And the fende saide:
'In what wise euer thei be louid, thei be ayenst the comaundement of
God.'   75
And whanne these enemyes were ouercome, the fende beganne
ayen malicious accusacionis saieng: 'It is wretin: "Yef thou do not to
wete to the wickid his wickednesse, y shal requere [his] blode of thi
honde." This man hathe not denounced worthili penaunce to the
sinfull.' And the holy aungel said: 'Whanne tho that heren and 80
despisen the worde of the prechour, the tongge of the doctour is lette
to speke whan he seith that his predicacion ys herde and dispised, so
that it aperteinithe to the wise to holde [h]is pees whanne it is no
tyme to speke.' And ayenst the withsaieng of the fendes the bataile
was right stronge, so ferforthe thei come before the aungel of oure 85
Lorde and that the good hadde ouercome the wicked. And thanne
this holy man was bysette with right gret light.

And as Bede saithe, one of the aungelis bade hym beholde the
worlde. And thanne he turnid hym and sawe a derke vale and .iiij.
fyres in the eyre aboue that were ferre that one fro that other by 90
certayne space. | Thanne the aungel saide: 'These ben the .iiij. fyres f. 230ᵛᵃ
that brenne the worlde. The furst is the fire of lyenge, for in baptime
alle men behight to renounce the fende and to all his werkes and thei
fulfell it not. The secounde ys [of] coueitise, that is whanne the loue
of richesse of the world is sette before the richesse of heuene. The 95
thridde is dissencion, whanne a man dredithe not for to trouble the
soule of hys neyghboure by veyne thingges. The fourthe is
wickednesse, whanne thei lede to dispoile the most feble and for

67 fende] fendes E   69 contrarie] contray H1   world] worlde *with* r *on erasure* H1,
add and D   70 he] *add* hath D   Louithe] lowethe *with* w *changed to* v H1   therein ys]
þere is yn H1   74 wise] *add* þat H1D   louid] belouyde H1   77 accusacionis]
excusacions *changed to* accusacions H1   78 y] *om.* D   his²] *om.* ED   80 And] *add*
than H2   holy] *om.* D   81 lette] let't'e H1   82 speke] preche D   ys] *add* 'not' H1
dispised] dispisith D   83 it¹] *om.* D   his] is E   84 fendes] ffatai *followed by short*
space D   bataile] baile D   87 was] *add* al H1D   right] *om.* H1   88 And] *ins.* H1
one of] *om.* H1A1   91 Thanne] And þan H1D   92 that . . . of] *om.* H1   93 to²]
om. H1D   94 fulfell it not] fullfilled not H1, be nat fulfillid D   of] *om.* E, *add* þe H1
95 of¹] *add* þe H1   richesse] *add* and D

to do frauude to hem for not.' And after that tho fires beganne to
100 aproche and wexe togederes into one and neighed hym wonder faste.
And thanne he dredde hym and saide to the aungel: 'For this fire
[shal neigh] me'. And the aungel ansuered: 'That that thou hast not
alight shal not brenne the, for this fire examinithe men after her
merite, for right as the bodyes brenne by vnlefull wyllis, right in the
105 same wise he shall brenne by payne of dette.'

Atte the laste he was brought ayen to hys propre body, weping his
frendes, wenyng that he had be dede. And he lyued a while after and
endid hys lyff in preisable werkys.

Here endithe the lyff of Seint Fursyn, and nexst begynnithe the lyff of Seint Michael, Cap^m. .C.xxxviij.^m

The holi solempnite of Seint Michael ys callid apering, dedicacion,
victorie and mynde.

The apering of this aungel is in mani maners. The furst is whanne
he apered in the mounte of Gargan, for that is a mountaigne in Poyll
5 that hight Gargan and is byside the citee that ys called Sispent. And
f. 230vb in the yere of oure Lorde .iijC.|.iiij^xx.x. ther was in that citee of
Sispent a man that hight Garganus, that after sum bokes toke his
name of that mountayne, or ellys that the mountayne shuld take his
name of hym. And this man was right riche and hadde gret
10 multitude of shepe and nete. And as thei fedde hem abought the
costes of that hill, it fell that a bole lefte her felawship of bestis and
stied up to the hight of the hill and come not ayen home with his
felawshipp. And thanne the lord toke gret multitude of seruauntes
and made hem to seche hym ouer al, and at the last he was founde in
15 the hight of the mountayne bysydes the entre of a pitte. And thanne
the maister was meued for that he was go so astraied and shotte an
arwe atte hym, but anone the arwe turned ayen as it hadde be with a
wynde and smote hym that shotte hym. And tho of the citee were

99 do frauude to] defraude D   not] no`u3't H1   102 shal neigh] neighid EH1
that] om. D   not'] ins. H1   104 wyllis] will H1   108 hys] add blessid H2
preisable] profitable H1

EH1DH2A1A2; D has damage caused by excision from 1–3 and breaks off after 3
whanne   1 Michael] Mighell Michael H1   4 mounte] monthe with -he del. H1
6 Lorde] ins. H1   that] þe H1H2   8 or ellys . . . mountayne] om. H1   11 her . . .
bestis] his fellawis H2   15 the mountayne] that hille H2   16 maister] master with
aster del. and ayster inserted H1, lorde H2   was'] on erasure H1   that] om. H2   astraied]
astraie H2   17 atte] ayens H2

troubled with this thing and went to the bysshop and asked how thei
shuld do of this newe wonder thinge. And he enioined hem that thei 20
shulde faste .iij. dayes and praie to God. And whanne that was do,
Seint Michael apered to the bisshop saieng: 'Wete it wel that this
man is smyte with his dart by my will. I am Michael the archaungel
that will worship this place in erthe and suerly kepe it, and therfor y
haue proued that y am keper of this place by the shewyng of this 25
thinge.' And anone the bisshop and tho of the citee went a procession
to that place but thei durste not entre in but abode withoute in her
praiers.

The secounde apering was the yere of oure Lorde .vijC. and .x. in
a place that is called of the tombe, bysides the see, that is .vj. myle 30
fro the citee of Abriacency, that Seint Michael apered to the bisshop
of that citee and comaunded hym that he shulde make | a chirche in f. 231ra
the forsaid place and, as it was made in the mount of Gargane, that
he made it in the same wise in the name of Seint Michael and
halowid it in the mynde of hym. And the bisshop dredde hym of the 35
place where he shulde make it, and he bade hym that he shulde make
it there as he fonde a bole that was hidde with theues. And yet he
dredde of largenesse of the place, and he comaunded that he shulde
make it of the largenesse that he shuld fynde of the going about [of
the fete] of the bole. And there were .ij. roches that no mannys might 40
hadd power to meue. And than Seint Michael appered to a man and
comaunded hym to go to the said place and remeue tho .ij. roches.
And whanne the man come thedir he remeued the .ij. roches as
lightly as thou thei hadd weied nothinge. And whanne the chirche
was edefied there, Seint Michael leide a pece of the stone of marble 45
upon the whiche he stode. For as moche as in that place there was
gret lacke of water, thei made a well in a stone bi the techinge of the
aungel, and anone there ranne oute so gret habundaunce of water
that vnto this day it lastithe. And this apperinge is halowed solemply
in the said mountayn and in the same place in the .xviij. day of 50
Nouembre.

20 shuld] shul Hı   23 man] *add* that H2   dart] *add* is H2   27 her] *om.* Hı
29 .vijC.] .CCC. H2   30 called] *add* the place HıH2   .vj.] .vij. H2
31 Abriacency] Abriency H2   the²] to Hı   33 mount] mounth *with* h *erased* Hı
33–4 that he made it] so that was made H2   36–7 and . . . it] *om.* HıH2   38 and
he] For Mighelle H2   39 largenesse] *add* of the place H2   going] *add* in E
39–40 of the fete] *om.* E, the feete H2   44 thou] *om.* Hı   thou thei] he H2
45 pece] pytte H2   46 place] *punct. after* place Hı   47 gret] moche H2
47–8 the aungel] an angel Hı, Seint Mighelle H2   48 and] *add* þan Hı
50 mountayn] mounteynes H2

And there fill in that place a thinge worthi to be tolde for miracle.
That place is all environed with the Gret See, but on Seint Michael
Day she makithe weye to the peple. And as right gret felawship of
55 men went to the chirche, yt fell that a woman with childe ny her
deliueraunce was in [the] felawship. And whanne thei retourned, the
wawes come with gret strengthe so that the felawshippe for drede
fledde to the see side, but she was wrapped and take in the flodes of
f. 231rb the see, for she was so gret she might | not flee. But Seint Michael
60 the archaungel kepte the woman al hole so that she hadde childe
amonge the wawes of the see, and toke her childe in [her] armes and
gaue it sucke, and went oute ayen whanne the see withdrow hym al
hole and sounde with gret ioye of her childe.

The thridde aperinge come in the tyme of Seint Gregori the pope.
65 For whanne that same pope hadd ordeined the Grete Letanies for
the pestilence that was thanne and hadde right deuoutely praied for
the peple, he sawe stondinge the aungel of God upon the castell that
was called the mynde of Adryane, wyping his swerde that was all
blody. And thereby Seint Gregori understode þat his praiers weren
70 herde of oure Lorde, and thanne he made in that place a chirche in
the worship of Seint Michael and into this day the castell ys called
the castell of the holy aungell. [And] another apering was made in
the mount of Gargane whan he apered and gaue victorie to hem of
Sispont, and that day is halowed the .viij. day of Iuyn.

75 Another apering is made in the Storie Parted in Thre in a place
biside Constantinople where the goddesse Vesta was worshipped but
[it] is now otherwise, for there is made a chirche in the same place
and is called the place of Michael bicause of a man that hight
Aquilyn, whiche man was take with a brenninge feuer caused of gret
80 habundaunce of rede colere. And the fesicianes gaue hym [suche] a
drinke [for he] was so sette afire, by whiche drinke he fell in suche a
castinge that he might broke nother mete ne drinke. And in this wise
he was nigh dede, and thanne he made hymselff to be brought to that
f. 231va place and hoped | wele ther to receiue hele or sone to be dede. And
85 thanne Seint Michael apered to hym and bade hym that he shulde do

54 makithe] make'th' þe H1   to] vnto H1   as] om. H1   55 H1 punctuates after
chirche   56 the¹] om. E, that H2   57 with] add so EH1   58 side] om. H2   she]
this womman H2   in] with H1   60 hole] sauff H2   61 her²] om. EH1   67 the²]
an H1   68 all] so H2   72 aungell] add Seint Mighelle H2   And] om. E
73 mount] mounthe with he erased H1   77 it] om. E   78 of¹] add Seinte H2
80 fesicianes] Phicicien H2   suche] so that EH1   81 for he] om. EH1   afire] add with
the feuer H2

make hym a confeccion with honi, wyne and pepir, and that he shulde wete therein his mete that he ete as for his sauuce, and so he shulde be perfitly hole. And so he was, notwithstonding that after reson of phisik it ys holde contrarie to yeue drinkes that be hote to hem that be colerik, and in this wise saithe the Storie Parted in 90 Thre.

Secoundeli, this fest is called Victoriest. And the victori of that archaungel Michael is in mani maners bothe of hymselff and of other aungels. The furst is the victorie that he gaue to hem of Sispont in this manere. In a tyme after the fyndinge of this place, the peple of 95 Naples were atte that tyme paynimes and thei ordeined an hoste to fight in bataile ayenst hem of Syspont and of Bonyvent. So that, bi the counsaile of the bisshop, the cristen token truys of .iij. dayes that thei mighte fast tho .iij. dayes and beseche helpe and grace by the merites of her patron Seint Michael. And the thridde night Seint 100 Michael apered to the bisshop and saide hym that her praiers were herde, and behight hem the victorie and bade hem to go upon her enemyes on the fourthe hour of the day. And whanne thei beganne to renne upon her enemyes the mount of Gargan beganne gretli to tremble, and an houge tempest arose and al the hight of the hill was 105 couered with a thicke derkenesse in suche wise that .vjC. [h]ere aduersaries deieden by the shotte of cristen men that come from aboue oute of the eyre by vertu of the aungel. And thanne the remenaunt lefte her errour of her ydolatrie | and bicame cristen and f. 231vb submitted hem to the faithe. 110

The secounde victorie of Seint Michael was whanne he putte oute of heuene the dragon that was Lucifer with al his and alle tho that folued hym, whiche thinge is shewed in the Apocalipse wher it is saide: 'The bataile is made in heuene.' For whan Lucifer coueited to be evene with God, the archaungel Michael that bare the signe of the 115 heuenli oste came and chased Lucifer fro hevene and enclosed hym in derkenesse into the day of dome. For thei be not suffered to duelle in heuene neither in the soueraine partie of the erthe, for that it is a

86 wyne, pepir] *trs.* H1   87 shulde] *add* do H1   he] to *del.* 'he' H1
93 archaungel] *add* seint H2   other] *om.* H1   95 peple] men H2   96 paynimes]
paynyres *with* res *del.* 'mes' H1   98 of²] for H2   98–9 that . . . dayes] *ins.* H1
99 tho] *om.* H2   100 And] *add* he *del.* H1   103 the¹] *ins.* H1   105 hill]
mounteine H2   106 thicke] wicked H1   suche] *add* a H1   here] yere E, yere *changed*
to 'of' þere H1, men H2   107 of . . . men] *subp.* H1   113 Apocalipse] Apocalipses E
115 archaungel] angell H1   116 heuenli] holi H1   oste] goste *changed to* ooste H1
fro] *add* þe holi H1   117 into] to H1

placc clcrc and delectable, ne for to be among vs lest thei shulde
120 turment vs to sore. But thei be in the eyre betwene heuene and erthe,
so that whanne thei loke upward and beholde the ioye that thei lost
thei be turmented with grettest sorugh, and whanne thei beholde
dunward thei see soules stie up to heuene from whennis thei fell, and
thanne thei be turmented with grettest peyne of enuye. But by the
125 sufferaunce of God thei descende amonge us, and as it is shewed to
sum holy men, thei fle often tymes among us as flies and fulfell the
eyre without nombre. Wherof Hamon saith: 'As oure philisofers
sayen and oure doctours sayen, that the eyre is as full of fendes as the
sonnebeme is full of motes.' And though it be so that there be so
130 many, as after the sentence of Origene, thaire power is right litell,
and so litell that he that hathe be ouercome with any holy man, he
may neuer tempte hym ayen with that same vice in whiche he hathe
be ouercome.

The thridde victorie that the aungels haue euery day of fendes is
f. 232ra whanne thei fight for us a|yenst hem and deliuer vs from her
136 temptacionis. And thei deliuer us in thre maners. Furst in refrei-
ninge the might of the fende, as the apostell saithe of the aungel that
bonde the fend in the souerein desert. And this binding is not ellys
but that he refreinithe his might that he wolde haue ouer vs.
140 Secoundely thei deliuer us in refreyning oure couetise, the whiche
thinge is signified in Genesy in the .xxxij. chapitre wher he saithe
that the aungel touched the synow of Iacob and anone it dried up.
Thriddeli thei emprintin in oure hertes the mynde of the passion of
oure Lorde. And that is signified in the Apocalips in the .vij. chapitre
145 wher he saithe: 'Wyl ye not for to noye the erthe nother the see
nother the trees into [the] tyme we haue signed the servauntes of
God in her forhedes.' Also in Ezechiel the .ix. chapitre he saithe:
'The signe of thau shal be in the forhedes of weylinge men.' The
figure of thau is made in manere of a crosse, and he that is marked
150 therwith dare not drede hym of the smityng aungel. Wherfor it is

119 delectable] delitable H2   be] add here H2   120 to] om. H1   122 grettest]
right grete H2   sorugh] add and peine H2   123 up] vpward H1   124 grettest]
grete sorowe and H2   But] add offten tyme H2   125 and] ins. H1   127 Hamon] A/
man H1   128 sayen¹] seith H1   129 that there be so] om. H1   131 and so litell]
om. H1   hathe] om. H1   with any] by an H2   132 tempte] tempest H1
134 victorie] add is H1   haue] had H2   of] add þe H1   135–6 from . . . us] om. H2
136 us] add first H1A1   Furst] ins. H1   141 in²] om. H1   .xxxij.] .xij. H2
142 anone] ins. H1   143 emprintin] emprented H1   145 for] subp. H1   to] om. H1
146 the²] om. E   signed] signified H1   148 thau] þat del. 'hem' H1, hem H2
149 thau] þat H1, hem H2   he] ins. H1   150 dare] so with a on erasure H1

saide in the same place: 'Upon whom thou seest the signe of thau loke thou sle hym not.'

The fourthe uictorie is the whiche the archaungel Michael shal haue of Antecrist whanne he shal sle hym. For thanne the gret prince Seint Michael shal arise, as he saith in Daniel in the .xij. chapitre, 155 and he shal stonde ayenst Antecrist as a mighti defendour and a protectour of hem that be chosin. And after that, as the Glose saithe, Antecrist shal feyne hym to be dede and hide hym thre dayes, and after that he shal apere and saie that he is risen from dethe to lyff, and than bi his wichecrafte the fendes shull bere hym up into the 160 ayre as though | he stied up bi his owne vertu, and all the peple seing f. 232rb this shul worshippe hym with gret meruaile. And whan he shal be sette in his sege upon the Mount of Olyuete in that place wher oure Lorde stied up into heuene, Seint Michael shal come and sle hym. Of whiche bataile and victorie hit is understonde after Seint 165 Gregorie, the whiche is saide in the Apocalips, wher he saithe: 'Bataile is made in heuene, Michael and his aungels.' This worde of trebil bataile is vnderstond of that bataile that he hadd withe Lucifer whanne he droue hym oute of heuene, and of the bataile that he hathe with fendes that turment us, and of this laste. 170

This sollempnite is called also dedicacion, for in that day the said place in the mount of Gargane was halued bi reuelacion, and in this wise. Whanne thei were returned to Sispont from the discomf[i]ture of her enemyes and haddin had so noble a victorie, thei dredde to entre into the forsaide place and to halwe it to the archaungel. And 175 thanne the bisshop went to haue counceil of the pope that hight Pelagien. The pope saide: 'Yef the chirche shal be dedied, it were most acording that it were done in that same day that the victorie was done in, and yef it like otherwise to Seint Michael, we most requere his wille upon that matere.' And thanne the pope and the bisshop 180 with the peple of the citee fasted .iij. dayes, and Seint Michael apered thanne to the bisshop and saide: 'Ye haue none nede to dedie þat y haue edefied, for y that made the chirche haue halowed it', and comaunded hym that the day foluynge he shulde entre into the place

151 the²] þis H1   thau] taw H1, the crosse H2   153 the¹] om. H1   162 hym] hem H2   164 into] to H1   167 Bataile] The bataile H1   heuene] add of H2 170 hathe] ins. H1   with] add the H2   and] add also H2   and . . . laste] 'þe' last of H1 171 also] om. H1   said] seinte his H2   173 discomfiture] discomfuture E, disconfute H1   174 victorie] add yit H1   177 The . . . saide] and seide to hym H2   dedied] edefied H2   were] is H1   178 acording] conuenient H1   181 the¹] om. H1 184 the¹] om. H1   the²] þat H1

f. 232va with the peple and that thei shulde haunt | it with praiers and that
186 thei shulde make hym her special patron, and gaue hem tokin of the
forsaid consecracion, and that was that thei shulde stie up bi a
posterne towarde the est, and there thei shulde fynde the pase of a
man prented in the marble. And thanne the bisshop in the morwtyde
190 with gret peple come to the place and entred withinne and fonde a
gret caue and .iij. auuters, of whiche two were sette towardes midday
and the thridde was in the est right worshipfully, and thei were
couered al with rede manteles. And the sollempnite of masses were
halued and the peple had take and receiued her housill, and alle
195 returned with gret ioye to her propre places, and the bisshop lefte
there prestes and clerkes for to serue the place with diuine seruice.
And withinne that chirche there springethe up clere water and
delicious that the comune peple drinkithe, and mani diuerse siknesse
be heled with that water. And whanne the pope herde these thingges
200 he ordeined for to halw þat day in the worship of all the blessed
aungels and for to kepe it thorugh[oute alle] the worlde.

      Here endithe the lyff of Seint Michael, and nexst begin-
      nithe the lyff of Seint Ierome, Cap^m. .C.xxxix.

Seint Ierome was sone of a noble man that hight Bede born of the
castell Discrodoni that is in the ferrest ende of Damaske and of
Pa[n]onnie. And he beinge right yonge of age went to Rome and
lerned and stint not till he was perfitely taught in the letteres of
5 Greke, Latin and Ebrew. And his doctour of gramar hight Donat,
f. 232vb and for rethorik he hadde Vic|torin the aduocate, and he was night
and day ocupied in divine scriptures, and drowe it vnto hym
coueytously and after he poured it oute habundantly.
      And as he writithe in a pistle to Eustace that on a day as he hadde
10 redde coriousli Plato, for that the wordes lyked hym not in the bokes
of prophetes, he was aboute mid Lente take with a brenninge feuer,
and brought so lowe therewith that he was euene atte the dethe. And

188 shulde] shul H1   the pase of a] a place of H2   189 prented] perputid H2
the¹] *om.* H2   191 auuters] *add* therein H2   192 were] wered *with* d *erased* H1
193 couered] *ins. after* all H1   194 and¹] *add* 'whan' H1   and³] *subp.* H1
195 ioye] *add* retourned ayenne H2   197 and] *add* right H2   199 pope] peple *del.*
'pope' H1   200 the²] *om.* H1   201 oute alle] *om.* EH1

EH1H2A1A2; D resumes at 46 *that was* (for *that is*)   3 Panonnie] Pavonnie EH1
yonge] stronge H2   8 coueytously] vertuously H1   after] aftirwarde H2   poured]
pointed H1

as thei ordeined for the seruice of his deyeng, he was sodenli
rauisshed in iugement before God and it was asked hym what he
was and of what condicion, and he saide frely that he was a cristen 15
man. Thanne the iuge saide to hym: 'Thou failest full vntruli, for
thou art a citronyen and not cristen, for there as thi tresour is there is
thin herte.' And Ierome helde his pees. And thanne the iuge
comaunded that he shulde be right sharpeli bete. And thanne he
cried and said: 'Lorde, haue merci on me.' And tho that were 20
abought the iuge praied and mekeli besought the iuge that he wolde
haue merci on that yonge man. And he suore and saide: 'Lorde, yef
euer y rede in ani of tho seculer bokes y forsake the.' And thanne he
was lefte and foryeue bi his othe, and awoke and turned to lyff
sodenli, and his visage was al wete of teres and the trases of his 25
betinge apered bitwene his shuldres right pitously. And fro thennis
forwarde he redde the diuine bokes with as gret studi as he had redde
before the bokes of paynemes.

And whanne he was .xxix. winter olde he was cardinal and preste
in the Chirche of Rome, and whanne Lyberien pope was dede 30
Ierome was chose for to be pope. But whanne he be|ganne to f. 233ra
blame the dissolucion of prestis and of monkis and of the clergie,
thei beganne to haue hym in gret haterede and for to lye in awayte of
hym, and as Iohn Belet saithe, thei dede hym grete despite for the
clothinge of a woman. For as he rose in a night to Mateins as he 35
hadde in custume, he fonde that his enemyes had leyde bisydes his
bedde the clothinge of a woman, and he went yt hadde be his owne
and clothed hym therwith and went to the chirche. And his enuious
enemyes hadde do this to hym bi cause [that] men shulde deme that
he hadde kepte a woman in his chaumbre. 40

And whanne he sawe that, he thought to eschewe her malys and
went to Gregorie thanne bisshop of Constantinople. And whanne he
hadde lernid of hym holy scripture he went into a desert, and he
tolde to Eustachien how grete thingges he suffered there for the loue
of oure Lord. For whanne he was in that gret desert and in that wast 45
solitude that is so drie forscorched bi the hete of the sonne that she
yeuith to the monkes right a drie duellynge place, 'thanne went and

15 a] om. H1   19 right] om. H2   24 bi] om. H1   turned] add ayenne H2   25 wete
of] bi wette with H2   26 right] om. H2   fro] from with m subp. H1   27 redde¹] on
erasure H1   31–2 to blame] om. H2   33 hym] om. H1   of] for H1   35 For as] And
for H1   38 the] om. H1   39 that¹] om. EH1   41 he¹] Ierome H2   44 the] om. H1
46 solitude] solicitude H2   that is] that was H2   forscorched] scorchid D   the¹] add grete
H1D   46–7 she yeuith] shineth H1   47 thanne] Thei H1   went] add I D

supposed y for to be in the delytes of Rome, and my membris so
forscaldid that the drought hadd made hem to be right in like manere
50 as the skynne of a man of Ynde, and y was euer in sorugh and in
weping, and whanne dede slepe ouercome me that y might no lenger
refuse it, y leid my drie bones to the bare erthe. Of metys and of
drinkes y helde my pees, for tho that languisshen usyn only colde
water, and for to take ani sodeyn mete hit were to hem lecherie, and
55 y was ofte felaw with scorpions and wilde bestes, and notwithstonding al this the firy dartis of lecherie growed in my colde bodi and in
f. 233ʳᵇ my flesshe. And thanne y wept | continuely and daunted my prouude
flesshe with fasting wokis and dayes. And ofte tyme the day and the
night y cesed not to bete my breste, that restfulnesse and pesibilte
60 might be youen from oure Lorde. And y dradde my propre sel[le] as
knower of my thoughtes, and therfor reuenging me of myself y
passed allone the desertis. And as y toke oure Lorde to witnesse that
it semid to me as y hadde be in the felawship of aungels al tho .iiij.
yere that y dede there my penaunce, and thanne y returned ayen to
65 the place of Bethlem where as a wise beste y offered me for to duelle
in the creche of oure Lorde.' And thanne his closed bible that he had
made with gret studie and other bokes, he redde hem fastinge from
the morw to the evin. Mani disciples he gadered to hym for to
laboure with hym in [the] translacions of scriptures. .lv. yeer and .v.
70 monthes he laboured in holy ocupacion and was clene uirgine into
the laste ende of his lyff. And notwithstondinge that his legende
saithe that he was virgine, he wrote in this wise to Palmacion of
hymself and saide: 'Y shall bere uirginite with me to heuene, and not
for that y haue it, but for that y wondre that y haue it not.'
75   And atte the laste he might not rise for werinesse of so gret
trauaile, that there he laie in his bedde he hongid a corde bi a beme
that he might drawe hymself up therby whan he shulde arise for to
do the Office of the Chirche as he might.
        In a day after Euesong tyme, as Seint Ierome satte with his
80 bretheren for to here an holy lesson, there come sodenly amonge hem

48 the] om. H1   so] ins. H1   49 to] for to H1   52 of] om. H1   54 take]
make D   55 with scorpions] to serpentis D   56 growed] so with gr on erasure H1
58 And] ins. H1   day] daies H1   59 night] nightes H1   60 y] ins. H1   dradde]
add in H1   propre] om. D   selle] self EH1D (celle P2)   62 toke] take D   that] as del.
'that' H1   63 to] om. H1   al tho] And þe H1   65 for] om. H1   66 creche]
chirche H1   67 redde] herd del. 'he redde' H1   68 he] be H1   hym] hem changed
to hym H1   69 the] om. EH1 D   70 ocupacion] occupacions D   72 this wise to]
his life the D   72–3 of hymself/and saide] trs. with of ins. H1   75 the laste] ins. H1
77 arise] add & del. to H1   78 the¹] om. H1   of] in D   80 hem] om. D

into the chirche | a lyon holtinge sore. And whanne the bretheren f. 233va
sawe hym thei fledde, alle saue Ierome allone that arose and went
ayenst hym as to his gest. And anone the lyon shewid hym his fote
that was hurte, and thanne he called his bretheren and comaunded
hem that thei shulde wasshe his fete and that thei shulde diligently 85
seke where the wounde was. And whanne thei hadd so do, thei fonde
that the sole of the lyon[s] fote was sore hurte with thornes, and
thanne this holi man dede his diligence and cure for to hele it, and
whanne it was hole he duellid still with hem as a tame beste. And
whanne Seint Ierome sawe this, he considered and thought that God 90
of his goodnesse hadd not only sente this lyon to hem for helynge of
his fote but for sum other profit that shulde falle to hem bi hym,
[thanne he ordeined hym] an office bi the acorde of his bretheren and
that was that he shulde lede an asse to pasture and kepe her diligently
from wolues and fro all other harmes. This asse serued for the 95
bretheren for to bere her wode, and as this lyon was ordeined to do
so he dede. He waited truly upon the asse and as a good sheparde
went with her and came and wolde in no wise parte from her and was
to her a true defendour, and certaine tymes atte oures acustumed he
wolde bringe home the asse for to haue her bothe refeccion and 100
bringe her to the felde ayen.

And in a tyme as the asse went in her pasture and the lyon was
faste aslepe, there passed by her marchauntes with cameles and sawe
the asse allone and toke her and ledde her forthe with hem. And
whanne the lyon awoke and fonde not his felawe, he went roringe 105
here | and there, and whanne he sawe that he coude in no wise finde f. 233vb
her he came al sorufulli to the yates of the chirche and durst not for
shame entre withinne as he was wont. And whanne the bretheren
sawe that he was latter come thanne he was wont and withoute the
asse, thei went that he hadde bi nede of hunger ete the asse and 110
wolde not yeue hym his mete as he was wont to haue, but saide to
hym: 'Go and ete that other partie of the asse and fulfell thi glotenie.'

And for that thei wolde wete whedir he hadd done this euell dede

82 hym] the lyon D   saue] *add* oonelie D   85 that . . . shulde] to H1   87 lyons]
lyon E   88 man] *add* Seinte Ierome D   and¹] an'd' H1   89 it] he D   92 hym]
this lyonne D   93 thanne . . . hym] *om.* E, 'and so he ordeyned hym' H1   94 to] *add*
his D   96–7 do so] kepe the asse D   97 He] so and D   98 went] *twice once del.*
H1   99 atte] and D   100 her bothe] *trs.* H1   refeccion] refeccions H1
104 forthe] *om.* H1   hem] him *changed to* hem H1   105 roringe] *add* vp and downe H1
106 whanne] *ins.* H1   that] *ins.* H1   107 chirche] monasterie D   108 wont] *add* for
to doo D   109 latter] late'r' H1   110 that he hadde] *ins.* H1   bi] for H1
113 that] *om.* H1

or none, thei went into the pasture for to wete yef thei coude finde
115 ani partie of the asse or ani shewinge of her dethe, and thei fonde no
maner thinge and thei tolde so to Seint Ierome. And he comaunded
hem that thei shuld leye upon the lyon the office of the asse, and
thanne thei went and gadered wode and leyd [it] upon the lyon, and
he bare it mekely.

120   So in a day as he hadde do his office, he went oute to the feldes
and beganne to renne bothe here and there, desiringe for to knowe
where the asse his felaw was bicome. And thanne he sawe afer
marchauntes that came with cameles charged, and the asse went
before hem, for the manere of that contrei was that whanne men
125 went in ferre contre with cameles thei wolde make an hors or an asse
to go before for to make hem to go more right in her waye, and he
shulde bere a corde abought his necke for to drawe hem. And
whanne the lyon hadde knowin the asse he beganne to rore upon
hem and ranne upon hem so fersly with horible voys that the cameles
130 were all afraied, and he constreined hem alle charged as thei were to
go right to the celle. And whanne the bretherin sawe this thei tolde
f. 234ʳᵃ [it anone] to Seint Iero|me, and he bade hem to make purueiaunce
for her gestis and wasshe her fete and yeue hem mete and abide and
see the will of God upon this werke.

135   And thanne the lyon beganne to renne thorugh the chirche meri
and gladde as he was wont, and laye hym downe before eueri brother
and fawnid upon hem with his tayle and made gret ioye. And
therwith come one to Seint Ierome and saide that there were gestis
withoute the gate that wolde speke with hym. And whanne the abbot
140 come to hem anone thei fell downe on her knees at his fete and
besought hym of foryeuenesse, and he toke hem up goodly and
praied hem that thei wolde take her owne good and take none others.
And thanne thei praied hym humbli that he wolde take half her oyle,
and he refused it and wolde not. And atte the last with gret instaunce
145 he graunted to take a sertaine mesure, and thanne thei promessed
that thei wolde euery yere paie a certaine mesure to that chirche
whiles thei liued, and her heires after hem.

114 none] no Hɪ   115 shewinge] sheding Hɪ   118 it] om. EHɪ   120 So] And so
HɪD   to] into Hɪ   121 bothe] om. D   123 that] ins. Hɪ   124 that¹] þe Hɪ
125 in] into Hɪ   126 for] om. Hɪ   more] þe D   127 a corde] accord HɪD
129 fersly] fresshli Hɪ   130 he] the lionne D   131 right] add even D   celle]
monasterie D   132 it anone] om. EHɪ   to¹] it Hɪ   133 yeue] yafe D   abide] aboode D
135 meri] merili Hɪ   136 and gladde] om. Hɪ   wont] add to doo D   downe] add as he
wonte to doo D   139 the abbot] seinte Ierome D   143 that he wolde] to Hɪ   144 he]
ins. Hɪ   not] add take it D   146 paie] add such EHɪ   that²] þe Hɪ

And it was the custume of olde tyme that whoso wolde singe in that place he shulde not be lette, and for that cause the emperour Theodesyen besought the pope Damassien for to ordeine sum wise 150 [and] devout man that wolde ordeine for an Office and a Rule of that Chirch. And thanne he wost wel that Ierome was perfit in the tonge of Greke and of Latin and of Ebrewe and in alle cunnynge, and committed that souerain office to hym. And thanne Ierome deuised the Saughter by the feries, and deuised to eueri feri his propre 155 Nocturne and ordeined the *Gloria patri* for to saie in the ende of eueri psalme. And after that he ordeined resonabli the episteles and the gospeles and other | thinge pertinent to the Offis of the Chirche f. 234rb thorugh the cours of al the yere, and sent that ordenaunce fro Bedlem to the pope and to the cardinales, and he was gretly preised 160 of hem and his Office confermed in the Chirche perpetualy. And after that in that one side of the creche where oure Lorde laie, he made his graue, and whanne he hadd fulfelled .iiij^{xx}. yere and .viij. and .vj. monthes he slepte in oure Lorde and was beried there.

And it shewithe wel how Seint Austin had hym in gret reuerence 165 bi the episteles that he wrote hym, in one of the whiche he wrote unto hym in this manere: 'To his right dere frende and right pure bi honeste of lyvinge and right stronge and mighti embracer of charitee.' And elliswhere he writithe in this wise: 'Seint Ierome, holy preste, taught in the tonge of Latin, Grewe and Ebrewe and in 170 all holy writte into his last age, of whiche the nobilnesse of his faire langage shined fro the est into the west as the brightnesse of the sonne.' The blessed Prosper saithe also of hym: 'The holy prest Seint Ierome was in Bedlem sum tyme clere to the world and serued bi noble studie and kunnynge to alle the Chirche.' He saide also of 175 hymself to Ambigense: 'I enforced me neuer so miche fro my childehode to nothinge as for to eschewe a swellinge corage and a lyft up hede, callyng ayenst her the hate of God.' And: 'Y haue euer dredde the seure thingges.' And: 'With al myn herte y haue entended to the Chirche to hospitalite, and y haue resseiued gladly alle comers 180 and wesshe her fete, sauf onli heretikes.'

151 and'] a EHı   153 in] of Hı   157 episteles] Pistille D   the²] *om*. Hı
158 gospeles] Gospelle D   thinge] þinges Hı   pertinent] perteynyng Hı   Chirche] *add* and
that E, *add* and Hı   162 that one] the too D   creche] chirche HıD   where] w'h'ere Hı
163 fulfelled] *om*. D   166–7 in one … unto hym] *om*. D   167 unto hym/in this manere]
trs. with in to *for* unto Hı   right²] *om*. Hı   bi] and D   170 and'] *om*. Hı   175 and] all
Hı   178 up] *add* his Hı   179 And] *om*. D   herte] mynde D   180 Chirche] *add* and D
haue] *add* alleweie D   gladly alle] *om*. D   gladly alle/comers] *trs*. Hı

Hit is wretin also of Icrome bi Severus, that was disciple of Seint

f. 234va Martine and was | in his tyme in this wise: 'Ierome bysides the merite
of his faithe and the doweri of vertu was not onli lerned in Latin and
185 in Greke but also in the letteres of Ebrew. He was so taught that in
alle kunnynge there durst none make comparison with hym, the
whiche hadde continuel werre ayenst wicked men. The heretikes
hated hym, for he lefte neuer to werrei hem, the clerkes hated hym,
for he blamed euer her unthriftely lyff, but alle tho that were good, of
190 clerkes and other, loued hym and praised hym and ioyed of the
goodnesse of hym. And tho that demed hym an eretik, thei woxen
mad. He was euer besi in lesson or in bokes, wrytinge or redinge
night and day, continuelli ocupied.'

And as he writithe hymself he suffered gret persecusion of wicked
195 tunges, the whiche he suffered paciently as it shewithe bi a pistle that
he wrote to Assell: 'I yelde thankingges to God that y am wordi that
the worlde hate me, for y wote wel that me[n] comithe to hevene bi
defame and by good fame. And y desire that the nombre of
misbeleuers wolde pursue me for the name and the loue of Ihesu
200 Crist. Mi will is that the reproef of this worlde arise ayenst me more
feruently so that y might deserue to be preised of Crist and for to
haue the mede of his beheste in his blisse.' And he passed to oure
Lord God full of vertues the yere of oure Lorde .CCC.iiij^xx.xviij.

Here endithe the lyff of Seint Ierome, and nexst beginnithe
the lyff of Seint Remigius, Cap^m. .C.xl.^m

Seint Remige conuerted to the faithe, as it is saide, the kinge of

f. 234vb Fraunce and alle | his peple. The quene of that londe in tho dayes
hight Clotildo and she was a full cristen ladi and enforced her with al
her powere for to conuerte her husbond to the faithe, but she might
5 not in no wise. And whanne she hadde bore a childe she wolde haue
baptised it, but the kynge forbade her in all wise, but in no wise she
coude liue in reste till the kynge had graunted her that it were

183 his] this D   EH1 *begin quotation at* In this wise   187 hadde] *add* euer D
continuel] continualli H1   188 werrei] werre with D   189 tho . . . were] *om.* D
192 was] washh *with* -hh *erased* H1   besi] beseli H1   or²] *add* in H1   194 suffered]
suffreth H1   195 suffered] suffreth H1   as] And D   197 the worlde] þei wold
changed to þe wo`r´ld H1     men] me E, me`n´ H1   198 y] bi D   202 beheste] be left
changed to be hest H1   203 God . . . vertues] *om.* H1   the . . . Lorde] `þe ȝere´ H1

EH1DH2A1A2   1 Remige] Remy *changed to* Remigy H1   2 and alle] *ins. and add*
of H1   5 wolde] word *changed to* wold H1   6 her] it D   7 coude] *add* not H1

cristened. And as sone as it was cristened it deied. And thanne the kinge saide to the quene: 'Now it apperithe wel that Crist is but a symple god whan he may not kepe the lyff of hym that be his faithe might haue be lefte up into 't'his kyngdom after me.' And the quene ansuered and saide: 'I thanke my Lorde God with al myn herte, for hereby I fele and hope uerely that y am acceptable and loued of hym, for y wote wel that he hathe resseiued the furst fruytes of my wombe, and the kingdom without ende, whiche is moche beter thanne thine, he hathe youe to my sone.

And thanne she conseiued ayen and had another sone that she gate to be cristened with mani praiers as she gate the furst, and as sone as it was cristened hit felle so sike that no creature supposed lyff therof. And thanne said the kynge to the quene: 'Now suerli thi god is a feble god, that may not kepe the liff of none that is baptised in his name. And thou haddest a .M^l. and that thou woldest cristen hem, thou shuldest lese hem alle.' But notwithstondinge al that, the childe recouered and hadde perfite hele and regned after his fader. And this true blessed ladi enforced her in al that she might for to haue brought her husbonde to the faithe, but he refused it in alle wise. But it is saide in that other fest | that is after the twelfe tyde how the kinge was conuerted to the faithe.

And the forsaid kinge Cleovise whanne he was cristen he wolde endowe the chirche, and said to Seint Remigie that he wolde yeue as moche londe as he might ouerride while he slepte after None. And so it was done. But withinne the same grounde that Seint Remigie had gotin there was a mille, and as the seint went aboute to close his ground the milwarde putte oute the seint bi gret despite. And Seint Remigie saide to hym: 'Dere frende, lete it not greue the, though this mille serue us bothe.' But for al that he putte hym out, and anone one of the whelis of the mille beganne to turne contrariewise, and thanne he cried after Seint Remigie and saide: 'Seruaunt of God, come and lete us haue the mille togederes.' And he saide: 'It shal nother be thine ne myne', and anone the erthe opened and swolued in the mille all hole.

After this Seint Remegie knew that there shulde falle a gret famyne, and gadered togedre a gret quantite of whete, and the

10

15

20

25

f. 235ra

30

35

40

---

8 And . . . cristened] *ins. with* also *for* as H1   11 this] his D   12 ansuered and] *om.* D   19 supposed] *add* þe H1   25 in] *om.* H1D   26 but . . . wise] *twice, once del.* H1   34 milwarde] miller H1   39 come] *add* hiþer H1   he] seint Remigee D saide] *add* ayenne D

dronkin churlcs of thc cuntre scorned hym and his wisdom and sette
45 fire in his garneres. And whanne he wost it he come thedir and for
that he was of colde age and drow faste to Euesonge warde into
declyning of his lyff, he warmed hym with glad chere and saide that
fere was euermore good and holsom. But alweys tho that had do this
dede and al her kinrede after hem were brokin in here membres and
50 the women were gowtous. And in this wise it felle in that towne into
the tyme of Kinge Charles that chased hem oute and disparpled hem.
    And it is to wete that the feste of his passinge oute of this worlde is
f. 235rb in the monthe of Iani|ver. And this is said the fest of the translacion
of his holy bodi. For whan after his dethe his holy bodi was bore to
55 the chirche of Seint Timothe and of Seint Apoloneyr, he beganne to
peise so heuy whanne he was nigh the chirche of Seint Cristofere so
that vnnethes thei might not meve hym in no wise. And atte the laste
thei constreined and praied to oure Lorde that he wold vouchesauf
for to shewe hem whedir he shulde be beried in the chirche of Seint
60 Cristofre, in whiche chirche there rested a .M^l. reliques of seintes,
and anone thei lefte up the bodi lightly and beried it worshipfully.
And mani miracles encresed within that chirche so that thei most
encrese the chirche, and thanne thei made an oritarie behinde the
auuter, and wolde haue digged up the bodi for to haue beried it in
65 the oratorie, but thei might not meue the bodi in no wise. And
[thanne] thei went al to praier and woken till midnight, and in the
morutide whanne thei rose thei fonde the bodi in the place that thei
had made, borun thedir with aungels, and that was in the kalendes of
Octobre. And after that longe tyme in that same day he was sette
70 with all his shrine of seluer in a more riche shrine, about the yere of
oure Lorde .CCCC.iiij^{xx}. and .x.

45 whanne he] *ins.* H₁   46 that] *om.* H₁   colde] olde H₁D   48 fere] Feire H₁
euermore] euere D   alweys] alle D   49 her] þe H₁   here] þe H₁   50 the women]
þei H₁   gowtous] goutisshe (?) D   in this wise] thus D   that] þe H₁   into] vnto H₁
51 disparpled] disparkeled H₁   52 oute] *om.* H₁   54 of his] *twice, once subp.* H₁
whan] *om.* D   bodi²] *om.* D   57 vnnethes] *add* þat H₁   not] *om.* H₁
58 constreined] *add* hem D   and] *om.* H₁   59 for] *om.* H₁   whedir] where H₁
62 most] must H₁   62-3 most encrese] encresid D   63 chirche] *add* gretelie D
64 the] *add* holie D   66 thanne] *om.* EH₁   68 kalendes] kalenders H₁
70 seluer] *add* and H₁

Here endithe the lyff of Seint Remigie, and nexst beginnithe the liff of Seint Leodegari, Cap^{m}. .C.xlj.^{m}

Leodegare whiles he shined in vertues and disseruid to [be] bisshop
of Aclus, and whan Clotarie kinge of Fraunse was dede he was gretli
greued with the cure of the reaume, in so miche that bi the will of
God and bi the counsaill of baronis he made | Childeriche brother of f. 235va
Clotair, a couenable childe, kyng and crowned hym. But Eubronyen 5
wolde haue made kynge Theodorik, brother of that Childerithe, not
for the profit of the peple, but [for that] he was take fro his power
and was hatid of alle so that he dradde the wrathe of the kynge and of
the princes. And for that cause he asked l[e]ue of the kynge and
entrid into religion. And he graunted hym, and thanne [he] made 10
putte in warde Theodorik his brother, lest he shulde ymagine
anithinge ayenst hym and ayenst the reaume, and so by the holynesse
and good purueaunce of the bisshop alle thei were in ioye and pece.

In a litell while after, the kinge, empeired bi the counscile of sum
wicked folke, was meued to hate ayenst the servaunt of God, so that 15
[he] entended besily how that he might [couenablie] putte hym to
dethe. But Leodegar suffered alle full paciently and he helde all his
enemyes right as his frendes, and dede so moche towarde the kinge
that he dede the seruise afore hym on Ester Day in the citee where
he was bisshop. And that day it was tolde hym that the kinge had 20
ordeined for to perfourme the ordenaunce of his dethe. But he
dradde nothinge, but that same day dined atte the kingges borde, and
thanne he fledde his pursuer in suche wise that he went to the
chirche of Lucan and there he scrued God and to Eubronyen that
hidde hym there in abite of a monke in grete charite. 25

And thanne withinne a litell tyme after, the kinge deyed and
Theodorik was enhaunsed to the kingdom. For whiche thinge
Leodegare was meued by [the] wepinge of the peple and constreined
by comaunde|ment of his abbot for to retorne to his citee, but f. 235vb
Eubronyen renounced anone his religion and was made stuarde of 30
the kingges hous. And thow it were so that he was right euell
af[or]de, yet he beganne now to be moche worse after, and studied

EH1DH2A1A2   1 be] the E   2 Aclus] Achis H1   Clotarie] Clotaire þe H1
5 Clotair] *add* and H1   6 that] *ins.* H1   7 for that] *trs.* E   take] *om.* D   9 leue]
loue EH1   10 he²] thei E   12 anithinge] any þinges H1   13 and¹] *add* þe H1
14 after] *om.* D   16 he¹] *om.* E   couenablie] *om.* EH1   to] *add* a couenable EH1
23 suche] *add* a H1   26 litell tyme] while D   tyme] *ins.* H1   28 the¹] *om.* E
29 retorne] *add* ayenne D   31 thow] thought D   32 afore] aferde EH1D (*auant* P2)

with alle his might for to hate Leodegare and sent knyghtes for to take hym. And whanne Leodegare wost it he wolde haue escaped her
35 malys, and as he went oute of the towne in bysshoppes habit he was take of the knyghtes, the whiche drowe oute the eyen of his hede.

And thanne .ij. yere after that, Seint Leodegare with Garin hys brother that Eubronyen hadde exiled were ledde in despite of Eubronyen into the paleys of the kinge. And as Eubronyen scorned
40 the bisshopp he ansuered full wisely, and notwithstondinge that, Eubronien sent Garin for to be stoned with stones, and al a night he made lede the bisshopp barfote thurgh a rennynge water full of sharpe stones. And whanne he herde that he preised God in his turmentis, he made hys tunge to be cutte of, and after that he made
45 hym to be kepte in prison for to suffre nwe turmentes. But he loste neuer the worde, but entendid for to preche and to praie as he might, and tolde byfore how this Eubronyen and he shulde deye and whanne thei shulde deye. And thanne a gret light in manere of a crowne beclipped his hede so that many one sawe it. And whanne
50 any asked hym what thinge that was, he sette hym anone upon his knees in prayers and yeldid thankingges to God and councelled all that were there that they shulde chaunge her lyff into betyr.

And whanne Eubronyen herde that, he had enuie and sent .iiij. mordereres and comaunded that he shulde be biheded. And whanne
f. 236ra thei ledde hym | he saide to hem: 'It is no nede that ye trauaile
56 further, but dothe here the desire of hym that sent you.' And thanne .iij. of hem had so gret pitee that thei kneled downe and bisought hym foryeuenesse, and whanne the fourthe hadde byheded hym he was anone rauisshed with the fende and caste hymselff in the fire and
60 endid his lyff cursedly.

And thanne .ij. yere after, Eubrongen herde that that holy bodi was enlumyned and shined by gret miracles, and he turmented bi gret enuye sent a knight thedir for to wete the trouthe. And whanne this proude knight come thedir in grete dispite, he smote the tombe
65 with his fote and saide: 'Euel dethe take hym that beleuithe that this dede bodi may do myracles.' And anone he was rauisshed with

33 with alle his] as he H1D   34 haue] om. H1   37 Seint] om. D   41 a] þe H1
42 barfote] om. D   rennynge] add ryver of H1   43 herde] sawe D   44 he¹] Than
Eubronien D   of] out of his heede D   45 loste] leffte D   46 the] om. H1   worde]
add of god D   to²] om. H1   47–8 and³ . . . deye] om. D   50 thinge] om. D
52 that²] om. H1   55 is] add now H1   trauaile] add any D   58 hym¹] add of D
60 his lyff] ins. H1   61 after] add þat H1D   holy] om. D   65 that²] om. H1
66 dede] om. D

fendes and deied sodenly and worshipped the seint by hys dethe.
And whanne Eubranien herde that, he was thanne more turmented
with malice of enuye and enforced hym to quenche the renome of
that seint, but after that the seint hadde saide before and in suche 70
wise he slowe hymself with a swerde. And this seint suffered dethe
about the yere of oure Lord .vj.C.iiij^{xx}. in the tyme of Constantine
the ferthe.

Here endithe the lyff of Seint Leodegari, and beginnithe
the lyff of Seint Fraunceys, Cap^m. .C.xlij.^{m}

Fraunceys, seruaunt of God and frende to the right Lorde, was bore
in the citee of Asise and was made marchaunt wel nigh .xxv. yere
olde and wasted his tyme in vanite. And oure Lorde corrected hym
by beting of syknesse and chaunged hym sodenly in another man, so
that he beganne for to shine by sperit of prophecie. For in a tyme as 5
he was take of the Perses and was putte into a cruel prison, and alle
hys felawes were sori and hevy and he alone | was gladde and mery. f. 236rb
And whanne his felawes undertoke hym he ansuered and saide:
'Wetithe wele that y reioyse me for that y knowe wele that y shall
hereafter be worshipped as a seint of alle the worlde.'   10
   He went in a tyme to Rome bi cause of deuocion, and dede of alle
his clothes and clothed hym in a beggers clothinge and sate amonge
the pore men before the chirche of Seinte Petre and ete hastely right
as one of hem and gredely, and yet more wolde haue done yef the
shame of his knowleche had not take it fro hym.   15
   The olde enemy of mankynde enforced [hym] for to take awey his
purpos fro his gostly hele and shewyd hym a woman horribly
disfigured that was in the citee and sayd hym yef he lefte not that
purpos that he hadde take he wolde make hym lyke to her. But he
was comforted with oure Lorde and herde a voys that saide hym: 20
'Fraunceys take b[ite]r thingges for the suete and dispise thiself yef
thou coueite to knowe me.'
   He mette in a tyme a mesell, and such men be naturally dredde,

69 enforced] forced H1   70 suche] add a H1

EH1DH2A1A2L   E breaks off after 490 an; D breaks off after 185 upon the and resumes
at 431 neuer: L f. 339va omits 224 toke to 305 pouerte with no break in the text.   2 wel]
fulle D   3 olde] om. D   Lorde] ins. H1   4 in] into H1D   6 the] om. H1
14 and^1] add right D   yef] ner for D   15 had not take] þat toke D   16 hym] om.
EH1   17 fro] of H1   20 was] add anone D   21 biter] betir E   22 coueite]
add for H1   23 mesell] add also D   such . . . naturally] shoned that man bi naturelle D

but he bethought hym of the worde that was saide to hym fro God
25 and ranne to hym and cussed hym, and anone he disapeired. For
whiche thinge he went to the duellynge of pore men and of sike men
and kissed devoutly her hondes and gaue hem money.

He entred in a tyme into the chirche of Seint Damyan for to praie,
and the ymage of Ihesu Crist aresonid hym by miracle and saide:
30 'Fraunceys, go and make ayen my hous that is al destroied as thou
seest.' And from that houre the soule of hym was al moltyd and the
passion of Ihesu Crist was merveyllously fiched in his herte so that
he sette alle his entent for to repaire the chirche, and solde alle | that
f. 236ᵛᵃ euer he hadde and gaue the money to a prest, and he durst not take it
35 for drede of his kynne, and he caste it before hym in dyspisinge it as
duste. And thanne he was therfor takin of his fader and bounde and
yelde hym all his siluer and lefte [hym] al hys clothes and went al
naked to oure Lord and clothed hym with the haire. And thanne
went the seruaunt of God to a symple man, the whiche he toke in
40 stede of a fader, and praied hym [that] right as his fader dubled his
curses upon hym that in contrarie wise he wolde blesse hym. And his
bodely brother that sawe hym in wynter tyme couered with vile
cloutes tremblynge for colde and besily entendinge to prayer saide to
a felowe of his: 'Go to Fraunceis and bidde hym sell to the a
45 peniworthe of his suetinge.' And whan he herde it he ansuered
gladly: 'Y will sell it to oure Lorde.'

In a day as he herde in a chirche redde all the thinges that oure
Lorde taught to his disciples whanne he sent hem for to preche, and
anone he dressed hym with al his vertu for to kepe tho thinges, he
50 dede of his shone and his hosyn, and clothed hym with a vile cote
alone without mo, and toke a corde for to gerde hym in stede of a
gerdel.

He went in a tyme bi a wode in the tyme of snow and he was take
with theues, and thei asked hym what he was, and he said that he was
55 the messenger of God. And thei toke hym and threw hym in the
snowe, saienge: 'Lye there, thou churle messengere of God, for noble
and vnnoble, clerkes and laie men haue dispised the worlde for to
f. 236ᵛᵇ folw hym.' And the holy fader taught hem | the perfeccion of the

24 the] þat Hɪ   25 he] *on erasure* Hɪ   26 to] into Hɪ   31 and] in HɪD
36 duste] a durst *with* r *subp.* Hɪ   37 hym²] *om.* EHɪ   39 symple] sinfull Hɪ
40 that] L, *om.* EHɪD   curses] courses *with* u *subp.* Hɪ   43 cloutes] cloþes Hɪ   to¹]
add his Hɪ   44 the] *add* of his Hɪ   46 gladly] *add* and seid Hɪ   50 cote] clothe
Hɪ   51 a corde] *one word* ED   53 went] *add* also D   54 said] *add* hem HɪD
57 and laie] seie that D

gospell was for to be take in pouerte, and that men shulde go bi the
waye of sympilnesse. 60

And thanne he wrote to hymselff a rewle after the gospell and to
his bretheren, the whiche Pope Innocent confermed. And thennes
forwarde he byganne more brenningly for to shede the worde of God
and for to go aboute to castellis and to citees by merueylous feruour.

And there was a frere that semed outeward of meruaylous high 65
perfeccion, and he was so streite in kepinge of his silence that he
wolde not be confessed bi worde but by sygnes. And as eueri man
preised hym as a seint, this holy man Fraunceis came thedir and
saide: 'Bretheren, lete be youre preysinge for y see nothinge in hym
as yet that is for to preise, for it is to drede that this be done bi 70
feyninge of the fende. Lete hym be taught and charged to shriue
hym twies a woke by worde, and yef he do it not, it is but temptacion
of the fende and a foule deceit.' And thanne the bretheren counselled
hym for to shriue [hym], and he leide his fynger on his mouthe and
shoke his hede and shewed that in no wise he wolde be shriue. And 75
thanne within a while after he turned ayen as an hounde to his
vomyte and went oute of his ordre and ended his lyff cursidly.

Seint Fraunceis was in a tyme weri of goinge and as he rode upon
an asse, and his bewpere Frere Leonard that folued hym afote was
weri also, and as he walked he thought in his herte and said to 80
hymself: 'Thi kyn and [myne] were not felawes.' And anone the holy
man lyght downe of his [as]se and saide to the frere: 'Hit sitte not to
me to ride and ye to go afote, for thou art more worthier thanne y.' |
And thanne was the frere sore abasshid and kneled doune and asked f. 237ra
hym foryeuenesse. 85

In a tyme as he passed by a pl[ace] a noble ladi come in gret haste
ayenst hym, and she come so faste that vnnethes she might speke for
lacke of brethe, and he asked her what she wolde. And she saide:
'Praie for me, Fader, for y may not perfourme the purpos [of] my
gostely hele that y hadde begonne for my husbonde that lettithe me 90
and dothe to me gret aduersitee in the seruice of God.' And he said
to her: 'Doughter, goo forthe thi way, for thou shalt haue anone

60 simpilnesse] simples H1   61 after] of D   65 And] Also D   of] om. H1
high] bi H1A1   66 so] om. D   70 to²] om. D   be] ins. H1   73 deceit] add of þe
feende D   74 hym²] om. E, ins. H1   81 myne] my kyn E   82 man] add
Fraunceis D   asse] horse EH1   83 ye to] to the D   thou art] ye ben H1   86 he]
seint Fraunceis D   place] pleke E, planke H1   87 ayenst] to D   89 me] my changed
to me H1   of] for EH1   92 to her] to me ayenne D

comforte of hym, and saye to hym from God and from me that it is
now tyme of hele, and after tyme shal be of reson.' And whanne she
95 hadde do this message to her husbonde he was sodenly turned and
behight to God chastite.

In a tyme a pore laborere deied nigh for thruste in a wode and the
holy man bi his praiers gate a faire well springe for to comfort hym
with.

100 He in a tyme saide to a brother of his that was familier with hym
in grete counsaile bi reuelacion of the holy goste: 'There ys lyuynge
at this day a servaunt of God that, as long as he lyuithe, oure Lord
God wolle suffre no famyne come amonge the peple.' But withoute
drede it ys tolde that it fell so. But as sone as he was passed oute of
105 this world al that condicion was chaunged into the contrarie, for after
his holy passinge out of this worlde he apered to the same frere and
saide to hym: 'Lo, here comithe the famyn that oure Lorde wolde
neuer suffre to come whiles y lyued.'

In an Ester Day the freres of Greys had leyde her borde in deserte
110 more coriously thanne thei were wont and made redi thair [v]erres,
f. 237ʳᵇ and the | servaunt of God, whanne he perceiued this, he withdrowe
hym anone and toke the array of a pore man that was there and his
staffe in his honde and went oute atte the yates and abode at the
dore. And whanne the bretheren were atte the mete he cried atte the
115 dore, and praied for the loue of God that thei wolde graunte an
almesse to a pore sike pilgrime. And whanne the pore man was called
inne he sette hym downe upon the grounde and sette his disshe upon
the flore. And whanne the freres sawe hym thei hadd gret drede. And
he saide to hem: 'Y sawe the boorde arraied and made redi and gay
120 and y knewe wele that she was not sittinge to the pore that sought
thaire brede from dore to dore.'

He loued pouerte in hymself and in other, so that he callyd
pouerte allwey his ladi, but whanne he sawe ani mo pore men thanne
he was, he hadde anone enuye and drede lest he shulde be ouercome
125 with hym. On a day as he mette with a pore woman he shewed her to

93 hym²] add þu commest D   me] om. H₁   that it] and D   it] om. H₁   95 hadde]
ins. H₁   97 In] Also in D   98 man] add Fraunceis D   bi his praiers/gate] trs. H₁
springe] springinge D   for] om. H₁   99 with] þerewith H₁   101 of] add oure lorde
and D   105 this] the H₁   106 his] this D   same] ins. H₁   108 y] he D
109 of Greys] in grees H₁, in Grece D   110 verres] werres E   112 the array] him to
a poer aray H₁   113 his] twice D   atte] twice, once del. 'the' H₁   114–15 And . . .
dore] om. D   114 the³] ins. H₁   119 and²] om. H₁   120 she] it H₁D
119–20 that sought thaire] man that asketh H₁   123 mo] om. D   124 he¹] him self
H₁   125 hym] hem D

his felowe and saide: 'The pouerte of this woman dothe us gret shame
and blamed gretly oure pouertee. For as for my most richesse y chase
my ladi pouerte and [she] is clerer seyn in this woman thanne in me.'

In a tyme as a pore man passed by hym and he was meued to haue
gret pitee of hym, his felowe saide to hym: 'Ye, though ye see hym 130
pore, perauenture there is not a richer of his owne will in al this
province.' And thanne the seruaunt of God saide to hym: 'Anone
dispoile the of thi cote and yeue it to hym and yelde the gilty and
falle downe atte his fete.' And he obeied anone and dede so.

He mette on a day .iiij. women | resemblyng of visages in al thinge, f. 237ᵛᵃ
that salwed hym in this wise: 'Welcome my ladi pouerte', and anone 136
they vanisshed awey and were no more sein.

As he went on a tyme to the citee of Arette and a gret mortall
bataile was meuid withinne the towne, the servaunt of God sawe
upon the citee fendes that made gret ioye. And thanne he called his 140
felawe Siluestre and saide to hym: 'Go to the yate of the citee and
comaunde the fendes in Goddes behalf almighti that thei go oute of
the citee.' And thanne he went forth in gret haste and cried
strongely: 'Alle [y]e fendes go oute of the citee in the name of
God and by the comaundement of Fraunceis oure fader". And anone 145
thei went oute and alle the citezeins were anone acorded.

And [as] this Siluestre was yet but a seculer preste, he sawe in his
slepe a crosse ouergilte goinge oute of Fraunceis mowthe, of the whiche
the ouer ende touched heuene, and the armes of the crosse streched in
large brede of the worlde. And than th[is] preste was contrite and lefte 150
the worlde and folued perfitely the servaunt of God.

So as this holy man was in his praiers the fende called hym thries
bi hys name. And whanne the seint hadde ansuered hym, he said:
'There is not so gret a synne in this worlde but that God wolde
foryeue it yef he conuerted hym to his mercy, but he that sleithe 155
hymself bi harde penaunce shal neuer fynde mercy.' And anone the
seruaunt of God knewe bi reuelacion the deseit of the enemye, how
he laboured for to withdrawe hym from his gostely laboure. And

126 The] add grete D   127 oure] his D   most] grete D   128 she] om. E
clerer] 'more' clere H1   129 and] om. H1   131 will] cataill H1   135 mette] add
also D   138 As] And D   to] ins. H1   139 towne] add and D   God] add
Fraunceis D   140 upon] within D   made] add hym D   thanne] om. H1   141 to
hym] om. H1   142 almighti] om. D   144 ye] the EH1   147 as] om. E
150 this] the E   152 man] add Fraunceis D   153 hys] om. H1   the] add holie D
155 conuerted] wolde conuerte D   157 the enemye] add the feende D   158 for] om.
H1

whanne the enemy sawe that he might in no wise preuaile ayenst
160 hym, he tempted hym greuously with temptaciones of hys | flesshe;
f. 237vb and whanne he felt hymselff stered, he dede of his clothes and bete
hymself with right harde corde, seying: 'A, Syr asse, this behouithe
you to abide in this plite and for to be bete.' And whan he sawe that
this temptacion wolde not awey, he went oute and plunged hymself
165 in [a] vyneyerde full of snowe, and he made .vij. gret balles of snowe,
and proposed for to take hem into his body and saide: 'This grettest
is thi wiff, and of the[se] other .iiij., [ij] be thi sones and .ij. be thi
doughtres and these other .ij. here, that one is thi chaumbrere, that
other is thi yeman. Haste the for to clothe hem, for they deie for
170 colde, and yef the besynes that thou haste aboute hem greue the sore,
leue hem and serue [one] Lorde perfitely.' And anone the fende
departed al confused and Goddes seruaunt returned glorifieng God
into his selle.

So as he duelled in a tyme with Leon the cardinal bi his praier, the
175 fendes came in a night and bete hym right greuosly, and thanne he
called his felaw and saide to hym: 'These fendes be iaillours of oure
Lorde that he sendithe for to ponisshe the excesse[s] and offences,
but y canne not remembre me of none offence that y haue done but
that y haue bi the merci of God wasshed it awaye bi satisfaccion. But
180 perauenture thei be sent to me for to kepe me that y falle not, for that
y duell in the courte of gret lordes, the whiche thinge perauenture
engenderithe not goode suspecion to my pore bretherin, that wene
that y abounde in delites.' And thanne he arose hym up in the
morwtide right erly and went thennes.

185 Whanne he was in a tyme in his praiers he sawe upon the
coueryng of his hous assembled togederes a grete hepe of fendes
f. 238ra that ronnyn he|dir and thedir with gret trouble ande noise. And he
went oute and made ouer hym the signe of the crosse and saide: 'Y
charge you bi the name of God almighti that ye [des]sende downe
190 and do in me alle that shall be suffered you to do in me, and y shall
sustene pesibly, for y haue none so grete an enemy as is my bodi, and

159 enemy] feende D   162 corde] coordis D   this] þis it *with* þis *del*. H1, thus it D
164 awey] a vaile D   165 a] *om*. E   vyneyerde] a dyvine yerde *with* dy *del*. H1
166 grettest] grete tempest H1   167 of] *om*. D   these] ther E   .ij.'] *om*. EH1D (*les .ij*.
P2)   168 that one is] be þat oon H1   169 hem] him *changed to* hem H1
170 the²] hem D   171 one] oure E   177 excesses] excesse EH1   178 canne] am
del. 'can' H1   180 to me] *om*. D   for'] *om*. H1   falle] *on erasure* H1   180–1 that y]
itt fallith nat to me to D   187 ande] of H1   And] *add* whanne E   188 hym] hem
H2   189 dessende] sende EH1   190 do'] *add* charge H2

ye shull reuenge me right well of myn enemy and aduersarie as longe
as ye take veniaunce in my lyff.' And thanne thei vanisshed awey
[al] confused.

A frere that was felow to Fraunceis was in a tyme rauisshed and 195
sawe in sperit the glorious place of heuene wherinne he sawe mani a
riall and glorious sete, amonge whiche he sawe one withoute
comparison more brighter shininge thanne ani of the other. And as
he meruailed for whom this right noble sete was arraied and kepte,
he herde a uoys that saide: 'This sete was one of the princes that fell 200
bi his pride, and now it is made redi and kepte for meke Fraunceis.'
And thanne whan Seint Fraunceis come from his praiers he asked
hym and saide: 'Fader, how fele ye of yourself in youre [owne]
conceit?' And he ansuered: 'I am as me semithe right a gret synner.'
And anone the spirit come to the herte of the frere [and saide]: 205
'Beholde what was thine auision that thou saw, the whiche humilite
shall lefte up the right humble to the sete that was lost bi pride.'

The seruaunt of God sawe aboue hym seraphin crucified, the
whiche he printed in hym the signes of his crucifieng, that it semed
to hym that he was crucified, and that his hondes and his fete and his 210
side were marked with the woundes of the crucified, but he hidde
[these] token[s] as longe as he might that none shulde see hem. | And
not for that, sum there were that sawe hem in his lyff, and [at] his f. 238rb
dethe thei were sein of mani. And it was shewed by mani miracles
that these signes were trewe and verrei, of whiche miracles it 215
suffisithe to you two of hem to be saide here atte this tyme.

A man that hight Rogere was in Poyle before the image of Seint
Fraunceis and beganne to thenke and saie might it be trewe that he
was thus worshipped with suche a miracle, or whedir it is [a] uision
or that his bretheren haue contreued this fals ymage. And as he 220
thought this, he herde sodenly a sowne as it hadde be of a quarell
shot oute of an arblaste and therewith he felt hymselff greuously
wounded in the lefte honde, but the hurte apered nothinge in the

192 right well] om. H2   194 al] om. EH1   confused] add and taried not H1
197 riall and] ful H1   199 was] add ordeigned H1   200 was] is H1   203 owne]
om. E   204 ansuered] add and seid H1H2   205 and saide] om. EH1
206 auision] avision with a erased H1   humilite] humbelie H2   207 humble] om. H2
208–10 the whiche . . . crucified] om. H2   210–11 and his side] om. H2   212 these
tokens] this token E   And] but H1   213 at] om. E   214 it was] om. H1
215 signes] thingis H2   216 two] even H1   217 Rogere] add and D   219 a¹]
om. H1   it is] is it H1, it be H2   a²] in E   a uision] inuision E, illusion H1
222 arblaste] arowe blast H2   223 nothinge] not H2

gloue. And thanne he toke of his gloue and sawe in his honde a
225 wounde as it had be of an arrowe, of whiche there went oute so grete
strengthe of akinge and brenninge that almost he deied for sorw and
peine, and he repented hym and saide that he leued verrily the signes
of [the] blessed Fraunceis, and he was anone heled as he hadde .ij.
dayes praied to Seint Fraunceis and to his signes.
230   In the reawme of Castell a deuout man to Seint Fraunceis went
towardes Complie, and men laye in awaite for to slee another man,
and so this man bi ignoraunce was take in stede of that other and was
dedly wounded and lefte as for dede. And after that the cruel
mortherer stiked his swerde in his throte and lefte it there, for he
235 might not drawe it thennis, and went his waye. Men cried thanne
f. 238ᵛᵃ and ronnen here and there and com|pleined this man as for dede.
And as thei ronggen atte midnight to Mateins the freres belle, the
mannes wiff beganne to crie and saide: 'Arise up, Sire, and go to
Mateins, for the belle callithe the.' And anone he lefte up the honde
240 for to shewe that sum man shulde take awey the swerde oute of his
throte and anone, seinge all that were there, the swerde lepte aferre
right as it hadde be caste of a stronge championes honde, and anone
[he] rose up al hole and saide: 'The blessed Fraunceis came to me
and ioyned his signes to my woundes and anointed hem with the
245 swetnesse of his signes and sawdid hem merueilously with his
touchinge. And whanne he wolde go, y shewed hym that he wolde
take awey the knyff, for elles y might not speke, and he toke it and
threw it awey and thus he heled me with the touchinge of his signes.'
    The two right clere lightes of the worlde Seint Domenik and Seint
250 Fraunceis weren atte Rome before the lorde of Ostience that thanne
was pope, and this bisshopp saide to hem: 'Whi make ye not your
freres bisshoppes and prelates that be more worthe thanne other by
t[e]chinge and bi ensaumple?' And than was there gret strife betwene
the seintes for to ansuere, and humilite ouercome Fraunceis so that
255 he wold not putte hymselff forthe for to answere furst, and Domenik
that he obeied furst in answeringe and saide: 'Sire, oure bretheren be
lefte up in good degre yef thei knewe it, ne y shalle neuer suffre to

224 And thanne he] *twice* E   227 hym] *add* sore H1   228 the] *om.* E   as] *add*
sone as H2   232 other] *add* man H1H2   235 and] but H2   Men] then H2
237 atte] abou3t H1   to Mateins] *om.* H1   240 oute of] fro H1H2   241 seinge]
beyng H1, seienge H2   all] to alle thoo H2   243 he] *om.* EH1   245 sawdid]
sheueded H1, sowed H2   247 knyff] swerde H2   for] or H2   and¹] *om.* H1
248 the] *om.* H1   251 hem] him H1   253 techinge] touchinge EH1H2
(*enseignement* P2)   255 furst] *om.* H2

my power that thei shull haue other hope of dignite.' And Seint
Fraunceis ansuered after and saide: 'Oure bretheren be called
Menours for that | thei wolde not be called gretter.' f. 238vb

And thanne the blessed Fraunseis full of right gret sympilnesse 261
and humilite amonestid to alle creatoures to loue her creatoure. He
preched to the briddes and was herde of hem, and he handelyd hem
and planed hem, and thei durst not go fro hym withoute leue. And
the swalowes in a tyme songin while he preched, and he comaunded 265
hem to holde thaire pees. Ther was a bridde that satte vpon a fygge
tree before his selle and songe, and this holi man putte oute his
honde and called this bridde, and anone the bridde obeied and come
vpon his honde and he saide: 'Now singe, my suster, and preise thi
Lorde.' And thanne the bridde songe anone and went not from hym 270
tille he hadde leue.

He spared to touche lightes or lampes or candeles that he wolde
not defoule the fairenesse of his hondes. He went worshipfully upon
the stones in worship of hym that is saide a stone. He gadered the
wormes oute of the wey for thei shulde not be trode and defouled by 275
hem that passed bi the waye. He comaunded in wynter to yeue hony
to the bees for thei shulde not perisshe for hunger. He called alle
bestis his bretheren. He was replenisshed with meruailous ioye for
the loue of his creatoure. He behelde the sonne and the mone and the
sterres and he somoned hem to the loue of her creatoure. He 280
defended that the barboure shulde not make hym a gret crowne
saienge: 'Y will that my symple bretheren haue parte of my hede.'

A seculer man herde the seruaunt of God preche atte Seint
Severin, ande sawe bi the reuelacion of God that Fraunceis was
straught upon a crosse | made of two right clere and bright swerdes, f. 239ra
wherof that one cam from the hede unto the fete, and that other 286
streched from that one [h]onde to that other. Thanne he that hadde
neuer before knowing of suche a sight conuerted hym to God and
entred into the Ordre and ended his lyff blessidly.

So as Seint Fraunceis was sike in his eyen bi continuel weping, his 290

258 haue other] om. H2   hope] chope with c erased H1   of] add any othir degree or H2
262 creatoure] add Also H2   263 preched] teched H1   264 planed] pleied with H2
266 was] add also H2   267 man] add Fraunceis H2   268 the] þis H1
272 spared] add also H2   272 that] ins. H1   273 the . . . of] om. H2   274 He]
add went and H1   275 by] with H1   277 called] add also H2   278 was] add also
H2   283 God] add Fraunceis H2   atte] that H2   284 Severin] Se's'verin E
285 crosse] add and subp. H1   286 other] add swerde H2   287 honde] bonde E
288 knowing] knowelich H2   a] om. H1   a sight] sightis H2   289 and] add there H2
blessidly] om. H2

bretheren praied hym that he wolde refreine hym from wepinge, and
he ansuered and saide: 'The uisitacion of the light euerlastinge is not
to be put awey for loue of the light that we haue here with flies.' And
whanne his bretheren constreined hym that he shulde take medi-
295 cynes to his eyen and the surgyen helde an hote yren in his honde,
the holi man saide: 'My brother fyre, be to me atte this tyme
debonayre and curable; y praie oure Lord that made [the] that he
attempre thi hete to me.' And than he made the signe of the crosse
ayenst the fyre and thanne the fire was putte into the tendre flesshe
300 fro his ere into his eyelydde, and he felt neuer disese therwith.

He was strongly sike in the desert of Seint Vrban, and whanne he
felte that nature failed hym he asked after wyne, and thanne was
there none there, and thei brought hym water and he blessed it, and
it was anone conuerted into good wyne. The purte of that holi man
305 gate there that the pouerte of the desert might not, and as sone as he
hadde tasted therof he gate strengthe and hele.

He loued more to here blame of hymselff than preisinge, and
therfor whanne the peple lefte up in hym any matere of holinesse, he
comaunded to sum frere that he shulde priuily in his ere saye to hym
f. 239ʳᵇ sum vyleni and repreef | by defoulyng hym. And whanne this frere,
311 thus constreined ayenst his will, wolde calle hym churle, marchaunt
and vnprofitable fole, thanne he was gladd and wolde blesse hym and
saie: 'Now God blesse the for thi trewe sayenge, for thou saiest
wordes of verrei trouth and suche as it sitte me to here.' And the
315 servaunt of God wolde neuer take upon hym so gladly to haue
lordship as he wolde to be a soget, ne he wolde neuer comaunde so
moche as he wold obey, and therfor he lefte to be General and asked
ouer hym a wardein to whos will he wolde be submitted in alle
thingges. He behight alweyes obedience to the frere with whom he
320 went and helde it.

And whanne a frere hadd done anithinge ayenst the rule of
obedience and he hadd tokin of penaunce, alwey the seruaunt of

291 and] *om.* Hı   292 the] *om.* HıH2   293 loue of] *om.* Hı   296 the holi man]
Than Fraunceis H2   My] *om.* Hı   297 praie] *add* to H2   the] *om.* EHı   299 into] to
Hı   300 therwith] *add* affter H2   304 was] *om.* Hı   good] *om.* H2   purte] pouerte Hı
man] *add* Fraunceis H2   306 gate] *add* ayenne his H2   307 He] and Hı   308 the]
om. Hı   in hym any matere of] ony mater of him in Hı   309 to] that Hı   in] *ins.* Hı
310 by] *om.* HıL   by defoulyng] in the foulinge H2   this] þe Hı   312 wolde] *om.* Hı
313 saie] seyd Hı, *om.* H2   314 and] *om.* Hı   sitte] semeþ Hı   And] *ins.* Hı
314–15 the servaunt of God] this holie man Fraunceis H2   315 upon] on Hı   to haue]
om. Hı   317 lefte] last Hı   319 alweyes . . . frere] to be frere alwei obeciens Hı
322 tokin] take Hı, the tokenne H2   alwey] And also H2

God for to make other aferde wolde comaunde to caste the hode of
hym in the fire. And whanne he hadde leyn a litell while in the fire
he wolde comaunde to take it oute and yelde ayen the frere his hode, 325
and the hode was nothing blemisshed with the fire.

He went in a tyme bi the more of Venys and fonde a grete
multitude of briddes synging, and he saide to his felawe: 'Oure
sustres these briddes done praise her creatoure, go we in the myddes
of hem and synge oure Houres to the Lorde with hem.' And so thei 330
went in amonge the briddes and thei remeued nothinge oute of her
place for hem, but for as moche as thei might not here that one that
other for gret noyse of briddes, he saide to hem: 'My sustres briddes,
sesithe youre synging till we haue saide to oure Lorde dewe
preisyngges.' And thei helde her pees, and whanne he hadde saide 335
Laudes | he gaue hem leue to singe ayen, [and anone thei beganne to f. 239ᵛᵃ
singe ayen] after her custume.

He was in a tyme herborwed with a knight, and he saide to hym:
'Brother and dere oste, acorde the to that y shall tell the. Go and
confesse the of thi synnes, for thou shalt ete in shorte tyme 340
elleswhere.' And anone he graunted hym and ordeined his meyne
and toke penaunce of hele. And as sone as thei went to mete, the
knight his oste did deie sodenly.

In a tyme as he fonde a gret multitude of briddes, he saide to hem:
'My bretheren and susteren, ye aught moche to praise youre maker, 345
that clothid yow with fetheres and gaue you pennis to fle with, and
graunted you the purete of the eyre and gouernithe you withoute ani
cure or besinesse.' And the briddes turned her bek to hym and
spredd out her winges and dressed upward her hedes and her neckes
and behelde hym ententifly. And he passed bi the middel of hem so 350
that he touched hem with his cote, and thei neuer remeued oute of
her place til he yaue hem leue that thei shulde fle togederes.

As he preched in a tyme in the castell of Maury and he might not
be herde for cheteringe of swalues that made her nestes, thanne he
saide to hem: 'Mi sustres, it is tyme that y speke, for ye haue spoke 355
ynow. Holde youre pees till the worde of God be saide.' And thei
[anone] obeied and helde her pees.

323 God] add Fraunceis H2   for] om. H1   324 he] it H2   litell] om. H2
333 briddes²] om. H2   334 sesithe] sese ye H1   335 thei] add anone H2   saide] add to
H1   336–7 and...ayen] om. E   339 and dere oste] wilt thou H2   343 his oste] om.
H2   did deie] died H1H2   347 purete] pure hete H1   348 bek] billis H2   353 he¹]
Fraunceis H2   354 nestes] add and EH1   357 anone] om. EH1

As the seruaunt of God passed in a tyme thurgh Poile he fonde bi the waie a gret purs ful of money, and whanne his felaw sawe it he wolde
360　haue take it and youe it to the pore men, but he wolde not suffre hym in
f. 239ᵛᵇ　no wise and | saide: 'Sone, it aperteinithe not to the to take the good of others.' And whanne this other hasted fast, Fraunceis praied a while, and thanne he comaunded hym to take the purse wherin there was a gret addre in stede of siluer. And whanne the frere sawe that he
365　beganne to drede, but he wold obeye and toke the purse in his hondes and there lepe oute anone a gret serpent. And than the seint saide: 'Money is not ellis but a venemous serpent.'

As a frere was sore tempted, he thought in his herte that yef he hadd ani writyng of his holy faderes honde his temptacion wold
370　lyghtly passe awey, but he durst in no wise discouer this thinge. And in a tyme this holy man called hym to hym and saide: 'Sone, feche me parchemyn and ynke, for y will write sum preising of God.' And whanne he hadde wretin it he saide: 'Take this chartre and kepe it as longe as thou lyuest.' And anone all the temptacion went awey. And
375　this same frere, whanne Seint Fraunceis laie syk, beganne to thenke: 'Oure fader neighe[th] to the dethe, Lord, y shulde be gretly comfo[r]ted yef y might haue his cope after his dethe.' And sone after the holy man called hym and saide: 'Y yeue the my cote after my dethe that thou shalt reioyse of plein right.'

380　He was in a tyme herborwed in Lumbardie with an honest man that asked hym yef he wolde for the obseruaunce of the gospell ete of alle metis that were sette before hym. And he consented to the deuocion of the oste so that he ordeined a good capon for his mete. And as thei were atte the mete there cam an vntrewe man and asked
385　mete for Goddes loue. And as sone as that holy man herde that name
f. 240ʳᵃ　he sent hym a membre of that capon and that cursed | man kepte that yefte. And in the morw whanne that holy man preched, [he saide:] 'Lo, what flesshe this frere etithe that ye holde as a seint, for this same he gaue me yesternight.' But that membre of the capon was

358 As] Also H2　God] add Fraunceis H2　in a tyme] ins. H1　359 gret] om. H2
360 the] om. H1H2　361 the] add for H1　362 this other] his fellawe H2　fast] add
Seinte H2　363 hym] his fellawe H2　364 siluer] moneie H2　366 than] ins. H1
the seint] Seint Fraunceis H2　368 As] Also as H2　369 temptacion] temptacions
EH1　371 man] add Fraunces H2　374 temptacion] temptacions H1
375 thenke] add in his herte H2　376 neigheth] neighed E　377 comforted]
comfoted E　378 man] add Fraunceis H2　cote] so changed to cope H1　379 that]
than H2　reioyse] add it H1　right] trouthe H2　382 he] om. H1　385 that holy
man] Fraunceis H2　386 that¹] the H2　387 And] ins. H1　he saide] om. E, ins. H1
388 that] and H1　holde] add him H1　389 that] ins. H1

sein in the sight of all the peple an hole capon, so that he was blamed 390
as mad of all the peple. And whanne he sawe that, he was ashamed
and asked foryeuenesse, and thanne he that hadde mistake hym come
to his good thought and the flesshe to his propre fourme.

In a tyme as he satte atte the borde and thei made collacion of the
pouerte of the blessed Virgine, anone the seruaunt of God rose from 395
the borde and beganne to wepe and to sobbe sorufully and wette
hymself al in teres and beganne to ete the remenaunt of his brede
upon the bare erthe.

He wolde that gret reuerence and dignite were bore to the hondes
of prestes, to whom is youe for to make the sacrement of the auuter 400
oure Lordes blessed bodi. And thanne he wold saie ofte tyme: 'Yef y
shuld mete with a seint of heuene and that y mette with a pore
preste, y wolde turne from the seint and kisse the prestes hondes and
saie to the seint: "Abide me, for the hondes of this prest hathe
handeled the sone of lyff and thei passen sum thingges aboue 405
mankinde."'

He was made noble in his lyff by miracles, for the brede that was
brought to hym for to blesse yaue hele to all syknesse. He conuerted
water into wyne wherof a sike man receiued his hele.

And as he neighed to his last dayes and was greued with greuous 410
siknesse, he made hymself be layde upon the bare erthe and lete call
all his bretheren that were there, and whan thei were all present he
blessed hem alle and right as atte the Cene he yaf euery man a
morsell of brede, and taught hem as he was wont for to praise her
maker. | And the dethe that is horrible and noyous to all he taught f. 240rb
hem for to preise, and also in his owne persone he desired dethe to 416
come to hym and saide: 'My suster dethe, wolcome shalt thou be to
me.' And whan he come to his last houre he slepte in oure Lorde. Of
whom a frere sawe the sowle in manere of a sterre lyke to the mone
in quantite and to the sonne in brightnesse.   420

A frere that was ministre in the londe of laboure, as he was atte his
last ende and had lost his speche, he cried sodenly and saide: 'Abide
me, Fader, abyde, for y come anone with the.' And whanne the

390 in the sight] *om.* H2   the²] *om.* H1   391 mad] a madde manne H2
392 hym] this holie man Fraunces H2   396 wette] wepte H1, wente H2   397 and]
add þan H1   400 of ¹] *add* þe H1   the] *add* holie H2   402 and] *add* also H2
409 man] *add* drank and H1   410 he] this holie man Fraunceis H2   411 bare]
barthe *with* the *del.* H1   412 were] *add* there H2   413 atte] *ins.* H1   he] *ins.* H1
414 praise] praie se E   415 And] *add* also H2   is] *add* so H1   421 that] *add* hight
that E, *so marked for deletion* H1   422 his] *om.* H1

freres asked hym ho that was, he saide: 'Se ye not how oure fader
425 Fraunceis gothe to heuene?' And anone he slepte in pees and folued
the fader.

A ladi that hadd be devouute to the blessed Fraunceis deied, and the
prestes and clerkes were atte her bere for to do her seruice, and sodenli
she sette her upon her bere and called one of the preste [to her] and
430 saide: 'Fader, y wolde be shreue. Y was dede and shuld haue be putte in
a sorwfull prison for that y was neuer shriue of a synne that y shall now
telle you, but Seint Fraunceis praied for me and hathe gote me grace of
lyff for to shewe my synne and to haue foryeuenesse therof, and as sone
as y haue tolde it you y shall reste in pees.' And thanne she was shriuen
435 and assoyled and reste anone in oure Lorde.

The freres of Nice borwed a chare of a man, and he ansuered bi
despite and saide: 'I hadde leuer that y hadde flein you bothe with
youre Seint Fraunceis thanne y wolde lene you my chare.' But
afterward he come to hymself and repented of the blame and dredde
f. 240ᵛᵃ the wre[t]he of God. Anone [this mannes sone fell] | sike and deied.
441 And whanne he sawe his sone dede, he fell downe to the erthe and
turmented hymselff wepinge and crieng upon Seint Fraunceis and
saide: 'Y am he that synned, thou shuldest haue bete me. Yelde to
me, deuout synner, that thou haste take from me, blamyng the
445 wickedly.' And anone his sone quikened ayen and saide: 'Whanne y
was dede Seint Fraunceis ledde me a longe way in derkenesse, and
atte the laste he broughte me into a faire gardine and saide to me:
"Retourne ayen to thi fader, for y will no lenger holde the."'

A pore man owid to a riche man a quantite of siluer and praied hym,
450 for the loue of Seint Fraunceis, that he wolde graunte hym lenger
terme. And he ansuered hym proudely and saied: 'Y shal putte the in
such a place that Seint Fraunceis nor none other shal helpe the.' And
anone he bonde hym and kiste hym into a derke prison. And withinne a
while after Seint Fraunceis come and brake the prison and brake his
455 cheines and brought the man al hole to his propre place.

A knight that missaied of the miracle[s] of Seint Fraunceis and of
his werkes, in a tyme as he pleied at the dys, ful of wodenesse and of
misbeleue, and saide to hem that were there: 'Yef Seint Fraunceis be

424 how] *om.* H2   426 the] *add* holie H2   428 bere] burienge H2
429 upon her] on þe H1   to her] *om.* E   437 flein] slaine D   438 Seint] *om.* D
440 wrethe] wreche E   this mannes sone fell] he was E, he *changed to* his `son was' H1
443 me] *add* wherfor D   444 synner] seint D   448 Retourne] recover H1   lenger
holde] leng`er hold' H1   451 he] the riche man D   453 into] in H1
456 miracles] miracle E   457 of²] *om.* H1   458 and] *om.* D

a seint, .xviij. pointes come upon the[se] dys.' And anone cam there
in .iij. dys in euery .vj., and it fell so atte eueri caste .ix. tymes. And 460
thanne for to ioyne wodenesse to wodenesse he saide: 'Yef it be trewe
that he be a seint, my bodi be this day smiten with a swerde, and yef
it be not trewe, that y ascape all hole.' And whanne the game was
done, for that his praier was made in | synne, he saide wronge to a f. 240ᵛᵇ
newew of his, and he toke a swerde and smote hym thorugh the bodi 465
and slow hym.

Ther was a man that hadde so loste his thigh that he might not
meue it, and called upon Seint Fraunceis bi these wordes: 'Helpe me,
Seint Fraunceis, and remembre the of the deuocion and seruice that
y haue do to the, for y bare the upon my asse, and kessed thi fete and 470
thi hondes and now y deye for sorugh of gret turment.' And thanne
the seint apered to hym with a litell staffe that he helde in his honde
that hadd the signe of thau, and touched the place where the sore
was and anone the postume brake and he resseiued fulli hele, but the
signe of thau abode alwey still upon the place. And Seint Fraunceis 475
was custumed to ensele his letteres with that signe.

Ther was a maide in the mountaynes of Poill in a castell and her
fader and her moder hadde but her allone so that she was dede. And
the moder was right devout to Seint Fraunceis, but she was thanne
full of sorugh and that of right gret sorugh. [And] Seint Fraunceis 480
apered to her and saide: 'Wepe no more, for the light of thin eyen
that thou wepist is quenched, and it longithe to me for to yelde her
to the ayen bi thi praier.' And thanne the moder hauinge ful truste in
the seint wolde not suffre the bodi to be bore oute, but continuelly
callynge upon Seint Fraunceis she toke her doughter that hadd be 485
dede and lefte her up hole and sounde.

A litell childe in the citee of Rome was falle oute of a wyndowe to
the grounde, and thei called upon Seint Fraunceis and anone he was
restored to liff.

In the citee of Susse an | house fell vppon a childe and slowe it, H1 f. 302ᵛᵃ
and whan þe childe was leide vppon a bere for to be buried, the 491
moder | called vppon Seint Fraunces with all here deuocion, and H1 f. 302ᵛᵇ

459 these] the E   462 bodi be] bo'dy be' H1   464 made] om. D   465 and¹]
om. H1   467 so] om. D   that²] and D   469 the¹] om. H1   470 the²] om. H1
472 that he helde] om. H1   473 thau] þe crosse H1   and] add þan he H1   the³] he H1
475 upon] in H1   476 his] þe H1   477 in²...castell] om. H1   478 so] and so it
happid D   480 and ... gret sorugh] om. H1   And] om. EH1   482 that ... wepist]
om. D   quenched] add wherfor thou wepest D   485 callynge] callid D   488 anone]
om. D   489 restored] add ayenne D   490 Susse] add þat del. H1

abou3t midni3t þe childe cou[g]hed and arose vpp all hole and he [be]gan to preise God.

495   [Fr]ere Iames of Reate hadde passed a flode in a vessell and þe freres were go oute and he þat was last hasted for to go oute, [and] þe vessell torned vpsodown so þat he fell in þe depnesse of þe water. And þan þe freres preiden to Seint Fraunces for him, and he himself as he mi3t with deuocion, and anone þe frere began to go in þe 500 bottoume of the water as he wold haue do on dri grownde and toke þe vessell þat was plunged and drowe here to þe banke and he came owte. And his cloþes were noþing wete nor besemyng þat ony droppe of water hadde touched him.

[Here endith the lyfe of Seinte Fraunceis, and bygnneth the life of Seint Pelagien, Cap°. .C.xliij.°]

Pelagen was þe worþiest in þe cite of Antioche and she was full of riches and of al worldli goodes. She was right faire of bodi, noble of cloþing, veyn and variable of corage and vnchast of here bodi.

In a tyme as she went þorough þe towne in here grete quentises 5 þat þere was noþinge [þat] might be seyn vppon hire but gold and siluer and precious stones, [and] where euer she went she filled þe eyer with flauour of swete sauoures. And þere went bifore grete H1 f. 303ʳᵃ multitude of yong men and also of yong | wymmen þat were cloþed with right noble cloþing and riche. And an holi bisshopp that hight 10 Noyron, bisshopp of Leopoleos, þat is now called Damiette, passed bi þe cite and sagh hire, and þan he bigan to wepe right bitterli for þat she had more cure and besines to plese þe worlde thanne he hadde for to plese God. And he fell downe vppon þe pament and smote his visage to þe erthe and wet all þe pament with his teeres 15 and cried on hie and seid: 'Lorde, haue merci on me sinfull, for þe grete cure and besines of o sinfull womannys aray hath ouerpassed al þe wisdome in my life. Goode Lorde, lete not þe aray of þis wrecched woman confounde me before þe si3t of þ[i] dredfull mageste; she hath araied hireself with all here powere for to plese

493 coughed] couched H1   began] gan H1   494 preise] *add* oure lorde D 495 Frere] Sere H1   496 oute¹] *add* of the vesselle D   and²] *om.* H1 500 grownde] lande D

H1DH2A1A2; in D an excision has affected 54 *wicked* and 57–64 *not . . . Within   Rubric, supplied from* D, *is omitted by* H1 *with* Pelagen *written between the chapters by a corrector* 5 þat²] *om.* H1   vppon] of D   6 and²] *om.* H1   9–10 that hight Noyron] of Norlon D   10 now] *om.* D   12 he] she *with* s *erased* H1   18 þi] þe H1 19 all] *add* and *del.* H1

'to' erthly þinges, and I hadde purposed for to plese þe, endeles 20
God, [and] fore my negligence I haue not fulfilled [it].' And þan he
seid to hem þat were with him: 'I tell you in trouth þat God wol
bring þis woman in iugement ayenst vs, for as moche as she doeth
grete [besinesse] in peyntyng hire for to plese worldly louers, and we
forslouthe þe tyme for to plese þe heuenly spouse.'   25
     As he seid þies þinges and many oþer, sodeinli he fell on slepe,
and it semed him in his slepe þat he was at his masse and þat a
blakke dove al defouled fly besily abought him, the which | þan H1 f. 303rb
commaunded þat al þei shuld voide þat were not baptized, and anone
þe dowue vnappered. And aftre masse she came ayene and of þe 30
same bisshopp she was plunged in a vessell of water, and þan she
went oute white and clene and fly so hie þat she miȝt not be seyn,
than he awoke.
     And in a tyme as he went to þe chirche and preched, Pellegian was
present, and þrogh þe goodenesse and merci of God she hadde so 35
grete compunccion þat she sent the bisshopp lettres seying: 'Holi
bisshop þe seruant of God and tru disciple and I Pellagien þe disciple
of þe fende, if þou arte proued þe verri disciple of Crist, þat, as I
haue herd seid, came downe fro heven for sinners, vouchesaue for to
receyve me sinfull repentaunt.' To whom he sent ayene and seid: 'I 40
pray þe, dispise not my lownesse, for I am a sinfull man, but if thou
desire for to be savid, thou maist not se me alone, but among oþer
þou shalt se me.' And as she 'came' to him before moche peple, she
fell downe at his fete and wept bitterly and seid: 'I am Pelagien,
moder of wickednesse, þe flode of synnes, þe depnesse of perdicion. I 45
am the deuourer of soules. Many haue I deceyved, þe which nowe I
lothe hem all.' Than þe bisshopp asked here what was hire name. To
whom she seid: 'For my birthe I am called Pelagian, but for þe
pompe and pride of myn araie men callen me Margarete.' | Then þe H1 f. 303va
bisshopp benigneli receyving here, enyoyned here penaunce and 50
tauȝt here diligently in þe lawe of God and baptized here in holi
bapteme. The fende beyng þere present seying: 'O what violence I
suffre of this olde croked felawe! O þou violence! O þou 'olde'
wicked! Cursed be þe day in which þou were bore contrarie to me,
for my moost hope thou hast take fro me.'   55

20 to²] and erased 'to' H1, om. D   þe] om. D   21 and] om. H1   it] om. H1
24 besinesse] harme H1   25 þe²] oure D   28 dove] dowse D   al defouled]
diffilid D   30 dowue] dowse D   and of] to D   31 plunged] baptisid D
40 me] add to D   repentaunt] repentaunce D   43 him] om. D   48 For] fro D
49 araie] add alle D   53 olde] om. D

In a night as Pelagien slepte, þe fende come to hire and seid: 'O
lady Margarete, what euer harme haue I do to yow? Haue I not
araied þe with al riches and glorie? I prey þe tell me wherein I haue
displesed þe and I shal anone make þe amendes. But howeuer it be, I
60 beseche þe that þou forsake me 'not' lest I be made reproue to
cristen men.' Than she anone made þe signe of þe crosse and blewe
vppon him and he sodenly vanissh[ed] awey. And þe þird day aftre,
she gadered togidre all þat she had and departed it amonge poer
men. [And] within a while aftre, vnwyting of enybody, she stale awey
65 by niȝt and went to þe Mounte of Olyvete, and þere she toke þe abite
of an heremite and in a litull celle she closid hire and serued God in
grete abstinence. She was had in grete fame of al þe peple and Frere
Pelagien she was called.

Aftre þat a deken of þe bisshopps [þat] had cristened hire went to
Hı f. 303ᵛᵇ Ierusalem for to visite þ[e] holi place[s]. To | whom þe bisshop seid:
71 'Whan ye haue visited þe holi places, goeth and visiteth an holi
monke þat hiȝt Pelagien which is þe verry seruaunt of God.' And
whan he come thider she knew him anone, but he in no wise knew
hire, [for] she was [so] disfigured with penaunce. To whom Pelagien
75 seid: 'Ye haue 'a' bisshopp?' And he seid: 'Ye.' And þan she seid:
'Prey him to prey for me, for suerli he is a verri appostole of Ihesu
Crist.' Than he went his wey. And þe þirde dai he come ayene and
knocked atte hire doer, but þer was none þat answhered. He went
þan and opened a wyndowe and saw hire dede. And þen he ron to þe
80 bisshopp and told him. Anon þe bisshopp and his clerkes with all þe
monkes assembeled hem togidre for to do [þe] seruice for þat holi
man. And whan þei had brought þe body oute of þe selle, þei founde
þat she was a woman, and all þei gretely merveiling yafe þonkingez
to God and biried hire body worshipfully. 'Sche' deied þe .viij. day
85 of Octobre the yere of oure Lorde .CC.lxxx[x].

60 forsake] forsaine D   62 he] add seid subp. Hı   vanisshed] vanissh Hı
63–4 poer men] the poore D   64 And] om. Hı   69 þat²] om. Hı   70 þe] þat
Hı   places] place Hı   72 verry] om. D   74 for] om. Hı   so] om. Hı D
76 Prey] add for del. D   79 ron] add ayenn D   81 þe] om. Hı   84 body] om. D
Sche] add þat del. Hı   85 .CC.lxxxx.] .CC.lxxx. Hı

Here endithe the liffe of Seint [Pelagien], and next
beginneþ þe life of Seint Margarete, [Cap°. .C.xliiij.°]

Mergerete þat is seide Pelagien was a right noble and a faire virgine
ful of riches, and she was nobli and curiously kept of hire [freendis]
so þat she was taught to kepe all | gode maners, and she was so   Hı f. 304ra
ententif for to kepe honeste and chastite that she refused to be seyn
[of] men in all wise. And atte þe laste [she] was desired of a noble 5
yong man and bi þe accorde of oon and othir of here kyn all þinges
were ordeined þat longed to here fest of þe mariage with grete glorie
and grete richesse.

And whan þe day of þe mariage come þat þis yong man and þis
maide were assembled with right grete noblenesse before the 10
chambre [and] þat here kinrede made þan þe fest of [the] weddyng
with so grete yoie and solempnite, þis holi virgine enspired of God
considered how þe harme and losse of here virginite was bought with
[h]armefull reioysing. She fell downe to þe erthe in teeres and bigan
to þenke in hire herte þe recompense of þe [ioie of] virginite and þe 15
sorowes þat foloweth weddynges, so þat all þe ioies of þis world she
accompted hem for nought. And than þat nyȝt she kept hire from þe
felaship of hire husbond, and at mydniȝt she recommaunded hire to
God and kut of here here and cloþed here in mannys cloþing and
fledde ferre into a monasteri of monkes and called hereself Pelagien, 20
and þere she was receyved of þe abbot and taught diligently. And she
bare hereself ful holely and religiously.

And þen when þe ruler and þe keper of a nonri þat was þere fast
by was dede, | bi þe counseil of þe abbot he was made mastre of þe   Hı f. 304rb
abbey of nonnes þough it were so þat he refused it ful gretly. And as 25
he minstred to hem not oonli here bodeli necessitees but also þe
gostli pastes of hevenli fode withoute ony blame continuelli, the
fende havyng envie of þis grete vertu of him þought `how he´ might
put abak his goode name bi som obieccion of syn. And as he þouȝt he
parformed his cursed purpose, for a virgine þat dwelled withoute þe 30
yates did aduoutry bi þe instigacion of þe fende, so that here wombe
aroos þat she might no lenger hide it.

HıDH2AıA2; in D excision of an initial has caused damage to 4 *honeste*, from 27
withoute to 31 *wombe*, and from 54 *dying* to end.   *Rubric* Pelagien] Fraunceis Hı   Cap°.
.C.xliiij°.] *from* D   2 freendis] *om.* Hı   3 gode] *om.* D   5 of^1] amonge Hı
she] *om.* Hı   11 and] *om.* Hı   the] *om.* Hı   13 bought] brouȝt D
14 harmefull] armefull Hı   15 ioie of] *om.* Hı, *add* hir D   23 a nonri] the
fermorie D   25 ful] *om.* D

Then were al þe virgines so shamefaste and so dredfull, [and] all
þe monkes of þat oþer abbey, þat þei wist not what to do, and
35 wenden vereli þat Pelagien þat was prouost and famulier with þe
virgines hadde done þis and was condempned of all withoute
iugement. And þan he was put oute and he wist not whi and was
reclused in a pit within a roche. And þan þe moost cruell of þe
monkes was ordeigned for to minstre to him, and he serued him with
40 barli brede and water, and þat in right litull quantite. And whan þe
monkes hadde enclosed him þei went hire wey and left Pellagien
alloone þere. And he moost mekli and moost paciently susteyned and
Hı f. 304ᵛᵃ suffred all the wronges and was not troubled | in noþing, but euer
hertli loued and þonked God and conforted him in his chastite bi þe
45 ensaumple of seintes.

In þe laste ende whan she wist þat here dethe neghed she wrote
lettres to þe abbot and to þe monkes in this wise: 'I of noble kinrede
was called Mergarete in þe worlde, but for I wold eschue þe
temptacions of þe worlde, I called myself Pellagien. I am a man. I
50 haue not lied for to deceyue, for I haue shewed þat I haue vertu of
man, and I haue hadde vertu of þe cryme þat was put vppon me, and
I innocent þereof haue do þe penaunce. But I prai yow for as moche
as men knewe me not for woman, þat þe holy susteres mai beri my
bodi so þat þe shewing of me dying be clensing of my lyving, and þat
55 þe wymmen know þat I am a virgine þat thei iuged for a vouterer.'

And whan þe abbot herd þies þinges the monkes [and] þe nonnes
ron to þe pitte where she was reclused, and the wymmen knew þat
she was a woman and a pure virgine withoute touche of man, and
[þen] þei diden al penaunce for þe wronge þat þei had do to hire and
60 beried hire holi bodi worshipp[f]ulli amonge þe virgines.

Here endethe the life of Seint Mergarete. And next
bigynnethe the liffe of Seint Thais, [Capitulo .Cᵒ.xlv.ᵒ]

Thais, as it is red in the liffe of faders, was a comyn woman and she
Hı f. 304ᵛᵇ was | of so grete beute þat mani folowed hire and solden all hire

33 virgines] nonnes D   and²] of Hı, add also D   35-6 þe virgines] thoo nonnes D
36 þis] add deede D   37 he was] was Pelagien D   49 man] 'wom'man Hı, womman D
51 vertu of þe] twice D   cryme] so with y on erasure Hı   53 knewe] knowe D   for] as a D
56 and] of Hı   57 ron] wenten D   58 touche] touchinge D   59 þen] om. Hı
60 bodi] add right D   worshippfulli] worshippulli Hı

HıDH2AıA2; E resumes at 31 well; D breaks off after 17 ne   Rubric Mergarete] add
Icallid Pella⟨gien⟩ D   Capitulo .Cᵒ.xlv°.] from D   2 mani] add a man D

substaunce and put hem to pouerte. And tho þat loued hire foughten
many a tyme togidre for ielosye and slough eche oþer diuerse tymes,
so þat mani tymes bi here fytinges here house was full of blode [of] 5
yong men that drew to hire.

So in a tyme there was an holi man þat hight Payne and herd of
here wrechednesse. He went and toke vppon him seculer cloþing and
toke a shilling and went into a cite of Egipte and yaf hire þis shillyng,
þat is to sey .xij.d., as [though] he hadde yeve it bi cause of syn. And 10
'when' she hadde take þis money she seid to him: 'Go we into þe
chaumbre togidre.' And whan þei were in þe chaumbre she bade
hym go to bedde þat was preciously couered with a covertoure. Than
he seid to hire: 'Is þere no more secrete place herein þat we may go
to?' And whan she hadde ladde him by many diuerse places he seid 15
evere [þat] he was aferde to be seen. 'There is a place' she seid, 'þat
no man comeþ ne no man shall know vs but oonli God.' Than he
seid to hire: 'Knowest þou that God is and þat he seeth all þinges
clerli?' And she answhered and seid: 'I beleue þat God is and seeth
and knoweth all þing moost clerely.' Than seid þat blessid man: 20
'Thu seist þou knowest all þis, knowest thou not how he will
punyssh synners with endeles tormentes of hell and reward vertues
lyvers with soueraigne blisse in heven?' | And she seid: 'Al þis I H1 f. 305ra
knowe and beleue.' And þen he seid to hire: 'Sith þou knowest all
þis, whi hast thou perisshed so many soules? Wite it well þat þou 25
shalt 'not' oonli be dampned for thyn oonli synnes but thou shalt
yeve accountes bi peyne for all þo þat þou haste made syn.'

And whan she herde þis þing she kneled here downe to þe fote of
þe abbot Payn with bitter teeres and bisought him to resccyve hire to
penaunce, and she seid: 'Fader I wote well 'what' penaunce is, and I 30
wote | well that be thi praiers y may haue foryeuenesse. I aske the E f. 241ra
only the terme of .iij. houres and after that y will go whedir thou wilt
and will do and obeye whateuer thou comaunde me.' And whanne he
had graunted her the terme and assigned the place wher she shulde
come to hym, she went and gadered all her thingges togedre that she 35
hadde gote by synne, and bare hem alle into the middell of the citee

5 of] and H1   9 a cite of] *om.* D   þis shillyng] the that D   10 though] *om.* H1
it] *add* hir D   11 she¹] this Thais D   14 Is þere] ther is D   secrete place] *twice* D
16 þat¹] *om.* H1   place] *add* herein D   19 I] *add* knowe and H2   21 thou] *followed by*
erasure H1   26 not] *om.* H2   thyn] thou *changed to* thyn H1   27 bi peyne] *om.* H2
29 þe] this holie H2   to¹] that she myght H2   to²] *om.* H2   30 penaunce] *add* for hir
mysdoynge H2   wote] knowe H2   what] þat *del.* 'what' H1   30–31 what . . . well] *om.* H1
33 will] *om.* H1   me] *om.* H1   he] this holie Abbot H2   34 assigned] *add* hire H1

before alle the peple and brenned hem in [the] fire, sayenge:
'Comithe hider to me alle that haue synned with me, and sethe
how y brenne that the whiche ye haue youe to me.' And the pris of
40 the gold and of the [th]ingges was .vC. li.

And whanne she hadde brende it she went to the place that she
was assigned vnto by the abbot Payn. And there was a chirche of
virgines where he enclosed her in a celle and seled the dore with lede,
and the cell was litell and streite and lefte alonly but a litell wyndowe
45 bi the whiche thei might ministre to her her lyvinge. And the abbot
comaunded that thei shulde eueri day ministre to her a litell brede
and a litell water. And whanne the abbot shulde go, Thays saide to
hym: 'Fader, where wilt thou comaunde that y putte oute that the
whiche comithe oute of the condites of nature?' And he said: 'In thi
50 celle as thou art worthi.' And thanne she asked how she shulde praie
to God, and he saide: 'Thou art not worthi to nempne God ne that
the name of the Trinite be named bi thi mouthe, ne for to lefte up
thin hondes to heuene, for thi lippes be full of wyckednesse and thin
hondes full of wicked touchinges of felthe, but [loke] only ayenst the
55 orient in recordyng of this word: "Lord that formedest me, haue
merci and pitee of me."'

And thanne whanne she hadde be .iij. yere enclosed in this plite,
f. 241rb   the abbot remembrid hym and bethought | hym of her, and went
thanne to the abbot Antoni for to enquere wher God hadd foryeue
60 her her synnes and tolde hym the cause. And thanne Seint Antony
called his disciples and comaunded hem that thei shulde that night
wake and praie that God wold of his mersy declare the cause of the
abbot Paynes comyng. And thanne as thei praied withoute cesinge,
the abbot Paule that was the grettest of the disciples of Antony sawe
65 sodeinly a bedde in heuene arraied with precious clothes, that .iij.
virgines withe clere faces kepten. And these .iij. virgines were these:
the furst was drede of the peynes in hell, that withdrowe this Thays
fro her synnes; the secounde was shame that she hadd for her synnes
[that] she hadd done, [that] made her deserue pardon; the thridde
70 was loue of rightwisnesse that lefte her up to the soueraine place.

37 the²] *om.* E   38 hider] hiþer *changed to* hider H1   to me] *add* and H1
40 thingges] ringges EH1H2 (*choses* P2)   li.] pounde H2   45 her²] *om.* H1   47 Thays]
Thus she H2   47–8 to hym] *om.* H1   48 the] *om.* H1   49 thi] þe H1H2   52 name
of the] *twice* H2   bi] in H1   up] *add* to hym E   53–4 and . . . touchinges] *om.* H2
54 loke] *om.* E   56 of] on H1H2   57 .iij. yere/enclosed] *trs.* H1   58 hym¹] *om.* H1
60 her¹,²] *om.* H1   64 of the disciples] disciple H2   66 withe] *add* .iij. E   69 that¹]
om. E   that²] The .iij. EH1H2 (*qui* P2)   the thridde] and that H2

And whanne Poule hadd said that the grace of that vision was onli bi
the merites of Seint Antoni, an heuenli vois was herde that saide that
it was not by the merites of Antony but [by] the merites of Thays the
sinfull woman.

And in the morw whanne the abbot Paule hadd tolde this vision, 75
and that thei hadd knowe the will of God, the abbot Payne departed
thennes with gret ioye and went anone to the monasteri there she
was, and opened the dore of the selle. And she required hym that she
might abide still lenger. And thanne the abbot saide: 'Come oute, for
thi synnes be foryoue the of God.' And she ansuered and saide: 'I 80
take God to witnesse that sethe y entred into this selle I haue sette al
my synnes before myn eyen and, right as the brethe partithe neuer
from the mouthe and fro the nostrelles, right so my synnes passed |
neuer my sight, but y haue euer beholde hem and wepte for hem.' f. 241ᵛᵃ
To whom the abbot thanne saide: 'God hathe not onli foryeue the thi 85
synnes bi thi penaunce, but for thou hast hadd euer drede in thi
corage.' And thanne he toke her oute from thennes, and .xv. dayes
she lyued after, and thanne she rest in pees in oure Lorde.

And the abbot Effraym wolde in like maner conuerte a comune
woman. As that wreched woman drewe Seint Effraym to synne 90
foliously, he saide to her: 'Folu me,' and she folued hym, and whan
thei come in a place ther was grete multitude of men, he saide to here:
'Sitte downe, for y will haue to do with the [here].' And she saide to
hym: 'How may y do suche a synne before suche a multitude of men?'
And thanne he saide to her: 'Yef thou hast shame of man, how moche 95
more shalt thou haue gretter shame of God thi creatoure that knowithe
all hidde thingges?' And so she went from hym al confused.

Here endithe the liff of Seint Thays, and nexst beginnithe
the liff of Seint Denis, Capᵐ. .C.xlvj.

Seint Denis was conuerted to the faithe of the blessed apostle of
Ihesu Crist Seint Paule, and men saien that he was named Ariopagite

73 of] *add* Seinte H2   by²] *om.* E   75 tolde] seyne H2   76 knowe] knowelege
of H2   77 monasteri] celle H2   80 the] *om.* H1   82 neuer] *om.* H2
85 thanne] *om.* H2   thanne saide] seid Than H1   86 but] *om.* H2   88 in²] with
H1H2   89 And] *add* also H2   90 woman] *add* and H2   drewe Seint] entised the
abbot H2   92 thei] he H2   was] *add* a H1   93 to¹] *ins.* H1   here] *om.* E, *add* in this
place H2   95 he] she *with* s *erased* H2   96 shalt thou haue/gretter shame] *trs.* H1H2
97 so] *om.* H1

EH1T1H2A1A2L; E omits all beween 51 *speking* and 116 *heuene*; D resumes at 40 *shulde*
and is affected by a crease from 59–70 and 149–159

of the strete wher he duelled in the citee. And in that strete was the temple of Mart, for all tho of Athenes named euery strete after her
5 goddes that thei worshepeden in the same. And there as thei worshepeden the god of Mars thei called it *Ariopage*, and *Ario* is to saie the god Mars, and that strete wher thei worshipped [Pan] thei called it *[P]ariopage*, and so of other stretis.

And *Ariopage* was euer the gret excellent strete, bicause tho
f. 241vb whi|che were noble and worthi duelled therinne. And thereinne
11 duelled the scolers of artes and Denys that was a gret philisopher, and for the plente of his wisdom of the godhede that was in hym he was called Theosophe, that is to saie knowing of God. And Apolophanis was his felawe in philosophie. And in that tyme there
15 were the secte of Epicurus, that saiden that all the blessednesse of man was only in the delit of the bodi, and also there duelled the secte of Stociens that saide she was onli vertu of the soule.

And thanne in the day of the passion of oure Lorde, whanne derkenesse was made thorugh the world, the philisophres that were
20 atte Athenes coude not fynde in causes naturels the cause of this derkenes. For it was [no] naturel eclipse, bicause the mone was right ferre fro the region of the sonne, and the mone was thanne .xv. and so there was an unperfite distaunce in the sonne, and alweyes the eclips takithe not awey the light of alle the parties of the worlde, and
25 also she may not dure .iiij. houres. And it aperithe bi that [that] Luke saithe, the Euuangelist, that thilke eclips toke al the light awey in eueri parti thorugh the worlde for oure Lorde suffered peyne in alle his membris, and therfor was the eclips in Ethiope, in Egipte, in Rome, in Grece. And Orose witnessithe that she was in Grece and in
30 the end of Asye the Litell. And he saithe that whanne oure Lorde was nailed on the crosse, ther was made a gret tremblyng of the erthe thorugh the worlde, the roches and the mounteynes were kitte and clouen, right gret abundaunce of flodes fell in mani places more thanne was custumed before. [And] that day, from the .vj. houre the

3 strete²] *add* where he dwellid in the cite *followed by erasure* H2   4 Mart] Mars H1 of²] þat H1   5 in the same] *om.* H2   6 Mars] Martis H1, Mart H2   6–8 and *Ario . . . Pariopage*] *om.* H2   7 Pan] it thanne E, it H1   8 Pariopage] Ariopage EH1 (*Pariopage* P2)   9 strete] *om.* H2   bicause] *add* that H1H2   12 wisdom] *add* and H2   godhede] goodnesse H2   17 Stociens] Scociens H1H2   21 no] *om.* E 23 unperfite] on perfite H1   25 that²] *om.* E   28 Egipte] *add* and H1   29 And Orose] Andorose H1   30 Asye] Alicie H1   32 worlde] *add* for H2   33 clouen] *add* that H2   34 custumed] custome H2   And] *om.* EH1   that] *ins.* H1   from] From *beginning new sentence* EH1

sunne derked and lost his light thorugh | alle the parties of the world   f. 242ra
and in that orrible night there was neuer sein sterre [in] Egipte.   36

And this same recordithe Denis in a pistell to Apolaphanes, saieng: 'The worlde was derked comonly with blaknesse of derkenesse and sethe the onli diametre retorned purged. And whanne we had founde that it was thinge certeyne that the sonne shulde not 40 suffre such sorw and tristes, ne [we] mowe not yet haue perceiued the misterie of this thing bi oure gret wisdom: "O Apolophanes, mirour of doctrine, what shal y saie of these hidde thingges? Y putte hem fulli to the as to a diuyne mowthe that passithe mannes conseite." Than he ansuered and saide: "O goode Denys, the 45 chaunge of thinge[s] ben diuerse." And in the ende it is signified the [f]erie dyvine and the yere of the annunciacion that Poule oure doctour saide to oure deif eeres, and by the signes that crieden that y shuld recorde, I haue founde the might of the verite of God and y am deliuered from the snares of falshede.' And these ben the wordes of 50 Denis. And of this same he spekinge | to Policarpe and to   H1 f. 306rb Apoliphanes seith in his epistle: 'We tweyne were at [Heliopalin] | and we segh þe mone of heven [go] [disordenatli] and þe tyme was   H1 f. 306va not conable. And whan þey segh þis wondre with oþer many þat ben not declared here Denys and Apolyphanes went into Egipte for to 55 desire to lerne astronomye, and aftre Denys returned `aȝene'.

And þat þis eclips was in Asie witnesseth Eusebee in his Cronicle, and seith þat he radde in þe Di[c]tes of Euchiciens þat þere was a grete erthequake in Bethanie þat is a prouince of Azic the Litul and þere was þe grettest derkenesse of þe sonne þat ever had ben. For þe 60 houre of none of þe day was torned into derkenesse of þe niȝt also into perfite derkenesse. And he seith þat in Vicenne þat is a cite of Bethanie þe trembling of þe erthe caste downe þe houses. And it is redde in stories þat þe philosophres were brought þereto fore to sei þat þe god of nature suffred dethe or elles þat þe order of nature was 65 ouerturned or elles þat the elementes lied or elles had pite of god of

36 night] light H1   in²] thorugh E, þorogh oute H1   38 comonly] continuelli H1 39 sethe] om. H1, seith H2   retorned] add and H2   we] he H1   40 that it was] ins. H1 41 tristes] trestes H1, tristinesse D   we] om. E, ins. H1   44 fulli] holie D 46 thinges] thinge E   ferie] L, verie E, veri with v on erasure H1   48 deif eeres] differis D   49 verite] vertue D   50 falshede] falsenes D   51 of] om. H1 52 Heliopalin] holy Apolyn H1D   53 of] add and del. þe H1   go disordenatli] `goth disortinale' H1   54 oþer many] mani moo D   ben] were D   56 desire to] om. D 57 Cronicle] croniclis D   58 Dictes] dietes H1   59 erthequake] erþquaue D 60 For] bifore D   61–2 also . . . derkenesse] om. D   63 þe¹] add and del. tre on erasure H1

naturc þat suffrcd dcthe. And [it is] redde elleswhere that Denys said: 'This derkenesse and ny3t signifieth þat a newe and a verri light of þe worlde shal come.'

70   And þan þei of Athenes made to þat god an auter and set a title aboue it thus: 'þis is þe god vnknowe.' And in eueri auter of here goddes þe title was set aboue, shewyng of whom þe auter was dedied. And whan þei of Athenes `wold do sacrifise´ þe philisophres seid þat

Hı f. 306ᵛᵇ 'God hath | no nede of oure goodes, but knele ye downe bifore þe
75   auter of him and bisecheth him and preieth to him vmbeli for he secheth not þe offeryngges of sinners but þe deuocion of soules.'

And aftre that whan Seint Poule come to Athenes, the philo-sophres of Epicures and Stociens disputed and stroof with him, and som of hem seid: 'What wold þis sower of wordes mene?' And som
80   seyde: 'He wol be a newe bringer of tidinges of fendes.' And than þei ladde him into þe strete of philosophres for to examine him of his newe doctrine and seid to him: 'Thou hast brought to vs some newe þinges. We wold wete what þei were.' And þise philosophres of Athenes entended moost [to] here newe thinges. And þan [whan]
85   Seynt Poule had biholde þe auters he segh amonge þe oþer þe auter of [þe] god vnknowe, [and seid]: 'A, Sires philosophres, I anounce to yow þis god þat ye worshipp and ye wote not who it is. I tel you þat it is he þat made heven and erthe.' And þan he turned vnto Denys whom he segh most ententife to here dyvine trouthes and seid:
90   'Denys, what is this verri god vnknowen?' And Denys seid: 'This is þe verri god vnknowen þat is not shewed amongest þies oþer goddes. He is knowen of vs, but to yow he is vnknowen, and he shal come in þe worlde to come and regne in everlastingnesse.' Than seid Poule: 'Is he

Hı f. 307ʳᵃ a man onli | or a spirit?' And Denis seid: 'He is God and man, but he is
95   vnknowen for þat his conuersacion is aloonli in heven.' And þan seid Poule: 'þis is he that I preche of, þat discended fro heuen and toke mankinde and suffred deth and roos þe .iij. dai fro deth to liffe.'

And as Denys disputed with Poule, there passed bi aventure a blinde man befor hem. And anone Denis seid to Seint Poule: 'If þou
100   seist in þe name of þi Lorde: "Late þis blinde man haue sight," I shal

67 it is] is it *marked for trs.* Hı   72 dedied] edified D   79 mene] meve D
80 seyde] *with* y *on erasure* Hı   newe] *om.* D   82 him] *add* þat D   83–4 We wold
. . . thinges] *om.* D   84 to] L, of Hı   whan] *om.* Hı   86 þe] *om.* Hı   and seid]
om. Hı   87 worshipp and ye] *om.* D   88 he] Poule D   turned] *add* to hym *with*
to *subp.* D   91 vnknowen] *add* and he shal come D   92 knowen . . . is] *om.* D
vnknowen] *add* of you D   94 or] *add* els D   is] *add* boothe D   100 Late] þat D
sight] *add* and Hı

anone bileue [in] him so þat þou do it not by non enchauntement, for thou mightest kon suche wordes þat haue suche strengthe.' And Poule seid to him: 'I shall tel þe afore þe forme of þe wordes þat haue suche strength which I wol sai þat shul be seid, "In þe name of Ihesu Crist boren of a virgine, crucified and dede, þat roos ayene 105 and stied into heven and from þens shal come to iuge þe worlde."' And for þat al suspecion sh[uld] be put awey, Poule sei[d] to Denys þat he himself shuld sei þise wordes. [And whan Denys hadde seid þise wordes] to þe blinde man, anone he recouered his sight. And þan was Denys cristoned with Damar his wife and al his 110 housold.

And he was made a tru cristen man and was with Poule .iij. yere. And than he was ordeigned bisshop of Athenes, and there he was in predicacion and conuerted þat cite and grete parte of þat region to þe feith of Ihesu Crist. And it is seid þat Poule shewed him þat he segh 115 whan he was rauisshed into þe .iij. | heuene as Denis shewithe in E f. 242ra mani places. And bi that cause he spake so clerely of the gerarchies of aungels and of ordres and of disposiciones and of the office[s] of hem so that men wene not that he might lerne it of none other but yef he hymselff hadd be rauisshed into the .iij. heuene and that he hadde 120 there saien alle these thingges.

He was made noble bi the spirit of prophesie, as hit semithe bi a pistell that he sent to Seint Iohn the Euuangelist into the ile of Pathmos where he was sent into exile, and Denys prophesied that he shulde come ayen, [saieng]: 'Reioyse the, | verrcy loued, verrey f. 242vb frende, and louely and right loued, thou shalt be take oute of the 126 kepinge wher thou art in Pathmos, and thou shalt come ayen into Asie and shalt do there the good werkes of [the] l[i]vinge God, and thou shalt deliuer hem to tho that shull [come] after the.' And as it ys said and shewed in the Boke of Dyvine Names that he was atte the 130 passinge of the moste blessed Virgine Marie.

And whanne that he herde that Peter and Paule were in prison in Rome vnder Nero, he ordeyned a bisshopp vnder hym and went for to uisite hem. And whan thei were goodly passed to God and

101 in] *om.* H1   do] *om.* D   not] *om.* D   103 þe¹] *om.* D   þat] *add* I D
106 to] ayenn and D   107 shuld] shal H1   seid] *so with* d *erased* H1   108 sei¹] seid
H1   108–9 And . . . wordes] L, *om.* H1D   109 recovered] receiued D   116 .iij.]
dredde E   118 offices] office EH1   119 yef] *ins.* H1, *om.* D   121 saien] seyn
with ey *on erasure* H1   123–4 of . . . exile] *ins.* H1   124 prophesied] seide D
125 saieng] and EH1   126 right] *add* welle beloued D   128 the²] *om.* EH1
livinge] lovinge EH1   129 come] be E, go H1

135 Clement satte in the sege of Rome, after a space of tyme he was sent
by that same Clement into Fraunce, and there were in his felawship
Rustin and Eleutherie. And thanne he come to Paris and conuerted
there moche peple to the faithe and ordeined there mani chirches and
putte in hem diuerse clerkes [of diuerse ordres]. And thanne he
140 shined in so gret heuenli grace that, whanne the bisshoppes of ydoles
meued debate ayenst hym and the peple come for to haue destroied
hym, as sone as thei had beholde hym al her cruelte was gone and
thei wolde falle downe atte his fete where thei hadde so gret drede
that thei wolde flee before hym and durst in no wise abide hym.

145 But the fende that hadd envie and seigh euery day his power
decrees and [th]at the chirche lordshipped and had the victorie, he
stered thanne Domecien emperoure into so gret cruelte that he made
a comaundement that whosoeuer founde ani cristen man that he
shuld constreine hym to do sacrifise or ellis torment hym bi dyuerse
f. 242ᵛᵃ tormentis. | And thanne he sent the prouost of Rome that hight
151 Sisi[n]ien to Parys ayenst the cristen, and founde there the blessed
Denis prechinge to the peple, and anone he made take hym and
cruelli for to bete and shamfulli spitte on hym and dispised hym, and
lete binde hym harde and with hym [Rustyn] and Euletharie and was
155 brought before hym. And whanne he seigh that the seintes were
stable in the confession of oure Lorde he was full of anger, and
thanne come there forthe a gret matrone and tolde how that her
husbonde was foule deseiued with these enchauntours. And thanne
he was anone sent for and cruelly slayne with longe perseueringe in
160 confession of God. And the seintes were cruelli bete with .xij.
knightes, and thanne thei were bounde streiteli in cheines and
putte in prison.

And the day foluing Denys was putte on a gredyrne of yren and
streched oute al naked upon the colis and upon the hote flawme of
165 fire, and there he songe to oure Lorde: 'Thi worde is forciblement
embraced and thi seruaunt louithe it.' And after that he was sette
betwene two cruel bestes that were meued bi right gret hungre bi
longe fastinge. And as sone as thei ronne vpon hym he made the
signe of the crosse ayenst hem and thei were anone right tame. After

135 sege] sete D   sent] passid D   138 faithe] add of Ihesu criste D   139 of
diuerse orders] om. ED   141 debate] hate Hı   143 where] and D   144 before]
fro D   in no wise] nat D   146 that] atte EHı   the¹] 'þe' Hı   lordshipped] lordeship
Hı   151 Sisinien] Sisilien EHı   152 he] the provest D   154 harde] fast D
Rustyn] om. E, ins. Hı   156 stable] stabled EHı   159 he] Denys D   for] anone
bifore t⟨h⟩e iuge D   160 the] add tothir D

that he was caste in a brennynge furneys of brennynge fire, and the 170
fire quenched and he hadde none harme. And after that he was putte
upon a crosse and therupon he was turmented longe, and thanne he
was take downe and putte in prison with his other felawes and with
mani | other cristen. And as he songe there his masse and houseled f. 242ᵛᵇ
the peple, our Lorde appered to hym with gret light and gaue hym 175
his blessed bodi and saide: 'Right dere frende, resseiue me, for thi
gret guerdon is with me.'

After that he was presented to the iuge and was ayen putte into
nwe turmentis, and thanne the hedes of the .iij. felawes were smite of
in the name of the holi Trinite, and this was done bysides the temple 180
of Mercurie. And anone the bodi of [Seint] Denys arose up and bare
his hede [two] myle bi the ledinge of aungeles, and the light of the
godhede went before hym and bare hym fro the Mount Mart[r]e into
the place where he restith now bi his owne chois and bi purueaunce of
God. And so gret melodie of aungeles was herde there that mani of hem 185
that herde it beleued in God, and [L]arci the wiff of the pr[o]uost
Lybien [said] that she was cristen, and she was anone beheded and
baptised in her owne blode, and Lybien her sone was a knight in Rome
vnder .iij. emperoures. And sithe he turned ayen to Paris and was there
[baptised] and putte hymselff in the noumbre of religio[u]s. 190

And the wicked paynimes dredden lest that the good cristen wolde
berie the bodies of Seint [R]ustin and Elowthere, and comaunded
that thei shulde be caste into Seyne. And a noble ladi bade to dinere
with her tho that bare hem, and the whiles thei were atte the dinere
she stale the holi bodies and beried hem priueli in a felde of hers. 195
And after, whanne the persecusion cesed, she toke hem from thennes
and putte hem worshipfulli with the bodi of Seint Denys. And [thei]
suffered dethe aboute the yere of oure Lorde | .iiijˣˣ.x. in the .vj. yere f. 243ʳᵃ
of Domacien in the age of Denis .iiijˣˣ.x.

About the yere of oure Lorde .viijC.xxxij. in the tyme of Lowis 200
the kinge, his messages were sent fro Michel the emperour out of
Constantinenople and withe other thingges thei brought to Lowys,

170 furneys] add ful D   and] add anone D   172 longe] add time D
174 cristen] add puple D   179 the²] om. H1, thoo D   181 Seint] the saide EH1
182 his] add owne D   two] a EH1   183 Martre] Martee E   into] vnto D
185–6 hem that] om. D   186 Larci] darci E, Dari H1   prouost] pruost E
187 said] ins. H1, om. D (dit P2)   that she was cristen] was cristened D   188 her²]
his D   190 baptised] om. EH1D (baptisie P2)   of] add þe H1   religious] religiones E
191 cristen] add puple D   192 bodies] body H1   Seint] Denys D   Rustin] Austin E,
Rustyn with R on erasure H1   193 Seyne] Savie D   194 with her] om. D
195 holi] om. D   197 thei] L, om. EH1D   201 his] om. D

the sone of Charles the Gret, bokes of Seint Denis of the ierarchie of
aungels translated from Greke into Latine, and thei were resseiued
205 with gret ioye, and that night .xix. seke men were heled in his
chirche.

[S]o as Seint Ruyle the bisshop dede the sollempnite of the masse
at Arle, he recorded in the canon of the masse the names of the
marteres Denys, Rustin and Eleuther. And whanne he hadde saide it
210 he meruailed moche of hymselff, for he wend [verri]ly that thei hadd
lyued, [and also he meruailed] what hym ailed to reherce her names
vnwetyng of hymselff. Ande therewith apered .iij. doves to hym thus
meruaylinge, and stoden vpon the crosse of the auutre, and there was
wretin upon her brestes with blode the names of the martres. And
215 whan he hadd diligently beholde this he vnderstode that the seintes
were passed to God.

About the yere of oure Lord .vjC.xxxiij. as it is conteined in a
cronicle how that Dagebirt kinge of Fraunce, that reyned longe afore
Pipin, beganne to haue from his childehode gret reuerence to Seint
220 Denys, for whanne he dradde in that tyme the wratthe of his fader he
wolde anone flee to the chirche of Seint Denys. And whanne the
kinge was dede, it was shewed in a vision to an holi man that the
soule of hym was rauisshed in iugement and that many seintes
accused hym that he hadde dis[poil]ed the chirches. And so as the |
f. 243ʳᵇ wicked aungeles wolde haue rauisshed hym to the peynes of helle,
226 the blessed Seint Denys come thedir, and thanne he was deliuered bi
his comyng and askaped the peynes. And by grace he was returned to
lyff and dede penaunce.

The kinge Lowys discouered the bodi vndewly and brak of his
230 arme and stale it coueitously, and he turned anone in[to] madnesse.

And wetithe well that Ignacien bisshop of Reynes wrote in a pistell
that he sent to Charles that this Denys sent into Fraunce was Denys
Arroparexit so as it is saide aboue. And Iohn the Scotte witnessithe
the same in his epistell sent to Charles the same, ne reson witnessithe
235 [it] not bi the acounte of the tyme so as sum wolde withsaie it.

207 So] Lo EH1, *add* in a time D   as] *add* the EH1   208 at] of D   the⁴] *om.* H1
Rustin] Russyn H1   210 verrily] wisly E   210–12 for . . . hymselff] *ins. with*
wisly *changed to* wyssli *and om.* and also he meruailed H1   211 and also he meruailed]
L, *om.* ED   212 .iij. doves/to hym] *trs.* H1   217 is] *ins.* H1   223 many seintes]
trs. H1   224 dispoiled] distroied EH1   226 thanne he was] he was anone D
227 returned] *add* ayenne D   229 The] Also the D   bodi] *add* of seinte Denys D
230 into] in EH1   233 Arroparexit] Apaceit D   235 it¹] is EH1, *om.* D   not]
add and del. no H1

Here endithe the lyff of Seint Denys, and nexst beginnithe
the lyff of Seint Calixe, Capitulum .C.xlvij.ᵐ

Kalixe pope was martered the yere of oure Lorde .CC.xxij. under
Alisaundre emperoure. And bi the werkes of that emperoure the most
apparaunt partie of the citee of Rome was brent with fire of
vengeaunce and the lifte honde of the ydole of Iubiter that was of
golde was al ymolte. And thanne al the bisshopes of ydoles went to the 5
emperoure Alisaundre and required hym that the goddes that were
displesed might be apesed with sacrifice. And thanne as thei dede
sacrifice, in a Thrusday erly whanne the eyre was al clere .iiij. prestes
of the ydoles were slayne bi veineaunce with a clappe of thondre, and
the auuter of Iubiter was brent so that al the peple of Rome fledde | out   f. 243ᵛᵃ
of the walles of Rome.   11
    And whanne Palmachien wist that the pope hadde hidde hym with
other clerkes ouer the watre of Tybre, he required that the cristen bi
whom this euel fortune was falle to hem might be putte oute for to
clense the towne. And whanne he hadde power for to do this he hasted 15
hym for to go thedir with his knightes, and anone thei were al blynde,
and than Palmachien was sore afraied and denounsed this thinge to
the emperoure Alysaundre. And thanne the emperoure comaunded
that on the Wednisday all the peple shulde assemble for to do sacrifice
to Mercurie, so that thei might haue ansuere of hym vpon these 20
thingges. And as thei dede her sacrifice, a virgine of the temple that
hight Iuliane was rauisshed with the fende and beganne to crie: 'The
God of Kalixt is verrei trouthe and liff, that is wrothe and hathe
indignacion of oure filthes.' And whanne Palmachien herde that, he
went ouer the Tybre into the citee of Rauen to Seint Kalixt and made 25
hymselff to be baptised of hym, and his wiff and all his meyni.
    And whanne the emperoure herde that, he made hym be called
before hym and deliuered hym to Symplicien senatoure for to teche
hym with faire wordes, for that he was full profitable for the comune.
And Palmachien perseuered in fastynge, in orisones, and good werkes, 30
and thanne there come to hym a man that behight hym that yef he
might hele his wiff that hadde the pallesie he wolde beleue in God.

EH1DH2A1A2; H1 *has* Narracio *deleted in place of rubric*   1 Kalixe] Calixt H1D
pope] *del. and ins.* buschop E   .CC.xxij.] .CC. and .xij. D   5 ymolte] there moost *del.*
'imolte' H1   7–8 And . . . sacrifice] *om.* H1   12 pope] *add* 'Calixt' H1, *so* D
14 this] þat H1   16 thei] tweine *del.* 'thei' H1   20 haue] *add* an H1   25 ouer]
add water of D   27 herde] *ins.* H1   29 comune] commones D   31 to hym/a
man] *trs.* H

f. 243ᵛᵇ And thanne whanne Palmachien hadd preied, the wyffe | arose al hole
and she ranne to Palmachien and saide: 'Baptise me in the name of
35   Ihesu Crist that hathe holde myn hond and lefte me up.' And than
come Kalixt thedir and baptised her and her husbond and Simplicyen
and mani other. And whanne the emperoure herde it he dede sende for
to behede al that were cristened, saue that he made Kalixt lyve in
prison .v. dayes and .v. nightes withoute mete or drinke. And whanne
40   he saw after that he was more comforted and more glad thanne before,
he comaunded that he shulde eueri day be bete with staues, and thanne
he made for to binde a gret stone about his necke and caste hym oute of
a wyndowe into a pitte. And Astacien his preest toke [vp] the bodi oute
of the pitte and beried it in the [cemetorie] of Calopodien.

Here endithe the lyff of Seint Kalixt, and nexst begynnithe
the lyff of Seint Leonard, Capitulum .C.xlviij.

It is saide that Seint Leonard was aboute the yere of oure Lorde
[.vC.]. And he [was] lefte up from the fount of Seint Remigie
Archebisshoppe of Re[m]es and was taught bi hym in the holy
disciplines of hele. And the kinrede of Leonard helde the furst
5   place in the kingges paleis. And he was in so gret grace with the
kinge that all the prisoners that he visited were anone deliuered. And
whan the renoune of his name encresed, the kinge constreined hym
for to duelle with hym a grete tyme, vnto that he seighe couenable
tyme to yeue hym a bisshopriche. And he refused it and lefte alle,
10   desiringe for to be in desert, and thanne he come prechinge to
Orleaunce with Leo[f]ard his brother. And there thei lyued a litell
f. 244ʳᵃ tyme in a covent, and than | Leo[f]ard hadd desire to dwell allone in a
desert vpon the riuere of Leyre, and Leonard was taught bi the holy
goste for to go preche in Aquitaigne, and thanne thei cussed togedre
15   and departed. Thanne Leonarde preched there, and dede many
miracles, and he duelled in a forest nygh the citee of Lymogis, in
the whiche forest the kinge had an halle that was there ordeined for
hym whan he wolde hunte.

37 for] *ins.* H₁   38 Kalixt] *add* to H₁D   38–9 in prison/.v. dayes] *trs.* H₁
40 after] *om.* D   more¹] *om.* D   thanne] *add* he was D   41 staues] stones H₁
43 And] An`d´ H₁   vp] oute E   44 cemetorie] cuntrey E

EH₁T₁DH₂A₁A₂L; D breaks off after 115 *nothinge*; H₁ *has* Narracio *deleted in place of*
rubric   2 .vC.] *om.* EH₁, *space* D (.vᶜ. P₂)   was] *om.* EH₁   up] *om.* D   3 Remes]
Reynes EH₁   5 And] *add* also D   9 hym] *add* in E   11, 12 Leofard] leonard
EH₁   13 the] a H₁

It happed in a day that the kinge wolde go hunte in that forest and
the quene with hym that was gret with childe. And as thei were in the   20
forest the quene beganne to trauaile [of] childe in suche wise that she
was in perile of dethe, so that the kinge and al his meyne wepte and
sorued withoute comfort. And Leonard thanne passinge bi the forest
herde the voys of hem that wepten and was meued with pitee and
went thedir. And the king called hym and asked what he was, and he   25
saide that he was a disciple of Seint Remigye. And thanne the kinge
conceiued good hope in hym, for hym thought that he was taught of a
good maister. Thanne he ledd hym to the quene, and praied hym that
he wolde praie for the helthe of the quene and for the fruit of her
wombe so that God wolde yeue hym double ioye. And anone as he   30
hadde made his praiere God graunted hym his orison and gate of God
his request.

And thanne the kinge offered to hym golde and siluer, but he
refused alle and praied hym to yeue it to the pore and saide: 'Y haue
no ncdc of none of alle these thinges, it suffisithe me only to dispise   35
the richesse of this worlde and to serue God in this wode, and that is
alle that y de|sire.' And thanne the kinge wolde haue yeuen hym al   f. 244rb
that wode and he saide: 'Y will not haue it [alle], but as moch therof as
y may go about with myn asse, so moche y praie you to yeue.' And
thanne the kinge dede it gladly.   40

And thanne he made there a chirche whereinne he lyued longe in
abstinence, and tweie felawes with hym. And as the water was thanne
a myle from hem, he dede make a pitte al drie and felled it full of
water with his praiers. And he called that place Noble for that a noble
kinge hadd yeue it hym. And he shined there bi so mani miracles that   45
whosoeuer was in prison, as sone as he called his name and his helpe
his bondes were losed and he went freli and offered his cheines to
Seint Leonard. And mani of tho men duelled with hym and serued
there oure Lorde. And there were .vij. of his noble kinrede that leften
the worlde and comen and duelled with hym, and he deliuered to ech   50
of hem a partie of the wode and thei duelled with hym and drew many

19 go] *om.* D   21 of] on E   26 a] *om.* H1   28 he] the kinge D
29 helthe] helpe H1   30 anone] assone D   31–2 and . . . his] of godis D   35 none
of] *om.* D   only/to dispise] *trs.* H1   36 God] *add* in pees E, *add* oonli in pees H1
wode] forest D   37 that] *ins.* H1   desire] *add and del.* And þan the king wold haue
yoven him all þat wode and þat is al I desire H1   38 wode] forest D   and] *add* þan H1
alle] *om.* EH1   39 to yeue] haue D   40 thanne] *om.* D   dede it] grauntid hym D
41 he] leonarde D   longe] *add* time D   43 it] *add* vp H1D   47 losed] *add* anone D
went] *add* out D   48 And] *add* also D   51 hym] *add and del.* And he deliuered to
eche of hem a parte of þe wode H1

to vertues bi her ensaumple. And after, this [holi] man made noble bi many uertues passed oute of the worlde [to oure Lorde] in the .viij. ide of Nouembre. And whanne he hadde do there mani miracles, it
55 was shewed to the clerkes of the chirche that, for as moche as that place was to litell for the multitude of concours of peple that come thedir, that thei shulde make owher another chirche and bere the bodi of Seint Leonard thedir worshipfulli. And thanne the clerkes and the peple were alle tho thre dayes in fasting and in orisones, and in the
f. 244va thridde day thei sawe all the contre keuered | with snowe, saue onli the
61 place were Seint Leonard was rested in, that was all grene. And there was the chirche made and the holi bodi was bore thedir, and there moche multitude of irnes and cheines witnessin wel how grete miracles oure Lorde dede for hym and nameli to prisoners whos
65 tokenes hange befor his tombe.

The vicount of Lymagis had do made a gret cheine for to fere wicked men, and comaunded that she shulde be fyched in his toure, and ho that euer was bounde in that cheine he was putte to alle the distemperaunce of the eyre and he shulde not deie of one dethe but as
70 it were [of] a .M.¹ dethes. But so it fell that one of the seruauntes of Seint Leonarde was bounde with that cheine withoute ani deseruinge, so that almost he gaue up the spirit, and than, as he might, he vowed hymselff to Seint Leonard and besought hym that sithen he hadde pitee of other that he wolde haue pitee upon his seruaunt. And anone
75 Seint Leonard apered to hym in a white clothinge and saide: 'Drede not, for thou shalt not deie. Arise up and y shall bere this cheine with the to my chirche. Folow me, for y go before.' And thanne he arose and folowed Seint Leonard till he come to his chirche, and anone as he was before the yates Seint Leonard lefte hym there, and thanne he
80 entered into the chirche and tolde to alle folke what Seint Leonard hadd do to hym, and hangged that gret horrible cheine before his tombe.

Ther was a man that loued and worshipped the place of Seint
f. 244vb Leonard and was ful deuout and true vnto the seint, and so it | fell that
85 he was take of a tyraunt. And whanne the tyraunt hadde hym he beganne to thenke in this wise: 'How shal y do for this Leonard, for he

52 And] *add* þan H1   holi] noble EH1   53 to oure Lorde] *om.*   ide] *changed to* dai
H1   57 the] L, *add* holi EH1D   61 was] *om.* H1D   in] him H1D   63 grete]
mani D   66 made] make D   67 fyched] fried H1   68 the] *om.* H1   70 of¹]
om. E   74 of] on H1   75 Leonard] *add and del.* appered H1   77 Folow me]
twice EH1   79 he] this man D   80 entered] went H1   folke] þe puple D
81 and] *add* than thei D   his] the H1   84 true vnto] drewe to H1   86 for²] *om.* H1

losithe all maner yrnis and all the strengthe of yrne meltithe afore hym as wexe [tofore] the fire. Yef y putte hym in cheynes, anone Seint Leonard wol deliuer hym. Now y wote what y wyl do, y shal make a depe pitte in my towre and y shal caste hym withinne ouercharged 90 with yrnes, and thanne wol y [m]ake a cofre of tre aboue the pitte, and thereinne ther shul lye knightes armed. And though it be so that Leonard breke the cheines, he shall not mow entre under erthe, and thus y shal kepe hym till he haue paied me a .M.¹ shillinges.' And whan that he hadd done all that he thought, that man that was there 95 cried with al his power to Seint Leonard, so in a night Seint Leonard cam and turned the cophre vpsodoune and closed these armed knightes all witheinne right as dede men in her toumbe. And thanne he entered into the pitte with gret light and toke the honde of his deuout and true seruaunt and saide: 'Slepest thou or wakest 100 thou? Lo here Lenard that thou hast so moche desired.' And thanne he fulle of mereuaile saide: 'A Lord, helpe me.' And anone all the cheines tobraste and he toke hym upon his propre shuldres and bare hym oute of the toure. And thanne he walked with hym, talkinge as a frende to another, til he hadde brought hym to his owne hous. 105

As a pilgrime retorned from the visitinge of Seint Leonard, he was take in Almayne and enclosed in a depe pitte. And there he praied hertly to Seint Leonard and to hem also that helde hym in prison that | thei wolde for the loue of Seint Leonarde lete hym go, for he had f. 245ʳᵃ neuer offended hem. And thei saide but yef he bought hymself right 110 dere that he shuld ncucr oute. Thanne he saide pitously: 'Now be it betwene you and Seint Leonard, to whom y am al recomaunded.' And thanne the night foluyng Seint Leonard apered to the lorde of the castell and comaunded that he shulde lete go his pylgrime. And in the morutyde he went haue dremed and dede nothinge. The secound 115 [night] he come and comaunded the same, and yet he wolde not obeie. The thridde night Seint Leonard come and toke hym oute of the castell, and anone the toure and half the castell fell downe and slow all sauf the prince that hadde his hippes tobrostin and lefte hym so to his confusion. 120

88 tofore] ayenst EH1   91 make] take EH1   of tre] om. H1   95 he¹] this tiraunte D thought] couth and þough H1   there] add prisoner D   99 he] Seint leonard D 105 to¹] with H1   108 hertly] om. D   hym] hem H1   110 hem] to hym D   hymself] hym D   111 oute] add of prisoune D   Thanne] And þan H1   Now] om. D 112 whom] on erasure H1   114 comaunded] add him H1   115 haue] to haue H1, that he had D   116 night] om. E   he] Seinte Leonarde H2   come and] om. H2   yet] om. H1 he²] the lorde H2   obeie] add yit H1   119 lefte] lost H1

Ther was a knight enprisoned in Bretaigne that called ofte to Seint Leonard, the whiche anone apered before all and knowin to all and hougely abasshed, and he entred into the prison into alle the hous and braste the bondes and put hem in the knightes honde and ledd hym
125   thorugh [hem] all so that thei were sore all afrayed.

Ther was also another Leonarde of one maner profession and of one uertu, of whiche the bodi restithe in Corbigny. And as this Leonarde was prelate in a chirche, he was of so gret humilite that he was sene to be the lowest of hem alle, so that almost alle the peple
130   drowe to hym for his goodnesse. The enuious come to the kinge Clotarie and saide to hym that, but yef he toke good hede, the reaume of Fraunce shulde take gret harme bi Leonarde that gadered to hym
f. 245ʳᵇ   moche peple under the | coloure of religion. And thanne that right cruel kinge comaunded that he shulde be chased oute. And the
135   knight[es] that come to hym [were] so conuerted bi his wordes that [thei] behight to be his disciple[s]. And thanne the kinge repented hym and asked merci and putte hem oute that had so missaid of hym bothe fro her godes and her worshippes, and euer after he loued gretly Seint Leonard. And this same seint praied also to God that hosoeuer
140   were in prison and asked his helpe that he might haue deliueraunce.

And in a day as he was in his praiers, a gret serpent streched up from the fote of Seint Leonard unto his breste. Yet neuer for that wolde he leue his orison, and whanne he hadd ended his orison he saide: 'Y wote wel that fro the beginninge of thi makinge thou
145   turmentest mankynde as moche as thou maist, and therfor yef ani powere be youe ouer me, do to me as y haue deserued.' And whanne he hadde so saide, the serpent lepte downe thorugh his hode and fell dede atte his fote. Whanne he apesed .ij. bisshoppes that weren atte debate, he tolde before that he shulde passe to God the morw after,
150   and so he dede.

122 and²] *add* thei were H2   123 hous] houses H1H2   124 hym] hem H1
125 hem] *om.* E   sore all] *trs.* H1, sore H2   127 of whiche the] the which H1
129 almost] *om.* H2   130 goodnesse] goodis H1H2   The] And than alle the H2
enuious] *add* puple H2   come] *add* þan H1   134 oute] *add* of the reaume H2
135 knightes] knight E   were] was E   136 thei] he E   disciples] disciple E
138 and¹] *add* eke fro H1   139 seint] *add* Leonarde H2   140 deliueraunce] *add* was
anone H2   141 And] *om.* H2   142 Yet] ne H1   Yet neuer for] but for alle H2
146 me¹] *add* to H2   148 Whanne] And also in a time H2

Here endithe the lyff of Seint Leonard, and nexst beginnithe the lyff of Seint Luke, Capitulum .C.xlix.^m

Luke was of the nacion of Surrie and Antiochen bi art of phisik, and
after some he was one of .[the .lxxij.] disciples. Seint Ierome saithe
that he was disciple of the apostles and not of oure Lorde, and the
Glose upon the .xxv. chapitre of Exodi signefiethe that he ne | ioyned   f. 245va
hym not to oure Lorde whan he preched, but he came to the faith after   5
the resureccion, but it is rather for to holde that he was not one of the
[.lxxij.] disciples yef it were so that some went it. And he was of so
gret perfeccion of liff that he was right wel disposed and ordeined, as
to God, and to his neigheboure, to hymself, and to his office.

   And in tokene of these .iiij. manere of ordenaunces he was discriued   10
for to haue .iiij. faces, that is to saie, the face of a lyon, of a man, of an
oxe and of an egle. And eueriche of these .iiij. bestes had .iiij. faces and
.iiij. winges, as it is saide in Ezechiel in the furst chapitre. And for that
it shal be beter sein, lete us ymagen sum best that hadde a foure square
hede, and lete us ymagen in eueri quarter a visage, so that the mannes   15
face be afore, and in the right side the face of the lyon, and in the lefte
side the face of the oxe, and behynde the face of the egle. And for that
the face of the egle aperithe aboue the other for the lengthe of the
necke, therfor it was saide that that face was aboue. And eueri of these
.iiij. hadd .iiij. wynges, for yef we ymagin eueri beest .iiij. square, and   20
in eueri quarter be .iiij. corners, and in eueri corner ther was a penne.
And after the seintes, be these .iiij. beestes [be] signified the .iiij.
euuangelistes yef it were so that eche of hem had .iiij. faces, in
discriving, that is to saie, of the humanite, of the passion, of the
resurreccion and of the diui[ni]te of Godhede, notwithstonding that   25
these singuler thinges be singuleri sette to eueriche of hem. For after
Ierome, Matheu is figured in man for he was principali meued to
speke of | the manhode of oure Lorde; Luke was figured to an oxe for   f. 245vb
he deuised the presthode of Ihesu Crist; Mark was figured to a lyon
for he wrote most clereli of the resurreccion. For as sum sayn the   30

EH1H2A1A2L; D resumes at 225 *wisdom*   *Rubric* Leonard] Denys *del.* 'Leonard' H1
2 some] sone H1   the] *om.* EH1   .lxxij.] L, .lxxj. EH2, .lxxi'i' H1   4 ioyned] ioineth
H2   5 not] *ins.* H1   after] before H1   7 .lxxij.] .lxxj. E, .iiij^{xx}. and .xij. H2
10 manere of] maner'es' *with* of *erased* H1   10–11 of² . . . haue .iiij.] *ins.* H1
11 lyon] *add* and H1   man] *add* and H1   14–15 us . . . lete] *om.* H2   16 and¹] *om.*
H1   19 was²] *om.* H2   And] *add and del. in* H1   20 and¹] *add* eueri quarter be .iiij.
square and H2   22 the] these E   be¹] ben H2   be²] L, *om.* EH1H2   23 yef] yit
H2   24 the¹] he H2   passion] *add* and H1   25 diuinite] diuite E   of²] *add* the
H1H2   30 sum] *add* men E

faunes of the lyon lyen as dede vnto the thridde day but by the
brething of the lyon thei be arered the thridde day. And for that he
beganne to crie of predicacion, Iohn is figured as an egle that fleithe
most high than ani other brid for he wrote of the diui[ni]te of Ihesu
35 Crist. For Ihesu Crist was .iiij. thinges, he was man born of a uirgine,
he was a bole in his passion, a lyon in his resurreccion, an egle in his
ascencion.

And bi these .iiij. visages it is wel shewed how Luke was wel
ordeined and disposed in .iiij. maners. For bi the visage of man it is
40 shewed that he was ordeined rightfulli as to his neigheboure, how he
aught bi reson teche hym and drawe hym bi debonairte, and norisshe
hym bi fraunchise. For man is a beest resonable, debonair, and fre.

Bi the face of the egle was shewed that he was rightfull[i] ordeined
to God, for the ey of his understondinge behelde God by contempla-
45 cion, and the ey of his desire was [shar]ped to hym bi thought of
effecte, and his age was putte out bi new conuersacion. The egle is of
sharpe sight so that he will mightly loke ayenst the bemes of the sonne
withoute blenching, and whan he is high in the eyre he seithe wel the
fishes in the see. He hathe his becke gretli croked, that he be not lette
50 to gadre his mete, he whettith and sharpithe his becke atte a stone and
makithe hym couenable to the use of his eting. And whanne he is
f. 246ra broyled in the hote brenning of the | sonne he caste hymself with gret
strengthe into a welle, and there he takithe awey his age bi hete of the
sonne and chaungithe all his fetheres and takithe awey the derkenesse
55 of his eyen.

By the face of the lyon it is shewed how he was ordeined to
hymselveward, for he had noblesse bi honeste of maners and of holi
conuersacion, he hadd sotilte for to eschewe the lygingges in awaite of
his enemies, and he hadd sufferaunce for to haue pitee of hem that
60 were turmented. The lyon is a noble beest, for he is kinge of beestis.
He is sotel, for he defasithe the trace of his fete with his taile that he be
not founde whan he fleithe. He is sufferable, for he sufferithe
sumtyme the quartein.

By the face of the oxe is it shewed how he was ordeined as to his
65 office, the whiche is wretin in the gospell, for he prosedid morialli,

33 as] to H1H2   34 than] of H1H2   diuinite] diuite E   36 resurreccion] add
and H1H2   43 egle] add he EH1   rightfulli] rightfull E   45 sharped] L,
worshipped EH1, worshippe H2   47 mightly] om. H2   48 blenching] blemshing
H1H2   49 hathe] add also H2   51 couenable] vnuenable H2   52 hote . . . the]
repeat on next folio E   54 and²] also it H2   59 pitee of hem] put on him H1
64 the] om. H2

that is to saye bi moralite, for he beganne from the natiuite [of the
foregoer and of the natiuite] and the childehode of Ihesu Crist, and so
he proceded litell and litell unto the fulfellinge of the laste. He
beganne wisely, for he beganne after .ij. euuangelistes, so that, yef thei
hadde anithinge foryete or lefte behinde that he might write it, and 70
leue that whiche thei hadde sufficiauntli saide. He was taught in the
maners towarde the temple and sacrifices, as it aperithe in the
beginnynge, in the middil, and in the ende. The oxe is [a] moral
beest and hathe his clee clouin, wherbi discrecion is understonde, and
also he is a beest sacrifisable. 75

And verily he is [best] sheued in the ordenaunce of his lyff how this
Luke was ordeined in the forsaid .iiij. thingges. For he was ordeined as
to God furst. After Seint Bernard man is ordeined to God in .iij.
maners, that | is bi desire, bi thought, and bi entencion. The desire f. 246[rb]
shulde be holy, the thought clene, and the entencion rightfull. He 80
hadde holi desyres, for he was full of the holi goste. So as Ierome saithe
in the Prologe upon Luke. 'He went into Bethani full of the holi goste.'
Secoundeli he hadd holy thoughtes, for he was a pure uirgine in bodi
and in soule, in whiche the clennesse of his conscience is signified.
Thriddeli he hadde a rightwis entencion, for in all that euer he dede he 85
sought the worshippe of God. And of [these] .ij. laste thingges it is
saide in the Prologe upon the Dedes of [the] Aposteles: 'He was
withoute synne and duelled in virginite', and that is to the clennesse of
his thought, 'Bi whiche he loued the beter to serue God', and that was
to the worshipp of God as bi his rightfull entencion. 90

Secoundely he was ordeyned to his neigheboure. We be ordeined to
oure neigheboure whan we do to hym as we aught do. And after
Richard of Seint Victore seithe: '.iij. thinges ther bene that we shull
haue [to oure neighboure], that is power, oure knowyng, and oure
will, and the ferthe is added therto, oure dedes; oure power in 95
helpinge of hym, oure knowlache in counsellinge, oure wille in
desires, oure doyngges in seruices.' And as to these .iiij. blessed
Luke was ordinat.

He yaue furst his helpe to his neigheboure bi his power, and that

---

66 moralite] mortalite H1   66–7 of the foregoer . . . nativite] L, om. EH1H2   and[2]]
of H1   67 Ihesu] om. H1   70 it] om. H2   73 a] om. E   76 best] a beest
EH1H2 (mieulx P2)   All MSS end sentence with lyff   how] Nowe H2   85 a rightwis]
right a wise H1   86 these] this E   87 in] vppon H1   the[3]] om. EH1   89 to
serue] EH1H2   91–2 to oure neigheboure] ins. H1   92 as] that H1   94 to oure
neigheboure] L, ny EH1, nygh vs H2   knowyng] konnyng H1   96 hym] hem H2
knowlache] knoweng H2   98 ordinat] ordeigned H1

100 shewithe wel whan he ioyned hym alwey with [Paulc] in all his
tribulaciones and wold not departe fro hym but was helping to hym in
his predicaciones, as it is in the epistle of Paule in the secounde
f. 246ᵛᵃ chapitre to Timothes: 'Luke is only with me.' In that he | saithe 'with
me', he signifiethe that he was helper and defendour in that he gaue
105 hym comfort and helpe, and in that he saithe 'allone' is signified that
he ioyned hym to hym stably. And he saide in a chapitre to Corinthes:
'Ner he is not alone, but he is ordeined of th[e] chirches for to be
felowe of oure pilgrimage,' after his knowlache in councellynge.

And thanne yeuithe he his knowinge to his neigheboure whan he
110 writethe to hem the doctrine of the aposteles and of the gospell that he
knew. And of that berithe he hymself witnesse in his prologe, sayenge:
'Hit semithe me and y me sent, Theophile, for to write to the right
well fro the begynninge by ordre so that thou knowe the trouthe of the
wordes in whiche thou art taught.' And also it aperithe how [he yaue]
115 his cunynge in counsailez to his neigheboures by that worde that
Ierome saide in his Prologe, that is to wete that his worde is medicine
to the soule languisshinge.

Thriddely he yeuithe his will to the desires of his neigheboure, and
[it] aperithe by that he desirithe her hele euerlastinge, as Paule saithe
120 to the Colecens: 'Luke the leche grete you wel', that is to saie he
thinkithe in youre euerlastinge hele and desirithe it for you.

Ferthely he yaue vnto his neigheboure his dedis in hem seruinge,
and that aperithe bi that whanne he went that oure Lorde hadde be a
straunge man and receiued hym in his hous and dede hym all the
f. 246ᵛᵇ seruice of charite. For | he was felow to Cleophas whanne thei went
126 into Emaws, as sum men saien, and Gregori saithe in his Moralitees,
[though] it be so that Ambrose sey that it was another of whiche he
puttithe the name.

Thriddely he was wel ordeined as to hymself. And after Seint
130 Bernard thre thingges ther be that make a man right wel ordeined to
hymselfwarde and makithe hym holy, that is to lyue soberly, to werke
rightfully, and a meke witte, and as by Seint Bernard eueri of this is

100 hym] *om.* H1   Paule] you E   102 is] *add* seid H2   secounde] .iiij. H2
103–4 In . . . with me] *om.* H2   104–6 was helper . . . signified that he] *twice* E
105 saithe] seid H1   107 Ner] *om.* H2   he is not] is 'not' he H1   the] tho E
110 aposteles] Gospelle H2   gospell] Gospellis H2   112 sent] *add* to H2
113 knowe] knewe H1   114 he yaue] ye haue EH2   115 that²] of H1
116 saide] seying H1   119 it] that E   that] *add* þat H1   her] for H2   120 to¹] in
H1   Colecens] Collectens H1   122–4 seruinge . . . hym²] *om.* H2   123 that³] with
del. 'that' H1   126 into] vnto H1   men] *om.* H1H2   127 though] yef EH1
130 right] *om.* H2   132 and¹] *add* haue H2   and²] *om.* H2

deuyded in thre: to lyue soberli is to lyue chastely, compeynabli, and
humbly; the rightfull werkinges ys yef he be rightfull, discrete, and
fruitfull; rightfull bi good entencion, discrete bi mesure, fruitfull by 135
edificacion; the witte is meke whan oure faithe felith God to be
soueraig[n]ly good, so that by his might we beleue to be holpe of oure
infirmite, and that oure ignoraunce be corrected bi his wisdom, and
that by his goodnesse oure wickednesse be putte awey. And this saithe
Bernard.   140
    And in all these thinges was this blessed Luke wel ordeined and
disposed. For he hadde furst sobernesse in lyvinge in treble manere.
He lyued in continence and chastite, for, as Seint Ierome witnessithe
of hym in the Prologe upon Luke, he hadd neuer wyf ne childe. Also,
he lyued compainably, and that is signified in that is said of hym and 145
of Cleophas in the opynion before saide how twey disciples went that
day into Ierusalem; compainabli is bytokened in that thei were .ij.
disciples. Thriddeli, he lyued humbli, of whiche the humilite is
shewed in that he expressed the name of his felowe Cleophas, and
helde his pees | of his owne. And this come of souereayne mekenesse. f. 247ra
    Secoundeli he had rightfull dedes, for his dedes were rightfull bi 151
entencion, and that is signified in his orison where it is saide: 'He bare
in his bodi mortifyeng of his flesshe from delites goodly for thi loue.'
He was discrete bi attemperaunce, and therfor he was figured in
fourme of an oxe that hathe the cle clouin wherbi the uertu of 155
discrecion is expressed. He was fruitfull bi edificacion. He was nigh to
God, right nygh, for he was holde and loued as a dere frende, and he
was called of the apostle right that saide: 'Luke fisician, right dere
frende, grete[th] you.'
    Thriddely he hadde a witte, for he beleued and confessed in his 160
gospell God for to be [souerainly mighti], souerainly witti and
souerainli good. And of the two furst he saithe in the secounde
chapitre: 'Thei were al abassed and wounded in the doctrine of hym,
for the doctrine of hym was in his might.' And of the thridde it

    135 fruitfull¹] faithfull *corr. to* fruthfull H1   fruitfull²] faithfull *corr. to* fruthfull H1,
rightfulle H2   136 whan] *add* þat H1   137 soueraignly] soueraigly *twice* E   good]
god H1H2   139 this¹] thus H2   saithe] Seint H1   140 Bernarde] *add* 'seiþ' H1
141 And] *om.* H1   143 Ierome] *add* seith and H2   144 Also] And H1   147 is
bytokened] as bitokeneth H1   148 lyued] loued H1   150 owne] *add* name H2
153 in] *om.* H1   154 was¹] *add* also H2   155 cle] clawis H2   156 was¹] *add* also
H2   edificacion] *add* for H2   157 God] *add* and H2   157-9 and² . . . frende] *twice
once del.* H1   159 greteth] grete E, I grete H1   161 souerainli mighti] *om.* E   witti]
on erasure H1   162 good] *ins.* H1

165 aperithe in the .xviij. chapitre wher he saithe that ther is no good but
onli God.

The ferthe and the last he was right wel ordeined as to his office, the
whiche was for to w[r]ete the gospell. And in that appered how he was
ordeined in as moche as that gospell is made noble with moche
170 trouthe, she is full of gret profit, and she is embelisshed with gret
honeste, and is auctorised bi gret auctorite. She is furst ennobled with
gret trouthes, for there be .iij. trouthes, that is of lyff, of right[wis]-
nesse, and of doctrine. The trouthe of lyf is concordaunce fro the
honde to the mouthe, verite of rightwisnesse is concordaunce fro the
175 sentence to the cause, verite of doctrine is concordaunce of the thinge |
f. 247ʳᵃ to the understondinge. And this gospell is made noble bi these treble
ueritees, and bi that that this treble uerite is made noble in the gospell
shewithe Luke that Ihesu Crist had in hym the treble vertu and that
he taught hem to other. And he shewithe that God had this verite bi
180 the witnesse of his veritees bi the witnesse of his aduersaries, and so he
saithe in the .xxvij. capitre: 'Maister, we wote wel what thou saiest
and techest rightfully,' that is the verite of the doctrine;' and that thou
receyuest not the persone,' that is the verite of doctrine; 'but thou
techest in trouthe the waye of God,' that is the uerite of lyf, for good
185 lyf is the way of God. Secoundeli he shewithe in his gospell that Ihesu
Crist taught the treble ueritees. Furst he taught the uerite of lyf, the
whiche is in kepinge of the comaundementis of God, wherof it is
saide: 'That shalt loue thi lorde God of all thine hert *etc.* and do that
and thou shalt lyue.' And whanne a Pharise asked hym what he shulde
190 do for to haue euerlastinge lyff, oure Lorde said: 'Knowest thou not
the comaundementes, sle not, ne do not none avowtre *etc.*' He hadd
uerite of doctrine, wherfor he saide to sum that peruerted this trouthe:
'Alas to you Pharisees, that prechen the dymes and passin the
iugement and the reson of God.' And thriddeli the uerite of right-
195 wisnesse is sheued whan he saide: 'Yeldithe to Cesar the things that

165 good] god H1H2   168 wrete] wete EH1H2 (*escripre* P2)   appered] it
apperith H1H2   171 ennobled] envoulued H1   172–3 rightwisnesse]
rightfulnesse E   176 these] þis H1   176–7 bi . . . noble] *om.* H2
177 ueritees] vertues H1   uerite] vertues H1   in] *om.* H2   179 shewithe] shewed
H2   God had] hath *del.* 'god hadde' H1   this] þe *changed to* þys H1   verite] vertu H1
180 veritees] *add* and H2   181 .xxvij.] .xxvj. H1   182 verite] vertu H1, veritees
and H2   183 that] *ins.* H1   184–5 that . . . God] *ins.* H1   185 gospell]
Gospellis H2   186 the¹] þise H1H2   187 kepinge . . . of God] the
commaundementis of godis kepinge H2   189 and] *ins.* H1   hym] *om.* H1
191 not²] *om.* H1   *etc.*] and H2   192 wherfor] therefor H1   this] his H1
193 Alas] Wo H1   dymes] devynes H1H2   194 uerite] entente H2

bene of Cesar and that that longithe to God, yeldithe to God.' And
also he saithe in the .xix. chapitre: 'Tho be myn enemyes that wolde
not that y regne upon hem, bringe hem hedir and sle hem be|fore me.' f. 247va
And also he saithe in the .xiiij. chapitre, there as he spekithe of the
iugement that he shall saie to the reproued: 'Departe you fro me alle 200
that haue do wikkednesse.'

Secoundeli his gospell is full of profite, wherfor Poule and hymself
writithe that he was a leche, wherby it is signified that by his gospell
he arraiethe to us medicines right profitable. And ther be .iij.
medicines: curinge, keping and amendinge. And these treble medi- 205
cines shewed Luke in his gospell that the heuenli leche had arrayed
for us. The medicine curatif is she that curithe from siknesse, and that
is the penaunce that helithe al spirituel siknesse. And this medicine
saith he that the heuenli leche had made redi for us whanne he saide in
the fourthe chapitre 'Helithe the sorufull hertis and prechithe to the 210
captiues remission.' And in the .v. chapitre he saithe: 'Y am not come
to seke the rightfull but the sinfull.' The medicine amendinge is that
encresithe the hele, and that is for to kepe good counsaile. For good
counsaile makithe a man betir and more perfit. This medicine
shewithe he that the leche hathe arraied for us whan he saithe in 215
the .xviij. chapitre that a man shulde selle all that he hathe and yeue it
to the pore. The medicine preseruatif is she that kepithe from fallinge,
and that is eschuyng of occasiones of sinnes and of wicked felaw-
shippes. And this medicine [he] shewithe that the leche hadde take us
whanne he saithe in the .xij. chapitre: 'Kepe you from the mete of 220
Pharisees', and there he taught for to eschewe the compani of wicked.
Other yt may be saide that that gospell is fulfelled with moche profit,
for | as moche as all vertu of wisdom is conteined therin. And of that f. 247vb
saithe Seint Ambrose: 'Luke comprehendithe in his gospel alle the
uertues of wisdom and the storie saithe he taught whan he shewid the 225
incarnacion of oure Lorde to be made bi the holy goste. Wher Dauid
techithe naturell wisdom whanne he saide: "Putte oute thi sperit and
thei shull be made." Also whan he techithe derkenesse made in the

196 that²] om. H1   197 Tho] yee H2   wolde] will H1H2   200 alle] add ye H1
202 his] is changed to his H1   gospell] Gospellis H2   is] ben H2   profite] profites E,
prophecies H2   203 it] þat H1   is signified] signifieth H2   gospell] Gospellis H2
204–5 right . . . medicines] om. H2   205 curinge] cursinge with s erased H2
206 gospell] gospellis H2   210 the²] ye H2   211 captiues] capteynes with first e
subp. H1   213 kepe] add a H1   213–14 For . . . counsaile] om. H1   217 fallinge]
allinge H2   219 And] Of H2   he] om. E   224 comprehendithe] comprehendid H2
gospel] Gospellis H2   225 storie] story with y on erasure H1   227 wisdom]
wisdomes D   thi] my D

passion of Crist, and tremblynge of erthe, and that the sonne
230 withdr[ewe] his bemes. He taught morialli [whan he taught maners]
in these blessidnesses. He taught resonable thinges whanne he saithe
"Ho that is trew in litell will be trew in gret thinges." And withoute
these treble wisdomes the misterie of the Trinite ner oure faithe may
not be, that is to saie, wisdom naturell, resonable and morall.' And
235 this is that Ambrose saithe.

Thriddely his gospell is made noble by gret honeste, for the stile
and the manere of spekynge is right honeste and faire. Thre thingges
be conuenient and necessarie to that [that] men holde in her saienges
honeste and beauute, the whiche Seint Austin techithe, that is to wete
240 that it plese and that it apere and that it stere or meue. That it please,
he shulde speke gaily, and that it apere, he shulde speke apertely, and
that it shulde stere, he shulde speke feruently. And this manere had
Luke in writinge and in prechinge. Of the .ij. furst it is saide in the
.viij. chapitre to the Corinthes: 'We sent with hym a brother.' And the
245 Glose saithe: 'Barnabe or Luke of whom the preisinge is thorugh all
the chirches in the gospell.' And in that he saithe 'the preisinges of
hym' is signified that he spake gaily; in that 'he thorugh al the
f. 248ʳᵃ   chirches' is signified | that he spake opinli; and that 'he spake with
feruens of loue', it aperithe in þat that whanne he saide: 'Was not oure
250 hert brenninge with us whanne he spake with us in the way.' Fertheli
his gospell is auctorised bi the auctorite of mani seintes. What
meruaile was that she was auctorised bi auctorite of mani seintes,
for she was furst ordeined of the fader, wherof Seint Ierom saithe in
the .xxxj. chapitre: '"Lo here the dayes that comyn," saithe oure
255 Lorde; "Y shall make a newe comenaunt with the meyne of Israel and
of Iuda, not after the comenaunt that y made with her faders, but it
shall be the comenaunt that y made with the meyne of Israel." This
saithe oure Lorde: for after these dayes y shal yeue my lawe in the
boweles of hem.' And he spekithe pleinli to the lettre of the doctrine
260 of the gospell. Secoundeli, she is enforced with the sone, for he saithe

230 withdrewe] withdrawithe E   morialli] moralli HıD   whan . . . maneres] om. E
231 these blessidnesses] þise blessidnesse Hı, this blessidnes D   232 Ho] he Hı   in¹]
add a Hı   litell] add thinges E   233 ner oure] nor of D   236 the stile] to be stille D
238 that²] om. E   holde] held Hı   240 it³] that is to D   241 gaily] goodelie D
242 shulde¹] shul Hı   244 And] om. Hı   245 is thorough] 'is' þo'r'ugh Hı
249 of] his D   that] om. D   Was] Is Hı   251 mani seintes] seintis mani oone D
251–2 What . . . seintes] om. D   255 comenaunt] couant Hı   256 comenaunt]
couenauntez Hı   it] I't' Hı   256–7 her . . . with] om. D   257 comenaunt] couaunt
Hı   Israel] Israellis fadres but it shalle be the couenaunt þat I made with the meyne of
Israell and D

in that same gospell in the .xxj. chapitre 'heuene and erthe shul passe, but my wordes mowe not passe.' Thriddeli, it is enspired with the holy goste, wherof Ierome saithe in his Prologe upon Luke: 'He wrote this gospell in the parties of Akay bi the teching of the holi goste.' Fertheli he was before prefigured of aungeles. For he was prefigured 265 of that aungel of whiche the apostle saithe in the .xiiij. chapitre: 'Y sawe the aungel fleinge bi the middel of heuene and had the gospel perdurable'. Hit is saide euerlastinge, for she is made of euerlasting-nesse, that is Ihesu Crist. Fitheli this gospell was pronounced of the prophetes, the whiche Ezechiel the prophete denounced before that 270 gospel whanne he saide that one of the bestes had a face of an oxe, wherby the gospel of Luke is signified, so as it is aboue said. And | whanne Ezechiel saide in the secound chapitre that he hadd sein the f. 248rb boke that was wretin, withinne and withoute, and in whiche his lamentaciones were wrete *etc.*, bi that boke is understonde the gospel 275 of Luke, that is wretin withinne for to hide the misterie of [his] godhede, and withoute bi shewing of the storie in whiche the lamentacion of his passion is conteined and the sorw of the perdurable dampnacion, so as it shewithe in the .xj. chapitre there mani sorwes be sette. Sixtely the gospell was openid bi the Uirgine, for the blessed 280 Uirgine Marie kepte and helde diligently in her herte all these thinges for that she wolde after that shewe it to writers, so as the Glose saithe that all the thinges that were done and saide of oure Lorde God she knewe and withhelde in her mynde, so that whan the tyme of prechinge or of writinge come of the incarnacion, that she might 285 sufficiauntly and clerely shewe al to the writers requiringe all these thinges as thei hadde be done. For whiche thinge Seint Bernard assignithe the reson [whi] that the aungell of oure Lord denounced to the blessed Uirgine the conceyuinge of Elizabeth: 'The conceyuing of Elizabeth was denounced to Marie for that whan the comynge was 290 denounsed to her of oure saueoure, anone of his messenger that come before hym, that she shulde withholde the tyme and the ordenaunce of thingges so that after that she might beter shewe to the screueners and to the prechours the trouthe of the gospell. This is she that pleinly fro the begynninge was fulli taught of the misteries of heuene.' And 295

274 was] *add* in the secound chapitre D   withinne] *ins.* H1   276 his] *om.* E
277 storie] stories H1   279 the] his H1   282 Glose] Gospelle D   285 or] and
H1   286 al to] *trs.* H1   287 as] þat H1   288 whi] with EH1D (*pourquoy* P2)
289 conceyuinge] comyng *changed to* con‸ce′iuyng H1   the conceyuinge of Elizabeth]
om. D   289–90 The conceyuing of Elizabeth] 'þe conceyuinge' H1   291 of] *ins.* H1
anone] *add* oon H1, *om.* D   293 that²] *om.* H1

f. 248ᵛᵃ we aught | wel leue that the euuangelistes enquered of her mani
thinges and she made hem sertaine, and as it is leuid of Luke that he
hadde his recours to her as to the arke of the testament and was
certefied bi her of mani thinges, and namely of tho that longed to
300 herself onli as of the annunciacion of the aungel, the natiuite of oure
Lorde and of the other wherof he spekithe. Seuenthli the gospell was
shewed to hym bi the aposteles, for Luke had not be with Ihesu Crist
in al his dedes and his miracles and therfor he wrote his gospell after
that the aposteles whiche hadd be present denounsed and reported to
305 hym, so as he shewithe in his Prologe seieng: 'So as tho that had sein
fro the begynning and had bene ministres toke it me.' And therfor it is
custume to bere witnesse in double manere, that is of thinges sein and
of thinges herde, therfor seith Seint Austin that oure Lorde wolde
haue .ij. witnesse of thinges seyne, and that was Iohn and Mathi, and
310 of the .ij. thinges herde was Marke and Luke. And for that the
witnesse of thinges yseyne is more stable and more certain thanne that
whiche is of thinges herde, therfor seithe Seint Austin that the twey
euuangelies that bene of thinges herde be sette in the middel right as
more feble thanne the endes so that bi hem thei mow be born up and
315 enforced. In the .viij. the gospell is meruailous[li] aproued of Paule
whan he ledithe the gospell of Luke to the profe and confirmacion of
his [seyinges]. And as Ierome saithe in the Boke of Noble Men that
f. 248ᵛᵇ sum men haue suspecion that alweyes whan | Paule saithe in his
episteles 'after my gospel' that he signifieth the volume of Luke. And
320 he aproued it merueillously whan he wrote of hym and saide: 'Of
whom the preisynges in the gospel thorugh al the chirche'.

Men rede in the storie of Antioche that, whanne the cristen that
were there [were] seged with gret multitude of Turkes that dede to
hem gret sorw and peine bi hunger and mani other turmentes, that
325 whanne thei were pleinli conuerted to oure Lorde by penaunce, there
apered a man ful of light clothed in white clothinge in the chirche of
oure Ladi of Tripoly. And whanne thei asked hym what he was, he
saide that he was Luke that come from Antioche, wher oure Lorde
hadd assembled the knighthode of heuene with his aposteles and

299 tho] *add* thingis D   301 wherof] wherefor D   302 aposteles] appostulle D
305 seieng] seying *with* sey *on erasure* H1   308 therefor] Th`er'fore H1   310 for
that] so D   313 euuangelies] aungellis D   315 .viij.] *add* chapitre D   the²] *om.* H1
meruailousli] meruailous E   316 to] into H1   profe] prophete H1, profite D
317 seyinges] seintes E   319 gospel] gospellis D   320 of] to D   323 were²] *om.*
E, writen H1   326 clothinge] cloþes H1

martires for to fight with his pilgrimes ayenst the Turkes. And than 330
the cristen hardied hem and discomfited al the oste of Turkes.

Here endithe the lyff of Seint Luke, and beginnithe the lyff
of Seint Crissant, Capitulum .C.l.

Crissant was the sone of right a noble man that hight Polyn, but whan
the fader sawe that the sone was taught in the faithe of Ihesu Crist and
he saw that he might not call hym ayen to the ydoles, he comaunded
that he shulde be shette up faste and that .v. maydenes shulde be putte
to hym for to withdrawe [hym] with faire wordes. And thanne he 5
praied to God that he shulde not be surmounted with no flessheli
couctise bi none of these right wicked bestes, and anone these
maydenes were so ouercome with slepe that thei might | nother ete f. 249ʳᵃ
ne drinke, but as sone as thei were putte oute fro hym anone thei toke
bothe mete and drinke wel ynow.   10
    And thanne right a wise uirgine that hight Daria arraied as gaili as
she hadd be a goddesse praied that she might go in to Crissaunt and
that she wolde yelde hym to his fader and to the ydoles. And whan she
was entred Crissaunt reproued her for the gret pride of her clothing,
and she ansuered that she hadde not do it for pride but she hadde 15
clothed her so for to drawe hym to do sacrifise to the ydoles and for to
bringe hym ayen to his fader. And than Crissant under[tok]e her of
that she worshipped h[e]m as goddes, for thei had be in her tyme
wicked synners and haunted folisshe women, and Daria ansuered:
'The philisophers felyn the elementes bi the names of men.' And 20
Crissant seide: 'Yef ani worship the erthe as goddesse and another
erith it and tilithe it as a churle, to whom yeuithe more the erthe? Hit
is proued that she yeuithe more to the plowman thanne to hym that
worshippithe her, and so it is of the see and of the other elementes.'
    And thanne Daria was conuerted, and thei coupeled hem togederes 25
bi the grace of the holi goste and feyned hem to be togederes bi
flessheli mariage and conuerted mani a creatoure to God. For
Claudian, that before hadde be turmentoure to hem, thei conuerted
to the faithe of Ihesu Crist, and his wiff and his children and mani

330 ayenst] with HₗD   331 of] add þe Hₗ

EHₗDH2AₗA2   Rubric Luke] on erasure Hₗ   5 hym²] om. EHₗ   7 right] om. D
14 clothing] clothinges Hₗ   16 so] om. Hₗ   17 undertoke] so with toke on erasure
Hₗ, understode ED (reprist P2)   18 hem] hym EHₗD (les P2)   21 and] om. D
22 erith] er`e´the with -he subp. Hₗ   as] is D   23 proued] prouidid D   26 the
grace . . . bi] om. D   28 hadde be] ins. Hₗ

30 other knightes. And thanne after was Crissant enclosed in a stinking
prison by the comaundement of Munerien, but the stinke was anone
turned into a right suete sauour. And Darie was ledde to the bordell,
f. 249ʳᵇ but a lyon that was fled | oute of Lamficiacre came for to be porter of
the bordell. And thanne was there sent a man for to defoule the
35 uirgine, but he was take anone of the lyon, and thanne the lyon
behelde the uirgine as thou he wolde haue knowlache what she wolde
that [he shulde do] with hym. And she comaunded hym that he
shulde do hym none harme but lete hym go to her. And anone he was
conuerted and ranne thorugh the citee and cried that Daria was a
40 goddesse.

And thanne there were sent hunters for to take the lyon, and
whanne thei come thei fell downe to the fete of the uirgine and weren
conuerted of her. And thanne the prouost comaunded to make a gret
fire atte the entre of the bordel so that the lyon were brent with Daria.
45 And the lyon considered this and dredde hym and beganne to bray
and toke leue of the uirgine that he might go where he wolde withoute
harmynge to ani creatoure.

And as the prouost dede continuelli mani diuerse turmentes to
Crissant and to Daria and might in no wise misdo hem, atte the laste
50 ende tho maried withoute corrupcion were putte in a depe pitte and
weren stoned with stones and ouerpressed with erthe, and so thei were
made martires of Ihesu Crist.

Here endithe the lyf of Seint Crissant, and nexst beginnithe the passion of .xjM.¹ virgines, Capitulum .C.lj.

The passion of the .xjM.¹ virgines was halued in this manere. There
was in Bretayne a noble kinge and a cristen that hight Nothus or
Maurus that engendered a doughter that hight Vrsula. This doughter
f. 249ᵛᵃ was full of | gret wisdom and high beauute and full of uertuous
5 condicions, and the renome of her went ouer all. And the kyng of

30 after] afterward HᵢD   32 into a/right] trs. Hᵢ   bordell] add hous D
33 Lamficiacre] lomficiaire Hᵢ, Lamfiatre D   34 bordell] add hous D   sent] present D
36 he] she D   knowlache] knowleched with d subp. Hᵢ, knowelechid D   wolde²] add
and D   37 he¹] she with s erased Hᵢ   he shulde do] she wolde E   38 he] þat man D
39 ranne] renne ins. Hᵢ   and²] was del. `&ʹ Hᵢ   42 to] atte Hᵢ   uirgine] lyonne D
44 bordel] add hous D   Daria] þe aire Hᵢ   46 the] add blessid D   48 diuerse] ins.
Hᵢ   50 tho] þei Hᵢ

EHᵢTᵢDH₂AᵢA₂L; D breaks off after 83 Methos; Tᵢ breaks off after 159 gret
1 manere] wise D   4 high] hight Hᵢ   uertuous] vertues and good D
5 her] add beaute D

Englond, that was than right mighti to submitte to his lordshipp mani naciones, herde of the renome of this uirgine and seid hym thought he shulde be blessed in alle thinge yef he might couple this uirgine to his sone in mariage. And that yonge lorde had gret desire after her. And thanne thei sent a solempne ambassiatrie to the fader of the uirgine 10 with gret promesses and saide mani faire wordes, and therwith thei made gret manaces yef thei turned ayen werned to her lorde.

And thanne the kinge of Bretaigne beganne to be full of sorugh and care for that she that was made noble bi faithe of Ihesu Crist shulde be wedded to hym that worshipped the ydoles, and also he knew well 15 that she wolde in no wise consent therto, and in that other syde he dredde gretly the cruelte of the kinge. Thanne she that was enspired bi the holi goste did so moche to her fader that he consented to the mariage with such a condition that for to do her solace and comfort the kinge shulde sende to her .x. virgines of the most noble that might 20 be gete, and also to her and to eueri of the .x. virgines he shulde sende a .M.¹ uirgincs, and that he shulde yeue her terme of thre yere for to halw her uirginite, and that this yonge lorde shulde be baptised and in tho .iij. yere he shulde be taught sufficiauntly in the faithe so that bi this wise counsaile and by the strengthe of the condicion sette he 25 shulde withdrawe his purpos. And this yong lorde receiued gladli this condicion and hasted his fader | and he was anone baptised and f. 249ᵛᵇ comaunded that all tho thingges that the virgine hadde required were do in haste. And the fader of the mayden ordeined that his doughter that he loued moche, and all the other uirgines that had nede of the 30 comfort and of the seruice of men, that thei shulde haue with hem for to do hem seruice.

And thanne come there uirgines from eueri partie, and men also, for to see this grete companie. And mani bisshoppes come to hem for to bere felawship with hem in her pilgrimage, amonge whiche Pantule 35 bysshop of Luse was with hem, and brought hem to Rome and returned ayen with hem and receiued martirdom. Seint Gerasine, quene of Cecile, that had made of her husbond that was full cruel a meke lambe, and she was suster of Seint Moris the bisshop, and of Darie the moder of Seint Vrsula, to whom the fader of Seint Vrsula 40 had sent priue letteres of alle these thinges. Thanne bi the inspiracion

6 mighti] myghtelie D   7 hym thought] and bithouȝte D   11 thei] *om.* H1
12 made] *add* many D   werned] warde D   14 made] *om.* D   18 he] she D
21 the] tho H1   22 and] *add* also D   24 tho] þe H1   faithe] *add* of Ihesu criste D
26 And] But D   27 and²] that D   30 loued] bileued H1   34 And] *add* also D
39 and²] *add* suster D   41 Thanne] that D

of God she toke anone the waye with her .iiij. doughtres, that is to
saie, Babile, Iuliene, Victoria, and Aurea and her litell sone Adrigen,
that putte hymselff with his owne will to this pilgrimage for loue of his
45 sustres, and thus she lefte her reaume in the gouernaunce of one of her
sones and came into Bretaine, and fro thennis she sailed into Englond.
And bi the counsaile of that quene the uirgines were gadered of
diuerse nasiones and she was euer a leder of hem, and atte the last she
suffered marterdom with hem.
50   And thanne after the condicion sette alle thinges were made redi.
Thanne the quene opened her counsaile to the knightes in her
f. 250ʳᵃ felawship | and made hem all to swere that new knighthode.
Thanne thei beganne to make pleies of mani maners, now pleyes of
batayles, now renning, now leping, and they feined all manere of
55 pleyes to make, and for all that thei lefte not that thei hadde in purpos.
Sumtyme thei come from her plaie atte midday and sumtyme unnethe
atte euesonge tyme. And the barones and the gret lordes assembeled
hem togedres to see the faire games and all hadde gret ioye in the
beholdinge.
60   And atte the last whanne Vrsule had conuerted all the uirgines to
the faithe, thanne she and al her felawship toke the see, and for the
good wynde that thei hadd thei came in the space of a day to a porte in
Fraunce that is called Tiele, and from thennis thei come to Coleyne,
and there apered the aungel of oure Lorde to Seint Vrsula and saide to
65 here that she and all her noumbre shulde returne hole thedir ayen and
thanne there thei shulde resseiue crowne of marterdom. And from
thennis bi the techinge of the aungell of God they come towardes
Rome and thei londed atte the citee of Basyle and there thei lefte her
shippes and went to Rome on fote. And in the comynge of hem the
70 pope Ciriaques was gretly reioysed, for as moche as he was born in
Bretaigne and hadd amonge hem mani cosynes, and he and his clerkes
resseiued hem with gret ioye and worshipp. And that night it was
[reuelid] fro God to the pope that he shulde resseiue with tho uirgines
crowne of marterdom. The whiche thinge he hidde and kepte it to
75 hymself and baptised mani of tho uirgines that were not yet baptised.
f. 250ʳᵇ   And whanne he sawe couenable tyme that he had | gouerned the

42 waye] *add* and D   42–3 .iiij. . . . saie] she toke D   45 sustres] suster H1
the] *ins.* H1   of¹] *on erasure* H1   53 pleies . . . maners] *om.* D   now¹] newe D
55 make] *add* merthe D   63 Fraunce] *so subp. and erased* ʽalmaynʼ H1   65 her]
ʽhereʼ H1   66 there] *om.* H1   shulde] shul H1   67 thennis bi the] *ins.* H1   of
God] *om.* H1   69 And] *om.* H1   70 pope] *erased* D   73 reuelid] releuid EH1
pope] *erased* D   74 hidde] didde H1D

chirche a yere and certaine wekes after Peter the .xix. pope, he
purposed before all and shewed his purpos that he resigned the office
and the dignite. But as [all] withsaide hym and principaly the
cardinales that wendin that he hadd be so blinded that he wolde 80
haue l[ef]t his glorie of his astate for to folw sum of tho folisshe
women, but he wolde not acorde for to abide but ordeined an holi man
for to abide in his place that hight Methos, and, for as moche as he
lefte the sege of the pope ayenst the will of the clergie, the clerkes haue
putte oute his name of the cathologe of popes and al the grace that he 85
hadd deseruid in his office was take from hym for that holy felawship
of women. And thanne .ij. felon princes of the knighthode of Rome,
Maximyan and Aufrican, sawe this holi companie of virgines and how
that moche peple of men and women drow to hem, and dredde lest the
religion of cristen shulde encrece bi hem gretly. Wherfor thei 90
enquered diligently of her viage, and thanne thei sent messangeres
to Iuliane her cosyn, prince of the peple of Hynnorum, that he shuld
bringe his oste ayenst hem and that thei shulde assemble atte Coleyne
and there behede hem all for that they were cristen.

And the blessed Ciriaque went oute of the citee of Rome with the 95
blessed cumpani of uirgines, and Vincent prest cardinal, and Iamys
that was come oute of his cuntre of Bretayne into Antioche and helde
there .vij. yere the dignite of bisshop, the whiche had folued the pope
and was gone oute of the citee and made hym felowe to tho uirgines
and suffered martir|dom with hem. And Moris bisshop of Leuitane f. 250ᵛᵃ
the cite, that was vncle to Basile and to Iulyan, and Cyliciene bisshop 101
of Luce, and Cilicie bisshop of Rauen that thanne were come to
Rome, went forthe with these uirgines. And Otherin that was
husbond to the blessid uirgine Ursula was in Bretayne taught by
oure Lorde by the avision of an aungel that he shulde stere his moder 105
to be cristen. For in the furst yere that he was cristened his fader
deyed, and Etherin his sone was kinge after hym. And thanne as these
holi uirgines retorned hem from Rome, Etherin was taught of oure
Lorde that he shulde rise anone and go ayens his spouce and that he

77 pope] *erased* D   79 as all] L, *so on erasure* H1, as well E, alle D   80 wendin]
wendend *with final* -d *subp.* H1   81 left] lost EH1D (*laissee* P2)   tho] this H1, the D
82 abide] *add* in noo wise D   84 sege] seete H2   89 hem] him H1
90 religion] region H1   94 hem . . . cristen] alle thoo virginnes and othir cristen puple
H2   99 felowe] followe H2   100 with hem] *om.* H2   101 that] *om.* H1
102 Luce . . . of] *ins.* H1   103 Otherin] Oserin H2   104 blessid] bisshopp *del.* H1
106 be cristen] the cristen feith H2   yere] þere H1   cristened] baptisid H2
107 Etherin] *add* that E   after hym] *om.* H2   108 Etherin] *add* that E
108–9 of oure Lorde] anone H2

110 shulde with her resseiue crowne of marterdom atte Coloyne, the
whiche obeied to the techinge of God and made anone to baptise his
moder and [with her and] Florence his litell suster that weren thanne
cristen and with the bisshopp Clement [he] came ayenst these uirgines
and felawshipped hem with hem in marterdom. And Marcule bisshop
115 of Grece, and Constaunce his moder, and the doughter of Dorothe
kinge of Constantinople that had be wedded to the sone of a kinge but
he deied before the mariage and she vowed her uirginite to God, and
weren taught [bi] a vision and come to Rome and ioyned hem with
other virgines to martirdom.

120   And thanne all these uirgines with her bisshoppes come to Coloyne
and fonde that she was beseged, and whanne this cursed peple sawe
the multitude of these uirgines, that is to saye Hungres, men of
f. 250vb Hungry, | thei ronne upon hem with gret cry and wodenesse right as
wolues upon lambes and slowen alle the multitude. And whanne thei
125 come to Ursula, the prince of hem sawe her gret beauute, so gret and
so meruaylous, and was al abasshed and beganne to comfort her upon
the deth of the uirgines and behight her that he wolde take her to his
wyf. And whanne she hadde refused hym vtterly and dispised hym in
all wise, he shette atte her an arw and smote her thorugh the bodi, and
130 so she fulfelled her marterdom. And one of the uirgines that hight
Cordell was so hougely aferde that she hidde her al that night in a
shippe, but in the morw she suffered dethe with good will and
receiued crowne of marterdom. And after that, whan that her fest
was not halued for þat she suffered not dethe with that other, she
135 apered longe tyme after to a recluse and charged hym that the day
foluyng of the fest of the uirgines her fest were remembered.

    And thei suffered dethe the yere of oure Lorde .CC.xxxviij., but sum
men sayne that bi reson of the tyme it stondithe not that thei suffered
dethe in that tyme, for Cecile and Constantinople were not thanne
140 reawmes, but men wene more uerily that thei suffered dethe longe
tyme after whan Consta[ntine] was emperoure and that the Hynnes
and the Gothes dedin so grete cruelte ayenst the cristen in the tyme of
the emperour Marcian that regned the yere of oure Lorde .CCCC.lix.

112 with her and] L, om. EH1H2   that weren] ins. H1   113 cristen and with]
cristened of H2   he] L, and EH1H2   came] went H2   114 felawshipped] followid H2
with hem] om. H2   115 Constaunce] Constantine H2   118 weren] was H2   bi] in E
hem] hir H2   124 wolues] wollfes with ll on erasure H1   multitude] add of virgines H2
129 her^1] add with H2   her^2] add with an arowe H2   130 so] om. H2   135 apered]
add `a' H1   after] ins. H1   138 men] om. H2   141 Constantine] Constaunt EH1
Hynnes] hemmes H1

Ther was an abbot that praied to the abbes of Coloyne that she wolde graunte hym one of tho glorious uirgines bodies, and he hight 145 her that he wold | shrine her in a riche shrine and set her in his f. 251ʳᵃ chirche, but whanne he hadd his desire he kepte the body al an hole yere in a shrine of tree bisides the auuter. And atte the yeres ende, whanne the abbot and the monkes weren atte Matenis, atte midnight the uirgine arose from the auuter bodely and enclined her reuerentely 150 before the auuter and went thorugh the quere, seinge all the monkes that were there, the whiche were gretly abasshed. And than the abbot ranne to the shrine and fonde her al voide, and thanne he went to Coloyne and tolde the abbesse al that wonder bi ordre. And than thei went to the place wher they hadde take the body, and there thei fonde 155 the same. And thanne the abbot asked merci and besought that he might haue that holy bodi ayen, behoting right certainly for to do make hastely a precious shrine, but he coude not gete her in no wise.

Ther was a religious monke that had gret deuocion to these uirgines so that in a tyme as he was right sike there apered to hym a right faire 160 and a nobille uirgine and asked hym wher he knewe her. And he, al meruayled of that visyon, saide nay, he knew her not, and thanne she saide to hym: 'Y am one of the uirgines to whom thou hast so gret deuocion, and for that thou shalt haue guerdon yef it so be that thou wilt saie the orison of oure Lorde whiche is the *Pater Noster* .xjM.¹ 165 tymes for the loue and the worship of us, we shull be to the bothe keper and [defend]our atte the houre of thi dethe.' And whan she was parted he fulfelled her request as sone as he | might, and anone after f. 251ʳᵇ he called his abbot and made hymself to be anointed, and as men woke hym he cried sodenly: 'Fleithe, fleithe, and make place to the virgines 170 that comyn.' And whanne the abbot asked what he ment he told hym bi ordre the promisse of the uirgines, and thanne al they withdrow hem abak and come ayen within a while after and fonde hym passed to God.

---

145 hym] hir H2   tho] þe H1   153 her] it H2   156 same] holie bodie H2
157 right] hir H2   162 he] *on erasure* H1   166 the loue] *ins.* H1   the²] *ins.* H1
167 defendour] comfortour EH1   168 parted] *add* fro hym H2   172 bi] 'by' H1
173 and²] *add* there thei H2   to] *add* oure lorde H2

Here endithe the lyff of .xjM.[1] virgines, and nexst
beginnithe the lyff of Symonde and Iude, Capitulum .C.lij.

Symon Cananien and Iude Thadee were bretheren of Iames the Lesse
that was sone of Marie Cleophe that was wedded to Alphee. And
Iudas was sent bi Thomas the apostle to the kinge Abagar of Edisse
after the assencion [of oure Lorde].

5   And it is redde in the Storie that is called Ecclesiast that the forsaid
Abagar sent a pistle to oure Lorde Ihesu Crist in this manere: 'Abagar
the sone of Euchanie to Ihesus the blessed saueoure that aperithe in
the places of Ierusalem, greting. I haue herde of the [and of the] cures
that thou doest withoute herbes and medicines, that thou makest the
10   blinde to see and the lame to go, bi thi worde lepres be clensed and
dede men risen, the whiche thinge herde of the I wene in my soule
that thou be one of the goddes, that is that thou art God and come
downe from heuene to do this, or elles that thou be the sone of God
that doest these dedes. For whiche thinge y praie the wrytinge that
f. 251ᵛᵃ thou wilt trauaile so moche for to come to me | and hele my siknesse
16   with whiche y haue longe be trauailed and laboured. And y haue herde
how the Iewes grochin and murmerin ayens the. Come therfor to me,
for y haue a litell citee that shal suffise to us bothe.' And thanne oure
Lorde ansuered [bi] these wordes: 'Thou art blessed that hast leued in
20   me and sawest me not. It is wretin of me that tho that see me not shul
leue in me, and tho that see me shul not leue in me. Of that thou hast
wretin that y shulde come to the, hit behouithe me to fulfell that y
come for, and after that y am resseiued of hym that sent me y shall
sende to the sum of my disciples for to cure the and quiken the.' This
25   is wretin in the stori aforsaid.

And whanne Abagar sawe that he might not se God presentli, as it
is wretin in an olde storie, as Iohn Damacien witnessithe in his thridde
boke, he sent a paintour to Ihesu Crist for to haue the figure of his
uisage to that ende that sethe he might not see hym in his uisage, atte
30   the leste he might be comforted in his ymage. But whanne this
peintour come to hym he might not clereli behold hym for the gret

EH1H2A1A2L; D resumes at 153 *mete* and has damage from 194 *anone* to 196 *abasshed*
caused by excised initial   4 of our Lorde] *om.* EH1   8 and of the] *om.* E, *ins.* H1
10 H2 *punctuates after* go *and adds* And   12 that is] *add* or ellis H2   14 the] *add* bi
H2   18 litell] *om.* H2   19 bi] *om.* E, *ins.* H1   21 and tho . . . in me] *ins.* H1
22 shulde] shalle H2   24 the²] *add* of thi sikenes H2   25 aforsaid] aboue said H2
29 his] *add* propur H2   30 ymage] vesage H2   31 he] *add and del.* whan þis
peyntour come to him he H1

brightnesse of his visage and hym thought uerili that he might not take
the figure of hym. And [whanne] oure Lorde sawe this he toke of that
peintoure a lynen clothe and leide it upon his uisage, and the print of
his uisage abode therin. And thanne he sent it to the kinge Abagare that 35
so grctli coueited for to haue it, and it was conteined in that stori how
this uisage was discriued. She was wel eyed and wel browed and had a
longe visage and bowyng downe that was tokene | of sadnesse.   f. 251vb

And that epistle of oure Lorde is of suche uertu that in that citee of
Edisse no paynym may not come ne no tyraunt ne may there noy. For 40
yef any peple come upon that citee with force and armes a childe shal
be sette upon the yate and rede this epistele, and that same day other
the enemyes shull flee for fere other thei shull make pees with hem of
the citee. This was done, as men saien, in olde tyme, but sethenes that
citee hathe be take of the Sarizcnes and wasted for the multeplyenge 45
of synne [and so this benefite was loste].

And it is redde in the Storie Ecclesiast that whanne oure Lorde was
stied into heuene Thomas the apostlc sent Thadee that was called
Iudas to the kinge Abagar after the promesse of God. And whanne
they werc come to hym and that he hadd told hym that he was 50
messengere of Ihesu Crist whiche was behight hym, Abagar sawe in
the uisage of Thadee a merueilous and a deuine clerenesse. And
whanne he hadde beholde hym he saide: 'Uerily art thou the disciple
of Ihesu Crist the sone of God.' And therwith he [was] sore abasshed
and sore aferde [and] worshipped hym. To whom Thadee saide: 'Yef 55
thou wilt beleue in the sone of God thou shalt hauc all the desires of
thin herte.' And Abagar saide: 'Uerily I beleue and gladly wol y slee
the Iewes that crucified hym yef y haue power.' And as it is redde
ellyswhere that Abagar was lepre, and Thadee toke thc epistle of oure
Lorde and rubbed the uisage of Abagar therwith and he receiued 60
anone ful hele.

Iudas preched furst in Pount and in Mespotame, Symond preched
in Egipte, and from thennes cam streite into Perce, and there thei
fonde .ij. enchaun|tours, Zares and Arfaxat, the which Mathew the f. 252ra
apostle had chased oute of Ynde. And there thei fonde also the duke 65

33 whanne] *om.* EH1H2 (*quant* P2)   Lorde] *add* Ihesu Criste H2   this] *add* and
H2   35 his] þe H1   36 conteined] conceyved H1   38 tokene of] taken
for H2   40 noy] none ioie abide H2   42 other] *om.* H2   43 other thei
shull] or els H2   44 saien] seiden H1   46 and so this benefite was lost] *om.*
E, *ins.* H1   49 the¹] *om.* H1   53 Uerily/art thou] *trs.* H2, *punct. after* uerily
H1   54 was] *om.* EH1   55 and] he EH1H2 (*et* P2)   61 ful] parfite H2
62 Mespotame] *add* and H2

Varadath that was a duke of the kynge of Babiloyne, the whiche
shulde go into bataile ayenst the Iewes and he might haue none
ansuere of his goddes. And thanne thei went into another temple in
the citee, and there thei hadde ansuere that for the aposteles that were
70 comyn thei might yeue none ansuere. And thanne the duke made seke
hem and fonde hem and asked hem wherfor thei were come thedyr
and what thei were, the whiche ansuereden: 'Yef thou aske us of oure
kinrede, we be of Ebrew, and yef thou aske us of what condicion, we
be seruauntes of Ihesu Crist, and yef thou aske the cause of oure
75 comyng, we be come bi cause of hele.' To whom the duke ansuered:
'Whanne [y shall] be returned with victori fro the bataile y shall here
you.' To whom the aposteles saide: 'Hit is more conuenient that thou
knowe furst hym bi whom thou shalt haue uictorie and apese hem that
be rebelles.' And thanne the duke saide: 'Y see well that ye be more
80 mighti thanne oure goddes. I praie you tell me the ende of the bataile.'
And the aposteles saide: 'For that thou knowest that thi goddes be
lyers we comaunde hem that thei yeue the ansuere of that thou wilt
aske hem, so that whanne thei haue saide what thei canne we shull
preue hem lyers.'
85   And thanne the ydoles saiden that the bataile shulde be grete and
that moche of the peple shulde be ouerthrawe in bothe parties. And
[thanne] the aposteles beganne to laugh, and the duke saide to hem: 'I
f. 252rb   am aferde, and ye | laugh.' Thanne thei ansuered and saide: 'Drede
the not, for the pees is betwene you, for tomorw atte mydday the
90 messangers of Medis shul come and submitte hem in thi powere for to
haue pees.' And the bisshoppes of ydoles lefte up a grete laughing and
saide to the duke: 'Th[ese] here wolde assure the to that ende þat thou
shuldest folily leue hem and be take of thi enemyes.' And thanne the
aposteles saide: 'We saye not to the that thou shalt abide a monthe but
95 on sengil day, and thou shalt be ouercomer of all with pees.' And
thanne the duke made kepe bothe that one and that other so that bi

66 Varadath . . . a duke] *ins.* H1   Babiloyne] *add and del.* þat was called Varadath H1
67 into] *add* a H1   68 his] *om.* H1   69–70 aposteles . . . comyn] Appostulle that was
come thider H2   70 seke] *ins.* H1   71 hem¹] hym H2   fonde hem and] *om.* H2
hem wherfor thei were] hym whether and wherefore he H2   74 thou] þey H1   76 y
shall¹] *trs.* E, 'I' shal I *with second* I *subp.* H1   be returned] retourne H2   77 aposteles]
Appostull H2   79 see] shall *del.* 'see' H1   ye] I *changed to* y'e' H1   80 goddes] *add*
wherefor H2   me] *om.* H2   87 thanne] *om.* EH1   87–8 I . . . laugh] What seie yee H2
88 and¹] *om.* H1   thei] the appostullis H2   ansuered] *add* anon H1, *add* hem H2
89 is] *add* made H2   for tomorw] forto morw E, for to do morowe *with* do *del.* H1   atte]
and *del.* 'at' H1   91 And] *add* than H2   of] *add* the H2   92 These] this E, Th'e'is
H1   94 shalt] *add* nat H2   95 ouercomer of all] ouercome H2

issue of the thinge the sothe saier shulde be worshipped and the lyer ponisshed.

And whanne that thinge whiche the aposteles hadde saide before was falle the morw after, the duke wolde haue brent the bisshoppes of the ydoles, but the apostles lettid [hym] and saide that thei were not come for to slee the quicke but for to yeue lyff to the dede. And than hadde the duke gret meruaile that thei wolde not suffre hym to slee hem ner that thei wolde take none of his goodes, and so he brought hem to the kynge and saide: 'Syr kinge, y saie to the uerily that these here be goddes hidde in fourme of men.' And whanne he hadde al tolde of hem in presence of hys enchauntours, [anone the enchauntours] meued with enuye saide that thei were wicked men and purchasours of sotill malice ayens the reawme. And thanne the kinge saide to hem: 'Dere frendes, dispute with hem.' And the enchauntours saide: 'Yef thou wilt see how litell powere thei haue in oure presence, makithe to come hedir the best and | the fairest spekers that may be founde, and yef thei dore speke before us lete us be dispised in all thinges.'

And thanne there were brought forthe mani aduocatis and thei were anone made domme before these enchauntours so ferfortheli that thei might not bi sygnes shew that thei might not speke. And thanne saide these enchauntours to the kinge: 'For that thou shalt wete that we be goddes, we will suffre hem speke but thei shull not goo, and thanne we wole yelde to hem her goinge but thei shul see nothinge, and yet her eyen shull be opin.' And whanne thei hadde do all this, the duke ledde to the aposteles these aduocates all confused, and whanne these aduocates sawe the aposteles so euell yclothed thei hadde dispite of hem in her soule, to whom Simonde saide: 'Ofte tymes it fallithe that withinne coferes of golde wrought with precious stones there be full foule and vile thinges enclosed, and that withinne vile cofers of tre ben leyde [r]inges and precious stones. Behotithe that ye will renounce the ydoles and that ye will worship onli God invisible, and we shull make you the signe of the crosse in youre forhedes so that ye shull

Marginal line numbers: 100, 105, 110, f.252va, 115, 120, 125

97 shulde] shul H1   100 falle] add In H2   101 hym] om. EH1   104 his] hir H2   goodes] goedis (?) on erasure H1   106 hidde] om. H2   fourme] fo'r'me H1 106–7 al tolde] trs. H1   107–8 anone the enchauntours] om. E, so ins. preceded by & H1, add were H2   109–10 the kinge] he del. 'þe kynge' H1   110 And] add than H2 112 hedir] add before us H2   113 spekers] spekeres with -es del. H1, speker H2 117 bi . . . not] om. H1   122 to/the aposteles] trs. H2   all] that thus were H2 127 ringes] thinges EH1, fair thingis H2   Behotithe] wherefor yif yee wille bihote us H2 128 worship] om. H2

130 confounde these enchauntours.' And whanne thei hadde renounced
and were marked in the forhede with the crosse, thei entred ayen [to]
the kinge before these enchauntours, and thanne thei might in no wise
be ouercome with the enchauntours but thei confounded hem before
all the peple.

135 These enchauntours were angri and thei made to come gret |
f. 252vb multitude of serpentes, and thanne the aposteles came anone bi the
comaundement of the kinge, and thei filled her mantelles with these
serpentes and caste hem ayenst these enchauntours and saide: 'Meue
you not in the name of oure Lorde but that ye bi the rentinge and
140 bitinge of these serpentes shewe youre sorues by weylinges and
crienges.' And whanne these serpentes rentin and etyn the flesshe
of these enchauntours thei howledin as wolues. And the kinge and
other praied the aposteles that thei might deye with these serpentes,
and the aposteles ansuered that thei were sent for to bringe ayen from
145 dethe to lyf and not for to ouerthrowe fro lyf to dethe. And thanne
thei made her praiers and comaunded to the serpentes that thei shulde
take awey her venume that thei hadd shedde and retorne ayen to her
place, and the enchauntours feltin gretter peyne in the withdrawinge
of the venim than in the furst tyme whanne thei were bitin. And
150 thanne the aposteles saide to hem: 'Ye shull fele .iij. dayes these
sorwes, and in the thridde day ye shull be hole so that ye departe from
youre malice.' And whan thei hadd .iij. dayes be turmented withoute
mete or drinke or slepe, the aposteles come to hem and saide: 'God
lest not haue seruice enforced, and therfor arisithe up al hole and
155 gothe youre waye. Ye haue free power and will to do what ye wyll.'
And they perduringe in her malys fleddin from the aposteles, and thei
meued almost all Babiloyne ayenst hem.

After this the doughter of a duke conceiued a sone in fornicacion,
f. 253ra and whanne it was | wost she defamed an holy dekene and saide that
160 he hadde defouled her and that she hadde conceiued by hym. And as
her kynne wolde haue slayne hym, the aposteles came and asked
whanne the childe was born, and thei saide: 'This day in the furst
houre of the day.' Thanne saide the aposteles: 'Bringe hedir the childe
and bringe forthe the dekene that ys acused.' And whanne this

130 thei] these aduocates H2　　renounced] *add* the ydollis H2　　131 to] with EH1
133 before] *add* the kinge and H2　　138 these] þe H1H2　　139 ye] *add* 'þe' H1　　the
rentinge] rentinges H1, returnynge H2　　140 bitinge] bitinges H1, betenge H2
144 ansuered] *add* in EH1　　145 lyf², dethe²] *trs.* H2　　149 than] *add* thei diden H2
161 wolde] come for to D　　hym] that dekenne D　　162 This] the same D

was done the aposteles saide to the childe: 'Childe, telle us in the name 165
of oure Lord yef this dekene haue do this dede.' And the childe
ansuered: 'This dekene is a chast and an holi man ne he defouled
neuer his flesshe.' And whanne the kinrede asked who had do this
dede and praied the apostelis that they wolde aske the child, thei
ansuered: 'It sitte to us for to excuse the innocent and not to accuse 170
the wikked doer.'

In that tyme it fell that two cruel tygres that were closed in diuers
caues thei brake oute and devoured all tho that thei mette with. And
thanne the aposteles came to hem and made hem in the name of oure
Lorde as debonaire as ani lambes. And after, the aposteles wolde haue 175
departed from thennes, but thei were holde bi praiers and duelled
with hem a yere and .iij. monthes, and in that space of tyme the kynge
and mo [than] .lxM.¹ men withoute litell children were baptised.

And the enchauntours went to a citee that hight Samair where there
were .lxx. bisshoppes of [the] ydoles, the whiche thei meued ayenst 180
the aposteles so that whanne thei come there thei shulde make hem to
do sacrifice or ellis to slee hem al out. And whanne the aposteles
hadde | gone about all the prouince thei come to the saide citee, and f. 253ʳᵇ
anone the bisshoppes and all the peple toke hem and ledde hem to the
temple of the sonne, and the fendes beganne to crie: 'What will men 185
with us and to you aposteles of lyving God? Lo, here we be brent with
flawmes sethe the tyme that ye entred.' And thanne the aungel of oure
Lorde apered to the aposteles and saide to hem: 'Chese ye of two
thinges, one, that is, or that this men be dede al sodenli, or elles that
ye be martired.' To whom thei saide: 'We will that thou conuerte 190
these that be here and lede us to peyne of marterdome.' And thanne
all madin pees and the aposteles [saiden]: 'For that ye shull wel knowe
that these ydoles be full of fendes, we comaunde hem that thei go
oute, and euery of hem breke his fals ymage.' And anone two Ethiopes
blake and horrible and naked went oute of the ydoles, seyng al tho that 195
were there, wherof thei were gretly abasshed. Thei brake her ydoles
and went her way crieng horribly, and whanne the bisshoppes sawe
that, they ranne upon the aposteles and alle tohewe hem anone. And

165 was done] om. D   166 childe] deken del. 'child' H1   167 a] om. H1   ne]
for D   169 they] he D   176 holde] withholde D   178 than] om. E
180 the¹] om. E   meued] made H1, add gretlie D   184 anone] add alle D
187 flawmes] add of fire D   189 one that is or that] oon is that alle these with punct.
before oon D   al] om. D   190 ye] add wille D   191 and] or H1   192 saiden] om.
E, ins. H1   shull] add fulle D   195 seyng] seienge to H2 (D damaged)   196 were²]
add alle H2   Thei] the feendis D

in that same houre that it was right faire wedir ther come so gret
200 thunder and lighteninge that the temple was cutte in thre, and the .ij.
enchauntours were turned into cole with the stroke of the thunder.
And the kinge bare the bod[ies of the aposteles into the cite] and made
a chirche of meruailous gretnesse in the worshipp of hem.

And it is founde in mani places that Symond was fyched in the
f. 253va gibet of the crosse, the whiche thinge in the Boke of the | Dethe
206 [of the] Aposteles Isidre saithe, and Euseby in the Storie Ecclesiast,
and Bede upon the Dede[s] of the Aposteles, and Maister Iohn Belet
in his Somme witnessithe. And as thei sayn, whan he hadd preched in
Egipte, he came ayen and was made bisshop of Ierusalem after the
210 dethe of Iames the Lasse and was chosyn bi the acorde of [the]
aposteles. And it is saide that he areised .xxx. dede men. Whanne he
hadd gouerned Ierusalem many a yere into the tyme of Trayan þe
emperour vnto the tyme that Axit councellour was in Ierusalem, of
whom he was take and turmented and fixed upon the gibet of the
215 crosse, and the iuge and alle that were there meruailed gretly that so
old a man of an .C.xx. yere might suffre the turment of the crosse but
that it was another Simond that suffered the marterdom of the crosse.

And other ther be that sayen verily that it was another Simon, the
sone of Cleophas brother of Ioseph. And Eusabe bisshop of Cesare
220 witnessith it in his Cronicle, for Isid[o]re and Euseby corrected her
cronicles of that thei hadd saide before, as it shewithe bi Bede that
felithe the same in his Retracciones. Vsuardus witnessithe the same in
his Martiloge.

Here endithe the lyff of Symonde and Iude, and nexst
beginnithe the lyf of Seint Quintin, Capitulum .C.liij.

Seint Quintine was of noble kinrede of the citee of Rome, and he come
to the citee of Damyans doyn[g] mani miracles. And he was take of the
prouost of the citee bi the comaundement of Maximien and was betin
f. 253vb so long till tho | that bete hym were ouercome, and thanne he was

199 that²] om. D   wedir] add and anone D   201 turned] brent D   202 bodies
. . . cite] body EH₁   204 founde] founded EH₁   205 thinge] add is D   206 of
the] om. EH₁   207 Dedes] Dede EH₁   210 the³] om. EH₁   213 emperour] add
and also D   that] of D   Axit] add which was his D   councellour] councellours H₁   was]
and dwellid D   216 a] ins. H₁   217 that¹] om. D   217–218 that² . . . Simon]
om. D   220 it] om. D   Isidore] Isidre EH₁   221 thei hadd] twice, once del. H₁

EH₁DH₂A₁A₂   2 doyng] doyn E, douyng with u subp. H₁, add þere D

putte into prison. But the aungel of God vnbonde hym and he went 5
thorugh the citee prechinge to the peple.

And thanne he was take ayen and streched oute upon the
turnement called eculee unto his veynes brosten and betin with
rawe synues right longe, and sethe he was putte in grece and oyle
and in piche boylynge, and yet he scorned the iuge. And the iuge 10
made for to pore into his mowthe hote lyme, vinegre and galle, and yet
he was neuer meued for alle this. Thanne thei ledde hym to
Vermendoys, and there thei droue hym yn .ij. nayles thorugh his
hede downe into his thighes, and .x. nayles they droue in betwene his
nailes and his flesshe, and atte the last the prouost made hym to be 15
biheded and cast the body into the water.

And whanne he hadde be hidde there .lv. yere he was founde in this
wise of a noble ladi of Rome, for as she was contynuelly in orison she
was in a night taught bi an aungel that she shulde goo hastely to the
castell of Vermendoys and that she shuld seke the bodi of Seint 20
Quintine in that place and berie hym worshipfully. And whanne she
was come to the forsaide place with grete companie, as she made her
praier the body of Seint Quintine apered aboue the water right well
smelling and withoute corrupcion, the whiche she beried, and for the
sepulcre that she dede make worshipfully she that was blynde 25
resseiued [her] sight and edefied there a chirche and returned to
her propre place.

Here endithe the lyff of Seint Quintine, and nexst
beginnithe the lyff of Seint Eustas, Capitulum .C.liiij. |

Eustas that was called Placidas was maister of the cheualrie of Traian f. 254ra
the emperoure, and he was right besi in werkes of merci, but for al that
he was abondonid for to worship ydoles. And he hadd a wiff of the
same condicion that loued the werkes of merci, of the whiche wiff he
hadde .ij. sones the whiche he dede norisshe nobli after his astate. And 5
for that he was ententif to the werkes of merci he deserued for to be
clered and lighted and brought to the waie of trouthe.

5 hym] hem *changed to* hym H1   9 synues] zenues H1   11 pore] put D   hote]
add brennynge D   13 Vermendoys] Bermendois H1   13–14 hym . . . into] into his
heede twoo nailis doun to D   13 thorough] *add* all H1   18 was] *om.* H1
20 Vermendoys] Bermedois H1   22 was] *om.* H1   23 well] swete D
24 beried] *add* worshipfullie D   25 worshipfully] rialy D   was] *add* of *subp. and del.*
H1   26 her] the EH1   returned] *add* ayen D

EH1DH2A1A2LLa   3 was . . . for] usyd amonge La   4 of the . . . he] and they
La   6 to¹] in H1D   7 clered] clepid La   and lighted] lyghtned La

In a day as he went for to hunte he fonde a gret assemble of hertes,
among whiche he fonde one more fairer and gretter thanne ani of that
10 other, that parted from his felawes and lepte into the grettest desert of
the forest. And his other knightes ranne after the [other hertes], but
Placidas with al his powere enforced hym to folue and to take that gret
hert, and as the hert saw that he enforced hym so gretly for to folw
hym, he went upon an high roche. And thanne Placidas neyghi[d]
15 hym for to see how he might be take, and as he behelde the herte
diligentely he sawe betwene the hornes of hym the forme of the crosse
shininge more bright thanne the sonne and withinne the ymage of
Ihesu Crist that bi the mouthe of the herte, right as sumtyme he spake
to Balam bi the mouthe of the asse, saienge: 'O Placidas, whi pursuest
20 thou me? I am apered to the in this beste bi the grace of the. I am
Ihesu Crist that thou worshippest ignoraunte. Thi almesse be stied
up before me and therfor y come hedir so that bi this hert that thou
f. 254ʳᵇ huntest y shall hunt the.' And sum other saiǀen that that ymage of
Ihesu Crist that apered betwene the hornes of the hert saide these
25 wordes.

And whanne Placidas herde this he hadde right gret drede and light
adowne of his hors, and by an hour after he come to hymself and rose
hym up from the grounde and saide: 'Reherse ayen that thou saidest
to me and y shall leue the.' And thanne saide Ihesu Crist: 'Placidas, y
30 am Ihesu Crist that formed heuene and erthe, that brought forthe
light and deuided her from derkenesse, that ordeined the tyme and
the dayes and yeres, that formed man of the slyme of the erthe,
that apered in the world in flesshe for the hele of mankinde, that was
crucified and beried and arose the thridd day.' And whanne Placidas
35 herd that he fell ayen to the erthe and said: 'Y beleue, Lorde, that thou
art he that wrought all thinge of not.' [Than saide oure Lorde]: 'Yef

8 In] And in D, And so on La   assemble] semble D   9 fonde] sawe La
9–10 any . . . other] a nothir D   11 other hertes] hirde EH1, harte La   13 as] *om.* D
14 went] lepte La   neyghid] neyghinge D   16 the hornes of hym] his hornes La
hym] the hert D   the³] a La   17 the²] that the D, that an La   18 that] *add* spak D
herte] *add* spak La   19 to Balam/bi . . . asse] *trs. and add* as the byble telleth La
saienge] And sayd La   20 bi the grace] for grace and helpe La   21 almesse] almes
dedys La   22 hedir] hidre *with* h *on erasure* H1   23 other] *om.* La   24 these] the
forsaid La   26 whanne . . . this] *om.* D   27 by an hour after] hit was an houre after
or La   come] *add* ayenne D   and²] *add* than he La   28 saide] *add* to the hert D
30 Crist] *add* thi Lorde La   31 her] it DLa   that] and he that D, And I La   the tyme]
tymes La   32 that] I La   that formed] And I am he þat ordeined D   33 that¹] and
he that D, and I La   flesshe] *add* and blode La   that²] I La   34 crucified] *add* dede La
day] *add* and aftyrward stied into heven La   36 Than saide oure Lorde] *so ins.* H1, *om.*
ELa, *add* Ihesu Criste D

thou leue this, go to the bisshop of the citee and do the to be baptised.'
Than saide Placidas: 'Lorde, wilt thou that y hide this thinge fro my
wiff and fro my two sones?' And oure Lorde said: 'Saie to hem that
thei be clensed with the togedre, and thou come ayen hedir tomorw to 40
me so that y apere to the ayen and shewe to the what shall fall the.'
And whanne he was come to his hous and he hadde told this thinge to
his wyf, she cried and saide: 'My Lorde, y sawe hym also the night
that is passed, and he saide to me: "Tomorw thou and thine husbonde
and thi sones shul come to me," and thanne y knewe that it was oure 45
Lorde Ihesu Crist.' And thanne atte midnight thei went to the bisshop
of Rome that baptised hem with gret ioye, and he called Placidas
Eustas and his wiff Theospice and | his .ij. sones Agapite and f. 254ᵛᵃ
Theospice. And in the morw Eustas went for to hunte as he dede
before, and whan he come nigh the place he departed his knightes as it 50
were for to finde venison, and anone he sawe in that place there the
fourme of the furst vision, and anone he fell to the erthe before the
figure and saide: 'Lord, y beseche the that thou opene to me tho
thinges that thou hast behight me thi seruaunt.' To whom oure Lorde
saide: 'Eustas, thou art blessed for thou hast take the wasshinge of my 55
grace, for now thou hast ouercome the fende that had defouled the
and deceiued the. Now shall apere thi faithe, for the fend that thou
hast forsake is cruelly armed ayenst the, and it behouithe the to suffre
mani peynes for to haue the crowne of victorie. Thou must suffre gret
thinges that thou be made meke fro the high vanite of the worlde, and 60
thou shalt ayen be lefte up in diuine spiritualle thinges. Loke thou
defaile not and beholde not thi furst glorie, for it behouithe that by
temptaciones thou shalt be the secounde Iob, and whanne thou shalt
be made meke y shall come to the. Telle me now whedir thou wilt
suffre these temptaciones now anone or elles in the last ende of thi 65
lyff.' And he saide: 'Lorde, yef it behouithe for to be th[u]s, comaunde
anone þat these temptaciones come; but yeue me vertu of pacience.'
And oure Lorde saide to hym: 'Be stable, for my grace shal kepe

37 thou] *add* wilt Hɪ   this] *add* said Crist La   39 Saie . . . that] to hym D
40 the] *add* alle D   thou EHɪ] than D   41 so that y] and I shalle D   y] *add* may La
42 he¹] Placidas DLa   hadde told] tolde all La   45 thi] *add* twoo D   thanne] þat Hɪ
knewe] *add* welle D   that it] *om.* Hɪ   50 departed] *add* fro DLa   51 there] *om.* D
54 thi] thine owne D   59 mani] *add* thinges and La   60 that thou be made] for to
make the La   high] *om.* La   ayen] ayenward La   62 defaile] faile D   not²] *om.* D
thi] þe Hɪ   that] þe D   63 be] *add* made La   Iob] Ioue La   64 the] *add* wherfor D
me] *om.* La   65 temptaciones] turmentis D   anone] in the biginnynge D   66 he]
Eustas La   yef] *om.* Hɪ   behouithe] *add* me D   for to] *om.* La   thus] this EHɪ
67 come] *add* anone D   but] *add* lorde D, *add* than La

the and y shal kepe youre soules.' And thanne oure Lorde departed
70 and stied up into heuene. And Eustas returned to his hous and tolde
f. 254ᵛᵇ all | to his wiff.

And within a while after there come a dedly pestilence and assailed
his seruauntes and his chaumbreres and slow hem alle. And within a
litell while after that all his hors and al his bestes deyeden sodenly, and
75 after that sum þat were of his felawshipp entred by night into his hous
and robbed hym of all his golde and of alle his siluer and of alle other
thinge. And he and his wiff and his children thanked God of all and
fledde awey be night al voide of goodes, and for thei dredden shame
thei fledde into Egipte, and all his gret possession come to not bi
80 extorcion of wicked men. And the kinge thanne and the senatoures
sorueden gretly for the maister of knightes that was so noble for that
thei coude here no tydingges of hym.

So thanne as thei went forthe thei neighed to the see and fonde a
shippe and entred inne for to passe ouer. And the maister of the
85 shippe saw that Eustasis wif was right faire and he desired gretly for to
haue her, and whanne he hadd passed hem ouer he desired his mede
and thei had nothinge to paie hym, so that the maister comaunded
that the wiffe were witholde for the hire and so he wolde haue her with
hym. And whanne Eustas herde that he withstode as longe as he
90 might, but than the maister of the shippe comaunded his shipmen
that thei shulde [throw] hym in the see so that bi that he might haue
his wyf. And whanne Eustas sawe that he lefte his wiff full sorufulli
and toke his .ij. sones and went his way wepinge and saienge: 'Alas to
f. 255ʳᵃ me and to you, for youre moder is take [to] a straunge husbond.' | And
95 thanne he come bi a flode and for the gretnesse therof he durst not
passe it with bothe children, but he left that one on the riuer side and
bare that other ouer. And whanne he hadde passed the flode he sette

60 the . . . kepe] om. La   departed] add from him DLa   70 returned] add ayenne D
71 all] add this La   72 a] add litell La   after] om. D, add that La   73 And] om. D
74 while] add and D, om. La   hors and al his] om. La   his²] om. H1   75 þat were] om. D
76 golde and of alle his] om. La   siluer] add jewels La   of alle] om. La   77 all] add his
soonde D   78 of] from eny La   81 sorueden] sorweden with sorw on erasure H1
83 thei¹] Eustas and his wife D   went] add thus La   84 shippe] add redy to passe ouer La
inne . . . ouer] therin La   85 faire] a fayre woman La   desired] add right H1   86 hadd]
add led and La   passed] brouȝt D   ouer] add the see D   desired] add right H1, askid D
mede] add for his frauȝt D, add for his travaile La   87 hym] add for her passage La   that]
than D   88 witholde] add and kept still La   the²] his D   he] the shippe man D   her] add
stille D   89 withstode] add it D   91 throw] draw EH1   in] into H1D   93 saienge]
sighinge and seide D   94 you] add my sonnes D   to²] om. EH1   96 children] add at ones
DLa   but] And so he La   one] add childe La   riuer] heder La   97 that other/ouer] trs. La
ouer] add the floode D

his childe downe that he bare and hasted hym ouer for to fette that
other. And as he was in the middes of the water there come a wolfe
and rauisshed the childe anone that he had sette downe and fledde to 100
the wode. And as he was al oute of hope of hym and he went for to
fette that other, there come a lyon and toke that other and fledde so
that he might not atteine to take hym, for he was yet in the middel of
the water. And thanne he beganne to wepe and to rende his here and
wolde haue throw hymself in the water yef [the] grace of God had not 105
withholde hym.

And the shepardes sawe the lyon that bare the childe al quik and
folued hym with her houndes so that bi [the] dispensacion of God the
lyon lefte the childe al hole. And other [there] were that ereden the
londe and sawe the wolfe and ascried hym and deliuered the child al 110
hole fro hurtynge, and so bothe that one and that other, that is to saie
bothe the shepardes and the tyliers, norisshed up the children in her
owne houses.

And Eustas wist it not but went sorwfully wepinge and cryenge and
saide: 'Alas to me, for before this thinge y shined as a tre, but now y 115
am made naked of alle thinge. Alas, y was wont for to be enuironed
with multitude of knightes, and now y duelle allone, not so moche
that thei haue lefte me my sones. Lorde, y remembre me that thou
saidest to me that me behoued that y were tempted as Iob, but as | me f. 255rb
thinkithe that there is more done ayenst me than ayens Iob, for though 120
he were made naked of all his possessiones, yet he hadd a donghill
wheron he might sitte, and also he hadde frendes that hadde pite of
hym. I haue none of these thinges, but y haue wilde bestes myn

98 downe] *add* on the lande La   ouer] *om.* H1D   99 water] ryver H1
100 rauisshed] *add* aweie D   fledde] *add* fast La   101 hope . . . went] hym selfe for
sorowe and woo And as he was goyng than La   hym] hymselff and when he saw3e none
oþer bote D   for] forthe D   102 other] *add* child La   there] And bi þat he D   and']
om. D   that other] it La   fledde] *add* his weie D   104 and'] *add* alle D   105 throw
. . . yef] dreynt hym selfe ne had the La   yef] but yif D   the] L, *om.* EH1D
105–6 had . . . withholde] holpe La   105 not] *om.* D   107 the'] than D   and] *add*
anone thei D   108 the'] *om.* E   dispensacion] disposicion La   109 there] *om.* E
that] in the felde and La   110 wolfe and] *add* anone thei ronnen afftir hym and D, *add*
with the childe La   ascried] afferid D, astryed La   and³] so he D   111 fro] withoute D
hurtynge] *add* of the wolfe La   bothe] *om.* D   bothe . . . saie] *om.* La   other] *add* were
sauff D   112 the'] 'þe' H1   tyliers] tyllers H1   up] *add* bothe La   113 owne] *om.*
La   114 And] But D   it not] nothinge therof La   went] *add* in his wey La   and²]
om. D   115 as a tre] in prosperite La   116 duelle] am La   118 that . . . haue] is
D, as me is La   me'] *om.* La   my] *add* twoo DLa   sones] *add* wherfor D   me²] nowe of
D, *add* nowe La   119 me behoued] It behoueth me DLa   that y were] for to be D
Iob] *add* was D   121 naked] bare La   122 hadde] *add* many La   123 these] alle
the D   y haue] *om.* La   bestes] *add* be La

enemyes that haue take awey my children, and my wiff is take fro me
125 [and yeue] to another. Now, good Lorde, yeue rest to my tribulaciones and yeue a kepinge to my mouthe so that my herte faile not and
that y saie no wordes contrarie before thi visage.' And in that saienge
he went into a strete in the towne where [his] children weren
norisshed that wist not in no wise that thei were bretheren, and
130 there he was hired to kepe the feldes of men of the towne. And so he
kepte hem .xv. yere, and oure Lorde kepte his wiff so that straunge
men had neuer to do with her, but she was kepte withoute corrupcion.

      In that tyme the emperoure and the peple of Rome were gretly
turmented with her enemyes. And thanne thei bethought hem upon
135 Placidas that had mani a tyme nobli fought ayenst his enemyes, and
the emperour made gret sorw for hym and sent bi diuerse cuntreies
mani of his knightes and behight to hem that shulde fynde hym gret
richesses and worshippes. And two knightes that sumtyme had be
with hym in his viages come into that towne and into the same strete
140 where Placidas was, and as sone as Eustas sawe hem he knewe hem,
and thanne come to [his] mynde his dignite and he beganne to be
f. 255ᵛᵃ sorufull and saide: 'A, good | Lorde, graunte me also that sumtyme y
may see my wiff, for my sones y wote wel be dede with wylde bestes.'
And thanne come to hym a voys that saide: 'Eustas, haue faithe, for in
145 short tyme thou shalt resseiue thi worshipp and thou shalt haue thi
wyf and thi children.'

      And anone as he mette these knightes thei knew hym not, for thei
asked hym yef he knew ani straunge man that hight Placidas and hadd
a wiff and .ij. children, and he saide: 'Nay'. And alwey atte his request
150 they come to his hous and there he serued hem. And whanne he
remembered hym of his furst astate he might not holde hym from
wepinge. And than he went oute [and] wysshe his visage and returned
ayen for to serue hem, and thei considered hym and saide that one to

124 that] *add* I *del.* `they' H1   take¹] *om.* D   125 and yeue] *om.* E   yeue²] if H1,
add me D   yeue rest to] cese La   125–6 tribulaciones] tribulacion H1   126 a] me
D, me a La   128 went] come La   the] a La   where] whereinne D   his] her EH1
weren] *add* wele La   129 that¹] but he D   bretheren] there D   130 there] than D
131–2 straunge men] no strange man La   132 kepte] *add* clene La   withoute] *add* eny
La   133 that tyme] this same tyme it happed that La   135 his] her La
139 that] *add* same D, the same La   140 hem²] *add* wele La   141 come . . . his²] he
remembryd hym of his first La   his¹] *om.* EH1   142 A] *om.* La   also] *om.* La
143 my²] *add* twoo D   144 thanne] *add* there D   145 worshipp] *add* ayenne D
147 anone as] whan D   mette] *add* with D   149 And] but La   151 holde]
forbere D   152 and wysshe] awysshe E   visage] face La   153 considered] behelde
La   hym] *om.* D   saide/that one] *trs.* La

that other: 'This man resembelithe gretly to hym that we seke.' And
that other saide: 'Sikerly, he resembelith hym full moche. Now lete us 155
take hede whedir he haue a wounde in his hede that was yeue hym in
suche a bataile.' And thanne thei loked and sawe the signe of the
wounde and knewen verily that it was he that thei sought. And thanne
thei rysen up and custe hym and asked hym of his wiff and of his
children, and he saide that his children were dede and that his wiff 160
was take awey from hym. And thanne al the neigheboures ronne for to
see this thinge, for that the knightes tolden of his furst glorie and his
vertu, and thanne thei tolde hym the comaundement of the emperoure and clothed hym and ledde hym to the emperoure.

And whanne the emperoure wost of his comynge he went anone 165
ayenst hym, and whan he sawe hym he clipped hym and kissed hym
with gret ioye. And than | Eustas before all the peple tolde how it was   f. 255vb
fall hym bi ordre, and so he was ayen restabled to his furst worshipp
and astate and made ruler and gouernour of all the knighthode and
constreined hym for to take it upon hym. And thanne he tolde his 170
knightes and sawe that thei were fewe ayenst her enemyes, and he
comaunded that all the yonge men of [the] citees and townes were
gadered togedre to hym. And so it fell in that contre where his sones
were norisshed yaue .ij. men of armes. And thanne the duellers of that
cuntre ordeined these two yonge men [his] sones more couenable than 175
all other for to go with the maister of knighthode. [And whan the
maister] sawe [these two] yong men of so noble fourme arrayed with
honeste of good condiciones he wept strongly and ordeined that thei
shuld be the furst in his bataile.

And whan he hadde submitted his enemyes to hym he made his 180
oste for to reste .iij. dayes in a towne wher his wiff duelled in an ostrie.
And bi the will of God her .ij. sones were herborued in her hous

154 hym] Placidas D   155 full] *om.* La   156 a wounde] *om.* D   157 the
signe of] *om.* D   signe] marke La   158–9 that² . . . up] *om.* La   159 wiff . . . his]
om. La   160 dede] *add* with wild bestes La   161–2 al . . . the] thes La   162 for
that] and than D   tolden] *add* him La   164 hym¹] *add* and arayed him La
165 anone] *om.* La   167 before . . . peple/tolde] *trs.* D   168 ayen] *om.* D
restabled] restablisshid D, restored La   furst] *add* degre La   171 sawe] *add* welle DLa
thei] there D   fewe] feble H1   172 the²] *om.* E   173 to hym] *ins.* H1   fell] *add* þat
DLa   that contre] þe toune D, þe contre La   174 norisshed] *add* they La   yaue . . .
armes] were askid men D   174–5 that cuntre] þe toune D   175 his] La, *om.* EH1D
(*ses* P2)   sones] *add* of Placidas which were D, *add* that were La   176 knighthode]
kny3tis D   whan] than La   176–7 And whan the maister] *om.* E, ʻand þan þe maistre'
H1   177 these two] this and no E, *so with* þis *changed to* þes H1   men] *add* were La
177–8 arrayed . . . honeste] and La   with honeste] honestli and D   182 her²] the
same La

withoute knowynge what she was, so that in a day thei satte togederes
and spake that one to that other of her childehode. And thaire moder
185 that was there herde hem ent[ent]ifly, so that the elder saide to the
yonger: 'Whanne y was a childe y can remembre no further but that
my fader that was maister of the knightes had wedded my moder that
was right a faire woman and she hadd .ij. sones, me and another right
faire, and thei toke us and went bi night from oure hous and went into
190 a ship for to go y note neuer wheder. And whan we come oute of the
shippe oure moder [was] lefte behinde, but oure fader bare us with
f. 256 hym full sore wepinge, and whan | he come to a water he passed ouer
with my brother and lefte me upon the riuer syde. And whanne he
returned for to fette me, a wolf come and toke my brother awey, and
195 or he might fulli come to me a lyon come oute of the forest and bare
me to the wode. But shepardes deliuered me from the mowthe of the
lyon and so y was norisshed in that towne that ye knowe, and y might
neuer know what fell of my fader and of my brother.' And whan the
yongger brother herde this he beganne to wepe and to saie: 'Forsothe
200 as y haue herde y am thi brother, for tho that norisshed me tolde me
that thei had take me from a wulfe.' And thanne thei beganne to clippe
and to kisse and wepte eche on other.

And whanne her moder hadd herde al this, she considered longe in
herself whedir thei were her .ij. sones that had so ordinatli tolde that
205 was falle to hem. And that other day foluinge she went to the maister
of knightes and required hym saienge: 'Syr, y beseche you that ye wil
comaunde that y might be brought ayen into my contrei, for y am of
the cuntre of Romaynes and y am here a straunger.' And in that saieng
she saw in hym sygnes wherbi she knewe that he was her husbonde,
210 and thanne she might no lenger forbere but fell downe to his fete and
saide: 'Sir, y beseche you that ye tell me of youre furst astate, for y
wene that ye be Placidas maister of knightes, that by another name art
called Eustas, the whiche Placidas the saueoure of the worlde
conuerted, and hath mani a sore temptacion, and y that am thi wiff

183 what . . . was] eny of hem of oþer La   day] add as D   184 and] om. D   spake/that
one] trs. DLa   185 that was there] om. D   ententifly] entifly E, om. La   186 can
remembre] am remembred La, add me D   189 faire²] add children D   bi night] om. La
190 for to go] om. D   we] he D   191 was] om. EH₁La   192 whan he] as we La
195 fulli . . . lyon] ins. H₁   198 brother] moder H₁   199 herde] add all La   201 me]
add aweie D   202 eche] add one E   203 hadd] om. La   longe] add time D   205 day]
ins. H₁   207 might] om. D   be] ins. H₁   207–8 for . . . cuntre] ins. H₁   209 hym] the
La   knewe] add welle D   211 Sir] om. D   ye] add wille D   212 of] add þe H₁
213 Placidas] om. La   214 hath] add had D, add yove La   a] add tyme La   temptacion]
temptaciouns La   y] add here D   that] om. La   wiff] add that La

was take from the in the see and allwey oure Lorde hathe kepte me 215
from all corrupcion.' And whanne Eustas herde this thinge he
considered and knewe | that it was his wiff, and wepte for ioy and f. 256rb
cussed her and glorified God that comfort[ith] tho that be turmented
bi tribulacion.

And thanne his wif saide to hym: 'Mi lorde, where be oure .ij. 220
sones?' And he saide: 'Thei be slayne with wilde bestes', and tolde her
in what wise thei were loste. And she saide to hym: 'Yelde we
thankinges to God, for y beleue right as God hathe yeue us grace to
finde eche other, so he wille graunt us to finde oure children.' And he
said: 'Y haue tolde you that they be deuoured with wilde bestes.' And 225
she said: 'Y sate yesterday in a gardin and herde .ij. yonge men
reherce her childehode, and y beleue verily that thei be my sones.
Aske hem and they will tell you as y herde.' And thanne Eustas called
hem and herde the manere of her childchode and knew wel that thei
were his sones. And thanne he and the moder clip]ped hem and kissed 230
hem and made gret ioye. And alle the oste were fulfelled with
gladnesse and ioy of the findynge of his wiff and of his children and
of the victori of the barbarins. And thanne [whan he was] returned,
Trayen tho was dede and Adrian succeded after hym that was wors in
alle wickednesse, and what for the findinge of his wiff and his children 235
[and for the uictorie] he resseiued hym worshipfully and lete ordeine a
gret dyner. And the nexst day after he went to the temple for to
sacrifie for the uictorie of [the] barbari[n]s. And thanne whan the
emperour sawe that Eustas wolde not do sacrifice neither for the
victorie ne for the fyndinge of his wiff and of his children, he bade 240
hym in all wise that he shulde do sacrifice. To whom Eustas saide: 'Y

215 take] *add* aweie D   and allwey] a wey and La   216 corrupcion] correpcioun La
217 knewe] add welle D   it] she D   218 comfortith] comforted E   be] he La
220 oure] youre H1   221 saide²] *add* ayenne to hir D   be] *add* deede and D
222 saide] *add* ayen D   223 right] verelie D   223–4 to² . . . other] euche of vs to
fynde oþer right La   224 graunt] yeve La   225 said] *add* ayenne to hir D   be]
hathe La   227 that] *om.* H1   my] oure La   sones] *add* wherfor sir I praie you to D
228 you] *om.* La   229 her] þe H1   herde . . . and] *om.* La   that] *om.* H1
230 clipped] cleped E   hem] *om.* H1   231 and made] with D   231–2 And . . . ioy]
om. La   232 findynge] tidyngges & *subp.* fidinges H1   his¹] her lordis D   his children]
her twoo sones D   232–6 and³ . . . victorie] *om.* La   233 whan he was] L, was he
EH1, Eustas D   returned] *add* home ayenne and bi that time D   234 tho] the
emperoure D   235 and²] *add* of D   236 and for the victorie] L, *om.* EH1, and also
for his victorie that he had D   resseiued hym] was resseiued D   hym] hem La   and²] *add*
there thei D   237 he] this Adryan La   238 the²] *om.* EH1   barbarins] barbaries
EH1   238–9 the² . . . that] *om.* La   241 shulde] *add* go EH1   Eustas] *add* enswerd
ayen and La

worshippe oure Lorde Ihesu Crist and serue hym only.' And thanne

f. 256ᵛᵃ the emperoure fulfelled | with wratthe putte hym and his wiff and his
childeren in a place and lete go to hem a cruell lyon. And the lyon
245 ranne to hem bowinge downe his hede as in doynge worship to hem,
and thanne he parted fro hem. And thanne the emperoure lete ordeine
a beste of brasse and made hym glowinge hote of fire and comaunded
that thei were al quicke putte withinne, and thanne the seintes made
her praiers and [recomaunded hem to God and] entred into the oxe,
250 and there thei yelded up her sperites to Ihesu Crist. And the thridde
day thei were draw oute before the emperour, and thei were founde so
hole that none here of her hede was atamid with the fire. And cristen
men toke hem and beried hem in a right noble place and made aboue
hem an oratorie. And thei suffered dethe under Adrean that beganne
255 aboute the yere of oure Lorde .C.xx. in the kalendes of Nouembre.

Here endithe the liff of Seint Eustas, and nexst beginnithe
the sollempnite of Alle Seintes, .Cᵐ. .C.lv.ᵐ

The fest of Al Seintes was ordeined for .iiij. causes: furst for the
dedicacion of [a] temple, the secounde for the suplement of defauutes
done, the thridde for to putte awey necligence, the ferthe for to gete to
us the more lightly that we praie for.

5 This feste was ordeined furst for the dedicacion of [a] temple, for
whanne the Romaynes sawe that thei hadde lordshipp ouer alle the
worlde, thei made right an high temple and sette her ydole in the
middes, and al about that ydole thei sette her fals ymages of other

f. 256ᵛᵇ prouinces so that | all tho ydoles behelde right in the ymage of Rome.
10 And it was so ordeyned by the crafte of the fende that whanne a

242 serue . . . only] hym will I only serue La   243 with] add grete La   244 hem]
him La   245 bowinge] beryng La   246 he] the lionne D   the] add cruelle D
247 glowinge hote] hote glowynge of hete La   248 quicke] om. D   withinne] therin La
249 recommaunded . . . God and] om. E, ins. H1   oxe] beeste of bras D, add of brasse La
250 to] add oure lorde D   251 day] add after La   252 And] add than DLa
254 thei] thes martris La   Adrean] add the Emperoure La   that beganne] the emperour
D, add to regne La

EH1DH2A1A2L   DH2 have Augustine for Austin except H2 austine at 176, and
Grisosthome for Crisosthome, except D Crisosthome at 185.   Rubric nexst] om. DH2A2
sollempnite] Feest DH2A1A2   2 a] L, the EH1DH2A1A2   suplement] supplementis
A2   of²] add the DH2A2   defauutes] offencis A2   3 to³] om. L   5 a] L, the
EH1DH2A1A2   for] om. A1   7 worlde] add than A2   right] om. DH2   and] add þey
A2   ydole] ydollis DH2, ydols of goold A2   8 middes] add thereof A2   that ydole]
these ydols A2   ydole] ydollis DH2   her] the H2   of other] and euery A1   other] þoo L
9 prouinces] prouince A1   tho] þe L   tho ydoles] they A1   in] on A2   10 so] om. L
the¹] om. DH2A2   a] any A2

prouince wolde rebelle ayenst the Romaynes the ymage of that
prouince wold turne his bak to the ymage of Rome as in warnyng
that she turned awey from his lordship. And thanne anone the
Romaynes wolde go with gret strengthe into that cuntre and turne
hem ayen to her lordship. And yet it suffised not to the Romaynes that 15
thei had in her citee all the fals ymages of the prouinces, but thei made
to euery of these fals goddes a temple, right as though tho goddes had
made hem lordes ouer alle the prouinces. And for that all the ydoles
might not [be] in that temple, thei made right a grete temple and more
higher than all that other, and for to shewe the more her madnesse 20
thei dedyed that temple in the worshipp of all her goddes and named
it Pantheon, þat is as moche to saie as all goddes. And for more
deceyuinge of the peple the bisshoppes of the ydoles feyned that it
hadde be comaunded hem bi Cibile, a goddesse that thei called moder
of all her goddes, for that yef thei wolde haue the uictorie of all her 25
enemyes that thei shulde make a gret temple to all her sones.

And the fundement of that temple was caste bi a spere, so that bi
that fourme the perdurabilite of [the] goddes was shewed. And for
that [the] multitude of the voydinge of the erthe withinne was seine to
be not sustenable, as sone as the werke shewed a litell vpon the 30
grounde, thei fulfelled the creues within the erthe and medlid
therwith siluer, and thus thei dede till all the temple was fulfelled.
And | thanne thei gaue leue to tho that wolde come and take awey the f. 257ʳᵃ
erthe to take as for her owne all the money that thei coude finde with

11 prouince] add of alle the worlde A2   Romaynes] add Then L   13 turned]
turneth H1   turned . . . lordship] did rebelle ayenste room A2   lordship] lod schip A1
14 go] add anone A1   with . . . strengthe/into . . . cuntre] trs. with power for strengthe and
provynce for cuntre] A2   15 to¹] vnto DH2   suffised] suffiseth H1   16 the¹] tho
A2   ymages] ydollis DH2A1, goddis A2   the prouinces] euery provynce A2   prouinces]
province DH2A1   17 euery . . . goddis] eche god A2   though] om. DH2A2   tho] þe L
18 made] om. A2   the¹] tho A2   that all] trs. DH2   that] om. A2   the²] these A2
19 be] om. EH1, add worshippid L   made] did do make A2   right a] trs. A2   20 all]
any of DH2A2, om. A1   that] þe H1DH2A2   other] add templis A2   and] om. DH2A2
madnesse] paraph after madnesse DH2   21 dedyed] edified A2   that] the A1   temple]
add also DH2A2   her] om. A2   goddes] goodes A1   and] add thaye A2   22 as²] add of
A2   goddes] goodes A1   And] om. H2   23 bisshoppes] bishop A1L   the³] þer L
24 hem bi] of A2   bi] of DH2A1   a goddesse] of goodes A1   25 of¹] ouer DH2   for
that] om. DH2   that] om. A2   the] om. A1A2   all²] om. DH2   26 that] þan A2   to]
of DH2A1   to. . . . sones] om. A2   27 the] add foundacion and A2   bi¹] evyn rowned
with A2   28 the²] om. EH1L, her DH2   29 the¹] om. EH1   the²] om. H1
30 sustenable] sustentable DH2A1A2   30–1 vpon . . . grounde] aboue the erthe A2
31 creues] crevessis DH2   32 therwith] with A1, it with A2   thus] this A2   all] om.
A1A2   fulfelled] fulle finiysshid & made A2   33 to] add alle DH2A1   tho] alle A2
34 to] that þaye shulde A2   take] add away A1, add it A2   for] as A2   owne] add with A2
coude] cowe A2   34–5 with . . . erthe] there in A2

35 the erthe, and thanne come in gret haste gret companie of peple and
voided anone al the temple. And atte the laste ende the Romaynes
made a pyne tree of brasse ouergilte and sette it in an high place. And
as men saine all the prouinces were corue merueylously withinne this
pine tree, so that alle tho that come to Rome might see in that pine
40 tree whiche partie his prouince stode. And after a gret while that pyne
tre fell, and there abidithe yet in the highest place of the temple the
place where it was.

And in the tyme of Focas the emperoure, whanne Rome and the
peple had resseiued [the] faithe of oure Lorde, Boniface the fourthe
45 after Gregorie the grete about the yere of oure lorde .vjC. praied to
Focas the emperoure that he might haue this temple, and thanne he
made caste oute the filthe of all these ydoles. And in the .iiij. yde of
Maij he consecrat that temple in the worshippe of oure Ladi Seint
Marie and of alle martires, and now she is called of the peple Seint
50 Marie Rotounde. For thanne men made no sollempnite of confessours, and for that gret multitude of peple assembled atte that feste
and men might not finde lyuelode for the peple that came, the pope
Gregori ordeined this feeste for to be in the kalendes of Nouembre,
for there shulde be thanne gretter habundaunce of goodes whanne the
55 cornes were gadered and the vynes vendeged. And so he ordeined that
day to be halwed thurgh the worlde in [the] worship of all seintes. |
f. 257rb And so the temple that was made to alle the ydoles is now dedied to all

36 thanne] *add* there DH2A2   come] *add* theder A2   in. . . . peple] people a fulle grete
nombre A2   gret] *om.* H2   companie] companies DH2   36 the¹] *add* erthe oute of the
A2   the²] *om.* H1A1   atte. . . . ende] after that A2   ende] *om.* DH2   38 as] *add* som
A2   the] tho A2   corue] gravyn A2   38–9 merueylously. . . . tree] there in
mervelouslye A2   39 pine¹] *add* note DH2   to] into L   40 tree] *add* in L   his . . .
stode] was theiris DH2A1   40–1 whiche. . . . yet] there owne provynce and yet it
abidith A2   after . . . there] yit it DH2A1   41 yet] *om.* DH2A1   41–2 the place]
om. DH2A1A2   43 and] *add* alle L   43–4 Rome. . . . peple] the people of Room A2
44 the¹] *om.* EH1A1   Lorde] *add* ihesu cryste than A2   fourthe] *add* pope of þat name A2
45 to] *om.* A2   46 Focas] oure lorde A1   and] *add* he graunte it hym with gode wylle
and A2   47 oute] *add* alle DH2A1, *add* there of alle A2   of¹] and A2   these] the A2
48 that] the H2L   oure] *add* blessid A2   49 alle] *add* the EH1   she is] *trs.* DH2   of²]
add alle A2L   peple] *om.* L   50 Marie] *add* the DH2   men] thaye A2   made] make
A1, *add* there A2   50–1 confessours] confessiouns L   51 for that] because A2
that³] the DH2   52 men] *om.* A2   the¹] that A1   came] *add* to A1A2L   pope] *erased*
D, *add* therefore pope A2   53 this] þe L   feeste] *om.* DH2   for] *om.* A2   be] *add*
holde A2   54 there] þei H1   there . . . gretter] that tyme is grete A2   gretter] grete
DH2   of] *add* alle maner of A2   goodes] *add* and frutis for A2   whanne] than A2
55 gadered] *add* inne DH2   vynes] vyne A1, wynes A2   vendeged] vyndeined A1, also A2
so] þan A2   55–6 that day] this feest A2   56 thurgh] þorowe owte alle L   the
worlde] alle cristendome on that daye A2   the²] *om.* EH1   57 the¹] that L   to. . . .
the²] tofore to A2   alle] *om.* DH2A1   the²] *om.* DA1L   dedied] dedicate A2

seintes, and there as was the worshippinge of ydoles is now preised the multitude of seintes.

Secoundeli she is ordeined for to fulfelle thinges that bene 60 ouerpassed and lefte vndone, for we haue ouerpassed and lefte mani a seint of whom we haue not made nether solemnite ne her memorie. For we mow not make feste of eueri seint bi hymself, as wel for the multeplyenge of seintes that bene withoute nombre as for oure infirmite, for we be feble and mowe not suffice therto, [and also for 65 the shortnes of time, for the time might not suffice therto], as Ierome saithe in a pistle that is sette in his kalendre, there is no day excepte the day of the kalendes of Ianiuere, but there may be founde euery day made noble with .vM.[1] martires. And for that we may not make singuler festes of eucri seint, Ierome the pope hathe ordeined that we 70 shull worshippe hem all togederes.

And Maister William Daucere putte .v. resones in his Somme of the Office wherfor it was ordeyned that we shulde make sollempnite of seintes in erthe. The furst is for the worshippe of the Godhede, for whanne we do worshippe a seint we worship God in his seintes, and 75 we saie that he is meruailous in hem, for he dothe worship to seintes he worshippithe specially hym that hathe halowed hem. The secounde is for to haue helpe in oure infirmite, for bi oureselfe we gete none hele and therfor haue we nede of the praiers of seintes, and therfor we shull worshippe hem to that ende that we might deserue 80 her helpe. Hit is redde in the fourthe boke of Kinges | in the furst f. 257va chapitre that Bersabe that is expouned the pitte of fillynge, that is to saie the victorious Chirche, saide to her sone that he hadde gote the kingdom bi her praiers. The thridde cause is for the encresinge of

58 of] add al A1, add alle þe A2   preised] the preisinge DH2A1A2   the] with DH2, of A1A2   59 multitude of] alle A2   60 for] om. A2L   62 whom] which DH2A1L we] om. A1   not] om. A1A2   nether] add her L   ne] nor DH2A1A2   her] om. A2 memorie] add of þem A2   63 mow] can A2   feste] solempnyte A2   as wel] om. A2 64 multeplyenge] multytude A2   seintes . . . bene] them is A2   65 infirmite] add and A2   65–6 and² . . . therto] om. E, ins. with curtnes for shortnes H1   66 might] maye A2   as] add seinte A2   67 excepte] add sauff DH2   68 day²] add to be DH2 69 with] om. DH2   make] add a A2   70 festes] feest A2   Ierome] om. A1A2 71 shull] shuld H2   72 putte] puttith A2L   .v.] .vj. A1A2   his] the DH2 73 wherfor] where of H1DH2A1A2   make] add this daye A2   of] add alle A2 74 worshippe] worshippinge DH2   Godhede] godhode L   75 do] om. DH2 worshippe] add to A2   76 seintes] add for DH2, add and A2   77 he] and L hathe] om. A2   79 haue we] trs. A2   the praiers] praiere DH2A1   80 might] may H2   deserue] add to haue DH2   81 in the¹] four minims followed by the A1 fourthe] þird L   82 Bersabe] basabe with ba on erasure H1   83–4 gote/the kingdom] trs. H1

85 oure seuerte, so that bi the glorie of seintes that is purposed to hem in
her sollempnite, oure hope and oure sollempnite is encresed. And yef
dede[ly] men like to us now in suche wise be lefte up bi her merites,
hit foluithe that we mowe in the same wise, sethe the might of God is
not ne may not be lessed ne menisid. The ferthe is for the ensaumple
90 of oure folowinge, for whanne the feste is recorded we be called to
folw hem, so that bi ensaumple of hem we dispise erthely thinges and
desire heuenly thinges. The fifthe is for the dette of entrechaunginge
of neighburhede, for the seintes make feste of us in heuene, for the
aungeles of God and the holy sowles haue ioye of a synner that dothe
95 penaunce. And therfor it is right that like as thei make ioye of vs in
heuene that we make fest of hem in erthe. The sixt is for the
procuracion of oure worship, for whanne we worship seintes we
procure oure owne worshipp, for her sollempnite is oure dignite. For
whanne we worshipp oure bretheren we worship oureself, for charitee
100 makithe all thinges comune, and all thinges ben oures, heuenly
thinges, ertheli, and euerlasting.

And ouer these resones here, Maister Iohn Damacien puttithe
other resones in the fourthe boke in a chapitre, wherfor the seintes
and her bodies and her reliques shulde be worshipped, of whiche
f. 257vb resones | sum be take as to her dignitees, and sum for the preciosite of
106 her bodies. And the dignite of hem is in .iiij. maners, for thei be
frendes of God and sones of God. Of the secounde saithe the apostle
to the Romaynes: 'Yef so be that ye be sones, ye be heyres.' Of the
fourthe he saithe in this wise: 'How moche shuldest thou laboure for
110 to finde a leder, the whiche might bringe the to the kinge of
vndedlynesse and speke to hym for the. That is to saie that thei be
leders of grace of al mankinde and makin her praiers to God for the.'

85 oure] *om.* A2   87 dedely] L, dede EH1DH2A1A2   men] *add* that were A2   us]
add be DH2   be] we H1   up] *add* now H1   88 that . . . mowe/in . . . wise] *trs.* A2
mowe/in . . . wise] *trs.* DH2   sethe] see DH2A1A2, *add* þat L   God] *add* þat DH2A2
89 lessed] lessened A1   ne²] *add* in no wise L   ferthe] *add* cause A1A2   90 folowinge]
folowyng *with* w *on erasure* H1   the feste is] þeir festis be L   91 bi] *add* þe DH2A1A2L
ensaumple] sample A2   we] *add* maye A2   dispise] *add* alle A2L   and] *add* for to A2
92 desire] thesire H2   The] *om.* A2   the] *om.* L   entrechauninge] entrechauntyng
H1A2   93 feste] feestis A2   94 the] *om.* DH2   holy] *add* seyntes as L
95 penaunce] *add* for his synnes A2   therfor] *add* as A1   96 hem] *add* here DH2A2
for] of H1   100 thinges¹] thyng A1A2   and] for DH2, *add* than A2   ben oures] *om.*
DH2, *add* bothe A2   101 thinges] *add* and DH2   ertheli] *add* thingis DH2A1A2, *so ins.*
H1   and] *om.* DH2L   euerlasting] *add* thynges A1A2   102 here Maister] *om.* A2
103 the¹] hys L   wherfor] where he spekith of A2   104 and²] *add* al H1   105 for]
ins. H1   107 and . . . God] *om.* H1   108 heyres] eres *preceded by* y *changed to* P (?)
H1   109 fourthe] thrid DH2   111 the] *add* and *del* that is to saye A2   be] *add* the
A1   109–10 That is . . . for the] *om.* DH2   of²] to L   112 the] hem L

The other resones be take for the preciosite of her holi bodies, for
these holy bodyes were selers of Goddis, temples of Ihesu Crist; thei
were alabastre of spirituel oynement, wellis of lyff, membres of the 115
holy goste. For these seintes be the verrey celers of God bi whom he
pourithe oute the wyne of his grace thurgh all the worlde. Secondely,
thei be temples of Ihesu Crist, for God duellithe withinne hem bi
understondinge, wherof the apostle saithe: 'Wite ye not that youre
bodies be temples of the holy goste duelling in you?' And of that 120
saithe Crisostome: 'Man delitithe in edificacion of walles, and God
delitithe hym in the conuersacion of seintes,' wherof Dauid saithe:
'Lorde, y haue loued the beauute of thi hous.' But that beauute is not
made bi diuersite of marbre, but it is youen to lyuinge men bi
diuersite of grace. The beauute of marble delitithe the flesshe, the 125
beauute of graces quikenithe the soule, the ferst deceiuithe the eye,
that other understondithe euerlastinge edefienge. Thriddeli, thei be
alabastre of spirituel oynement, wherof it is saide: 'An oynement of
swete sa|uuour comithe of hymself, and this same yeuithe the reliques f. 258ʳᵃ
of seintes. And sethe water wellithe oute of the roche and of the harde 130
stone in desert, and also there ranne oute water of the asse cheke to
Sampson that was athriste, whi shulde it not thanne be credible but
that ther wellithe oute of the reliques of seintes oynementis well
smellynge? This knowen wel tho that kn[o]w the yefte and the vertu
of God and the worship of seintis that comithe only of hym.' Fertheli, 135
thei be wellys of diuinite, where he saith: 'Tho that lyue in trouthe
with fre prescience ben with God and bene to us welles of heuene.
Oure Lorde Ihesu Crist yeuithe to the reliques of his seintes benifices
in mani maners.' Fytheli, thei be membres of the holi gost. And this

113 other] tothir DH2   for² . . . bodyes] om. A1A2   114 selers] soleris A1
Goddis] god and L   of²] om. DH2   115 were] add þe A2   116 be] haue A2
celers] a seleris DH2, soleris A1   117 pourithe] aporiþ L   118 be] add the A2
duellithe] dwellid A1A2   bi] preceded by (?) two erased letters D   119 wherof] wherefore
H1   120 temples] temperles E, tempelers H1   121 Crisostome] Grisosthome H1
delitithe] delithe L   122 conuersacion] conuersion A2   124 bi¹] add þe L   marbre]
marbille A2L   125 flesshe] add and DH2A1A2   126 graces] grace A1A2L   soule]
soulis DH2A1   128 wherof] wherefore H1   wherof . . . oynement] om. A1
129 sauour] odoure L, add that DH2A1A2   130-3 And . . . seintes] om. L
130 sethe] suche DH2   roche] erthe A1A2   131 asse] asshe E, assh with h erased H1
132 but] om. A2   133 wellithe . . . seintes/oynementis] trs. A2   oynementis] oynement
DH2A1A2   well] right swete A2   134 wel tho] þey wele L   know] knew EH1
135 God] þe holigoost L   the] om. A2   only/of hym] trs. A2   136 thei] þe H1
wellys] welle A1, the welle A2   where] whereof A1A2L   lyue] ben A1A2   137 fre] the
DH2A1A2   with²] in L   138 Ihesu Crist] om. DH2A1A2   benifices] benefites
DH2A2   139 Fytheli] Ferthli H1, First A1A2   thei] tho DH2, tho that A1A2

140 reson assignithe Seint Austin in the boke of the Citee of God and
saithe: 'Thei be not to dispise but gretly to be worshipped the bodies
of holi seintes, of whiche whanne thei liued, the holi goste vsid hem as
a membre of his owne in all good werkes.' And the apostle saithe: 'Ye
seken the experience of hym that spekithe in me, Ihesu Crist.' And of
145 Seint Stephen it ys saide: 'Thei might not contrarie to the wisdom and
to the holi gost that spake.' Also Seint Ambrose in Exameron: 'This is
a precious thinge that men be made orgones of the voys of the
Godhede in her bodies [wherebi] thei shewe the heuenli worde.'

Thriddely this fest was ordeined for the clensing of oure necli-
150 gences. For yef it be so that we make feste of a fewe seintes, yet we do
it necligently and leue moche thinge that we shulde do bi oure
ignoraunce and necligence. And ther[for] yef we haue do in other
f. 258ʳᵇ solempnitees sympely and | necligently, at the lest we may in this
general feste fu[l]fell it and amende, and meke oureselff and purge vs
155 of oure defauute. And this reson is touched in a sermon that [is] this
day redde thurgh the Chirche, and as he saithe that it is ordeined that
in this day mynde be made of all seintes, so that bi as moche as
mannes freelte hathe do lasse thanne well bi ygnoraunce and bi
necligence other bi ocupacion of wordli thinges, in the sollempnite
160 of seintes that we worship bi the cours of the yere of hem of the New
Testament the whiche this day we gadre togederes for to fulfill that
whiche before we haue do necligently. These ben aposteles, martires,
confessours, virgines, and these .iiij. be signified bi the .iiij. parties of
the worlde, by orient the aposteles, by midday the [m]artires, bi the
165 northe the confessoures, and by occident the virgines.

140 the¹] a DH2   141 dispise] be dispysed A2   gretly] add for L   be worshipped]
worshipp L   142 of¹] add þe H1   whanne] than A1   hem] add there DH2A1A2
144 the] om. DH2   me] add þat is DH2A1A2   144–5 of² . . . saide] Seint Augustine and
Stephen seith DH2A1A2   145 not] ins. H1   to] om. L   145–6 and to] of DH2A2L
146 in] add his L   Exameron] add seith A1A2L   147 orgones] orygans A2   the²] this A1
148 wherebi] Verily EH1   149–50 necligences] negligence DH2A1A2L   151–3 and . . .
necligently] om. and ins. and leue moche thyng that we schul do (smaller hand) A1
151 oure] youre with y erased H1   152 therfor] ther EH1   haue] had L
154 feste] add by ignorance and negligence. And therfore if we haue done in other
solempnites simply and necligently A1   fulfell] fufell E, fu'l'fell H1   it] om. DH2A1A2
149 amende] add it H1DH2A1A2   155 defauute] defautes DH2A2L   is²] om. EDH2, ins.
H1   is/this day] trs. A2   156 the] alle holye A2   that¹] as L, om. DH2A1A2   157 so that
bi] for A2   mannes] mennes DA2   158 thanne] as L   and] as L   bi²] om. A2   159 in]
add which DH2A1A2   sollempnite] solempnytees A2   160 hem] add and L   the³] a H1
Testament] followed by paraph DH2   161 for] om. L   that] add the A1   before] om.
DH2A2   162 confessours] add and DH2A1A2L   163 signified] singnefied A2   the¹]
om. DH2   164 worlde] add that is A2   by¹] add the DH2A1A2   by²] add the A1   martires]
wartires E   165 and by] bi the DH2A1   by] add þe A2L

The furst difference is of the aposteles, of whiche the dignitee and
the excellen[ce] is shewed, for that they surmount all other seintes in
.iiij. thinges. Furst in soueraynte in dignite, for thei be wyse prinses of
the Chirche of Cristes peple; thei be mighti accessours of the iuge
perdurable; thei be swete shepardes of the shepe of oure Lorde. 170
Wherof Bernard saithe: 'It aperteinithe wel for to ordeine suche
shepardes and suche doctours to mankinde that were suete, mighti
and wise; swete that thei might resseiue us suetely and bi merci,
mighti for to strongely defende us, wyse for to lede us to the wey of
trouthe.' After, they surmountyn other seintes in souerantie of might, 175
wher Seint Austin saithe: 'God hathe yeue might and power | to the f. 258ᵛᵃ
apposteles ouer the fendes for to distroie hem, upon the elementes for
to meue hem, upon the soules for to assoile hem from synne, ouer the
dethe for to dispise hit, aboue the aungeles for to sacre the body of
oure Lorde. And thriddely for the prerogatif of holinesse, so that by 180
her grete holynesse and the plente of grace, the lyff and the
conuersacion of oure lorde Ihesu Crist shined in hem as in a mirrour,
and was knowen in hem as the sonne is bi his shininge and as the rose
is bi his sote sauour and the fire bi his hete. And of this saithe
Crisostome: 'Ihesu Crist sente his apposteles as the sonne sendithe his 185
bemes and as the rose sendith his sauour and as the fyre departithe his
sparkeles, and right as the sonne aperithe bi his bemys so bi the vertu
of he[m] is knowen the might of Ihesu Crist.' Firtheli is the bounte of
moche profit, of whiche profit Austin saithe: 'The most symple the
most ydiotis and the porest bene ennobled, be multeplied, be 190
illumyned, with right suete spekynge, with right noble cunninge,
and with meruaileous wisdom, with sollempne spekinge of auctours
and of doctours and be ioyned to Ihesu Crist.

166 is] *om.* A1   167 excellence] excellent EH1   for] *om.* A1   surmount] surmountid
A2L   168 soueraynte] *add* and DH2A2L   in²] and A1   169 accessours] assessoures L
171 Wherof] wherfore A1   for] *om.* DH2A1A2   172 suete] *add* and A1   174 mighti]
myghtely A2   wyse for] in weies DH2A2, in ways for A1   to³] in A2   175 After] *add* þat
DH2A1A2   surmountyn] suremountid A1A2   other] *om.* A2   176 wher] whereof
DH2A1A2L   176–7 might . . . power/to . . . apposteles] *trs. with* þat *after* apposteles A2
177 the¹] *om.* DH2A2   fendes] *add* and L   179 for¹] *om.* DH2A2   the²] *om.* DH2A2
180 for] *om.* A2   181 the¹] *om.* DH2A1A2   the³] *om.* A2   184 and] *add as* DH2   and
. . . hete] *om.* A2   185 as] and A1   186 sauour] savyoure A2   the²] *om.* DH2
187 sparkeles] sparkes A1   bemys] *add* and DH2A2   vertu] myght A2   188 hem] her E
hem is] his H1   might] vertue A2   Firtheli] *add* it DH2A1A2   189 profit²] *add* seynte A2
190 ydiotis] diotis L   the] *add* moste DH2A1A2   be¹] *om.* DH2A1A2   be²] and DH2A1
190–1 be illumyned] *om.* A2   191 suete] grete DH2A1A2   spekynge] *add* and A2L
with² . . . cunninge] *om.* A2   noble] grete DH2A1A2   192 with¹] *add* right LA2
sollempne] *add and del.* nite H1   193 and¹] *om.* A2   and of doctours] *om.* H1   and²] *om.*
DH2A1, that A2

195   The secounde difference is of marteres, of whiche the excellence is
shewed for that thei suffered in mani maneres, profitabeli, stably,
multiplyingly, for as moche as withoute [the] marterdom of blode thei
suffered thre other marterdomes. Wherof Seint Bernard saithe:
'There is .iij. marterdomes withoute blode shedinge, the furst is

f. 258ᵛᵇ   sparinge in plente, the whi|che Dauid hadde, wisdom in pacience, the
200   whiche Tobye sheued, and chastite yn youthe, of the whiche vsed
Ioseph in Egipte.' And after Gregori there be .iij. other marterdomes
withoute shedinge of blode. The furst is pacience in aduersite, wher
he saithe: 'We may be marteres withoute yren yef we kepe verili
pacience in oure will and haue compassion of hem that be in sorw and
205   tribulacion.' Wherof it is saide: 'He that hath sorw and compassion in
othres necessite berithe the crosse in his mynde,' and 'He that
sufferithe dispisingges and lo[u]ithe his enemy is a martir secretely
in his thought.'

    Secoundely, marterdom is profitable, the whiche profit is to [the]
210   marteres remission of synnes, plente of meritis and a resseyuinge of
euerlastinge ioye. And suche thinge haue thei bought with her
precious blode, and therfor it is called precious blode, that is to saie
full of pris. And Seint Austin saithe in the boke of the Citee of God of
the furst and of the secounde: 'What thinge is more precious [than]
215   dethe bi whiche synnes be foryoue and merites encresed?' And he
saithe upon Iohn: 'The blode of Ihesu Crist is precious withoute
synne, and yet he made her blode precious with the pris of his blode.
For but yef he hadde made the blode of his seintes precious, hit shuld
not be saide that the dethe of his seintes were precious befor hym.'
220   And Ciprian saithe: 'Marterdom is the ende of synnes, the terme of
perile, the duke of hele, maister of pacience, the hous of lyff.'

    194 whiche] whom A2   195 suffered] suffre A1   196 multiplyingly]
multiplying H1   the] om. EH1   blode] add shedyng A2   197 other] om. DH2A2
saithe] add that A1   198 There] This H1   is¹] ben DH2A1A2   200 sheued] had
A1   youthe] þought L   of] om. DH2A1A2   201 Gregori] add telleth H1   other] om.
DH2A2   202 wher] wherof A1L   203 verili] velely H1   204 and²] add in A2
206 othres] a noþere mannes DH2A2   necessite] necessites A1, add he A2   crosse] add of
cryste A2   207 louithe] lowithe EH1, loued A1   enemy] add he DH2A1A2   martir]
maner L   secretely] sikirlie DH2A1A2   209 the²] om. EH1   210 synnes] add and
A2   a resseyuinge] the areysing A2   211 thinge] thingis DH2A1   haue] hath H1
212 and . . . blode] twice once del. H1   214 than] in EL, in changed to þan H1
215 bi] add the A2   216 upon] add seint A1   217 he] thei DH2A1A2   with] by A2
218 yef] om. A2   218–19 hit . . . be] withoute synne A1   219 befor hym] in his
sight A2   hym] om. A1   220 saithe] add that DH2A1A2   synnes] seintes H1   terme]
tyme A1   221 perile] perellez H1DH2A2

Of the thridde saithe Seint Bernarde: 'Thre thinges ther be that maken the dethe of seintes precious, reste of | trauaile, ioy of no[v]elte, f. 259ra seuerte of euerlastingnesse.' And as to us the profit is doubeled, for thei be youe to us in ensaumple for to fight, wherof Crisostome saithe: 225 'Thou cristen man, thou art to delicat a knight yef thou wene to haue the uictorie withoute bataile. Fight therfor with mighti strengthe, fight cruelli in this bataile, considre the comenaunt, vnderstonde the condicion, knowe the knighthode. Considre the comenaunt that thou hast made, the knighthode wherto thou art youen and take the name 230 upon the. For bi this comenaunt all thei fighten, thei wynnen all bi this condicion, and thei haue the victorie bi this knighthode.'

Secondely, ye be youe us as oure patrones for to helpe us, for thei helpe us by her merites and her praiers. Of the furst saithe Seint Austin: ['A the] right gret pitee of God that woll that the merites of 235 martres be oure helpes! He examinithe hem for to teche us, he tobrekithe hem for to gadre us; he will that her turmentes be oure profites.' Of the second saithe Ierome Ayenst Vigilancien: 'Yef the aposteles and the martires whanne thei were in her lyvinge bodies might praie for other, how [yet] thei ought to be more corious after 240 the corownes and the victories. Moyses, o man only, gate foryeuenesse of God to .vjC. men armed, and Seint Stephen praied for his enemyes, and whanne thei be with God shulde thei be lasse worth to us? [Nay], God defende.' The thridde is that thei were ferme and stable in sufferinge, whereof Austin saith: 'The soule of a martir is the 245

---

222 Of] And of DH2A2   thridde] iiijth A1   Thre thinges/ther be] trs. A2   ther be] om. A1   223 of¹] or H2   precious] add þat is A2   novelte] L, nobelte EH1, nobulte and DH2A1A2   224 euerlastingnesse] everlastingis L   225 us] add as DH2A2 ensaumple] essaumple H1   226 to] om. A2   delicat a] trs. A2   227 bataile] add and del. fight þerefore withoute bataile H1   mighti] myght L   strengthe] add and DH2A2 228 comenaunt] add and A2   vnderstonde the] in margin in smaller hand with add and del. al they fighten in text A1   229 condicion] add and A2   229–30 Considre . . . knighthode] ins. H1   230 made] add and A2   231 the] add of del. A2   thei] þat DH2   fighten] add and A2   231–2 bi this] 'by' þies on erasure II1   232 condicion] condicions H1   bi] of DH2A1A2   233 ye] they A1   youe] add to DH2A1A2 234 and] add bi DH2A2   and . . . praiers] om. H1   235 A the] L, hathe EH1, he hath DH2A1A2   236 helpes] helpe DH2A1A2, helpe and A2   teche] add hem to L 237 tobrekithe] brekith DH2A1A2   gadre] gider A1   us] add and A2   will] wolde L 238 saithe] add seynte A2L   239 in her] here in the A2   240 for] add vs H2   DH2 paraph after other   how] ins. H1, om. DH2A2   yet] that E, ȝit on erasure H1   ought] add thei E, add and del. þei H1, might A2   be] add þe L   241 and the] and DL, of H2 victories] add of DH2A1   man only] synguler man A2   242 .vjC.] .vjC.Ml. A2 armed] of armes A1   and Seint] del. D   243 whanne] sith A2   be²] doo DH2, do nowe A2   243–4 worth to] for DH2A2   244 Nay] om. EH1A1L   that] om. A2   thei] add miȝt subp. H1   245 whereof] add Seinte DH2A2   a martir] martirs A2

suerde shinynge bi charite, sharpe bi verite and rightwisnesse,

f. 259rb braundisshinge | bi vertu of God fightinge, the whiche ouercomithe
the companye [of] ayensaiers in repreuinge hem, she smitithe the
wicked and castithe downe hem that be contrarie.' And Crisostme
250 saithe that tho that were turmented were strenger thanne the
turmentoures, and the toren membres with yren ouercome the
rentynge yrins.

The thridde differens is of confessours, of whiche the dignite and
the excellence is shewed in that thei knoulache God in .iij. maneres, bi
255 herte, bi mouthe and bi werke. The confession of the herte suffisithe
not withoute confession of the mouthe, so as Crisostme preuith in .iiij.
maneres. And as to the furst he saithe: 'The rote of confession is faithe
of the herte, confession is fruit of the faithe. And as longe as the rote is
quicke in the erthe it is necessarie that she putte oute her bowes and
260 her leuys, and yef she put hem not oute it is to suppose that she is
dried up in the erthe; and in the same wise whanne the rote of faithe is
hole in the herte she bringithe forthe alwey confession bi mouthe; and
yef confession of herte apere not in the mouthe understonde verily
that the confession is dried up in the hert. As to the secounde he saithe
265 in this wise: 'Yef it suffice the to leve with hert and not be shreuin
before man, that is to saye to a prest, thanne art thou untrue and a fals
ypocrite, for yef it were so that he leued not in herte, yet it shulde
profite to confesse Crist bi mouthe, and yef thou saie that it profitithe
not to hym that shriuithe hym withoute faith right as that profitithe

f. 259va not to hym that leuithe withoute confession.' | As to the thridde thus
271 he saithe: 'Yef it suffice to Crist that thou knowe hym yef thou be not
confessed before man, thanne it shulde suffice to the that Crist knowe

246 charite] *add* and A2   sharpe] sharpere DH2   verite] vertue A2   and] of
DH2A1A2   247 vertu] verite DH2A1, the veryte A2   God] good DH2A1   fightinge]
fiꞌgh'ting H1   248 of] *om.* EH1DH2   in] and H1L   hem] *om.* A2   smitithe] sendith
DH2 sleyth A1, shendith A2   the] *added in gap in another hand* D   249 Crisostme]
Crisꞌos'tome H1, Grisostome H2   251 turmentoures] tormentorꞌs' H1   the'] thei
H2   254 knoulache] know'le'che H1   maneres] marners H1   255 the] *om.* DH2
256 the] *om.* DH2A2   .iiij.] three DH2A1A2   257 And] *om.* L   258 the'] *om.*
DH2A2   confession . . . faithe] *om.* DH2A1A2   259 she] he H1   putte] sprede A2
260 is'] *add* for DH2A2   262–3 bi . . . confession] *ins.* H1   263 apere] appierid A2
264 confession] feyth A2   hert] *add* and DH2A2   265 Yef] *om.* A2   suffice] *add* to
DH2A2   the to] *trs.* A1   leve . . . hert] lyve and leve wiþ herte L, live here DA1A2, liue
bere H2   not] *add* to DH2A1A2   266 to²] vnto L   267 he] *om.* A1   leued] loued
H1, belevid A2   in] the DH2A2   in herte] that they herde A1   yet] *om.* L   it²] he
DH2A2, *om.* H1   shulde] shalle A2   268 that] *om.* L   269 not] na3t L   that
shriuithe hym] *om.* L   faith] *om.* A2   right] *add* so DH2A1A2   as that] as hit A1, it A2
that²] *ins.* D, *add* it DH2L   270 to'] *om.* A2   As] And as DH2A2   thus] this A1A2

the yef thou were not confessed before God; and yef it suffice the not
the knowleche of hym withoute more, neither it suffisithe hym not thi
faithe withoute more.' As to the fourthe he saithe: 'Yef the faithe of 275
thi herte had suffised only, God wolde haue made thine herte onli, but
God hathe made the an herte and a mouthe for to beleue hym with
herte and knowleche hym bi mouthe.' Thriddeli thei confessed [God
by] werkes. In what manere a man confessithe God or reniethe God
shewithe Seint Ierome and saithe: 'Ihesu Crist is wysdom, right-   280
wisnesse, verite, holinesse and strength. Wisdom is renyed bi folie,
rightwisnesse bi wickednesse, trouthe bi lesyngges, holinesse bi
unclennesse, strengthe bi febilnesse of will and alweies whanne we
be ouercome with uices and synnes we renie God; and in the contrarie
wise, as ofte tyme as we do ani good we knowleche God.'   285
    The fourthe difference is of virgines, of whiche the excellence and
the dignite is shewed in that they be spouses to the souerayne kinge,
and of that saithe Seint Ambrose: 'Who may haue gretter beauute
thanne the beauute of her that is loued of the kinge, aproued of the
iuge, halued of God, euermore wedded, euer hole and pure withoute 290
corrupcion?' Secoundeli for that she is felawshipped with aungeles
and lykenid [to] aungeles: 'Virginite surmountithe the condicion of
mankinde, bi the whiche man | is felawshipped with aungeles. And the f. 259ᵛᵇ
uictorie of virgines is gretter than that of aungeles, for the aungeles
lyuen withouten flesshe and the uirgines haue victorie in her flesshe.' 295
Thriddely for that thei be more noble thanne other good cristen men,
wherof Ciprien saithe: 'Virginite is floure of all the sede of the
Chirche, beaute and ornement of grace spirituel, ioy bounden with
worshipp and praisinge, a pure werke withoute corrupcion, ymage of
God, and yet more noble the holinesse of God the worthiest porcion 300
of the bestes of Ihesu Crist.' Fertheli for thei be set byfor tho that be

273 the not] nat the nat DH2   274 the] to H1   suffisithe] *add* to A2   not] *om.* A2
275 more] *add* and A2   the²] *om.* A2   277 herte, mouthe] *trs. and add* boþe A2
mouthe] *add* bothe A1   with] in L, without DH2, *add* thi A1, *om.* A2   278 herte] with
del. `hert H1, *om.* A2   and] *add* to A2   278–9 Thriddeli . . . manere] *twice once del.* H1
God by] L, goodly EH1DH2A1A2   279 confessithe] confessed A1
280–1 rightwisnesse] *add* and A2   283 bi] in D   284 synnes] *add* than A2
285 good] *add* thyngis A2   God] *add* and forsake the devylle A2   287 spouses] spousid
DH2A1A2   289–90 the iuge, God] *trs.* L   290 wedded] *add* and DH2A2   and
pure] *om.* DH2A2   291 felawshipped] felyship A2   292 and . . . aungeles] *ins.* H1
to] with EH1L   293–4 And . . . aungeles²] *ins.* H1   294 that] *om.* A2   of²] *add* the
DH2A2   for . . . aungeles] *om.* A1   295 flesshe¹] filth A1   in] of DH2A2   her] þe A2
296 for] *om.* L   that] *om.* A1   297 wherof] wherfor H1L   298 Chirche] *add* and
DH2, *add* and þe A2   and] *om.* H1, *add* an DH2, *add* the honourment and A2   ioy] *add*
and A2   299 corrupcion] *add* the A2   300 worthiest] worthi A1

maried, and that excellence that uirginite hathe to the regarde of hem
that be coupled by mariage apperithe bi comparison multipliengly, for
mariage fulfillith the wombe and uirginite the mynde. Austin saithe:
305 'Uirginite chesithe more fairer, that is rather to folow the lyff of
aungeles in her flesshe than for to encrece the nombre of dedli bodies
bi her flesshe.' Forsothe more plenteuous, more blesfull and more
fruitfull it is for to fulfill the mynde with purete thanne the wombe
with peynefull gretnesse, for that one bringithe forthe sones of sorw
310 and uirginite bringithe forthe sones of ioy and of gladnesse; wherfor
Seint Austin saithe: 'This continence is not barein but plenteuous; she
is moder of children of ioy, she fulfellithe the heuene with children.'
Ierome saithe that wedded folke fillen the erthe, uirginite fillithe
paradis, the ferst with gret labour and besinesse, the secounde with
315 gret rest and quietenesse. Gilbert saithe: 'Uirginite is restfulnesse
from besi cures, pees of the flesshe, the redempcion of uices,
f. 260ra lord|shippe of vertues.' Mariage is good but uirginite is beter, and
Ierome writithe to Palmachien and saithe: 'Suche difference is
betwene wedding and uirginite as is betwene not [to] synne and to
320 do wel, and as betwene good and betir.' Continence in mariage is
likened to thornes, uirginite to roses. Ierome writithe to Eustas: 'I
praise weddingges, but that is for y wolde gadre the roses among the
thornes, the golde in the erthe, and of the quar[r]ei precious stones.
The fifthe for that thei ioye of mani priuileges. For the virgines shull
325 haue the crowne that is called auriole, thei allonli shull singe the newe

302 maried] martiren A1   the] om. DH2   303 multipliengly] multiplying A1A2
304 fulfillith] fillith DH2A1A2L   the mynde] denyeth it DH2A2, denyeth A1   Austin]
Seinte Augustine DH2A2   305 chesithe] closeth H1, add þe DH2A2   306 for] om.
A1 307–8 more plenteuous . . . fruitful/it is] trs. DH2A1A2   307 blesfull] blessidful
A1   308 for] om. L   fulfill] fille DH2A1L   309 peynefull] pensifful del. 'peynful'
A1   for] so DH2A1A2   forthe] add the DH2A2   309–10 sorw . . . of¹] om. L
310 forthe] add the DH2A2   of²] om. H2   wherfor] where of DH2A1A2L   311 she]
suche DH2A1A2   312 is] add the DH2A2   of] add þe DH2A2   ioy] add and of
gladnes A1   fulfellithe the] fulfylled A2   313 Ierome] Seinte Ierome DH2A2   folke]
men and wemen A2   fillen] fulfillen DH2A2   erthe] add and DH2A2   fillithe] fulfillith
DH2A2, om. A1L   314 besinesse] add and DH2   315 restfulnesse] fulnesse H1
316 flesshe] add is DH2A1A2   the²] om. A1   uices] add and DH2A2   317 vertues]
vertuouse H1, add and A2   and] om. L   319 wedding, uirginite] trs. L   as] add it H1
betwene] om. A2   to¹] om. EH1L   and] add as A1   to²] om. DH2   320 as] add is DH2
in] of A1   321 to¹·²] vnto DH2A2   thornes] add and DH2A2   Eustas] add and sayeth
A2   322 the¹] om. DH2A2   the²] om. A2   323 quarrei] quartei E   324 fifthe]
frist is DH2A1A2   thei] ye H1   ioye] ioyne EH1   the] om. DH2A2   shull] shulde H2
325 auriole] add and DH2A2   allonli] al in on A1

songe, thei shull be clothed all in one clothinge with Ihesu Crist euer ioyeng, and folow euer that holi lambe whereuer he go.

Fertheli and last the fest was ordeined for to gete more lightli oure praiers; bi that that we worshipp in that day all the seintes generally, right so [thei] praie for us all togederes, and in suche wise we shull 330 gete the lightloker the mersi of oure Lorde. For yef it is vnpossible that the praiers of mani shulde not be herde, hit is more impossible that the praiers of all seintes shulde be unherde. And this reson is touched whanne thei sayen in the orison of this day: 'Lorde, yeue us by the multeplied praiers of thi seintes the desire[d] habundaunce of 335 thi meke merci.' And the seintes praie for us bi merit and bi will; bi merit whanne her merit helpithe us, bi will whan thei will that oure will and desires be fulfilled, and that do thei not but for to fulfell the will of God.

And in this day all the seintes assemblyn for us to praie, as it is 340 shewed in a vision that befell the secounde yere that this fest was ordeined. | In the same day ther was a clerke of Seint Petres chirche f. 260ᵛᵇ that hadde bi deuosion visited all the auuteres of the chirche and hadde asked helpe of all seintes, and atte the laste he come to the auuter of Seint Petre and there he reste hym a litell and sawe this in a 345 vision. Hym thought he sawe the kinge of kinges sittinge in the highest sege with multitude of aungeles about hym. And thanne the Uirgine of uirgines came crowned with right a shinynge crowne and there folued her a multitude of uirgines without nombre and of

326 songe] add and DH2A2   euer] add more DH2A2   327 ioyeng] ioynyng L
folow euer] trs. A2   folow . . . that] folowyng þe L   that] the H2   whereuer]
whersoeuer DH2A1A2, add þat A1L   328 last] leste A2   the] this DH2A1A2L
gete] add the DH2A2   328–9 oure praiers] that we praye for A2   329 that²] om.
H1A1A2   in . . . day/all . . . seintes] trs. with this for that and om. the A2   generally]
generalle DH2   330 so] add in þat L   thei] om. EH1   and] om. L   shull] schulde
A1   331 lightloker] li3tlyer L, sonner DH2A1A2   is] be DH2A1A2   vnpossible]
impossible DH2L, inpossible A1A2   332 shulde] shull H1   impossible] vnpossible
DH2A1L   333 praiers] prayer A2L   all seintes] many seyntes L, many A1
shulde] shull H1   be unherde] not be herde A2   334 whanne . . . sayen] om. A1
in] om. A2   335 the¹] thi DH2   multeplied] multyplying A2   thi] alle A2
seintes] add for DH2A1A2   the desired] L, thei desire EH1DH2A1A2   336 bi¹,²]
add theyr L   merit] merites L   337 merit] meritis DH2A2   helpithe us] twice A1
338 will] lorde del. A1   and¹] add oure DH2A1A2L   do thei] trs. A2   for] om. A1A2L
340 And] add þat A1L   this] that DH2A2   for us to] and DH2A2   is] om. H1
341 yere] add aftir L   that²] after A2   342 the] that A2   Petres] Peter A1
343 bi] add the E   344 all] add the H2   the¹] om. DH1A1   345 litell] while
DH2A2   in a] om. A2   346 Hym] He A2   thought] add þat A2   of] add all H1A2
347 sege] sete DH2   with] add gret A1   of] add alle A2   348 crowned] om. L
right] om. L   349 there] her H2   her] om. A1   a] add grete A2   of²] om. A2
349–50 without nombre/and of continentis also] trs. and om. of A2

350 continentis also. The kinge arose ayenst hem and made hem sitte in
a sege that was nigh hym. And after that there come a man clothed in
a chamel skin, and gret multitude of auncien men with hym that
folued hym full worshipfulli. And after that there come another
clothed in an abite as a bisshopp, and a gret multitude folued hym in
355 like habite. And after that there come a multitude of knightes
withoute nombre that a grete cumpany of diuerse men folowed, and
thei all come before the throne of the kinge and worshipped hym on
her knees. And thanne he that was in habit of a bisshopp beganne
Mateins and all that other meiny folowed hym. And this clerke was
360 ledde bi an aungell in this uision and tolde hym that in the furste
cumpanie was oure Ladi Uirgine Marie the moder of God, and he that
was clothed in the skynne of a chamell was Seint Iohn the Baptist with
the patriarkes and the prophetes, and he [that was] clothed in habite of
a bisshopp was Seint Petre with the aposteles [and] the knightes were
f. 260ᵛᵃ the martres, the other confessours | the whiche come all before the
366 kinge to yelde hym thankinge for the worshippe that thei resseiued
this day thurgh the worlde of dedely men and for that thei might praie
for all the worlde. And after that the aungel ledde hym into another
place and shewed hym there women and men, sum in beddes of golde,
370 sum ioyenge in diuers delites. Sum other there were pore and naked
and other begging for her [brede]. And this place he tolde hym was
purgatorie; tho that habounded in welthe were tho that were socoured

350 continentis] EL *punct. before* also   also] *add* than DH2A1, *add* and than A2   hem¹]
hir A2   hem²] hir DH2A2   351 a sege] an seete DH2   clothed] *om.* A1   352 a]
om. A2   chamel skin] camelis skynne DH2A2   and] *add* a A2   353 full] *om.* DH2
full worshipfulli] right mekely A2   another] *add* companie DH2A1A2   354 an] the
DH2A2   as] of DH2A1A2   a bisshopp] bysshops A2   and] the DH2   a²] *om.* A2
multitude] *add* þere A2   folued] folowinge DH2A1   354–5 hym . . . habite] after one
of þem A2   355 habite] *add* as a bisshopp H1   a] *add* grete DH2A2   356 that] and
DH2H1A1A2   folowed] folowyng A1, *add* them A2   357 kinge] iuge A1   on] vppon
DH2A2   358 he] *om.* H2   in] *add* the DH2A2, *add* an A1   359 that] the A2L
meiny] *om.* A1   hym] hem A1   this] the A1   360 bi] with A1   in¹] to A2
361 oure] *add* blessid DH2A1A2   Ladi] *add* the DH2   Uirgine Marie] *om.* A2   God]
crist L   362 skynne . . . chamell] chamel skyn L, camels skynne A2   the²] *om.* DH2A2
363 the²] DH2A2   that was] is E, `þat is´ H1, *so* L   in] *add* the DH2A2   364 a]
om. L   was] *add* a bisshopp E, *so and del.* H1   the¹] *om.* A2   and] *om.* EH1A1L
365 the²] *om.* EH1L   the³] *om.* L   366 thankinge] thankingis DH2A2, thankes A1
worshippe] worshipes A1   that] *om.* L   resseiued] *om.* A1   367 thurgh] *add* alle
DH2A1A2   368 into] to DH2A2   369 there] *add* boþe A2   women, men] *trs.* A2L
golde] *add* and DH2   370 ioyenge] ioynyng L   delites] *add* and DH2A2   there] *om.*
A2   371 other²] some DH2A2   brede] grete E, poverte L   And] *add* the angelle saide
A2   he] the aungelle DH2   he . . . was] is A2   372 habounded] habundyn A2   were²]
we A1

habundauntli bi gret helpe of frendes, the pore were [tho] that were foryete and had no comfort of her frendes. And than he comaunded hym that he shuld tell all this to the pope so that after the Fest of All 375 Seintes he shulde ordeine the Day of Alle Soules so that general praiers temperell might be made for hem in that day whanne thei might haue no speciall.

Here endithe the [feste] of All Seintes, and nexst beginnithe the [commemoracion] of All Soules, Capitulum .C.lvj.^m

The mynde of all trewe soules passed oute of this worlde is ordeined bi the Chirche to be made on this day so that thei mowe haue generall helpe where thei mowe haue no speciall, as it is shewed in the uision beforesaide. Petrus Damyan tellithe that in Cecile in the yle of Vulcan Seint Odile herde the fendes crienge and roring sore for that the 5 soules of hem that were passed were taken out of her handes bi almesse and by orisones, and therfor he ordeined that after | the Feest f. 260vb of All Seintes the rememberaunce of the dede shulde be made in all chirches. The whiche thinge was aproued after of all the Chirche. And here we may specialli touche of .ij. thinges, furst of the purgacion of 10 the soules, and after of the suffrages.

As to the furst, it is to touche [of] .iij. thinges, furst what be thei that be purged, secoundeli bi whom thei be purged, the thridde wher thei be purged. [It is to wete that there be thre maner of kyndes of hem that be purged.] 15

The furst be tho that deien bifore that they haue do satisfaccion of the penaunce that was enioined hem, notwithstondinge that thei hadd so gret contricion of herte that it had be sufficiaunt for to haue putte awey her synne, thei shulde haue freli gone to euerlastinge liff yef it hadde be so that thei hadde not fulfelled her satisfaccion, for 20

373 habundauntli/bi . . . frendes] *trs.* A1   habundauntli] gretelye A2   bi] with þe L, with DH2   gret] *om.* A2   of] *add* þer A2   frendes] *add* and DH2A2   tho] *om.* EH1, they A1L   374 her] *om.* A2   he] the aungelle DH2A2   comaunded] bade A2   375 that . . . shuld] *om.* A2   this] these thyngis A2   377 temperell] *ins.* H1, temperalli DH2A1A2, seperally L

EH1DH2A1A2L   E breaks off after 405 *oute*; D breaks off after 68 *purgatorie* and resumes at 348 *in the Dedes*   *Rubric* feste] liff EH1   commemoracion] day EH1   1 mynde] commemoracion D   3 speciall] *add* helpe D   4 Damyan] Damasien D   5 Odile] Idole H1   6 hem] men H1   7 almesse] *add* deedis D   9 Chirche] chirches H1   12 of] *om.* EH1   13–15 the thridde . . . purged] *ins.* H1   14–15 It . . . purged] *om.* E   17 thei] *add* haue EH1   18 had] *om.* H1   19 yef] thou3 D   20 be . . . hadde] *twice* H1

contricion is right gret satisfaccion for synnes and right gret puttinge
awey of hem. And of that saithe Seint Ierome: the lengthe of tyme is
not so moche worthe before God as the lengthe of sorw, ne abstinence
of metis is not so uailable as mortificacion of vices. But tho that haue
25 not suche contricion and deien before the fulfelling of her penaunce,
be greuousli ponisshed in purgatorie of all that thei hadde do litell
penaunce in this liff. For God that knowithe the manere and the
mesure of peynes and of synnes, puttithe to payne sufficiaunt for to do
awey [v]tterly synnes so that none abide unponisshed. Wherfor the
30 peynes that be enioined other thei be gretter or egale or lasse. Yef she
be gretter that that he hathe more done shall turne hym to encrece of
ioy and glorie, and yef she be egal thanne she suffisithe hym to the |
f. 261ʳᵃ remission of synnes, yef she be lasse thanne that faillithe shall be
fulfelled with the vertu of the might of the Godhede. The thridde,
35 whiche be tho that descendin into purgatorie, thei be suche as bere
with hem wode or heye or stuble. These be tho that with that that thei
loued God thei had propre carnell loue to her richesses, to her wiwes,
to her children, to her maners and [to her] possessiones, but alwey
thei loued most God, and tho be purged in purgatorie after the
40 manere [of] her [louinge] longe or shorte, so as the wode hathe more
substaunce to endure more, or lasse as hey is of lesse substaunce and
as towe [that is of lesse substaunce or leste], so thei shull be broiled.
And Seint Austin saithe though that [the] fire be not perdurable yet is
she merueilously greuous so that she [surmou]ntithe all the peynes þat
45 euer was suffered in this worlde; for so grete turmentis were neuer
suffered in the flesshe yef it be so that mightli martires suffered
turmentis.

The secounde is, to wete bi whom thei be turmented or ponisshed
or bi what manere ponisshinge, she is done bi the wicked aungeles and
50 not bi the good, but the good aungeles turment not tho that be good,
but the good aungeles turmentin the wicked aungeles, and the wicked
aungeles turmentin the good cristen sowles. And hit may goodly be
bileued that the good aungeles uisiten ofte and comforten her

23 as] *add* is D   24 metis] *add* It D   as] of D   26 hadde] haue Hɪ
29 vtterly] bitterly E, bit / ʿvʹtterli *with* bit *del.* Hɪ   32 and¹] ʿ&ʹ Hɪ   34 might of
the] *om.* D   The thridde] Thridlie D   36 or¹] and D   that¹] nat D   that³] *om.* D
37 God] *add* yit D   38 to her³] *om.* EHɪ   40 of] or EHɪ   louinge] L, *om.* EHɪD
shorte] *add* abidinge D   wode] woʿrlʹde Hɪ, worlde D   41 lasse] *add* and D   hey] *add*
or tow3 D   41–2 and . . . so] *om.* D   42 that . . . leste] L, *om.* EHɪ   43 the] L,
om. EHɪD   44 surmountithe] L, turmentithe EHɪD   46 yef] thou3 D   mightli]
myghtie D   49 aungeles] aungelle D   50–1 but . . . aungeles¹] aungelle D   but . . .
good] *ins. with* for *for* but Hɪ   51 aungeles²] *ins.* Hɪ

bretheren and her felawes and counsaile hem and stere hem to suffre
in pacience. And also thei haue another remedie of comfort in that 55
that thei knowe certeinly that thei shull come to ioye and to glorie, but
this certeinte is | lasse thanne of hem that be in the cuntrei of ioye, and f. 261rb
more than of hem that lyuen. For the certeinte of hem that be in ioye
is withoute ani doute abidinge or withoute ani drede neuer to lese it,
but the certeinte of hem that be in the waye is contrarie. The certainte 60
of hem that be in purgatorie is as a mene for thei abide to haue ioy
withoute ani drede, and thei haue free will confermed neuer mowe to
synne no more. And thei haue also another comfort for thei hope
alwey that there is done for hem bothe almes and praiers. And
perauenture it is more credible that this ponisshinge is not made bi 65
the wicked aungeles but bi the diuine rightwisnesse of God.

To the thridde thinge, that is to wete where thei be purged, thei be
purged in a place bisydes hell that is called purgatorie, and this is after
the opinion of mani wise men, yef it be so that there be mani other
that semyn that it is in the eyre in a brennyng rounde place. But alwey 70
bi the divine dispensacion of God there be diuerse places ordeined for
diuers and mani other causes, whiche is as for light ponisshinge or for
her hasti deliueringe or for oure techinge or for the synne done in the
place or for the praier of sum seint.

Furst for [her] light ponisshinge, as it hathe be shewed to sum and 75
after the saienge of Seint Gregorie that sum sowles be ponisshed in
the shadowe.

And after for her hasti deliucraunce, for that thei mowe reuele to
other her nede and requere her helpe and in suche wise come more
hasteli oute of peyne, as it is redde | how that Seint Thebaud hadde f. 261va
suche a brenninge in his legge that there might nothinge kele it ne 81
comfort it with no refresshinge of no medicines. And in a tyme
fissheres that fissh[ed]en in the see, in stede of a fisshe thei drow up a
gret gobet of yse, and whanne thei had it thei were glad therof
concideringe the grete dissese of her holy bisshopp and hopeden that 85
the colde therof shulde lysse his grete brenninge hete. And so thei
brought it to hym and it was to hym a souerain comfort. And in a tyme

57 certeinte] certeyn H1D   thanne] om. D   58 certeinte] certein H1   60 certeinte]
certein H1   contrarie] add to D   certainte] certein H1   61 purgatorie] add for it D   as]
om. D   62 confermed] om. D   66 diuine] diuinite of the D   67–8 thei be purged]
om. H1   69 so] om. H2   70 rounde] grounde or H2   72 light] lighter EH1
73 her] þe del. `her´ H1   synne] same H2   75 her] the EH1   light] lighter EH1
78 for¹] om. H2   80 of] add the H1   as it] It H2   81 kele] hele H2   81–2 ne comfort
it] nothir noo comforte H2   83 fissheden] fisshen EH1   85 holy] om. H2

the bisshopp herde the vois of a man that semed withinne that gobet
of yse, and he coniured hym that he shulde tell hym what he was. And
90 he saide: 'Y am a soule that for my synnes am turmented in this pece
of yse, and y might wel be deliuered yef thou woldest saie for me .xxx.
masses and continue eueri day till thou hast done.' And he toke it
upon hym and beganne to saie, and whanne he had halff done and
arraied hym for to go to the auuter, the fende putte suche dissencion
95 in the citee that all the men of the citee foughten. And than the
bisshopp was called for to staunche the debate, and thanne he dede of
his [vestimentes] and lefte to saie his masse. Thanne the morw ayen
he biganne the seruice, and whanne he hadd saide the .ij. parties it
semed to all the peple that a gret oste hadd beseged the citee so that he
100 was constreined bi drede to leue the remenaunt of his masse. And in
the morw whanne he beganne his seruise ayen and hadde all done sauf
the last masse that he wolde begynne, sodenly all the towne and all the
f. 261vb bisshoppes place was | take with fire. And whanne his servauntes come
and tolde hym that he must leue his masse for the chirche was al afire
105 ouer hym, he saide: 'Yef al the towne shulde be brent y wol not leue
my masse atte this tyme.' And as sone as he had saide his masse, anone
the yse was molte and the fire that thei went had be seyne was al gone
as fantasie withoute doynge ani harme.

Thriddely for oure instruccion, that is that we mowe knowe how
110 gret peyne ther is arraied to synners after this deth of the bodi. Hit
befell atte Parys, so as the chaunter of Paris tolde, that ther was a
scoler of his fell sike and shulde deie, and the chauntour praied hym
that after his dethe that he wolde come to hym ayen and telle hym of
his astate. And withinne a fewe dayes after he apered to hym in a cope
115 of parchemyn al forwretin with deceiuable argumentis and it was all
withinne full of flaumes of fire. And the chaunt[er] asked hym what he
was, and he saide: 'Y am that same that am come ayen to you.' And
thanne the chaunt[er] asked hym how it was with hym, and he saide:
'This cope that y bere upon me weiethe hevier thanne any melstone
120 and she is youe me to bere for the veyne glorie that y hadde in my
argumentis sophistiqes, that is to saye deceiuables; the skynne semith
light to bere but the flaumes withinne turment me sore and brennith

92 hast] haddist H2   he] than the bisshop H2   97 vestimentes] clothes EH1
99 he] the bisshop H2   102 towne] cite H2   105 Yef] though H2   towne] cite H2
106 anone] om. H2   111 chaunter] Chaunceler H2   112 chauntour] Chaunceler
H2   115 forwretin] two words EH1, for wreþin H1   116 chaunter] chauntre EH1,
Chaunceler H2   117 saide] add that EH1   am come] ame H2   118 chaunter]
chauntre E, Chaunceler H2

me cruelli.' And whanne his maister saide that he trowed not that the
peynes were so grete but that thei were lighter thanne he made of, the
spirit saide to hym: 'Streche oute youre honde that ye may fele the   125
lightnesse of my peyne.' And whanne the maister | hadde putte oute   f. 262ra
his honde, he lete falle a drope of [his] suete upon his honde and that
drope perced his honde lightlier thanne ani arowe so that he felt
merueilous turment. And thanne he saide hym: 'Y am all suche.' And
thanne the chaunt[er] was so sore aferde for the cruelte of this peyne   130
that he lefte the worlde and entred into religion.

Fertheli for the synne that is do in places, so as Seint Austin saithe
that sumtymes the soules be sette in the places wher thei synned, and as
it aperithe bi this ensaumple that Seint Gregorie tellithe in the fourthe
boke of his Diologes, that there was a preste þat haunted diuerse tymes   135
a bath, and whanne he come thedir he fonde euer a man that he knewe
not redi for to serue hym. So it fell in a day that for guerdon of his
seruice he gaue hym a loef blessed, and he ansuered hym wepinge:
'Fader, wherfor yeue ye me this thinge? Y may not ete and this brede is
holi. I was sumtyme lorde of this place, and whanne y was dede y was   140
sent hedir for to serue for my synnes, but y praie the that thou offre up
to God almighti this loof for my synnes. And wete wel whanne thine
orison shall be herde thou shalt not finde me here whanne thou comest
to wasshe the.' And thanne the prest offered up to God sacrifice an hole
woke, and whan he come thedir he fonde hym not.   145

Fiftly for the orison of sum seint, so as it is redde that Seint
Pa[trike] asked in a place a purgatorie for sum, and of that thou shalt
finde in the storie before in this place.

And as to the thridde thinge, that is of suffrages, ther be therinne to
con|sider .iij. thinges: furst of the suffrages that be do, secoundeli of   f. 262rb
hem to whom thei be do, thriddeli of hem for whom thei be do.   151

As to the suffrages that be do, it is to knowe that .iiij. manere of
suffrages be done that profitithe gretly to the dede, that is to saie,
orison of good folke and of frendes, almesse yevinge, and masses
singinge [and fastinge].   155

And of that þat the orisones of good men profite hem, it shewithe in
the ensaumple of Paschasion, of whom Gregorie spekithe in the

127 he] the spirite H2   his²] the EH1   129 hym] to his maistir H2
130 chaunter] chauntre E, Chauncelere H2   this] his H2   134 in the] *twice once del.*
H1   145 woke] loofe H2   thedir] *add* ayenne H2   147 Patrike] Paule E, *so changed*
to Patr`i´ke H1   148 the] a H2   in²] of H2   149 therinne] *om.* H2
150 consider] be considered EH1   151 thriddeli . . . do²] *ins.* H1   154 yevinge]
doynge H2   155 and fastinge] L, *om.* EH1H2   156 þat] *om.* H2

fourthe boke of his Diologes, and tellithe how that there was a man of
gret holinesse and of gret rightwisnesse. And in that mene tyme there
160 were .ij. chosen for to be popes, but after the Chirche acorded to that
one of the tweyne, and this Paschasius as bi errour susteyned alwey
that other and stode in this entent vnto the dethe. And whanne he was
dede and his bere stode ouer his sepulcre couered with a clothe, there
was a man brought thedir that was uexed with a fende, and as sone as
165 he had touched the clothe he was al hole. And longe tyme after that
Seint Germane bisshopp of Campane, so as he went to wasshe hym in
a bathe for to haue hele, he fonde there Paschasian dekene that was
there and serued. And whanne he sawe him, he dredde hym gretly
and enquered what that so grete a man and so holy dede there. And he
170 saide that he was there for none other cause but for that he hadde
holde more thanne reson was in the cause beforesaid. And thanne he
saied hym: 'Y praie the, praie hertely to God for me, and thou shalt
knowe whanne that thou shalt be herde whanne thou comest hedir
f. 262va and that thou findest me not.' And thanne the | bisshopp praied for
175 hym and came thedir after, but he fonde hym not.

And Petre abbot of Clune saithe that there was a prest that eueri
day songe a masse for alle cristen soules, and he was acused to [the]
bisshopp and suspended of his office. And as the bisshopp went on a
day to the sollempnite of an high feest thorugh a chircheyerde, the
180 dede bodies arose ayenst hym and saide: 'This is the bissop that hathe
take from us oure prest; certis, but yef he amende it, he shall deye.'
And thanne the bisshop assoiled the prest and songe gladli after for all
soules.

And also it aperithe that praiers of the quicke bene agreable to hem
185 that be dede bi that that the chauntour of Paris tellithe, that there was
a man that eueri tyme whan he passed thurgh a chircheyerde, he
wolde saie this psalme De Profundis for all cristen soules. And in a
tyme as he came thurgh a chirchyerde he was folued with his enemyes
for to haue be slaine, and anone the dede bodies arose, and eueri of
190 hem holde an instrument whiche he hadde used and wrought with in
his lyff and defended the man that used to praie for hem and chased
his enemies al abasshed and full of fere.

And the secounde manere of suffrages is for to yeue almesse, and

171 he] Paschasien H2   175 came] add ayenne H2   after] om. H2   176 Clune]
Clunie H1, Clevie H2   177 the] his EH1   180 saide] add in this wise H2
182 prest] add ayenne H2   all] add cristen H2   185 chauntour] Chaunceler H2
187 Profundis] add clamaui H2   190 with in] withinne E   191 chased] add aweie H2

that helpithe to hem þat be passed hennes as it aperithe in the boke of
Machabeus, bi that that Iudas a mighti man made a collacion and sent 195
.xij. dragmes of siluer into Ierusalem for to be offered for the synnes of
the dede. And men may knowe how gretli the almesdedes auaile by
the ensaumple that Seint Gregori tellithe in the fourthe boke | of his f. 262ᵛᵇ
Dialoges. There was a knight laye as dede without, spirit of liff, and
withinne a while he come ayen into the bodi and tolde that he hadde 200
sayen in sperit. He saied he sawe a brigge, and under that brigge ther
was a flode foule and horrible and ful of stinke, and ouer that brigge
there was a faire medwe ful of suete floures, and in that medwe ther
was assembeled a cumpani of faire peple clothed al in white and thei
were al norisshed with the swetnesse of the sauour of tho faire floures. 205
And the brige was suche that yef ani of the ministres wolde passe
ouer, he shulde falle in that horrible lake, and sum of that other passed
ouer safly ynow til thei come to this delitable place. And this knight
sawe a man that hight Pers that was withoute the brigge bounden and
ouerleyd with gret wight of yren, and whanne he asked hym whi he 210
was there, it was ansuered hym of another that saide: 'He sufferithe
this peyne for this cause. Whan he liued, yef ani man were deliuered
hym for to [do] ueniaunce he dede it more for cruelte thanne for ani
obedience.' And also he tellithe that he sawe a pilgrime that passed
ouer that brigge as he hadde lyued in this worlde clenli fro synne. And 215
he sawe another that hight Stephen that, as he wolde haue passed this
brigge, his fote slode so that he fell half ouer and so he hinge. And
thanne ther come right horrible and blake men and with all her might
thei enforced hem for to haue drawe hym downe, and other right faire
creatoures come and drow hym up bi the armes. And as this striff 220
lasted the knight that | sawe these thinges awoke of his traunce and f. 263ʳᵃ
wist not whiche partie had the beter. But this we mow understonde
that his wicked dedes strofe ayenst his almesse dedes. For bi tho that
drew hym upwarde hit apered that he had loued almesse, and bi that
other it apered that he had not perfitly contraried the synnes of the 225
flesshe.

And that the thridde manere of suffrages, that is to wete the holi
sacrement of the auuter, profitethe to hem that be dede it aperithe bi

195 collacion] collage H2   196 dragmes] dragones H1   197 the dede] add men H2
And] add also H2   200 while] add affter H2   into] to H2   201 He . . . sawe] om. H2
203 suete] om. H2   in that medwe] om. H2   204 a] add faire H2   of faire peple] om. H2
207 of that other] there were that H2   208 delitable] delectable H1   212 liued] lyueth
with th del. 'd' H1   213 do] om. EH1   224–5 loued . . . had] om. H2   225 perfitly]
gretelie H2   227 that¹] om. H2   that²] om. H2   228 dede] add For H2

mani ensaumples. And that tellithe Seint Gregorie in his Dyaloges
230 that, as a monke of his that hight Iustus whanne he come to his ende
he confessed that he hadd hidd .iij. pens of golde and wepte full sore
this trespas and so he deied. And thanne Seint Gregorie comaunded
to his brethren that thei shulde berie his bodi and his .iij. pens with
hym in a donghill ,saieng: 'Thi pecunie be with the in perdision.' And
235 notwithstondinge this Seint Gregorie charged one of his bretheren
that he shulde eueri day singe a masse for hym .xxx. dayes togedre.
And whanne he had fulfelled his terme, he that was dede apered to a
brother. And he asked hym how it was with hym and he saide: 'It
hathe be full euel with me til this day, but now thanked be God y am
240 well for this day y haue resseiued my hosill.'

And this sacrifice of the auuter profiteth not onli to the dede but it
profit[it]he also to tho that lyuen, as bifell to a man that was with mani
other in a roche wher thei digged for siluer, so that the roche fell
f. 263rb sodenly | upon hem and slow mani other, sauf one ther was that to
245 ascape he putte hymself in a creues of the roche but in no wise he
might not come oute. And hys wiff went that he had be dede and lete
eueri day a masse be songe for hym, and eueri day she offered for hym
a lofe and a potte of wyne and a candell. And the fende that had enuye
to her apered bi thre dayes continuinge [to her] in forme of a man and
250 asked her whedir she went. And whan she hadd tolde hym he saide to
her: 'Thou goest for not, for the masse is done.' And so she lefte the
masse thre dayes unseid. And after that another man digged siluer in
the same roche, and as he digged he herde a uoys withinne the roche
that saide: 'Smite softe, for y haue a gret stone ouer myn hede.' And
255 thanne he was aferde and called mani other to here this uoys, and
digged ayen, and thanne thei herde ayen the same uoys. And thanne
thei wentin nere and saide: 'What art thou?' And he saide: 'Smitithe
faire and softeli, for there is a gret stone ouer myn hede and is in point
to fall on me.' And thanne thei digged softeli bysydes til thei come to
260 hym and drew hym oute al hole. And thei enquered of hym how he
hadd lyued so longe there, and he saide that eueri day ther had be
offered to hym a lofe and a potte [of] wyne and a candell, sauf thre

232 so] *add* atte laste H2   234 pecunie] penaunce H2   237 a] his H2   241 And]
Wherfor H2   242 profitithe] profithe E   lyuen] viuen H2   243 fell] *add* doune H2
244 mani other] hem alle H2   244–5 to ascape he] escapid that H2   246 went] *add*
wisly E H1   249 to her] *om.* E, *ins.* H1   251 not] no'u3't H1   252 unseid] *add* bi the
feendis seienge H2   digged] *add* for H2   253 uoys] noise H1   255 he] this man H2
uoys] noyse H1   256 herde] *add* the hurde H2   ayen] *om.* H2   uoys] noyse H1
257 Smitithe] smyte it H2   259 bysydes] *om.* H2   262 of] *om.* E

dayes that he was nigh perisshed for defauute. And whanne his wiff
herde this she had gret ioye and knew wel that he hadd | be susteined   f. 263ᵛᵃ
with her offeringe and that the fende had deceiued her tho thre dayes   265
that she hadde not do singe th[e] masses.

And as Peter abbot of Clune witnessithe this thing that he tellithe,
it befell in the towne of Ferre in the diocise of Gramele that a shipman
was fallen in the see and a prest praied for hym and saide special
masses for hym, and he come oute of the see all hole. And whanne it   270
was asked of hym how he askaped, he saide that whanne he was in the
middell of the see and evene atte the dethe, there come a man to hym
and toke hym a lofe. And whanne he hadde ete it he was wele
recomforted and recouered his strengthes and was take into a shippe
that passed bi, and thanne it was founde that atte that houre that the   275
prest sange for hym that he hadde that lofe that was to hym so gret
comforte.

And that the fourthe manere of suffrages profitithe to hem that be
passed, whiche is fastinge, Seint Gregori in spekinge of this and of
other thre witnessithe and saithe: 'The soules of hem that is passed be   280
assoiled in .iiij. maneres, bi the oblacion of prestes, bi the praiers of
seintes, bi the almesse of frendes, and bi the fastinge of her kynne.'
For the penaunce done of her frendes is gretly worthe to hem, as a
solempne clerke and doctoure tellithe, that ther was a woman whan
her husbonde was dede fell in gret dispeire lest she shulde fall in   285
pouerte. And the fende apered to her and saide that [yef] she wolde do
as he wolde haue her he wolde make her riche, and she behight | hym   f. 263ᵛᵇ
to do as he wolde. And he enioined her that all the men of the chirche
[she] shulde resseiue into her hous and make hem for to do
fornicacion, and that she shulde bi day resseiue pore folke and bi   290
night putte hem oute withoute ani good hem doinge, and that in as
moche as she might that she wolde lette the seruise of God bi her
iangelinge, and that she were neuer confessed of none of these thinges.
And so atte the laste, whanne she neighed her dethe, her sone exorted
her and counsailed her to be shriuen, and thanne she discouered alle   295
her gouernaunce to her sone and tolde hym that she might in no wise
be confessed and also that her confession was not worthe. But as her

266 do] for to H1   singe] seie H2   the] L, tho EH1, om. H2   267 Clune] Cleuie
H2   274 recouered] add ayenne H2   276 sange] add his masse H2   279 in
spekinge] spekith H2   this] om. H2   280 thre] add and H2   284 that] om. H2;
EH1H2L begin a new sentence   286 yef] om. E, ins. H1, and H2   289 she] L, that E,
þat 'sche' H1   resseiue] add hem H2   290 fornicacion] add with hir H2   bi¹] add a H1
folke] add into her hous H2   297 But as] and than H2

sone laye sore upon her and saide that he wolde do the penaunce
hymselff for her, she repented her, and her sone sent for a preste in al
300 haste. But before that the preste might come the fendes apered to her
so horribly that she deyed for fere. And thanne the sone confessed to
the prest the synnes of his moder and toke upon him .vij. yere
penaunce, and whanne he had fulfelled yt he herde his moder that
yelded hym thankingges for her deliueraunce.

305   And also the pardones of holi Chirche is gret auaile to hem, wherof
it fell that a legat sent from the sege of Rome praied to an noble man
that he wolde go ride to the Abigeys in the seruice of the Chirche, and
he gaue indulgence and pardon to his fader that was dede and this
good man duelled there al a lente. And whanne he hadde do this his
310 fader aperid to hym more brighter thanne the sonne and thanked hym
herteli for his deliuer|aunce.

f. 264ra   And to [the] thridde, it is to wete for whom these suffrages be done,
it is for to be considered therein be .iiij. thinges. Furst what thei be to
whom thei mow profite, secondeli wherfor it shall profite [hem],
315 thriddeli to wete wher it shall profite to all egaly, fertheli how thei
mowe knowe the suffrages that be do for hem.

Of the furst, what thei be to whom thei mow profite, it is to knowe
as Seint Austin saithe, alle tho that be passed oute of this worlde,
either thei be right good or right euell or meneli good. And the
320 suffrages done for tho that be right good is for to yelde thankingges for
hem, and tho that be [done] for the [euell] bene to the comforte of
hem that lyuen, and for tho that be meneli good it is to hem clensynge.
The right good be tho that anone fleen to heuene and be quitte of the
peynes of purgatorie and of hell. And there be .iij. manere of suche
325 men, children nwe baptised, martires, and perfit men, and it be tho
that perfitly meintaigne the loue of God, the loue of her neigheburgh,
and good werkes, and coueite not to plese the worlde but God only.
And yef atte ani tyme thei haue do veniall synnes, it is wasted and
purged in hem bi the feruour of charite right as a droppe of water is in
330 [a] furneis, and therfor thei bere nothinge with hem that aught to

298 her] add for to doo it H2   299 her¹] add for E, add and H1, add and than H2 (elle
P2)   sent] went H1   300 that] or H2   might] om. H2   303 yt] his penaunce H2
304 her] om. H2   305 holi] the H2   hem] add that ben passid H2   306 that¹] of
H2   sege] seete H2   Rome] add and H2   312 the] om. E   313 considered] add
`þat´ H1, so H2    be²] add or H2      314 hem] om. E, `hym´ H1   315 to²] add hem H2
317 be] add or H2   knowe] wite H2   319 thei] om. H1   321 done] om. E, ins. H1
euell] quicke EH1   the²] om. H1   322 be meneli] be bemeneli H2   323 the] om.
H1   326 her] þe H1   neigheburgh] neghbourghs H1   327 but] add oure lorde H2
330 a] om. E, ins. H1

/

brenne. And ho that wolde praie for ani of these .iij. maneres or make
or do ani suffrages for hem, he shulde do to hem iniurie for he dothe
iniurie to a martir to praie for hym. But yef ani praie for a right good
man of whiche thei drede whedir he be in purgatorie or none, thanne
her praiers is a yelding of thankinges | and thei shull turne to the profit f. 264rb
of hem that praie, after that that Dauid saithe: 'My orison shall be 336
conuerted into my bosum.'

And to suche maner men the heuene shal be anone opened whanne
thei passen hennes and thei shull suffre none of the fires of purgatorie.
And that is signified bi the thre to whom it was openid. Hit was furst 340
opened to Ihesu Crist whanne he was baptised, and of that saithe
Seint Luke: 'The heven was open to Ihesu Crist baptised and
praienge.' Wherbi it is signified that the hevene is opened to hem
that be baptised, be thei litell or full growe, so that yef thei deye thei
shull flee to heuene withoute ani lettinge, for bapteme is clensinge of 345
all synnes original and dedly bi the vertu of the passion of Ihesu Crist.
Secoundeli it was opened to Seint Stephen that was stoned, where he
saithe in the Dedes of [the] Aposteles: 'I sawe the heuene open.' In
that it is shewed that it is open to alle martires whiche flee thedir as
sone as thei be passed [hennes]. Thriddeli it was opin to Seint Iohn 350
that was right perfit, wher it is saide in the Apocalipse: 'Y behelde and
lo the dore is opin in heuene.' Wherbi it aperithe that [it] is opin to
perfit men þat haue in all thingges fulfelled her penaunce and thei
haue nothinge in hem in veyne, and yef there be it is wasted anone by
the brenninge of charite and the heuene is opin to these .iij. maner of 355
peple so that thei mowe entre anone for to regne perpetually.

The right wicked be these that be anone plunged in the fire of helle,
for the whiche yef it be know there shulde none make no suffra|ges for f. 264va
hem, as Seint Austin saithe: 'Yef I wost that my fader were in helle, y
wolde no more praie for hym thanne for a fende in helle.' But yef ani 360
suffrages be do for sum that be dampned, of whiche men wost not how
it were, it shulde in no wise profite hym neither for his deliueraunce
ne for to gete hym any grace, as Iob saithe: 'in helle there is no
redempcion.'

331 ho] 'w'ho H1   maneres] manere puple H2   332 do] *om.* H2   333 a right] *trs.*
H1   335 thankinges] *add* to God H2   shull] shuld H1   336 praie] *add* And H2   that³]
om. H2   344 or] *add* moche H2   348 the²] *om.* EH1   350 hennes] *om.* EH1   Iohn]
add the Euaungelistis D   351 Apocalipse] apocalipses E   Y . . . lo] biholde and see D
behelde] behold H1   352 it²] *om.* E   354 in veyne] voide D   356 peple] men D
357 fire] fires EH1   358 none . . . suffrages] noo suffragis be made D   359 were]
where E   362 were] stant with hem D   shulde] shalle D   neither for] of D

365 Tho that be meneli good be tho that haue with hem sumwhat for to
brenne, as wode or heye or towe, or that thei were ouertake with dethe
before the[i] dede her penaunce in this worlde. And thei be not so
good but that the[i] haue nede of suffrages of her frendes, and thei be
not so euell but that it profitithe hem. And the praiers that is made for
370 hem is clensinge of hem. And these be tho to whom onli suffrages
shulde profite. And for to make the[se] suffrages the Chirche hathe
acustumed to kepe .iij. dayes, the .vij. the .xxx. and the annuel. The
.vij. is kepte that the soules come to hele of rest euerlastinge and that
the synnes þat thei haue do by .vij. dayes may be foryeue hem, or ellis
375 the synnes that thei haue do in the body that is of .iiij. complexiones
with the soule that hathe .iij. uertues be foryoue hem. The trentale is
kepte bi thries .x., for as moche as thei haue offended ayens the
Trinite bi the brekinge of the .x. comaundementes of the lawe that it
may be foryoue hem and thei purged bi this. The anniuersarie is kept
380 for that thei shulde come fro the yeres of wickednesse to the yeres of
f. 264vb euerlastingnesse. And right as we ha[low]e | eueri yere the Fest of All
Seintes in her worship and to oure profit, right so we halow eueri yere
the anniuersarie of All Soules to her profit and oure deuocion.

The secounde thinge is to wete yef suffrages shulde profite hem. It
385 is to knowe that thei shull profite hem bi .iij. resones. Furst for the
reson of vnite, for thei be one bodi with hem of the Chirche binethe
laboringe and therfor her goodes owen to be comune. Secoundely bi
reson of dignite, the whiche thei deserued whanne thei liued þat these
praiers shulde profite hem, for thei holpe to other and it is wel worthi
390 that men helpe tho that haue holpin. Thriddely [bi] reson of necessite,
for thei be in state wher that thei mowe not helpe hemself.

As to the thridde, for to wete whedir it helpe egali to all, it is to wete
that yef these praiers be made speciali thei profite more to hem for
whom thei be made thanne to ani other; and yef thei be made for the
395 comune, thanne thei profite most to hem that haue deseruid hem in
this lyff, that it shulde profite hem; and yef thei be made egaly thei
profite most to hem that haue most nede.

The ferthe, how thei mowe knowe that suffrages be made for hem,
after Seint Austin thei mowe knowe in .iij. maneres. Furst bi dyuine

367 thei¹] the EH1   dede] deied did D   368 thei¹] the E   370 is . . . hem] *om.* DA1
371 shulde] shulle D   these] the EH1   373 to hele] nat to helle D   hele] ʒeres *on erasure*
H1   of] *add* the D   374–5 by . . . do] *om.* D   376 .iij.] .viij. D   hem] him H1
381 halowe] haue EH1   384 shulde] shull H1   385 shull] shuld H1   386 hem] *ins.*
H1   390 bi] *om.* EH1   391 in] *add* suche D   392 As . . . for] but it is D
392–3 it² . . . that] and D   398 made] doone D   399 .iij.] foure D

reuelacion, whanne God luste to shewe hem suche a thinge; 400
secoundely bi shewinge of good aungeles, for ther be aungeles that
be alwey with us and considre al that we done, and thei mowe anone
descende to hem and anounce to hem anone. Thriddely bi shewinge
of soules that gone fro hennes and go thedir, for the soules that passe
oute | of þis worlde mowe shewe to hem suche þinges and oþer. Hɪ f. 333ʳᵇ
Ferthli, þei mowe wite it bi prefe and bi reuelacion, fore whan þei fele 406
hemself aleged of here peyne thei knowe wel þat þere be praiers made
fore hem.

Thirdeli, it is to wite wheþer þe praiers of hem þat be evell mai
profit as well `as´ of tho þat be good. But it is to knowe that if praiers 410
shuld profit thei must be made of hem that be in charite. For if þey be
made bi hem þat be wicked thei profit not. Where it is redde þat as a
knyght lay in his bedde with his wife and þe monc shone clereli þat
entred into þe chambre bi þe creue[i]s, he merveil[ed] hin grctcli fore
man þat is a resonable creatoure `þat he wold not obey his creatoure´ 415
whan þe vnresonable creatures obeied so bisely. And | þan he begaṅ to Hɪ f. 333ᵛᵃ
myssai of a kniȝt that was dede þat had be pryve with him, and anon
þe knight entred into þe chambre and seid: 'Mi frende, haue no euel
suspecion of me but foreyeve me if I haue synned in þe.' And whan he
asked him how it was with him he seid: "I´ am tormented with diuerse 420
peynes, and namli for þat I [v]ioled a chirchyerde and wounded a man
within and dispoiled him of his cope. And þat cope weie[th] hevyer
þan a grete mountayne miȝt do.' And he praied him þat he wold do
prai fore him. And whaṅ he asked him wheþer he wold þat suche a
preeste shuld prai fore him, the dede answhered noþing but shoke his 425
hede as in refusing. And than he asked him wheþer he wold þat suche
an heremite praied for him. And þan he seid: 'I wold fayne þat he
wold pray fore me.' And whan þe quyk knight hadde behight him þat
he shuld prai for him, þe dede seid: 'And I tell þe þat þis day .ij. yere
þou shalt dye.' And so he parted from him, and þe knight chaunged 430
his life into better and slept in our Lorde.

Wherefore it is seid þat suffrages made bi þe wicked mow not
profite but yif it be werkes of the sacramentez, as for to sing masses,

401 good] go`o´d Hɪ   404 for . . . that] and D   405 oþer] add thingis D
411 shuld] shul D   414 creueis] creuers Hɪ, crevessis D   merveiled] merveilyng Hɪ
416 creatures] om. D   419 if] om. D   421 violed] fioled Hɪ   422 weieth] L,
weied HɪD   hevyer] add vppon me D   423 do²] om. D   424 wheþer he wold]
om. D   426 he wold þat] om. D   427 praied] shulde praie D   he¹] the deede D   I]
he D   wold] add fulle D   428 me] hym D   429 dede] add knyght aunswerd and D
433 be] add bi the D

þat may not be violed by no wicked ministre, or elles yef þat þe `dede´
435 ne left only goodes fore to dispose by som wicked ministre, and he
shuld anone haue disposed it and lete it fall, as it is redde that it befell |
Hι f. 333ᵛᵇ to anoþer. Turpyn þe archebisshop of Reynes telleth þat þere was a
knight in bataile with Charles þe Grete, and he praied to a cosyn of his
þat if he deied in the bataile þat he wold sell his horse and yif þe price
440 þereof to poer men. And so he was dede, and þat oþer coueited þe
horse and withhelde [him] `to´ himself. And within a litull while aftre
he þat was dede appered to þat oþer as clere as any son and seid to
him: 'Goode cosyn, thou haste made me suffre peyne bi .viij. daies in
purgatorie fore my horse of which þe price shuld haue be yove to poer
445 men. But nowe hast þu not well quite þe to me, for þis same day
fendes shull haue þi soule to hell and I go purged to þe kindom of
God.' And þan þere was a cry herd sodeinly in þe heyre as of lyons
and of beres and of wulfes and bare him anone þens.

Here endeth þe commemoracion of All Soules, and next
biginneþ þe lyves of þe .iiij. Crowned Marters, [Cap.
.C.lvij.]

The Foure Crowned Marters weren Seuer, Severin, `Carpofor and
Vyctorine´, and þei were beten bi þe commaundement of Dioclisian
with gobettes of lede till þei were dede. And as men coude not finde
here names, þei were longe tyme aftre reveled bi dyvyne reuelacion,
Hι f. 334ʳᵃ and þerefore it was ordeigned þat here memorie | shuld be remembred
6 vnder þe names of .v. oþer marters, Claudian, [Castor], Symphorian,
Nichostrati and Simplicien. And þies marters knewe al þe craft of
kerving, and Dioclicien wold haue made hem to corue him an idole,
but þei wold not, ne þei wold do sacrafice to none. And þan bi þe
10 commaundement of Dioclisian þei were put in tonnes of lede and cast
into þe se abouȝt þe yere of oure Lorde .ijC.iiijˣˣ.vij. And
Malch[iad]es pope ordeigned þies .iiij. to be worshipped vnder þe
names of þies .v. and for to be called `corowned´ before that here
names were founde or known. And þough it were so þat here names

436 fall] be vndisposed D   440 he] this knyght D   þat oþer] the cosynne D
441 withhelde him] withhelded Hι   to] from del. `to´ Hι   445 But nowe] wherefor D
446 shull] add come and D   447 as] add it had be D

HιDH2AιA2   Rubric Cap. .C. lvij.] om. Hι   6 .v.] .iiij. D   Castor] om. HιD (Castor
P2)   7 Nichostrati] Nicho strati Hι   8 to] add haue Hι   9 not] make hym noone D
none] add ydolle D   12 Malchiades] Malchadies Hι   .iiij.] add martiris D   13 .v.]
.iiij. D   corowned] add martiris D   14–15 or knowen . . . aftreᴵ] and D

were founde aftre, yet were þei alwey aftre called by vsage the .iiij. 15
Corowned Marteres.

Here endeth þe liffe of þe .iiij. crowned marters, and next
biginneþ [the life] of Seint Theodore, [Cap. .C.lviij.]

Theodore suffred marterdome vnder Dioclisian and Maximien in þe
cite of Marme Vicanore. And whan þe prouoste bade him do sacrafice
and torne ayene to his first knighthode, Theodore answhered and
seid: 'I ride to Ihesu Crist þe son of God and my God.' And þan seid
þe prouost: 'Hath þi God a son?' And Theodore seid: 'Ye, sothli.' 5
And þe prouost seid: 'Yn what wise may we knowe him?' And
Theodore seid: 'Ye mai bothe knowe him | and go to him.' And H1 f. 334rb
þan he gaue terme to Seint Theodore fore to sacrafice in þe temple of
Mars by ny3t, and þe seint entred and set a fire within and brenned
vpp all þe temple. And þan he was accused of a man þat hadde sayne it 10
so þat he was take and set in prisoun fore he shuld dei fore hungoure.
   And oure Lorde Ihesu Criste appered to him and seid him:
'Theodore my seruaunt, haue gode hope and feith, fore I am with
þe.' And þan þere come to him a grete company of men cloþed in
whight and þe dores closed and began to singe with him. And whan þe 15
kepers saw þis, þey were aferde and fledde here way. And whan he
was take oute from þens, and men stered him to do sacrafice, he seid:
'Though ye bren me in fire and waste my bodi with diuerse
tormentez, shal I neuer reny my God as long as þere is spirit of life
in men.' And þan by þe biddyng of þe prouost he was honged vppon a 20
tre and cruelli al torente with hokes of iren þat his ribbes appered.
And þan þe prouost seid to him: 'Theodore, wilt þou nowe be with vs
or with þi God?' And he answhered: 'I haue be with my Lorde God
Ihesu Crist and am and euer shall be.' And þan þe prouost bade þat he
shuld be brente in þe fire til he gaue vp his spirit, but his body abode 25
withoute ony brennyng, abought þe yere of oure Lorde .CC.iii^xx.vij.

15 aftre²] *om.* D   16 Marteres] *add* and so alle weie contenued foorthe D

H1DH2A2; E resumes at 27 *with*; D breaks off after 16 *aferde*   *Rubric* marters]
marterteres H1   the life] *om.* H1   Cap. .C.lviij.] *om.* H1   1 marterdome] dethe D
3 and torne] he turned D   knighthode] *add* and D   answhered and] *om.* D   4 ride]
turne ayenne D   6–7 And . . . him¹] *om.* D   8 he] the prouest D   terme] leve D
9 þe] than D   seint] *add* Theodore D   within] *add* the temple D   12 Ihesu Criste]
om. D   14 grete] *om.* D   of men] *om.* D   16 here way] aweie H2   17 men] *om.*
H2   him] *om.* H2   21 his] *add* bare H2   23 answhered] *add* and seide H2   God²]
om. H2

E f. 265ra And than all were fulfilled | with a gret suetnesse of sote sauour, and a vois was herde that saide: 'Come to me my dere, and entre into ioie of thi Lorde.' And mani men sawe the heuene opin.

Here endithe the liff of Seint Theodore, and nexst beginnithe the liff of Seint Martin Capitulum .C.lix.^m

Seint Martin was bore in the castell of Salurie of Panononience, but he was norisshed in Ytaile with his fader that was maister of the knightes under Co[n]stantine and Iulius Cesar. And Martin rode under hem, but not with his will, for fro his childehode he was
5 enspired with God, and whan he was of the age of .xij. yere he fledde to the chirche maugre hys kynne and required that he might be made nwe in the faithe, and fro thennes he wolde haue entred into desert yef siknesse hadde not lette hym. And as the emperours hadde ordeined that the sones of [auncien] knightis shulde ride in stede of her faderes,
10 Martin was that tyme but .xv. yere olde and was comaunded to be a knight, and thanne he wolde haue be but a seruaunt and yet Martin wolde serue hym ful ofte and do of his shone and wipe hem.

In a tyme [of winter] Martin passed bi the citee of Damiens and mette with a pore man al nakid to whom no man gaue nothinge. And
15 thanne Martin drowe oute his swerde and cutte his mantell and gaue that one parte to the pore man for he hadde not ellis to yeue and clothed hymself with that other [parte]. And that night foluinge he sawe Ihesu Crist clothed with that partie of his mantell that he hadde
f. 265rb youe to the pore man and | spake in this wise to the aungeles biside
20 hym: 'Martin yet new in the faithe [hathe clothed me with this clothinge].' Of whiche thinge this holi man was not left up in veyn glorie but knewe therebi the gret bounte of God, and [whan] he was of .xviij. yere [of] age he was baptised, and behight that he wolde renounce the dignite for to be iuge of knightes and all the worlde as
25 sone as the tyme of hys prouost were fulfelled, and so he helde forthe knighthode .ij. yere.

EH1H2A1A2L   D resumes at 112 that   1 of²] add the Diocise of H2
Panononience] Panonomence H1, bronobenience H2   3 Constantine] Costantine E
4 hem] hym H2   6 maugre] maugre with -ugre del. `gre' H1   8 emperours]
emperour H2   9 sones] soules with 1 erased H1   auncien] so on erasure H1, austin E,
Augustine H2 (anciens P2)   knightis] om. H2   13 of winter] om. EH1   17 parte]
om. EH1   19 aungeles] aungelle H2   20–1 hathe . . . me/with . . . clothinge] trs.
EH1   21 man] ins. H1   22 therebi] there H2   whan] om. EH1   23 of] om.
EH1   24 the¹] that H2   and] add also H2   25 prouost] prouost`ri' H1

And in this mene tyme the barbaryns entred into Fraunce with
stronge honde. And Iuliane emperoure that shulde fight ayenst hem
gaue gret good to his knightis, but Martin þat wolde no lenger medle
of no suche knighthode refused his yeftes and saide to the emperoure: 30
'I am a knight of Ihesu Crist and therfor it longithe not me for to
fight.' And than Iulian was wrothe and saide that it was not for grace
of the religion that he renounced knighthode but for cowardise that he
durst not abide the bataile. And Martin ansuered bi gret hardinesse:
'For that thou holdist this a cowardise and not trew faithe, y shal 35
tomorw al unarmed be bifore the bataile, and y shall be kepte bi uertu
of the crosse and not bi shelde ne bi helme, and y shall passe all sure
thorugh the bataile [of the enemyes].' And thanne it was comaunded
that he shulde be kepte unarmed ayens the enemyes so as he had saide.
But in the morw the enemies sent messangeres that thei wolde yelde 40
hem and her goodes. Wherof it is no drede but that bi the victoric of
this holi man this victorie was made withoute shedinge of blode.

And from thennes for|warde he lefte fulli all wordeli knighthode f. 265va
and went to Seint Hillari bisshop of Peiters and he made hym colet,
and thanne he was taught bi God in a vision that he shulde uisite his 45
fader and his moder that were yet paynimes. And he went thedir and
he saide hym that he shulde suffre mani thinges. And so as he went
ouer the mountaynes he fell into the hondes of theues, and as one of
the theues left up an axe for to haue smite hym Martin susteined his
stroke with his right honde. And thanne the thefe toke hym and bonde 50
his hondes bihinde hym and toke hym to another to kepe, and whanne
the theues asked hym whedir he were not so[re] aferde Martin
ansuered and saide that he thought hymselff neuer so sure, for he
wost wel that the merci of God was euer comynge with tribulaciones
and temptaciones. And thanne he beganne to preche to [the] theef and 55
conuerted hym to the faithe of Ihesu Crist. And thanne the theef
ledde Martin to the [high] wey and lyued an holi liff after that.

And whanne he hadd passed Melan, the fende apered to hym in
mannes forme and asked hym whedir he went. And he ansuered hym:

29 no lenger] nat H2   30 suche] add thingis ne H2   refused his] wolde nat take
H2   31 not] add to H1H2   33 religion] add but EH1   38 of the enemyes]
om. EH1   39 kepte] add alle H2   42 man] add Seinte Martine H2   46 yet]
þere H1   And] add so H2   47 hym that] om. H2   48 one of] sone as H2
50 thefe] theevis H2   52 sore] so E   53 thought hymselff] was H2
55 the] om. E   56–7 the theef, Martin] trs. H2   57 high] right EH1
59 mannes forme] the fourme of a man H2   and] add he L   whedir] wheþer H1, add
that H2L   he] Martine H2   hym] and seide H2

60 'Thedir that oure Lorde wolde. And the enemy saide ayen: 'Whereuer
thou go y shall euer be ayenst the and contrarie to the.' And Seint
Martin saide: 'Oure Lorde is myn helper, y drede nothinge that thou
maist do to me.' And anone the fende vanisshed awey.

And thanne he went forthe and conuerted his moder, but his fader
f. 265vb abode still in his errour. But whanne the eresie of the Ari|ans encresed
66 so that almost there was none contrarie to hem but he allone, thanne
thei toke hym and bete hym and droue hym oute of the citee, and he
returned to Melan and there he made a chirche for hym, but he was
putte oute [by] the Ariens and went with a prest alone to the Ile of
70 Galumer. And there he toke [to] his mete among other herbis the sede
of an herbe þat was enuenemyd that hight *eleboru*[s], and whanne he
felt that he shulde deye and was in perile, he chasid oute the venym bi
praier and bi the vertu of orison.

And than he herde that the blessed man Hilarie was returned from
75 exile and went ayenst hym, and thanne he ordeined a chirche biside
Peyters. And there was with hym one that was [nwe] in the faithe
whiche he had in kepinge, and as he went a litell waye oute of his
chirche and come ayen he fonde hym dede withoute bapteme. And
thanne he toke the bodi and bare it into his celle, and there he kneled
80 downe and praied with so gret deuocion to God that he deseruid to be
herde, and the man arose fro dethe to liff. And as that same man
diuerse tymes after that as the sentence of dampnacion shulde haue be
youe upon hym, two aungeles saide to the iuge: 'This is he that
Martin is plege for.' And thanne he was conuerted ayen to the bodi
85 and was deliuered quicke to Seint Martin. And also he restored
another mannes lyff that had hanged hymselff.

And sothely whanne the peple of Toures had no bisshopp, thei
required hym gretly [that he wolde take it vpon hym], but he refused
f. 266ra it. But there was one that was contrarie euer | to hym for that he used
90 foul clothinge and not faire of [vi]sage. [And there was] one special[y]
was ayenst hym þat hight Defensor. And as the lector was not present,

60 Thedir] whider H2   And] *add* than H2   enemy] feende H2   Whereuer] whider
that euer H2   61 and . . . the] *om.* H2   65 But] And H2   66 contrarie to] that
contraried H2   he] Martine H2   69 by the] L, with the EH1H2 (*des* P2)   70 to]
om. EH1   herbis] H1 *starts new sentence* The sede   71 *eleborus*] Eleborue E   75 a
chirche] chirchis H2   76 nwe] *om.* EH1   82 diuerse . . . the] *om.* H2
82–3 sentence . . . dampnacion/shulde . . . youe] *trs.* H2   be youe] `be sone´ H1
84 he] his soule H2   conuerted] committid H2   85 and] *add* so H2   deliuered] *add*
ayenne H2   86 another . . . lyff] ayen to life a man H2   88 that . . . hym] *om.* EH1
89 But there] For H2   to] ayenst H2   90 of visage] of usage EH1, *om.* H2 (*de voult* P2)
And there was] but/but E, But H1   specialy] special E, *add* that H2

another toke the Sawter and redde the furst psalme that he fonde, and
in that psalme was this vers: 'God hathe made perfit thi preising bi the
mouthes of children and of sowkers, for that thou shuldest distroie the
enemy defensour.' And so that Defensour was chased oute of towne. 95
And thanne was Martin ordeined bisshopp, and for he might not
endure the noise of the peple he ordeined a chirche .ij. myle from the
citee, and there he lyued in gret abstinence with .iiij^{xx}. disciples, of
whiche mani citeis chosen bisshoppes.

And as he duelled there a bodi was beried there in a chapell that was 100
worshipped as a martir, and Seint Martin coude finde nothinge of his
liff nor of his merites, and in a day as he come upon his sepulcre he
praied to oure Lorde that he wolde shewe hym of what merites he
was. And than he turned upon his right side and sawe a blacke shadow
bisides hym, and thanne Martin coniured hym, and he tolde hym that 105
he was a theef that for his wickednesse was dede. And thanne Seint
Martine made distroie the auuter.

Hit is redde in the Diologe Sever and Gall, disciples of Seint
Martine, that there be mani thinges that Seuer lefte of the liff of Seint
Martin that be fulfelled in the Dialoge. So it happed that Seint 110
Martine went in a tyme to Valentynien emperour for sum nedefull
thinge, and the emperour knewe well that he wolde aske hym | a   f. 266rb
thinge that he [wolde] not graunte hym and lete shette his dores
ayenst hym. And Martin suffered onis or twies to be wernid for to
entre, and thanne he wrapped hymself in an heire and sprenged 115
hymselff with asshes and made hys flesshe lene al a weke with fasting.
And thanne he was taught bi an aungel for to go to the paleis and ther
was none that withsaide hym so that he went to the empero[ur]. And
whanne the emperour sawe hym he was [w]rothe for he was entered
into hym and wolde not arise ayens hym til the fire hadde al couered 120
his chaumbre riall. And whanne he felt the fire behynde hym he arose
al wrothe and confessed that he hadde felt the uertu diuine, and
beganne to clippe the seint and graunted hym all his request withoute
ani askinge and offered hym mani yeftes, but Martin wolde none
resseiue.   125

93 vers] add `Ex ore infancium et lactencium' H1   95 so] om. H2   99 chosen] add
her H2   100 in] ny H1   104 turned] retourned H2   105 and^2] add þan H1
108 Diologe] add that H2   109 Martine] add seiden H2   110 happed] add in a time
H2   112 wolde] kepte EH1   115 entre] add into the wallis and the paleis of the
emperour D   116 al] om. D   118 emperour] emperorie E   119 wrothe] rothe E
120 al] add ouer E   124 hym] add more EH1   mani] in H1   none] not H1

And in that same Diologe it is rcddc how hc areised the thridde
dede man. For whanne a yonge childe was dede his moder praied
Seint Martin with mani teres for the reysinge of her sone fro dethe to
liff, and he was that tyme in the middell of a felde where there were
130 mani paynimes, and there he kneled downe and made his praiers, and
the yonge man arose up al hole bifore hem all, and all the paynimes
were conuerted to the faithe of Crist for shewynge of this glorious
miracle.

To this holy man obeied sensible thinges as fire and water. For as
135 he had comaunded to sette fire in the temple, the flawme was driue
f. 266ᵛᵃ with the wynde upon an hous that was ioyned to the | temple. And he
stied up on the heling of the hous and stode ayens the flawmes. And
anone the flawme returned ayenst the strengthe of the wynde so that
men might see the fightinge of the elementes. Also ther was a shippe
140 that perisshed in the see, and a marchaunt whiche was there and was
not cristened, and cried and saide: 'The god of Seint Martin helpe us.'
And anone the tempest sesed and the see was faire and clere.

And also thinges lyuinge and growinge obeied hym, as trees. For he
destroied in a place a right olde tree that was dedied to the fende, and
145 as Martin wolde haue rent hym downe the churles of the cuntre wolde
not suffre hym, til atte the laste one of hem saide to Martin: 'And thou
wolt nedes haue hym downe we shull hewe hym and thou shalt
resseiue the falle of hym, and yef thi god be with the as thou saiest
thou shalt ascape wel ynow.' And he graunted gladli hereto. And
150 thanne thei hew downe the tree and bonde hym in suche wise as he
might fall upon Martin. And whan he beganne to fall he made the
signe of the crosse ayens hym and the tre turned anone into that other
partie and slow almost all the churles that were there. And thanne
other were conuerted whanne thei sawe this miracle.

155 And also mani unresonable bestes obeied hym, for as it is wreten in
the same Dialoge that houndes folued an hare, and he comaunded
hem that thei shulde leue her foluinge, and thei lefte anone. A serpent
passed ouerthwart a flode and Martin saide to the serpent: 'I
f. 266ᵛᵇ comaunde the in the name of God that thou turne ayen.' | And
160 anone the serpent returned thorugh the worde of the seint and went

129 he] seint Martein D   131 all²] than D   132 of '] add Ihesu D   for] add þe
HıD   this] his Hı, the D   134 To] And also to D   man] add seint Marteine D
139 the¹] om. Hı   140 there and] thereinne which D   141 and saide] om. D
143 also] add alle D   obeied] add to D   144 was] om. D   146 not] ins. Hı   And]
If Hı   150 as] that D   151 he¹] the tree D   157 lefte] add of Hı
158 ouerthwart] ouer D   160 returned] add ayenne D

into another riuer, wherfor Seint Martin wepinge saide: 'Alas, serpentis understonde me wel, but men wolle in no wise understonde me ne here me.' In a tyme as a hounde abaied upon the disciples of Seint Martin, the disciple turned to the hounde and saide: 'I comaunde the in the name of Seint Martin that thou holde thi 165 pees.' And anone the hounde helde [his] pees as though [his] tunge had be smite of.

The blessed Martin was of gret humilite, for he mette in a tyme with a lepre atte Paris and that an horrible one to se of all men, and he cussed hym and blessed hym and he was anone clene. He was neuer 170 sayne that he satte in the chirche, and whanne he was in his celle he sate in an olde cheiere of .iij. fete. And yet he was of so grete a dignite that he was clepte the heir and felawe of aposteles, and that was for the grace of the holy goste that descended into hym in liknesse of fire right as into the aposteles, and the aposteles uisited hym ofte tyme as her 175 disciple.

And also it is redde in the same Dialoge that he satte in a tyme allone in his celle, and Seuer and Gall abode hym longe withoute the dore, and thei were ouertake with gret fere for thei herde mani men speke togedre withyn his celle. And whanne thei hadde tolde this to 180 Martin he saide to hem: 'Y praie you that ye speke to no creature hereof, for Anneis, Tecle and Marie were with me, not only now but ofte tymes bene and comen to uisite me.' And Petre and Poule come ofte tymes to uisite hym.

He was of gret pacience, | for he kept so gret pacience in alle thinge f. 267ra that he that was souerayne prest was often tymes hurte with his 186 clerkes withoute that he ponisshed h[e]m therfor, and therfor thei dredde hym not of his charite. For there was neuer man that sawe hym wrothe, ne neuer man sawe hym nother wepe ne laugh, ne he hadde nothinge in his speche but Ihesu Crist, nor in his herte but 190 pitee, pees and merci. Hyt ys redde in the same Dialoge that Martin was in a tyme clothed in a sharpe clothinge of blew, and with a gret

162 wolle] *add* not H1   162–3 understonde . . . me²] *om.* H1   166 hounde] houndes EH1   his¹] her EH1   his tunge] thaire tunges E   168 The] Also the D 169 that] *add* right D   170 He] Also he D   171 that he satte] sitte D   and] but D 173 was¹] *ins.* H1   of] *add* all H1   for] throu3 D   174 into] 'in'to H1   175 into] in H1D   178–9 hym . . . dore] withoute longe tyme for hym D   179 men] *om.* D 180 hadde] *om.* D   to] *add* seint D   181 that ye] to D   182 for] *ins.* H1 183 bene] *om.* H1, bifore D   to uisite] and vesitid D   184 hym] me also D 185 for . . . pacience²] *om.* D   187 withoute that] natwithstondinge D   hem] hym EH1 189 hym¹] *add* neþer H1   man] noone that] D   nother] never H1, *om.* D   he] *om.* H1 191 that] *add* seint D

blacke mantell that hanged downe abought hym on eueri side, and so
he rode upon his asse, and horse [that] came ayenst hym were so
195 aferde of hym that thei [th]rewe downe the men that were upon hem
to the erthe, and than thei for anger toke Martin and bete hym
greuously. And he abondonid hymself alwey to hem for to resseiue
gladly al that thei wolde do to hym, and thei enforced hem more and
more for to bete hym that he felt not her strokes but dispised hem.
200 And her bestes were so ouercome that thei might no more rise ne
remeue thanne a roche nether for betinge ne for drawinge, into the
tyme that thei turned hem to Seint Martin and confessed her synne
that thei hadd do bi ignoraunce, and praied hym of merci and of leue,
and anone the bestis arose and went forthe a gret pas.
205   He was of so gret continuaunce in praier that there was neuer hour
ne moment but that he praied or redde or studied, ne for none
ocupacion that euer he releced his mynde from praier, for right as it is
the custume of smithes of yren that in the mene tyme that thei werken
for sum reles of her laboure thei smiten upon the anefelde, right so
f. 267rb Martin whanne he wrought ani outwarde werke he praied | euer
211 inward.
      He was so harde and sharpe to hymselff, as Seuerus [wrote in a
pistell] to Eusebie, that as Martin come into a place of his diocise his
clerkes had ordeined hym a bedde filled ful of strawe, and whanne he
215 was leide therin he dradde hym for the softenesse therof, for it was not
his custume to lye softe but upon the harde erthe and a coueringe of
an heire upon his bedde. And thanne he was meued and rose hym up
and threwe oute all the strawe of his bedde and leide hym downe upon
the erthe. And abought midnight al that strawe was on a light fire, and
220 Martin arose and went to haue scaped, but he might not for he was al
enuironed with the fire that it brent his clothes. And thanne he turned
hym to his acustumed orison and made the signe of the crosse and
abode in the middell of the fire withoute ani harme, and he felt the
flawmes of the fire wel smellynge, the whiche he hadde felt before

194 that] *om.* E   195 threwe] drewe E   197 abondonid] abowed don D   alwey]
om. D   198 hem] him H1   199 that] and yit D   but] ne D   hem] *add* nat D
200 And] but D   so] *om.* D   201 thanne] but as a D   202 Seint] *om.* D
203 leue] love D   205 He] Also he D   so] *om.* D   205–6 hour ne moment] moment
of an houre D   206 ne for] nothir þere was D   209 for] *om.* D   thei] while that
some D   210 ani] *add* þing H1   212–13 wrote/in a pistell] *trs.* EH1   213 as]
om. H1   215 for²] *om.* H1   217 an] *om.* H1   bedde] heede D   218 bedde] *add*
And þan he was meued and roos him vpp H1   219 on a] vp on D   221 enuironed]
add alle about D   it EH1] he D   221–2 turned hym] returned D   223 abode] *add*
stille D   223–4 withoute . . . fire] *twice* H1

hote brennynge. And thanne the monkes were gretly meued and 225
ronnen thedir and fonde Martin in the middes of the flawmes
withoute ani disese felyng whiche thei wende to haue founde al
wasted with the fire.

He was ful pitous to al tho that offended hym, and to all tho that
wolde conuerte hem he receiued hem euer in his bosum of pitee. And 230
whanne the fende undertoke Martin for that he receiued to do
penaunce that were for a tyme, he ansuered hym and saide: 'O thou
most cursed best, yet yef thou woldest leue to turment mankinde as
thou doest and that thou woldest repent of thi wickednesse, y truste so
moche in the mercy of God that y wolde aske merci for the.' 235

He hadde euer gret pitee for the pore. | Hyt is redde in the forsaide f. 267ᵛᵃ
Dialoge that Seint Martin went in a tyme to chirche and a pore man
folued hym. And Martin comaunded to his archedeken that he shuld
clothe the pore man, and whanne he sawe that he taried to longe for to
clothe hym he entred into the sextrie and dispoiled hymself and 240
clothed the pore man with his clothinge and bade hym go his waye in
all haste. And as his archedeken hasted hym faste for to begynne the
seruice, Martin saide that he might in no wise go till the pore man
were clothed ayen. He ment of hymself, but thei understode hym not
bicause thei sawe hym couered with his cope and wist not that he was 245
naked under, and therfor thei cared not for the pore. And thanne he
saide ayen: 'Whi broght ye not a clothe to the pore so that now ye
hadde had no nede to clothe me pore?' And thanne he, ashamed and
constreined, went to the market [and with .v. d] bought hym a sori
sh[o]rte cote, and in anger [th]rewe it downe atte the fete of Seint 250
Martine. And he clothed hym therwith priuili, and the sleuis therof
come to his elbowes and the lengthe therof come unnethes to his
knees, and so he went to singe his masse. And as he was atte the masse
a gret light of fire descended upon his hede and was sayne of mani that
were there. And for this cause he was called euen and felow with the 255
apposteles. And to this miracle ioynithe Maister Iohn Belet and saithe
that whanne Seint Martin left up his hondes atte the masse as the
custume is, the sleuis of his aube slode up to his elbowes so that his

227 disese] di⟨.⟩see *with illeg. letter del.* H₁   229 He] Also he D   232 that were]
om. D   233 most] *om.* D   236 for] of H₁, vppon D   239 to¹] so D
240 hym] *om.* H₁   242 as his] than the D   And . . . faste] *om.* H₁   faste] *om.* D
246 therfor] *om.* D   cared] taried H₁   247 not] *om.* D   to the pore] for the pore
man D   that] than D   247–8 so that . . . pore] *ins. with* now ye *trs.* H₁   248 pore]
om. D   249 and/with .v. d] *trs.* E   hym] *om.* D   250 shorte] sherte an olde E
threwe] drewe E   252 come¹] *add* but D   258 the sleuis of] *om.* D

armes were al naked. And thanne were there brought hym bi miracle
f. 267vb .ij. | sleuis of golde wrought with precious stones, the whiche aungeles
261 brought hym and couered his armes couenabli ynow. In a tyme he
sawe shepe shoren and saide: 'These shepe haue fulfelled the
comaundement of the gospell, for she hadde .ij. sydes and she
hathe youe that one to hem that had none, and in this wise shulde
265 we do.'

He was of gret power to caste oute fendes, for he putte hem oute
mani tymes of mennes bodies. Hyt is redde in the same Diologe that a
cowe was turmented with a fende and enforced her to confound
moche peple, and as Seint Martin and his felawship dedin a viage this
270 wode kowe come renninge ayenst hem, and thanne Seint Martin lefte
up his honde and comaunded her to stonde stille, [and she stode stille]
withoute meuynge. And thanne Seint Martin sawe the fende that satte
upon her backe and blamed hym and saide: 'Go thennes, thou best of
dethe, and leue for to turment this beste that noiethe nothinge.' And
275 anone he fledde awey, and the best kneled downe atte the fete of the
seint and atte his comaundement she returned mekeli to her felawship.

He was of gret sotilte in knowinge of fendes. He was so seinge in
hem that whereuer thei went he sawe hem. For sum tyme thei shewed
280 hem to hym in liknesse of Iouis or of Mercurie or of sum mani other
wherinne thei wolde transfigure hem, but he knewe hem anone and
wolde blame hem eueriche bi his name. Hyt fell in a tyme that the
fende apered to hym in liknesse of a kinge clothed in purpre and
crowned and arraied with shone of golde and apered to hym with
f. 268ra frendely | speche and gladde chere, and whan bothe had holde her
286 pees a while the fende saide to hym: 'Martin, whi dredest thou to leue
in me whanne thou seest that y am Crist?' And thanne Martin taught
bi the holy goste said: 'Oure Lord Ihesu Crist said not so that he
wolde come in purpre nor in a crowne shyninge, and therfor y shall
290 neuer leue that Ihesu Crist be come but yef he come and be in the
habite and in the fourme that he suffered dethe on, and that the signe
of the crosse be borne before hym.' And with that worde he vanisshed
awey and lefte the celle full of stinke.

Seint Martin wost longe before his passing out of this worlde, and

260 sleuis] cleves Hı   266 was] add also D   270 kowe] knowe with n subp. Hı
271 and she stode stille] om. E   275 he] the feende D   275–6 the seint] seint Marteine D
278 of¹] add so D   He² . . . so] and in D   280 of sum] in D   other] add wise D
287 taught] þoȝt Hı   289 a] om. Hı   290 but yef . . . be] om. D   291 and¹] but D
292 he] the feende D   294 Seint] Also seint D   wost] add welle D

tolde it to his bretheren. And in the mene tyme as he visited the 295
diosise of Dol for to apese discorde that was there, and as he went, he
sawe in a caue a manere of briddes that aspied the fisshes and toke
hem, and thanne he saide: 'This manere of fendes is for to aspie foles
and for to take the vncunnynge and to devoure hem that thei haue
take.' And [t]hanne he comaunded hem that thei shulde leue the water 300
and that thei goo into the cuntreies of desert, and anone thei
assembled hem togedre and went to the wodes and to the hilles.

And thanne he duelled a while in that diocise and beganne to feble
in his bodi and tolde to his disciples that he shulde deie. And thanne
all saiden: 'A fader, whi leuest thou us, to whom wilt thou leue us al 305
discomfort? The rauesshinge wolues will assaile thi bestes. Haue
routhe and pitee upon thi flocke and leue us not with[oute] oure
shepard.' And thanne he was meued bi her weping, and praied weping
and saide: 'Lorde, yef y be yet necessarie to thi peple | y refuse not the f. 268rb
laboure; thi will be do.' Unnethes he wost whiche was the beste, for in 310
that one syde he was lothe to leue hem and in that other side he wolde
not longe be seuered from Ihesu Crist. And [w]hanne [h]e hadde be a
whiles turmented with the [f]eueres, his disciples praied hym that thei
might leye a litell strawe in his bedde wher he laye upon an heire and
in asshis, and he saide to hem: 'Sones, it longithe not to a cristen man 315
for to deie but upon an heire and in asshes, and yef y hadd sheued
other ensaumple y had synned.' And he hadde allwey his hondes and
his eyen toward heuene and his sperit was neuer relesed from praier,
and as he laye alweyes upright his bretheren praied hym that he wolde
remewe a litell, and he saide: 'Bretheren, lete me, lete me more for to 320
beholde heuene thanne the erthe so that the sperit be dressed to oure
Lorde.' And as he saide that, he sawe the fende that was come, to
whom he saide: 'What doest thou here, thou cruel beest? Thou
fyndest no dedly thinge in me, the bosum of Abraham shall resseiue
me.' And with that worde he gaue up his sperit to oure Lorde vnder 325
Arcadien [and Hungrien] that beganne about the yere of oure Lorde

296 and] Also anothir time D   297 in a caue a] a grete companie in D   fisshes] add
in the riuere D   298 hem] add and deuourid hem D   This] add is the D   is] om. D
300 thanne] whanne E   301 thei¹] ins. H1   303 he] Marteine D   feble] add fast D
305 us¹] add and D   to whom . . . us] ins. H1   306 discomfort] add For D   bestes] add
wherefor D   307 flocke] folke D   withoute oure] with oure E, with oute with t on r H1,
a D   310 do] add for D   H1 punct. after Unnethes   wost] add nat D   312 whanne
he] thanne we EH1   313 feueres] reueres E, reuerence H1   316 sheued] add none
EH1   320 lete me²] 'no' H1, om. D   for to] om. D   321 the¹] om. H1   the²] my D
322 as] than D   324 me] add for D   326 and Hungrien] of Hungrie E

.CCCC. and .xl. and the yere of his lyff .iiij^{xx}.viij.; and the uisage of
hym shined as it hadd be glorified and the vois of aungeles was herde
of mani that songe there.

330   And tho of Peiters assembled there as well as thei of Tours for to be
atte his passinge, and ther was gret altercacion betwene hem. For the
Peyteuynes saide: 'He is oure monke, we require to haue hym.' And

f. 268va that other partie saide: 'He was take fro you and youe | to us bi God.'
And atte midnight alle the Peyteuynes slepten and tho of Towres

335   putte oute the bodie bi a wyndow, and so he was caried upon Leyre by
water with gret ioye to the citee of Tours.

And as blessed Seuer bisshop of Coloyne in a Sondaye after
Mateins, as he uisited all the holy places in that hour that this holy
man passed oute of this worlde, he herde aungeles synginge in heuene,

340   and thanne he called his archedeken and asked hym yef he herde
anithinge, and he said that he herde nothinge. And the bisshop bade
hym that he shulde herke diligently, and he beganne to streche up his
necke and to dresse hym upon his toes and lened upon a staffe. And
thanne the bisshopp made his praiers for hym, and thanne he saide

345   that hym thought that he herde uoyses in heuene. Thanne the
bisshopp saide: 'That is my lorde Seint Martine that is passed oute
of this worlde, and aungeles bere hym now to heuene. And the fendes
were atte his passinge, but thei fonde nothinge in hym and went
thennis all confused.' And the archedeken acounted the day and the

350   houre, and thanne he knewe uerily that Seint Martin passed the same
houre.

And Sever monke that wrote the lyff of hym, as he slepte lyghtly
after Mateins, Seint Martin apered to hym clothed in an aube, the
uisage clere, his eyen sparkelynge [ful] bright, his here as of purpre

355   coloure, holdinge the boke in his honde that this Sever had wretyn of
his lyff. And whanne he hadde yeue hym his blessinge he sawe hym
stie up into heuene, and as he wolde haue stied up after hym he
awoke. And anone the messengeres come that saide that that same
night Seint Martin was passed.

327 lyff] *om.* D   uisage] passinge D   329 that songe there] *om.* D   331–2 the
Peyteuynes] thoo of Peiters D   332 monke] *add* wherefor D   we] he H1   334 alle
the Peyteuynes] þoo of Peyters D   335 bi] of seint Marteine at D   338 that^1] the
same D   339 man] *add* seinte marteine D   341 that . . . nothinge] Nay D
342 that he shulde] *om.* D   herke] herken H1D   he^2] than the Erchedekenne D
345 hym] *ins.* H1   352 lyghtly] in a nyght D   354 ful] L, for EH1D   bright]
brightnes D   357 hym] hymselff EH1   358 And] *om.* H1   358–9 that^2 . . .
passed] Seint Marteine passid the same nyght D

In that sa|me day Seint Ambrose bisshop of Melan songe [his] f. 268vb
masse, and he slepte upon the auuter betwene the lesson and the 361
prophecie and the pistle, and there durste none awake hym, and the
[sub]dekene durst not rede the pistle withoute his leue. And whanne
he had slepte .iij. houres he saide: 'The houre passithe and the peple
abidithe and be anoyed. Syr, comaundithe that the clerke rede the 365
pistell.' And he saide to hem: 'Bethe not wrothe, for Martin my
brother is passed to God and y haue do the Office of his passinge
hennes, but y might not make an ende of the laste orison so ye haue
hasted me.' And thanne thei assigned the day and the houre and fonde
wel that Seint Martin was passed thanne and go to heuene. 370

Maister Iohn Belet saithe that the kynges of Fraunce were wont
sumtyme for to bere his cope whanne thei went to bataile, and for that
thei kept this cope thei were called chapeleynes.

And after the passinge of hym the ycrc [.lxiiij.] whanne Seint
Perpetuel hadd encresed his chirche largely for to bringe thedir the 375
bodie of Seint Martine, than thei fasted ones or twyes and thanne
thries in wakingges and in praiers, but thei might in no wise remeue
his sepulcre. And as thei wolde haue lefte of there apered to hem right
a faire auncien man and saide to hem: 'Whi tarie ye? Se ye not how
Seint Martin is redi for to helpe you yef ye wolde sette to hondes?' 380
And thanne he sette on honde[s] with hem and lefte up the holi body
anone and leide hym there as he is now worshipped. And thanne he
anone disparbeled. This translacion was made and done in the monthe
of Iuyll.

And it is saide that there was thanne .ij. felawes, that one was a 385
crepill and that other was blinde. The crepill shewed the waye to the
blynde and the | blinde bare the crepill, and these .ij. bi her trewant f. 269ra
beggynge gate moche money. And thei herde how mani sike men were
heled bi the presence of Seint Martine, and for that thei wolde not be
heled but liue forthe in miserie that thei might haue and use her 390
truandise in begging, thei went fro that place and went to another
chirche where thei supposed that that holy bodi shulde not come. And
as thei fledde thei mette the holy bodi bi the waye vnwetynge hem,

360 his] the high EH1   362 prophecie and the] *om.* D   and³] and so E, ne D
363 subdekene] dekene E   his leue] the leue of hym D   364 he saide] than thei seide to hym
Sir D   365 clerke] subdeken D   366 he] than Ambrose D   368 ye haue] haue 'ye' H1
369 assigned] markid D   370 thanne and go] that time D   372 sumtyme] *om.* D   to²]
add any D   373 this] his D   374 .lxiiij.] .iiijˣˣ.iiij. EH1   378 lefte of] liffte it vp D
right] *om.* D   379 ye¹] *add* so D   381 hondes] honde EH1   383 disparbeled]
disparkeled H1, vanisshid D   392 chirche] place D   393 bodi] *add* of seint Martine D

and God whos goodnesse is infinit and geuithe frely his goodes to hem
395 that desire hem not, heled this .ij. ayenst her will and of her hele thei
were full sori.

And as Seint Ambrose saithe of Seint Martin in this wise: 'He
distroied the cursed errours and enforced the baneres of pitee, he
areysed the dede and droue oute fendes of bodies that thei hadde
400 beseged, and aleged bi remedie of hele tho that were trauailed bi
diuerse siknesse. And he was founde so perfit that he clothed Ihesu
Crist in his pore man, and the clothinge that the pore man hadde
receiued, the Lorde of all the worlde clothed. O blessed largesse that
couered the diuinite. O glorious dividynge of clothinge that clothed
405 bothe a kinge and a knyght. O inestimable yefte that deserued for to
clothe the Godhede. Lord, thou yeuest hym worthely the rewarde of
thi confession, thou puttest under hym worthely the cruelte of [the]
Arryens, and he dredde not the turmentes of [the] pursuours of thi
faithe for the desire that he had to martirdom. What shall he resseiue
410 for the offeringe up of all his hole bodi and sowle sethe he for so litell a
quantite of a litell clothinge deserued for to clothe God, and to see
God. In suche wise he gaue medicine to hem that hoped in God that
sum [h]e heled by praier and sum bi comaundement.'

f. 269rb   Here | endithe the liff of Seint Martine, and nexst
beginnithe the liff of Seint Brice, Capitulum .C.lx.^m

Brice was deken to Seint Martine and had gret enuie to hym. In a
tyme as a pore man asked gode of Seint Martine, Brice saide to hym:
'Yef thou wilt scorne this fole, loke up to heuenewarde as he dothe, for
he lokithe euer upwarde as a mad man.' And whanne the seint hadde
5 youe to the pore that he asked, the holi man called Brice and saide to
hym: 'Semithe the that y am mad?' And he denied it for shame, and
Martin saide to hym: 'Haue y not herde it? Were not myn eeres atte
thi mouth whanne thou saide it opinly? I telle the that y haue graunt
of oure Lorde that thou shalt succede after me, but wete it well that

395 not] *om.* D   hele] *ins.* H1   400 bi²] with H1D   402 man] mantel H1
403 clothed] *add* hym D   blessed] blesfulle D   404 couered] coueredist D
407 worthely] *om.* D   the²] *om.* EH1   408 not] *om.* D   the²] *om.* EH1   thi] þe
changed to þy H1   410 his] þis H1   412 God¹] *add* and H1D   413 sum¹] *om.* D
he] be E

EH1DH2A1A2L   3 this fole] *om.* D   up] vpward D   4 the seint] seint
Martine D   5 pore] *add* man D   man] *ins.* H1   6 am] *om.* D   7–8 myn, thi]
thine, my D

thou shalt sustene in thi bisshopriche mani contrarie thinges.' And 10
whanne Brice herde these wordes he dede but scorne hym and saide:
'Haue y not tolde you that this is but a fole?'

And than after that Seint Martine was dede Brice was chosin to be
bisshopp, and fro thennes forwarde he gaue hym al to praier, and
thow it were so that he were prowde of beringe yet he was euer chaste 15
of bodi. And whan he was in the .xxx. yere of his bysshopriche there
was putte upon hym a lamentable crime, for a religious woman that
wasshed his clothes conceyued and bare a childe. And thanne all the
peple gadered togedre atte his yate with stones and saide: 'We haue
longe suffered thi wreched vnclennesse for the pitee of Seint Martine, 20
but we will no lengger kisse thi defouled hondes.' But he denyed this |
strongely and saide: 'Bringe forthe to me the childe.' And whanne thei f. 269ᵛᵃ
had brought it to hym the childe was but .xxx. dayes olde, and Brice
saide to hym: 'I coniure the in the name of the sone of God that thou
saie afore all this peple whedir y be thi fader and gate the.' And the 25
childe saide: 'Thou art not my fader.' And thanne the peple wolde
haue made hym aske ho hadd be the childes fader, and he ansuered
and saide: 'That longithe not to me; y haue do that longithe to myn
acuse.' And the peple cried and saide that he had do that bi
enchauntement and saide: 'Thou shalt not thus falsly haue the 30
lordship ouer us under colour of holinesse.' And thanne for to
make his purgacion he bare brennyng colys in his lappe to the
tombe of Seint Martine, and his clothes were nothinge hurte with
the fire, and than he saide: 'Right as my clothes be clene fro
brennynge of the fire, so is my body clene from corrupcion of 35
woman.' And yet for al that the peple leuid hym not, but bete hym
and dede hym gret iniurie and putte hym oute of his dignite for that
the worde of Seint Martine might be fulfelled.

And thanne Seint Brice went wepinge to the pope and duelled
there .vij. yere, and purged hym of that he had mystake hym ayenst 40
Seint Martine. And the peple made Iustinien bysshoppe, and sent
hym to Rome to defende the bisshopriche ayenst Brice. And as he
went he deyed in the citee of Verseaux. And thanne the peple made
Armonium bisshoppe in stede of hym. And in the .vij. yere Brice
returned ayen bi the auctorite of the pope and toke his herburgh .vj. 45

11 saide] *add* to the puple D   14 praier] praiers E   15 of bodi] *om.* D
21 But . . . denyed] and than he wondrid vppon D   23 to] *om.* H1   24 hym] the
childe D   25 the²] *ins.* H1   26 fader] *add* that gate me D   27 the] *ins.* H1   he]
Brice D   31 lordship] worshipp H1   38 might] *add* nat D   41 Iustinien]
Iusticion D   44 Armonium] Armoun H1D   45 the¹] *om.* H1   .vj.] .vij. D

myle from th[e] citee. And Armenyen putte oute that night his spirit.
f. 269vb And Brice knewe it | bi diuyne reuelacion and saide to his men that
thei shulde arise and haste hem for to go with hym to berye the
bisshopp of Tours that was dede. And as Brice entered atte one yate,
50 thei bare the dede bisshopp bi another yate, and whanne he was beried
Brice toke his see and was after that bisshoppe .vij. yere and lyued a
preisable lyff, and in the .xlvij. yere of his bisshopriche he passed to
oure Lorde.

Here endithe the lyff of Seint Brice, and nexst beginnithe
the lyff of Seint Elizabeth of Hungry, Capitulum .C.lxj.

Seint Elizabeth was doughter of the noble kinge of Hungry, and yef
she were right noble bi kinrede she was moche more noble bi faithe
and religion, and her right noble kinrede she ennoblisshed bi
ensaumple and clered it bi myracle. She embelisshed it by grace of
5 holinesse, for the auctour of nature lefte her up in manere aboue
nature. Whanne this mayde, norisshed in delices reals, renounsed alle
childisnes and putte her ful in the seruice of God, wherein it aperithe
clerely how her tendre childehode enforced in symplenesse and how
she beganne bi suete deuocion that fro thennes forward she beganne
10 for to custume her in good custumes and for to dispise the playes of
vanitee and for to flee the prosperitees of the worlde and for to profite
alwey in the worshippe of God.

And whanne she was but .v. yere olde she wolde so ententifly abide
in the chirche for to praie that unnethes her felawes and servauntes
15 might take her thennes. And whanne she mette with any of her
felawshipp or chaumbreres, she wolde folue as in game towarde the
f. 270ra chapell, for she wolde haue occasion to entre | into the chirche. And
whanne she was entered she wolde knele downe and lye flatte on the
pament, and yef it were so that she hadde atte that tyme no knowynge
20 of letteres, yet she wolde opin the Sawter ofte tyme before her for to
feyne that she radde, and that none shulde lette her as though she
were ocupied. And whan she was amonge other maydenes of her
astate for to pleie, she wolde considre wel the manere of the pleie that

46 the] this EH1   51 see] seete D   after] affore *changed to* aftere H1   bisshoppe]
add þere D   53 Lorde] *add* god H1

EH1DH2A1A2L; D breaks off after 409 *grace*   3 ennoblisshed] envolnysshed H1
4 embelisshed] ennoblisshid D   7 childisnes] childenes D   11 for to profite] she
profitid D   13 so] *om.* D   14 and] ne hir D   16 folue] *om.* D   17 to entre]
om. D   20 yet] þat H1   21 feyne] haue D   22 whan] *ins.* H1

she might euer bere worship to God under that occasion. And in the
pley of rynges and of other games she sette her souerayne truste euer 25
and hope in God. And of alle that she wan or of the goodes she hadde
in any other wise, she beinge yonge maide she gaue the tenthe parte to
pore maidenes and ledde hem ofte tymes with her for to saie her Pater
Nostris and ofte tyme into the chirche for to grete oure Ladi.

And as she encresed bi age of tyme, so encresed she bi deuocion, for 30
she chase the Uirgine Marie moder of God to her souerayne ladi and
to her aduocat, and Seint Iohn the euuangelist for to be keper of her
uirginite. And in a tyme there were scrowes leide upon the auuter, and
in euery scrowe there was wrete the name of [an] apostle, and euery of
that other maydenes toke at auenture suche as fell hem, but she made 35
her praier and thre tymes she toke that [that] she desired wherinne
was wrete the name of Seint Petre, to whom she had so grct dcuocion
that she werned nothingc that askcd anithinge in his name. And for
that [the] good auentures of the worlde shulde not deseiue her, she
withdrow eueri day sumthinge of her propertees. 40

And as sone as she toke plesaunce in ani game, anone she | wolde f. 270rb
leue the remenaunt and saie that her luste no lenger to plaie, but saie
to her felawshippe: 'Y leue you the remenaunt for God.' She went
neuer gladly to caroles but withedrowe other as moche as she might.
She dredde euer to were fresshe araye but she loued to go honestly. 45

She had ordeined herselff for to saie a sertaine nombre of orisones,
and yef she were ocupied that she might not saie hem or that she were
constreined bi her women for to go to her bedde, she wolde wake and
saie hem to God in her bedde. This holy mayde worshipped all the
solempne dayes so gretly that she wolde suffre nobodi to lase her 50
sleuis for none occasion till the sollempnite of the masse were done
and fulfelled. She herde the Office of the Chirche with so gret
reuerence that whannc thc gospell was radde or whanne the sacrament
was lefte up, she wolde take of her broches of golde and the cercle of
her hede and leye it on the grounde. 55

And in this mene tyme that she kepte thus holily her uirginite, she

24 the] *om.* H1   25 of²] *om.* H1   euer] *om.* D   26 the] any D   27 any]
om. D   29 tyme] *add* she ladde hem D   30 bi . . . encresed] *ins.* H1   tyme] *add*
and D   she²] *om.* D   31 Marie] *add* to be D   34 an] L, *om.* EH1D   35 but she]
and Elizabeth D   36 that²] *om.* EH1   wherinne] *add* þere D   38 nothinge] *add* 'to
noo creature' H1   that . . . anithinge] to any creature D   39 the¹] *om.* EH1
44 gladly] *om.* D   other] hir D   45 honestly] *add* Also D   47 yef] *om.* D   or that]
also and D   were] was H1   49 This] Also this D   mayde] *add* Elizabeth D
52 Office] voice D   54 the cercle] sercle *with loop perhaps for* s H1, serclis D   55 it]
om. D   56 holily her] hir holie D

was constreined for to entre into mariage bi her fader, that gretly
desired for to haue fruit of her, notwithstonding that it was ful gretli
ayenst her will, but she durst not withsaie the comaundement of her
60 fader. And thanne she avowed to God and behight her trouthe to
Conrat, an holi man that was her confessour, that yef she might
ouerlyue her husbonde that she wolde kepe perpetuel continence.
And thanne she was wedded to Landegraue of Thoringe as the reall
might wolde, and the devine ordenaunce had ordeined for that she
f. 270ᵛᵃ shulde bringe moche of her peple to the loue | of God.
66   She was so feruent in praier þat she wolde go priuely to the chirche
before ani of her meni so that she might bi her secrete praier gete sum
grace of God. She wolde full ofte arise anight to praie whanne her
husbond wolde full hertely praie her to lye still. She ordeined a ladi
70 that was more familier with her thanne other that yef so were that she
were ouertake with slepe and passed her hour that she shulde take her
bi the fete softely for to awake her. So in a tyme bi auenture this ladi
wolde haue take her by the fote and toke her husbonde bi the fote, that
he awoke sodenly, and anone he considered the thinge as it was and
75 lete it passe wisely. And for she wolde offre good sacrifice to God with
her praier, she wette her body ofte with habundaunce of teres; and she
shedde hem ioyously and withoute chaungynge any semblaunt, so that
ofte tymes she wepte with sorw and ioyed with sorw.
    She was of so gret humilite that for the loue of God she leyde in her
80 lappe a sike man with horrible uisage and stinkinge hede, and she
wysshe his uisage and his hede and clipped of the filthe from his hede,
wherfor her women lough her to scorne. Alwey in the Rogacion Dayes
she wolde folow the procession barfote and wolwarde, and in tyme of
prechinge she wolde sitte with other pore folke. She wolde not arraie
85 herself with precious stones as other dede in the day of the
Purificacion, ne clothe her with no clothe of golde, but bi the
ensaumple of the Uirgine Marie she wolde bere her sone in her
f. 270ᵛᵇ armes and a lambe and a | candell and offre it up mekely so that therby
she shewed that the bobaunce and iapes of the worlde were for to be
90 putte awey. And whanne she come home she wolde yeue to a pore
woman the clothinge that she had wered that day.

57 into] add a H₁   58 ful] om. D   59 not] in no wise D   61 yef] om. D
63 Landegraue] lawdegrave D   65 shulde] wolde D   66 She was so] and D   þat]
om. D   68 anight] at mydnyght D   70 thanne] add any D   73 that] and H₁
75 it] om. H₁   76 ofte] offten times D   77 shedde] had D   78 with¹] add grete D
and . . . sorw²] om. H₁D   83 procession] processyon with y over e H₁   84 other]
om. D   not] om. H₁   85 with] add `no´ H₁   88 offre] offered H₁   89 and] of D

She was of so gret humilite that bi the consent of her husbond she putte her in the obedience of Maister Conrat, a pore man and litell of degre, but he was of noble science and of perfit relygion, so that she dede with ioy and reuerence whateuer he comaunded her for to haue 95 the merite of obedience and of God that was obedient unto the dethe. Hyt fell in a tyme that she was called for to go to [a] prechinge, and in the mene tyme come the Marquis of Losenge wherbi she was lette and went not. And her confessour helde hym not paied, wherfor he wolde not relece her of her obedience before that she were dispoiled into her 100 smocke with sum of her women that were gilty with her and that he made hem wel betin.

She was of so gret abstinence that whanne she satte with her husbonde atte the mete really serued with mani messis, the symple brede shulde suffice her. She was so rigorous to herself that she laye al 105 pale and lene. Maiste[r] Conraud defended her that she shulde touche none of her husbondes metis of whiche she had not hole conscience. And she kepte his comaundement with so gret diligence that whanne other abounded in delices she ete with her chaumbreres the comune boystous metis. In a tyme as she was trauailed with goinge, thei 110 brought to her husbonde diuerse metis that were gotin of true conquest, but she refused hem and toke | her refeccion of harde f. 271ra brede tempered with water. And for this cause her husbonde opposed her, with whiche she lyued with her chaumbreres that consented to her purpos. And her husbond suffered al in pacience and saide that 115 full gladly he wolde haue lyued in the same wise ner drede of gruchinge of his peple.

And so she that was in the state of souerain worship and glorie coueited the astate of souerayne pouerte, to that ende that the worlde had no parte in her and that she were uerrey pore as oure 120 Lorde Ihesu Crist was. And whanne she was allone with her chaumbreres she wolde clothe herself in vile clothinge and sette an olde pore veile upon her hede and saye merily: 'Lo, thus y will go whanne y am in the state of a wedowe.' And though she were right abstinent and streite to herself, she was full free and large to the 125 pore so ferforthely that she wolde suffre none in nede duellinge

94 and] *ins.* H1   she] 's'he H1   96 and . . . obedient] *om.* D   97 in¹] on H1
a²] *om.* EH1   98 lette] let *followed by erased letter* H1   99 not²] *add* wel H1   he] she
H1   103 was] *add* also D   so] *om.* D   105 so] *om.* D   106 Maister] Maiste E
her] *ins.* H1   107 hole] hold H1   113–15 opposed . . . husbond] *om.* D
123 veile] vile H1   Lo] *om.* D   124 a wedowe] wydowedhode D   126 suffre] *om.* D

about her, but gaue largely to hem all, for she entended to all her power to the .vij. werkes of merci.

In a tyme she gaue to a pore woman an honest clothinge, and
130 whanne this pore woman sawe that she hadde so noble a yefte she hadd so gret ioye therof that she fell downe to the erthe as dede. And whanne blessed Elizabeth sawe that, she sorued gretly that she hadde youe her so noble a yefte, dredinge lest she hadde be cause of her dethe, and thanne she praied for her and she arose anone al hole. Mani
135 tymes she wolde spinne wolle with her chaumbreres and therof she wold do make clothe, so that bi her owne propre labour that she gaue to the chirches she might resseiue glorious fruit and yeue good ensaumple to other.

f. 271rb   In a tyme that her husbond Landegra|ue was gone to the court of
140 the emperor that was thanne atte Cremone, she assembeled in a garner all the whete of the yere and ministred to eueriche that come thedir from all parties, for it was thanne right gret dirthe thorugh all the cuntre. And mani tymes whanne siluer failed her she wolde sell of her arraye for to yeue to the pore, but for nothinge that she gaue, the
145 garneres were neuer lessed of corne that was in hem.

She made a gret hous under the castell whereinne she might resseyue and norisshe gret multitude of pore folke, and eueri day she visited hem, sparing for no corrupcion of euel eyre ne for no manere of foule siknesse, but wasshed hem and wiped hem with her
150 owne hondes and with her kerchefes whanne she lacked other clothes. And also she norrisshed up in that hous the children of pore women so benignely that all thei called her moder.

She [dede make] the sepulcres for the pore folke whanne thei deyed and went deuoutely to her deyinge and halpe to berie hem with her
155 owne hondes in the clothe that she hadde do made, and mani tymes she wolde bringe the shete that she laye inne herselff for to berie dede bodies therinne.

And amonge al these thinges the deuocion of her husbonde is gretly to preise, for thou it were so that he was gretly ocupied, yet alwey he

127 her^1] *om.* H1   all^1] *om.* D   to^2] with D   her^2] *om.* H1   129 to] *om.* H1
132 sorued] scorned *del.* 'sorowed' H1   134 thanne] whan D   and^2] *add* þan D
135 spinne] s`p´ynne H1   136 do] *om.* H1   137 chirches] *add* so þat D
139 Landegraue] Lowdegrave D   139–40 the court . . . atte] *ins.* H1   143 of] all
H1   144 nothinge] alle D   146 made] *add* also D   castell] *add* walle D
147 and norisshe] *om.* D   153 dede make] made EH1   154 halpe] *add* deuoutelie D
155 made] make D   156–7 dede bodies] hem D   158 these thinges] this D
159 he^1] it H1

was deuout in the seruice of God, and for as moche as he might not 160
hymself personely e[n]tende to inwarde thinges, he hadde yeue power
to his wyff to do all that she might do to the worshippe of God and to
the helthe of sowles.

And blessed Elizabeth hadde gret desire that her husbonde shulde
leue all voyde | all wordeli ocupacions and with all his power and f. 271ᵛᵃ
might go and defende the faithe of God, and so she drow hym bi meke 166
and debonaire praiers that he wolde visite the Holi Londe. And he full
vertuously aplied to all goodnesse and went thedir. And whanne he
was there, that noble true and deuout prince full of feithe and
deuocion yelde up his sperit to oure Lorde God and receiued glorious 170
fruit of his werkes. And thanne she with gret deuocion resseiued the
state of weduhode. And whanne the dethe of her husbonde was
publisshed thorugh all Frise, sum of her husbondes meyne helde her
but a fole and a wastour of goodes and putte her ungoodli oute of the
heritage. And for that her wisdom were more clere and that she might 175
be sure of the pouerte that she had longe desired, she went her be
night into a pore manys hous and leide herself in a place there as
hogges lay, and she yaue thankinges to God with all her hert. And atte
Mateins tyme she went to the hous of Frere Menours and praied hem
that thei wolde thanke God for her tribulacion. And the day foluyng 180
she herself come with her litell children to the place and the hous of
her enemy, and thanne he deliuered to her a streite place to duell inne.
And whanne she sawe that she was hougely greued with her hoste an
ostesse, she gret and kissed the walles and saide: 'Y wolde faine take
my leue of men but y finde none.' And so constreined by necessite she 185
sent her yonge children here and there for to norisshe in divers places
and returned her to her furst place. And as she went there ther was a
streite way wher | men passed upon stones and the myre was right foul f. 271ᵛᵇ
and depe vnder and all aboute, and as she passid she mette with an
olde woman to whom she had do moche good before, that wolde yeue 190
her no wey but shoued her in the myre, and sche felle downe in the
dippest of the myre, and thanne as she might she arose and wiped her
clothes and lough.

In a tyme as she was besily praied of religious persones for to go

161 personely] personabli D   entende] ettende E   165 all²] and D   169 true]
om. D   170 oure Lorde] allemyghti D   174 of¹] add mennes D   175 And for]
tille D   178 atte] ins. H1   181 litell] om. D   183 hougely] ho'u'gely H1
187 her¹] add ayenne D   188 streite way] strete D   upon] ouer D   194 was] ins.
H1   praied] praienge D

195 into her cloistre and she went withoute lycence of her confessour and
whanne she come home ayen he made her to be bete so cruelly that
thre wekes after the traces apered. She was of so gret humilite that she
wolde not in no wise suffre that her chaumbreres called her ladi but
that thei shulde speke to her as to the lest and lowest in her hous. She
200 wold sumtyme wasshe the disshes and the vessell of the kichin and
wolde hide her that her chaumbreres shuld not lette her, and she
wolde saye: 'Yef y coude haue yfounde a more dispisable lyff y wolde
haue chose it.' She chase the beter partie as Mari dede. She helde
special grace in shedinge of teres and for to see heuenly visiones and
205 for to enflaume other to the loue of God.

In a day of Lent as she was in the chirche, she beheld towarde the
auuter ententifly right as her mynde hadde be rauisshed, and in that
tyme she was comforted and replenysshed with diuine reuelacion.
And thanne she retorned to her hous and prophesied of herself that
210 she shulde see Ihesu Crist in heuene and anone [as] she was leide
downe for febilnesse in her womannes lappe, she beganne to loke up
f. 272ra to hevenwarde and she fell into so gret | a ioye that she beganne to
laugh right hertely. And whanne she hadd endured in this gladnesse a
gret while she was sodenly chaunged into wepinge. And thanne ayen
215 she loked into heuene and anone she was turned into her furst ioye,
and whanne she closed her eyen she beganne to wepe, and she ledde
this lyff into Cumplyn tyme and abode in diuyne uisiones. And
thanne she helde her pees awhile, and afterwarde she saide: 'A Lorde,
wilt thou be with me and y with the? Lorde, y will neuer parte from
220 the.' Thanne after that her chaumbreres asked her whi she hadd so
laughed and wepte, and she saide: 'Y sawe the heuene opin and my
Lord Ihesu Crist that enclined hym towarde me, and y was of that
auysion gladde and wepte f[or] the departing, and he saide: "Yef thou
wilt be with me, y shall be with the," and y ansuered as ye herde.'
225 Her orison was of so gret uertu that she drow other to good, as it
apperithe bi a yonge man, the whiche she called to her and saide:
'Thou liuest a dissol[u]te lyff, wilt thou that y praie for the to God?'
And he saide: 'Y w[old] full gladly,' and required her therof. And
thanne she went to orison and the yonge man praied also for hymself,
230 and withinne a while the yonge man beganne to crye: 'Cesithe, good

199 and] or the D   202 coude] myght D   dispisable] deceiuable D   203 She
chase] se del. 'chase' HI   204 to] ins. HI   210 as] om. EHI   214 ayen] om. D
216 wepe] wype HI   219 Lorde] om. D   221 opin] om. D   223 auysion] vision
right D   for] from EHI   225 good] god HI   227 dissolute] dissolate E, desolate
HI   228 wold] will E   and¹] add y EHI   230 Cesithe] add þe HI

ladi, cesithe.' But she praied continuelly more feruently, and he beganne to crie: 'Cesithe, ladi, for y beg[y]nne to faile, so y brenne.' And he was take with so grete an hete that he swette and smoked and caste his clothes fro hym as a mad man, and threwe his armes abrode as he hadde be oute of hymselff so that men ranne to hym and halpe to 235 dispoile hym, and the hete that come fro hym was so grete that unnethe thei might endure to touche | hym. And [whanne Seint f. 272rb Elizabeth hadde ended her praier, he] ganne to aswage and came ayen to hymselff and entered into the ordre of Frere Menours.

After this an abbas that was of her kyn had compassion of her 240 pouerte and ledde her to a bisshop that was her vncle, the whiche resseiued her with gret ioye purposing fully for to wedde her ayen, the whiche purpos a gentill woman of hers herde that hadd auowed chastite with her. And with gret sorw and wepinge she tolde hit her ladi Seint Elizabeth, the whiche comforted her and saide: 'Trustithe 245 in oure Lorde, for loue of whom y haue auowed perpetuel chastite, and he will kepe my purpos and dissolue all mannys counsaile. And though my vncle will profer me mariage, y shalle discent with my sowle and ayensaie hym with my worde. And yef y see none other remedie, y shall cutte of myn owne nose and make myselff so 250 defourmed that eueri man shall haue abhominacion of me.' And as she was ayenst her wyll sent to a castell bi the bisshopp her uncle, there to abide till he hadde purueied for a mariage for her, she with wepinge teres recomaunded her chastite to God.

In this mene tyme bi the ordenaunce of God the bones of her 255 husbonde were brought from biyende the see, and anone the bisshoppe sent for her for to mete deuoutely with hem. Thanne the bisshop and she resseiued these bones with solempne procession and grete deuo- cion and sheding of teres, and thanne she turned her to God and saide: 'Y yelde the thankinges, my Lorde God, that thou wolt fouchesauf for 260 to comfort me thi wreched creatoure with the bones of my dere husbond. Thou knowest, Lorde, that yef | y loued the, and yet for f. 272va thi loue y forsoke his presence gladly and stered hym for to go to the holy londe. And though it hadde be delectable to me for to haue lyued

231 But] add euer D   232 beganne to crie] cried ayenne D   begynne] beganne
EHiL   234 his] om. Hi   235–6 halpe . . . hym¹] dispoilid hym out of his cloþis D
237 to] om. Hi   237–8 whanne . . . he] L, om. EHi, then it D   240 had] add grete
Hi   244 hit] add to HiD   247 he] om. D   purpos . . . mannys] om. Hi
248 discent] dissende D   249 and] om. Hi   250 so] om. D   252 bi] to Hi
256 anone] add And del. Hi   259–60 saide . . . the] yeldid D   260 my] to our D
262 yef] om. D   264 to me for] om. D

265 with hym [with such condicion to haue go abeggid with hym] in the
porest wise thorugh the worlde, yet y take witnesse of the that y wolde
not ayenst thi will beye hym ayen with the lest here of myn hede, nor y
wolde not calle hym ayen to be a dedly man. And therfor, Lorde, bothe
hym and me y recomaunde fully to thi grace.'

270   And thanne, for she wold not lese the fruit of an hundredfold the
whiche is youe to hem that kepe the perfeccion of the gospell, she
toke the clothinge of religion, the whiche she chase to be rude and
foul and abiecte, kepinge perpetuel chastite after the dethe of her
husbonde, beclippinge perfit obedience and wilfull pouerte. Her abit
275 was despisable, her mantell of the foulest gret russet, and her gowne
of another vile coloure, her sleuis toren and clowted with olde
clothe.

Her fader that was kinge of Hungri [herde] how that his doughter
was falle in so gret mischef and nede. He sent an erle to her for to
280 bringe her home to hym into her owne cuntre, and whanne he come
there as she was he founde her sittinge mekely in this most symple
array spynninge, the whiche for shame and confusion and houge
wonderinge cried and saide: 'Alas, ho sawe euer a kingges doughter
sitte in so vile an abite and do so foule an ocupacion as for to spinne
285 wolle?' And as he laboured with all his power for to haue brought her
to her fader she wolde in no wise consent therto, seinge that she hadde
leuer lyue in uerrey pouerte thanne for to abounde in all the richesse
f. 272vb of | the worlde. And that her soule might al passe to God and none
impediment be to her deuocion, she praied to God that he wolde putte
290 in her herte dispisinge of all temporall thinges and withdrawe her
herte from the loue of her children, and that she might with sadde and
stable herte be content with all tribulacion and afflixiones. And
whanne she hadde made her praiers, she saide to her seruauntes:
'Oure Lorde hathe herde my praier, for y acount all temporall thinges
295 but as felthe and myre, and y loue no more myn owne children thanne

265 with² . . . hym] *so with* abeggid/with hym *trs.* H1, *om.* E   266 yet] þat H1
267 beye] be with D   270 for] whan D   not] *ins.* H1   hundredfold] hundred folke tho
with k *subp.* `d´ H1   274 beclippinge] bi clippinge D   275 the foulest] foule D
278 herde] seie EH1   279 mischef] pouerte D   280 owne] *om.* H1   281 as she
was he founde her] she was founde H1   sittinge] *add* there H1, she sate D   282 array]
add that myght be D   the whiche] Than the Erle seynge hir in this araie D   houge]
ho'u´ge H1   285 as he] than this Erle D   286 fader] *add* but D   288 al]
oonelie D   289 impediment] *add* myght D   deuocion] *add* and so the erle went home
ayenne daielesse. Also D   290 in] *ins.* H1   herte] *ins.* H1   her²] þe H1
291–2 with . . . herte] be sadde and stable in hert and that she myght D   295 as] al H1,
om. D   loue no] beleue 'noo´ *with* be *del.* H1

the children of other mennes, and y recke of no peyne ne repreef ne dispisinge, and now y fele that y desire nor loue nothing but God.'

Her confessour Maister Conraude wolde mani tymes put upon her heui and contrari berdonis, and that it semed that she loued most she wolde voide from her felawshipp so fertortheli that .ij. yonge men 300 right good and true that were norisshed with her of childehode, wherfor there was many a tere shedde on bothe sides. But this he dede to breke her wille and that she shulde dresse all her affecciones to God, and that none of her seruauntes shulde bringe ayen to her mynde her furst worldely glorie that she hadde be inne. In all these 305 thinges she was founde gladde and obedient and sad and pacient that she might possede her soule in pacience and be made faire with the uictorie of obedience. And ofte tymes she wold saie: 'Yef y drede a dedly man thus moche for the loue of God, how moche am y bounde to drede God the heuenli iuge, and therfor y haue chose to be 310 obedient to a pore begger, my maister Conrade, [and] lefte riche bisshoppes, that therby y might kitte utterly | from me all comfortes of f. 273ʳᵃ temporall thinges.'

She was continuelly ocupied in the werkes of merci. There was deliuered to her .v. hundred marke for her dower, wherof she 315 departed half to the pore and with that other half she made an hospitale. And for that cause she was called a wastour of goodes and all thei called her fole and leude, and she humbly and gladly suffered all these iniuries and tribulaciones. And whanne the hospitall was made, she ordeined herself in her owne persone for to be seruaunt to 320 all the pore folke in the hospitall. And she bare her so humbely and so mekely in this seruise that she wolde bi night bere the sike bodies to her priuies for to ese hem and bere hem ayen to her beddis. She wisshe her clothes and clensed hem from all filth and vermyn. She hadde lepres and kepte hem and wisshe hem and wiped her woundes, 325 and she dede in her propre persone all that longed to hospitalite.

And whanne she had no pore folke, thanne she wolde spynne wolle that was sent her from an abbey that was there ny and yeue the pris therof to the pore. And thanne whanne she hadd thus longe tyme

297 nor . . . God] more loue of God than of any othir thinge D   298 confessour] add was D   Conraude] add that D   wolde] add put D   her] add many D   299 it] she D 302 he] Conrade D   309 moche¹] om. D   the] so with h on erasure H1   311 and] hathe EH1   314 was¹] add also D   merci] add For D   315 her¹] add atte a time D dower] duree D   317 And] om. H1   320 owne] add propur D   322–3 the sike . . . bere] ins. H1   322 bodies] bodie`s´ D        323 beddis] add Also D        325 wiped] add hem and D        326 propre] owne D        327 wolle] add `þat´ D   329 to] `to´ D

330 abidde in gret pouerte she resseiued other .v. hundred marke for her
dowri, the whiche she departed ordinatly to the pore. And thanne she
lete make an ordenaunce that hosoeuer remeued of his place in
preiudice of other whanne she yaue her almes, that her here shulde
be cutte of. So that bi fortune there come a maide that hight
335 Radegunde, whiche maide had a wonder faire here. She passed
therbi not for to haue almesse but for to uisite her suster that was
f. 273rb sike. And thanne she was brought to Seint | Elizabeth as a trespasour
of the ordenaunce, and she comaunded anone that she shulde cutte of
her here, and the maide wepte and ayensaide [it] as moche as she
340 might. And as a man that was there saide that she was innocent, Seint
Elizabeth saide: 'Atte the hardest, she shall not [a] good while go to no
caroles for to shewe her here.' And thanne Seint Elizabeth asked her
whedir euer she hadd purpos to the lyff of hele, and she ansuered that
yef the loue of her here hadde not bene she hadd a grete while gone
345 take the abite of religion. And thanne saide Seint Elizabeth: 'Hit is
leuer to me that thou hast loste thin here thanne my sone were made
emperoure.' And anone the mayde toke the habite of religion.

Whanne the tyme neighed that God had ordeined that she that
hadd despised the dedely kingdom shulde haue the kingdom of
350 aungeles, she leide her downe in her bedde and turned towarde the
walle. And tho that were there behelde her, and thanne ther was herd
a suete melodye comyng fro her, and one of her chaumbreres asked
her what it was, and she answered and saide: 'Ther come a bridde
betwene me and the walle, and he sange so suetly that he meued me to
355 singe also.' And in that siknesse she was euer gladde and in orison.
The last day of her passinge she asked of her women: 'What wolde ye
do and the fende come?' And anone she began to cry thre tymes:
'Flee, flee, flee,' as she had chased the fende from her. And thanne she
saide: 'Midnight neighe[th] in whiche tyme my lorde Ihesu Crist was
360 bore. Hit is tyme that my Lorde God call hys frendes to his
f. 273va weddinge.' Thanne oure Lorde Ihesu Crist | apered to her saieng:
'Come, my beloued and entre into the tabernacle of thi Lorde God.'

331 the whiche] *om.* D   332 ordenaunce] *add* amonge the pore folk D
333 yaue] ȝaue *with* ȝ *on erasure* H1   338 anone] *om.* D   339 ayensaide]
withseide D   it] her EH1   340 that was] *om.* D   341 a] *om.* E   345 of] *add* þe
H1   347 anone] than D   348 tyme] *add* come and D   neighed] neʼyʼghed H1
349 shulde . . . kingdom²] *om.* H1   353 answered and] *om.* D   bridde] *add* that come E
354 meued] made D   355 also] with hym D   356 passinge] *add* hens D
357 And] *om. and end sentence at* anone H1   358 flee²] *om.* H1   359 neigheth]
neighed EH1   360 God] Ihesu criste D   362 beloued] welbeloued D

And in this wise she slepte in oure Lorde the yere of oure Lorde .M^l.CC.xxvj. And thanne the grettest multitude of briddes were sayne upon the chirche that euer were seyne, and thei beganne so suetly to 365 singe that the melodie was so gret that no herte might thenke it, and it semed that thei were come for to do the seruice of her. And thanne her bodi was leyd .iiij. dayes on the erthe or she were beried, and she was euer full of suetnesse and no corrupcion neighed her. And thanne her body was leyd in a monument that anone after welled oyle, and thanne 370 ther fell many faire miracles [at her tombe after her dethe].

In the parties of the diocise of Saxonie ther was a monke that hight Hemer, and he was falle in so gret a siknesse that he cried and wold suffre no creatoure to haue reste aboute hym. And in a night there apered to hym a worshipfull[e] ladi clothed in white that bade hym 375 that he shulde auowe [hym] to Seint Elizabeth yef he wolde haue hele. And the night foluinge she apered ayen. And thanne bi the counsaile of his abbot he made there a uowe. The thridde night she apered to hym and made a crosse upon his shuldre and he resseiued perfit hele. And whan the abbot and the prioure come to hym thei hadde gret 380 meruaile and thei dredde gretly of the fulfellyng of this uowe. And the prioure saide that often tymes under the lyknesse of good there come illusiones of the enemy, and counsailed hym to be confessed of his auowe. And the night foluyng | that same persone apered to hym and f. 273vb saide: 'Thou shalt alwey be sike till thou haue performed thin avoue.' 385 And anone his siknesse toke hym. And than bi the licence of his abbot he fulfelled his auowe and was anone perfitely hole.

A maide asked drinke of her seruaunt, and she toke her drinke and saide: 'The deuel mot thou drinke.' And she dranke, and her thought that brennyng fire entered into her body, and she sualle as grete as a 390 barell so that eueribodi might see that she was demoniak. And .ij. yere she was in this astate, and thanne she was ledde to the tombe of Seint Elizabeth and had there full hele.

Herman, a man of the diocise of Tholose was holde in prison, and he with gret deuocion praied and called to Seint Elizabeth for to be his 395 helpe. And the night foluing she apered to hym and comforted hym gretly, and in the morw sentence was youe ayenst hym so that he was

363 in^1] om. H1D   Lorde^1] add in D   365 seyne] add bifore D   and] add than H1
368 .iiij.] three D   369 neighed] noyed H1   370 welled] add out D   371 at . . .
dethe] om. E   375 worshipfulle] worshipfully E   376 hym] om. E   378 apered]
add ayenne D   383 enemy] add þe feende D   386 hym] add ayenne D   388 A]
decorated O H1   seruaunt] seruauntis D   she] thei D   393 full] parfite D
394 Herman] om. D   man] add that was D

hanged. And th[anne] the iuge gaue leue to his kinrede to take hym downe, and thei bare hym dede and praied to Seint Elizabeth, and he
400 arose fro dethe to lyue [anone] before hem all.

A childe was falle into a well and drowned, and anone one come to drawe water and fonde hym dede and drow hym oute. And thanne he auowed hym to Seint Elizabeth and he was restored to his furst hele.

Also another mayde drowned in a water. She was yolde ayen to lyf
405 bi her merites.

Frederik that was a cunnyng man in the crafte of suymming bathed
f. 274ʳᵃ hym in a water and scorned a pore man that Seint Elizabeth | hadde youe sight to. And thanne the pore man saide: 'That holy lady that hathe do me grace wol venge me on the so that thou shalt neuer come
410 thennis on lyue.' And anone he lost his strengthe and might not helpe hymself, but sanke downe to the botum of the water as a stone and was drowned and drawen oute dede. And thanne sum of his neigheboures auowed hym to Seint Elizabeth and she yelde hym ayen to lyff.

Theodorik a man was greuously sike in his knees and in his thies so
415 that he might not goo, and thanne he auowed that he wolde seke the toumbe of Seint Elizabeth, and he made .viij. dayes iourney thedirward. And thanne he was there a monthe and fonde no remedye and went ayen to his hous. And thanne hym thought in his slepe that a man sprenged water upon hym, and he awoke and was all angry and
420 saide: 'Whi hast thou cast water upon me?' 'Y haue,' he saide, 'wette the, and leue wele this wetynge shall be thi profit.' And thanne he arose al hole and gaue thankingges to God and to Seint Elizabeth.

Here endithe the lyff of Seint Elizabeth the kinges doughter of Hungri, and nexst beginnithe the lyff of Seint Cecile, Capitulum .C.lxij.

Seint Cecile the glorious uirgine was of the noble kinrede of Rome, and fro her cradell she was norisshed [in] the faithe of Ihesu Crist, and she bare alwey the gospell of oure Lorde hidde withinne her herte, ne

398 thanne] thow E, though H1   400 anone] *om.* E   401 anone] *om.* D
402 hym¹] the childe D   oute] vp D   403 restored] *add* ayenne D   404 mayde]
add was D   a] *om.* H1   406 Frederik] Fˊrˊederik H1, Foderik D   412 oute] up H2
413 Elizabeth] *add* and . . . thedirward *misplaced from* 416–17 EH1H2   she] *om.* H2
416–17 and . . . thedirward] *misplaced in* 402 *above* EH1H2   419 all] fulle H2
420 me] *add* And EH1   Y haue/he saide] *trs.* H1   421 thi profit] profit to the H1H2

2 EH1H2; D resumes at 108 (*And*) *his breste* and writes *Palmachien* for *Almachien*
throughout.   1 glorious] nobul H2   2 in] at E   3 hidde] *om.* H2

she seced neuer night ne day for to worshipp ne for to praie to oure
Lorde, and her praier was specialli that oure Lorde wolde kepe her 5
uirginite. |

But atte the laste [her] frendes wolde nedes wedde her to a noble f. 274rb
yonge man that hight Valerian. And whanne the day of weddinge cam,
Seinte Cecile clothed [her with] the heire nexst her tendre flesshe, and
aboue that she arraied her with precious clothes of golde. And whanne 10
the instrumentes smeten she songe to oure Lorde and saide: 'Mi
blessed Lorde God, y beseche the that myn herte and myn bodi bi thi
grace may be kepte vndefouled and that y be not deceiued.' And she
dede faste .iij. dayes in recomaundinge her to oure Lorde.

And thanne come the night that she shulde entre into the chaumbre 15
with her spouse, and whan thei were togedre allone she aresoned hym
in this wise: 'O right suete and loucly yonge man, y knowe a counsaile
that y shulde tell you yef that ye wolde sucre to me not to discouer me,
but kepe it counsaile with al youre powere.' And thanne Valerian
suore that he wolde not discouer her for nothinge. Thanne saide she 20
to hym: 'I haue an aungel of God to my loue, and he kepithe my body
with so gret loue and tendernesse that yef he might fele ye wold
touche me bi ani vnordinat loue he wolde smite you in suche wise that
ye shulde lese the floure of youre age, and yef he knew that ye loued
me with pure loue he will loue you as wel as me and shewe you his 25
loue.'

And thanne Valerian, taught bi the will of oure Lorde, saide: 'Yef
ye will that y leue you, shewe me that aungell, and yef y may truly
knowe that he be an aungell y will do that ye require me.' To whom
Cecile ansuered and saide: 'Yef ye beleued in the verrey God and were 30
baptised ye might se hym, but while ye stonde | in this blindenesse ye f. 274va
may not, wherfor y shall sende you into the ile that is called Apyen,
the whiche is a myle from Rome, and ye shull saie to the pore men
that ye shull finde ther: "Cecily hathe sent me to you that ye shul
shewe me Vrban the holy man, for y haue a secrete counsaile to telle 35
hym fro her." And whanne ye see hym, tellithe hym al that y haue
tolde you, and doute you not but whanne ye shull be baptised of hym
ye shulle see the aungell that y haue tolde you of.'

4 ne^1] and H2   ne for] and H2   5 kepe] ins. H1   7 her^1] om. E   9 her with]
om. EH1   11 songe] seide H2   oure] add blessid H2   11–12 and . . . God] om. H2
18 to^1] ins. H1   me^1] add that ye wolde H2   19 but] and H1   it] add in H2
22 fele] add þat H1H2   23 ani] om. H2   27 oure Lorde] god H2   28 leue] loue
H2   32 ile] ins. H1   34 shull] shulde H1, om. H2   shul] shulde H2   37 but
whanne ye shull] whan that ye H2

And thanne went Valerian to the bisshopp Vrban that was hidde
40 withinne the sepulcres of dede men for drede of the gret persecucion
that was thanne ayenst the cristen religion, and tolde hym all the
wordes of Cecile. And whanne Vrban herde hym he helde up his
hondes to heuene and saide: 'O thou Lorde Ihesu Crist, the sower of
rightwis counsaile, resseiue the sede that thou hast sowed in thi yonge
45 servaunt Cecile. For, blessed Lorde Ihesu Crist, Cecile thi yonge
maide seruithe the as bee to the hony euer in encresinge, for her
husbonde that she toke as a lyon she hathe sent hym to me as
debonaire as a lambe.' And anone there apered betwene hem an
auncien man clothed al in white clothes that held a boke in his honde
50 wretin with letteres of golde. And whanne Valerian sawe hym he fell
downe for drede as dede, and anone this auncien man lefte hym up
and redde to hym that that was wrete in the boke aforesaid, whiche
sentence was thus: 'O God, o bileue, one bapteme, one is God and
fader of all and is aboue all and in us all.' And whanne he hadde redde
55 thus he saide to Valerian: 'Leuist thou that this is true, or doutest thou
f. 274vb   yet?' And Valerian ansuered: 'Ther is nothinge | vnder heuene so wel
to beleue.' And anone he vanisshed awaye, and thanne Valerian
resseiued bapteme of Seint Vrban.

And whanne he hadd done he turned ayen and fonde Seint Cecile
60 in her chaumbre spekinge with the aungel, and the aungel helde in his
honde .ij. crownes of roses and of lelies. And whanne Valeryan sawe
the aungel he fell ayen downe for drede, and the aungell benigly toke
hym up and said: 'Valeryan, for thou hast goodly leued the profitable
counsaile of thi wiff, oure Lorde hathe sent the here one of these .ij.
65 crownes for to be of sewte of thi wiff. Wherfor loke thou kepe these
crownes with herte and body withoute defoulynge, for y haue brought
hem to you from paradys bi the comaundement of almighti God, ne
thei shull neuer fade ne neuer lese her odour, ne thei mowe not be saie
of none but yef thei haue charite. And, Valeryan, for thi mekenesse
70 oure Lorde hathe comaunded me to saie to the that loke what thou
desirest of hym he wille graunte the.' And thanne Valerian with
souerayne gladnesse saide: 'Worship and ioye be to oure souerayne

45 for . . . Cecile] *om.* H2   thi] þe H1   46 as] *add* a H1H2   47 lyon] H2
punctuates after lyon   she²] And she H2   48 debonaire as a] a debonaire H1, `a´
debonair H2   49 clothes] cloþing H1   51 lefte] toke H2   52 that²] *om.* H2
53 thus] this H2   54 is] *om.* H2   59 Seint] *om.* H2   60 the aungel²] he H2
61 Valeryan] Valerie *changed to* Valerian H1   62 toke] kept H1, tokoke H2
63 leued] loued H1   64 here] *om.* H1   67 ne] that H2   67–8 ne thei shull]
twice E   69 haue] had H1   70 me] *om.* H1

Lorde of his gret merci done to me, wherfor ye[f] it like his high
goodnesse to do me suche grace y wolde beseche hym to shewe his
gret merci to a brother of myn that he might come oute of his 75
blyndenesse and see the clere wey of trouthe.' The aungel ansuered
and saide: 'It likethe to oure Lorde that ye haue required, wherfor ye
shull bothe come to hym bi the peyne of marterdom.'

After this Tyburcyan, brother of Valerian, entered into the
chaumbre of his brother, and as he entered he felt a gret sauour of 80
suetnesse of roses that he was al astonied and saide: 'I meruayle gretly
that y fele in this tyme suche sauour | of roses and lelyes, for though f. 275ʳᵃ
myn hondes were full y might not fele so gret a sauour of suetnesse as
y do. Truly, my dere brother and suster, y knowlache to you that y
fele me so refresshed with this suetnesse that y am sodenly alterat and 85
chaunged.' To whom Valerian saide: 'Dere brother, we haue crownes
that thin eyen mow not see of coloures of roses and of lelyes, and right
as thou felist the sauour and maist not see hem, thou shalt see hem
and thou wilt beleue.' Than Tyburcien saide: 'Is this a dreme that y
here, or is this true that thou saiest, Valerian?' And Valerian saide: 90
'We haue be into this tyme in a dreme, but we be now in the verrei
trouthe.' And thanne Tiburcien saide: 'Where hast thou lerned thus,
brother?' And Valerian saide: 'The aungel of God hathe taught me,
the whiche thou might see with thine eyen yef thou were purified and
haddest clene forsake all the ydoles.' 95

This same myracle of crownes of roses witnessithe Seint Ambrose
in his Preface and saithe: 'Cecile was so utterly fulfelled with the yefte
of the holy gost that she despised the worlde and toke upon her the
peyne of marterdom, and of that is witnesse the confession of Valery
her husbond and of Tyburcian his brother, the whiche [oure Lorde] 100
crowned bi the honde of the aungel with the smellyng floures. And the
virgine led these men to ioye, and the world might clerely perceiue
how myche the deuocion of chastite is worthe.' These be the wordes
of Seint Ambrose.

Thanne Seint Cecile shewed hem clerely that all the ydoles were 105

73 of] for H1   yef] yet E   80 a gret] so grete a H1H2   81 roses] *add* and of
lilies H2   82 tyme] *add* of the yere H2   84 suster] *add* wherfor H2   85 alterat]
al torent H1   86 saide] *add* my H2   brother . . . haue] *om.* H2   we haue] *trs. and
marked for reversal* H1   88 thou . . . hem] *ins.* H1   89 beleue] *add* in Ihesu Criste H2
90 is this] it is H2   91 in] but H2   92 thus] þis H1   99 Valery] Valeri'an' H1,
so H2   100 oure Lorde] were E   101 the²] an H1   smellyng] *add* of H2   And] *add*
Cecile H2   102 and] wherfor H2   might clerely] may H2   103 the¹] clere is H2
is worthe] *om.* H2   105 hem] Tiburcien H2

defe and doume and withoute any wyt. Thanne ansuered Tyburcien:
f. 275ʳᵇ 'Truly ho so leuithe not that ye saie is wors | thanne an vnresonable
beest.' Cecile hering hym with gret ioye she kissed his breste and
saide: 'This day y knowlage the to my brother, for right as the loue of
110 God hathe ioyned to me thi brother, right so the forsaking of ydoles
hathe made me thi cosin. Go now, my dere brother, with thi brother
for to resseiue purificacion so that thou may see the uisage of
aungeles.' And thanne saide Tiburcian to his brother: 'I praie you,
tell me to whom ye will lede me.' And Valerian saide: 'To the
115 bisshopp Vrban.' And Tyburcian saide: 'Is that Vrban that so mani
tymes hathe be condempned, the whiche is hidde in priue places and
yef he might be founde shulde be brent, and we with hym yef it were
knowe that we went to hym? And thus whan we shull seke the
dyvinite that is hydde in heuene we shul[l]e renne in the brennyng
120 wodenesse of tyrauntes here in erthe.' Thanne saide Seint Cecile: 'Yef
there were no mo lyues but this one, bi reson we shuld drede to lese
hit, but there ys a beter lyff that may not be [loste], the whiche the
sone of God hathe tolde us. For all the thinges that be made the sone
engendered of the fader made, and all thinges made the holy gost
125 comithe from the fader and quickenithe. And this same sone of God
techithe us that there is another lyff.'

Thanne saide Tyburcian: 'Truly this is a gret meruaile to me that
ye aferme o God to be, and now ye shewe us to be thre goddis.' Cecile
ansuered and saide: 'Right as in the wisdom of one man be thre
130 thinges, that is cunynge, mynde and vnderstondinge, right so in one
f. 275ᵛᵃ being of diuinite bene thre persones.' And | thanne she beganne to
preche of the comynge of the sone of God into this worlde, of his most
blessed lyvinge, and of hys peinfull passion. For she saide that
Goddes sone suffered for to be take and bounde that mannes soule,
135 whiche was [holde] and bounde in synne, might go atte large; he that
was most blessed suffered to be cursed for that cursed man shulde
resseiue blessinge; he suffered to be dispised [for to bringe men] oute
of the despite of the fende; he suffered his precious hede to be

106 any] *om.* H2   ansuered] *om.* H1   Tyburcien] *add* 'seid' H1   108 she] *om.* H2
kissed] *add* hym and H2   111 with thi brother] *om.* H1   112 may] myght D
113 aungeles] the aungelle D   114 the] *add* holy EH1   117 founde] *add* he H1D
it] we D   118 we shull] he shuld H1   119 shulle] shulde EH1   in] into D
121 one] allone D   122 loste] lefte EH1   123 the thinges that] these D
128 ye¹] þe H1   130–1 one being] obeyng H1   132 comynge] konnyng *with last*
minim of 'nn *erased* H1   134 soule] *add* the H1   135 holde] take E   137 for . . .
men] *om.* E   138 the¹] *om.* H1

crowned with sharpe thornes for to deliuer man fro the capitall
sentence of dampnacion; he resseiued bitter galle for he wolde restore 140
man to his suete taste; he was dispoiled for he wolde keuer oure
nakidnesse of oure furst fader; he was hanged on a crosse for that he
wolde take awey the trespas and the outrage of the tree of lyff.
Whanne Tyburcien herde all this he saide to his brother: 'A, my dere
brother, haue pitee of me and bringe me to that blessed man so that y 145
may resseiue purificacion.' And than Valerian ledde hym to Vrban,
and whanne he was baptised he sawe often tymes the aungel of God
and hadde of hym anone what he desired.

And thanne Tyburcian and Valerian departed for the loue of God
her goodes to pore men largely, and beryed the holy bodies that 150
Almachien the prouost slow for cristen faithe. And whanne this
tyraunt perceiued that, he lete call hem before hym and asked hem
ho made hem so hardy to bery the bodyes that be dampned to the
dethe for her felonyes. And Tyburcien ansuered: 'My will were that
we were seruauntes to hem that thou set|tist so litell by, for thei haue f. 275ᵛᵇ
dispised that that semithe to be and is not, and haue founde that that 156
is not sayne to be and is.' The provost saide: 'What thinge is that?'
And Tyburcian saide: 'That that is sayn to be and is not, is all that that
is in this worlde that bringithe men to no beinge, and that that is not
sayne to be and is, ys the lyf of rightwysse men, whiche is euerlastinge 160
ioye.' Than saide the prouost to Tyburcian: 'I trow thou saiest not
thus in irnest or elles thou art not well with thiselff.'

And thanne he comaunded Valerian to come before hym and saide
to hym: 'Valerian, y suppose that thi brother is not well with hymself,
and therfor thou must ansuere more wisely.' Thanne saide Valerian: 165
'It semithe to me that ye be to gret folis that refusen the ioyes and
coueiten peynes. For y haue sayne in tyme of gret frostes children and
ydell folke renne and plaie upon the yse and scorned workemen and
laboreres, but whanne somer come that the glorious fruit were ripe,
thanne the laboreres reioysed hem and tho that scorned hem wepte, 170
and so fare ye now. Ye laughe and scornen us for we suffre
tribulacions and laboures, but in tyme to come whanne ye shull
weyle and sorw we shull haue for oure mede euerlastinge ioye.'
Thanne saide the prouost: 'What, wenist thou that we noble princes

175 shull hauc cuerlasting wepinges and ye vile persones perpetuel ioye?'
And Valerian saide: 'Ye be men and not princes, born in youre tyme
for to deye hastely and shull yelde acountes to God more thanne any
other of lower degre.'

f. 276ʳᵃ   Than saide the prouost: 'Wherto tarie we so longe | in wordes?
180 Offerithe sacrifices to [oure] goddes and gothe quite.' And the seintes
ansuered: 'We yeue eueri day sacrifice to almighti God.' And the
prouost saide: 'What is his name?' And Valerian saide: 'Thou might
not serue his name though thou might fle with wynges.' And the
provost saide: 'Is not Iubiter the name of a god?' And Valerian saide:
185 'That is the name of a mansleer and of a vowtrere.' Thanne saide the
tyraunt: 'And this were trwe, than were all the worlde blinde and thou
and thi brother shulde only knowe the trouthe.' To whom Valerian
saide: 'We be not allone, for gret multitude of men withoute noumbre
haue receiued this holynesse.'

190   And thanne were these seintes putte in prison in the kepinge of
Maximyan, to whiche he saide: 'O beauute of youthe, whi haste ye
thus faste to youre dethe that go therto with as good will as though ye
were bode to a feste.' To whom Valeryan saide: 'Yef thou wylt behight
vs that thou wilt beleue in God, thou shalt see us after oure dethe.'
195 And Maximyan saide to hem: 'Yef it be true that ye saie, y shall
confesse hym only God that is of suche power.' And thanne
Maximian and all his housholde beleued in God and were baptised
of Seint Vrban that come thedir priuely.

    And whanne the dawnynge of the day apered, Seint Cecile come to
200 the prison to comfort hem and cried with a lowde voice to hem and
saide: 'Ye knightes of Ihesu Crist, puttithe aweye the werkys of
derkenesse and clothe you with the armes of light.' And than the
seintes were ledde .iiij. myle from the citee to the ydole of Iubiter, and
f. 276ʳᵇ   whanne thei wolde in no wise do sacrifice thei were beheded | in the
205 same place. And Maximian swore truly that whanne these holi seintes
were martered he sawe a gret multitude of aungeles about hem and
her sowles go oute of her bodyes as faire virgines oute of her
chaumbres, and the aungeles beringe hem up to heuene. And whan

---

175 perpetuel] euerlastinge D   177 shull] shuld Hı   thanne] add to Hı
179 the prouost] þei Hı   180 to oure goddes] to goddes E, om. Hı   183 serue]
disserne D   185 a vowtrere] one word E   187 shulde] shul nat D   192 good]
add a Hı   193 a] add grete D   195 hem] hym D   199 dawnynge] drawing
Hı   200 to comfort] and comfortid D   201 Ye] The Hı   203 from . . . to]
thens to a cite where D   Iubiter] add was D   204 were] add anone D   207 go]
om. Hı

Almachie[n] herde that Maximian was cristen, he made hym to be
bete with scourges knotted with lede so longe till he gaue up the 210
sperit.

And than Almachien toke all her goodes and sent for Cecile as for
the wyff of Valerian, that she shulde come and do sacrifice or elles
resseiue sentence of dethe. And whanne she herde this message she
armed her gladli with the signe of the crosse and recomaunded her 215
holy to her souerayne Lord Ihesu. And whanne the peple and her
seruauntes sawe that so noble and so faire a mayde putte herself frely
to the dethe, thei wepte and cried that it was pite to here. To whom
Cecile saide: 'O ye yonge peple, bethe of good comfort, for y le[s]e not
my youthe but y chaunge it into betir; y yeue myrre and receyue 220
golde; I leue a foule habite and receyue a precious clothinge; y yeue a
litell corner and y receiue a large and a right [cler] place. O good lord,
yef any man wolde yeue shillynges for a peny, how ye wolde high you
fast thedirward. Whi take ye none hede, thanne, how oure blessed
Lorde takithe a symple thinge and yeuithe an hundred folde? Leue ye 225
not this that y saie?' And thei ansuered: 'We beleue it, and also we
bileue verrily that Ihesu Crist is verrey God that hathe suche a
servaunt.' And thanne Cecile sent priuely for Vrban, | and there were f. 276ᵛᵃ
baptised atte that tyme .iiijC. and mo.

And thanne the tyraunt Almachien called Seint Cecile to hym and 230
saide to her: 'Of what condicion art thou?' And she ansuered and
saide: 'Y am of noble kinrede.' And Almachien saide: 'Y aske the of
what religion?' And Cecile saide: 'Thi demaunde hathe a lewde
begynnynge that wenist y conclude .ij. ansueres vnder one
demaunde.' And Almachien saide: 'Fro whennes comithe to the this 235
gret [presumpcion to ansuere me in suche wise?' And she saide: 'Of
verrei] conscience and of stedfast faithe.' Thanne Almachien saide:
'Wost thou not of what might y am?' And Cecile saide: 'Yes, full well,
for youre might is in your bely that is full of wynde, and yef it were
pricked a litell with a nedill, all youre might wolde sone fade.' 'What,' 240
saide Almachien, 'Thou begannest with iniuries and so thou perseuerist.' Cecile saide: 'Iniurie is not saide but bi deceiuable wordes.

209 Almachien] Almachiel E   210 knotted] knokked H₁   gaue] yeldid D
212 Almachien] the Prouest D   as for] *om.* D   219 lese] leve, E, beleue H₁, leefe D
(*pers* P2)   220 into] *add* þe H₁   222 y] *om.* H₁D   a¹] *om.* H₁   cler] gret E
223 wolde¹] wille D   224 blessed] *om.* H₁   226 ansuered] *add* and seiden D
232 Almachien] than the Provest D   236–7 presumpcion . . . verrei] *om.* EH₁D
237 Almachien] the Proueste D   238 Cecile] *add* answerid and D   Yes] þes H₁
239 for] *om.* D   240 a litell] *om.* D   241 begannest] biginnest D

Shew me the iniurie yef y haue spoke vtterly, or ellis amende thiselff
sayeng malice. For we that knowe the holi name of God mow not
245 denie hym, for it is moche beter to deye goodly thanne for to lyve
wickedly.' And Almachien saide: 'Whi spekest thou with so gret
pride?' She ansuered: 'As y tolde the ere, hit is no pride but sadnesse
of faithe.' Thanne Almachien saide: 'A, thou wreche, wost thou not
well that it is in my might for to yeue the lyff or dethe?' Cecile
250 ansuered: 'Y shall preue anone that thou hast made a gret lesinge
ayenst the comune trouthe, for thou mayst take awey the lyff of hem
that be quicke, but thou maist not yeue no lyff to hem that be dede,
and thanne art thou a ministre of dethe and not of lyff.' To whom
f. 276ᵛᵇ Almachien saide: | 'Holde thi tunge and do awey thi madnesse and
255 sacrifie to oure goddes.' And Cecile saide: 'Y trowe thou hast loste thi
sight, for tho that thou saiest be goddes we see all that thei be stones.
Putte forthe thin honde and fele but yef thou may see.'

Thanne Almachien, fulfelled with wodenesse, comaunded that she
shulde be ladde to his hous, and there al a night and al a day he made
260 her stonde in a bathe contynuelly boylinge. And she felt neuer disease
of hete but satte as fresshe as she had sitte in a medue of suete floures.
And whanne Almachien herde it he comaunded that she shulde be
biheded in the bathe. And the bocher smote .iij. strokes and might in
no wise smite of her hede, and for it was the custume that tho that
265 shulde be byheded shulde not haue the ferthe stroke, he lefte her there
half dede [and] all blody. And she ouerlyued .iij. dayes and gaue all
that she hadd to pore men, and all tho that she hadd conuerted to the
faithe she recomaunded to Seint Vrban, saieng: 'Y haue required the
space of .iij. dayes for to recomaunde hem to her blessednesse, and
270 also for that thou shalt sacre myn hous into a chirche.' And atte the
ende of .iij. dayes she offered up her blessed soule to the high blesse
of heuene, where it was resseiued with souerain worshipp and ioye
of al that blessed court. And Seint Vrban beried her body amonge
the bysshoppes and halowed her hous into a chirche as she hadde
275 praied hym. And she suffered dethe and fonde euerlastinge lyff about
the yere of oure Lorde .CC.xxiij. in the tyme of the emperour
Alysaundre.

243 haue] had Hi   246 Almachien] A'l'machian Hi   246–7 with . . . pride¹] so
proudelie D   247 She] And Cecile D   ansuered] add and seide D   250 ansuered]
seide D   252 not] om. Hi   257 and] om. Hi   260–1 disease of] om. D
261 fresshe] fresshly HiD   as²] add thou3 D   262 herde it] sawe þat D
264 custume] add þere D   265 he] but D   266 and¹] om. EHi   ouerlyued] livid
affter D   271 .iij. dayes] the thridde daie D   high] holi Hi   273 body] om. D

Here endithe the lyff of Seint Cecile, and nexst beginnithe
the lyff of Seint Clement, Capitulum .C.lxiij.^m

| Clement bisshopp was bore of noble kinrede of Romayns. His fader   f. 277ra
hight Faustin and his moder Melchiane. He hadd .ij. bretheren, of the
whiche that one hight Faustin and that other Faustinien. And so as
Machidiane his moder was of merueilous bewte of body, the brother
of her husbonde loued her vnordinatly. And as euery day he 5
turmented her bi continuel speking and with al the laboure that he
coude for to haue drawe her to his cursed entent, she wolde neuer
consent but rather haue deied thanne for to assent to so foul a dede.
And so she lyued in sorugh and gret trouble, and for to discouer this
malys to her husbonde she durst not for drede of debate betwene the 10
two bretheren.

And thanne she thought as for to eschewe these periles that it was
best to her to flee the contre till tyme that he hadde foryete his foule
and vnordinat loue that he hadd to her. And for she wolde haue leue
of her husbond therto she feyne[d] wilyli a dreme and saide: 'Hit was 15
shewed me tonight in a vision and comaunded me that y shulde go
oute of the citee of Rome with my .ij. sones gemelles Faustin and
Faustynien, and that y be oute into tyme that y be comaunded to come
home ayen, and but y do this y shall deye with my .ij. children.' And
whanne her husbonde herde this he dradde hym sore and anone sent 20
his wyff into Athenes and hys .ij. children with her with gret meyne
and goodes to gouerne her with. And the fader withhelde Clement hys
yongest sone with hym for to be his comfort, and he was that tyme .v.
yere olde.

And as the moder say|led thorugh the see with her .ij. children, in a f. 277rb
night the shippe tobracke by tempest and she was throwen into the see 26
amonge the wawes, till atte the last the wawes cast her up on a rocke,
and so she ascaped and went that her .ij. sones hadd be pershed and
sought hem as she coude and might. And whanne she coude not fynde
hem quicke ne dede she braied and cried as a woman oute of herselff 30
and wolde take no comfort of no creatoure. And thanne ther come to
her mani women for to comfort her tellyng her fortunes that thei hadd

EH1DH2A1A2L; D breaks off after 245 his   2 Faustin] `f'Austin H1   3 as]
om. D   4 his] her D   of body] so þat D   5 as] *om.* D   7 haue] *om.* D   entent]
add but D   8 consent] assent H1D   10 malys] *om.* D   15 feyned] feynes E
19 but] *add* if H1D   this] thus D   20 anone] *om.* D   21 his wyff] hir out D   hys]
hir D   27 till . . . wawes] and D   28 went] *add* vereli D   29 coude²] *twice* E
not] in no wise D   30 dede] ded`de' H1

resseiued, but in no wise she wolde recciue no comfort. And than
there come a woman amonge other and saide that she hadd loste her
35 husbonde in the see and for loue of hym she wolde neuer be maried,
so that sumwhat she comforted her and thei bothe togederes gate her
lyflode with laboure of her hondes. But withinne a while her hondes
fell in suche a plight that she might not werke, and that woman that
hadd herborued her fell in a palasie that she might not come oute of
40 her bedde. And thanne was Machidiane constreined for to gete hem
lyvinge bi begging, and in this wise she fonde her ostesse.

And whan the yeer was passed after that she was gone oute of the
cuntre with her .ij. children, [her husbond] sent messengeres to
Athenes to here how thei ferde, but he that he sent returned no
45 more ayen. Thanne he sent other messengers that retourneden and
saide that thei hadd founde nothinge. And thanne he lefte Clement his
sone in kepinge and went to seke his wiff hymselff and his children,
f. 277ᵛᵃ and went into a shippe, and | cam not ayen. And so was Clement .xx.
wynter an orphanyn that neuer he herde of his fader ne moder ne of
50 his bretheren. And he sette hymself to studie in bokes and became a
[souerayne] philosophre. And he desired and enquered curiously in
whiche manere he might knowe the vndedlynesse of the soule, and for
that he haunted often tymes the studie of philisophres. And whanne
he herde that [thei] concluded in her disputisons that the soule was
55 undedly he was ioyful and gladde, and [whanne] thei concluded that
she was dedly he was al confused.

And so atte the last, whan Barnabe come to Rome for to prech the
faithe of Ihesu Crist, the philosofers scorned hym right as thei wolde
haue done a madde man. And after that sum sayne Clement was one
60 of the furst that scorned Barnabe, for he made to hym this question in
dispit and saide: 'What is the cause that a litell worme hathe .vj. fete
and two wynges to flee with, and an olyfaunt that is a right gret beste
hathe but .iiij. fete and yet he hathe no wynges?' To whom Barnabe
saide: 'Fole, y might right lyghtly ansuere to thi question yef thou
65 asked it bi cause to knowe the trouthe, but it shulde be a rude thinge
to tell you anithing of creatures whan ye vnknowe in all thinge her
creatour, and for that ye knowe hym not it ys right that ye erre in his

35 loue] *ins.* H₁   39 hadd] *om.* D   fell . . . palasie] was in suche plite D   come]
rise D   40 Machidiane] Machidy`an´ *and add* and *del.* H₁   43 her husbond] he EH₁
44–5 no more] not D   45 retourneden] *add* ayenne D   47 his²] *add* twoo D
51 souerayne] worthi E, *om.* D   52 vndedlynesse] vndeedelie livis D   53 the] to H₁
54 thei] L, he EH₁D   55 whanne] *om.* EH₁   55–6 he . . . confused] *om.* D
56 dedly] *add* `þan´ H₁    64 question] conquestion D    67 creatour] creat`o´ure H₁

creatures.' These wordes toke gretly in the herte of Clement, so that
he was [informed] of Barnabe in the faithe of Ihesu Crist and
resseiued it and went anone to Seint Petre into Iude, and he resseiued 70
hym and taught hym perfitly the faithe and shewed hym clerely the
vndedlynesse of the soule. |

And in that tyme Symond the enchauntour had .ij. disciples, that is f. 277vb
to wete Aquyle and Vicene, and whanne thei knewe his falsnesse thei
forsoke hym and [w]ent to Seint Petre the apostle and weren hys 75
disciples.

And as Seint Petre asked of Seint Clement of what kynrede he was
come, he tolde hym al by ordre how it was fall bi his moder and bi his
fader and by hys .ij. bretheren, and as he supposed he saide his moder
and his .ij. bretheren weren drounid in the see and his fader either 80
dede for sorw or cllis drowned in the see. And whanne Seint Petre
herde this he might not restreine hym from wepinge for pitee and
compassion.

In a tyme as Seint Petre went into the yle where Machidian duellyd
that was the moder of Clement and in that yle there were pelours of 85
glas of houge lengthe. And as Seint Petre and other wondered upon
this thing, he sawe Machidiane go abeggyng, and Seint Petre blamed
her for that she went [so] about and wolde not werke with her hondes.
And she ansuered and saide: 'Syr, y haue not only the forme of
handes, for thei be bynome me so that y fele hem not, and it 90
forthinkithe me that y hadde not drowned myself in the see so that
y leued not.' And Seint Petre saide: 'What is that thou saiest? Wost
thou not wele that the soules of hem that slee hemself be greuously
ponisshed?' And she said: 'And y wost certainly that the soules lyued
after the dethe, y wolde gladly slee myselff for that y might see my .ij. 95
sones one tyme.' And thanne Seint Petre asked her the cause of so gret
sorw, and thanne she tolde | hym al her fortune afore rehersed. And f. 278ra
Seint Petre saide to her: 'Y haue with me a yonge man that hight
Clement that tellithe al that ye haue tolde how it befell his fader and
his moder in the same wise.' And whan she herde that she was so 100
abasshed that she fell nigh in swounynge, and whan she come to

68 in the] *om.* D of] *om.* D   69 informed] L, *om.* ED, 'bro3t' H1   in] turned
into D   70 it] anone bapteme D went anone] anone he was sent D   71 hym¹] *ins.*
H1   75 went] sent E, *so changed to* went H1   to Seint] *twice* E   80–1 and² . . . see]
ins. with aftre *for* either H1   82 restraine] constreine D   85 pelours] pereiles D
88 so] *om.* E   about] abought *changed to* aboute H1   90 thei be] I haue lost hem and
beth D   me] *om.* D   92 leued not] had not lyued H1   that] *add* þat D
94 certainly] *om.* D   101 come] *add* ayenne D

herself she said, sore wepinge: 'Y am his moder.' And thanne she
kneled downe before Seint Petre and besought hym that she might in
haste see her sone. And Seint Petre said to her: 'Whanne that thou
seest thi sone, abide a while til we be oute of the yle with the ship.'
And she behight hym that she wold. And thanne Seint Petre toke the
woman by the honde and ledde her into the shipp wher Clement was.
And whanne Clement sawe Seint Petre that he helde a woman bi the
honde he beganne to laugh. And as sone as she behelde verrili her sone
Clement, she might no lenger forbere but ranne to hym and clipped
hym and cussed hym and he, sore ashamed of her, putte her of right
angerly, wenynge that she were madde. And thanne said Seint Petre:
'What doest thou, my sone Clement, dredest thou not thy moder?'
And whanne Clement herde that, [and knewe her], he behelde her and
beganne to wepe bitterly and fell downe before her. And thanne bi the
comaundement of Seint Petre, her ostesse that laye syk on the palasye
was brought forthe and he heled her anone. And thanne the moder
asked of Clement how his fader deyed, and he saide: 'He went to seke
you and come no more ayen.' And whanne she herde that she [sighed]
sore wepinge and comforted her other sorwes with that | gret ioye that
she had of her sone.

In this mene tyme come in Vicene and Aquile, and whanne thei
sawe that woman thei asked what she was, and Clement tolde hem and
saide: 'This is my moder that God hathe yeue me bi the merites of
Seint Petre my lorde.' And thanne Seint Petre tolde hem al by ordre,
and whanne Vicene and Aquile herde this thei lefte up her hedes with
gret meruaile and were all abasshed and saide: 'O Lorde and God of
all thinges, wher this be trwe that we here, or [is it] a dreme?' Than
saide Seint Petre: 'Yef ye be in your right mynde these thinges be
verrey trewe.' And thanne thei saide: 'We be Faustin and Faustinian
that oure moder wende to haue be perisshed in the see.' And thanne
thei went for to cusse and clippe thaire moder, and she meruailed
gretly what thei were. And thanne Seint Petre saide: 'These be thi
sones Faustin and Faustinian that thou wendest had be perisshed in
the see.' And thanne she swouned for ioye, and whanne she was

f. 278rb

105

110

115

121

125

130

135

104–5 Whanne . . . sone] yif thou wilte se thi sone þu must D   105 with the] and come
to D   108 that he helde] holde D   114 whanne] om. D   and knewe her] om. E
118 asked] add hym D asked/of Clement] trs. D   119 ayen] add home D whanne . . . that]
om. D sighed] saide E Hi D (souspira P2)   120 wepinge] add Haue I lost myne husbonde D
comforted] than in comfortinge of D with that] had D   120–1 that she had] ayennewarde D
125 my lorde] om. D   128 is it] trs. ED   130 thei] Vicene and Aquile D   131 in the see]
om. D   133 saide] add to hir D   135 thanne] 'than' whan Hi whanne she] om. Hi

awaked she said to hem: 'Tell me how ye ascaped.' And thei saide:
'Whanne oure shippe was brokyn [we were bore forth on a borde, and]
other shippemen fonde us and toke us into her ship and chaunged
oure names and solde us to an honest woman that hight Iustyne, that
helde us as her sones and sette us to scole. And after we sette oureself 140
to philosophie, and thanne we went with one Symond an enchauntour
that was norisshed with vs. And whan we knew his falsnesse we
forsoke hym and lefte hym and were made disciples of Seint Petre.'

And the day foluyng Seint Petre toke the | .iiij. disciples with hym, f. 278ᵛᵃ
Clement, Vicene and Aquile, and went into a more secrete place for to 145
praie. And right a worshipfull auncien man, but full pore as he semed,
aresoned hem in this wise: 'Frendes, haue pite of youreself, for y
considre youre gret folye under the liknesse of pitee. For there is no
god, ne no worshippinge, ne no prouidence [whiche] anythinge dothe
but only fortune and engendrure that doth all, for y haue founde it 150
myselff in the see wher y was taught in the discipline of mathesis more
thanne other. And therfor lesithe youre tyme no lenger, for, praie ye
or praie ye not, that shall befall you that is ordeined to fall bi destyne.'
And Clement behelde hym and his herte bare that he hadde saine hym
bifore that tyme. And whanne Clement, Vicene and Aquile had 155
disputed longe with hym bi the comaundement of Seint Petre and
had shewed hym by opin resones what prouidence was, and euer as
they talked to hym thei called hym fader by reuerence. And atte the
last Aquile said: 'What nede is that we call hym fader, sethe we haue
in comaundement that we shull call no man fader upon erthe?' And 160
after that he behelde the auncien man and saide: 'Be not displesed,
fader, thou y blamed my brother that he called the fader, for we haue
in comaundement that we shull call no man bi no suche name.' And
whan he hadde so saide, all tho of the felawshipp beganne to laugh.
And he asked hem whi thei lough, and Clement saide: 'For that thou 165
doest that thinge that thou blamest other for in callynge this olde man
fader.' |

And whanne thei hadd longe disputed of prouidence, th[e] olde f. 278ᵛᵇ

137 we . . . borde] L, a borde EHɪ, wee cauȝte a boorde and heelde fast thereon D
and] *om.* EHɪ   138 shippemen] *add* come and D   141 we] *on erasure* Hɪ
146 And right] Than D   a] *add* worþi D   man] *ins.* Hɪ   147 of] on HɪD
148 gret] *om.* D   149 worshippinge] worshipp D   whiche] with E, wich Hɪ
151 the see] these D   the² . . . of] *om.* D   mathesis] Mathasis *with* as *on erasure* Hɪ
153 to fall] you D   157 was] *on erasure* Hɪ   158 thei . . . fader] *ins.* Hɪ
160 call] *ins.* Hɪ   fader] *add* but *subp.* Hɪ   162 brother] bretheren D   he] þei D
164 hadde] *om.* Hɪ   168 the] this E

man said: 'Y wolde bileue prouidence to be, but myn owne conscience
170 deuiithe it, for y knowe my destine [and the destine] of my wiff. Now
wol ye here the destine of my wyff and ye shull see what fel to her. She
hadd in her natiuite Mars with Venus upon the middell, and she
hadde the mone in the waninge in the hous of Martis and in the ende
of Saturnus, and this auenture makithe avouutereres and makith hem
175 loue her owne seruauntes, and makithe hem to go into straunge
cuntreis and for to be drowned in waters. For as my brother tolde me,
she loued hym furst, and for he wolde not consente to her she turned
her loue luxuriously in her seruaunt, there [w]e aught not to blam[e]
her for her destyne made her do it.' And [thanne] he tolde hem how
180 she hadde made hym a dreme, and how in going to Athenes she
perisshed with her children. And as his children wolde haue go to
hym and discouered to hym al the manere, Seint Petre defended hem
and saide: 'Abide till me lust.' And than saide Petre to hym: 'Yef y
shew to the this same day thi wiff right true and chaste and thi thre
185 sones, wilt thou leue that destine ys anythinge?' And he ansuered and
saide: 'Right as it is inpossible thinge to shewe me that thou behotest
me, so it is inpossible anithing to be ouer destyne.' Thanne said Seint
Petre: 'This here is Clement thi sone, and these other twey be thi
gemels Faustin and Faust[inien].' And [thanne] the olde man fel in
190 gret meruaile and was longe tyme as withoute lyff, and [thanne] his
sones came to hym and kissed hym and dreddin lest he hadde be
f. 279ʳᵃ dede. | And whanne he was come ayen to lif and herde all the
auenture, thanne come his wiff rennyng and crienge: 'Where is my
lorde and my husbond?' And as he herde her he ranne to her and
195 streined her fast in his armes.

And as thei were in this ioye togedre ther come a messenger that
tolde how that Apion and Ambyon whiche were gret freendes to this
olde man Faustynien were herborwed with Simon Magus, and he
hadde ioye of her co[m]ing and went to uisite hem. And anone a
200 messenger said that the mynistre of Cesar was come into Antioche for

169 but] for D   170 and the destine] *om.* E   170–1 Now wol ye] and ye shulle D
171 see] hire D   167 upon the middell] in the myddis D   173 hadde] bare *del.*
'had' Hᵢ   175 and] *add* also D   177 for] *add* loue Hᵢ   he] she *with* s *erased* Hᵢ
178 we] she E, for 'I' Hᵢ   blame] blamyd E   179 thanne] *om.* E   181 children¹]
twoo sones Gemellis D   as] all Hᵢ   182 manere] *add* and D   defended] diffendinge D
183 saide²] *add* Seint EHᵢ   185 thou] *add* than D   188 here] *om.* D
189 Faustinien] Faust EHᵢ   thanne] *om.* EHᵢ   190 thanne] *om.* EHᵢ   191–2 lest
. . . dede] *twice* D   192 lif] hymselff D   196 this] *add* grete D   198 man] *add*
And than afftir this D   Faustynien] *add* and his wiffe D   199 coming] conning E
199–200 a messenger] minestre D   200 the mynistre] a messanger D

to seke all the enchauntours and to ponisshe hem with dethe. And
thanne Symond, bicause he hated the sones of Faustinien for the[i]
hadd lefte hym, he emprinted his figure in the uisage of Faustinien,
that hosoeuer that sawe hym went it had be Symon Magus the
enchauntour. And this dede Simon for that the ministres of Cesar   205
shulde haue take hym and sleyn hym in his stede. And thanne Symon
went fro tho parties. And whanne Faustinien come to Seint Petre and
to his sones, the sones were abasshed that sawe hym in the visage of
Symond and [herde the voys] of her fader, but Seint Petre alonly sawe
his visage in his naturel kinde. But his wyff and his sones fledde hym   210
and blamed hym, and he said to hem: 'What ailithe you to fle me and
blame me as ye do? Am y not youre husbond and youre fader?' And
thei saide: 'We fle the for the visage of Symon Magus aperithe in the.'
Thanne he wepte and sorued and said: 'Alas y haue but one day be
knowe of my wyff and of my children.'   215
     And Symon Magus while he was in Antioche he hadd gretly
defamed Seint | Petre and saide that he was an enchauntour ful of   f. 279ʳᵇ
malys [and] a mansleer, and he hadd meued so the peple ayenst Seint
Petre that thei thought verrily to sle hym yef thei might take hym.
And thanne saide Petre to Faustinien: 'For as moche as thou semest to   220
be Symon the enchauntour, go into Antioche and excuse me befor all
the peple of thinges that Simon saithe of me in his persone.' And
thanne went Faustinien into Antioche and assembeled all the peple
togedre and said: 'Y Symond denounce to you and confesse that y
haue be deceiued of all that y haue said of Petre the apostle, for he is   225
nother traitour ne deceiuour nor enchauntour, but he is sent for the
hele of [the] peple. Wherfor yef y say any euel of hym after this tyme
that ye ponisshe me as a wycked traitour, and y do now my penaunce,
for y knowe well that y sayd euell, and therfor y counsaile you that ye
l[e]ue hym so that ye and your citee perisshe not.' And whanne he   230
hadd said al that Seint Petre had comaunded hym [and] turned the
peple to Seint Petre, Seint Petre come to hym and made his praier and

202 thei] the E   204 hosoeuer] ho þat euer H1   207 went] fledde D   tho] þe H1
Petre] add ayenne D   208 sones¹] add and whan D   sones²] add saw3 hym thei D   that]
and wende that he had Symon Magus whan thei D   208–9 of Symond] but thei D
209 herde/the voys] trs. EH1   but] And whan D   213 the¹] add fadir D
217 defamed] dispised D   218 and¹] om. EH1   so/the peple] trs. H1   219 hym]
seinte Petre D   220 saide] add seinte D   221 Symon] add magus D   225 deceiued]
add of all þat I haue be deceiued del. H1   227 the] om. E   say] haue seide D   228 y] add
wille D   229 y²] add haue D   euell] evel on erasure H1   230 leue] loue EH1D (croyez
P2)   231 and] he EH1   232 peple . . . and¹] puplis hertis ayen to love seinte Petre and
than retourned ayenne to seint Petre and than seinte Petre D

toke al the semblaunce of Symond fro hym. And thanne the peple of Antioche receiued Seint Petre full debonairly with gret worship and

235 so haunsed hym into the cheier of a bisshoppe. And whanne Symond herde that, he went thedir and assembled the peple and saide: 'Y meruaile me gretly that sethe y haue taught you the true comaundementes of hele, and bode you kepe you from that fals traitour Petre, and now ye haue not only herde hym but ye haue haunsed hym into

f. 279va the chaier | of a bisshop.' And thanne all the peple with houge crie

241 saide to hym in gret angre: 'Thou art not but a monstre out of kinde. Saidest thou not that thou repentest the that thou ha[dde]st saide so moche euell of hym and thou woldest now caste us downe with the.' And thanne thei dede hym mani dispites and dro[fe] hym oute of the

245 towne. And Clement tellithe in his boke al these thinges of hymself and putte it withinne his stori.

And after this, whanne Seint Petre come to Rome and he sawe that his passion neyghed, he ordeined [Clement] for to be bisshopp with hym. And whanne Seint Petre prince of aposteles was dede, Clement

250 that was a man purueied toke kepe of the tyme [to] come so that bi this ensaumple eueriche wolde chese a successour with hym in the Chirche of God, and for to possede the sentuari of God bi heritage. He lefte the sege to Lyne, and after that to Clere, but sum will saie that Lyne and Clere were not souerayne bisshoppes but only for the

255 helpers of Seint Petre the apostle, for whiche thing thei were putte in the cathel[o]ge of bisshoppes. And after that Clement was chose and constreined for to be in the se[g]e, and he shined so bi the arayeng of good maners that he plesed cristen, Iewes and paynimes. He had in writinge by name the pore of eueri religion, and tho that he halowed bi

260 bapteme he wolde not suffre to begge in comune.

And whanne he hadd sacred an holy uirgine that was nece to Domicyen the emperour, and had conuerted to the feithe Theod[o]re

f. 279vb the wyff of Cisicien | frende of the emperoure, and she hadd behight for to be in the purpos of chastite, Sicisien hadde fere and drede of his

265 wyff and entred after her into the chirche for to wete whi she haunted so moche the chirche. And whanne Seint Clement had saide the

233 toke] add aweie D   Symond] add magus D   fro hym] om. D   234 debonairly] deuoutelie D   235 Symond] add magus D   237 true] om. D   240 the¹] on erasure H1 houge] hugh H1   241 not] om. H1   242 haddest] hast E   244 drofe] drow E 245 towne] cite D   248 Clement] om. EH1   249 of] add þe H1   250 toke] to H1 the] add cite and of the H2   to] om. E   253 sege] seete H2   253, 254 Clere] so changed to Clete H1   256 cathaloge] cathelege E   257 sege] L, see E, so changed to seet H1, seete H2 259 name] add alle H2   pore] add and H2   262 Theodore] Theodre E

orison and the peple ansuered: 'Amen', Sisinyen was made blinde and
doume. And thanne he saide to his seruauntes: 'Take me fro hennys
anone and putte me oute.' And thei ledde hym aboute the chirche but
thei coude fynde no dores. And whanne Theodore sawe thei went so 270
ma[se]dly about, she went her waye wenyng that her husbond might
haue saien her. But atte the laste she came and asked what it ment that
thei went so aboute, and the seruauntes saide to her: 'Oure maister
wolde here and see that longithe not to hym, and therfor he is made
blinde and [dou]me.' And thanne she went to her praiers and praied 275
that he might go oute of the chirche. And whanne she hadd praied she
went to the seruauntes and saide: 'Gothe hennes and lede my lorde to
his hous.' And thei anone ledde hym home.

And thanne Theodore tolde Seint Clement what was fall to hym,
and thanne the seint come to hym bi the praiere of Theodore and he 280
fonde his cycn opin, but hc might not see ne here nothinge. And
thanne Seint Clement praied for hym and he receyued hering and
sight, and whan he sawe Clement nere he was ny madde for anger, and
went that he hadde be deceiued, and comaunded his seruauntes to
take Clement and holde hym faste and saide: 'He hathe made [me] 285
blynde bi his | wichecrafte for he wolde come to my wiff.' And thanne f. 280ra
whanne thei wende for to haue bounde and drawin Clement and his
clerkys, thei drow stockes and stones. And thanne said Seint Clement
to Sisinien: 'For [that] thou saiest that stockis and stones be goddes,
therfor thou hast deserued to drawe stockis and stones.' And he that 290
wend uerily that Seint Clement had be bounde said: 'Y do slee the by
cruel dethe.' But Clement went his waye unhurte and praied
Theodore to cese not for to praie for her husbond to oure Lorde
that he might be visited with his grace. And Seint Petre thanne apered
to Theodore praienge and saide: 'Thi husbond shall be saved by the 295
for to fulfell that my brother Seint Paule saide: "A man of mysbeleue
shall be saued by his true wiff."' And in that saienge he went his waye,
and anone Sisinien called his wiff to hym and praied her to praie for

267 ansuered] *add* and seide H2   Sisinyen] Sisinen *changed to* Sisinien (?) H1
268 doume] doumbe *del.* `deef' H1   271 masedly] madly E   275 doume] lame EH1
she] Theodore H2   276 he] hir husbonde H2   277 praied] *add* that hir husbonde
myght goo out of the churche H2   went] come H2   278 anone] *add* went out of the
churche and H2   279 hym] hir husbonde H2   280 the seint] Seint Clement H2
of] *add* seint EH1   283 nere] ny *del.* H1, *om.* H2   285 He hathe] that he had H2
me] mo EH1, hym H2   287 thei] the seruauntis H2   and drawin] *om.* H2
288 drow] bounden H2   289 that¹] *om.* E   291 Y do] I *with* `wol' *on erasure* H1,
that he wold H2   the] hym H2   296 Seint] *om.* H2   saide] *add* the EH1
298 Sisinien] Sysinyen *changed to* Sysicyen (?) H1

hym and that she wold call Seint Clement. And whanne he was come
300 he taught hym in the feithe and baptised hym with .CCC. and .xiij. of
his meyne, and mani noble men and frendes of the emperoure
bileuedin in oure Lorde by this Sisinien.

Thanne the erle of Sacrum gaue moche money and meued gret
noyse and discorde ayenst Clement. And thanne Mamertyn the
305 prouost of the citee of Rome might not suffre this discorde but
made Clement be brought before hym. And as he undertoke hym and
assaied for to drawe hym to his entent, Clement saide [to hym]: 'Y
wolde thou woldest drawe thiselff to reson, for yef many houndes
haue abaied ayenst us and haue sumwhat biten us, yet mow thei not
f. 280rb take from | us but that we be men resonable and thei be houndes
311 unresonable. This discencion that is arise[n] bi folys shewithe well
that thei haue no thinges certain nor trewe.' And thanne Mamertin
wrote to Traiane the emperour of Clement, and he ansuered that
other he shulde do sacrifice or ellys he shulde be sent into exile into a
315 desert that is ouer the see ny the citee. And the prouost saide to
Clement wepinge: 'Thi Lorde and thi God that thou hast worshipped
purely helpe the.' And thanne the prouost toke hym a shippe and all
his necessitees, and many clerkes and laye men folued hym into the
exile. And the prouost fonde in that yle mo thanne .ijM^1. cristen men
320 that were dampnid and sent thedir for to cutte the marbre oute of
roches. And as sone as they sawe Seint Clement they beganne to
wepe, and [he] comforted [hem] and seid: 'Oure Lorde hathe not sent
me to you be my meritis for to make me partener of youre crowne.'
And whanne he had vnderstonde bi hem that thei bare her water .vj.
325 myle upon her shuldres, he saide to hem: 'Praie we all to oure Lorde
Ihesu Crist that he opin in this place here the veynes of a well, and
that he that smote the stones in the desert of Synay yeue to us
renninge water so that we be ioyed of his benefetis.' And whanne he
had made his praier he sawe a lambe that lefte up the right fote and
330 shewed to the bisshopp the place, and none sawe hym but he alone.
And thanne he understode that it was Ihesu Crist, and went to the

300 .xiij.] .xvj. H2   301 and mani] *om.* H1   306 he] *om.* H2   307 to¹] *add*
haue H2   to hym] *om.* E   310 be²] *add* as EH1   311 arisen] arise E
313 ansuered that] sent hym worde ayenne H2   314 be sent] sende hym H2
318 laye] lewd H2   319 the prouost] Clement *on erasure* H1   cristen] *ins.* H1, *om.* H2
320 were] *add* cristenne which were H2   322 he] thei E, thei *with* t *and* i *erased* H1
hem] hym E   323 me¹] *add* hidir H2   meritis] *add* 'but' H1   324 whanne] than H2
325 shuldres] *add* than H2   326 here] *om.* H2   328 we] *add* mowe H2   329 up]
ins. H1   330 the bisshopp] Clement H2   hym] the lambe H2

place and saide: 'In the name of the fader and of the sone and [of the] holy gost | smite in this place.' And whanne he sawe that none wolde f. 280ᵛᵃ smite, he toke a picoys and smote a stroke lyghtely under the fote of the lambe and anone a well of water went oute, and thanne all ioyeden 335 in God. Thanne said Seint Clement: 'The comynge of flodes gladithe the citee of God.' And for the renome of this thinge myche peple went thedir and .vC. and mo receiued bapteme of hym in a day and distroied the temples of [the] ydoles. And in one yere thei edified to God .lxxv. chirches in that prouince. 340

And .iij. yere after, Traian emperour that beganne the yere of oure Lorde .lvj. herde this thinge. He sent thedir a duke, and whanne the duke sawe that thei wolde all gladly deye for the loue of God, he lefte all that multitude and toke alonly Clement, and bonde an ankre to his necke and caste hym into the see and saide: 'Thei shul neuer worship 345 hym as god.' And all the multitude of peple were atte the see side. And thanne Cornelien and Phebus the disciples of Clement comaunded all the peple to praie to oure Lorde that he wolde shewe hem the bodi of that holy martre, and anone the see departed by .iij. mile so that men might go into the see bi drie londe. And 350 thanne the peple went inne and there thei fonde an habitacle made as a temple of marbre that God had arayed, and there thei fonde the body in a cheste and the ancre bisydes hym. And hit was shewed to his disciples that thei shulde not take the bodi fro thennes, and eueri yere in the tyme of his passion the see will departe bi the space of | .viij. f. 280ᵛᵇ dayes .iij. myle and yeue drye wey to all the comers. 356

And so it happed in a tyme atte this sollempnite a woman with [her] litell child went to that place. And whanne the solempnite of th[e] fest was fullfelled the childe slepte, and the sowne of waters was herde comynge. And the woman was aferde and forgate her childe and 360 fledde to the see syde with the multitude of peple. And after, she bethought her of her sone and beganne to make gret sorw and lamentacion and ranne as a mad woman to the see for to beholde yef she might haue seyn hym floter upon the wawes. And whanne she sawe that she coude nothinge see ne finde, she retorned her and was al 365 that yere in gret sorw and heuinesse. The yere after, whanne the see

332 of the³] L, *om.* EH₁, the H₂   335 went] come H₂   339 the²] *om.* EH₁
344 to] about H₂   345 into] 'in'to H₁   347 the] were *on erasure* H₁   of] *add* seint
H₂   352 the] *add* holie H₂   355 will] wold H₁   356 wey] londe H₂
357 her] a E   358 the²] that EH₁   361 after] than H₂   363 ranne] þan H₁, *add*
alle about H₂   woman] *add* went H₁   for . . . beholde] *om.* H₂   364 floter] flote H₂
wawes] watir H₂   365 sawe that she] *om.* H₂   her] *add* ayen H₂

was opin ayen, she went before all other and come to the place for to wete yef she might anithinge finde of her sone. And whanne she was sette in praier before the auuter of Seint Clement, she rose her up and
370 sawe the childe in the place wher she had lefte hym slepinge. And she went nere wenynge to take up the body withoute the soule. But whan she sawe hym slepinge she woke hym and toke hym up in her armes al hole before all [the] peple, and she asked [hym] where he had be al that yeere, and he saide he wost neuer, for as hym thought he had
375 slepte but one night.

One bisshoppe of Hostiens tellith that in the tyme that Mighell the emperour gouernid newly the empire of Rome, ther was a preste that hight Philisophre come to Cossone and asked of hem of the cuntre of
f. 281ra things that be tolde in the stori of Seint Clement. And for that | he
380 was not of that cuntre but a straungere thei wolde not tell hym, but saide thei knewe nothinge therof, and also bycause of the synnes of the peple the water had longe tyme cesed for to withdrawe hym. And in the tyme of Martin emperoure the chirche had be destroied with barbaryns and the cheste with the body of the martir was all wrapped
385 in wawes of the see for the synnes of the duellers there. And thanne this preste had gret meruaile of all these thinges and went to a litell citee that hight Georgi and went to the bisshop and to the clerkes with al the peple for to seke holy reliques in the place where thei hoped that the body of this holy martir was. And there thei diggedin and songyn
390 ympnes and psalmes, and thanne by the diuine reuelacion thei fonde the holy body with the ancre bisydes hym and thei bere it to Cressone. And after, this prest come to Rome with the body of Seint Clement, and there God shewed many a glorious miracle for hym and the body was sette in the chirche that is now called Seint Clement. And it is
395 redde in a cronicle that the see dreied in that place and that the blessed Cerile bisshoppe of Moriane brought the holy bodi to Rome.

367 went] add thidir H2   371 the¹] add dede E   372 woke him, toke . . . armes] trs. H1   373 the] om. E   hym] om. EH1   376 One] A H2   that²] of H2
377 emperour] add that H2   378 hem] oone H2   380 thei] he H2   381 thei] he
H2   384 the²] add holie H2   the martir] Seint Clement H2   387 to²] add alle H2
388–9 that the . . . was] to fynde the holie martir H2   389 martir] man H1   and] add
founden and EH1   392 this] add the H1H2   393 shewed] sheweth H1
396 Cerile] Celeri H2

Here endithe the lyff of Seint Clement, and nexst beginnithe the lyff of Seint Grisogone, Capitulum .C.lxiiij.[m]

Grisogone was take and putte in prison bi the comaundement of
Dyoclisian, and Seint Anastace fonde hym his lyuinge. And than her
husbond putte her in a streite prison and she [s]ent to Grisogone that
taught her in the faithe these thin|ges writin: 'To the holy confessour   f. 281[rb]
of Ihesu Crist Grisogone,   Anastace: cursed be the dedes of [m]in   5
husbond that y haue take, but by the will of God y am kepte from his
bedde by dissimulacion of siknesse, and night and day folw and
embrace the steppes of oure Lorde Ihesu Crist. But this greuithe me
sore, that my wreched husbonde spendithe my patrimonie in the
worshipp of ydoles and of other filthes, and hathe putte me into   10
greuous prisone as y were an enchaunteresse or cursed for to make me
lese the temperall lyff, so that now there is nothinge lefte with me but
that my wreched body, seruaunt to the spirit, is leyde doune for to
deye. And though it be so that y glorifie me in this dethe, yet am y
gretly troubled in my thought that my richesses that y ha[d] ordeined   15
to God be wasted in foule thinges. Fare well, in the kepinge of oure
Lorde, thou blessed seruaunt of God, and haue mynde on me.' And
Grisogone ansuered in this wise: 'Doughter, take hede that thou
groche not for no wronge that is done to the in this lyff, be it neuer so
contrarie to the, for in suffering paciently thou maist not be deseiued   20
yef thou be preued. Pesible tyme shall sone folu, and thou shalt see the
florisshing light of God after this clowdi derkenesse, and after this
tyme colde and frosty shall come the tyme softe and lusti. Fare wel in
God, and praie for me.'

And as the blessed Anastace was so sore constreined in prison that   25
unnethes she receiued a loef in .iiij. dayes and that she went verily to
deye, she wrote another lettre to Grisogone in these wordes: 'To the
confessour of | Ihesu Crist Grisogone, I Anastace enforme you that   f. 281[va]
the ende of my bodily lyff is come, wherfor remembre the of me, so

EH1H2A1A2   3 and] for that H2   sent] went EH1H2 (enuoya P2)   4 faithe]
add and than H2   writin] she wrote H2   5 Grisogone] add y, E, add & H1H2 (text as
P2)   Anastace] add seide H2   be] bi H1   min] thin EH1   7 dissimulacion]
simulacion H2   10 of¹] add his EH1   11 enchaunteresse] Enchauntour H2
12 nothinge] om. H2   with] om. H2   13 that] om. H2   spirit] add that is H2   leyde]
le'i'dde with first d subp. H1   15 had] haue EH1   17 on] of H1   19 wronge]
thinge H2   20 thou] del. 'in' H1   21 and] ins. H1   22 derkenesse] sikenesse H1
23 tyme¹] add of H2   frosty] frost H2   tyme²] add of H2   lusti] add somere H2
27 to Grisogone] om. H2   the] add holy H2   28 enforme] enfor'me' H1

30 that whanne the soule shall parte from my body that he receiue it for
whom y suffre all these tribulacions, the whiche bi the mouthe of this
olde woman.' And thanne he wrote to her ayen in this wise: 'Hit is
sittinge that derkenesse go alwey before the light, and that hele come
after siknesse, and that the lyff be after the dethe. All the aduersitees
35 of this world be enclosed under an ende, and all the prosperites also,
so that despeir haue no lordship ouer the sorufull ne pride haue no
lordshipp ouer hem that be gladde. This is a see wherinne the shippes
of oure bodies sailen and oure soules haue the office of rowers under
the gouernaunce of the bodi. And the shippes that be well fastenid and
40 bound with harde cheines passen wel withouten ani brekinge thorugh
the strong wawes of the see, and other that haue but feble iointours of
tre be full ofte in perile for to drowne. But the, seruaunt of God, haue
thou [in] thi mynde the uictori of the crosse and arraie the to the
werke of God.'
45   And thanne Dyoclician, that was in the parties of Aquile and slow
cristen peple, comaunded that Grisogone shuld be brought to hym.
And thanne he saide to hym: 'Grisogone, take the power of the
prouost[e] and do sacrifice to oure goddes.' And he ansuered: 'Y
worshipp only one God of heuene and y despise thi goddes and thi
50 dignite as myre.' And thanne was sentence youe upon hym and he was
f. 281ᵛᵇ ledde into a place where he | was beheded the yere of oure Lord
.CC..iiij^{xx}.vij. And Seint Ely prest beried the hede and the bodi.

Here endithe the liff of Seint Grisogone, and nexst
beginnithe the liff of the blessed virgine Seint Katerine,
Capitulum .C.lxv.ᵐ

Here beginnithe the right excellent and most glorious liff and passion
of the right blessed uirgine Seint Katerine, whiche bi dissent of lyne
was of the noble kinrede of the emperours of Rome, as it shall be

30 he] my lorde Ihesu criste H2   31 whiche] *add* thinge is seide H   32 olde] *om.*
H2   35 also] *add and del.* that despeir H1   36 so] *om.* H1H2   36–7 the . . . ouer]
ins. H1   42 But] *add* to H1   43 in] *om.* EH1H2 (*en* P2)   mynde] *add* of H2
45 slow] *add* there H2   47 hym] *add and del.* Grisogone shuld be brought to him H1
48 prouoste] prouost EH1   oure] *add* lorde H1   49 despise] *add* alle H2   50 as]
and thi stinkinge H2   myre] mirroure H1   52 the¹] his H2   and the bodi] of the body
H1, *om.* H2

EH1H2A1A2LKT2; D resumes at 71 *ferforthely*, breaks off after 485 *drede you*, and
resumes again at 624 *philosophie*; A1 breaks off after 577 *before* (end of MS); T1 begins at 256
ansuered   1–2 and² . . . uirgine] of LK   1 and passion] *om.* T2   2 right] *om.* T2
Katerine] *add* and of hir passion T2   3 kinrede] kinredis K

declared more pleinly hereafter bi a notable cronicle, whos most blessed
lyff and conuersacion was wretin of the solempne doctour Athanasius 5
that knew her birthe, her kinrede, her lyff and conuersacion. And that
same Athanasius was one of her maistres in her tendre age or she was
conuerted to the faithe, and after her holy conuersion she conuerted
that same Athanasius by her holy prechinge and bi her merueilous
werkys that oure Lorde wrought in her. And after her martirdom he 10
was made bisshopp of Alisaundre and was a glorious peler of holy
Chirche bi the grace of oure Lorde and bi her holy merites.

As we finde bi credible cronicles that in the tyme of Dioclician and
Maximian so gret and cruell tyranni was shewed in the worlde, and
not only to cristen but also to the paynimes, so that mani a rewme that 15
was soget to Rome putte awey the yocke of her seruage and rebelled
opinli, amongc whiche the reaume of Ermonie was one that most
mightili withstode the tribuct that longed to the empire of Rome.
Wherfor there was chosin to apese that | rebellion a lorde of gret f. 282ra
dignite of the counsaile that hight Constancius, which before all other 20
was manli in armes and therto right discrete and full of vertues, the
whiche lorde whanne he come into Ermonie he staunched so bi his
manly and vertuous gouernaunce the rebellyon that he deserued the
loue of his enemyes, and moreouer that the kinge and all the peple
desired that he shulde wedde the doughter and eyre of that londe.   25

And whanne this was done, within a while after, the king of Ermeni
deyed and Constancius was crowned kinge of that londe, the whiche
withinne a while after had a sone bi the quenc, for whom was made
gret lamentacion of all her peple. After whos dethe he returned ayen
to Rome for to see the emperoure and also to see and knowe how his 30
lordshippes were gouerned in tho parties. And in that mene tyme

4 notable] nobille LK   5 the] *add* notable and T2   6 kinrede] *add* and LK
and] *add* hir H2T2   8 faithe] *add* of crist L   after . . . conuersion] aftirward through hir
holie conuersacion H2T2   conuersion] conuersacion H1   9 that] þe LK   her²] the
H2T2   11 made] *om.* H2T2   glorious] myghty and a holy T2   of²] *add* all T2
12 her . . . merites] the holie meritis of Seinte Katerine H2, the holy mene of seint katerine
T2   13 bi] *add* the T2   that] *om.* L   14 Maximian] *add* that H2T2   and¹] a LK
15 to¹] *add* the H2T2   the] *om.* H2T2   17 opinli] *add* ayens the empire H2, *add* ayenst
the emperoure T2, *add* aȝens Rome L   18 mightili] mighti H1   empire] emperour T2
LK   19 there] *om.* H2   was] *so on erasure* H1   that] grete L, *add* grete K   19–23 a
lorde . . . rebellyon] *twice* T2   20 dignite] *add* and H2T2   23 the¹] þat T2
rebellyon] *add* so H2T2L   24 the²] his H2T2   25 and] of the kinge the which was
H2T2   that] the H2   26 of Ermeni] *om.* H2T2   27 that londe] Ermonie H2T2
28 quene] *add* 'which was cleped Costis and anon after that died the qwene' H1, *add*
wheron she deied H2, *add* wherof she deyed T2   29 her] þe LK   30 see², knowe]
trs. H2T2   31 mene] *om.* LK

come tydingges to Rome how that the Gret Bretayne that now is
called Englond rebelled ayenst the empire of Rome, wherfor it was
sein amonge all the counsaile that it was necessarie to requere
35 Constancius the kinge of Ermenie to take upon hym to dresse that
rebellyon, the whiche request he goo[d]ly hath graunted and drow
hym in haste towarde tho parties.

And in his comyng he ruled h[y]m so bi his gret vertu and prudence
that he pesibly sodued the londe to the empire, and moreouer he was
40 so acceptable to the kinge of Bretayne whiche hight Coel, and to all
the peple of that londe, that with one voys thei haue required the
kinge to yeue hym his doughter and his eyre in mariage, whiche was
holy Seint Elyne that fonde the crosse. And the kinge Coel right glad |
f. 282ʳᵇ of this request agreyd hym fully therto and made betwene hem a
45 solempne mariage. Within a whiles after he gate on her Constantyne,
whiche was after emperoure bi processe of tyme. Not longe after deied
Constancius the fader of Constantin in tho parties, and Constantines
sone bi right of his moder was crowned kinge of Bretaigne that now is
called Englond. And Costes the kinge of Ermeni and the furst sone of
50 Constancius hathe wedded the kinges doughter of Cipre and his eyre,
of whiche as it shall be declared hereafter was brought forthe Seint
Katerine, whiche holy Seint Katerine as ye may here was of the noble
kinrede of the emperoure Constantine and of the nacion of Bretones,
the whiche deliuered Rome fro the tyrannie of Maxens.

55 Now foluithe the beginnynge of Seint Katerine the yere fro the
incarnacion of Crist .CC. that is to saye ouerpassed, there regnid in
the londe of Cipre a noble and a prudent kinge that hight Costus, the
whiche of bodely shappe was most semely and goodly aboue al other,
and in richesse most plenteuous, and in all good condiciones none lyke

34 all] *om.* H2T2   was] were LK   necessarie] *add* for LK   35 the¹ . . . Ermenie]
om. LK   dresse] `re´dresse H1, *so* H2T2, apese K   36 goodly] gooly E   hath] *om.* L
37 in haste] fast LK   towarde] to L   38 hym] hem E   prudence] wisdome H2T2
sodued] *two words* E, sow/dewed H1, so endewid H2T2, devided so L, so devided K   the¹]
that H2T2   empire] *add* ayenne H2T2   40 so] *om.* T2   Bretayne] *add* the H2
41 that¹] the H2T2   42 hym his doughter] his doughter to hym T2   his²] *om.* K
43 holy] ooneli H2T2   the¹] *add* holie H2T2   Coel] *add* was H2T2   44 request] *add*
and H2T2   made/betwene hem] *trs.* T2   45 mariage] *add* and H2K   Constantyne]
add þe LK   emperoure/bi processe of tyme] *trs.* K   bi . . . tyme] *add* and H2
47–8 Constantines sone] Constantine H2T2K   48 was] *add* here T2   49 and]
erased H2   50 hathe] had T2L   and his] þat is H1   eyre] heris T2   51 of] *add* þe
LK   as it] *om.* H2   52 whiche] with *changed to* wiche H1   Seint Katerine] virgyne T2
the] *om.* H1   53 nacion] naciones H1   55 of] *add* the life of T2   Katerine] *add* in
H2T2   56 there] he H1   58 and] *add* moost H2T2

hym. A quene he had lyk hymself in all vertuous gouernaunce, with 60
whom he lyued a blesfull lyff in as moche as longed to the worlde,
excepte that bothe he and his wiff liued after the right of paynimes and
worshipped ydoles. This kinge, for he wolde haue his name spredde
thorugh the worlde, he made a citee in the whiche he reised a temple
in the worshipp of the fals goddes that the blinde worlde worshipped 65
atte that tyme, and he named this citee Costi. Proce|ding thanne f. 282ᵛᵃ
forthe, the tyme and the langage of the peple sumwhat chaunged and
so thei chaunged the name of the citee and called it Famacosti,
kepinge alweyes the fame of the kinge.

In this citee he and the quene lyued in all worldely prosperite as 70
ferforthely as [her] hertes coude thenke. And right as the faire and
sote rose springithe amonge the thornes, right so betwene the
paynimes was brought forthe the precious spouse of Crist the holy
uirgine Seint Katerine. Whanne this holy child was born hit was so
faire of visage and so shaply of body that all hadde meruaile in [the] 75
beholdinge therof, and bi that tyme she come to .vij. yere of age she
encresed so in high bcauute and stature that all hoped that saw her
that in tyme to come she shuld be ioy and preisinge of the lond of
Cipre. Whanne .vij. yere were passed and that she was strenger of
body she was sette to scole, wherinne she profited so wonderfully that 80
aboue all tho that euer were of her age she resseiued merueilously all the
crafte and cuninge of all the .vij. sciences. And no wonder thou she
dranke plenteuously of the well of wisdom, for she was ordeined in
tyme to come to be a techer and an enformer of euerlastinge wisdom.

The kinge Costes her fader, hauing so grete ioye of the gret 85
wysdom of his doughter, lete ordeine her a tour in his paleys with

60 hymself] to hym H2T2   vertuous] goode L   61 blesfull] blessid H2T2L
62 that] *om.* H2   after the right of] in the lawe after T2   right] lawe H2, rightis L
63 This] The LK   65 the¹] *om.* H2   the²] *om.* LK   worlde] world *on erasure* H1
66 atte] H1 *starts sentence with paraph* At   Proceding thanne] *trs.* H2T2   67–8 and so]
so that H2T2   68 Famacosti] Fama Costi H2   69 alweyes] euere H2T2   fame]
name K   the²] *add* cite and of the T2   70 worldely] *om.* LK   as¹] *ins.* D   71 her]
om. E   the faire and] a faire and a H1   and] *add* þe LK   71–2 and sote/rose] *trs.* DT2
72 amonge] *add* the breris and DT2   so] *om.* H1   the¹] these twoo DT2K, þies H1L
73 the³] þis LK   75 shaply] shappi H1   all] *add* peple T2   the] *om.* E   76 therof]
of hir T2   of age] old L   77 high] *om.* LK   and] *add* in LK   all] *add* men T2
78 that] *om.* LK   come] *add* þat K   be] *add* the H1DLK   ioy and] the ioye and the
prayer and T2   and] *add* the DLK   79–80 strenger . . . was] *om.* L
80 wonderfully] vnderfulli H1, wondirly LK   81 euer] *om.* LK   were] *ins.* H1
82 sciences] science H1   86 The] Than this D, This T2   her fader] *om.* DT2   so]
om. K   85–6 the . . . doughter] her wisdom L, his doughtris wisdom K
86 doughter] *add* þat he T2

diuerse studies and chaumbris that she might be atte her owne leyser in her studie and none to lette her but whanne her luste. And therto he ordeined to awaite upon her .vij. the best and hyest maystres of
f. 282vb cunnyng that might be founde in the worlde as in tho par|ties. And
91 withinne a while that these maistres had be with thilke yonge lady Katerine, she encresed so merueilously in high wisdom that tho clerkes that were come to teche her and enforme her were full glad to become her disciples and to lerne of her. Thus withinne fewe yeres
95 whanne this glorious virgine was .xiiij. yere olde her fader the king Costus deied, and she was lefte as quene and eyre after hym. And the states of her londe come to this yong quene, and besought her that ther might be a parlement atte the which she might be crouned and receiue her homage, and that suche rule and gouernaunce might be
100 sette in her yong begynning that pees and prosperite might folw in her reaume. And than this yonge quene thanked hem goodly and graunted hem her askinge.

The tyme come that this parlement was begonne, and this yong quene crowned with gret solempnite with a riall fest and gret ioye to
105 all her peple. Whanne the fest of the coronacion was ended, as the quene sat on a day in her parlement, her moder bisydes her and al her lordes about her, a lorde arose bi the full avys of her moder and of all her lordes and comunes and kneled hym downe before the quene hauyng these wordes: 'Right `high´ and mighti princesse and oure
110 most soueraine lady in erthe, like youre souerayne nobilnesse to wete that y am comaunded bi the quene youre moder and bi all youre lordes and comunes to requere youre highnesse to graunte hem that leue and grace that thei might go ordeine vnto you sum noble kinge or prince that might rule you and youre reawmes and [us] all in pees and
f. 283ra reste, like as the noble | kyng youre fader and oure soueraine lorde
116 dede before you, and that we might reioyse gracious lyne of you, the

88 her¹] *om.* H1, *add* owne D   none] no body T2   her³] she LK   91 that] *om.* K thilke] that DT2K   91–2 thilke . . . Katerine] her L   93 her¹] *om.* K   94 fewe] *add* daies and H1   95 glorious] *om.* LK   the] *om.* DT2K   97 her¹] the DT2 98 the] *om.* H1K   99 that] *om.* LK   might] *om.* L   100 in] *om.* T2   101 this] þe T2   quene] maide DT2   hem] hym riȝt K   graunted] graunteth H1 101–2 thanked hem . . . hem] grauntid hem goodeli DT2   105 as] and DT2 106 on] in H1LK   in] at LK   107 about] besides T2   avys] a vice D   108 her] þe LK   and¹] of þe londe with þe will of þe K   the quene] her K   109 high] *om.* H1 princesse] princes H1DL   110 like] *add* it vnto T2, *add* it K   souerayne] sovereynte and K   113 go] do H1, *add* and DT2   114 you and] *om.* K   reawmes] reawme K us] in E, *om.* T2   and³] *add* in K   115 like] right LK   oure] youre H1   soueraine] *om.* DT2   116 gracious . . . you] graciouslie of your line D   lyne] life T2K

whiche is oure most desire and shall be oure most ioy, withoutc
whiche ioy we lyue in gret sorw and heuinesse, besechinge youre high
excellence to tendir oure desir and to graunte us of youre high grace a
gracious ansuere.'   120

   This yong quene, hering this request of her moder and of all her
lordes, fill in gret trouble in her soule hou she might ansuere to kepe
her moder and her lordes in reste and to kepe her chastite, for all her
ioye had euer be to kepe her body and her soule from all corrupcion.
And she hadd so gret and so perfit a loue to that vertu of chastite that 125
she hadd leuer suffre the dethe thanne for to blemisshe it in any wise.
But for to vttre her conseyt so sodenly her thought it was not for the
best, and therfor with a so[b]re chere and a debonayr loke she
ansuered in this wise to this lorde: 'Cosin,' she saide: 'Y thanke my
lady my moder and all my lordes and comunes of the gret loue and 130
tendirnesse that thei haue to me and to my rewmes, trusting fully that
though there be no gret haste as touching this matere of my mariage,
that there may be no maner perile in me concidering the gret wisdom
of my ladi my moder and of you all, with gret thought and kindenesse
that ye haue shewed me and my reawmes, trustinge fulli of youre good 135
continuaunce. Wherfor we shull not nede to seke a straunge lorde to
rule us and oure reawmes, for us thinkithe us able ynow, with youre
good trouthe and wisdom, to gouerne us and oure rewmes and you all
in suche pees and reste as the kinge my lorde [and] fader lefte you.
Wherfor y praie you all | to cese of this matere atte this tyme and f. 283rb
spekithe of suche materes as ye thenke is most nedefull and spedefull 141
to the good rule and gouernaunce of oure reawmes.'

   And whanne the quene had ended her tale, the quene her moder
and all the lordes were so abasshed of her wordes that thei wost not
what to saie, for thei considered wel by her worde[s] that she was in no 145

117 oure] your *with y erased* H1   118 gret] moche DT2   121 quene] *add*
Katerine DT2   123 for] of H1   124 had] hath T2   euer] *add* more T2   be] *add*
bysy T2   all] *om.* T2   125 gret and so] *om.* LK   of] *om.* D   126 the] *om.* K
blemisshe it] blemsshid D   127 her thought/it was] yt was as she þought L, *trs.* K
128 sobre] sowre E, soure *changed to* sobere H1   a²] *om.* L   130 and²] *add* my L
131 rewmes] reme LK   131–2 that though] *twice* E   133 that] *om.* LK   be/no
maner perile] *trs.* D   maner] *add* of DT2, *om.* LK   gret] *om.* H1   wisdom] *add* þat ye
haue shewed me T2   135 youre] *om.* D   136 shull] *om.* D   nede to] *om.* LK
strange lorde] straunger DT2   137 reawmes] reame D   us able] *om.* DT2
138–9 all in] *trs.* D   139 suche] good D, *om.* T2   and¹] *add* good T2   reste] *add* and D
lorde] *om.* DT2   and²] youre E, *so del.* '&' H1, *om.* D   you] *add* inne D   140 you]
me and you bothe T2   141 ye thenke] *om.* DT2   thenke is] þynkeþ L   is most] *trs.* H1
most] *twice* E   142 rule and] *om.* LK   143 the¹] *add* yonge DT2   quene¹] *add*
Katerine DT2   144 all the] alle hir D, hir T2   145 wordes] worde E

will to be wedded. Thanne stode there up a duke of her londe that was
her uncle, and kneled to her with humble reuerence and saide to her
in this wise: 'Mi right souerain ladi, savinge youre high and noble
discrecion, this ansuere is full heuy to my lady youre moder and to us
150　all your humble liege men withoute ye take beter avys to youre right
noble and discrete herte. Wherfor y shall meue you of .iiij. notable
thinges that the gret god hathe endowed you with before all erthely
creatures that we knowe, the whiche must nedes cause you to take a
lorde and an husbonde that the plenteuous yeftes of kinde and of grace
155　mow springe of you bi succession of right lyne into the generacions,
whiche fruitfull generacion must cause all youre liege peple an infinite
ioye and gladnesse and the contrarie therof gret sorw and heuinesse.'
　　'Now, good vncle,' saide that yonge quene, 'what be tho .iiij.
notable thinges that ye preise us so gret of?' Thanne saide the duke:
160　'Madame, yef it like youre high nobilnesse y will declare hem to you
shortely.' 'Vncle,' she saide, 'saie what you luste. Y will here you
gladly.' Thanne saide the duke with gret reuerence: 'Madame, the
f. 283va　furst notable point is this, that we know [that] you | comyn downe of
the worthiest blode in erthe. The secounde is that ye be the grettest
165　enheriter that liuithe this day of woman. The thridde is that in
cunynge and wisdom ye passe al other. The ferthe that as in bodely
shappe and high bewte was neuer none saie like vnto you. Wherfor,
madame, methinkes that these .iiij. notable thinges must nedis
constreine you to encline to oure ententys.'
170　　　Than this yonge quene with right a sadde loke: 'Now vncle, sethe
God and kinde hathe wrought this grete vertues in us, we be moche
more bounde to loue hym and plese hym, and we thanke hym
humbely of all hys gret yeftes. But sethe ye desire in all weyes

146 wedded] maried DT2, *add* and D　　Thanne] *add* there D　　148 right] *om.* D
noble] notable T2　　149 my lady] my *subp.* H1　　150 humble] *om.* D　　151 and]
add hye LK　　meue] *add* to DT2　　152 endowed] endewid LK　　all] *add* other T2
154 and an] to youre DT2　　155 the] *add* governaunce and also K　　158 that] this D
yonge] *om.* D, goode LK　　quene] *add* Katerine D　　159 notable] *om.* LK　　us so gret
of] vs so gretelie D, to vs so gretly T2, so gretely of LK　　160 high] *om.* T2　　will] shalle
LK　　161 saie] *om.* D　　you luste] ye liste and LK　　163 notable] *om.* LK　　know
that] knowin EH1, knowe welle þat DT2　　you] *add* be DT2　　downe] *om.* DT2, *add*
lynyally K　　165 enheriter] anheritid D, aduerted (?) T2　　166 and] *add* in D
ferthe] *add* is LK　　that] *om.* H1, is D　　as] *om.* LK　　167 saie] seen LK　　vnto] *om.*
DLK　　168 madame] *om.* LK　　methinkes] vs þenkes H1, vs thinkithe DT2LK
169 ententys] entente D　　170 Than] *add* seid DT2　　yonge] noble DT2　　quene] *add*
Katerine DT2　　loke] *add* seide LK　　171 this] so DT2　　171–2 we be . . . bounde]
the moche more we be bounde D　　173 in] *om.* T2　　weyes] wise K

that we consent to youre entent as of oure mariage, we lete you plainly
wete that, like as ye haue discriued us, we will discriue hym that we   175
will haue to oure lorde and husbonde. And yef ye cunne gete us suche
one we will be his with all oure herte, for he that shall be lorde of myn
herte and myn husbonde shal haue tho .iiij. notable thinges in hym
ouer all mesure so ferforthe that all creatoures shull haue nede of hym
and he nede of none. For he that shal be my lorde must be of so noble   180
a blode that all kinges must worshipp hym, and therwith so gret a
lorde that y shall neuer dere thenke that y made hym a king, and so
riche that he passe all other in richesse, and so full of bewte that
aungeles haue ioye to beholde hym, and so pure that his moder be a
uirgine, and so meke and benigne that he canne gladly foryeue all   185
offence done to hym. Now | haue y discriued hym that y desire to haue   f. 283vb
to my lorde and husbond, goth sekithe hym, and yef ye may finde
suche one we will be his with all oure herte yef he will fouchesauf.
And finaly, but yef ye gete suche one we shull neuer take none and
takithe this for a full ansuere.' With this she caste her eyen adoune   190
mekely and helde her stille. And whanne the quene her moder and her
lordes had herde this there was gret sorw and heuinesse, for thei saw
well that ther was no remedy in that matere.

   Thanne saide her moder to her with an angri voys: 'Alas, doughter,
is this youre grete wisdom that is talked of so ferre? Moche sorw be ye   195
like to do me and all youres. Alas, ho sawe euer any woman fourge her
an husbonde with wordes? Suche one as ye haue deuised was neuer
none, ne neuer shal be, and therfor good doughter, leue this gret foly
and do as your noble eldres haue do afore you.' Thanne saide this
yonge quene to her moder with a pitous sighinge voys: 'Madame, y   200
wote well bi verrey reson that there is one moche beter thanne y canne
deuise hym, whoso hadde grace to fynde hym. And but he bi his grace
finde me, trustith fully that y shall neuer haue ioye, for y fele bi gret

174 we] y T2   oure] youre D, om. T2   176 ye cunne] oon H1   us] om. DT2
177 his] add wife DT2   of] add al H1   180 he^{1}] om. D   must] shall LK   noble]
notable H1LK   182 shall] shuld K   183 in] om. T2   and] add also DT2
184 ioye] add of hym DT2   to] and LK   185 uirgine] mayde L   and] add so D
all] add þe LK   186 offence] offencis DT2   187 and^{1}] add my DT2   goth]
add and DT2   may] can DT2   188 his] add wiffe DT2   he] ye H1   189 but
yef] but H1, wiþ owte LK   190 adoune] doun to the erthe DT2   191 her^{3}] þe
LK   192 was] add a L   heuinesse] add amonge hem L   193 that^{1}] om. LK
195 talked] callid LK   196 do] add to LK   any] om. DT2LK   her] add suche
LK   197 deuised] descrived with scriv (?) on erasure H1   198 ne] om. T2
gret] om. L   200 quene] add Katerine DT2   202 but] add if T2
203 shall] 'schal' H1   shall neuer] trs. K

reson that there is a trewe wey that we be clene oute of, wherfor we be
205 in derkenesse. And til light of grace come we mowe not see the clere
wey, and whanne hym lest come he shall voyde al the derke clowdes of
ignoraunce and shewe hym clerely to me that myn herte so feruently
desirithe and louithe. And yef so be that hym lust not that y fynde
f. 284ʳᵃ hym, [yet] reson co|maundithe to kepe hole that is vnhurte. Wherfor y
210 beseche you humbly, my ladi and my moder, that ye ne none other
neuer meue to me of this matere, for y behote you pleinly that for to
deye therfor y shal neuer haue other but only hym that y haue
discriued, to whom y shall truly kepe all the pure loue of my herte.'
With this she rose her up, her moder also and all her lordes, fro the
215 parlement with gret sorugh and lamentacion, and toke her leue and
went her wey. And the yonge quene [went] vnto her paleys, whos
herte was so sette on fire with this husbonde that she hadde so
discriued that she coude nothinge thenke ne do, but all her mynde and
all her entencion was only in hym, wherfor she studied and mused
220 continuelly how she might finde hym, but it wolde not be as yet, for
she had no menis therto, notwithstondinge that he was full nigh her
herte, for he it was that had kindelyd in her herte a brennynge fire of
loue that shuld neuer be quenched for no peyne ne tribulacion,
whiche was wel sene after in her right glorious passion.
225 But now y leue this yonge quene as for a tyme, sittinge in her paleis
continuelly thinkinge and ymageninge how she might finde this nwe
spouse, with mani a tere of elongacion and mani a sori sigh for her
blinde ignoraunce. And y shall turne, as oure Lorde will yeue me
grace, [how oure Lorde] by special miracle cleped her [vnto] bapteme
230 in a singuler manere that neuer was herde before ne sethe, and after
how he wedded her visibly in a glorious manere shewing her
f. 284ʳᵇ souerayne tokenes of singuler loue that were neuer shew|ed before

204 trewe] *om.* DT2   we be . . . wherfor] *twice* E   wherfor] for LK   205 clere]
right LK   206 hym lest] *add* for to D, he lyste to L, he list K   derke] derknes of L
207 feruently] *om.* LK   209 yet] that EH1   211 neuer/meue to me] *trs.* DT2
matere] mariage D   that¹] *om.* L   213 shall] *om.* T2   kepe] *add* me with DT2
214 she] the yonge Quene Katerine DT2   her¹] *om.* K   up] *add* and DLK   also] *om.* T2
her³] þe LK   lordes] *add* went T2   fro] of LK   216 went²] *om.* EH1   219 all] *om.*
DT2K   221–2 her herte] *om.* D   222 for . . . herte] *ins.* H1.   224 was] *add*
riȝt K   after] *om.* T2   right] *om.* T2   225 yonge] *om.* T2   quene] *add* Katerine DT2
as] *om.* DT2   226 nwe] *om.* H1   227 with] bi D   of] *add* lamentacion and DT2
sori] sore DLK   228 And] *add* nowe D   oure Lorde] god DT2, my lorde LK
229 how . . . Lorde] *om.* E, *ins.* H1   vnto] *om.* EH1   bapteme] *add* and H1   231 he]
þat oure lorde DT2   visibly] merely LK   232 singuler] *om.* L, sovereyn K   were]
was D

ne sethe to none erthely creature, sauf only to oure Ladi his most blessed moder.

Bisydes Alisaundre a serteyne space of myles, ther duellyd an holy 235 fader in desert that hight Adrian, whiche holy fader had serued oure Lorde in that desert the space of .xxx. wynter in gret penaunce. And on a day as he walked afore his celle in his holy meditaciones, there come ayenst hym the most reuerent lady that euer ani erthely man behelde, and whanne this ermite behelde her excellent astate and high 240 bewte aboue kinde he was so astonied and adradde that he fell downe as dede. Thanne this blessid ladi, seing his gret drede, called hym goodly bi his name and saide: 'Brother Adriane, drede you not, for y am not come to you but for youre right gret worshipp and profit.' With that she toke hym up mildely and comforted hym and saide in 245 this wise: 'Adrian, ye must go in a message fro me into the citee of Alisaundre and into the paleis of the yong quene, and go to her and saie her that that lady gretithe her well whos sone she chase to her lorde and husbonde, sittinge in her parlement with her moder and all her lordes about her, where she had grete conflict and bataile in 250 keping of her virginite. And tell [her] that that same lorde that she chase there is my sone that am a clene virgine, and he desired her bewte and louithe her chastite amonge all virgines in erthe, and bidde her withoute tarienge that she come with the allone to this place and she shall be newe clothed, and thanne she shal see hym and haue hym | 255 to her euerlastinge spouse.'   f. 284va

The hermite heringe all this ansuered dredfulli in this wise, saieng: 'A, blessed ladi, how shulde y do this message, for nother y knowe the citee ne the waye. And what am y, thow y knowe it, for to do a message to the quene? Her meyne wil not suffre me come to her 260 presence, and though y dede she will not leue me of my message but putte me in dures as though y were a faitour.' 'Adrian,' said this blessed ladi, 'drede thou not, for that my sone hathe begonne in her

233 to¹] in H1   most] om. T2K   236 that] om. LK   237 holy] om. T2
239–40 man behelde] creature might beholde LK   240 ermite] holie man DT2   astate]
state LK   241 and adradde that he] þat he dredde and LK   242 his . . . drede] þis D,
this grete drede T2   243 you] þe LK   244 right gret] om. DT2   245 mildely]
mekely LK   246 this] add maner L   fro] for LK   246–7 the citee of Alisaundre]
Alisaunder þat grete cetee L   247 and¹] om. LK   the²] a LK   248 her¹] om. LK
chase] hath chose D   251 her²] om. E, ins. H1   that²] twice E   252 clene] clere LK
and] For DT2   desired] desirith DT2L   257 The hermite] add Adrian DT2   258 A]
om. LK   shulde] shalle DLK   259 do] add suche LK   260 the] a H1   me] add to
DLK   261 though] om. LK   will] wolde DLK   me] add nat D   262 a] add very K
Adrian] thenne T2   263 ladi] add Adrian T2   thou] you D, þe K   in] vppon D

must nedis be performed, for wete it well that she is a speciall chosin
265　vessell of grace before all erthely women that now lyuen. Wherfor
tarie not ne drede not, for bothe ye shull knowe the waie into the citee
and into her paleis also, and ther shall no creature take hede of you.
And whanne ye come into her paleis takithe good hede whiche dores
opene ayens you, and enterithe in hardely till ye come to this faire
270　yong quene whom ye shull finde allone in her studie besieng full sore
to finde bi her wittis that that will not be. Wherfor my sone hath
compassion of her laboure, and for her good will she shall be so
specialli with his grace there was neuer none like her outetake myn
owne persone that am his chosin moder. Wherfor, Adrian, high you
275　fast, and bringe me my dere doughter that y loue with al my herte.'
　　Whan Adrian had resseiued this message he laide hym flat downe
before this souerayne lady, saieng in this wise: 'All worshippe and ioie
be to myn soueraine Lorde God youre blessed sone and to you, and to
f. 284ᵛᵇ　youre wyllis be fulfelled y go atte youre comaun|dement.' He rose
280　hym up and highed hym faste towarde the citee of Alisaundre, and
passid the deserte and [so] forthe til he come into the citee and so went
forthe into the paleis, and as he had lerned so he dede. He entered in
atte the dores that he sawe opin, and passed from chaumbre to
chaumbre till he come vnto her secret studie wher no creature usithe
285　to come but herself allone. And whanne he entered in atte the dore he
sawe wher satte the fairest creature and the most goodly that euer
creature behelde, and she was so sadde in her studie that she herde
hym not vnto the tyme that he kneled hym downe bisides her and
beganne his message in this wise.
290　　'Madame, the endeles might of the fader almighti, the wisdom of
his sone al witty, and the goodnesse of his holy goste, .iij. persones and
one God, be with you now in youre studye.' And whanne this yonge
quene herde a mannes vois bisides her and sawe an olde fader al

　　264 wete] I woote LK　　　265 erthely] om. DT2　　　266 tarie not ne drede not]
drede þe not ne tarie not LK　　for] but H1　　　267 into her] also to the D　　also] om. D
you] add and del. and whan he come into here paleis also and þer shal no creature take hede
of you H1　　　268 into] to D　　hede] om. D　　　dores] doore is LK, dore T2
270 besieng] add hir DT2　　　271 be] add as yit DT2　　　272 for] om. T2
273 specialli] specialle LK, add endewed DT2　　grace] add þat DT2LK　　　273–4 myn
owne] my LK　　　275 and] to H1　　　277 before] by T2　　　278 youre..sone] om. DT2
you] add my soueraine ladie his moodir DT2　　and to²] om. DT2LK　　　279 youre wyllis]
your wille D, his wille T2　　He] Than he DL　　　281 so¹] om. ED　　into] 'in'to H1, to
DLK　　　282 He] and D　　　283 dores] dore T2　　　284 vnto] into D, to LK　　usithe]
vsyd DLK　　　285 in] add there T2　　　286 euer] add any T2K　　　287 sadde] hard T2
288 hym²] om. DT2LK　　　289 beganne] add to sey L　　　291 and¹] om. LK　　his²] the
T2LK　　　292 now] om. D　　yonge] om. D　　　293 quene] add Katerine D

forgrowe in her studie with an olde sclauein upon hym, she was gretly
astonied and ferde and wondred of [t]his sodein cas aboue mesure, for 295
she knewe well that she hadde shette her dores to her, wherfor she
saide with a dredfull voys: 'What be ye that thus meruailously
comythe into my studie where no man vsithe to come [in] by ani
enchauntement?' 'Nay madame,' he saide, 'but as a messenger that is
sent.' 'And, good Sir,' she saide, 'who was so hardi to sende you so 300
homly into oure preui studie to us?' 'Madame,' saide this olde fader,
'the quene of all quenes and ladi of all ladies, the floure of all bounte
and of bewte of all women.' 'Good Sir,' she saide, 'wher duellithe this
lady that ye preise | thus gretly? For we neuer herde speke of suche   f.285ra
one.' 'Madame,' he saide, 'her duellynge is in her sones kingdom wher 305
euerlastinge ioy regnithe.' 'And, good sir,' she saide, 'ho is her sone?'
'Madame,' he saide, 'the kinge of blisse.' 'Nou this is to me,' she saide,
'a gret meruaile that she is so gret in all dignite and her sone so mighti
as ye sayne, and sendithe so symple a messengere as ye bethe.'
'Madame,' he saide, 'it is the properte of that ladi to loue and cherise 310
most tho that refuse hemselff and all erthely thing for the loue of her
sone, and for this cause she sendithe me to you. She gretithe you well
as her doughter by that tokene that whanne ye satte in youre
parlement, youre moder and youre lordes about you, in kepinge of
youre uirginite ye discriued you an husbond wherfor youre moder and 315
all youre lordes were in gret heuinesse. But for ye were so stronge in
that conflict and bataile that ye refused all erthely kinges, she sent you
worde that ye shulde haue an heuenly kinge whiche was born of a
clene virgine and is kinge of all kinges and lorde of all lordeshippes, to
whos comaundement obeiethe heuene and erthe and all that is therin. 320
This same lorde is her owne derrest sone, whiche she conseiued bi the
vertu of the holy goste and bare hym withoute wemme of her virginite

294 in] within T2   sclauein] s`c′lauayn H1   295 of] vppon D   this] his E, his *changed
to* this H1   296 shette] *add* fast H1   to her] *om.* T2   297 meruailously] wondirfulli DT2
298 no] *om.* DT2   man] men T2   vsith] *add* nat D   come] *add* but yif he come in DT2   in]
om. E   299 enchauntement] *add* þen L   Nay madame/he saide] *trs. and add* not L   but] I
come to you DT2   300 And] Now D   300–1 so homly] *om.* LK   301 fader] man H1
302 all¹] *om.* H1   all³] *om.* LK   bounte] bountees T2   302–3 bounte, bewte] *trs.* H1
303 of²] *om.* H1D   304 thus] so DT2LK   we] *add* had T2   neuer herde] *trs.* LK   speke]
om. T2   306 euerlastinge ioy] euer ioye lastinge D   sone] *add* he seide to her L   307 he
saide] *om.* L   the] ke H1   Nou] þen L   this is to me/she saide] *trs.* LK   she saide] *om.* H1
308 that] *ins.* H1   so¹] *om.* T2   sone] *ins.* H1   309 and] as L   bethe] *add* þen he saide L
310 he saide] *om.* L   312 She] and DT2   314–15 in kepinge . . . you] *twice once del.* H1
316 all] *om.* D   for] þat LK   317 kinges] þinges H1   318 shulde] shull H1D
319 lordeshippes] lordes T2K   321 her owne] that same ladies DT2   derrest] dere DT2
322 wemme] vem *on erasure with* `wem′ *above* H1

[with] souerain worship and ioye that neuer was felt of woman ne
neuer shall after, wherfor she sent you to saie by me that ye shulde
325 come allone to my sell with me, and there shull ye see that blessed
lorde and that blessed Lady that abyden youre comyng with gret ioye
and gladnesse.'

Whan this yonge quene herde hym speke so clerely of hym that she
f. 285rᵇ hadde so be|sili sought with mani a feruent desire, she was so
330 brennyngly sette afyre with the desire of his presens that she forgate
all questiones and all her astate and meyne, and rose her vp mekely
and as a debonair lambe folued this olde Adrean thorugh her palays
and the citee of Alisaundre and so thurgh the desert. And in her
walkinge she asked hym mani an high question, and he ansuered her
335 sufficiauntly and enfourmed her in all the pointes of the faithe, and
she receiued plenteuously his doctrine and informacion and vnderstode hym merueylously. And thus walked this olde man Adryan and
this yong quene after hym thorugh the deserte to and fro thei wist not
whedir, wherfor Adrian was a sori man for he hadd utterly loste his
340 sell. He coude in no wise finde the waye thedir and therfor he was in
gret heuynesse, saieng by hymselff: 'Alas, whedir y be deseiued,
whedir this auysion be turned to illusion? Alas, shal this yong ladi
perisshe here amonge wilde bestis? Now, blessed lady, helpe now, for
y am almost in despaire and al my sorw is for this yonge lady that so
345 mekely hathe lefte and forsake all that euer [s]he hadde and obeyed
youre comaundement.'

And as he sorued by hymselff this yong quene perceiued hym and
asked hym what he ayled that he sorwed so. And he ansuered and
saide: 'Truly, ladi, it ys for you and for nothing ellys, for and y shulde
350 deye y canne not fynde my sell, ne y wote whedir y haue brought you,

323 with] wit E   324 to saie] woorde DT2   326 lorde . . . blessed] om. DT2
abyden] abideth DT2   326 gladnesse] add And DT2   327 quene] add Katerine D
speke] add thus D   330 the] om. H1   331 her¹] om. LK   and²] add alle hir D
and³] om. T2LK   332 and¹] om. DLK   folued] folowinge DL   olde] add man K
her] 'þe' T2   333 and¹] add throuȝ DT2   so] om. LK   the²] om. LK   334 her]
add fulle L   335 in] om. LK   336 and¹] add his DT2   337 man] om. LK
338 quene] add Katerine D   after hym/thorugh the deserte] trs. and om. the LK   not]
neuer DT2   340 sell] add for DT2L   He] and K   thedir] thidirwarde DT2
341 by] to DT2   deseiued] add or DT2   342 auysion] avision with a erased H1,
vysyon K   to] into LK   343 perisshe here] be perisshid DT2   here] om. D   helpe]
add me T2   344 al] om. H1D   my] add moost DT2   345 and forsake] om. LK
euer] om. K   she] he E, 's'he H1   obeyed] obeieth vnto DT2   347 he] this Adrian
DT2   348 he¹] hym H1DT2   349 for²] om. DT2   350 wote] not H1, add nat
DT2LK   whedir] whither with wh on erasure H1, add that D

ne what y shall do alas y wote not.' 'Fader,' she saide, 'bethe of good
comfort and hauithe trewe faithe, for trustithe fully that that lady
[that] is so good sent neuer | for us to perisshe us here in this f. 285ᵛᵃ
wildernesse. Fader,' she saide, 'what mynstre is that y se yender that
is so riche and so faire?' And Adrian loked up and saide: 'Where see 355
yee that?' 'Yender in the est,' she said, and he wyped his eyen and
behelde and sawe the most glorious mynstre that euer man sawe. And
whanne he hadde seyn that, he was full of ioye and saide to her: 'Now
blessed be that God that hathe visited with so perfit faithe, for there is
that place wherinne ye shull resseiue so gret a worshipp and ioye that 360
ther was neuer none like you sauf only the quene of all quenes.' 'Now,
good fader,' she sayd, 'high you faste that we were there, for there is
all my desired ioye.'

Within shorte tyme thei neighed to this glorious place, and whanne
they come to the yate there come ayenst hem a glorious cumpany all in 365
white with chapelettis of white lelyes on her hedis, and the excellent
beauute was so gret that neyther this yonge quene Katerine ne Adrian
might beholde hem, but all rauisshed fell downe before hem with gret
drede. Thanne one that was more excellent thanne another spake furst
and said to this yonge quene: 'Stonde up, oure dere suster, and 370
welcome with all oure hertes, for bi thi gret mekenesse and pure
chastite oure worshippe and ioye shal be gretly encresed, wherfor be
ye gladde in oure Lorde, for all virgines shull preise you. Come forthe
with vs to that souerayne lorde that will werke in you meruaylous
werkes of loue.' And thus thei passed forthe with gret ioye and 375
sollempnite till thei come to the secounde yate. And | whanne thei f. 285ᵛᵇ
entered in there come ayenst hem a moche more glorious cumpani
withouten ani comparison clothed all in purpure with fresshe
chapelettys of rede roses vpon her hedes. And whanne this yong
quene sawe hem she fell downe flat before hem with gret drede and 380
reuerens, and thei benigly comforted her and with a gladde chere said

351 not] *add* where I am D, *add* what to do ne where y am T2   352 faithe] *add* with
you DT2   for] and LK   353 that] *om.* E   here] *om.* DT2   354 wildernesse] *add*
Then D, *add* but K   Fader/she saide] *trs.* D   mynstre] ministre *changed to* monistre H1
that¹] *add* þat DT2LK   that²] *add* the whiche D   355 saide] *add* to hir T2
357-8 And . . . seyn that] then T2   358 hadde seyn] sawe D   359 that] *om.* D
visited] *add* 'ȝow' H2, *add* you DT2   362 fader] *add* Adrianne D   she sayd] Adrian T2
364 to this] that DT2   367 ne] nothir D, *add* þis L, neiþer þis K   368 might] *add*
not L   might beholde] myghold T2   with] *on erasure* H1   369 drede] *ins.* H1
371 and] *add* thi DT2   372 worshippe, ioye] *trs.* K   374 that¹] the D
376 thei²] *add* come and L   377 in] withinne DT2, *om.* K   moche] *om.* DT2
380 quene] *add* Katerine D

to her in this wise: 'Drede you not, oure dere suster, for there was
neuer none before you hertlyer welcome to oure soueraine Lorde and
to vs thanne ye be, and therfor ioye ye in oure Lorde, for ye shull
385 resseiue oure clothinge and oure crowne with so gret worshippe and
ioye that all seintes shull ioye in you. Come on now faste, for the
Lorde of ioye abidithe you with gret desire of youre presens.'

Thanne this yonge quene with trembelyng ioye humbely passed
forthe with hem as she that was so rauisshed with gret ioye and
390 meruaile that she hadde no worde to saye aught to all that was saide to
her. And whanne thei were entered into the body of the chirche, she
herde a merveilous melodye of suetnesse which passed all hertis to
discriue, and therwith she behelde a riall quene stonding in state with
gret multitude of aungeles and seintes about her. The beauute and the
395 richesse of this quene might no herte thinke ne penne write, for it
excedithe eueri mannes mynde. Thanne this noble cumpani of
martires with the felawshippe of uirgines that ladde this yong
quene betwene hem fill doune prostrat before this riall emperesse,
and with soueraine reuerence saide in this wise: 'Oure most soueraine
f. 286ʳᵃ lady, quene of heuene, emperesse of hell, | ladi of the worlde, moder of
401 oure soueraine Lorde king of blisse, to whos comaundement obeiethe
all heuenly creatoures and erthely, likithe you to wete, blessed lady,
that atte youre comaundement we present you here oure dere suster
whos name is specialli wretin in the boke of euerlastinge lyff,
405 besechinge youre most benigne grace to resseiue her as youre seruaunt
and chosin doughter, and to make a perfit ende of that werke that oure
soueraine Lorde almighti God your most blessed sone and ye haue
meruailously begonne in her.'

With that, that glorious emperesse with a glad and [a] reuerent
410 chere loked upon hem and saide: 'Bringe my beloued doughter to me
that y may speke with her.' And whanne this yong quene Katerine
herde the wordes of that most soueraine quene, she was so fulfelled
with heuenly ioye that she lay a gret while as dede. Thanne this holy
felawshipp toke her mekely up and brought her to this quene of blisse,

384 vs] *add* alle D   387 with] *add* right D   388 quene] *add* Katerine D
388–9 humbely/passed forthe] *trs.* DT2   389 so] *om.* DT2   390 aught] *om.* DT2
393 state] hir estate DT2   394 the] *om.* H1   395 ne] *add* noo DT2K
396 excedithe] excedit H1, excedid K   eueri] eny D   400 lady] *om.* D   of³] *add* alle D
emperesse . . . hell/ladi . . . worlde] *trs.* DT2LK   402 erthely] alle erthelie creatures
DT2   403 that] *om.* LK   atte] *om.* H1   405 most] *om.* D   406 that werke] all
T2   409 that²] the D, þis LK   a²] *om.* E   410 Bringe] *add* me DT2   my] me
changed to my H1   412 that] the D   414 of blisse] *om.* T2

to whom she saide: 'Mi dere doughter, right welcome to me, be 415
stronge and of good comfort, for ye be specially chose among all
women to be souerainly worshipped with the loue of my sone.
Katerin, doughter, haue ye mynde how ye discriued you an husbonde
sittinge in youre parlement where ye hadde a gret conflict and bataile
to defende youre maidenhode?' Thanne this yong quene, knelinge 420
with most humble reuerence and drede saide: 'A, moste blessed lady,
blessed be ye aboue all women, I haue mynde how y chase there a lorde
full ferre fro my knowlage. But now, good ladi, bi his mighti merci
and youre speciall grace he hathe opened the eyen of my blind |
ignoraunce so that y see the clere waye of trouthe. Wherfor, most f. 286rb
blessed ladi, y beseche you with al my herte that ye do me merci and 426
grace and yeue me hym that ye haue behight me, that my herte louithe
and desirithe aboue all thinge, withoute whom y may not lyue.' With
these wordes all her spirites were shette up so faste that she laye as
dede. Than this noble quene of grace with suete wordes comforted 430
and said: 'Drede not, my dere doughter, for it shall be right as ye
desire, but ye lacke one thinge that ye must nedis haue or ye come into
the presence of my sone, for ye must be clothed with the sacrement of
bapteme, wherfor come on, for all thinge is redi.'

   Ther was a fonte in that chirche solempli arrayed with all that 435
longithe therto. Thanne this quene of ioye called Adrian to her, the
olde fader, and saide to hym: 'Brother, this werke longithe to you that
be a prest. Baptise my doughter, and loke ye chaunge not her name, for
Katerine she shall hight forthe, and y shall holde her to you myselff
and be her godmoder.' Thanne Adrian baptised her, and whanne she 440
was clothed ayen, this heuenly quene saide to Katerine: 'Now, my
owne doughter, be gladde and full of ioye, for now the lackith
nothinge that longithe to the wiff of an heuenly spouse. Come now
with me, for y shall bringe you to my Lorde and to my sone that
abidith you with gret ioye.' Thanne was this yonge quene Katerine so 445
full of ioye that none herte coude expresse the suetnesse that she felt.

415 me] *add* and D   416 be] *om.* H1   417 women] *add* for LK   418 ye¹]
add nat DT2   421 humble reuerence] humylite L, humbilnes K   A] *om.* LK
422 aboue] amonge DT2   a] that DT2LK   lorde] *add* þat was T2LK   423 mighti]
grete K   424 the] myne DT2   425 y] *add* may DT2   429 that] as H1
430 comforted] *add* hir DT2   432 or] *add* that D   433 for] *om.* DT2
434 wherfor] *add* my dere doughter DT2   436 longithe] longid DT2L   this] þe LK
of] *add* heven and of T2   the] that D   439 forthe] *om.* DT2   to you/myselff] *trs.* H1
440 godmoder] goode moodir D, *add* And LK   441 was] *add* thus DT2   ayen] *om.*
DT2   442 for] *om.* LK   the lackith] ye lak DT2, *trs.* LK   443 heuenly] *add* kyng
and T2   444 to²] *om.* K   445–6 so/full of ioye] *trs.* L

She went forthe with this quene of ioye till thei come into the quere,

f. 286ᵛᵃ and as thei entered inne so gret | a suetnesse come ayens hem that it
passed all hertis to thenke it. With that she behelde the semliest yonge

450 kinge stondinge atte the auuter crowned with a riche crowne, havinge
aboute hym multitude of aungeles and of seintes. And whanne his
blessed moder sawe hym she leide her downe prostrat and toke the
crowne fro the hede and saide to hym with humble reuerence: 'Most
souerayne worship and ioye be to you, kinge of blisse, my Lorde, my

455 God and my sone, like youre most hynesse to wete that y haue
brought you here as youre will is youre humble seruaunt and
hondemaide Katerine, that for youre loue hathe refused and forsake
all ertheli thinge and is comen allone atte my sendinge with olde
Adrian, foryeting all ertheli good and astate, trusting fully to my

460 promesse. Wherfor y beseche you humbly, my soueraine Lord God
and my derest sone, that ye of youre endeles goodnesse fulfell my
promesse.'

Whanne this souerayne kinge had thus herde his moder, he toke her
goodly up and saide to her: 'Mi dere moder, ye know right wele that

465 all youre desire is my full will, and y haue desired her to be knette to
me in perfit mariage amonge all the virgines that lyue now in erthe.
Wherfor, Katerine, come hedir to me.' And whanne she herde hym
name her, so grete a suetnesse entered into her soule that she fell
downe as dede lyeng before hym. With that he gaue her a nwe

470 strengthe that passed kinde and said to her in frendely wise: 'Katerine,
doughter, cunne ye finde in youre herte to loue me best before all
thinge?' And she, beholdinge that blessed uisage that aungeles haue

f. 286ᵛᵇ continuelly ioye to beholde in, saide: 'A, most suet|test and most
blessed Lorde, so haue y do and shall whiles y lyue, ne neuer loued y

475 thinge but only you and for you.' Thanne saide that blessed king:
'Katerine, yeue me youre honde,' and she with soueraine ioye offered
hym her honde. And thanne that glorious king saide [to her]: 'Y take
you to my wedded wiff, be[hot]inge you truly neuer to forsake you
while youre lyff lastithe. And after youre present lyff y shall bringe

448 inne] *add* they felt T2　it] *twice* E　　450 havinge] and T2　　451 hym] *add* a
grete T2K, *add* a L　of²] *om.* K　　453 the] hir DK　humble] *add* chere and K
455 like] *add* to D, *add* it to T2, *add* yt L　458–9 thinge . . . erthli] *om.* K　　465 and] for
DT2　　466 now/in erthe] *trs.* K　　468 into] within D　469 a nwe] *om.* T2
471 before] ouer DT2, afore LK　473 continuelly] continuelle L　in] *om.* LK　saide]
om. K　suettest] *add* lorde D　most²] *om.* DT2　　474–5 ne . . . for you] for I loued
neuer noo þinge so moche as you oonelie DT2　　477 to her] here EH1, *add* here D, H1
punctuates here. I　　478 you¹] the D　behotinge] besechinge E

you to endeles lyff, where ye shull duell with me in blisse withoute 480
ende, in tokin wherof y sette this ringe vpon youre finger whiche ye
shull kepe in rememberaunce of me as oure weddinge ringe. And now
my dere wiff, be gladde and stronge of faithe, for ye must do gret
thingges for my name and resseiue moche turment and peyne and a
gret stroke on youre necke, but drede you not, my dere wyff, for y 485
shall neuer parte from you but comfort you and strengthe you.'

Than saide this humble spouse: 'A, most blessed Lorde, y thanke
you with all myn hert of all youre gret mercies, beseching you, my
soueraine Lorde, that ye make me worthi to be of youre lyueray, that
suffered so moche for me, and that y may [in sum thinge] be like you 490
that all myn herte louith and desirithe aboue all thinge.' With this,
this glorious kinge bade Adrian do on his vestimentes and go to masse
and saie the seruisc ouer hem as longithe to the custume of weddinge,
and that souerayn Lorde of blisse helde his spouse bi the honde
knelynge with her all the masse tyme before Adrian.   495

A, lorde, what ioye and blisse was felt in that blessed virgines soule!
Al that tyme was neuer no suche ioye felt before outake her ioye that
conceiued and bare the souerayne ioye and blisse whiche was his most
blessed moder. | All the spirites of heuene ioyed of this mariage so f. 287ra
feruently that it was herde the same tyme as thei kneled togederes how 500
thei songe this vers: *Sponsus amat sponsam Saluator uisitat illam*, and
that with so gret a melodie that no herte might conceiue it. This was a
solempne and a singuler mariage. Ther was neuer no suche herde of in
erthe, wherfor this glorious virgine is worthi to be gretly worshipped
and loued among all the uirgines that euer were in erthe. And whanne 505
this masse was done, this heuenly kinge saide to her: 'Now, my dere
wiff, tyme is come that y must go ayen fro whennes y come. Y haue
fulfelled all youre desire, and yef ye desire ani more y am redi to
graunte you what ye luste haue of me. After my departinge hennis ye
shull abide here .x. dayes till ye be perfitly taught all my lawes and all 510
my will. And whan ye comen home ye shull fynde youre moder dede.

481 wherof] here of D   482 oure] your DLK   483 gladde, stronge] *trs.* D   of]
in the D   485 on] in LK   488 of . . . mercies] *om.* H2   490 suffered] suffreth
H1   in sum thinge] *om.* EH1   thinge] thingis H2T2   492 his] thi H2T2
493 saie] sei *and one letter erased* H1   hem] us H2T2   494 of blisse] *om.* H2T2
honde] *add* and H1   495 tyme] while H2   496 blessed] *om.* L   497 tyme] *add* I
trowe there H2T2   no] *om.* H1   before] *add* þat tyme LK   outake] oute 'take' H1
498 and²] *add* kynge of K   blisse] blissid lord L   500 the] þat H1   502 that¹]
om. K   a] *om.* H2K   503–4 in erthe] merthe H2   507 Y] and LK   508 desire²]
list LK   am] *add* a H1   509 luste] *add* to H1H2LK   departinge] partinge H2LK
hennis] *om.* T2   510 shull] must H2T2   till] *add* þat K   be] *ins.* H1

But drede you not, for ye were neuer missed there all this tyme, for y
ordeined one in youre stede that all wenyn it be youre owne persone,
and whanne ye come home ayen she shall voyde. Now fare wel, my
515 derest wiff.' And with that she cried with a gret and [a] piteous voys:
'A, my souerain Lorde God, and all the ioye of my sowle, haue mynde
upon me.' With that he blessed her and vanisshed awey from her
sight, and for sorw of this partinge she fell downe in swowninge so
that she laye a large hour withoute sperit of lyff.

520 　　Tho was Adrian a sori man, he wepte and cried on her that it was
pitee to see or here. So atte the laste she awoke and lefte up her eyen
f. 287ʳᵇ and sawe nothinge aboute her but a litell | olde sell and Adrian
wepinge besides her, for all was gone that there was, bothe mynstre
and paleys and alle the comfortable sightes that she hadde sayne, and
525 specially he that was cause of all her ioye and comfort. Now is her
herte brought in so gret mornynge that she canne nothinge do but
wepe and sigh, till atte the laste she behelde the ringe of oure Lorde
sette on her fingre, and thanne she swownid ayen and she kist it an .C.
tymes with mani a pitous tere. And Adrian comforted her in his best
530 wise with many a blessed exhortacion, and she toke mekely all his
comfortes and obeied hym as her fader and duellid with hym the tyme
that oure Lorde assigned her til she was sufficiauntly taught all that
was nedefull to her.

　　And whanne tyme come she went home ayen to her palays, and as
535 sone as she might she made all her meyni to resseiue bapteme, and
.iiij. yere after this she helde her housholde in her paleys with full
cristen gouernaunce. All her ioye was euer to speke or to thenke on
her Lorde and her spouse, ther was nothinge ellys in her mynde but
his worshippe and his praisinge. Many a creature conuerted she to
540 hym. In this mene tyme she was neuer ydell, but continuelly ocupied
in his seruice full of charitee, for all her ioye was to drawe creatures to

513 wenyn] wenden H2LK　　　it] add had H2T2LK　　　owne] owe H1, om. T2
514 she] he on erasure H1, ye T2　　shall] add sone H2　　515 a²] om. E　　516 mynde]
add euere H2T2　　me] add and H2　　518 for] add the L　　sorw] sorowynge K
partinge] departyng LK　　swowninge] swowne H2　　so] om. LK　　519 that] ins. H1
of] and LK　　520 he] and H2K　　521 here] add and H2LK　　awoke] add of hir
swownynge H2T2　　523 wepinge] om. T2　　there was] were there K　　525 cause]
om. K　　526 in] into H1H2　　canne] couthe H2LK　　527 wepe] wepte LK　　sigh]
sighed LK　　of] þat T2　　530 exhortacion] exaltacion H2　　she] this noble virgine
Katerine H2T2　　531 comfortes] comforte H2　　536 this] om. H2　　537 euer] om.
H2T2　　538 ellys] om. H2T2　　but] add by LK　　539 his¹ . . . praisinge] her feithe
sche convertyd K　　his¹,²] her L　　conuerted she] om. K　　540-1 continuelly . . . his]
contynued in goddis K

hym. And thus y lete her duelle in her paleis fulfelled with al manere
of vertues and graces as the full dere and singuler spouse of almighti
God.

In this mene tyme the emperoure Maxencius, that was full enemy 545
to Goddes lawe and a cruell tyraunt, concidered the grete noblesse of
the citee | of Alisaundre and ordeined hym to come thedir with f. 287ᵛᵃ
multitude of peple to do a solempne sacrifice. And whanne he was
come he made all the peple to assemble, bothe pore and riche, for to
do sacrifice to the ydoles, and the cristen that wolde not do sacrifice he 550
made hem to be cruelly turmented. This yonge quene Katerine was
thanne of age of .xviij. yere, duellinge in her palays full of richesse and
of seruauntes. And as she satte in her studie in contemplacion of her
most dere lorde and truest spouce, she herde houge noyse of songe
and instrumentis and gret crienge of bestis, and wondered gretly what 555
it might be and called a messenger anone and bade hym go and bringe
her worde anone what it ment. He did her comaundement and come
ayen in haste and tolde her all the manere therof. And whanne she
hadde herde it she fell in so gret a sorw for the vnworshipp of her
Lorde and uerray spouse that her thought she might not endure it, 560
wherfor in gret haste she rose her up foryetinge herselff and all wordly
astate and made the signe of the crosse in her forhede and went
stre[i]te to the emperoure. And whanne she come thedir and behelde
in euery syde, she sawe mani a cristen man meued to do sacrifice for
drede of dethe, wherfor she was hougely greued in her soule. She 565
gothe her hardely thorugh the p[r]ece, and all tho that behelde her had
meruaile of her gret beauute and lefte her sacrifice for to folow here
mani one of hem, and for to beholde her.

And whanne she come to the emper|oure she loked upon hym with f. 287ᵛᵇ
[a] sadde chere and saide vnto hym in this wise: 'Emperoure, the 570

542 with] of LK   545 In this] And than in this H2T2   enemy] of envie H1
546 a] om. H2   tyraunt] add he T2   concidered] consider H1   noblesse] nobylnesse
H1T2   546–7 grete . . . the] noble and rialle H2T2   547 and] add he H2   come]
go L   with] add grete LK   549 come] add þedir L   assemble . . . for] om. H2
550 sacrifice] sacrafices H1   551 cruelly turmented] add and H2, trs. K   551–2 was
thanne] was T2, trs. LK   552 of ᵗ] add the H2   of age] om. L   yere] add age L
duelling/in her palays] trs. K   full of] wiþ grete K   552–3 and of] add her E, add her
del. H1   553 of ¹] many K   554 houge] ho'w'ge H1, moche T2, grete LK
555 and²] add she H2L   556 hym] hem K   go and] om. LK   557 anone] om. LK
560 her thought] she thought þat LK   561 her] om. LK   up] add and LK   wordly]
erþely L   562 went] add hir H2   563 streite] strette E   thedir] thidre as correction
H1   564 in] on LK   565–6 She gothe her] and wente L   566 thorugh] through
out alle H2   prece] pece E, p'r'ece H1   had] add grete H2T2K   567 gret] excellent
T2, om. K   568 one] om. LK   570 a] om. E   wise] add Sir LK

dignite of thin ordre and wey of reson shulde meue me to salwe the yef
thou were the creature of heuene, and that thou woldest call thi corage
fro thi fals goddes. Whi hast thou now assembled this multitude of
peple as in veyne for to wors[h]ippe the madnesse of ydoles? Art thou
575 not ashamed of thi blindenesse? Thou meruailest gretly of this temple
that is made with mannes honde and of the precious ornamentes that
shal be as poudre before the wynde. Thou shuldest rather, and thou
haddest ani resonable witte, meruaile of heuene and of erthe and of all
thinges that be conteyned therinne, the sonne, the mone, the sterris,
580 how thei serue fro the begynninge of the worlde unto the ende, thei
rennyn night and day to the occident and comyn ayen by the orient
and thei be neuer weri. And whanne thou hast perceiued all these
thinges, aske and lerne ho is the fourmer and maker of all these
thinges. And whan thou haste knowe hym, bi his grace thou shalt
585 finde none like to hym, for he is almighti and therfor hym only
worshipp and glorifie, for he is only almighti God and none but he,
kinge of kinges and lorde [of all lordshippes and of] all creatoures.'
And thanne she began to declare to hym the incarnacion and the
merueilous goodnesse of the sone of God, wherfor the emperoure was
590 al abasshed and coude not ansuere her, but atte the last he saide: 'And
thou, woman, suffre us to ende oure sacrifice, after that we shull
f. 288ra ansuere the.' And thanne he comaunded that she shulde be | brought
into his paleis and kepte with gret diligence. And all that herde her
hadde gret meruaile of her gret wisdom and passinge beaute, for she
595 was faire before all women that lyued. And so she apered to hem all
that loked on her, and specially the cristen that were constreined to do
sacrifice for drede of dethe toke suche corage to hem in the
b[eh]oldinge of her sadnesse and reuerent beauute that thei hadde
leuer haue suffered dethe thanne to forsake her faithe.
600   After, whanne the emperoure come to his paleys, he sent for this

571 and] bi H2T2   shulde] shal H1   572 call] *ins.* H1   573 this] *add* grete
H2T2   574 for] *om.* K   worshippe] worsippe E   the] thi H2T2, *add* fals K
576 the] *om.* H1   577 wynde] *add* and LK   rather] *add* pas H2   579 conteyned]
conceiued H2   sonne, mone] *trs.* K   581 night] 'nith' H1   by] to H1   582 neuer]
'n'euer H1   583–4 of all . . . thinges] þerof and of alle oþer thinges T2   585 hym
only] al oonly hym LK   585–6 and . . . almighti] *om.* H2T2   587 and¹] *om.* K   of
all lordeshippes and of] ouer EKL, of H1, of alle lordes and lordships and of T2
588 she] this Katerine H2   and] *add* of H2   590 saide] *add* to hir H2   And]
om. H2   591 sacrifice] *add* and H2   593 all] *add* thoo H2   her] *add* þey L
594 and] *add* of hir H2   595 that lyued] *om.* H2T2   597 suche] *add* a H2L
598 beholdinge] boldinge E, 'be'holdyng H1   599 haue suffered] suffir LK
600 After] H2T2 *punctuate and add* And

yonge quene and saide to her in this wise: 'Maide, we haue herde of youre eloquence and meruaile of youre gret wysedom, but we were occupied in sacrifices that we might not tende to you. Wherfor y aske you now of what kinrede ye be come.' And she ansuered and saide to hym: 'That y shall answere the shall not be bi auauntinge of pride but 605 only for loue of trouthe. I am Katerin, doughter of the kinge Costis, and though y were bore and norisshed in purple and taught in the liberall artis, y haue all wordely thinge refused and yeue me frely to oure most souerayne Lorde Ihesu Crist, that is verrey God and man, wherfor the goddes that ye worshippen be verrey [v]eyne and fals and 610 withoute ani profit, ne thei mow socour none in tribulacion ne deliuer none in perile.' Thanne saide the emperoure to her: 'Yef it be so as thou saiest, all the worlde failithe and thou only sayest sothe. And all trouthes shull be confermed bi the mouthes of .ij. or [.iij.] witnesse, for though thou were an aungell or an heuenly vertu, yet me aught not 615 to leue the allone, and so | miche lasse that thou art a freel woman.'   f. 288rb She ansuered and saide: 'Emperoure, y praie the that thou suffre thi madnesse to be ouercome, that so grete encomberaunce of perturbacion be not in the corage of the that holdest thiselff so mighti. For yef thou wilt be gouerned bi gode corage thou shalt be a kinge, and ellys 620 truste me fully that thou shalt be a thralle. Wherfor labourest thou to embrace us in thi dedly sotelteys with thin ensaumples of philosopherres? Thei auaile the not, and thei hurte us not, but and thou wilt be a meke disciple y shall teche the true philosophie, wherbi thou maist lerne to knowe thi God and thi maker and to rule thiselff and to 625 regne as a worthi kinge.'

And whanne the emperoure sawe that he couthe in no wise ansuere to her by wisdom, he parted awey fro her with gret wonder and sent anone his letteres to all the gramarians and rethoriens that thei shulde come to his presens in gret haste vnto the citee of Alisaundre, and yef 630

601 quene] add Katerine H2   602 and] add I H2T2   meruaile] add gretelie H2
603 tende] tent H1   you] yowre speche L   604 you] om. LK   605 not be bi] be
noo LK   606 of ¹] add the H1   the] om. H2LK   607 in²] add alle H2LK
609 most souerayne/Lorde] trs. and add god H2   Ihesu . . . man] lorde and kinge H2T2
610 veyne] feyne EL, so changed to veyne H1, feyned K   and²] om. H2LK   611 ani]
om. H2T2   ne¹] for H2T2   none] add that ben H2T2   612 none] add þat been T2
her] Katerine H2   614 shull] shuld H1H2   confermed] conformyd L   or .iij.] LK, or
E, om. H1H2T2   616 leue] loue changed to leue H1   617 saide] add Sir K
618–19 perturbacion] turbacion H2, tribulacion T2   620 shalt] add not erased H1
621 that] om. H2LK   a] om. H2   622–3 philosopherres] philosophy LK   623 but
and] and if H1   629 anone his] om. LK   rethoriens] rethoricience L, rethorience K,
retoriciencez T2   630 and] om. D

thei might ouercome an eloquent uirgine he wolde rewarde hem with
merueilous yeftes. And so there were brought .l. maistres that
surmounted all dedli men in worldely wisdom, and whan thei come
to the presens of the emperoure thei desired to knowe the cause of her
635 comynge. Thanne the emperoure saide: 'We haue a maide none like to
her in souerayn wisdom, and she labourithe to confounde all oure
lawes and saithe that oure goddes be fendes, and yef ye may ouercome
her y shall sende you home into youre cuntreies with gret worshipp.'
f. 288ᵛᵃ Thanne one of hem that was of gret presumpcion | saide: 'This is a
640 wonder counsaile of an emperoure, for to ouercome a yong frele
mayde he hathe called to hym the wisest of the worlde from so ferre
parties, whanne one of the symplest children that we haue might
ouercome her lightly.' Thanne saide the emperoure to hem: 'Y might
haue constreined her to haue do sacrifice, but y hadde leuer that she
645 be ouercome bi youre argumentis.' Thanne said the maistres: 'Late
bringe her forthe, and whanne she is ouercome bi her foly she shall
well knowe that she sawe neuer erst wise men.'

And whanne the glorious uirgine knewe the strife of this disputison
that abode her, she recomaunded her all to oure Lorde her souerayne
650 spouse with full truste of his promesse, and thanne an aungel apered
to her and bade her drede not but be strange and stable of faithe, for
she shulde haue a gret uictori and bringe hem all to the crowne of
marterdom. Than was her soule full of ioye, yeldinge souerayne
worshipp and thanke to her souerayne Lorde and trewest spouse. And
655 whanne she was brought before the emperoure and the maistres, she
saide to the emperoure: 'This is a faire iugement of a lorde, to sette .l.
maistres ayenst a symple mayde and behote hem gret guerdon for her
uictori, and me allone ye constreyne to dispute with hem withoute
hope of guerdon. But my Lorde Ihesu Crist that is verray guerdon to

633 all] *om.* DT2   in] and T2   634 presens of the emperoure] Emperour
presence K   637 saithe] s`e′ith H1   638 with] *add* riȝt L   worshipp] worshippis
DT2   640 emperoure] *add* that DLK   yong] *om.* LK   641 hathe called] callith D
of] *add* all K   so ferre] the ferthest DT2   642 might] may LK, *add* haue DT2
643 to hem] *om.* LK   644 haue²] *om.* T2K   644-5 that . . . ouercome] to oercome
her LK   645 the maistres] that maister DT2   649 all] *om.* LK   650 with] *om.*
T2   an aungel] þe aungelle L, þe aungel of god K   651 but] *add* seide D   of] in the D
652 she] ye DT2   shulde] shulle D   hem all] alle these maisters DT2   653-4 souerayne
. . . thanke] thankingis and soueraine worshipp DT2   654 her souerayne] our LK
and²] *add* her LK   655 and] *add* all DT2   656 of] for H1   to sette] þat settith L,
þat sette K   657-8 and behote . . . uictori] *twice once del.* H1   658 ye] *add* grante no
þynge but L   constreyne] *add* me for L, *add* for K   659 of] and *del.* `of′ H1
guerdon²] g`we′rdon *ins. on erasure* H1

all tho that striuen for hym shall be only with me and my parfit 660
guerdon.'

Thanne the maistres begonne and saide that it was impossible that
God had be made man or that he shulde mow suffre dethe. And than
that blessed virgine shewed hem bi | holy scripture that there was   f. 288ᵛᵇ
nothing inpossible to God, and also she shewed hem that paynimes   665
hadd saide it long before or it was done, for Craton had saide it, and
Sibile also saide that he was blessed that shulde hange high on a tree.
And whanne the virgine had shewed hem by opin preues her
blyndenesse and declared her goddes veyne and fals, these maistres
were so abasshed and wost not what to saie, but helde hem still. The   670
emperoure seinge this was fulfelled with gret wratthe and beganne to
blame hem sharpely that thei wolde suffre hemselff to be ouercome
with a simple mayden. Thanne one that was maister ouer all that other
saide: 'Sir emperour, wetithe right well that there was neuer none that
might holde hym ayenst us but he were ouercome anone, but this   675
mayde in whiche the sperit of God spekithe yeuithe us so gret
meruaile that we haue no reson to saie ayenst Ihesu Crist, and therfor
we knowlage us sadly that but ye cunne yeue us prouable sentence of
the goddes that we haue worshipped unto now we be all conuerted to
Ihesu Crist.'   680

And whanne the tyraunt herde this he was al sette afyre in
wodenesse, and comaunded thei shulde be brent in the middes of
the citee. And thanne this holy uirgine comforted hem and stabled
hem to suffre marterdom and taught hem diligently the faithe. And
thanne thei sorued that thei shulde deye withoute bapteme. The holy   685
uirgine ansuered hem and saide: 'Drede you not, my dere bretheren,
for the sheding of youre blode shal be acounted you for bapteme.
Blesse you with the figure of the crosse and ye shull be crowned with
me in heuene.' And whanne thei were caste in the middell of the |
flawme thei yelde up her soules to God that neither her clothes ne her   f. 289ʳᵃ
here were tamed with the fire. And whanne the cristen had beried her   691
bodies, the tyraunt spake to the virgine and saide: 'A, thou right noble

662 the maistres] thei T2   663 made] add a LK   shulde mow] trs. LK
667 shulde] shulle D   668 whanne] ins. H1   669 her] þe K   670 so] sore L   and]
that thei DT2   helde] ins. H1   672 hemselff] add so feble DT2L   673 ouer] of hem
DT2   that other] om. DT2   678 knowlage] knowe LK   that but] wiþ owte LK   but] add
if H1DT2   prouable] profitable DT2, probabille L   682 comaunded] add anone that D
be] add alle DT2   685 bapteme] add and DT2K   686 uirgine] add Katerine D
687 acounted] add to K   for²] as K, add youre DT2   689 middell] add and del. of þe
mydle H1   the²] om. H1   691 cristen] add men T2   692 right] om. D

uirgine, haue pite of thi youthe and thou shalt nexst the quene be
called lady in my paleys, and thin ymage shall be made in the middes
695 of the citee and worshipped of all as goddesse.' To whom the virgine
saide: 'O thou most fole, leue of to saie suche thinges, for it is
wickednesse to thenke on hem, and y haue tolde the pleinly and yet do
that y am holy youen to my Lorde Ihesu Crist as his spouse. He is my
ioye and all my loue and all the swetnesse of my sowle, wherfor
700 neither faire wordes ne drede of turnementes may not parte me from
hym.' And thanne he, fulfelled with wodenesse, comaunded that she
shulde be dispoiled and betin with sharpe scourges and put into a
streite prison and ther to be turmented .xij. dayes withoute mete or
drinke.

705   In the mene tyme the emperoure rode oute for certaine ocupa-
ciones, and the quene had grete desire to see this holy uirgine, wherfor
in a night she toke with her the prinse of knightes and went priuely to
the prison wherinne this holy virgine was. And whanne she come
thedir she sawe so gret a light withinne the prison that her thought
710 that all erthely light was but derkenesse thereto, and therewith she
sawe glorious aungeles that benignely anointed the woundes of that
glorious uirgine. And thanne this blessed virgine beganne to preche to
the quene the ioyes of heuene with so suete and so devout wordes that
f. 289ʳᵇ she conuerted her to the faithe, and she bade her | to be stronge for she
715 shulde resseiue the crowne of marterdom, and so thei spake togederes
till midnight. And whanne Porphirie hadde herde all her talkynge, he
fell downe to the fete of the virgine and resseiued the faithe of Ihesu
Crist with .CC. knightez. And for that the tyraunt hadde comaunded
that she shulde be .xij. dayes withoute mete or drinke, almighti God
720 her soueraine Lorde sent to her a white dowue fro heuene that fedde
her with heuenly mete.

And after that, oure Lorde Ihesu Crist hymselff came to her with
multitude of aungeles and of virgines and saide to her: 'Mi dere
doughter and true wyff, knowest thou me thi maker, for whom thou

693 nexst the quene/be] *trs.* L   695 virgine] *add* Katerine D   696 suche] *add*
voide DLK   697 and'] *om.* DLK   tolde] *add* to Hı   698 that] *om.* D   my Lorde]
om. Hı   701 he] *add* alle DLK   she] 'sche' Hı   702 betin] alle tobete LK
sharpe] *om.* LK   into] in LK   703 streite] strong K   ther] *om.* LK   .xij.] .vij. LK
withoute] *add* oþer K   708 wherinne] where L   virgine] *add* Katerine D   709 her]
she L   710 all] *add* þe K   therewith] also LK   712 blessed] glorious DK   virgine]
add Katerine D   713 the quene] *add* of K   so²] *om.* Hı   717 fete] foote L   and]
add he K   718 knightez] *add* with hym DT2   720 soueraine Lorde] *trs.* L   heuene]
hevid L   722 hymselff] *om.* DT2   723 aungeles, virgines] *trs.* L   of²] *om.* LK
724 thou me] nat thou D, thou not T2   for] of *changed to* for Hı

hast take upon the this laboure and traueilous bataile?' And whan she 725
behelde her souerayne Lorde and herde hym speke she fell downe to
his fete with souerayne ioye and saide: 'A, my derest and most
souerain Lorde, how shulde y not but yef y knewe you that haue
shewed me so mani graces and bene all the souerayne ioy [and
suetnesse] of my soule. A, blessed Lorde, how all my spirites haue 730
sore longed after you. And, good Lord, with al my herte that is truly
youres y thanke you of the high goodnesse of these victories that ye
haue youe me, and y am redy, my Lorde and my God, with all the will
of my soule for to receiue for the loue of youre holy name all the
turnementis that may be thought to me. Wherfor, my suettest Lorde, 735
haue mynde upon me.' And thanne oure Lorde with a blessed and a
gladde uisage saide to her: 'Drede you not, my dere wiff, but be
stronge and of good comfort, for y shall truly be with you in all your
bataile and neuer parte from you.' | And with this he blessed her and f. 289ᵛᵃ
vanisshed awey fro her syght. And thanne so gret a suetnesse bode in 740
the prison after his departing that none herte might thenke it.

And whan the emperoure was returned ayen, he comaunded that
this virgine shulde be brought before hym. And whan he sawe her
shine in high beauute that he went hadd be disfigured by ouer
fastinge, he went that sum of her kepers hadde fedde her, and was 745
oute of hymselff for angre, and comaunded that the kepers shulde be
turmented. And thanne said this holi virgine: 'Truly y toke no mete of
mannes honde all this tyme, but my Lorde Ihesu Crist hathe
norisshed me.' Thanne saide the emperoure to her: 'Y praie the,
faire virgine, sette it sadly in thi herte that y shall tell the, ne ansuere 750
vs not by suche voyde wordes, for we will not holde the as a
chaumbrere, but ye shull haue ladishipp in oure reawme as a quene
of souerain beauute.' To whom the virgine ansuered: 'Now, emperoure, y praie the vnderstonde me well, and iuge truly whether aught y
rather chese the almighti kinge euerlastinge most faire and most 755

728 not] *om.* L, do K   729-30 and suetnesse] *om.* EH1   730 A] and L, also
and K   731 sore] *om.* L   732 you of the] yowre T2   of these] and LK
734 youre] þy LK   735 Wherfor] *add* my sperite is glad and I beseche the K
736 with] *on erasure* H1   737 to her] *om.* LK   740 bode] *add* stille DT2
741 his departing] þis partyng L, his partinge DK   742 returned] *add* home T2   ayen]
om. LK, *add* home D   743 this] þe LK   virgine] *add* Katerine D   744 in] *add* so D
went] *add* verelie D   746 the] hir DT2K   747 virgine] *add* Katerine D, *add* to þe
emperour L   749 saide/the emperoure] *trs.* K   750 tell the ne] and D   751 vs
not] me L, *om.* K   752 as] *om.* H1   753 To whom] *om.* K   the virgine] Katerine
DT2   ansuered] *add* and seide DT2, *add* hym K   755 rather] *om.* DT2

glorious, other a foule dedly donghill most full of horrible wrechidnesse.' And than the emperoure full of wrathe with despite saide to
her: 'Chese in haste of .ij. thinges, other to do sacrifice or ellys to
suffre greuous turnementis and perisshe.' Thanne she ansuered:
760 'Tarie not to what turnementis [thou wilt], for y desire to offre to
God my blode and my flesshe as he offered hymselff for me. He is my
souerein Lorde and my God and all the desire of myn herte.'

f. 289vb   Thanne was | there a cruell tyraunt that for to plese the emperoure
taught hym how he shulde lete ordeine .iiij. whelys of yren environed
765 with sharp nayles, and .ij. of the ouer whelys shulde renne ayenst the
.ij. nether whelis bi gret violence so that thei shulde all torende
anithinge that were sette betwene hem. And than this holy virgine
praied oure Lorde that he wolde by his gret might distroie this
turment to the preysinge of his name, so that the peple seinge his
770 might and vertu might be conuerted bi that myracle. And anone as the
uirgine was sette in this turment, the aungell of oure Lorde was sent
and all tobraste this turment with so gret a violence that it slow .iiij.
thousand paynims. The quene that stode in her toure and behelde all
this was smiten with gret sorw, and in gret haste come downe and
775 blamed hem sharpely of so grete cruelte. And the emperoure hering
this of her was full of wodenesse and comaunded that but yef she
wolde do sacrifice she shulde haue her brestes rent [of] with yren
hokis, and after that her hede to be smite of. And as she was ledde to
her marterdom she praied Seint Katerine that she wold praie oure
780 Lorde for her. And than Seint Katerine saide: 'Drede thou not, right
well beloued quene of God, for this day ye shull resseiue an
euerlasting kingdom for this fayling kingdom, and ye shull haue an
endely kinge to youre husbond full of goodnesse and beauute for this
foule and corrupte dedly that ye haue had before.' And this blessed
f. 290ra quene was full of sadde faith and comaunded the turmentoures | to do
786 that thei were bodin. And than thei ledde her oute of the citee and

756 other] or LK   most] *om.* LK   full] foule DT2   757 with] and of DT2   with
despite] fulle dispitously LK   758 or ellys] or L, oþer K   ellys] *om.* DT2L
759 greuous] grete K   and] *add* so DT2   answered] *add* and seid T2
760 turnementis] *add* that DT2   thou wilt] *om.* EH1, *add* put me K   763 that
for] *om.* DT2   765 .ij. of the] the two D   the²] *om.* LK   766 nether] *add* er L
767 anithinge] euery thyng L   virgine] *add* Katerine D   769 preysinge] prassing
changed to praysing H1   770 anone] as sone as D   772 tobraste] to brake DT2
773 paynims] *add* And K   774 with] *add* so D   775 hem] hym K   so] that DT2K
776 that] *om.* LK   777 of] *om.* E   779 wold] shuld H1   praie] *add* to DT2K
780 saide] *add* to hir DT2   thou] you D, þe K   783 endely] heuenly *on erasure* H1,
eternalle DT2, endles L   784 dedly] husbonde DT2, *add* kyng L

with tonges of yren thei rent of her brestes and smote of her hede, and
Porpheri stale the body and beried it the day foluynge.

Whanne the body of the quene was asked, and that the emperoure
comaunded that diuerse men shulde be turmented to tell the trouthe, 790
Porphirie come before all the peple and said: 'It am y that haue beried
[the body of] the seruaunt of Crist.' Thanne Maxence for wo beganne
to grinte with the tethe and to tremble as a wode man and cried
dredfully: 'O thou cursed caytef, see here Porphiri that was only the
keper of my soule and comfort in all my disesis now is deceiued.' And 795
whan he had saide these wordes to his knightes, thei ansuered all and
said: 'Porphiri hathe do wisely, and we all be truly cristen as he is and
redy for to deye for the loue of Ihesu Crist.' And thanne the
emperoure drunkin in wodenesse comaunded anone that all her
hedes shulde be smite of and her bodies caste to houndes. And 800
thanne he called holy Seint Katerine to hym and saide: 'Thow it be so
that thou hast made my wiff to deye bi thi wichecrafte, yef thou wilt
repent the thou shalt be the furst in my reawme as soueraine quene,
and yef thou wilt not thou shalt deye anone.' To whom she saide: 'Do
on anone what thou hast thought, for y am redi to suffre al that thou 805
canst ymagine for the loue of my Lorde God.' And thanne he gaue
sentence ayenst her and comaunded that she shulde be byheded.

And anone she was ledde oute to the ordeined place, and whanne
she come thedir she kneled her downe and lefte up | her eyen to f. 290ʳᵇ
heuene and praied to oure Lorde God saieng in this [wise]: 'O thou 810
most blessed Lorde Ihesu Crist, blessed king, that art the worship and
the ioye of uirgines, hope and hele of true beleuers, I beseche you my
Lord God that whosoeuer haue mynde upon my passion, be it atte his
dethe or in any necessite, that thei call myn helpe that thei mow haue
comfort and profit of her praiere and be herde of her askinge.' And 815
than a uoys was herde from heuene that saide to her: 'Come on, my

788 LK *punctuate after* beried it   789 and that] *om.* DT2   emperoure] kynge LK
792 the body of] LK, *om.* EH1, the quene DT2   of²] *add* ihesu DLK   wo] wrathe LK
793 the] his DK   794 see] lo T2   only] *om.* LK   795 now] *add* he K
797 wisely] riȝt wisely L   truly] trewe K   799 drunkin . . . wodenesse] *om.* L
800 shulde be] *ins.* H1   bodies] body'es' H1   802 that] *ins.* H1   thi] *om.* H1
wichcrafte] wrecchid craffte DT2   wilt] *om.* H1LK   805 redi] *add* for L
808 oute] *om.* LK   to] vnto K   809 her¹] *om.* D   810 heuene . . . saieng] god of
hevyn prayyng to hym L, god of heuene praiyng K   wise] *om.* E, *add in margin* The
peticion graunted by godde to Sceynt Katerine H1   812 uirgines] virgininis D
beleuers] bileue DT2   813 that] *add* yee wolde graunte vnto L   whosoeuer] whom so
ever L   814 in] at LK   814–15 haue comfort] be comfortid K   815 and¹] *add*
have K   praiere] praieris D   816–17 my faire loue] *add* and D

faire loue, my dere wyff, the yates of heuene be opened ayenst the, and
y behote the all tho that worship thi passion shulle haue heuenly
comfort, and whom thou praiest for shull not perisshe.' And thanne
820 her blessed hede was smyte of, and in stede of blode ther came oute a
gret streme of mylke. And aungeles toke the holy body and bare it to
the Mount of Synay more thanne .xx. iourneys thennes, and there thei
beried it worshipfully.

But for as moche as it was not knowe wher her bodi was become
825 there was gret sorw and lamentacion among the cristen and saide
among hem: 'Alas the most clere light of oure faithe full of wisdom
and the verrey temple of the holy gost is gone fro us.' But in this grete
heuynesse y leue hem and returne to shewe you as y finde it wretin
how that right precious and that holy body was found, the whiche
830 holy body as it ys wrete was an hundred yere and .xxx. hidd from the
knowlage of cristen peple. And whanne oure Lord luste to shewe the
peple the gret plente of his mercy, he graunted us that holi relique in
this wise.

f. 290ᵛᵃ   In the region of the desert of | Mount Synai there were mani cristen
835 heremites that were enflawmed with souerayne deuocion to that holy
virgine, wherfor by comune assent thei haue ordeyned a chapell
wherinne this holy spouse of Crist might contynuelly be worshipped
in [with] worthi preisingges. This chapell was ordeyned bi the
disposicion of God not ferre fro the hyest coppe of the hill, wher
840 fast by was the place where the busshe dede growe that oure Lorde
lust to apere in to Moyses. In this saide chapell these holy heremites in
gret abstinence and deuocion lyueden a glorious lyff, wherfor the
aungell of God apered to hem saieng these wordes: 'Youre effectuel
deuocion Gode hathe beholde from heuene, wherfor he hathe
845 ordeyned to graunte you this grace that by you shall be founde and
knowin the holy body of the glorious virgine Seint Katerine to his
souerain worshipp, and therfor arisithe and foluithe me. And though
it be so that ye see not me, the shadowe of the palme that y bere in

817 opened] open D   the²] you D   818 the] *om.* DT2   820 in stede] in the
stede D   821 And] *add* the D   to] into LK   822 .xx.] *add* daies H1DK   823 it]
add ri3t L   824 as¹] *add* so D   826 faithe] *add* and D   827 the¹] *om.* H1
828 to shewe you/as y finde] *trs.* L, *as* L *but om.* you K   it] *add* is D   829 that²] *om.*
DK   830 yere/and .xxx.] *trs.* DL   832 holi] *om.* L   834 of²] *add* the LK
836 haue] *om.* L   837 wherinne] in þe whiche L   holy] *add* seynt Kateryn and L,
om. K   of] *add* Ihesu D   838 in] *om.* LK   with] whithe E, which D   839 coppe]
coop H1   840 busshe] tree K   dede growe] grewe K   841 in to] vnto D   these]
the D   in²] wiþ LK   843 saieng] and seid D   845 this] þat LK   847 arisithe]
add vp D   848 me] *add* yit L   the²] þis D

myn honde shall neuer departe from youre sight.' These ermytes went
forthe and folued the aungell till thei come to the place wher vnnethe 850
any creature might entre for streitenesse of the waye and sharpenesse
of rockes. And whanne thei come euene to the coppe of the hill thei
sawe not the aungell, but thei sawe so euydently the shadowe of the
palme that it semed that all the place was full of the shadowe of the
leues of the palme, wherby thei come to the place where this holy 855
body hadd leyne an hundred wynter and .xxx. in a stone, the flesse
dreied up for | lengthe of tyme, but the bones were so conpact and f. 290ᵛᵇ
pure that they semed even kepte by the cure of aungeles.

Thanne thei with gret ioye and reuerence toke up this holy body
and bare it doun to the chapell that thei hadde made. And this semid 860
not done withoute gret miracle, for the place where she laye inne was
so stikill and so streite and so daungerous to come to that vnnethes
any mannes mynde coude ymagine how it might be done. Whanne
this holy body was brought in this chapell with gret solempnite, thei
ordeyned thanne the feste of the inuencion of that holy virgine, the 865
whiche day of the inuencion is kepte of the deuout cristen there-
aboutes in tho parties, and the tyme thereof is about the Inuencion of
the Holy Crosse. This holy place oure [Lorde] lust to worshipp by
gret myracle, [for] of tho holy bones that an hundred wynter had layne
and dried in the coppe of the hill, plente of oyle welled oute largely, 870
whiche oyle is of so gret vertu that it yeuithe hele to all manere of
siknesse as it ys knowen to mani a deuout pilgryme which haue uisited
that right holy and devout place.

This holy virgine suffered dethe under Maxence the tyraunt that
beganne in the yere of oure Lorde .CCC.ix., and it ys conteyned in the 875
Inuencion of the Crosse how Maxence was ponisshed for this feloni
and for other.

850–3 till thei . . . aungell] *twice* H1   852 of¹] *add* þe K   853 so] *om*. DT2
854 was] had be D   856 wynter] *om*. DLT2   .xxx.] *add* yere DLT2   858 even]
euenli DT2   the] *om*. H1   aungeles] aungelle L   861 not] *ins*. H1   where . . . inne]
wherein she laie D   862 stikill] litille L   so²] *add* thikke and so DT2   863 mannes
mynde coude] man cowde or my3t LK   864 in] into K   865 virgine] *add* Seint
Katerine D   866 the¹] *om*. H1   inuencion] *add* of that holy virgine E   868 Lorde]
om. E   lust] *om*. DT2   869 myracle] meraclis D   for] *om*. E   tho] the DLK
hundred wynter] .C. and .xxx. wyntir L   871 yeuithe] is euere DT2   hele] helth T2
of²] *om*. K   872 siknesse] siknessis D   which haue] þat hath LK   873 and devout]
om. K   874 the tyraunt] the emperoure DT2   in] *om*. H1DLK   875 .CCC.ix.]
CCC and xix DT2   and] as LK   876 feloni] foly T2   877 for] *add* many L

Here endithe the lyff of Seint Katerine, and nexst beginnithe the lyff of Seint Saturnyne, Capitulum .C.lxvj.^m

f. 291ra Seint Saturnyne was ordeined bisshopp ouer the disciples of the apposteles and was sent | into the citee of Toloce. And as he entred into the citee the fendes cesed to yeue answere, and thanne saide one of the paynemes that thei shulde not sle Saturnyne lest thei shulde haue
5 none ansuere of her goddes. And thanne thei toke Saturnyne that wolde not do sacrifice and bonde hym bi the feet and drow hym into the high tour of the Capitoyle bi the grees, and thanne thei [thre]we hym downe to the erthe so that hys hede al tobrast and the brain went oute, and so he fulfelled his marterdom.
10 Ther was another Saturnyne, the whiche the prouost of Rome helde longe in prison, and after that he made hym be lefte up in the turment that is called ecule and lete bete hym with scourges and with the synues of bestes, and set fere in hys sydes and brenned hym as he hanged, and thanne toke hym downe and made his hede to be smyte of
15 about the yeere of oure Lorde .CC.iiij^xx. vnder Maximien.
And yet ther was another Saturnine in Aufrik, brother to Seint Saturnyne and of Seint Renouele and of Seint Felicite and Seint Perpetuel that were his sustres that were of noble kinrede that suffered dethe al togedre, of whiche the passion is done in other
20 tyme. And whan the prouost sawe that in no wise thei wolde do sacrifice to the ydoles he lete putte hem in prison. And whanne the fader of Seint Perpetuel herde it he come to the prison weping and saide: 'Alas, doughter, thou hast vnworshipped and shamed alle thi kinrede, for there was neuer man of thi kinred putte in prison til now.'
25 But whanne he wost that she was cristen, he ronne to her and wolde haue shoued oute her eyen with his fingeres.
And the blessed Perpetuel sawe a uisyon whiche she tolde on the
f. 291rb morw to her felawes. 'I sawe,' | she saide, 'a laddre of golde of right meruailous highnesse that was dressed euene to heuene, and it was so
30 streite that ther might but one stie up atte ones. And knives and suerdes were fiched in the lefte side, and in the right side sharpe alles, that tho that stiedin up might nother loke on the right side nor on the

EH1DH2A2L　　　　2 Toloce] *so changed to* Tolos H1　　　　6 hym bi the] his D
7 threwe] drowe E　　　9 fulfelled] `ful'filled H1　　　12–13 with the] *om.* H1　　　13 set]
lete H1　　　16 ther] þes H1　　　24 neuer] *om.* D　　　kinred] kyn H1D　　　26 shoued]
put D　　　27 on] in H1　　　30 but one] noo man D　　　31 side²] *om.* H1

lefte syde, nother hedir ne theder, but streight up to heuene. And a
dragon of right horrible forme laye under, so that eueri creature was
aferde to stie up for drede. And thanne y saw [a satire] that stied an 35
high and behelde us and saide: "Drede ye not this dragon, but stiethe
up suerly?"'

And whanne alle had herde this thei gaue thankingges to God, for
thei knew that thei were called to marterdom. And thanne thei were
presented to the iuge, and whanne thei wold not do sacrifice he made 40
Saturnyne be parted from hym and from the women and putte hym
with men and saide to Felicite: 'Thou haste an husbonde?' And she
saide: 'So y haue, but y reke not of hym.' And he saide: 'Woman, haue
pite of thiself, for thou art quicke with childe.' And she saide: 'Do
with me as thou wilt, for thou shalt neuer drawe me to thi purpos.' 45
And thanne the kinrede of this Perpetuel and her husbonde come to
her and brought with hem a litell childe sucking, and whanne her
fader sawe her stonde before the iuge he fell doune before her and
saide: 'My right suete doughter, haue pite on me and on thi sorufull
moder and on thi wreched husbond that may not lyue after the.' And 50
she stode withoute ani chaunginge. And thanne the fader leide the
litell babe in her necke, and the fader and the moder cussed her
hondes and saide: 'Ha|ue pite on us and liue with us.' And thanne she f. 291ᵛᵃ
threwe the childe from her and putte hem awey and saide: 'Partithe
from me, ye enemyes of God, for y knowe you not.' 55

And than whanne the prouost sawe her stabilnesse he made bete
hem right longe and thanne putte hem ayen in prison. And thanne the
seintes, full of sorugh for Felicite that was gret with childe, praied for
her, and she began to trauaile and brought forthe a quicke childe. And
thanne one of the knaues that kepte hem saide to her: 'What wilt thou 60
do whanne thou comest before the prouost that art now so greuously
turmented?' And Felicite ansuered and saide: 'I suffre now paine for
myselff, and thanne God shal suffre for me.' And thanne thei were
drawe oute of the prison and were dispoiled and ledde bi the places.
And thanne thei lete renne lyones to hem, the whiche deuowred Satir 65
and Perpetuel, and Felicite and Renouat were slaine with libardes, and

33 but] *add* euen D   34 under] vndirnethe D   35 drede] *add* of that dragon D
a satire] *space with ins. paraph* E, *one word erased* H1, oone D (*vng satirel* P2, *satyrum* LgA)
39 thanne] anone D   41 hym¹] hem D   from²]*add* alle D   42 and] *add* than the
iuge D   43 he] she H1   44 saide] *add* to hym D   51 thanne] 'þan' H1
53 saide] *add* to hir D   55 ye] the D   56–7 bete hem] hem to be beten D
61 prouost] *om.* H1, iuge D   65 lete . . . whiche] *om.* D   65–6 Satir and] *om.* D
66 and¹] *om.* H2   Renouat] the remenaunte D

Seint Saturnine had his hede smite of with a swerde about the yere of
oure lorde .CC.lvj. vnder Valerian and Galyan emperoures.

Here endithe the lyff of Seint Saturnyne And nexst
beginnithe the lyff of Seint Iames the martir. Capitulum
C.lxvij.

Seint Iames the martir that is called Intercise was noble bi kinrede but
moche more noble bi faithe, and he was of the region of Perce of the
citee of Elapene, and had right a cristen wiff. And he was wel knowen
with the king of Perce, and was wel renomed amonge the princes and
f. 291vb   one of the | furst. And so it fell that for grete lou[e] he had to the kinge
6   he was deseiued and brought for to worship the ydoles. And whanne
his moder and his wiff herde this thei were full of sorugh and wretin
letteres to hym in this wise: 'Thou hast lefte hym that is lyff in
obeying to hym that is dedly, and in plesinge hym that shall be but
10   asshes and poudre thou hast left and loste the euerlastinge suetnesse;
thou hast chaunged trouthe into lesinge, and in obeyeng to hym that is
dedly thou hast forsake the iuge of quicke and dede; and therfor know
thou wel that from hennes forwarde we shull be straunge to the, ne we
shull neuer duelle with the in no wise.' Whan Iames had redde these
15   litteres he wept bitterly and saide: 'Yef my moder that bare me and
my wiff that is wedded to me be thus made straunge to me, how
moche more is God made straunge to me.'

And whanne he had be strongely turmented for his errour within
hymselff, there come a messenger to the prince that saide that Iames
20   was cristen. And thanne the prince called hym and saide: 'Telle me,
art thou become Nazarien?' And Iames saide: 'Ye, uerily y am
Nazarien.' And the prince saide: 'Thanne art thou an enchauntour.'
And Iames saide: 'Nay, that am y not.' And as he thanne manaced
hym of mani turmentis, Iames saide: 'Thi manaces trouble me
25   nothinge for it is but wynde blowing upon a stone, thine wodenesse
passith anone thorugh myn eres.' And than the prince saide to hym:

66 empereroures] *add* Here endeth the Boke of the life of Seintes called in latyn legenda
aurea compiled and drawen into englissh bi worthi clerkes and doctours of Diuinite suengly
aftre þe tenure of þe latin H1

EDH2A2L   *Rubric* martir] *add* callid Intercise D   5 loue] lou E   8–9 in
obeying] and obeied D   9 but] *om.* D   10 and loste] *om.* D   14 redde] herde D
14–15 these litteres] þis lettir D   16–17 how . . . to me] *om.* D   18 be] *add* thus D
21 become] *add* cristen and a D   Ye uerily] *om.* D   am] *add* become a D   23 as he
thanne] than the prince D   24 mani] *add* diuers D

'Fare not thus unordinatli with thiselff lest thou perisshe bi greuous dethe.' Thanne Iames saide: 'It is not that whiche shulde be called dethe but it is a slepinge, for withinne a litell while | men risithe ayen.' f. 292ra
And the prince saide to hym: 'Let not these N[a]zariens deceiue the 30 that saine that dethe is but a slombre, for the gret emperoures dreden it.' And thanne Iamys saide to hym: 'We drede nothinge the dethe, for we hope to goo from dethe to lyff.'

And thanne the prince gaue sentence ayenst Iamys bi the counsaile of his frendes that he shulde be dismenbrid membre from membre for 35 to make other aferde. And thanne sum had pite of hym and wept, and he saide: 'Wepithe not for me for y goo to lyff, but wepithe for youreself to whom euerlasting turmentis bene arraied.' And thanne the turmentoures cutte of the membre of the right honde, and thanne he cried and saide: 'Deliuerere of Nazariens, recciue the braunche of 40 the tree of thi mercy, for the ouergrowen braunches be cutte of hym that [t]ilithe the vyne for to springe the betir and for to bere more plenteuously fruit.' And thanne the bocher saide: 'Yef thou wilt consent to the prince, y shall spare the and geue the medicines to hele the.' And thanne Iamys saide: 'Hast thou not sene the stocke of the 45 vine, that whanne the bowes be cutte awey how that the knotte that abidithe in his tyme eschaufith hym with the erthe and cast[eth] oute the fresshe springes thorugh all the places of the cuttingges? And thanne yef the vine be cutte for that she shulde springe and bere the beter after, how shulde not thanne springe [more] plenteuosly man in 50 the faithe that sufferithe for Ihesu Crist that is verrey vyne?'

And the bocher cutte of another fynger, and Iamys saide: 'Lorde, receiue another bowe of the tree that thou plantist with thi right honde.' And he cutte of another finger, and Iames saide: 'Y am deliuered from thre temptaciones and y shall blesse the fader, the | 55 sone and holy gost, and y shal confesse the Lorde with the .iij. f. 292rb children that he deliuered from the furneis of fyre, and synge thi name, Ihesu Crist, in the cumpanye of marteres.' And than was the .iiij. fyngre cutte of, and he saide: 'Lorde, the saueoure of the sones of Israel, that in the ferthe blessinge was pronounced, receiue of thi 60

29 is] *add* but D   30 Nazariens] Nzariens E   31–2 for . . . it] *om.* D
37 saide] *add* to hem D   39 the turmentoures . . . thanne] *om.* D   42 tilithe]
cilithe E   for to springe] þat springith D   47 in] *om.* D   eschaufith]
escheweth D   casteth] L, cast ED   50 how] whi D   more] *om.* E
53 receiue] *add* nowe D   54 he] the bocher D   another] the thrid D   saide]
add nowe D   59 he] Iames D

seruaunt the confession of the fourthe fynger right as of Iuda.' And
whanne the .v. was cutte of he saide: 'My ioye is fulfelled.'

And thanne the bocher[s] saide: 'Spare thi soule that thou perisshe
not, and greue the not thou thou haue loste one honde, for there be
65 many that haue but one and haue full gret worshippes and richesses.'
And the blessed Iamis saide to hem: 'Ye know wele that whanne the
shepardes begynne to shere her shepe he takith not only awey the
right syde and leue the lifte syde. Thanne yef the lambe that is but an
vnresonable beest wol lese al her flees, how moche more y that am a
70 resonable man shulde not be glad to be alle dismembred for God.'
And thanne went the cursed felonis to the lefte honde and cutte of his
litell fynger, and thanne Iamis saide: 'Lorde, yef thou be gret thou
woldest be made litell for us, and therfor y yelde to the body and soule
that thou boughtest with thi precious blode.' [And than the .vij. finger
75 was] cutte of, and he saide: 'Lorde, y haue said .vij. tymes preisingez
to the this day.' Thei cutte of the .viij., and he said: 'Ihesu Crist was
circumcised the .viij. day.' And thanne the .ix. was cutte of, and he
saide: 'Atte the .ix. houre oure Lorde Ihesu Crist hanginge in the
crosse toke his sperit to his fader, and therfor, Lorde, y confesse me to
f. 292ᵛᵃ the in the peyne of the [.ix.] finger | and yelde to the thankingges.'
81 And whanne the tenthe was cutte of he saide: 'The .x. nombre is in
the comaundementis of the lawe.'

And thanne sum of hem that were aboute hym saide: 'Yet dere
frende, confesse oure goddes only before oure prince so thou may
85 lyue; yef it be so that thi hondes be cutte of, there be full wise leches
that canne ese the of thi sorwes.' And thanne saide Iames to hem:
'Goth hennis fro me, for there shal neuer fals dissimulacion be founde
in me, for there nis no man that sette his honde to the plow and
lokithe bacwarde that is couenable to come to the kingdom of God.'
90 And thanne the bochers had despite and cutte of the too of his right
fote, and Iames said: 'The fote of Ihesu Crist was persed and blode
come oute therof.' The secound was cutte, and he saide: 'Lorde, this
day is grete to me aboue all dayes, and what meruaile for this same day
y shall fully go conuerted to the mighti God.' The thridde too was
95 cutte of and caste before hym, and Iames in smylinge saide: 'Thou

62 .v.] add fynger D   saide] add Nowe D   63 bochers] L. bochere E, bocher's' D
70 for] add þe loue of D   74–5 And . . . was] There .vij. fyngers were E   76 the¹]
om. D   .viij.] add fynger D   77 the .ix. . . . of] thei cutte of the .ix.ᵇᵉ fynger D
80 .ix.] om. ED (ix.ᵉ P2)   81 tenthe] add fynger D   he] Iames D   82 the¹] add .x. D
83 of hem] om. D   Yet] right D   85 yef] and thou3 D   91–2 and¹ . . . cutte] and
than thei cutte of þe secounde too D   92 therof] add than thei cutte of D

thridde [too] go to thi felawes, for right as the grein of whete yaldithe
moche fruyt so shalt thou with thi felawes and rest the in th[e] last
dayes.' The ferthe was cutte of, and he saide: 'My sowle, whi art thou
sorufull, and whi troublist thou me? Y hope in hym that is my God for
that y confesse me to hym is the hele and comfort of my chere.' The 100
fifte was cutte of, and thanne he saide: 'Now y begynne to saie
preysinges to oure Lorde for that he hathe made me worthi to be a
felaw of his servauntis.'

Thei toke thanne the lefte fote and cutte of the litell too, and thanne
Iamis saide: 'Thou litell too comfort the, for grete and litell shul | haue f. 292vb
one resurreccion, ne the lest here of the hede shal not be lost, and thou 106
shalt not be departed fro thi felawship.' And after the secounde was
cutte [of, and than] Iamis saide: 'Distroiethe this olde hous, for a more
noble is arraied.' And thei cutte of the thridde, and he saide: 'Bi suche
cuttinge shall y be purged of vices.' And than thei cutte of the fourthe, 110
and Iames saide: 'Comfort me, God, for my soule trustithe in the.'
And thanne thei cutte of his right fote, and he saide: 'Now y offre a
yefte to an heuenly kinge for whom y suffre.' And thanne thei cutte of
hys lefte fote, and thanne [the] blessed Iames saide: 'Lorde, thou art
he that doest mervailes, enhaunce me and saue me.' Than thei cutte of 115
the right honde, and he saide: 'Lorde, thi mercies helpen me.' And
thanne thei cutte of the lefte, and he saide: 'Lorde, thou art he that
louest the rightwis men.' And thanne thei cutte of his right arme, and
he saide: 'My soule preise oure Lorde; y shal preise oure lord in my
lyff and singe to my God as long as y shall be.' And thanne thei cutte 120
of his lefte arme, and he saide: 'The sorwes of dethe hathe beclipped
me, and y shal thenke on oure Lorde ayens hem.' And thanne thei
cutte of his right legge bi the thigh. And thanne [the] blessed Iamis,
greued bi right gret sorugh, cried and saide: 'Lorde Ihesu Crist helpe
me, for the waylingges of dethe haue beclipped me.' 125

And thanne he saide to the bochers: 'Oure Lorde will clothe me
with nwe flesshe that youre hondes may not touche.' And [thei]
contynued for to dismembre hym. And whanne thei had rested hem

96 too] finger E felawes] add noo fors D 97 the²] tho E 98 ferthe] add too D
98–9 sowle . . . and] sorowfulle too D 101 fifte] add too D he] Iames D
104 Thei] the bocheris D 106 one] a D ne] for D 107 secounde] add too D
108 of and than] om. E 109 thridde] add too D 110 fourthe] add too D
111 Iames] he D soule trustithe] trust is D 112 he] Iames D 114 the] om. E
115 mervailes] add for to D 117 lefte] add honde D 121 he] Iames D
123 the²] om. E 124 Crist] om. D 127 And] but for alle that D thei] om. E
128 for] stille D

they come ayen and cutte of his lefte legge vnto the thigh, and thanne
130 the blessed Iamis cried and saide: 'Lorde, enhaunce me halff quicke,
thou that art lorde of quicke and dede; y haue no fingers for to streche
f. 293ra up to the, nor no hon|dis to ioyne to the; my fete be cutte of and my
knees, so that y may not bowe hem to the. Y am as an hous fallen
wherof the pelers be take awey. Lorde Ihesu Crist, enhaunce me, and
135 take my soule to the oute of this prison.' And whanne he had so saide,
the bochers smote of his hede. And cristen men come priuely and stale
the body and buried it worshipfully, and he suffered dethe in the fifte
kalendes of Decembre.

Here endithe the liff of Seint Iames surnamed Intercise,
and nexst beginnithe the liff of Seint Pastor abbot,
Capitulum C.lxviij.

The abbot Pastor was mani yeres in gret abstinence in desert and
turmented his flessh bi right longe tyme and shined bi right gret
holinesse of religion. He had a moder that desired full gretly to see
hym and his bretheren yef she might in ani wise, and in a day as he
5 and his bretheren went to [the] chirche she come to hem. And whanne
thei sawe her thei fledde from her and entered into her selle and closed
the dore after hem. And she stode atte the dore and cried with gret
weping, and thanne Pastor come to the dore and saide to her: 'What
criest thou, here olde woman?' And she vnderstode the voys of hym
10 and cried lowder and saide: 'Y wolde see you, my sones. Whi shulde y
not see you? Am y not youre moder that bare you and gaue you sucke
and am now al hore for age.' And thanne her sone saide to her:
'Whether will ye see vs, in this worlde or in another worlde?' And she
ansuered: 'Yef y see you not here, shal y see you elliswhere?' And he
15 saide: 'Ye moder, yef ye mowe forbere us here a litell while for
Goddes loue, ye shull see us and be with us euer after.' And thanne
f. 293rb she parted gladly and saide: 'Y wolde gladly forbere a litell short | ioye
for so longe foluinge ioye.'

The iuge of that contre wolde nedis see abbot Pastor, but he might
20 in no wise, and thanne he toke his susteres sone as thowgh he hadde
be a misdoer and putte hym in prison and saide: 'Yef abbot Pastor will

131 thou that] for thou D   134 awey] add wherefor D

EDH2A2L   3 full] om. D   4 wise] add fynde hem D   5 the] om. E
6 selle] celles D   7 the dore] her dores D   14 ansuered] add and seide D   he]
Pastor D   17 parted] add thens D   18 longe] add a D   21 abbot] om. D

come and pray for hym, y shal deliuer hym.' And than the moder of the childe come weping to his selle and praied hym to helpe her sone, and whanne she coude gete none ansuere ther of hym she saide to hym with gret violence: 'Now yef thi bowels be harde as yren and that thou art not meued to haue pitee of anithinge, atte the leste yet haue pite of thin owne blode that is myn sone.' And thanne Pastor sent her worde and saide: 'Pastor engendered neuer childe.' And so she parted thennes with gret sorugh. And than the iuge saide: 'Atte the leste late hym comaunde bi worde and he shal be deliuered.' And the abbot sent hym worde: 'Examyne the cause after the lawe, and yef he be worthi to deye late hym deye anone, and yef not do as it likithe the.'

He taught his bretheren and saide: 'It is not necessarie a man to concidre and kepe hymselff and for to haue discrecion with the workes of solitarie lyff. There were .iij. persones, Noe, Iob and Daniel. Noe representi[th] the persone of hym that possede nothinge, Iob the persone of tho that be troubeled, and Daniell the persone of tho that be discrete. Yef a monke hate .ij. thinges, he may be fre thurgh all the worlde, and that ys flesshely couetise and vein glorie. Yef thou wilt finde pees in this worlde and in the worlde that is to come, say in alle cases: "What am y?" and "Iuge no man."'

As a brother of a congregacion | had offendid, the abbot bi counsaile of a solitarie man putte hym oute awey, the whiche for sorugh and weping fell nigh into dispaire. Abbot Pastor made hym to be brought to hym, whom he comforted benignely, and sent to the solitarie man saieng: 'Hering of the, y desire to see the, and therfor labour and come to me.' The whiche whan he was come, Pastor saide: 'There were two men that eueriche of hem had a dede bodi of his owne, and that one of hem forsoke his owne dede body and wepte the dede body of that other.' Whanne the solitarie man herde this and vnderstode it, he was conpunct in his wordes.

And thanne thei asked hym of that worde: 'That sh[all] wrathe his brother withoute cause', and he saide: 'Of all the thingges that thi brother will greue the withe, angre the nothinge til he putte out thi right eye, and yef thou do thou wratthist the withoute cause. But yef any wolde parte the from God, thanne wrathe the with hym.'

And thanne he said furthermore: 'He that compleinithe hym is no

30 abbot] *add* Pastor D   32 not] þou wilt nat so D   34 with the workes] *om.* D
36 representith] representid E   38 fre] *om.* D   47 was] saw3 D   49 and . . .
body] *om.* D   52 shall] shulde E   54 greue] wrath D   angre] *add* wherefor angre D
57 furthermore] *add* that E

monk; nor he that holdithe malice in his herte is no monk; nother he
that is wrathfull is no monk; nother he that yeldithe euel for euel is no
60 monke; and he that is a proude man or a iangeler is no monke. He that
is a verrey monke is alweies humble, softe, full of charite, and in all
wayes and in all places he hathe the drede of God before his eyen that
he offende not. For yef there be thre togederes of whiche that one
restithe well, and that other is sike, and the thridde seruithe hym with
65 pure wille, these thre be like in one werke.'

A brother compleined hym that he had mani thoughtes and that he |
f. 293ᵛᵇ perisshed in hem, and he putte h[y]m oute into the ayre and saide to
hym: 'Strecche out thi lappe and take the wynde.' And he saide: 'Y may
not.' And that other ansuered: 'No more maist thou de[u]ie but that
70 diuerse thoughtes wol entre, but thou shuldest euer contrarie to hem
yef thei be noght and withstonde hem that thei abide not with the.

Here endithe the lyff of Abbot Pastor, and nexst beginnithe the lyff of Abbot Iohn, Capitulum .C.lxix.ᵐ

The abbot Iohn, whan he had .xl. winter be in desert with Episien,
Episien asked hym how moche he profited. And he ansuered and
saide: 'As long as y haue be solitarie there was neuer sonne that sawe
me etinge.' And Episien saide: 'Nother me slepinge.' This thinge
5 lykly almost is redde in the Liff of Faders, for whanne Episien bisshop
gaue in a tyme flesshe for to ete to Hillari the abbot, he saide to hym:
'Fader, holde me excused, for sethe y toke this abite y ete neuer mete
in ydelnesse.' And the bisshop saide: 'And sethe y toke this abite y
suffered neuer no slepe that was contrarie to me, nor y slepte neuer as
10 longe as y was contrarie to ani other.' And thanne saide Hillari:
'Fader, foryeue me, for thou art beter thanne y.'

Abbot Iohn wolde haue lyued as aungeles done, and entended
alwey to God withoute ani other thinge doing, and dispoiled hymselff
and was all a woke in desert. And whanne he was nigh dede for hunger
15 and was all forstungin with bees and with waspis, he returned to the
dore of his brother and knocked. And he asked who was there, and he
saide: 'Y am Iohn.' The brother ansuered and saide: 'That art thou

58–9 nother . . . monk] om. D   60 He] For whoo D   63 offende] offendid D
67 hym] hem E   69 ansuered] add and seide D   deuie] denie (?) E

EDH2A2L   1 winter] yere D   7 mete] om. D   8 And] add Episien D
abite] om. D   14 all] add nakid D   a woke] awoke E   16 knocked] add thereate D
17 Iohn] add thi brothir D   The brother] and he D

not, | for Iohn is become an aungell and duellithe no more amonge f. 294ra
men.' And he saide: 'Uerily it am y.' But he wolde not opin to hym,
but lete hym be turmented there all night till on the morugh. And 20
thanne he opened the dore and saide: 'Yef thou be a man, it is nede
that thou laboure ayen for to be fedde, and yef thou be an aungell
wharto sekest thou to entre here?' And thanne he saide: 'Foryeue me
brother, for y haue synned.'

And whanne he deied his bretheren praied hym that he wolde leue 25
hem in stede of heritage som worde of hele in shorte wise. And thanne
he sighed and saide: 'Y dede neuer yet myn owne propre will, nor y
dede neuer thing to other but y dede it myselff.'

Here endithe the lyff of Abbot Iohn, and nexst beginnithe
the lyff of Abbot Moyses, Capitulum .C.lxx.m

Moyses saide to a brother that asked of hym a sermon: 'Sitte stille in
thi celle, and he shall teche the all that is nedefull.'

So as an auncien man that was sike wolde go into Egipte for he
wolde be greuous to his bretheren, the abbot Moyses saide to hym:
'Go not, for yef thou doest thou shalt fall into fornicacion.' And he 5
was wrothe and saide: 'My body is dede, whi saiest thou so?' And
whanne he was go, thei sawe a uirgine that by grete deuocion seruid
hym, and whanne he was hole he defouled her and she bare hym a
sone. And whanne the childe was bore the olde man toke the childe in
his armes and come on an high festfull day into the chirch of Siche 10
and praied hem that prayeden there and saide: 'See ye here this
childe? Wete ye well for certaine that this is a sone of inobedience.
Take ke|pe to youreselff, bretheren, for y haue made this childe in f. 294rb
myn age. Praiethe for me.' And thanne he went ayen into his celle and
recouered ayen his furst astate. 15

And as there was another olde man saide to another: 'Y am dede,'
he ansuered hym ayen and saide: 'Truste not to thiself as longe as
thou duellist in thi body, for yef thou se[in]e that thou art dede the
enemye of mankinde is not dede.'

A brother that had synned was sent to [the] abbot Moyses fro his 20

19 saide] add ayenne to hym D   to hym] the dore D   20 morugh] morowetide D
23 he] Iohn D   26 hele] ese D   27–8 nor . . . other] om. D   28 y dede] that I
wold haue doo D   it] add to D

EDH2A2L; D has initial excised affecting 1–7   2 teche] yeue H2   5 doest]
goo D   fall into] doo D   11 and saide] om. D   14 age] add wherefor D
16 And as] Also D   17 saide] om. D   18 seine] seme ED (dit P2)   20 the] om. E

bretheren, and he toke a basket full of grauell upon his backe and
come to hem. And thei asked hym what that was, and he saide: 'It be
my synnes that renne after me and y see hem not, and this day y am
sent for to iuge the synnes of a straunger.' And whanne thei herde this
25 thei spared that brother.

A likli thinge is redde of an holy fader the abbot Prioure, for as the
bretheren spake of a brother that was gilty, he helde his pees. And
than he toke a sacke full of grauell and leide [it] behynde hym, and
before hym he bare a litell, and they asked hym what it ment. 'This
30 sacke that is full of grauelle behinde me be my synnes that y bere
behinde me and not considre hem ne sorw not for hem, and this litell
grauel that is leide before me be the synnes of my brother that y
considre allwey and iuge hem, but y shulde allwaye bere myn owne
synnes before me and thinke allwaye on hem and praie to God to
35 deface hem.

[Here endithe the lyff of Seint Moyses, and next beginnithe the lyff of Seint Arsenye. .C.lxxj.]

Of Seint Arsenye the abbot it is write that as he was maister in the
paleis [of] a prince, he praied hertly God that he wolde dresse his
f. 294va wayes to he hele of his sowle, so that in a tyme | herde a voys that saide
to hym: 'Arseni, fle the felawship of men and thou shalt be saued.'
5 And whanne he herde this he toke monkes clothinge, and thanne he
herde a voys that saide ayen: 'Fle and holde the still and lyue in pees.'

And men rede in the same place as for to coueite reste there were
.iij. bretheren that were made monkes, the furst chase for to labour for
to bringe hem that were in discorde to vnite and pees, the secounde
10 chase to visite the sike, the thridde chase to rest in desert. The furst,
that trauailed for to apese hem that were in debate, might not plese all
parties but was ouercome bi werinesse and annoye, and he come to the
secounde and fonde hym all mate and failed in corage and might not
performe that he had vndertake. And thanne by acorde thei come to
15 the thridde that was in desert. And whanne thei hadde told hym her
tribulaciones, he putte water in a cuppe and saide: 'Take hede how

23 y¹] om. D   26 the²] his D   28 it] om. E   29 a] but D   they] than þe
bretheren D   30 is] was D

EDH2A2L; D has initial excised affecting 78–86   All MSS omit rubric   1 Of . . .
abbot/it . . . write] trs. and preceded by Also D   2 of] with E   6 ayen] add to hym D
still] add in this abite D

this water is troubeled.' And thanne after he saide: 'Now loke how it is
faire and clere.' And whanne thei loked withinne thei sawe her visages
in the water. And thanne he saide to hem: 'Right so it is of hem that be
in the noyse of the worlde, thei mow not see her defauutes for the 20
noyse of the peple, but yef thei wolde reste hem allone [in] silence thei
shulde sone se her synnes and defauutes.'

In a tyme a man fonde hym eting herbes as a beste all naked. He
ranne after hym that fledde and saide: 'Abide me, for y folw the for the
loue of God.' And he ansuered and saide: 'And y fle the for the loue of 25
God.' And thanne for wery he caste of his clothes, and thanne he that
was pursued abode and saide: 'Whan thou hast caste from the the
matere | of the worlde y wol abide the.' And than he praied hym to tell f. 294vb
hym how he might lyue to saue his soule, and he ansuered and saide:
'Fle men and holde thi pees.'   30

Ther was a noble ladi of Rome that come for to see the abbot
Arsenien bi gret deuosion, and Theophile the ershebisshop praied
hym that she might see hym, but he ne wolde graunte it in no wise.
And atte the last [s]he went to his sell and fonde hym withoute his
dore and kneled her downe at his fete. And he toke her up in gret 35
angre and saide: 'Yef thou wilt se my visage now beholde it.' And she
for shame and drede durste not beholde hym. And thanne he saide to
her: 'How is it that thou that art a woman durst take upon the so gret a
viage? Now thou shalt go ayen to Rome and telle other women that
thou hast saie the abbot Arsenien and thei shul come also for to see 40
me.' And she saide: 'Yef God geue me grace to come to Rome y shall
suffre no woman [to] come to the, but atte the leste y praie the to praie
for me and haue continuel mynde on me.' And he saide: 'Y praie to
God that he take fro myn herte the mynde of the.' And whan she
herde that she was right sori and came to the citee and beganne to 45
tremble with the feuer for heuinesse. And whanne the bisshop woste
it he went to comfort her, and she saide: 'Alas, y deye for sorugh.' And
the ershebisshop saide to her: 'Wost thou not that thou art a woman
and the enemy ouercome holy men by women, and therfor he praied
so? But truste wel that he praiethe alwey for thi soule.' And so she was 50
comforted and returnid to her propre place with ioye.

17 Now] om. D   21 in] to E   23 hym] hem D   25–6 And¹ . . . God] om. D
26 wery] werinesse D   33 she] he D   34 she] he E   37 hym] it D   39 that]
howe D   40 for to] and D   41 God] add wille D   42 suffre] doo D   to¹] om. E
46 whanne] add Theophile D   47 saide] add to hym D   48 not] add welle D
49 enemy] add the feende offten time D   51 returnid] add ayenne D

And it is redde also of another fader in the whiche whan his disciple
f. 295ra saide to hym: 'Fader thou | art woxe in gret age, late us go duelle nere
the worlde,' [and] thanne the abbot saide: 'Late us goo there no
55 women be.' The disciple saide: 'Where is that place that women be
not but yef it be in deserte?' And he saide: 'Thanne bringe me into
desert.'

Arsenien all the dayes of his liff, whanne he wrought with his
hondes, he had a lynen clothe in his bosom for the plente of teres that
60 ranne so fast fro his eyen. And al the night he vsed to wake and to
praie, and in the morwtyde whanne verrey necessite of werinesse drof
hym to slepe he wolde saie with heuinesse: 'Come wicked seruaunt,'
and thanne he wolde take a litell slepe sitting. And he wolde saie
thanne an houre of slepe were sufficiaunt to a monke yef he were a
65 continuel fighter ayenst vices.

Whanne the fader of Arsenien was dede, whiche was a gret senatour
and noble, he lefte gret heritage to Arsenien, and Magistren brought
the testament to Arsenien, and he toke it and wolde haue broke it.
And Magistren fel[le] adowne atte his fete and besought hym that he
70 wolde not breke it, for yef he dede he shulde lese his hede whanne he
come home. And thanne Arsenien said: 'Y am dede before hym
though he be now dede. Whi wolde he sende me this testament and
make me his heir?' And thanne he sent it ayen and wolde not take no
part therof.

75   In a tyme a voice come to hym and saide to hym: 'Come and y shal
shewe the the werkes of men.' And thanne he ledde hym into a place
and shewed hym a man of Ynde that hewed wode and made a grete
burden, so grete that he might not bere it, and alwey he hewed and
leide on his burdon and thus he dede longe tyme. And after that he
f. 295rb shewed hym another man that clensed a lake and caste all the | water
81 in a cisterne persed, and all the water that he caste into the cisterne
ranne ayen into the lake, and euer he laboured to fell the cisterne. And
after that he shewed hym a temple and two men on horseback that
bare a tre ouertwarte and wold entre into the temple, but thei might
85 not. And thanne he expounid it and saide: 'These be tho that beren as
it were the birthen of iustice with pride and meke hem not, and
therfor thei duelle without the hous of God. He that cuttithe the wode

52 also] *om.* D   in] *om.* D   54 and] thanne E   55 place that] *om.* D   56 he]
the Abbot D   Thanne] *om.* D   58 Arsenien] *add* seide *del.* had D   69 felle] feld E
79 thus] so D   80–1 and . . . persed] *om.* H2   82 ranne] *add* out H2   86 of] *add*
the E

is the man that hathe mani synnes and dothe away none by penaunce
doing but puttithe alwey wickednesse vpon wickednesse. He that
drawithe oute the water is the man that dothe good werkes, but for as 90
moche as euell werkes be medeled with hem he lesithe his [good]
werkes.'

And atte Euesong tyme in the Saterday he left the sonne byhynde
hym, and kneled and helde up his hondes to heuene til on the Sonday
on the morw that the sonne come ayen before his visage, and this he 95
abode all the night. And this is yfounde in the Lyff of Holy Faders.

Here endithe the lyff of Abbot [Arsenye], and nexst
beginnithe the lyff of Agathen, Capitulum .C.lxx[i]j.^{m}

Agathen bare .iij. yere a stone in his mouthe for he wolde lerne to kepe
silence. And as another brother entred into the congregacion, he saide
to hymselff: 'Thou and an asse be o thinge, for an asse whanne he is
bete spekithe not but [suffrith] wronge withoute anithing ansueringe,
and right so dost thou.' And another brother was putte fro the table 5
and ansuered nothinge, | and after he was asked upon that and he f. 295va
saide: 'Y haue set in my herte that y am felaw to an hounde that
whanne he is chased he gothe his waye oute.'

And in a tyme it was asked of Agathan in what vertu was most
laboure and [he ansuered and] saide: 'Y trowe that there is none so 10
gret a laboure as for to praie to God, for the enemy laboureth
continuelly for to breke his orison, for amonge other laboures a
man hathe sumtyme reste, but he that praiethe hathe continuelly nede
of gret strife.'

A brother asked of Agathon how he shulde duell amonge his 15
bretheren, and he saide: 'Right as thou dedist the furst day, and take
to the no trust but drede and sufferaunce, for there is no more perilous
passion thanne is fole assuraunce, for she is moder of all passiones.
And kepe the well fro wrathe, for yef a wrat[h]full man might reise a
dede body it shulde not plese God for his wrathe.'   20

A brother that was all angri saide to hymselff: 'Yef y were allone y
shulde not so sone be stered to wrathe.' And in a tyme as he felled a

89 but] ne D   alwey] aweie D   vpon wickednesse] *om.* D   91 good] *om.* E

EDH2A2L   *Rubric* Arsenye] Moyses ED   .C.lxxij.^{m}] .C.lxxj.^{m} E   3 be] *add* of D
4 suffrith] softely E   5 table] batelle D   6 upon that] of oone D   9 was^{2}] is D
10 laboure] *om.* D   he ansuered and] *om.* E   11 enemy] *add* the feende D
13 continuelly] continuelle D   15 A] Also a D   18 fole] fulle D   19 yef]
thou3 D   wrathfull] wratfull E

potte with water and bare it home, he shedde oute all the water bi the way. He went thanne ayen and filled his potte, and shed it oute ayen.

25 The thridde tyme he went, and shedde it ayen, and than he, meved with gret angir, brake his potte. And thanne he avised hym in hymselff and sawe well that he was deceiued of that same fende of yre and of angir, and saide: 'Now y am bi myselff y am ouercome with angre. Y shall turne ayen to my congregacion, for y see well that ouer all is

30 laboure and in all places is nede of pacience and of the helpe of God.

f. 295vb There were two bretheren | contrarie wise that longe tyme duelled togedre and wost not what chidinge was, for thei were neuer mevid to w'r'atthe. And on a tyme that one of hem saide to that other: 'Lete us make strife betwene us two as men of the worlde do.' And that other

35 ansuered: 'Y wote not how striff is made.' Thanne saide the furst: 'Here is a sacke betwene us sette. Chalenge thou that it is thin, and y will saie that it is myn and so shull we begynne to striue.' Thanne saide the furst: 'This sacke is myn,' and that other ansuered: 'Thin mot it be, take it with the and go thi way,' and so thei departed

40 withoute striuinge.

The abbot Agathon was wys in vnderstondinge and slow in laboure, scars in etinge and in clothinge. He saide of hymself: 'Forsothe y slepte neuer atte my wille as longe as y bare anithinge ayens my brother, ne y lete neuer no[ne] slepe that had ani cause ayens me.'

45 Whanne Agathon shulde dye he helde hymself .iij. dayes withoute movinge, holding his eyen opin. And whanne his bretheren stered hym he saide: 'Y am before the iugement of God.' And thei saide: 'And hast thou drede?' And he saide: 'Y haue laboured with all the vertu that y had for to kepe the comaundementis of God, but y am but

50 a man full of freelte and wete not whedir my werkes haue plesed God or no.' And thei saide: 'Trust thou not tho werkes that thou had do for God?' And he saide: 'Y will not presume tofor that y come to the iugement of God, for the iugement of God is otherwise thanne the iugement of man.' And as thei wolde haue asked hym more, he saide

55 to hem: 'Shewe ye to me youre charite and spekithe no more to me, for y am ocupied.' And after that he hadde saide that he yelde up the sperit with ioye into the hondes of oure Lorde.

---

23 shedde] *add* it D   all . . . water] *om.* D   25 and¹] *add* fillid his potte and D   it] *add* out D   26 hym in] *om.* D   28 y²] and D   31 wise] *om.* D   that] *add* had D   36 thou that] þereon and seie D   38 ansuered] *add* and seide D   44 none] no E   47 hym] hid D   saide²] *add* to hym D   48 thou] *add* noo D   51 tho] to the D   had] hast D   55 charite] chartre D

Here | endithe the liff of Agathen, and nexst beginnithe the   f. 296ra
lyff of Barlaham the ermite, Capitulum .C.lxx[i]ij.^m

Barlaham, of whiche Iohan Damascien made the storie with gret
diligence, in whom the devine grace wrought so that he conuerted to
the faithe Iosaphat the kinge.

And as in tho dayes all Ynde was replenisshed with cristen peple
and devout monkes, there rose up a mighti kinge that dede gret 5
persecucion ayens the cristen and namely to monkes, his name was
Auenour. So it befell that a frende of the kingges and one of the furst
in his paleys was taught by the divine grace and lefte the hall riall for
to entre into the ordre of monkes. And whanne he herde it he was
wode for angre and made hym be sought thorugh all the desert so that 10
vnnethis he was founde, and thanne he was brought before hym. And
whan the kinge behelde hym in so vile a cote and made all pale and
lene for hunger, that was wont to shine in riche clothinge and precious
metis with all plente of richesse, he saide to hym: 'O thou fole of thi
witte, whi haste thou chaunged worship into velanie? Thou hast made 15
a childes play.' And thanne he saide to hym: 'Yef thou wilt here a
praier of me, do thin enemyes awaye fro the.' And thanne the kinge
asked hym ho were his enemyes, and he saide: 'Yre and couetise, for
they empeche and lette the trouthe [that it] may not be sayne ne
herde. And drawe into wysdom and equite that thou maist here that is 20
for to be saide.' The kinge saide: 'Be it as thou haste deuised.' And
thanne he saide: 'The foles dispise tho thinges that bene as though
they were not, and thei enforcen hem for | to take thingges that be not f. 296rb
as yef they were. And he that hathe not tasted of hem that be, he may
not vse of the swetnesse of hem, and he may take no trouthe of thinges 25
that be not.' And whanne he had shewed mani thinges of the
incarnacion, the kinge saide: 'Yef y had not behight the atte the
begynning that y shulde putte away wrathe fro my counsaile, y shulde
right sone sette fire to thi flesshe. Go thi way fast and fle fro my sight
that y se the no more, for and y do y shall destroie the in the worst 30
wise.' And thanne the servaunt of God went his waye with gret sorugh
for that he had not suffered no marterdom.

EDH2A2L; D breaks off after 395 *beter*   *Rubric* C.lxxiiij.^m] .C.lxxiij.^m E   4 Ynde]
Iudee D   replenisshed] replevisshid D   5 gret] moche D   9 he^1] the kinge D
16 hym] the kinge D   18 Yre] *add* and wratthe D   19 that it] L, *om.* ED
20 And] ne D   drawe] *add* the D   and] ne D   23 hem . . . take] to make D
24 yef] *om.* D   were] *add and del.* not D   he^1] whoo D   25 and] *add* so D   may] *add*
not D

In this mene tyme that the kinge had no childe bi his wiff longe
tyme, atte the laste he hadde a sone and was called Iosephath. And
35 thanne the kinge assembled a gret multitude of his peple for to do
sacrifice to her fals goddes for the birthe of his sone. And thanne he
assembled .lv. astronomeres for to enquere what shulde falle of his
sone. And they ansuered all that he shulde be grete and mighti in
richesses, and one that was more wys thanne another saide: 'Sir King,
40 this childe that is born shall not be in thi kingdom, but he shall be in a
beter withoute comparison. And wetithe verily that y wene that he
shall be of [the cristen] religion [the which] thou pursuest.' And he
saide not this of hymselff but by inspiracion of God.

And whanne the kinge herde this he dred hym gretly and lete make
45 the citee withoute right a noble paleis, and thereinne he sette his sone
for to duelle, and sette aboute hym the fairest yonge peple that he
f. 296ᵛᵃ coude chese, and comaunded hem that thei | shulde neuer name
before hym nother dethe nor age ne siknesse ne pouert nother
nothinge that in any wise might yeue hym heuinesse, but alwey
50 bringe to his mynde ioyous thinges so that his thought were euer
ocupied with gladnesse, so that he shulde neuer thenke on nothinge
that were to come. And as sone as any of his mynistres were sike,
anone the kinge comaunded that thei shulde be remeued and an hole
man sette in his stede, and also he bade that no man were hardy to
55 name Ihesu Crist afore hym.

And in that tyme there was with the kinge a man that was priuily
cristen, and he was the furst amonge the noble princes that were about
the kinge. And in a tyme as he went an huntinge with the kinge, he
fonde a pore man that was hurt in the fote with a beste lyeng in the
60 ground, and praied this knight that he wolde resseiue hym for he
might do hym profit in sumthinge. And thanne the knight saide: 'Y
wolde receiue the gladly, but y canne not wete whereinne thou
mightest profite me.' And thanne the pore man saide: 'Y am a leche
of worde, for yef ani man be hurte in worde y canne hele hym.' The
65 knight sette not by that he saide, but for the loue of God he toke hym
and heled hym.

And so within a while after there were enuyous men that sawe that
this knight was gretly cherisshed with the kinge, and accused hym to

37 .lv.] *om.* D   38 all] *add* and seiden D   he] the childe D   42 the cristen *om.* E
the which] of cristen peple that E   44 make] *add* hym E   46 sette] *om.* D
54 were] *add* so DL   56–7 man . . . cristen] cristen man preuelie D   60 hym] *add*
and helpe hym D   64 hym] *add* but D   65 he saide] *om.* D   but] And than the
knyght seide D   65–6 toke . . . heled] wolde receiue hym and hele D

the kinge and saide that he was not only turned to the cristen faithe
but also he laboured for to withdrawe hys rewme fro hym to that ende 70
he hadde stered all his felawshippe for to do the same. 'And yef ye
will | knowe the trouthe hereof, calle hym to you in gret counsaile and f. 296vb
telle hym that this lyff is not and sone ended, and therfor ye will leue
the glorie of this worlde and become a monke, whiche before this
tyme ye haue so cruelly pursued bi ygnoraunce, and thanne ye shull 75
see what he will ansuere you.' And whanne the kinge had all saide
after her avys, this knight that knew nothinge of her treson, beganne
to wepe for ioye and comended the kinge gretly in hys purpos and
counsailed hym to do it in [as] gret haste as he might. And whanne the
kinge herde hym speke in suche wise, he went that all had be trwe that 80
he had herde and was fulfelled with gret wrathe, but yet he ansuered
hym no worde.

And than this knight perceiued that [the kinge] had take his wordes
amys. He went home and remembred hym that he hadde a leche of
wordes and went and tolde [hym] all this tale by ordre. And he 85
ansuered and saide: 'Wete it well that the kinge supposithe verrily that
ye be aboute to take his rewme from hym. Now dothe after my
counsaile: arise anone and goo shere thin hede and clothe the with the
haire and do on the the habite of a monke and go tomorw right erly
vnto the kinge, and whanne the kinge will aske the what that 90
amountithe, thou shalt ansuere: "My lorde, y am redy for to folw
the, for yef the waye that ye desire to go be harde, yef y be with you it
shall be lyghter [to you], for right as ye haue had me in prosperite
right so ye shull haue me in aduersite. Y am al redy, wherto tarie ye?" '
And whanne the kinge had herde all this he was hougely meruailed 95
and reproued the vntrewe saiers and lo|ued hym and dede hym gretter f. 297ra
worship thanne euer he dede before.

And thanne the kinges sone whiche was norisshed in the paleis
come to a perfite age and was souerainly lerned in all wisdom, and
meruailed gretly whi his fader kepte hym so in close, and called to 100
hym one of his most familier servauntes, and in counsaile he asked
hym of this thinge and saide that he was in grete heuinesse that he
might not go oute, so that nother mete ne drinke dede hym no good.

72 to] bifore D   73 this] his D   therfor] *add* saie that D   75 haue] *add* see E   bi]
add youre E   78 hys] *add* good D   79 in . . . haste] as hastelie D   as] L, a E   83 the
kinge] his lorde E   85 hym] *om.* E   tale] *om.* D   87 Now] wherefor D   91 ansuere]
add and seie D   93 be] *add* þe more D   to you] *om.* E   in] *add* youre D   94 in] *add*
youre D   96 loued] bilevid D   gretter] grete D   97 worship] *add* more D   98 the^2]
add 'kingis' D   103 so that nother] in so moch þat his D   dede] myght doon D

And whan his fader herde that, he was hevy and sori and anone lete
105 ordeine horses and a fresshe felawship for to ride with hym and to
disporte hym. And in a tyme as this yonge lorde went to disporte hym,
a lepre and a blynde man come ayens hym, and whanne he saw hem he
was sore abasshed and asked one of his servauntes what hem ayled,
and he tolde hym that it were passiones that fell to men. And he asked
110 hym whedir tho passiones fell to all men, and he saide: 'Nay.' And
than he asked whether men knewe which thei were that so shulde
resseiue th[o] passiones or ellis that it come to hem by fortune, and he
ansuered: 'What is he that may knowe the auentures of men?' And
thanne he beganne to be pensef for the vncustumable thinge of that
115 sight. And whanne he knewe that sum suche passiones come by
lengthe of longe lyff, he asked what shulde be the ende, and thei saide:
'Dethe.' And he saide: 'Is the dethe ende of all or of sum?' And
whanne thei saide that all must deye, he asked in how mani yere this
shulde falle, and thei saide in .iiij^{xx}. yere or in an hundred and all that
120 foluithe the dethe. And whanne this yonge lord had conceyued all this
f. 297rb he was in gret thought and discomfort, but alwey be|fore his fader he
shewed glad chere, but souerainly he desired to be dressed and taught
in these forsaid thinges.

And in that tyme there was an holy monke that duellyd in desert, a
125 man of perfite lyff and holy conuersacion, his name was Balaham. And
this holy man knewe in sperit what was done about the kinges sone,
and toke the habite of a marchaunt and came to the citee and spake
with the kinges yongest sone, and saide that he had a precious stone
that gaue lyght and sight to the blinde, heringe to the defe, spekinge to
130 the dou[m]e, and yeuithe wisdom to foles. 'And therfor bringe me to
the kinges eldest sone and y woll gladly sell hym this precious stone.'
This yonge lorde saide to hym: 'Thou semest a man of gret wisdom
but thi wordes acorde not therwith, neuer the latter and y had
knowlage of that stone and that it were proued that thou saiest, y
135 wote well that thou shuldest haue right gret worship and thanke of the
kinges sone.' And he saide: 'My stone hathe such a vertu that he that
hathe none hole sight and that kepithe not pure chastite lesithe the
vertu that he shulde resseiue bi the sight therof, and y am a fesisyan

104 whan] *add* the kinge D   109 that²] *ins.* D   110 he] the seruaunt D
111 he] this yonge lorde D   112 tho] the E   113 ansuered] *add* and seide D
114 he] this yonge lorde D   115 sum] *om.* D   116 asked] *add* hym D   the ende]
than D   119 hundred] *add* yere D   122 glad] good D   128 yongest] yonge D
130 doume] dounne E   133 thi wordes] I D   therwith] *add* but D   135 right]
om. D   136 he] than Balaham D   saide] *add* to this yonge lorde D

and y se well that thi sight is not clene, but y vnderstonde that the
kinges eldest sone hathe right chaste eyen, right faire and right hole.' 140
And than he saide: 'Yef it be so, shew it not to me, for y haue no hole
sight but defouled with synne.' And he tolde this to the kingges sone
and he sent for hym anone.

And whanne he was entred and had receiued hym with gret
reuerence, Barlaham saide to hym: 'Sir, thou hast wel done, | for f. 297ᵛᵃ
thou hast not take hede of my litelnesse that aperithe outewarde. 146
Thou hast done as a noble kinge dede that rode in his chare all of gold
and mette with pore men with clothes totorn, and anone he wente
downe of his chare and dede hem gret reuerence and kissed hem, and
his barones were euell apaied, but thei durst not saie nothinge to 150
hymselff but pleined to his brother and saide that the kinge had done a
gret thinge ayenst his mageste, and than the brother undertoke hym of
this thinge. And the kinge had this custume that whanne he wolde
deliuer ani man to dethe, he wolde sende before his yate a criour with
a trumpe that was ordeined therto. And so the same night that he was 155
vndertake he sent the crioure with the trumpe to his brotheres yate
and made sowne the trumpe. And whan his brother herde this he was
full of sorugh and oute of all comfort of his lyff and slepte no slepe all
that night. In the morw he made his testament and clothed hym in
blacke and came wepinge, he and his wiff and all his children, to the 160
paleis of the kinge. And the kinge made hym come to hym and saide to
hym: "A, fole, yef thou hast herde the message of thi brother to whom
thou wost wel thou hast not offended, and thou dredest so moche,
how shulde y not thanne drede these messengers of oure Lorde God
whom y haue so greuously offended, whiche messengers signifien the 165
dethe miche more thanne the trompe atte thi yate, and also thei shewe
me the dredfull cominge of the iuge." And after this he dede ordeine
.iiij. chestes, and the tweyn he lete couer with golde and | filled hem f. 297ᵛᵇ
withinne with rotin dede bonis, and that other tweine he anointed
withoute with piche and filled withinne with precious stones, and 170
thanne lete call before hym the gret maistres that he wost wel that
hadde compleined of hym to his brother, and made sette these .iiij.
cophers before hem and asked of hem whiche of hem were most

140 faire] *add* and clere D   right] *om.* D   141 he] this yonge lorde D   142 but]
þei ben D   he] *add* went and D   kingges] *add* oldist D   sone] *add* his brothir D
144 had] was D   hym] *om.* D   146 outewarde] *add* but D   147 as] like D   dede]
om. D   149 kissed hem and] askid hym yiff D   152 the brother] he D   hym] the
kinge D   153 the kinge] this D   160 wepinge] *add* bothe D   161 to¹] bifore D
164 how] whi D   167 dede] lete D   168 he] thereof D   170 withoute] hem D

precious, and thei saide that tho that were arraied with golde were of
175 more pris. And thanne the kinge comaunded that thei shulde be
opened, and right gret stenche come oute of hem. And thanne the
kinge saide to hem: "Thei be like hem that be clothed with precious
clothinge withoute and withinne be full of stinke of synnes." And
after that he made for to opene that other tweyne, and right suete
180 smelle come oute of hem. And thanne the king saide: "These be like
to the pore men that y worshipped so moche, for though thei were
clothed in vile vestimentis thei shinid inwarde with suetnesse of all
vertues. And ye take none hede of that [is] outwarde and considre not
what is withinne, and ye haue do to me right as that kinge dede, for ye
185 haue graciously resseiued me."'

And thanne Barlaam beganne a long sermon of the creacion of the
worlde and of the trespas of the furste man and of the incarnacion of
Ihesu Crist, and of the day of iugement and of the guerdon of good
and euell, and blamed gretly tho that serued to the ydoles and putte
190 suche an ensaumple of her foly, and saide: 'An archer toke a bridde
that hight a nytingale, and whanne he wolde sle hym a voys was youe
to the bridde and saide: "Certis, thou maist not fell thi bely with me, y
am so litell, but yef thou wilt lete me goo y shall teche the .iij. |
f. 298ra wisdomes wherewith thou maiste gretly profite." The man was sore
195 abasshed whanne he herde the bridde speke, and in hope of these .iij.
wisdomes he lete hym goo. And thanne the bridde saide: "Stody
neuer to take that thinge that may not be take, and be neuer sori of
thinge loste withoute recouere; leue neuer thinge that is not to leue."
And whanne the bridde was fre from hym aboue in the eyre he saide:
200 "Alas, thou wreched man, how thou hast had this day euell counsaile
and how thou hast loste this day a grete tresour, for y haue in myn
entrayles a precious stone as gret as [the] eye of an ostriche." And
whanne the man herde this he was sori, and enforced hym to take this
bridde ayen, and saide: "Come into my hous and y shall yeue the all
205 that the nedithe and lete the go worshipfully." And thanne saide the
nytingale: "Now knowe y well that thou art a fole. For thou hast not
profited in nothinge that y haue taught the, for thou art sori that thou
haste loste me, and yet y am withoute recouere and yet thou aspiest

179 tweyne] cheste D   182 vestimentis] *add* yit D   183 none] *om.* D   is] ye
see E   and] but ye D   191–2 a voys . . . Certis] there was youen hym a vois that
certes seide D   192 bely] bodie D   me] *add* for D   193 but] and D
197 take] late D   199 fre] ferre D   202 a] *add* grete tresour a D   the] an E
207 nothinge] no wise D

for to take me, and ouer that thou wenist that there be in me a gret
precious stone and all my body is not so grete as an ostriches eye."   210
And right in this wise do tho that worshippen ydoles and putte her
truste in suche false goddes that thei haue made with her hondes and
saie that thei be her kepers and defendours.'

And thanne he beganne to dispute ayen the false delites of the
worlde and the vanitees and brought thereto mani ensaumples and   215
saide: 'Tho that lyuen and desiren her bodely delites, they letin her
evyn cristen deye for hunger. It farithe bi hem as it ferde by a man
that fledde before an vnicorne | for drede lest he wolde devoure hym.   f. 298rb
And as he fledde he fell in a depe pitte, and as he was fallyng he caught
a tre with his hondes and set his fete vpon a sliding place. And thanne   220
come there .ij. mise, that one blacke that other white, that withoute
cesinge thei gnewe the rote of this tree that the rote was nigh atwo.
And he sawe in the botum of that pitte a grete dragon castinge oute
fire with opin mouthe for to devoure hym, and vpon the place where
his fete lenid he sawe the hedis of .iiij. serpentis that come oute of that   225
place. And thanne he lefte up his eyen and sawe a litell honi hanging
in the braunches of that tree, and for[yat the] perill that he was inne
for a litell of the swetnesse that he atasted. The vnicorne is dethe, that
euer foluithe man and coueitithe to take hym, and the pitte is the
worlde, that is full of all wickednesse. The tree is the lyff of eueri   230
creature, that bi the houres of the dayes and of the nightes wastithe
allway, and the myes signifien men. The slidinge place where the .iiij.
serpentes appered bene the bodies that bene made of [the] .iiij.
elementis, by the whiche the ioynning of membris be corrupte in
vnordeined bodies. The horrible dragon is the mouthe of hell, that   235
coueitithe to devoure all creatoures. The bowe of the tree is the
deceiuable worlde, bi the whiche men be so continuelly deceiued that
they take none hede of the perile thei bene inne.'

Furthermore, he tolde that he that louithe the worlde is like to a
man that hadde .iij. frendes, of whiche he loued the furst as moche as   240
hymselff, the secounde a litell lasse thanne hymselff, and the thridde
as litell or not. Hit fell so that he | was fall into gret perill and was   f. 298va
somened for to apere before the kinge. This man was in gret sorw and
drede and went to his furst frende and praied hym of helpe and

215 mani] add faire E   216 lyuen] liveden D   227 foryat the] for that E, for that
the D (oublia le P2)   inne] add was D   228 of the] om. D   233 the²] om. E
236 bowe] bowes D   tree] trees E   239 louithe] lovid D   the worlde] twice D
240 moche] welle D

245 rehersed hym how he had allwayes loued hym. His frende ansuered
hym and saide: 'I wote not what the eylithe. Y haue other frendes with
whom y must this day disporte me that from hennes forwarde shull be
my frendes, but yet y wol yeue the a thinne clothe to couer the with.'
And thanne he al confused went to the secounde frende and required
250 hym his helpe. And he ansuered: 'Holde me excused, for y haue so
moche ado that y may not go with the in this strife. Neuertheles, y
shall bringe the to the dore of the paleis and thanne turne ayen to myn
hous and take of my propre nedis.' And thanne this man, full of
sorugh and in dispaire, went to the thridde frende and saide to hym
255 with shamefast chere: 'Y haue no reson to speke to the bicause y haue
not loued the as y shulde do, but y am in tribulacion and withoute
frendes, wherfor y beseche the to haue pite on me and helpe me.' And
he ansuered hym with glad visage and saide: 'Suerly y haue not
foryete the litell good that ye dede to me, and therfor y knowlage me
260 to be youre true frende, and y shall goo before the kinge and praie for
the.' The furste frende is the possession of worldely richesses, for
whiche men putte hem in mani a perile, but whanne the dethe
comithe he leuithe hym nothinge but an olde clothe to berie hym
inne. The secounde frende is his wyff, his children, and his kyn, the
265 whiche wol bringe hym to his pitte and thanne turne ayen to her |
f. 298vb owne besinesse. The thridde is faithe, hope and charite with
almesdedes, the whiche alwey whanne we go oute of the body thei
go euer before us for to praie to the kinge for us.'

And yet acordinge to this purpos, he saide that it was the custume
270 of a gret citee that eueri yere thei wolde chese a straunge man to be her
prince, and all that yere he hadde full powere to do what he wolde and
lyued in gret richesses and in gret delites, and wende euer to haue
stonde in that plight. But sodenly atte the yeres ende thei wolde arise
ayenst hym and dispoile hym of all his richesses and lede hym naked
275 thorugh the citee and thanne exile hym into an yle where he shulde
n[oth]er finde mete ne clothe but was forpined with hunger and colde.
And thanne thei wolde lefte up another, and so atte the laste thei chase
one that knewe her custumes, and in the mene tyme he sent all that
yere right gret tresour into that yle withoute nombre, and whanne the
280 yere was fulfelled he was sent thedir, and whanne that other that were

247 shull] shulde D   248 couer] hile D   251 strife] add but D   252 thanne]
add I wolle D   253 take of] doo D   254 and¹] add nygh D   255 shamefast]
shamefulle D   256 am] add nowe D   260 true] om. D   262 a] add grete D
264 inne] with alle D   273 wolde] add all E   276 nother] neuer E   279 right]
om. D

there persheden for hunger and colde he abounded in gret delites. This citee is the worlde. The citezenes be the princes of derkenesses that drawe vs bi fals delites of the worlde, and the dethe comith wherof we take none hede, and so we [be] sent into exile into a place of derkenesse; the tresours that be sent before be made [bi] the hondes of 285 pore men.

And whanne Barlaam had diligentely taught the kingges sone so that he wolde forsake his fader for to serue hym, Barlaham saide: 'Yef thou do this, thou shalt be like to a yonge man to whom a noble man wolde haue yeue a wiff of gret noblesse, but he refused it and fledde. 290 And he sawe a pore | virgine in a place that laboured and praised God f. 299ra with her mouthe, to whom he saide: "What is that, thou maiden that art so pore, and thou labourest as faste to yeue thankinges to God as though thou haddest resseiued grete goodes of hym." And she ansuered and saide: "Right as a litell medicine dothe often tymes 295 awey a gret siknesse, right so gret thankingges for litell yeftes is made a gret yeuer of gret yeftes; for tho thinges that be witheoutc bc not oures, and therfor y haue resseiued of hym gret yeftes, for he made me to his ymage and hathe yeue me reson and vnderstondinge and called me to his glorious blisse; and for so mani gret yeftes am y contynually 300 bounde to preise [hym]." And thanne whanne this yonge man sawe this wisdom of her he asked her of her fader that he might wedde her. And the fader saide: "Thou maist not haue my doughter, for thou art a sone of riche and noble men, and y and my doughter be pore." And whanne he praied effectualy, he saide: "Y may in no wise yeue the my 305 doughter for to lede her in thi faderes house, for she is myn only doughter." And he saide: "Y will duell with the and acorde with the in all thinges." And thanne he toke of his precious vestement and clothed hym in the clothinge of the olde pore man and toke his doughter to his wyff and duelled with [her] fader and lyued simply as 310 he dede. And whanne the olde man had longe proued hym, he ledde hym into his chaumbre and there he shewed hym gretter richesse thanne euer he had sayne before and gaue hym all that richesse.'

And than saide Iosephat: 'This narracion touchith me, y suppose thou hast tolde it for me. Now good fader, tell me where ye | duelle f. 299rb and how mani yeres olde ye be, for y will neuer be departed from you.' 316

282 citezenes] add thereof D   derkenesses] derkenes D   284 be] om. E
285 before] add hem D   bi] om. E   293 yeue] yeelde D   297 gret¹] om. D
300 glorious] om. D   301 hym] om. E   310 her] his E   314 me] twice D
315 good] goo oolde D   316 be departed] departe D

And he saide: 'Y haue .xlv. yere duelled in the desert of the londe of
Sennar.' And Iosephath saide: 'Fader, it semithe me that thou hast
more thanne .lxx. yere of age.' And thanne he saide: 'Yef thou aske
320 after the yeres of my natiuite, thou hast wel acounted, but y acounte
hem not in the nombre of my lyff, and specially tho that y spended in
the vanite of the worlde; for y was thanne dede to God, so that y
acounte not the yeres of dethe to the yeres of lyff.' And as Iosephath
wolde haue folued hym into desert, [Barlaam saide]: 'Yef thou do thus
325 y shall not haue thi felawship, and also y shall be cause of persecucion
of my bretheren, but whanne thou shalt see couenable tyme thou shalt
come to me into deserte.' And thanne Barlaam baptised the kingges
sone and taught hym right well in the faithe and returned ayen to his
sell.

330   And after that [whanne] the kinge wost his sone was cristen he was
in gret sorugh. And a dere frende of the kingges comforted hym in
this wise and saide: 'Sir Kinge, y knowe right well an olde felawe that
is wonder like to Barlaam in all thinges; he shal feyne as though he
were Barlaam and defende the faithe of cristen men, and after that he
335 shall suffre hymselff to be ouercome and repele all that he hathe
taught, and so shall youre sone turne ayen to you.' And thanne the
kinge toke gret strength for to take Barlaam and toke this heremyte
and feined that he had take Barlaam. And whanne the kingges sone
herde that Barlaam was take he wepte bitterly, but after he knewe by
f. 299ᵛᵃ devyne reuelacion | that it was not he.
341   And thanne the kinge went to his sone and saide: 'Sone, thou hast
putte me in gret sorw, thou hast vnworshipped myn age, thou has
derked the light of myn eyen; whi hast thou do so? Thou hast forsake
the worshippe of my goddes.' And he ansuered hym and saide:
345 'Fader, y haue fledde derkenesse and am turned into ly[ght], y haue
fledde erroure and knowe trouthe, and therfor trauaile not for not, for
thou maist neuer withdraw me from Ihesu Crist. And right as it is
inpossible that thou touche the highnesse of heuene with thine honde,
or ellys thou might make drie the Gret See, wetithe wel that also sone
350 thou mightest do this thinge.' And thanne saide his fader: 'Ho hathe
wrought me all this euell but only myselff that haue norisshed the so
gloriously that neuer fader kepte his sone so tenderly. Wherfor thi

318 Sennar] Samar D   319 he] Balaham D   323 as] *om.* D   324 Barlaam
saide] L, *om.* E   324–7 Barlaam . . . deserte] *om.* D   328 sone] *add* Iosaphat D
330 whanne] *om.* E   337–8 and . . . Barlaam] *om.* D   342 sorw] *add* for D
343 Thou hast] *add* and whi hast þou D   344 he] Iosaphat D   345 lyght] lyff E
346 not¹] *om.* D   349 Gret] *om.* D   wetithe] wite it D

pride and wicked will hathe made [the] wode ayenst me. With good
right the astronomers in thi birthe saide that thou shuldest be proude
and disobeisaunt to thi kinrede, and therfor, but yef thou wilt now 355
obeie me, thou shalt no lengger be my sone but [in] stede of thi fader y
shall be thin enemy and y shall [do] to the that y dede neuer to
enemy.' To whom Iosephat saide: 'Fader, what ailithe the to wrathe
the so greuously, is it for y am made a prince of the good? What fader
is that that is sori of the welthe of his sone? Y shall no lenger calle the 360
fader yef thou be contrarie to me, but y shall pursue the as a serpent.'

And thanne the kinge departid from hym in gret wrathe and tolde
Arache his frende alle the hardenesse of | his sone, and he counsailed f. 299vb
that he shulde saie to hym no sharpe worde, for a childe is sonner
drawe by softe wordes thanne bi harde and sharpe. The day foluing 365
the king came to his sone and beganne to clippe hym and cusse hym
and saide to hym: 'Right suete sone, the worship of myn age, now
good sone, drede thi fader, wost thou not what good it is to obeye to
thi fader and make hym gladde? And in the contrarie wise, what synne
it is to wratthe thi fader and make him sori, for tho that wrathe her 370
faders perisshen wyckedly.' To whom Iosephath saide: 'It is [tyme] to
loue and tyme to hate, tyme of pees and tyme of bataile, and therfor
we shuld in no wise obeie to hem that wolde take us fro God, be it
fader or moder.'

And whanne the fader sawe the sadnesse of his sone he saide to 375
hym: 'Sethe y see thi folie and that thou wilt not obeie me, come and
wete truly that Balaham that hathe deseiued the is in prison fast
ybounde. We shull assemble togedre oure men and youres with
Balaham, and y shall sende that all the Galyens shull come withoute
drede, and thei shull begynne to dispute, and yef youres and Balaam 380
haue the betir we shull beleue with you, and yef oures haue the betir
ye shull turne to vs.' And this liked well to the kingges sone. And
whanne all was ordeyned with hym that named hymself Balaam how
he shulde furst defende the faithe and afterwarde suffre hym to be
ouercome, Iosephat turned hym towardes Nater that feyned hymselff 385
to be Balaam and saide: 'Balaam, thou wost wel how thou hast taught

353 the] L, this E, me thus D   354 right] ED *end the sentence here*   355 now]
om. D   356 in] *om.* E   357 do] *om.* E   359 the good] allemyghti god D
362 tolde] *add* it to D   363 counsailed] *add* þe kinge D   365 harde and] *om.* D
sharpe] *add* woordis D   367 hym] *add* My D   Right] *om.* D   368 good sone] *om.* D
369 thi] the D   370 thi] the D   371 tyme] to me ED (*temps* P2)   372 and
tyme¹] time and D   378 togedre] *add* alle D   380 yef] *add* ye and D   382 sone]
add Iosaphat D   383 named] callid D   384 hym] hymselff D

f. 300ʳᵃ me; yef thou defende that lawe that thou haste | tought me y shall
abide in thi doctrine unto the ende of my liff, and yef thou be
ouercome y shall right sone venge in the myn iniurie, for with myn
390   owne hondes y shall draw out the tunge of thin hede and yeue it to the
houndes so that thou shalt not dore another tyme putte a kinges sone
in erroure.'
   And whanne Nater herde this he was sori and sore aferde, for he
sawe that he was fall in the pitte that he had made hymselff, and
395   thanne he avised hym and thought that it was beter to holde the partie
of the kinges sone in eschewinge of the dethe, sethe that the kinge had
bidde hym hardely for to defende the faithe withoute ani drede. And
thanne one of the maistres saide: 'Thou art Balaam that hast deceiued
the kinges sone.' And he ansuered and saide: 'Y am Balaam that haue
400   not sette the kinges sone in erroure, but y haue brought hym oute of
erroure.' And thanne saide the maister: 'Sethe that so noble and
meruailous men haue worshipped oure goddes, how durst thou dresse
the ayenst hem?' And he ansuered: 'Tho of Caldee and of Egipte and
of Grece erreden and saide that the creatures were goddes, [and the
405   Caldees saide that the elementes were goddes] that be made to the
profit of man, and so thei haue made hem sogetis to hem, and therfor
thei be corrupte with mani passiones. And also the Caldees wenin that
cursed men be goddes, as Saturne that thei sayne he ete his sones and
that he cutte of his menbris and caste hem in the see and that therof
410   was Venus born, and that he was bounde and caste into hell bi Iupiter
his sone. And thei saye that Iubiter was kinge of other goddes and that
f. 300ʳᵇ he transfigu|red hym often tymes in forme of a beste for to do
avoutrie. For sumtyme Mars was her husbond and sumtyme
Adonis. The Egipcians worshipe[d] bestis, a calf and a pigge. And
415   the cristen worship the sone of the right high kinge that descended
from heuene and toke mankinde.' And so Nather beganne right
mighteli [to] defende the faithe of cristen folke, and shewed forthe
so [many] resones that all the other maistres were abasshed and woste
not what to ansuere.
420   And thanne Iosephat hadde gret ioye of that oure Lorde had
defended the trouth by hym that was enemye of trouthe. And
thanne the kinge was full of angre and comaunded that the counsaile

      390 owne] *om.* D   396 sone] *add* Iosaphat H2   403 and¹] *om.* H2   Egipte] *add* of
Erogon H2   404 erreden] *om.* H2   the¹] *om.* H2   404–5 and² . . . goddes] *om.* E
405 be] he H2   408 goddes] *om.* H2   411 saye] *add* also H2   412 transfigured] *add*
seyn E   in] *add* for in E, in to the H2   414 worshiped] worshipen E   bestis] *add* as H2
416 so] *add* this H2   right] *om.* H2   417 to] *om.* E   418 many] L, mighty EH2

shulde be departed as thou he wolde in the morw trete of the same matere. And thanne Iosephat saide to his fader: 'Lete my maister be with me this night so that we may make collacion togedre for to make oure ansuere tomorw, and lede youre maistres with you and take youre counsaile with hem, for yef ye lede my maister withe you ye do me no right.' For whiche thinge he graunted hym Nator in hope that he wolde deceiue hym. And whanne the kinges sone and Nator were togedre, Iosaphath saide to hym: 'Wenist thou that y kn[o]w the not? Y wote right well that thou art not Balaam, but thou art Nator the astronomer.' And thanne Iosephath preched hym the weye of helthe and conuerted hym to the faithe and sent hym into desert, and there he was baptised and lyued the lyff of an holy heremite.

And thanne there was an enchauntour that hight | Theodas that had herde these thinges and came to the kinge and saide that he wolde make hym turne to the lawes of his goddes. And the kinge saide to hym: 'Yef thou do it y will in worship of the make an ymage of golde and offre therto sacrifices as to my goddes.' Thanne saide the enchauntoure to the kinge: 'Putte awey all tho that be aboute thi sone, and sette aboute hym faire yong women well arraied, and comaunde hem that thei go neuer from hym but that thei serue hym and continuelly be with hym; and y shall sende a wicked sperit to enflaume hym, for there is nothinge that may so sone deceiue a yonge man as the beauute of a woman.'

And thanne he tolde this ensaumple. 'Ther was a kinge that had but a sone, and the [wise] phisiciens saide that yef he saw sonne or mone withinne .x. yere that he shulde lese his sight. And thanne this childe was norisshed withinne a roche that was in a depe pitte and, whanne the .x. yere were passed and he was brought oute, the kinge comaunded that all thinges of diuerse kindes shulde be brought afore hym that he might knowe hem and the names of hem. And thanne there was brought before hym horses and iuelles, golde and siluer and precious stones, and mani other thinges and tolde hym the valu of euerithinge. And whanne thei brought before hym women gaily arraied he asked besily what thinges they were and, for they wolde not telle hym in haste, he was full of sorw and anguisshe. And

425

430

f. 300va
436

440

445

450

455

426 oure] *om.* H2   427 for] and H2   428 he] the kinge H2   430 know] knew E   432 of] *add* trouthe and of H2   helthe] helpe H2   437 hym] his sone H2 the¹] his H2   of . . . goddes] *om.* H2   438 worship of the] the worshipp H2 441 women] *add* and loke that thei be H2   443 sende] *add* the E   444 that may so sone] sooner mai H2   447 wise] wiff E   phisiciens] philosophers H2   457 haste] *add* what thei were H2

thanne the maister squier that was about the king saide to hym in his
f. 300vb   borde: "It be fendes that deceiue men." And thanne | the kinge asked
460   hym what thinge he hadde most ioye of, of all that he had saine, and
he ansuered and saide: "Fader, my desire coueitithe nothinge so
moche as the fendes that deceiue men." And therfor, [Sir] kinge, trust
verily that [nothinge] shull ouercome thi sone but women that mowe
allwey stere hym to lycherie.'

465   And thanne the kinge putte from hym all his servauntes and putte
aboute hym faire yonge women well arraied that shulde alwey be
aboute hym and stere hym to iape and to plaie, and thanne the wicked
sperit was sent for to enflawme hym, and this yonge man felt gret
meuinges and brenninge steringges inwarde, and these maydenes
470   made hym a cruell bataile outewarde. And whanne he felt hym in this
sorufull plite, he recomaunded hym all to God and resseiued dyvine
comfort, and all the temptacion went awey.

And thanne the kinge sent to hym a faire yonge maide that was a
kingges doughter and she was orphelyn. And thanne the servaunt of
475   God Iosephath beganne to preche her, and she saide to hym: 'Yef thou
wilt saue me and departe me from the worshippinge of ydoles, ioyne
the to me by mariage, for cristen peple dispise not mariage, for her
patriarkes and prophetis and Peter the apostell had wyues.' And
thanne saide Iosephath: 'It is for not that thou tellist me this, for yef it
480   be lefull cristen men to wedde wyues, it is not lefull that tho that haue
avowed chastite for to wedde wyues.' And thanne she saide: 'Now be
it as thou wilt, but yef thou wilt saue me, graunte me a lytell bone, that
thou wilt lye with me one night, and y behight the that tomorw y shall
f. 301ra   be made cristen, for as ye cristen | saien that the aungeles in heuene
485   haue ioye of a synner that dothe penaunce, and therfor graunte me
only this thinge and thou shalt haue me sauf.' And thanne she
beganne gretly to stere his soule and his consciens.

Thanne saide the fende to his felawes: 'See ye not how this yonge
maide hathe do more thanne all we? Now lete us helpe her forthe, for
490   now is tyme couenable.' And whanne this holy yonge ma[n] felte
hymselff in so gret ch[etiu]ite that couetise of the flesshe ouer

458–9 his borde] game H2   459 It] these H2   460 hym] his sone of H2   of ¹] om.
H2   462 Sir] om. E   463 nothinge] they E   but] so soone as H2   468 for] om. H2
and] so that H2   470 this] add sorugh and E   471 resseiued] add anone the H2
472 the temptacion] his temptaciouns H2   476 worshippinge] add of goddis H2
481 Now] om. H2   482–3 but . . . wilt] om. H2   484 cristen²] add men H2   486 me]
om. H2   488 yonge] om. H2   489 we] add where for H2   490 holy yonge man] L,
Iosaphat H2   man] L, maide E   491 so] om. H2   chetivite] chastite E

laboured hym and that he desired the sauinge of that maide bi the techinge of the fende, in gret sorw and wepinge he putte hym to praier, and atte the last he fell aslepe. And thanne he sawe in a vision that he was brought into a faire medw full of faire suete floures where 495 the leues of the trees made a suete sowne as thei were blowe with [an] agreable wynde, and thennes come a delicious savour and the fruit of that place was right faire to beh[olde] and right delictable in the taste, and there were seges of golde and siluer arrayed with precious stones [and beddes richely arrayed] and a faire clere water ranne thorughe 500 that place. After that he entred into a citee whereof the walles were of fin golde and shined bi merueilous clere light, and he sawe in the eyre sum that songe a songe that neuer ere of dedly bodi herde none suche, and it was saide: 'This is the place of hem that be blessed.' And as thei wolde haue ledde hym thennes he praied that he might abide still 505 there. And than thei saide to hym: 'Thou shalt hereafter come hedir with gret laboure yef thou maist suffre it.' And after that he was ledde into a place wheras all derkenesse and horrible stinke was, and thei saide: 'This is the place for tho | that be wicked.' And whanne he was f. 301rb awaked, the beauute of that mayden and of all other was to hym more 510 stinkinge thanne ani careyne.

And as the wicked spiritis come ayen to Theodore and [he] blamed hem, thei saide to hym: 'We did all that we might and troubeled hym sore as longe as we fonde hym withoute signe of the crosse, but whanne he was arraied with that signe he turmented vs sore.' And 515 thanne Theodore come [to] hym [with] the kinge and hoped to haue peruerted hym. But that enchauntour was take of hym that he went [to] haue takin, and was conuerted and resseyued bapteme and lyued after a pesible lyff. And thanne the king was oute of all hope, and bi the counsaill of his frendes he lefte his sone half his rewme. And 520 though he had leuer go into desert with al his desire, yet for to encrese the cristen faithe he resseiued the kingdom a certaine tyme and lete make chirches and lefte up crosses in his rewme and conuerted the peple to Ihesu Crist. And atte the laste the fader consented to the resones and predicaciones of his sone and resseiued the faith of Ihesu 525

493 fende] add he was H2A2   wepinge] add and H2   496 sowne] swowne H2   an] om. E   497 and¹] add from H2   498 beholde] L, be had EH2   the taste] that state H2   499 seges] seetis H2   500 and beddes . . . arraied] om. E   508 stinke] stinkinge H2   509 whanne] thanne changed to whanne E   510 more] mooste H2   512 he] om. E   514 but] and H2   515 vs] add right H2   516 to¹, with] trs. E   518 to] om. E   520 his¹] om. H2   520–1 And though] but H2   521 go] to haue goone H2   with] and that was H2   desire] add but H2

Crist and bapteme, and lefte his kingdom to his sone and toke hym to the werkes of penaunce and ended his lyff p[r]eysably.

Iosephath warned ofte tyme the kinge Barachiell that he wolde flee into desert, but he was euer withholde of his peple. But atte the laste
530 he went his way, and as he went thorugh the desert he mette with a pore man and he gaue hym his habit ryall and abode hymselff in a pore cote. And the fende arraied ayenst hym mani harde batailes. Sumtyme
f. 301ᵛᵃ he wolde renne vpon hym with | a swerde drawen, thretinge hym to smite but yef he wolde leue the desert. Sometyme he wolde apere to
535 hym in liknesse of a wilde beste and renne upon hym for to devoure hym, and he wolde mekely saie: 'Oure Lorde Ihesu is myn helpe, y drede nothinge that thou may do to me.'

And this Iosephath went .ij. yere thorugh the desert and might not finde Barlaam. And atte the laste he fonde a pitte in the irthe, and
540 there he stode atte the dore and cried and saide: 'Fader, yeue me thi blessinge, holy fader blesse me.' And thanne Barlaham herde his voys and rose hym vp and come oute and kissedin and clippedin togedre with gret ioye. And thanne Iosephath tolde to Barlaam alle [the] thinges that were fall to hym, and he preised and thanked God. And
545 Iosephath duelled there mani yeres in gret pacience [and] full of vertues. And whanne Barlaam had fulfelled his dayes he reste in pees about the yere of oure Lorde .iiijC.iiijˣˣ., and Iosephath lefte his rewme the yere of his age .xxv. and ledde the lyff of an hermite .xxxv. yere, and rested in pees full of vertues and was buried with Barlaam.
550 And whanne the kinge Barachiel herde this thinge he come to the place with gret cumpanye and toke the bodies and bare hem with gret sollempnite to his citee, and mani a miracle God wrought for the holy bodies to his worship and preising. Amen.

526 lefte] *add* alle H2   toke hym] bitoke hymselff H2   527 preysably] L, peysably E, Pecibulli H2   529 his] *om.* H2   535 in liknesse] *om.* H2   wilde] *om.* H2   for to] as he wolde H2   536 Ihesu] *add* Criste H2   538 this] thus H2   541 fader] *add* I praie the to H2   543 the] *om.* E   545 and¹] *om.* E   546 fulfelled] *add* alle H2 547 and] *add* so H2   551 the] *add* holie H2   552 sollempnite] worshipp H2   the] thoo H2

Here endithe the lyff of Barlaham, and nexst beginnithe
Pelagien with the gestis of Lumbardes, Capitulum
.C.lxx[i]iij.^m

Pelagien pope was of gret holynesse and gouerned hym preisably in
the sege of Rome, and in | his end he rested in oure Lorde fulle of   f. 301vb
good werkes. But this was not Pelagien successoure of Seint Gregore
but another that was before hym. And after this Pelagien was pope
Iohn, and to that Iohn succeded Benedicte, and after hym come   5
Pelagien and thanne Gregorie. And in the tyme of this Pelagien come
the Lumbardes into Ytalie, and for mani knowe not this stori y haue
sette it here as it is conteined in the stori of Lumbardes, and Paule a
maister of the storie of Lumbardes made it, and it is founde true by
mani cronicles.   10
    He saithe that there was a multitude of peple of Germani went oute
bi sailinge in the Grete See towardis Septemtrion fro the yle of
Shandynare and envyronid mani londes and dedin grete bataîlcs. And
atte the laste thei come into Pavonie and durst not passe ouer and
ordeined there for to laye her sege. And thei were furst called   15
Humiliens and sethe thei were called Lumbardes. And as thei were
ʒet in Germani, Agilmus that was kinge of Lumbardes fonde .vij.
children bisides a well that [had be] caste there of a misgouerned
woman for to be drowned. And whanne the kinge had found hem by
case of auenture he meruailed gretly, and with the ende of his spere he   20
turned hem and one of the children toke the kingges spere in his
honde. And whanne the kinge sawe that, he was abaisshed and lete
take hem up and norisshed hem, and he called the grettest of hem
Lanceon and saide hoso liued shulde see hym right gret and mighti.
And so it felle that after whanne the kinge was dede the Lumbardes   25
made hym her kinge.
    And in that same tyme in the yere of the incarnacion .CCCC.iiij^{xx}.
as a bisshoppe that was of the secte of Ariens, as Erope | saithe, wolde   f. 302ra
haue baptised one that hight Barbe and saide: 'Barbe, y baptise the in
the name of the fader by the sone with the holy goste,' and wolde   30

EDH2A2L; D resumes at 692 *anone* and has losses from 744 *before* to 754 *Constantinople*
caused by excision of an initial; H2 breaks off after 363 *for* (*so* H2) and resumes at 479 *passed*;
Pope has been erased throughout H2; when DH2 are not available variants from L and A2
are recorded   *Rubric* .C.lxxiiij.^m] .C.lxxiij.^m E   2 sege] seete H2 *and passim*
6 thanne] afftir hym come H2   12 fro] for H2   18 had be] he had E   20 case]
cause H2   22 lete] *add* anone H2   27 incarnacion] *add* of our lorde H2
28 secte] sette H2   29 haue] *om.* H2

shewe that the holy goste were lasse thanne the fader, and sodeinly the holy water vanisshed al away and he fledde to the chirche for to be baptised.

And in that tyme florisshed Seint Marke and Seint Gildard
35 bretheren of one wombe and born in one day and in one day, [and made bisshoppes in one day], take of Ihesu Crist.

And before that tyme, as it ys saide in a cronicle, about the yere of oure Lorde .vC.lxviij. they had of custume for to haue right longe berdes. And as thei sain that [whan] the discover[er]s shulde come to
40 aspie hem Albyon comaunded to all [the] women that thei shulde vnbinde her here and putte it about her chinnes, so that thei that shulde come to aspie hem shulde wene that thei were all men, and therfor was it saide after of these Lombardes that the name come of longe berdez. And other saine that whanne thei shulde fight with the
45 Wandelyens thei went to a man that had the sperit of prophete and praied hym to blesse hem and that he wolde praye that they might haue the victori. And by the counsaile of his wiff thei sette hem atte his wyndowe where he worshipped towardes the orient and thei putte her here aboute her chynne[s] in stede of a berde, and whanne he
50 openid his wyndowe he cried and saide: 'What be these longe berdes?' And than his wiff praied hym that he wolde yeue the victori to hem to whom he hadde youe the name. And thanne thei entred into Ytalye and toke nigh honde alle the citees and slow all the duellers in hem, and .iij. yere thei beseged Pavie and atte the laste thei toke it. And the
f. 302rb kinge Albion hadde | suore that he wolde slee all the cristen. And as he
56 shulde entre into Pauie his hors kneled downe before the yate of the citee and he might not make hym arise for constreininge of spores nor for nothing bifore that by the counsaile of a cristen man he had chaunged his othe. And fro thennes come the Lumbardes to Melan,
60 and withinne a litell while they putte vnder hem all Ytalye saue Rome and Romagronolye that was called so for it was another Rome, for she helde euer with Rome.

And whanne the kinge Albion was atte Cremone and had made a gret feste, he comaunded that his cuppe whiche he hadde do make of

32 al] om. H2   35–6 and³ . . . day] L, om. EH2   38 right longe] om. H2
39 whan the] L, was the E, what H2   discoverers] discovers E   shulde] om. H2
40 the] om. E   that thei] om. H2   43 Lombardes] add is E   44 longe] om. H2
45 of] add a E   47 thei sette hem] that sette hym H2   48 thei] these men H2
49 chynnes] chynne E   51 wolde] shulde H2   53 citees] cite H2   in hem] om. H2
57 hym] add to H2   for] add noo H2   60 while] time H2   62 Rome] the reame H2
64 cuppe] cuppis H2   make] made H2

the kinges hede were brought hym. And he dranke and yaue it 65
Roseamond his wiff and saide: 'Haue and drinke with thi fader.' And
whanne Roseamonde wist it she had gret hate to her husbonde the
kinge. And the king had a duke that misused a gentill woman of the
quenis, and she in a tyme went oute, and the quene went into the
chaumbre of this woman and sent for the duke in her name, and whan 70
he had do his will with her she said to hym: 'Wost thou what y am?'
And he saide: 'Ye, suche a woman, my love.' And she saide: 'That am
y not, but y am Roseamond the quene, and thou hast do suche a
thinge with me that other thou shalt [s]le Albyon the kinge or he shall
slee the, for y will that thou venge me of hym that hathe slaine my 75
fader and hathe made a cuppe of his hede and made me to drinke
therof.' But he wolde in no wise behote her to do hit, but he
promessed her that he wolde ordeine one to do it. And than |
whanne he shulde come that shulde do the dede she toke all the f. 302va
kingges armure and bonde his suerde fast in his scauberk that he 80
might in no wise drawe it oute. And as the kinge slepte in his bedde
this homicide enforced [hym] to entre into the chaumbre, and the
kinge perceiued it and lepte oute of his bedde and toke his suerde, but
he might not drawe it oute, so he defended hym longe til atte the laste
he that was strongly armed ouercame hym and slowe hym. And 85
thanne he toke the tresour of the paleis and went with Roseamond
into Rauene. And whan Roseamond was in Rauenne she sawe a
semely yonge man that was provost of the towne and coueited to haue
hym to her husbonde and gaue venym to her husbonde, and whanne
he felt the bitternesse of the venym he comaunded Roseamonde to 90
drinke the remenaunt. But she refused it and he drowe oute his suerde
and constreined her to drinke, and so the[i] perisshed bothe togederes.

And thanne the Lumbardes made a kinge that hight Adorolik that
was baptised and toke the faithe of Ihesu Crist, and thanne thereafter
a quene that hight Cheudeku, that was right a cristen woman that 95
made a faire oratorie in Madotee. And Gregori expouned to her the
bokys of the Dyologes, and she conuerted her husbonde to the faithe
of Ihesu Crist that hight Agissulphe, and he had be furst duke of
Thaurmuse, and after he was kinge of Lumbardes, and she made hym
haue pees with the emperoure and with the Chirche. And the pees was 100

· 66 thi] twice H2   70 this] add gentille H2   71 thou] add nat H2   72 saide²]
add ayenne to hym H2   74 sle] fle E   79 he] she E   82 hym] om. E
83 suerde] add in his honde H2   84 oute] add of the skabart and H2   longe] as longe as
he myght H2   89 her²] add owne H2   92 drinke] add it H2   thei] the E
94 thereafter] afftir H2   97 bokys] boke H2   100 the³] om. H2

f. 302vb made betwene the Romaynes and the Lumbardes the | day of the Fest
of Seint Geruase and Seint Prothase, and therfor Seint Gregori
ordeined [to singe] in the office of her masse *Loquetur dominus
pacem etc.* And in the Natiuite of Seint Iohn the Baptist the pees
105 was all confermed. And that Chewdelyn had special deuocion to Seint
Iohn, and saide that bi the meritis of hym her peple were conuerted,
and in his worship she made an oratorie in Madote, and thanne it was
reueled to an holy man that Seint Iohn was patron and defender of her
peple.
110   And whanne Gregori was dede Sabin succeded after hym, and
Bonefas succeded to Sabin and was the thridde, and Boneface the
ferthe come after the thridde, and bi the praiers of hym Focose the
emperoure gaue to the Chirche of Ihesu Crist the temple of Pantheon
aboute the yere of oure Lorde .vjC. and .x. And he had ordeined by
115 the praiers of Boneface the thridde that Rome shulde be cheef and
hede of all other chirches, for before that the chirche of Constan-
tynnople wrote hymself to be [the] highest of all other. And whanne
Focas was dede Eracles regnid about the yere of oure lorde .vjC.
and .x.
120   Machomete the fals prophete and enchauntour deceiued the
Agariens and the Ysmaelitis, that is to saie [the] Sarisenes, in this
wise, as it is redde in a cronicle and in a storie of hym. There was a
clerk renou[m]ed that was atte Rome that might not haue in the court
the worship that he desired, and fledde by despite in the parties
125 beyende the see and drow to hym moche peple bi simulacion, and
there fonde Machomete and tolde hym god and lorde of all the peple.
And [he] norisshed a dove and putte whete and other mete in the ere
f. 303ra of Machomete, | and the dove shulde stonde upon his shuldre and take
mete oute of his ere. And he was so acustumed therto that eueri tyme
130 that he sawe Machomete he wolde flee upon his shuldre. And thanne
the clerke called the peple and saide that he wolde make hym lorde
and maister of all that the holy goste wolde shewe, and vpon his
shuldre he wolde alight in lyknesse of a dove. And thanne he lete oute
the dove priuily and he anone fleye [on] the shuldre of Machomete
135 that was there amonge the peple and putte his becke in his ere. And

103 to singe] *om.* E   104 *etc.*] *om.* H2   105 Chewdelyn] Cheudeku H2
107 his worship] the worshipp of hym H2   111 to] afftir H2   115 thridde] fourth
H2   117 the] *om.* E   120 deceiued] *om.* H2   121 the²] *om.* E   123 clerk]
add that was H2   renoumed] L, renounced E, renomeied H2   126 there] *add* he H2
and¹] *add* thei H2   hym] *add* as for H2   127 he] thei E   129 he] this dowfe H2
131 clerke] clerkis H2   132 all] *om.* H2   134 on] in E

whanne the peple sawe this thinge they wende verily that it had be the
holy goste that had descended vpon h[y]m for to denounce hem the
worde of God. And in this wise deceiued Machomete the Sarisenes,
and thanne they obeyed all to hym and assayledin the kingdom of Pers
and all the parties of the orient into Alisaundre.   140

But it is more levely credible thinge that shal be saide after. For
Machomete feyned propre lawes and lyed, [for] he said that he had
resseiued the lawes by the holy goste that lyght vpon hym in forme of
a dove, and the peple saw often tymes how this dove came to hym.
And in his lawes he putte sum thinges of the Olde Testament and sum   145
of the Newe, for whanne he was in his furst age he haunted in Egipte
and in Palestin and was a mercer and ledde chameles, and was gretly
conuersaunt with the Iwes and with cristen men of whom he hadde
lerned bothe the olde lawe and the newe. And in that wise be Sariseins
circumcised after the custume of the Iewes and thei ete no porke. And   150
whanne Machomete assigned hem the cause that thei shulde ete | no   f. 303rb
porke, he saide that after Noes flode whanne all the worlde was
drowned the swyne were made of the donge of cameles, and therfor it
is to be eschewed of all the world for it is an vnclene beste. And also he
acordithe with cristen men in one thinge, for he bileued in one God   155
almighti, maker of all thinges. And so this fals prophete medlyd trwe
thinges with fals thinges. He saide that Moyses was a gret prophete,
but Crist he saide was souerayne and most grettest prophete of all
prophetis. He saide that he was bore of the Virgine Marie withoute
sede of a man, but by vertu devyne. And he saithe in his boke that is   160
called Alkaron that whanne Crist was a childe he made briddes of
slyme of the erthe, but he medelid venim with his wordes for he saide
that Ihesu Crist was not verrily dede ne rose not up, but that it was
another that he had made in liknesse of hym.

There was a lady that hight Dygam that was lady of a province that   165
hight Crotayne. She sawe this man how he was gouernour of the peple
of Sarisenes and wende that the dyvine mageste had be hidde in hym,
and she was a wedwe and toke hym to her husbonde, and so
Machomete was prince of all that province. And so by fals shewingges
he deceiued not only that lady but he deceiued Iwes and cristen men,   170

136 it] he H2   137 hym] hem E   141 levely] *om.* H2A2   thinge] *add* to bileue
H2   142 for] tofore E, therefore and H2 (*Car* P2)   143 lawes] yifftis H2
150–2 And . . . porke] *om.* H2   155 acordithe] accordid H2   156 so] thus H2
159 saide] *add* also H2   withoute] *add* the E   160 is] was H2   165 was²] *add* a H2
169 all] *om.* H2   170 and] *add* also H2

so that he saide hem opinly that he was Messias that was promessid in
the lawe. And after this Machomete bygganne to falle downe often-
tymes by the passion of his foule euell. And whan Cadycam his wiff

f. 303va wist this, she was | full of sorugh that she was wedded to a persone
175 that hadde so foul an euell. And he pesed her bi such wordes and saide
that he loked oftentyme upon the aungell Gabriell spekinge to hym,
and that he might not suffre the right grete shyninge of hym but fell
downe and was all a[ni]entised for the tyme, 'so that y may not sustene
myself,' the whiche thinge his wiff leued, and so dede mani other that
180 it was true.

And it is redde [elles]where that a monke that hight Sirgus taught
Machomete, for he was an heretike Vastorien, wherfor he was putte
oute from other monkes and went into Araby, and there he mette with
Machomete. And it is redde in other places that it was an archedeken
185 that was in Antioche, and as sum sayne he was [a I]akobyn, that
preched the circumcision and saide that Crist was not God but an holy
man only, that [was] conceiued bi the holy goste, born of a virgine.
And that beleued the Sarisenes. And this Sergius taught to Machomete mani thinges bothe of the newe lawe and of the olde. And
190 Machomete whanne he was orphelyn of fader and of moder so that he
was in his childehode vnder the cure of an vncle of his and by longe
tyme he worshipped ydoles with the peple of Arabye, so as he
witnessith in his Alkaron, for he saithe how that God sai[d]e to
hym: 'Thou were orphely[n] and y resseiued the, thou were in erroure
195 of ydolatrie and y halpe the oute thereof, thow were pore and y made
the riche.'

All the peple of Arabye worship[ed] Venus for her goddesse, and
f. 303vb yet it comithe therof that Sarisenes holden the | Friday in gret
worship, right as the Iwes done the Saterday and cristen men the
200 Sonday. And whanne Machomete was enriched with the goodes of the
wedue Cadygam he lifte hymself in so gret pride that he thought to
vsurpe to hym the rewme of Arabie. And whanne he sawe that he
might not do it bi strengthe, only that he was dispised of his
felawshippe that hadde euer be grettest with hym, he made hymself

171 Messias] Messus H2   174 to] add suche H2   178 anientised] amentised (?)
EH2   179 thinge] add Cadigan H2   180 was] add verelie H2   181 elleswhere]
where EH2 (ailleurs P2)   185 that was] om. H2   sum] add men E   a Iakobyn]
Arakobyn E   187 was] om. E   189 olde] add lawe H2   193 saide] saithe E
194 orphelyn] orphely E   196 riche] add And that time H2   197 worshipped]
worshipin E   203 that] than H2   204 made] add hym H2   204–5 hymself a
prophete/and feyned] trs. and add of H2

a prophete and feyned gret holynesse so that he might submitte to 205
hym bi his feyned fals holynesse tho that he might not by strengthe.
And thanne he toke for to byleue the counsaile of Serdyus that was a
sotel man, and lerned of hym priuely all that he shulde do and
rep[or]ted it to the peple, and saide that it was Gabriel that had
enformed hym. And so by feyned falsnesse of a prophete he helde all 210
[the] lordship of all that peple, and all byleued in hym by her fre
wylles or for drede of the swerde. And this ys rather to be holde true
thanne that of the dove.

And for that Sergius was a monke, he wolde that Sarisenes vsed the
gouernaunce of a monk, it is to wete a covyll withoute an h[oo]de, and 215
that in the gyse of monkes they shulde make mani knelingges and that
thei shulde werche ordinatly. And for that the Iewes worship[ped]
towarde the occident and the cristen towardes the orient, he wold that
his secte shulde worship toward midday, and all these thinges the
Sarisenes do yet. 220

And Machomete publysshed mani lawes that Sergeus taught hym,
and he lerned moche of Moyses lawe. For the Sarisenes wesshe hem
ofte and namely whan thei shull worship and praie, and | thanne thei f. 304ʳᵃ
wasshe all her menbres of her bodyes generaly for they wolde praie
more clenly. And in praieng thei confesse one God that hathe no pere 225
lyke vnto hym, and that Machomete [is his] prophete. And thei faste
euery yere an hole monthe, and whan thei faste thei ete not til night
come but fast all the day, and fro that tyme of the day till the sonne go
downe they dore nother ete ne drinke ne be with his wiff. And fro the
sunne go downe into the tyme betwene night and day they mowe duly 230
ete and drinke and duelle with her wywes. The sike men be not
constreyned therto, but it is comaunded hem that bycause of the
conisaunce they shull go euery yere to Ametys and praie there, and
thei shull go al aboute couered with vestimentis that be not sowed and
caste stones betwene her thies for to stone the fende. And thei saie 235
that Adam made that hous for all his children, and that it was a place
of orison to Abraham and to Ismael, and thei saie that Machomete
toke this hous to hym and to all his peple. Thei mow ete of all manere

209 reported] repented *changed to* reported E   211 the] that E   that²] the H2
her] *add* owne H2   212 wylles] wille H2   drede] fferde H2   215 it] that H2
hoode] hede E   216 in] afftir H2   217 worshipped] worshipen E   219 toward]
add the H2   220 do] *add* it H2   221 And] *add* this H2   223 and²] or H2
225 confesse] confessed H2   226 Machomete] Machometes E   is his prophete]
prophete E, the prophete H2 (*est prophete de celi* S)   faste] fastid H2   227 faste] fastid
H2   til] *add* it were H2   228 come] *om.* H2   fast] fastid H2   230 duly] oneli H2

of flesshe sauf porke and blody flesshe. Eueriche [man] may haue .iiij.
240 wyves wedded to h[y]m, and they mowe refuse and take into the
thridde tyme, but the fourthe tyme they may not. But they [mowe]
haue concubynes as mani as hem luste and putte hem from hem as
often as hem luste so that they be not with childe. And also they mowe
take wyves of her owne kyn for to encrece her kynrede of her blode so
245 that they be constreined thereby to strenger loue thanne is the loue of
frenshipp. Whanne he shall aske possession of another, it behouithe
f. 304rb that | the asker proue that he is innocent by his othe. And whanne thei
be founde in avoutrie thei be stoned togederes, and whanne thei do
fornicacion thei be bete .iiij^{xx}. tymes.
250   Machomete saide that it was denounced hym of the aungell Gabriel
that God had graunted hym that he might take other mennis wyfes for
to engendre men of vertu and prophetis. And one of his servauntis
had right a faire wiff and he defended her that she shulde not see his
lorde, and in a day he fonde her spekinge with hym and anone he
255 putte her fro hym. And Machomete resseiued her and putte her with
his other wyfes. And thanne he dredde the murmur of the peple, and
feyned that there was a writinge sent vnto hym from heuene,
wherinne it was conteined that yef ani refused his wiff, that she
shulde be wiff to hym that resseiued her; and yet the Sarisenes kepe
260 this in her lawe. He defended to drinke wyn.
          And as he afermed, oure Lorde graunted paradys to tho that kepte
his comaundementis and other of the lawe, that is to saye the place of
delites environid with renning wateres, in whiche paradys thei shull
haue seges perdurables; thei shull not haue to grete hete, ne to grete
265 colde, and they shull vse of all manere metis, and finde anone before
hem suche as thei will desire. Thei shull be clothed with clothes of
silke of all manere coloures, thei shull be ioyned with right faire
virgines, and they shull haue all manere delites. And the aungeles
shull come as botelers with vessels of golde and of siluer, and in the
f. 304va vessels of golde he shall geve hem | melke and in [the] vessels of siluer
271 he shall yeue hem wyne, and thei shul saie: 'Etithe and drinkithe in
gladnesse.'
          And Machomete saide to hem that thei shulde haue .iij. flodes in
paradis, one of melke and one of honi and the thridde of wyne and

---

239 man] *om.* E   240 hym] hem E   241 mowe] *om.* E   242 hem^3] hym H2
245 thereby] thereto H2   246 he] any H2   250 Machomete] Also Machomete H2
260 defended] *add* also H2   261 as] *om.* H2   afermed] *add* also that H2   264 to^1]
noo H2   ne to] nothere H2   270 the] *om.* E   274 the thridde] oone H2

right precious spices, and thei shull see the right faire aungeles that be 275
so gret that fro that one eye to that other there is the space of a dayes
iourney. And tho that will not beleue in God and in Machomete he
shall haue the peynes of hell withoute ende. And hoso will beleue in
God and in Machomete atte the day of his deth, with what synne that
he be bounde, whanne Machomete that shall come to the day of dome 280
he shall be saued. And the Sarisenes wrapped in derkenesse afermed
that Machomete the fals prophete of prophecie aboue all other
prophetis, and aungels obeied to hym and kepte hym. And thei
saine that before God made heuene or erthe the name of Machomete
was before God. And thei lyen vpon hym, for thei saie that the mone 285
come to hym and he restreined her in his hondes and deuided her in
two parties and after ioyned her ayen. And thei saine also that a lombe
was offered to hym in flesshe and spake to hym and saide: 'Loke thou
ete me not, for there is venim withinne me.' But notwithstonding
that, mani yeres after that there was yeue hym venym wherof he 290
deyed.

But now we wol returne to the storie of Lumbardes, for in that
tyme the Lumbardes weren wonder contrarie to the Chirche of Rome
and to the empire, though it were so that thei had resseiued the faithe
of Ihesu Crist. And thanne Pepyn [that was] the grettest | prince in the f. 304vb
kingges hous of Fraunce was dede, and Charles his sone come after 296
hym and dede mani batailes and had gret victories, and [left] .ij. sones
princes of the hall riall, that is to saie Charles and Pepin. But Charles
lefte the nobelnesse of the worlde and was monke atte Cassinionse,
and Pepin gouerned worshipfully the hall riall. And for the king 300
Cheldre was [not] profitable but symple, come Pepyn for to [t]ake
counsaile of the pope Zakarie wher he shulde be kinge that did
nothinge [but] bere the name, or he that did all the laboure that
longed to a kinge. And the pope ansuered that he that shulde haue the
name of the kinge that gouern[ed] well the rewme. And the Frenshe 305
men were made hardi vpon this ansuere and made Pepin her kinge
and enclosed Childeriche in a monasteri about the yere of oure Lorde
.vijC. and .xl.

276 eye] ere H2   277 Machomete] add atte daye of his dethe H2   283 obeied]
add it E   290 venym] om. H2   295 that was/the grettest prince] trs. E   297 left]
lost E   299 was] bicome a H2   300 worshipfully] rially L   300–1 for . . .
symple] than Cheldrich shulde haue be kinge but he was but a symple man to gouerne the
halle rialle. Than H2   301 was . . . profitable] he was profitable gouerned worshipfully
the halle ryall E   take] make E   303 but] L, om. EH2   304 ansuered] add and seide
H2   305 that . . . the^3] shulde gouerne his H2   governed] L, gouernithe E

And thanne was Astulpho the kinge of Lumbardes and had
310 dispoiled the Chirche of Rome of his possessiones and of his
lordshippes; Stephene the pope that come after Zakarie, come and
required helpe of Pepin kinge of Fraunce ayenst the Lumbardes and
came hymselff into Fraunce. And thanne Pepin assembled a gret oste
and come into Ytalye, and beseged the kinge Astulphe and wanne
315 hym and ouercome hym and had of hym .xl. hostages, that he yelde to
the Chirche of Rome alle that he had take fro yt and neuer more to
wexce here. But whanne Pepin was gone, Astulfe did nothinge [of]
that he had behight, and a litell while after as he rode an huntinge he
deyed sodenly, and Desyer come after hym.

320   And in that same tyme that Theoderik kinge of Gothis gouerned
f. 305ra Ytalye bi the comaundement of the | emperoure Phelip consulte and
patricien, of whom this Theoderik was gendered, and that [C]helderik
was an eretik of the secte of Ariens, and that Phelip gouerned the
comune of Rome and defended the senatours ayenste Theoderik. And
325 Theoderik had sent Boys into exile to Pavye, and there he made the
boke of Consolacion and there he deyed. His wyff that hight Helpes,
whiche as thei sayne made the ympne of Peter and Paule: *Felix per
omnes*. And she made the subscripcion of her toumbe in this wise: 'I
am Elpes of the cuntre of Cecile, and maried and norisshed was out of
330 my contrei and that made loue, and y rest now in holy place not as a
straunger, and confesse the tro[n]e of the euerlastinge iuge.' And
Theoderik deied sodenly about the yere of oure Lorde .vjC.iiij^xx. and
one.

Dagoberde kinge of Fraunce, as it is conteined in a cronicle, that
335 longe tyme afore Pepin had regned, began fro his yougthe to haue
Seint Denis in gret reuerence, for whanne he dredde the wrathe of his
fader Loterie he wolde fle anone into the chapell of Seint Denis. And
whanne he was made kinge he loued hym and worshipped hym gretly.
And after whan he was dede it was shewed to an holy man in a uisyon
340 that his sowle was rauisshed and sette in iugement, and that mani
seintes aposed hym of that he had robbed her chirches. And as the
wicked aungels wolde haue rauisshed hym and ledde hym to peynes,
the blessed Seint Denis come and deliuered hym by his praiers. And
perauenture his sperit come ayen to his body and dede penaunce. The

311 lordshippes] *add* Than H2   315 he] *add* shulde H2   yelde] *add* ayenne H2
317 wexce] vexe H2   of] after E   318 had] *add* promisid and H2   320 same] *om.*
H2   322 gendered] engendrid H2   Chelderik] thelderik E   326 and ... wyff] And
there he heedid his wiffe H2   331 trone] trouthe E   341 aposed] appechid H2

kinge Lowys discouered the body of Seint Denis with lasse reuerence 345
than he shulde and brake the bone of his | arme and bare it awey f. 305rb
coueitously, and anone he waxe madde.

In that same tyme Bede a worshipfull man [and] a prest was a clerke
in Englonde, and though it be so that he be acounted in the cathologe of
seintes, yet he is not called of the Chirche Seint, but worshipfull, and 350
that by double reson. The furst is for the right gret age of hym he was
blynde, and he hadde a leder that ledde hym by townes and castelles
where he preched the worde of God in eueri place. And in a tyme as he
was ledde by a grete valey full of grete stones, hys leder in scorne saide
that there were assembled a grete peple to here hym preche, [and than 355
he beganne to preche] right myghtely. And in the ende whanne he
conclused and saide: '*Per omnia secula seculorum*,' anone all [the] stones
cried with high vois: 'Amen, worshipfull fader.' And this [is] one cause
whi he is called worshipfull fader. Another cause there is that after hys
dethe a right devout clerke of his coveyted to make [a] vers to sette 360
aboute his toumbe and beganne in this wyse: 'Here stant the fossa' and
wolde haue determyned in this wise: '*Sancti Bede ossa*.' And the vers
wolde in no wyse acorde, and for werinesse he went to his bedde. And
in the morw as he loked upon the toumbe he sawe where was wrete
about the toumbe with the handes of aungels this vers: *Hac sunt in fossa* 365
Bede uenerabilis ossa. And so was the name of Seint turned into
worshipfull. The body of hym is worshipped deuoutely atte Gonys.

In that tyme, about the yere of oure Lorde .vijC. Rachordes kinge
of Frise shulde be baptised and was b[r]ought to the funtstone, and
whanne his one fote was withinne, he asked whether there | were mo f. 305va
in heuene or in helle of his predecessours and of his peple, and thei 371
sa[i]de that there were mo in hell. And thanne he pulled oute his fote
ayenne and said it was a more holy thinge to go with the more party
rather thanne with the lasse, and so he was deseiued of the fende that
behight hym temperell worshippes and goodes ynow of the worlde 375
withoute ani comparison. And withinne .iiij. dayes afterwarde he
perisshed sodinly with euerlasting dethe.

348 and] *om.* E   349 he] it H2   be²] *add* nat H2   350 yet] that H2
355 grete] *add* companie of H2   355–6 and than . . . preche] *om.* E   356 ende] *add*
of his sermon H2   357 conclused] concludid H2   the] ste E   358 is] *om.* E
359 is²] *add* tolde H2   360 of] *om.* H2   a] *om.* E   363 acorde and for werinesse]
make there a trewe verse and so he was werye of laboure and A2   for] so H2   364 loked
upon] knelid before A2   where was] *om.* A2   366 worshipfull] *add* fader A2
368 Rachordes] boturdus A2   369 was brought] L, was bought E, came A2
372 saide] sade E   hell] *add* thanne in heuene E   376 ani comparison] nommbre A2
.iiij.] .iij. A2

In the [champaine] of Ytalye bothe whete barly and rye fell from
heuene as reyne.

380   Men sayne that in that tyme about the yere of oure Lorde .vijC. and
.xl. whanne the body of Seint Benet hadde be born to Florence, and
Seint Scolastica his suster was bore to Teromane, Charles the monke
of Cassinence wolde haue bore the body to Cassine, but by myracles
that were shewed of God he was deuied.

385   In that same tyme ther was gret tremblyng of erthe bi the whiche
the citee[s] fell downe, and the citees that were in the mountaynes
were brought downe into the valeyes all hole with the duellers
withinne mo thanne .vjM^l.

The body of Seint Pernell the doughter of Seint Peter was brought
390   thedir and it was wrete vpon her toumbe: 'This is the right well
beloued Pernell my doughter.'

And as the pestilence was in that cuntre, tho of the cuntre by the
teching of cristen men clipped her hedys lyk crosses, and for that
bicause of that signe hele was graunted hem, they vse continuelly that
395   manere of shering yet.

And thanne after mani gret victories the kinge Pepin deyed and
f. 305vb Charles the Grete succeded | after hym in his kyngdom. And in his
tyme Adrian the bisshopp sate in the sege of Rome and sent
messengeres to Charles the kinge to require hym of hel[p]e ayenst
400   Desyer kinge of Lumbardes that turmented gretly the Chirche right
as Astulf his fader had done. And Charles obeyed to the pope and
came into Itayle with a gret oste, and he seged mightly the gret cite of
Pavye, and there he toke Desyer and his wiff and his children and his
princes and exiled hem into Fraunce and restored to the Chirche all
405   the rightes that the Lumbardes had take awey. And in that tyme Amys
and Amylon were right noble knyghtz in the kinges court, but they
were more noble bi faithe and by vertu in the sight of Ihesu Crist, of
whiche [men] rede mervailous dedis, that fell atte Mortayne where
Charles surmounted the Lumbardes. And there was failed the rewme
410   of Lumbardes, for thei had no kinge sethe but hym that the
emperoure wolde assigne.

And thanne went Charles to Rome, and the pope assembled a sene

378 champaine] companie E   380 in . . . about] it was in A2   383–4 but/by . . .
God] trs. A2   385 erthe] add quauys A2   386 citees] L, citee EA2   388 mo. . . .
vjM^l.] om. A2   395 yet] add into this daye A2   399 helpe] helthe E   401 obeyed
. . . and] om. A2   404 Chirche] add of Room A2   405 the rightes] om. A2
407 and . . . sight] om. L   408 men] L, mot E, add we A2   409 failed] fynysshid A2
412 a sene of] the cyte with A2

of an .C. bishoppes and .liij., in whiche cene the pope gaue Charles the right for to chese the pope and for to ordeyne the sege of Rome, and graunted hym for to clothe the bisshoppes and the ershe- 415 bisshoppes in his province byfore they were sacred, and hys sones were made kinges and anointed at Rome, that is to saie, Pepin king of Ytalye, Lowys kyng of Gascoigne. And thanne floured Alcion, the king Charles maister. And Pepin wolde haue lordship ouer his fader, and he was ouercome and made a monke. 420

And about the yere of oure Lorde .vijC.iiij^{xx}. and .iij., Hyrene the emperesse moder of Constantine, there was a | man that digged in a f. 306ra longe walle, and as it is redde in a cronicle he fonde an arche of stone and a man lyenge withinne and letteres writen in this wise: 'Crist shall be born of Marie the Virgine and y beleue in hym. Vnder Costantyne 425 and Hirene the emperesse, O sonne, yet thou shalt see me ayen.'

And whan Adrian was dede Leon was sette in the sege of Rome, a noble man and worshipfull in all thinges. And the frendes and kynne of Adrian were sory that he was [enhauns]ed in that wise, and as he redde the Grete Letanies they stered the peple ayenst hym so that thei 430 ranne vpon hym and drowe oute his eyen and his tunge oute of his hede. But God by myracle restabled bothe sight and tunge ayen, and thanne he fledde to Charles and he putte hym in his sege ayenne and ponisshed tho that were gilty. And thanne the Romaynes by steringe of the pope about the yere of oure lorde .vijC.iiij^{xx}. and .iiij. Charles 435 lefte the empire of Constantinenople, and he was made emperoure and was crowned by Leon the pope and was made cesarien and augustien bi the acorde of all.

In the tyme of this Charles the Office of Seint Ambrose was gretly lefte and that of Seint Gregory was solempnely publisshed, and the 440 auctorite halpe it gretly for, as Seint Austin saithe in the boke of Confessiones, Seint Ambrose had gret persecucion of Iustine the emperesse that was of the eresie of Ariene and was awaited in the chirche, he and his clerkes, and therfor he ordeined to singe ympnes and psalmes after the custume of hem of the orient so that the peple 445 shulde be made wery by synnes of that errour, and sethe after it was ordeined thorugh all the | chirches. And thanne Seint Gregorie come f. 306rb

415–16 and the ershebisshoppes] *om.* A2   421 Hyrene] heren L
422 emperesse] emperours A2   Constantine] Constantynoble A2   there was] ordeyned
A2   427 Leon] Lowys A2   the] his L   428 and^1] *add* a L   429 enhaunsed]
chaufed E   432 restabled] restorid A2   433 to] *add* the kyng A2
436 emperoure] *add* of Room A2   437 cesarien] nazarien A2   438 acorde]
councelle A2   446 by] *add* there A2

after and chaunged mani thingges and putte to and toke awey as hym thought best, for the holy faders might not anone se all thinges that
450 perteyned to the beauute of the Office, but diuerse faders ordeyned diuerse thinges. For they had .iij. begynnynges. For she had sumtyme begynnynge atte the lessones as she hathe yet the holy Saterday, and thanne after, Selestine pope ordeined to saie psalmes atte the begynninge of the masse, and Gregori ordeined that in the begyn-
455 ninge ye shull saie a vers of that psalme that was wont for to be al songe. And sumtyme clerkes songen rounde aboute the auuter and songin acordingly togedre, and of that it was called *chorus*, but F[l]amatyne and Theodore ordeined that they shulde singe on eueri syde, on the quere one syde [o] verse and that other side another
460 verse. Seint Ierome ordeyned psalmes, episteles and gospelles and the Office of the day and of the night. Gelosyes and Gregorie putte to the songe the orisones [and] the lessones, and ordeyned the graiell, the tracte and alleluya before the gospell. Pelusie and Gregorie ordeined the *Gloria* to be songe in the masse, and Hillarie putte to *Gloria in*
465 *excelsis, Laudamus* to that that foluithe. And the abbot of Seint Galle made furst the sequences with alleluya. Aryen the Contracte of Thewthonik made *Sancti spiritus assit nobis gracia*, and *Simond Bariona*. Pers bisshop of Canpostell made *Salue regina*, but Sycheberde saith that Robert the kynge of Fraunce made *Sancti spiritus assit*
470 *nobis gracia*, the sequence aforesaid.

f. 306ᵛᵃ   And as Turpin tellithe that Charles was faire | of body but his lokinge was cruell. He was of .viij. fote of height, his face was a large pawme [and an half] longe, [his berde was a pawme longe], his forhede was a fote large. He wolde cleue a man on horsebacke atte one stroke
475 and the horse to the gerthis. He wolde breke .iiij. horshone lightly with his hondes. He wolde lefte [an] armed [man] at all peces aboue his hede; he wolde ete an hare and a gose and .ij. hennes atte a mele. He dranke litell wyne with water; he was alwey so litell a drinker atte his mete that he passed neuer thries drinkinge. He dede mani gret
480 batailes, and atte the laste he made Ihesu Crist his eyre and ended his lyff preisably.

And Lowys his sone succeded after hym in the empire, that was right a debonair man, about the yere of oure lorde .viijC. and .xv., in

455 ye] she A2   wont] vsid A2   458 Flamatyne] Famatyne E   Theodore] oþer A2
459 o] a E   462 songe] add of A2   and¹] L, *om.* EA2   464–5 *Gloria . . . Laudamus*]
in excelsis deo A2   465 that²] *om.* A2   467 Thewthonik] betonyke A2   472 .viij.]
.vij. A2   473 and an half] *om.* E   his berde was a pawme longe] *om.* E   476 an
armed man] armed E   479 dede] *add* also H2   481 preisably] pesibullie H2

the tyme of whom the bisshoppes and the clerkes leften her gilte
gerdeles and her disgises and arrayes that they vsed before. And 485
Theodulff bisshop of Orlyaunce was acused to the emperoure
vntrewly and was sent into prison in Angers. And as it is conteyned
in a cronicle that on Palmes Sonday whanne the procession passed
before the hous where he was in prison he opened his wyndowe, and
whan he herde that thei were still he beganne to synge this right faire 490
vers that he had made, *Gloria laus etc.*, to the emperoure, that anone
toke hym oute of preson and restabled hym to his dignite.

The messengers of Michell the emperoure of Constantinenople
brought yeftes to Lowes the sone of Charles the Gret, among whiche
yeftes they brought the bokys of Seint Denis of the Ierarchie of 495
Aungeles translated out of Grewe into Latin, and he res|seiued hem f. 306^vh
with grete ioye; and twenty sike men were heled that night in the
chirche of Seint Denis.

And whanne Lowys was dede, Lothaire helde all the empire, and
Charles and Lowys bretheren madin werre ayenst hym, and in a 500
bataile there was so gret slaughter of bothe parties that there was
neuer no suche sayne in the londe of Fraunce. And in the ende there
was made couenaunt that Charles shuld regne in Fraunce and Lowis
in Almayne and Lotheyre shulde regne in Ytalye and in the partie of
Fraunce that is called Loreyne. And after this he lefte to Lowys his 505
sone that was emperoure by the waye after hym and become a monke.

And it is saide in another cronicle that Serge was pope that tyme,
but he was called before Swynes Mouthe, but his name was thanne
chaunged and called Serge. And fro thennes forward it was ordeined
that popes shulde chaunge her names for as moche as oure Lorde 510
chaunged the name of hym that he chase to be apostle, for right as his
name is chaunged so shulde he chaunge his lyff into the lyff of
perfeccion, and also that he whiche is chosen to that perfeccion be not
defouled with no foule name.

In the tyme of this Lowys in the yere of oure Lorde .viijC. and .vj. 515
it is saide in a cronicle that in [the] parisshe of Magontin the wicked
spirites betin the houses and the walles as it had be with hamours, and
spakin opinly in sowing discordes, and turmented men in suche wise
that in what hous thei entered anone the hous brent. And whanne the
prestes saide [the] Letanies thei threwe stones atte hem and made 520

491 *etc.* to] And than H2   that²] *om.* H2   492 hym²] *add* ayenne H2   495 they]
he H2   496 of] *add* the E   516 the¹] *om.* E   518 sowing] swouninge H2
520 the] *om.* E

mani one of hem couered with blode. And in a tyme he lough and
saide | that whanne thei caste holy water about he hidde hym vnder
the cope of a preste that was his owne familier felawe and acused
[hym] that he hadde synned with the emperours doughter.

525   In that same tyme the kynge of Bogie was conuerted to the faithe
and alle his peple. [He] was of so gret perfeccion that he made his
eldest sone kinge and toke the abite of the monke. But his sone
gouerned hym so wrechidly that he toke ayenne the lawe of the
paynimes, and thanne his fader toke upon hym knighthode ayen and
530 pursued his sone and toke hym and putte hym in prison and toke ayen
his abite.

It is saide that in Itaile it reyned blode .iij. dayes. In that same tyme
come into Fraunce langustus right cruell, that had .vj. wynges and .ij.
longe fete and tethe harder thanne any stone, and flyen bi cumpanies
535 right as the cumpanye of armed men by the space of a iourne, and thei
helde .v. or .vj. myle of lengthe and deuowred all that was grene of
grasse or of trees, and thei come to the see of Bretayne and there they
were drowned in the see by strengthe of wynde and the hete of the see
caste hem up ayen upon the londe. And thanne was the eyre so
540 corrupte of the corrupcion and stinke of hem that therof come so gret
a pestilence that almost the thriddde parte of the peple dyed.

And after that was emperour Oton the furst. And after that Oton
the furst was Oton the secounde. And whanne [the] Ytaliens had
many tymes broken the pees of hem and of Romaynes, he made a gret
545 and a generall fest of comunes. And whanne they were atte the dynere
he beclipped hem alle with men of armes, and thanne he made his
compleint and named the gylty bi writyng and beheded hem all anone |
right there, and to all the remenaunt he made grete feste and grete
chere.

550   And Oton the thridde come after hym the yere of oure Lorde
.ixC.iiij^{xx}. and .x. and was named the mervaile of the world. And as it
is saide in a cronicle that his wiff loued an erle of his, but he wolde not
assent to her. And thanne she did so gret a wickednesse that she
defamed hym to the emperoure so that he was beheded withoute
555 havinge ani audience. But before his deyeng he praied his wiff that she

521 one] *om.* H2   he] thei H2   522 he] thei H2   hym] hem H2   523 a preste]
preestes H2   his] her H2   524 hym] *om.* E   526 He] *om.* E   527 toke] *add*
hymself H2   534 flyen] flowen aboute H2   535 the cumpanye] companies H2
540 therof] ther H2   542 that²] *om.* H2   543 the³] *om.* E   544 hem and of] the
H2   550 hym] *add* aboute H2

wolde shewe hym innocent bi beringe of an hote yren. And so it fell on a day that the emperoure sate in his iugement for to do right to wedwes and to orphelyns. And thanne come this wedu with the hede of her husbonde betwene her armes and asked with what dethe he aught to deye that had slayne a man wrongfully. And the emperoure 560 saide that he shulde haue the hede smite of. And thanne she saide: 'Thou art he that hast slayne myn husbonde bi the fals monestynge of thi wiff and he verrey innocent, and for to proue that y saye sothe y shall bere the hote yren.' And whanne Cesar sawe this he was all abasshed and yelde hymselff vnto the womannes hondes for to be 565 ponisshed after her will, but alwayes bi the praiers of bisshoppes and other lordes the emperoure toke terme of .x. dayes and thanne of .viij. and thanne of .iij. til the matere were examined and the trouthe knowen. And whanne he knew all the trouthe he lete brenne his wiff all quicke and gaue the woman that was wedw .iiij. castelles for 570 redempcion, the which bene in the bisshopriche of Lune and thei be called the termes of dayes.

And after regned Harre that was duke of Bouer in the yere a .M.[1] and .ij. and wedded | his suster that hight Galle to the kinge of f. 307va Hungry. And he was that tyme panim, but by grace and by vertu she 575 conuerted hym and alle his peple to cristen faithe, and his name was Stephen. And he was after of so perfit and so holy religion that God wrought for hym mani glorious miracles. And that Harre and Ragand his wiff were virgines and ledden heuenly lyff and resten in pees.

And after that Conrade came, a duke of Fraunce, and wedded the 580 nece of that holy Henre, the whiche a confessour of his that was a Iacobyn enpoisoned in yevinge of the sacrement. And in that tyme was ysayne in heuene a beme full of brenninge fyre and was right grete aboue the sonne and she was saine fall from heuene to the erthe. This emperoure putte sum of the bisshoppes in prison and made brenne 585 the subarbes of Melan. And on Whitsunday as the emperoure was crouned in a litell chirche hit thundred so gretly and so horribly that sum went out of her mynde and sum deied for fere. And Brune the bisshopp that sange the masse saide that he sawe Seint Ambrose about the secrete of the masse that thretenid the emperoure. 590

In the tyme of this Conrate the yere a .M.[1] and .xxv., as it is saide in

556 hym] that he were H2   562 husbonde] *add* wrongefulli H2   564 Cesar] the emperour H2   sawe] *add* and hurd H2   566 but . . . the] And than atte H2 569 And . . . trouthe] *om.* H2   573 yere] *add* of our Lorde H2   580 came] *om.* H2 and] *om.* H2   588 Brune] brent H2   591 yere] *add* of our lorde H2

a cronicle, Lympole an irle and his wiff fledde into a forest for drede of
the wratthe of the emperoure and hidde hem in a pore hous. And as
the emperoure went for to hunt in that forest the night come upon
595 hym so that he must abide in that pore hous. And there the lady that
trauailed ordeyned for hym as well as she might, and that night she
f. 307vb bare a sone. And thanne a voice come to the emperour | and saide:
'Conrant, the childe that is now bore shall be thin ayre.' And whanne
he arose in the morwtyde he called to hym .ij. squiers of his and saide
600 to hem: 'Go ye and take that childe from the moder and sle hym and
bringe me the herte of hym.' And thei went in gret haste and toke the
childe from the moders lappe. And whan thei sawe it of so faire a
forme they had pitee and were meued with merci and leide it upon a
tree for it shulde not be deuoured with bestes, and slow an hare and
605 bare the herte to the emperoure. And that same day a duke passed
thorugh th[at] forest and herde a childe that cried and bade that it
shulde be brought to hym, and for that he had no sone he made it be
bore to his wiff and made it be norisshed and feyned that he hadde
engendered it and called hym Harre. And as he was well norisshed he
610 encresed and was right well taught and a faire speker to all and
gracious in his gouernaunce. And whanne the emperoure sawe that he
was faire and wys, he asked hym of his fader and made hym duell in
his courte, and whanne he sawe that this childe was so gracious and
preised of alle he dredde that he shulde regne after hym, and leste it
615 were he that he had comaunded to slee, he wrote letteres to his wiff
with his owne honde in this wise: 'As dere as thou haste thi lyff as sone
as thou haste these letteres sle this childe.' And as the messengeres
went there as he was herburghed in a chirche and was wery and fill
aslepe upon a benche and his purs that his letteres were inne hyng
620 downe bysides hym, and a preest that was corious for to knowe [w]hat
f. 308ra was withinne opened the purse and | sawe the letteres seled with the
kingges sele and opened the letter and redde it, and dredde the gret
felonie and chaunged it sotelly there as he saide: 'Thou shalt slee this

592 Lympole an] Lympolyan the H2   595 the] that H2   that³] *om.* H2
596 trauailed] *add* of childe H2   599 morwtyde] morninge H2   603 it] the childe
H2   605 bare] brought H2 And] *add* as E   606 that¹] the E bade] *add* anone H2
it] the childe H2   608–9 and feyned . . . norisshed he] and so the childe H2
609 well] faire H2   611 in his] of H2   614 alle] *add* the puple H2 dredde] *add*
gretelie H2 and] *om.* H2   615 he³] And than the emperour H2 letteres] *add* anone
H2   617 thou haste] this childe bringe you H2 sle this childe] *add* anone that he be
slaine H2 sle] *add* hym E   617–18 as² . . . herburghed in] than he sent forthe this
childe amessage to his wiffe with the lettris And so he went forthe and come into H2
620 what] that E   623 felonie] velony H2

childe', 'Thou shalt yeue oure doughter to hym to wyve.' And whanne
the quene hadde resseiued this lettre and sawe it seled with the kinges 625
sele and wretin with his owne honde, she called the princes and
halwed the weddinge and gaue hym her doughter to wive. And this
wedding was made at Pays. And whanne it was saide to the emperoure
how the weddinge of his doughter had be sollempnely done, he was
hougely abaisshed and knewe the trouthe of tho .ij. squiers and of the 630
[duke] that fonde the childe and of the preest. And thanne he
perceiued well that a man shuld not contrarie to the will of God ne
to his ordenaunce, and thanne he sent for the childe and aproued hym
as his gendre and ordeined hym to regne after hym. And in the place
where this childe Harre was bore he founded a noble chirche, and the 635
forest is called atte this day Oursyne.

This Harri putte oute of his courte alle iogeloures and gaue to pore
men al that wont to be youe to mynstrales. In his tyme there was so
grete discorde in the Chirche that thre soueraine bisshoppes were
chosen. And a preest that hight Gracian gaue gret plente of moncy to 640
the thother and thei lefte hym the sege and he was pope. And as Harri
the emperoure come to Rome for to apese the discorde, Gracian went
ayenst hym and offered to hym a crowne of gold for that he shulde be
gracious to hym, but he passed by lyghtly and feyned as he were well
and assembled a | sene, in whiche Graci[an] was convicted of symoni f. 308rb
and putte downe and another sette in his place. Notwithstondinge in a 646
lettre that he wrete to the emperise Mauude that that preest that was
to symple, whanne he had gote the sege bi money to that ende that he
contraried to the discorde, he knewe after his errou[r]e and bi the
am[on]estinge of the emperoure he d[e]posed hymselff. 650

And after this emperoure was emperoure Harri the thridde. And in
his tyme Brune was chose pope and was called Leon, and as he went to
Rome to take the sege he herde the voys of aungeles singing: 'Oure
Lorde saithe: "Y am he that know the thoughtes of pees."' This
Brune made the songe of mani seintes. And in that tyme the Chirche 655

626 princes] add of the londe to hir H2   629 be] add so E   630 and¹] add
than bi devine grace he H2   and²] add also H2   631 duke] hert and of hym E
preest] add that chaungid his lettris H2   he] the emperoure H2   632 a] om. H2
634 as his gendre] of his engendrure H2   637 This] add same H2   alle] om. H2
638 that] add was H2   mynstrales] hem H2   641 and²] add so H2   644 by]
add hym H2   well] add apaied H2   645 and] add And than Herry the emperour H2
sene] add of bisshoppis H2   Gracian] Gracie E   647 that that] this H2   that⁴] om.
H2   648 sege] seete of Rome H2   649 discorde] add and H2   erroure]
erroue E   and] om. H2   650 amonestinge] amestinge E   deposed] disposed E,
dispoilid H2 (deposa P2)

was gretly troubeled [bi one] Beringer that affermed [that] the body
and the blode of oure Lorde were not verily but by figure in the
sacrement of the auuter, ayenste whom Lanfrank the prioure of
Betens wrote full nobly, and he was born in Pavye and was maister
660 to Ansel[m] ershebisshopp of Caunterbery.

And after this was Harri the fourthe and in his tyme floured
Lanfrank prioure of Betens. And Ansel[m]e come to hym fro
Burgeyne for his doctrine that was full of vertues and of wisdom,
and he was prioure after hym. And in that tyme was Ierusalem take of
665 the Sarisenes and recouered ayen by the cristen men.

And the bones of Seint Nicholas were born to Bere, and of that it is
saide amonge other thinges that whanne they songe a nwe stori of
Seint Nicholas in a chirche that was of the Holy Crosse and was soget
to the chirche of Oure Ladi of Terentene, the freres praied fast her
f. 308ᵛᵃ prioure that thei might singe that | nwe stori, but he wold in no wise
671 graunte hem. And yet more hertly thei praied hym, and he in gret
anger bade hem go her waye for thei shulde in no wise haue leue of
hym. And in a feste of Seint Nicholas whanne all the bretheren had
saide her Mattins, Seint Nicholas apered visibly and right dredfully to
675 the prioure and drow hym bi the here oute of the dortour and beganne
to singe *O pastor eterne*, and atte eueri note he smote a smarte streke
upon the prioures backe with a rodde and songe that anteme
melodiously to the ende. And thanne the prioure cried so loude
that he awoke all the freres and was bore to his bedde as [half] dede.
680 And as sone as he come to hymselff he saide: 'Gothe and singithe the
nwe stori of Seint Nicholas fro hennes forwarde.'

In that tyme the abbot of the covent of Melosyne and .xxj. of the
monkes went for to duelle in desert for to kepe the more streitely the
profession of her rule, and there they hadde a nwe ordre.
685 Hildebronde prioure of Cluni was made pope and was called
Gregori. And whanne he was in Ordre of Menours and he was sent
as a legat, he ouercome merueilously the ershebisshop of Ebronence of
symoni. For as that ershebisshop hadde corrupte all his accusoures so
that he might not be ouercome, [that] the legat comaunded hym he
690 shulde saie *In nomine patris et filij*, but he might not saie *et spiritus*

656 bi one] LA2, *om.* EH2 (*par* P2)   that²] *om.* E   657 of oure Lorde] *om.* H2
figure] signe H2   659 Betens] Obetens E   660 Anselm] Anselyn E
662 Betens] Obetens E   Anselme] Anseline E   669–70 fast her prioure] *om.* H2
670 prioure] praieris H2   671 yet] than H2   gret] *om.* H2   677 prioures backe]
bak of the priour H2   679 half] *om.* E   680 saide] *add* to his bretheren H2
682 of¹] and H2   of the²] *om.* H2   686 in] *add* the H2   689 that] *om.* E

sancti. [What merueile!] For he hadde synned ayenst the holy goste. [And than he confessed his synne and was deposed, and anone he confessed with clere voys the holy goste.] And this miracle tellithe Brune in a boke that he made to Mauude the emperesse.

And whanne this Harre was dede than regned Harre the fifth the 695 yere .M^l.C. and .vj., the whiche toke the cardinales. And in that tyme Seint Ber|narde and his bretheren toke the religion of Cisteaux. In the f. 308vb parisshe of Lige a sowe bare a pigge that had the visage of a man, and a chekyn of an henne hadde .iiij. fete.

And to Harri succeded Lotharie, in whos tyme a woman of Spaine 700 bare a monstre that had double body and ioyned that one body ayenst that other, [and] that before was fourme of man in all fetures and that behinde was forme of a woman in alle manere fetures and propertees.

After this regned Conrade the yere a .M^l.C.xxxviij. And in that yere passed the holy doctour Hugh de Seint Victore, that was right 705 excellent in all sciences and devout in religion, of whom it is ysaied that whanne he was in his laste sikenesse whanne he might broke no mete he asked wel devoutely for to resseiue the sacrement. And thanne his bretheren for to apese hym brought hym a symple oste as yef it hadde be the sacrement, and anone he knewe it in sperit and 710 saide: 'God foryeue it you, bretheren, why wol ye deceyue me? This is not my Lorde that ye bringe me.' And thanne thei went all abasshed and fette hym the verrei body of oure Lorde Ihesu Crist, and whanne he sawe hym he lefte up his hondes and saide: 'Now go ye, sone to the fader, and the sperit to God that made hym.' And whanne he had so 715 saide he gaue up hys sperit and the bodi of oure Lorde disapered. Eugeni abbot of Seint Anastace was made pope, but he was putte oute of the citee for that the cenatours hadde chose another, and thanne he wente into the parties of Fraunce and sent Bernarde afore hym for to preche the waie of oure Lorde and dede gret miracles. And in that 720 tyme florisshed Gilbert the Patriarke.

Frederik | nevew of Conrand was emperoure the yere .M^l.C.liij. f. 309ra And in his tyme florisshed Pers Lumbarde bisshop of Parys [that] glosed the Sentences and the Sawter and the Pistoles of Paule full

691 What merueile] *om*. E, *add* was H2   692–3 And than . . . holy goste *om*. E
696 yere] *add* of oure lorde D   699 chekyn] *add* come of D   700 to] afftir this D
701 ayenst] to D   702 and^1] *om*. E   fourme of] fourmed affter D   703 forme of]
fourmed affter D   704 After . . . Conrade] In D   yere^1] *add* of oure lorde D   708 the]
add holie D   709 thanne] *add* oone of D   711 me] *add* for D   713 oure Lorde] *om*. D
719 sent] seint E, *add* seint D   721 Patriarke] *add* and D   722 Frederik] *add* the D
was emperoure] *om*. D   yere] *add* of oure lorde D   723 that] and E

725 profitably. And in that tyme there were .iij. mones sayne and in the
middell of hem the signe of the crosse, and but a litell after the[re]
were sayne .iij. sonnes also. And thanne was Alisaundre made pope
rightfully, and ayenst hym was chose .iij. popis, Octavion and Iohn
Cremon and Iohn Stremen, and thei were worshipped in the sege bi
730 the fauour of the emperoure. And that discorde dured .xviij. yeere,
and in that tyme the Almaynes that were duellinge in Tuscan for the
emperoure of Rome, thei sailed the Romaynes that were atte Mount
Port, and slow so mani from none to euesonge tyme that there were
neuer so mani thousandes of Romaynes slayne, yef it be so that in the
735 tyme of Hanyball there were so many slaine that there were .iij. lepes
filled with ringges that were take of the lordes fingres that were slayne,
the whiche Haniball bare into Cartage. And mani of the dede were
beried atte Seint Stephenes and atte Seint Laurens, and it was wrete
upon her toumbe that they were .xx.^{ti} tymes .xM^l.xvjC. and an halff.
740 And whanne Frederik the emperoure visited the holy londe, as he
wysshe hym in a flode he was drowned.
        And Harri his sone was emperoure after hym the yere .M^l.C.iiij^{xx}.
and .x. And in that tyme there was so gret thundringges, lyteninges
and reynes that neuer before had be sene no suche, for the heylestones
745 fell as gret as a gose eye and in her fallinge they destroied bestes and
men, vynes and trees. And ravonis and other briddes were saine with
f. 309rb brondes of fire in her mou|thes fleinge thorugh these tempestes
settinge houses afire. And this Harre was alwey a tyraunt ayenst the
Chirche of Rome, and therfor whanne he was dede the [pope]
750 Innocent [opposed] ayens Phelip his sone that he shulde not be
emperoure, and helde the partie of the duke of Sasoigne that made
hym to be kinge of Almayne at Ays. And in that tyme mani barones of
Fraunce went ouer the see for to deliuer the holy londe, and thei toke
Constantinenople.
755   In that tyme beganne the ordre of Frere Prechours and of Frere
Menoures. Innocent the thridde sent messengeres to the kinge of
Fraunce for to ass[a]yle the londe of Albiones for to putte awey the
eretikes, and he toke hem and brent hem all. And after that Innocent

---

726 litell] while D   there] the E   728 was] were D   and Iohn] trs. D
729 Stremen and they] Iohn and Cremon D   sege] seete D   731 for] add bi cause of D
732 thei sailed] the assailid D   736 slayne] add atte þat tyme D   737 dede] add
bodies D   739 .x.M^l.] add and bi .x. tymes D   742 yere] add of oure lorde D
745 a gose eye] ges eyren H2   destroied] add many H2, lost by damage D   746 men]
many D   748 afire] `a´fire D   749 pope] om. E   750 opposed] appased E,
appesid D   751 duke] dukedome D   756 thridde] om. D   757 assayle] assoyle E

Oton was crowned emperoure and was made swere that he shulde
kepe the right of the Chirche, and anone he dede ayenst his othe and 760
dispoiled the Chirche. And therfor he was acursed and putte oute of
the empire. And in that tyme florisshed Seint Elizabeth the kinges
doughter of Hungri that Landegraue had wedded, the whiche amonge
other miracles she areysed mani dede bodyes to lyff and gaue sight to
many that were blynde and specially to one that was born blynde. 765
Whanne Oton was deposed Federik his sone was chose [emperour]
and Honoure the pope corowned hym. And he made right noble lawes
for the fraunchise of the Chirche and ayenst the eretikes. And he
abounded aboue all other in glorie and in richesse, but he vsed hem
wickedly and in pride and was a tyraunt ayenst the Chirche. He putte 770
two cardinales in prison, he dede take the prelatis that pope Gregori
hadde [made] to assemble at the counsaile, and therfor | was he cursed f. 309ᵛᵃ
of that pope. And thanne deied Gregory that was greued by mani
tribulaciones, and there was made pope Innocent the .v.ᵉ, borne of
Gene, that assembled a counsaile atte Lyones where he deposed the 775
emperoure. And than was the sege voyde and yet hedir is voyde.

Here endithe the forsaid gestes, and nexst beginnithe the
Dedicacion of the Chirche, Capitulum .C.lxx[v].ᵐ

The dedicacion of the chirche is solempnely halowed amonge all other
festes of the Chirche and for that the double feste of the chirche or
temple, that is to saie materiall or spirituel, and therfor it is to be seen
shortly of the dedicacion of this temple that is double.
As to the dedicacion of this materialle temple, thre thinges be for to 5
be considered; furst wherfor it is dedied or sacred, secoundely how it
is sacred.
The auuter is furst sacred to .iiij. thinges; furst for to sacrifie to
God, as it is saide in Genesy in the .viij. chapitre: 'Noe edified furst an
auuter to oure Lorde and toke of all the briddes and all the bestes of 10
the worlde and offered hem up on the auuter.' And that sacrifice that
we do upon the auuter is the bodi and the blode of Ihesu Crist that we
sacrifice in mynde of the passion of oure Lorde after that he vs

764–5 to many] twice E   766 emperour] kinge E   768 and] om. D
769 aboue] bifore D   770 Chirche] add for D   772 hadde] om. D   made] om. E
774 .v.ᵉ borne] veborne E, Verbon D (vᵉ. ne P2)   776 hedir] add to D

EDH2A2L; D 1–19 is partly illegible because of a crease, and D breaks off after 199
impression   Rubric C.lxxv.ᵐ] .C.lxxiiij.ᵐ E   1 other] the D   3 seen] seide D
11 up] om. D   11–12 And . . . upon] for D

recomaunded and saide: 'Dothe this in mynde of me.' We haue thre
15 myndes of the passion of oure Lorde: that one mynde is the passion of
oure Lorde; that other is [ymagined] in figure, and that is whanne we
see the ymage of Ihesu Crist and other ymages that be in the chirche
f. 309vb in | rememberaunce of God and of his seintes for to stere the deuocion
of the peple, for thei be as bokes to lay men, and these two myndes be
20 but one. The seconde mynde is but one in worde, and that is the
passinge of Ihesu Crist preched, and that mynde is made to the
heringe. The thridde mynde is the passion of Ihesu Crist transfigured
in this sacrement that is verily soule, body and blode of Ihesu Crist,
and this mynde is made as to the taste. And thanne yef the passion of
25 Ihesu Crist that is wretin embrasith the will and yef she [be] preched
enbr[a]se hym, thanne moche more strongely shulde enflawme this in
whiche she is enprentid so signifi[auntli].

Secondely for to calle the name of oure Lorde, and of that saithe the
Genesy in the .xij. chapitre: 'Abraham edified an auuter to oure Lorde
30 that there apered to hym, and there he called the name of oure Lorde.'
And this vocacion or callynge shulde be called and made after that the
apostle saithe to Timotheus, or by praiers that be made for to take
awey eueles, or by orisones made for to gete goodes and for to encrece
hem and for to kepe hem. The furst that is made upon the auuter is
35 properly saide the masse, for that Ihesu Crist is sent fro heuene. And
messe is properly saide for to sende, and atte the masse Ihesu Crist is
sent from his fader, and sacred that same oste, and she is sent by that
same from us to the fader that he praie his fader for us. And of that
saithe Seint Hugh de Victore: 'That holy and sacred oste may well be
40 called messe, for furst she is sent from the fader to vs by incarnacion,
f. 310ra and sethe it is sent of vs by | halwinge.' And we therewith bi that
oblacion that praiethe for vs. And it is to wete that the masse is songe
in thre langages, that is in Grewe, Ebrwe and Latin, and also for to
signifie that alle langages shulde preise God. The tonge of Latin is the
45 pistoles and the gospeles; the Grewe is the *kyries* that is saide .ix.
tymes so that we may come to the .ix. ordres of aungeles; of the Ebrw
is the Alleluya, Osanna and Sabaoth.

14 We] And we shulde D   16 that other] The secounde that D   ymagined]
magnified E   19 thei] the ymagis D   lay] lewde H2, *illeg.* D   20 in worde]
innwarde D   22 passion] passinge E   transfigured] translatid D   25 be] *om.* E
26 enbrase] L, enbrose E, to D   27 signifiauntli] signifiethe ED {*signifiement* P2)
36 atte] *om.* D   41 we therewith] *om.* D   45 and] *add* the tunge of D   gospeles]
add The tunge of D

Thriddely it is sacred for to synge, and therof saithe the boke of
Ecclesiaste in the .xlvij. chapitre: 'Ho yaue hem might ayenst the
enemyes and made hem to be putte awey from the auuter and made 50
the syngers to synge, and thei yaue a suete melodie in her sowne.' And
he saithe melodyes in wepinge after that Hugh de Sancto Victore
saithe thre manere of sownes there ben that maken .iij. melodies.
There is a sowne by smitinge, by wynde, and bi synginge. The
touchinge and the smitynge longith to the harpe, and to orgonis the 55
blowing, and to the voys the syngynge. And this concordaunce of
singinge may be assigned to the concordaunce of good maners, for in
the touchinge of the harpe men maye reporte the werke of the honde,
and in the blowinge of orgones the devocion of the thought, and to the
songe of the voys the techinge of the worde; but in that, what 60
profitithe the suetnesse of the songe withoute the suetnesse of the
herte? She brekithe the voys, but the wille kepithe the concordaunce
of the voys and the concordaunce of good maners, | so that by f. 310rb
ensaumple he acordithe to his neygheburgh, and bi his good will he
acordithe to God, and by obedience to his maister. And this is treble 65
manere of musik that is reported to the treble difference of the
Chirche, so as it is saide in the boke of the Office of the Chirche, for
the Office of the Chirche is made in psalmes, in songe, and in lessones.
The .v. manere of musik is made by touchinge of fingeres as in the
sawtry or in lyke instrumentis. The seconde is the voys and that 70
perteinithe to lessones, and therof saithe Dauid: 'Singithe to hym in
beringe vp your voys.' The thridde, that is made by blowinge,
longithe to the songe of the trumpe, and thereof saithe Dauid:
'Preisithe hym in the sowne of the trumpe.'

The temple or the chirche is sacred for .v. resones. The furst is for 75
that the fende and all his power be putte oute, wherof Seint Gregore
tellithe in his Dialoge that as a chirche of the heresye of the Ariens was
yelde to cristen men, and thei blessed and halued the chirche and
brought inne of the relikes of Seint Fabyan and of Seint Sebastian and
of Agathe, and all the peple were gadered togederes, the peple herde 80
sodenly an hogge renne to and fro bytwene her legges and sought the
dores of the chirche and might not be seine of none, and alle had gret
mervaile. | But oure Lorde shewed to hem that it was the foule sperit f. 310va
that duelled in that place and was gone oute. And that night was made

52 in] and D   57–63 for ... maners] *twice* E, *so with* hert *for* harpe *and om.* but ...
maners D   58 werke] werkis D   60 worde] *add* of God D   61 of the songe]
om. D   62 kepithe] helpeth D   81 an hogge] oone D

85 a gret noyse aboue the helinge of the chirche, as though men had
ronne thereon, and the secounde night was made a gretter noise, and
the thridde night was made so dredfull a noyse as though the chirche
shulde haue be throwe adowne. And thanne the wicked sperit parted
and neuer apered thereafter in no wise, and that sowne that was so
90 dredfull signified that for certaine he was constreined for to go oute of
that place the whiche he had longe withholde.

Secondely she is sacred for that that tho the whiche that fleen to the
chirche for socour in ani bodely perile, that thei shulde be saued. For
the chirche defendithe the gilty fro blode and that he shalle not lese
95 lyff ne membre, and therfor fledde Ioab to the tabernacle and toke the
auuter.

Thriddely she is sacred for that orisones shulde be lefte up there,
and that is signified in the boke of Kingges in the .viij. chapitre, for
whanne the temple was dedied Salamon saide: 'Ho that euer shall
100 praie to the in this place thou shalt enhaunce hym into thi tabernacle
of heuene and thou shalt be to hem debonaire.' And we shull worship
God in the chirche towardes the Est for .iij. causes. The furst is that
we shewe that we desire oure contre, secundely that we beholde Ihesu
Crist crucified, thriddely that we shewe that we abide that iuge to
105 come. For Daniel saithe: 'God planted paradys in the hous of the
orient, fro which he putte oute man exiled for he passed his
f. 310vb comaundement and made hym duelle before paradys towar|de the
occident. Before that he sought other cuntre, and therfor we beholde
to that chirche and worship God towarde the orient. He was born an
110 hye, and so the aposteles worshipped hym, and so he shall come as
thei sawe hym goinge to heuene, and so we worship hym towardez the
orient in abidinge his cominge.

Ferthely she is sacred for that preysinges be there yolden to God.
And this thinge is done in the .vij. Houres of Matenis, Prime, Tierce,
115 Sixt, and None, Euesong, and Complyn. And thou it be so that God is
to be worshipped in all the tymes of the day, but that oure infirmite
may not atteyne therto, hit is ordeined that in these Houres we shulde
praise hym specially for that in sum thinges these Houres be more
priuileged thanne other. For atte midnight, whanne Matenis be songe,
120 Ihesu Crist was born and was take and dispised of [the] Iwes. And in

86 a gretter] anothir D   89 apered] come D   95 toke] to D   99 dedied]
edified D   101 of heuene] om. D   106 fro] for D   oute] om. D   110–11 and² . . .
hym¹] toward the orient in abidinge his D   114 Prime] add houres D   115 Sixt] add
and E   118 specially] worshipfullie D   these] his D   120 the] om. E

that same houre he dispoiled hell. So as it is saide in Mitraly he dispoiled atte midnight in takinge midnight largely, that is to saie before the day. For atte Matenis before the day he arose and atte the Houre of Prime he apered, and sum sayne that he shall come to the day of dome atte midnight. Wherof Seint Ierome saithe: 'I wene that thinge whiche the aposteles haue saide shall be bifore the day, for the vigile of virgines of Estre before midnight thei mowe not leue Matenis for the peple abidinge the cominge of Ihesu Crist. And whanne that tyme shall be come men aught haue se[wr]te that all makin the fest the day.' And we synge to God in that oure preisinges, for that we yelde hym thankingges for his natiuite, for his takinge [and] of the deliueraunce of [the] holy aposteles, so that we may besyly and coriously abide the tyme | of his cominge.

And the ⟨La⟩udcs bc ioyned to the Matenis for that in the morutyde he drowned the Egipcians in the see, and also he made the worlde and arose, and atte that our we yelde praisinges to God so that we be not drowncd in the see of this world with the Egipciens.

In the Houre of Prime Ihesu Crist came to the Temple and the peple assembled about hym, as Luke saithe in the .xxj. chapittre. He was atte that houre presented to Pilate, and atte that houre arisinge he apered to the women, and that is the furst hour of the day. And therfor we yelde praysinges and thankingges to God so that we mowe folw hym and yelde to hym the furst fruites of all oure werkes in the begynninge of the day.

Atte the Houre of Tierce Ihesu Crist was crucified with the tonges of Iewes and was bounde to the pilere and scourged before Pylate and, as it is saide in storie, that the blode aperithe yet vpon the pilere of his betinge, and in that same houre was the holy gost sent to the aposteles.

In the sixt houre he was nayled upon the crosse and derkenesse was made thorugh all the world, and atte that hour he was atte the dyner the day of the ascencion with his disciples.

Atte the Houre of None Ihesu Crist yelde up his sperit and Longius persed his side, and the cumpanie of the aposteles had in custume for to assemble hem togederes for to praie, and Ihesu Crist stied up into heuene. And for these worshippes praisen we God in these Houres.

Atte the Houre of Euesonge Ihesu Crist ordeined the sacrement of his body and of his blode togedre, and wysshe the fete of his aposteles

---

122 hell] hem D   Mitraly] Matiralli D   129 sewrte] serwte E   the fest the] feeste þat D   131 and] *om.* E   132 the] *om.* E   140 presented] represented E 141 women] woman D

and dissiples, and he was take downe of the crosse and born to the
f. 311rb sepulcre, and that | tyme he shewed hym to the disciples in pilgremes
160 clothinge. And for these thinges atte that [Houre] the Chirche
yeldithe thankinges to God.

Atte Complyn tyme Ihesu Crist suette droppes of blode, and atte
that tyme his monument was made to be kepte, and there he rested
hym. Whanne he was risen he denounced the pees to his apostoles,
165 and of these thinges we yelde thankingges to God. And upon this
saithe Seint Bernarde how we shulde yeue thankinges to God: 'My
bretheren,' saide he, 'whanne ye wol do sacrifice to God in sacrifise of
praisinges, ioynge in mynde to thi wordes, and thi will to thi witte and
gladnesse to thi will, and sobirnesse to thi gladnesse, and mekenesse
170 [to] fre will.'

Fiftely she is sacred for to ministre there the sacrementes of the
Chirche. And the chirche is as the table of God, in the whiche the
sacrementis be comuned and ministred. And sum sacrementes be
ministred to comers, as bapteme; and sum be youe to hem that gone
175 oute, as the laste anointinge; and sum be youe to duellers, as ordres;
and sum fight and sum falle, and to hem is youe penaunce; other
contrarien, and to hem is youe hardinesse of corage for to strengthe
hem, and that is by confirmacion; and to sum there is youe mete to
sustene hem, and that is by resseyvinge of the sacred body of oure
180 Lorde Ihesu Crist; and sum tyme thei take aweye the occasion that
thei falle not in synne, and that is by ioyning togeders in mariage.

Secundely it is to wete how she is sacred, and furst men shull
knowe of the auuter and after of the chirche. And mani thinges
perteine to the sakeringe of the auuter.
f. 311va   Furst men makin .iiij. crosses in the .iiij. cor|ners of the auuter with
186 holy water, and she is avironed mani tymes al about and with ysope
springed. And after, the encense is brent within the auuter, and after
anointed with creme, and thanne it is couered with blacke clothe. And
that representith hem that go to the auuter. For they shulde haue furst
190 charite in .iiij. maners, that is thei shulde furst loue God and thanne
hemselff and her frendes and her enemyes. And that betokenithe the
.iiij. crosses in the .iiij. corners of the auuter. And of these .iiij. corners
it is saide in Genesis in the .xxviij. chapitre: 'Thou shalt des[te]nde to
orient to occident to septemtrion and to midday.' Other the .iiij.

160 Houre] L, tyme ED   162 droppes of] water and D   163 monument]
commaundement D   167 ye wol] wille ye D   170 to] *om.* E   will] *add* and so seith
seynt Bernard D   193 destende] desornde E   194 Other] and D

crosses be made in the .iiij. corners signifie that Ihesu Crist saued bi 195
the crosse the .iiij. parties of the worlde. Or elles that we shulde bere
the crosse of Ihesu Crist in .iiij. maneres, that is in the herte bi
thenkinge, in [the] mouthe bi confession, in the body by mortefienge,
and in the face by continuel impression.

Secundely thou shalt haue cure and thei shulde wake; [and] that 200
betokenithe the environinge of the auuter, for they synge thanne: 'The
waytes of the citee shull finde me,' for thei shulde wake upon hem that
be committed to hem. And therfor puttith Gilberde the necligence of
prelates amonge the vnordinat thinges and saithe: 'It is a foule thinge
but moche more perilous a blynde archer, a lame messenger, a 205
necligent prelate, and an vncunnynge doctour, and a domme crier.'
Or ellis .vij. consideraciones that [we] shulde haue towardes the .vij.
vertues of Ihesu Crist[is] humilite and we shulde environe hem ofte.
The furst vertu is that he that was riche was | made pore; the seconde f. 311vb
that he was leyde in the creche; the thridde that he that was soget to 210
his kinrede; the fourthe that he bowed his hede vnder the power of his
servaunt; the .v. that he sustenid his disciple that was a theef and a
traitour; the .vj. [that] before a fals iuge he helde his pees as a debonair
lambe; the .vij. that he praied for hem that crucified hym.

Thriddely thei shulde haue mynde of the passion of Ihesu Crist, 215
and that betokenithe by the sprynginge of the water that betokenithe
the .vij. shedingges of the blode of Ihesu Crist. The furst was in his
circumcision, the seconde was in praienge, the thridde was in
scourgynge, the fourthe was corowninge with thornes, the .v. was
with naylinge of his hondes, the .vj. the naylinge of his fete, the .vij. 220
was openinge of his side. And these springinges of blode were made
with ysope of humilite and of vnestimable charite. Ysope is an herbe
hote and moist and the auuter is environed .vij. tymes in tokeninge
that in bapteme the .vij. yeftes of the holy goste be youen. Or by these
.vij. yeftes be signified the .vij. comyngges of Ihesu Crist. The furst 225
was from heuene to the wombe of his moder, the secunde from the
wombe into the crache, the .iij. fro the crache to the worlde, the .iiij.

195 crosses] *add* þat D   198 the¹] *om.* E   200 and²] *om.* E   201 for] when
H2   202 me] men H2   205 perilous] *om.* H2   206 and¹] *om.* H2   207 we]
it E   208 Cristis] crist E   210 he¹] *add* that E   that³] *om.* H2   212 servaunt]
seruauntis H2   213 that] *om.* E   216 water] autiere H2   betokenithe²] signifieth
H2   218 in¹] *add* his H2   in²] *add* his H2   219 was¹] *add* in his H2   220 .vj.]
add was in H2   221 was] *add* in H2   springinges] springes H2   222 with] in H2
224 yeftes] *add* of the holie goost H2   227 wombe] *add* of his mooder H2   crache¹'²]
churche H2

fro the worlde to the gibet of the crosse, the .v. fro the crosse to the
sepulture, the .vj. fro the sepultre to hell, the .vij. fro hell whanne he
230 arose and stied into heuene.

Ferthely thei shulde haue brenninge orison, amerous and devoute,
and that is betokened bi the encense that is brent upon the auuter.
f. 312ʳᵃ And than it hathe vertu to stie up bi the light|nesse of the smoke and
for to comforte bi his qualite, and for to ioyne bi that it glewithe, and
235 for to comfort for that it is aromat, that is to saie well smellynge. And
right so is the orison that stiethe vp to God bi true mynde; she
comfortithe the soule as for the gilt passid in geting medicine; she
constreynithe as for that is to come warnes; she confermithe as to the
present in getinge defence and kepinge. Other it may be saide that
240 devout orison by the encence that she pertenithe that she stiethe to
God. Of that [it] is saide in Ecclesiast: 'Orison of humilite yevithe
suete smellinge to God whanne she gothe oute of an herte enflawmed.'

Fifthely thei shulde haue shyninge of conscience and odour of good
renome, and that is signified by the creme that is made of oyle. They
245 shulde haue pure conscience so that thei might saye with the apostle:
'Oure glorie is the witnesse of oure conscience, and also is good
renome,' wherof the apostle saithe to Timothes: 'Hit behouithe that
thei haue good witnesse of hem that beth without forthe.' And
Grisostom saithe that clerkes shulde not haue in hem no manere of
250 soylour, nother in worde nor dede, nother in thought, nother in
opynion, for they shulde be the vertu and the beauute of the Chirche,
and yef they be wicked thei defoule all the Chirche.

Syxtli thei shulde haue clennesse of good werkes, the whiche is
signified bi the white clothes with which the auuter is couered. The
255 vsage of coueringe and of clothinge was founde for to couere and kepe
warme and for to arraye ordinatly. And right so good werkes couerin
the nakidnesse of the soule, wherof the apostle saithe: 'Clothe you
f. 312ʳᵇ with white clothing | so that the nakednesse of youre confusion appere
not.' Hit arraiethe the soule with honeste, wherof the apostle saithe to
260 the Romaynes: 'Clothe you with clothinge of light.' Hit enchawfithe
or enflawmithe to charite, wherof it is saide: 'Be not the clothingges
hote and warme.' For it shulde be lytell worthe to hym that gothe to

230 into] vp to H2   236 true] vertue H2   238 that] add that H2   240 that
she²] and H2   241 it] that E   243 of¹] in H2   244 They] þat L
245 shulde] shulle H2   246 witnesse] swettenesse H2   is²] his H2L   248 without]
add forthe E, add feithe H2 (dehors P2)   250 soylour] soile H2   worde nor] om. H2
256–7 good . . . couerin/the nakidnesse . . . soule] trs. H2   258 confusion] confession
H2

the auuter for to haue an high dignite and a defamed lyff. 'Hit shulde
be an horrible thinge for to haue an high sege and a lowe lyff, and
souerayne degree and lowe astate, a sadde visage and light in werkes, 265
mani wordes and fewe dedes, noble auctorite and a fleinge corage.'
Secundely we shulde take hede how the chirche is sacred, for
thereto perteinithe mani thinges. [For] the bisshop gothe aboute .iij.
tymes, and atte eueri tym that he comithe by the yate he hurtithe with
his crosse and saithe: '[Ye] princes opin youre yates.' And the chirche 270
is blessed withinne and withoute with holy water, a crosse of asshen is
made upon the pauement, and of sonde in travers of the corner
towarde the orient vnto the corner occident, and the a b c is wretin
withinne with letteres of Greke and Latin; crosses there be made in
the walles of the chirche and they be anointed with creme. 275
Now it is to wete that these .iij. [go]inges aboute the chirche
betokenithe the thre goinges about that Ihesu Crist made for the
halwinge of the Chirche. The furst was whanne he come from heuene
to the worlde, the secunde was whan he descended from the worlde
into helle, the thridde was whanne he come and arose and stied up 280
into heuene. Other the [thre] goinges about shewen that the Chirche
[is] | sacred in the worship of the Trinite, or elles for to signifie the f. 312ᵛᵃ
thre astates of hem that be for to be sacred bi the Chirche, that be
virgines and continentis and tho that be maried, the which be signified
in the disposicion of the materiall chirche, so as Richarde of Seint 285
Victore shewithe. For he saithe that the seintwarie is streiter thanne
the herte and the hert more streiter than the body, for the ordre of
virgines is more worthi thanne of the continentis, and the ordre of
continentis is more worthi thanne the mari[ed].
The secunde thinge, [that] is that he hurtithe at the dore, 290
signifiethe the treble right that Ihesu Crist hathe to the Chirche
wherby she shulde be openid to hym, for she is his bi creacion, by
redempcion, and by promesse of glorifienge. And of this treble right
saithe Anselme: 'Certis Lorde, for that thou madest me y aught [to] be
all thine, and for thou hast behight me so grete thinges all my loue 295
aught to be thine, and for that thou art gretter than y for whom thou

263 defamed] defoulid H2   264 sege] seete H2   268 For] Furst EH2 (Car P2)
269 yate] yatis H2   270 Ye] The E   272 corner] corneres EH2 (angle S)
274 there] om. H2   276 goinges] thinges E   276–7 the chirche . . . that] om. H2
280 up] om. H2   281 thre] L, thridde EH2   goinges] goynge H2   shewen] shewinge H2
282 is] om. E   286 shewithe] seith H2   288 thanne] add the ordre H2   289 the] add
ordre of H2   maried] mariage E   290 that'] L, om. EH2   292 his] om. H2   293 this
treble right] these treble rightis H2   294 to] om. E   296 y] om. H2

woldest yeue thiselff [and to whom thou behightest thiselff,] y owe to
the more thanne myselff.' And of that [that] the bisshopp crieth .iij.
tymes: 'Opin youre yates *etc.*' signifiethe the treble puissaunce that he
300 hathe in heuene, in the worlde, and in helle.

And that [she] is .iij. tymes sprenged withinne and withoute
signifieth .iij. causes. The furst is for to putte oute the fende, for
holy water hathe propre vertu for to chase oute fendes. And therfor it
is saide in the blessinge of the water: 'For that this water be made
305 blessed for to chase awey alle the power of the fende and for to race
awey the might of that enemy with his wicked and cursed aungeles.'
And thou aughtest knowe that holy water is made of .iiij. thinges,
f. 312ᵛᵇ water, salt, wy|ne and asshin, whiche thinges puttin oute the fende
and chase hym awey. By water is signified shedinge of teres, by the
310 wyne is signified spirituel gladnesse, and bi the salte is sheued ripe
discrecion, and by the asshes is sheued depe and lowe mekenesse.

Secoundely she is dedyed for to clense her from all erthely thingges
that ben corrupte by synne, and for she wolde be clensed from all
filthe she is sprenged with holy water so that she be clene and pure.
315 And that was signified in the olde law that all were clensed bi water.

Thriddely she was sacred for to putte awey all cursinge from the
erthe that was atte begynninge cursed with his fruit for that man was
deceiued bi his fruit. The water was not cursed and therfor sum sayne
that oure Lorde ete fisshe, for it is not founde that he ete flessh but
320 only of the paschall lambe, and that was in ensaumple for to fulfell the
comaundement of the lawe. And therfor that all cursednesse shulde be
take awey the chirche is ysprenged with holy water.

Ferthely the a b c is wreten in the pament in Latin and in Greke,
and that betokenithe the comunyon of that one and of that other
325 peple, or it signifiethe the scripture of that one or of that other
testament, or ellis the articles of the faith. For the scripture of letteres
Grewe and Latin that were made in the table of the crosse
representithe the faithe made bi Ihesu Crist in the crosse. And for
that is that crosse ledde and made in travers of the corner of the orient
330 into the corner of the occident, for to signifie that he that furst was
right was made lifte and that he that was made in the hede was made

297 and . . . thiselff] *om.* E   298 that²] *om.* E   299 *etc.*] *om.* H2   301 she]
see E   sprenged] sprongen with holie watir H2   304 water¹ . . . this] autier that is H2
305 the fende] feendis H2   race] rache H2   307 thou aughtest] that we ought to H2
309 By water is signified] watir signefieth H2   313 for] *om* H2   wolde] wille H2
316 was] is H2   318 his] *om.* H2   321 therfor] for H2   324 and that] *om.* H2
329 ledde] leide H2   330 for to signifie] signefieth H2

in the tayle, and so in the contrarie. And so it representith the scripture of bothe testamentes that | was fulfelled in the crosse by f. 313ra Ihesu Crist, for he saide whanne he deied that all was fulfelled. And the crosse is travers for that one testament is contenid in that other, 335 for all the lawe is in a whele.

Thriddely crosses be peinted in chirches for .iij. resones. The furste for to fere the fende, for whanne thei see the signe of the crosse fro whennes they were putte oute thei flee and be aferde and dore not entre, for thei drede gretly the signe of the crosse. And of that saithe 340 Grisostom that: 'In what place they see the signe of the crosse thei flee, for thei drede the staffe wherwith thei haue be wounded.' Thriddely it representith the articles of the faithe, for the pauement of the chirche is the fundament of the faithe, the letteres that be thereinne wretin be the articles of ourc faithe bi the whiche the rude 345 and thc wicked in the faithe be taught; thei aught acounte hem as asshes [and] duste, after that Abraham saithe in Genesis: 'How dare y speke to my lorde that am but poudcr and asshes?' Secundely to shewe the signe of the victori of Ihesu Crist, for the crosses be signes and baneres of Ihesu Crist and of his victori, and therfor crosses be 350 peinted for to shewe that the place is dewly soget to God. Thriddely for to represent the aposteles men vsen to sette .xij. lightes before the crosse that bi the faithe of the crucified thei enlumined all the worlde, and anointed with creme of bapteme for oyle betokenithe clennesse of conscience and baume signifiethe odour of good lyff. 355

And it is to knowe that the chirche or the Temple was as men sayne soyled bi .iij. persones, [that is] by Ieroboam, bi Nabizardan, and by Antiochus. For as it is redde in the boke of Kinges, Ieroboam dede make two calues of golde and putte that | one in f. 313rb Iudee and that other in Bethell that is saide the hous of God; and 360 this did hc for couetise. And bi that is signified that by the couetise of clerkes the Chirche of God is gretly defouled, the whiche auarice regnithe gretly in hem. Wherof Seint Ierom saithe that: 'Fro the lest vnto the grettest thei foluen all auarice.' And Seint Bernard saithe the same: 'The whichc wilt thou yeue of these prestis that 365 tenden not more for to voide the pou[r]ses of her sogettis thanne for to take awey her synnes?' The calues be her sones and her neuewes that thei settin in Bethel, that is in the Chirche of God. The chirche was defouled bi Ieroboam after that is saide before, and

333 scripture] cripture H2   334 And] in H2   346 aught] om. H2   347 and]
or E   351 dewly] due and H2   357 that is] om. E   366 pourses] pouses E

370 so is the Chirche gretly defouled whanne she is edefied with
couetise of vsureres and theues.

Wherof it is redde that an vsurere had founded a chirche with
rapinesse of his vserie, and praied a bisshopp that he wolde dedye his
chirche. And as the bisshop dede the office of the dedicacion, he sawe
375 the fende sittinge in a chaier bysides the auuter in the abite of a
bisshop, and saide to the bisshop 'Whi dediest thou my chirche? Y
charge the for to cese, for thou hast not to do here, for the right
longithe to me for she is made with vsurie and fals takin good.' And
than the bisshop and all his clerkes were foule afraied and fledde awey,
380 and anone the fende distroied all that chirche with horrible noyse and
cry, with thunder and lighteninge and horrible tempest.

Naburzardan, as it is redde in the .xxv. chapitre of Kinges, brent
the hous of God for he was prince of the cokes, and that is signified
[to] hem that servin to glotenie and lecherie and makin of her wombes |
f. 313ᵛᵃ her goddes, after that the apostle saithe that her wombe is her god.
386 And Hugh de Seint Victore shewithe how her wombe is [her] god and
saithe: 'Sumtyme men were wonte to make temples to God, dresse up
auuters and ordeine ministres for to serue and for to sacrifice bestes,
and for to brenne encence. But now the wombe and the kichin is the
390 temple, the table is the auuter, the cokes be ministres, the bestis
sacrified ben the sodin and rosted flesshes, the encens is the odour of
the sauours.

The kinge Antiochus was the most proude and coueitous man that
was in his dayes and in his tyme, and defouled the chirche of God as it
395 is redde in Machabeus, and bi hym is signified the pride that wallithe
in preestis and the coueitise of hem that desire not to do profit to
sowlis but for to haue lordshippes of goodes, and thei defoule the
Chirche of God. Of whiche pride and coueitise saithe Seint Bernard:
'They go worshipped with the goodes of oure Lorde and thei bere
400 hym no worshipp; thei go euery day as golyardes in shininge clothinge
and in riall abite, thei bere golde in her brideles, in sadelis and in her
sporis [and] moche more shining harneys than other men; and therfor
right as the hous of God was defouled bi these thre, right so was she
dedyed by other thre. Moyses made the furst dedicacion, and
405 Salamon made the secunde, and Iudas Machabeus the thirde; bi

373 dedye] dedifie H2   376 dediest] edifiest H2   378 takin] gooten H2
384 to¹] bi E   386 her²] om. E   387 were wonte to] did H2   dresse] and dressed
H2   388 ordeine] ordeined H2   390 the table] tabernacle H2   auuter] add of H2
391–2 of . . . sauours] and the sauour thereof H2   395 wallithe] walketh H2
400 golyardes] a galondis H2   402 and¹] om. E   405 Machabeus] add made H2

whiche thinge is signified that we shulde haue in the dedicacion of the
chirche humilite that was in Moyses, wysdom that was in Salamon,
verrei confession of faithe that was in Iudas Machabeus.

After that it behouithe to | see the dedicacion of the gostly temple, f. 313vb
the whiche temple we be, that is to saye the assemble of all good 410
cristen. And this temple is made of quik stones, as Seint Petre saithe:
'Late vs edifie whiles the stones be quicke.' This temple is made of
stones polisshed, whereof it is songe: 'The iointures be made of stones
polisshed'. Hit is also made of squared stones, that is to saie of faithe,
hope, and charitee, and good werkes, that bene all egall, so as Seint 415
Gregori saithe: 'As long as thou lyuest thou hast hope, for as longe as
thou beleuest thou hopist sumthinge, and thou louist as longe as thou
beleuist, and as longe as thou beleuest, hopist and louist, so longe thou
werkest in hem.' In this temple the auuter ys the hertc, and upon this
auuter thre thingges owen for to be offered to God. The furst thinge is 420
the fire of euerlastinge loue, so as the apostle saithe: 'The fyre of loue
shall be euerlasting and shall neuer faile in the auuter of the hert.' The
secunde thinge is the encense of orison well smellinge, so as it is said
in Parlipomenon to Aaron and to Fynees [that] offered encens vpon
the auuter of holocaustis, that is to wete the auuter of sacrifices, where 425
men brenden thinges well smelling and precious. The thridde thinge
is sacrifice of rightwisnesse, and that is the offeringe of penaunce in
sacrifice of perfit loue, and in calves of mortefyeing of the flesshe; and
of this seithe Dauid: 'Thou shalt resseiue the sacrifice of rightwisnesse.'   430

This spirituel temple whiche we be is the temple of God right as
that other [material] temple. For furst the souerane bishop Ihesu Crist
whanne he findithe the dore of the temple clos he gothe about thre
tymes, that is | whanne he bringithe to mynde the synne of the f. 314ra
mouthe, of the herte, and of the werke. And [of] this treble goinge 435
aboute saithe [he] as to the furst: 'Y haue environed the citee', that is
to saie the herte. As to the secunde saithe Ysaie: 'Take thin harpe',
and as to the thridde: 'The comune woman is youen in foryetinge.'

Secundely he smitithe .iij. tymes the dore of the hert that is close
for it shulde be opened to hym, and he smitithe it by the stroke of 440
benefetes, of counsaile and of discipline. And of this treble stroke it is
saide in the Prouerbes: 'To the wicked y haue streched oute myn

415 all] *om.* H2   424 that] L, *om.* E, thei H2   432 material] tarstrical E
temple] *add* is H2   435 mouthe] *add* and H2   of³] *om.* EH2   436 he] *om.* E
437 harpe] happe H2   438 woman] women H2   440 of] *add* his E

honde *etc.*' As to the benefites youen, he saithe: 'Thou hast despised
all my counsailes' to hem that he hath enspired with the yefte of
445 counsaile, and: 'Thou hast despised the stroke of my blaminge' to
hem that he scourgithe. Or this treble goinge aboute is made whanne
he sterithe to resonable knowlache of synne and to angri sorugh for
synne and for to venge hem upon hymselff, by bitter contricion, bi
pure and opin confession and bi satisfaccion of penaunce doinge.
450   Thriddely he sprengithe the spirituel temple .iij. tymes with water,
and these .iij. manere of wetynges betokenithe .iij. manere of teres.
For as Seint Gregori saithe the thought of an holy man shulde be
confused with sorw in consideringe where he was, where he shal be,
and where he is and where he is not. Where was he but in synne, and
455 where is he but in iugement, and where shall he be but in
wrechidnesse, and where is he not but in glorie. Whanne he shedithe
thanne the teres of the herte in consideringe that he was in synne and
shall be in iugement for to yelde reson for the synne, than is that
f. 314rb temple onis sprenged with | water. And whanne he is contrite and
460 wepithe for the wrechidnesse wherein he is, thanne is the temple
sprenged the secunde tyme. And whan he wepith for lacke of the ioye
that he hathe not, thanne he sprengithe the temple the thridde tyme.
And thou must vnderstonde that wyne, salt and asshes be medeled
with this water, for by the wyne in the water is vnderstonde the
465 humilite of Ihesu Crist, in that he toke mankinde. And by the salt is
vnderstonde the holynesse of his lyff, that yeuithe suete savour to all
tho of his religion. By the asshes is vnderstonde his passion. And with
these .iij. thinges we shulde moist and wete oure hertes, the whiche
bene the blessinge of his incarnacion by whiche we be called to
470 mekenesse and humilite, the ensaumple of his holy conuersacion by
whiche we be enformed to holynesse, and the mynde of his passion bi
whiche we be meued to charite.
     Ferthely in the temple of the gostly herte is wrete the a b c other the
spirituel scripture. And this scripture is treble, the thinges of eueles
475 done, the witnesse of divine benefetes, the accusacion of [his] propre
misdedes. And of these .iij. thinges saithe the apostle to the
Romaynes: 'The men that haue lawe they do naturaly the thinges
that bene of the lawe; tho that haue no lawe be lawe to hemselff; tho
that shewen the werke of the lawe wretin in her herte,' that is the

448 hymselff] hemselff H2, *add* for E   450 .iij.] .iiij. E.   451 wetynges]
wateringis H2   473 the³] in H2   474 treble the] *trs.* H2   475 his] the E

furst; 'The witnesse of her conscience' is the secounde; and 'He that 480
bethenkithe hym in his herte for to acuse hym' is the thridde.

Fifthely the crosses shulde be peinted with[in] this temple, that is
to wete that he shulde haue the sharpenesse of pe|naunce, and this f. 314ᵛᵃ
sharpenesse aught to be anointed and haue light of fire, for thei shulde
not only suffre in [pacience] but with good wille. And of that saithe 485
Seint Bernarde: 'He that is manaced with drede of Ihesu Crist berithe
the crosse in pacience, he that profiteth in hope berithe it gladly, but
he that berithe it in charite enbracithe it brennyngly. And mani men
beholde youre crosse that beholde not your anointyngges.'

And he that hathe these thinges in hym shall be the temple of God 490
and shall be full[i] worthi that God duelle in hym by grace so that he
may duelle with hym bi glorie, the whiche he vs graunte that lyuithe
and regnithe by all the worlde of worldes. Amen.

Here endithe the Dedicacion of the Chirche, and nexst
beginnithe the Advent, Capitulum .C.lxxv[j].

The comyng of oure Lorde that is called Advent is made by .iiij.
wokes to signifie that there be .iiij. comynges. The furst coming is in
flesshe, the secunde in dethe, the thridde in thought, the fourthe in
iugement. And the last woke is vnnethe ⟨ende⟩d for that the glorie of
seintes that shall be youe hem that laste Sonday shall neuer faile. And 5
therfor the furst response of the furst Sonday of Advent, for to
acounte the *Gloria patri*, conteinithe .iiij. verses to that ende to signifie
the forsaid .iiij. cominges.

And though it be so that there be .iiij. comynges, yet the Chirche
makithe speciall mynde but of .ij., that is to saie of the comynge in 10
flesshe and of the iugement so as it is in the Office of that tyme. And
for this cause the faste of Aduent hathe sum parte of ioye and | sum of f. 314ᵛᵇ
wepinge, for by the comynge into flesshe the faste is saide of ioye, and
by reson of the cominge in iugement the fast is [sai]de of wepinge.
And for to shewe this thinge the Chirche singithe thanne sum songes 15
of ioye, and that is for [the] cominge of mercy; and she takithe awey
su[m] songes, and that is for the cominge of the cruell iugement.

480 The] *om.* H2   481 in . . . for] here H2   482 crosses] crosse H2   within]
with E   485 pacience] penaunce E   486 with] *add* the H2   491 fulli] full E

EH2A2L; E breaks off after 135 *said*, after which variants in A2L are recorded.   *Rubric*
.C.lxxvj.] .C.lxxv. E   1 that] *om.* H2   Advent] *add* and H2   4 for] so H2
5 hem] *add* and H2   10 .ij.] .iiij. E   11 and] *add* of the commynge H2
12 sum²] *add* parte H2   14 saide] made E   16 the] *om.* E   17 sum] such E

And unto cominge into flesshe it may be saie thre thinges: the furst
is [the] couenablete of the cominge and the necessite and the profit.
20 The couenablete is vnderstonde furst of the partie of the man that was
furst ouercome in the lawe of kinde by defauute of goodly knowlache.
For in tho dayes thei fill in right wicked erroures of idolatrie, and
therfor he was constreined to saye: 'Lorde yeue light to myn eyen.'
And after that [come] the lawe that comaundithe in whiche [he] was
25 ouercome by non power as he before criethe and saithe: 'There is none
that fulfellithe but there is that comaundithe.' And this he is only
taught, but he is not deliuered fro synne, nother holpe by [any] grace
for to do well, and therfor was he con[s]treined for to saie and chaunge
his spekinge: 'There is none that comaundithe but that fulfellithe.'
30 And thanne come the sone of God couenably whanne man had be
ouercome with ignoraunce and vnmight, for yef he had come before
perauenture man wolde haue saide that he had be heled bi his propre
merites and by that he shulde not take his medicine aggreably.

Secondely she is vnderstonde bi the partie of the tyme wherof the
35 apostle saith to the Galathas in the .vij. chapitre: 'He came in the
f. 315ᵃ plente of tyme.' And Seint Austin saithe: 'Mani men saien: | "Why
come not Ihesu Crist before?" And it is ansuered for that the plente of
tyme was not come, bi the attempering of hym by whom the tymes be
made. And whanne the plente of tyme was come, he came that same
40 that deliuered vs of the tyme. And we deliuered of the tyme be now
come to that euerlasting[n]es where there is no tyme.'

Thriddely it is vnderstonde bi the partie of the wounde and of the
vniuersal siknesse, for whanne the siknesse was vniuersall hit was
most couenable to putte therto an vniuersall medicine. Wherof Seint
45 Austin saithe that the gret leche came whanne that siknesse laye
thorugh the worlde. Wherfor the Chirche shewithe in .vij. antemys
that be songe in the Aduent before the Natiuite, and shewithe the
multeplyeng of his siknesse. And for eueriche he requirithe the
remedie of medicine, for before the cominge of the sone of God in
50 flesshe we were ignoraunt and blinde, and bounde by bonde to the
peynes euerlastinge, seruaunt of the fende, bounden with wicked
custume, wrapped in derkenesse, chased from oure cuntrei. And

19 the¹] *om.* E   24 come] L, *om.* E, that H2   that²] *om.* H2   he] *om.* E
26 this] thus H2   27 any] L, my EH2   28 constreined] contreined E   31 had]
add be H2   32 his] *add* owne H2   36 men] *om.* H2   38 attempering] temptinge
H2   whom] *add* whiche attemptinge H2   the tymes] time H2   40 of the¹] *add* same
H2   41 euerlastingnes] euerlastinges E

therfor we haue nede of a doctoure, of a redemptour, of a deliuerere, of an outedrawer, of an enluminour and of a saueoure.

And for that we were vncunninge we hadde nede to be taught, and 55 therfor we crie in the furst anteme: 'O wisdom that comithe oute of the mouthe of the most hiest, come and teche us the waye of wisdom.' But litell [auail]id it that we were taught but yef that we were bought, and therfor we requere to be bought by hym whanne we saie [in] the secounde anteme: 'O Adonay duke of the meyne of Israel, come and 60 beye us in the might of thi right arme.' And what shulde auaile us oure te|chinge and oure beyenge yef we shuld alwey be kepte and f. 315rb holde in captiuite, and therfor we require to be deliuered whanne we crie in the thridde anteme: 'O rote of Iesse, come and deliuer vs and tarie not.' But what shulde auaile to vs wreches yef [we] were bought 65 and deliuered and not vnbounde of all oure bondes so that we might goo fre where we wolde? And therfor we require to be take oute of the [bondes] of synne whanne we crie in the fourthe anteme: 'O keie of Dauid, come to vs and take vs oute of preson sittinge in derkenesse and in the shadwe of dethe.' And for that tho that haue longe tyme 70 bene in derkenesse haue no clere sight, for her eyen be derked therfor, after the deliueraunce of the prison we require to be enlumined that we mowe see where we shulde goo. And therfor we crie in the .v. anteme: 'O orient shiner of euerlastinge light, come and enlumine tho that sitten in derkenesse and in the shadwe of dethe.' And yef we were 75 taught, bought, vnbounde and enlumined, what shulde availe vs but yef we shulde be saued? And therfor we require to be saued in .ij. antemes foluinge and saie: 'O kinge of men, come and saue vs that thou madest of the slyme of the erth;' 'O Emanuel duke and berer of oure lawe, Lorde oure God, come and saue us.' 80

The profit of his coming is assigned of mani seintes in mani maners, for as Luke saithe in the .iiij. chapitre that oure Lorde was sent and come for .vij. profites, and he saithe: 'The sperit of oure Lorde upon me etc.' Other he saithe bi ordre that he was sent to the comfort of the pore, to hele tho that were sike, to deliuer tho that were holde in 85 prison, to teche the vn|cunnyng, to foryeue synnes and for to beye all f. 315va mankinde and for to yeue guerdon to hem that deserued it.

Seint Austin puttithe .iiij. profites of his cominge and saithe: 'In

58 availid] L, shewid EH2   taught . . . were] om. H2   59 in] om. E   64 rote] Rooce H2   65 we] om. E   65–6 bought and] om. H2   68 bondes] hous E, hondis H2   73 shulde] om. H2   77 .ij.] .vij.the H2   78 and1] the H2 80 oure1] the H2

this wicked worlde what thinge aboundithe but for to be born, to
90 trauaile, and dethe? These be the marchaundises of this region, and to
these marchaundises he come downe. And for that all marchaundises
yevin and takin, he gaue that whiche he had and toke that he had not,
Ihesu Crist in this marchaundise yaue and toke. He toke that
haboundithe here, that is for to be bore, trauaile, and deye, and
95 yaue for to be bore ayen, for to rise, and for to regne eternaly. This
marchaunt come to vs for to take riot and geue worship, to take dethe
and to yeue lyff, for to take pouerte and to yeue glorie.'
    Seint Gregorie puttithe .iiij. causes or profites of his cominge and
saithe: 'All the proude that were come of the sones of Adam studiedin
100 for to haue the prosperitees of this worlde and to eschew contrarie
thinges, for to flee reprofe and to folw glorie. And thanne come oure
Lorde amonge hem born in flesshe, coueitinge aduersitees and
dispisinge prosperitees, byclippinge reproues and fleing glorie. And
Ihesu Crist came that was abydyn and taught nwe thinges, and in
105 techinge he dede meruailous thinges and in doinge meruailes he
suffered mani sorughes and dissesis.'
    Seint Bernarde putte otherwise and saithe: 'We be trauailed with
.iij. wicked siknesses, for we be light to deseyue, feble for to werke,
and frele for to withstonde. Yef we will deserne betwene good and
f. 315vb euell we be deseiued; yef we assaye | to do wele we faile full sone; yef
111 we enforce vs to withstonde [eu]yll we be sone ouercome. And therfor
the cominge of oure saueoure was necessarie so that he duellinge in vs
by faithe enlumyne oure blindenesse, and in duellynge with vs helpe
oure sykenesse, and in beinge with us defend oure freelte.'
115 The secounde comyng is to the iugement, and therinne be two
thinges to be sein, that is the thinges that be before the iugement and
the thinges that be after the iugement.
    The thinges that be before the iugement be .iij. thinges, furste
dredfull signes, and thanne the fals begylinge of Antecrist, and the
120 right gret strengthe of fyre. [The] dredfull tokenes that shull be before
the iugement be sette in Luke in the .xxj. chapitre: 'There shull be
signes in the sunne and in the mone and in the sterres and houge
grevaunces to men. The .iij. furst signes be determined in the
Apocalipses in the .vj. chapitre that saithe: 'The sonne is made
125 right as a gret sacke of here and the mone is made as blode and the

    93 this] his H2   99 studiedin] subeiden H2   103 glorie] glories E
111 euyll we] L, wyll we E, we wille H2   112 duellinge] dwellid H2   113 faithe]
add and H2   120 The] Soche E   124 .vj.] .vij. H2   125 gret] om. H2

sterres shull fall upon the erthe.' The sunne is saide derke for as
moche as he is depriued of his light, as he were saie wepinge for the
deyinge of men, or as for the comynge of the gretter, that is the
brightnesse of Ihesu Crist; or ellys for to speke by symilitude, for
Seint Austin saithe that the vengeaunce shall be so cruell that the   130
sunne dare not beholde it; or for to speke for the propre significacion
for the sunne of rightwisnesse Ihesu Crist shall be so derke that there
shalle none dore knowlage hym. The heuene that is called Aeren and
the sterres that be called Asuly that haue similitude of ster[r]es and
thei be said | ben the sterris that f[a]llen fro heuen afftir the commoun   H2 f. 252ᵛᵇ
opinioun whan Ausli descendi[th], for the scripture conf[o]rmeth to   136
the comoun manere of spekinge. And than namelie shalle be made
such [im]pressioun that the qualite of the fire shalle habounde, and
that shalle oure Lorde doo to feere the synfulle. Or els the sterris ben
seide to falle for that thei put out flawmes of fire, or ellis for many   140
prelatis whiche be seyn to be prelatis of the Churche shulle falle, or
ellis for that thei withdrawe her light that thei be nat seene.

Of the fourthe signe that there shalle be greuaunce to men seith
Seinte Marke in the .x[x]iiij. | chapiter: 'Than there shalle be   H2 f. 253ʳᵃ
tribulacioune that there was neuer none gretter from the biginninge   145
of the worlde.'

The .v.ᵗᵉ signe shalle be confusioune of the see, for some wene and
seine that the see shall perisshe withe hugie brekinge of his frist
qualite, afftir that the Appostulle seith in the .xxj. chapiter: 'The see
shalle no more be;' or ellis some othir seyn it schalle be for that he   150
shalle [not] be lifft vp withoute grete murmour .xl. cubitis aboue alle
the mountaines of the worlde and sith she shalle be aba[s]id ayenne.
Or plainli to the letter afftir Gregorie: 'Than shalle there be made a
newe see that neuer was hurde and there shalle be troublinge of
wawes.'   155

Seint Ierome fonde in the annelis of Ebrewes .xv. signes that shulle
be bifore the iugement, [but for to wete whether thei shull be]

128 is] *add* by E   133 shalle] *om.* H2   134 Asuly] Ausli H2   sterres²] steeres E
134–6 that haue . . . Ausli] *om.* A2   135 ben] *om.* L   fallen] fillen H2
136 discendith] descendid H2   conformeth] confermeth H2A2   138 impression]
oppression H2A2   141 whiche . . . prelatis] that shulde be A2   Churche] *add* be feynte
and A2   withdrawe] with withdrawe H2   143 greuaunce to] grete pressure in erthe
of L   144 .xxiiij.] .xiiij. H2   145 gretter] suche L   147 wene and] clerkis A2
148 hugie . . . of] grete brennyng fro L   150 ellis] after L   othir] *add* clerkis A2
seyn] *om.* L   151 not] *om.* H2A2   murmour] grucchyng A2   152 abasid] abatid
H2A2   157 the] *add* dome of A2   but . . . be] *om.* H2A2, *add* þe iugement L

continuelli or bitwene he deuisith nat, and he seith that the frist daie
the see shalle arise .xl. cubitis aboue the high hillis and he shalle be in
160 his place as a walle. The seconde daie he shalle discende so lowe that
vnnethis he may be sene. The thridde daie the w[hal]es of the see
shalle appere aboue the watir and thei shulle crie and rore up to the
heuen and God oonelie shalle vndirstonde her crie. The fourthe [daie]
the see and the lande shalle brenne. The .v.^te [daie] the trees and the
165 herbis shalle yeue a dewe like blood, and some seine that that daie alle
the briddis of heuen shalle assemble in a feelde, euery maner of foule
bi hymselff, and thei shulle taste of noothinge for drede of the nyȝe
commynge of the iuge. The .vj.^t daie the beeldingis shulle falle doun
[and] in that daie as it is seide, tempestes of fire shulle brenne and thei
170 shulle come fro the orient ayens the [f]ace of the firmament and thei
shulle renne euen to the occident. The .vij.^te daie the stoones shulle
smyte and hurtle togidirs the tone with the tothir in foure parties and
euerie hurtelinge ayens othir, and ther shulle noone vndirstand her
sowne but oonelie God. The .viij.^t daie the erthe shalle tremble
175 [generallie] and there shal be so grete mevinge that no creature shall
mowe stonde but falle doun to the erthe. The .ix.^te daie the
H2 f. 253rb　mountaines shulle be | made euen with the erthe and alle the coppis
of hillis shul turne into poudir. The .x.^te daie men shulle come out of
caues and renne about as wood men and noone speke to othir. The
180 .xj.^te daie the boones of deede men shulle arise and be vppon her
sepulcris, and alle the sepulcris fro the est to the west shulle ben
opened so that dede bodies mowe goone out. The .xij.^te daie the sterris
shulle fallen fro heuen, and alle thoo that turne and be stable shulle
cast out fire, and than shalle Asub be gretelie greued. And in this daie
185 men seie that alle beestis shulle assemble and thei shulle lowe
petuouslie and taste of noothinge. The .xiij.^te daie alle livinge
thinge shalle deie for to arise with the deede. The .xiiij.^te daie the

158 bitwene] *add* whilis L   deuisith] expressiþ L   frist] *add* and L   159 high]
hight of L   160 walle] valey A2   he] the see A2   161 be] *add* knowe and A2
whales] wawes H2L   163 heuen] *add* fulle petevouslye A2   daie] *om.* H2
164 daie] *om.* H2   165 a dewe . . . blood] blody dewe L   165–6 some . . . heuen]
foulis L   169 and^1] *om.* H2A2   170 face] place H2A2   the firmament] iugement
A2   171 euen] ayen A2   173 euerie . . . othir] *om.* L   hurtelinge] partie shalle
hurtylle A2   175 generallie] greuouslie H2A2   176 doun] anone A2
177 coppis] toppis A2   178 of^1] *add* þe L   come] arise L   179 wood] mad A2
180 deede] good A2   182 opened] opyn L   183 stable] *add* in god A2
185 men seie that] alle men and A2   shulle^2] *add* crye and A2   lowe] *add* right L
186 and] *add* dare A2   noothinge] *add* for drede of the iuge A2   187 with] *twice* H2
deede] *add* bodyes that died in alle the worlde before A2

heuen and erthe shulle brenne. The .xv.^{te} daie shalle be made a newe heuen and a newe erthe and alle shulle arise.

The seconde thinge that shalle be bifore the iugement shulle be 190 [the] fals bigilingis of Antecriste, for he shal enforce hym to disseiue the puple in foure maneris. Frist bi malicious techingis or bi fals exposiciouns of scripturis, for he shalle enforce hym to afferme bi scripturis that he is Messias bihight in the lawe and distroie the feithe of Ihesu Crist and ordeine his owne feythe. Whereof Dauid seithe: 195 'Lorde ordeine aboue [hem] the berere of the lawe,' and the Glose seith that it is Antecriste that is berere of the wickid lawe, and Danielle seith: 'He shalle yefe abhominacioun and discomforte.' [And] the Glose seith that Antecriste shalle be as in the time of oure Lorde right as God to take aweie the lawe of God. Secondelie he 200 shalle enforce hym to disseiue the puple bi meraclis werkinge. Danielle seithe in the secounde chapiter: 'Of whiche the commynge shalle be affter the werke of the feende in alle woordis and tokenes and fals shewingis.' Thridlie he shalle disseiue bi large yifftis. The Apocalips seith: 'He shalle [ye]ue powere in many thingis and he 205 shalle deuide the erthe to his plesaunce. And thoo that he may nat sub|mitte to his errour by dreede he shalle submitte hem bi H2 f. 253va turmentis.'

The thrid thinge that shalle be bifore the iugement is this: there shalle be right grete strengthe of fire, the which shall goo bifore the 210 face of the iuge. And oure Lorde shal sende frist this fire to renue the worlde, for he shal purge and renue alle the clementis, and right as the watir of Noes floode was, right so the fire shalle be more high than the montaines bi .xv. cubites, and so it is seide in the Maister of Stories for that the werkis of men myght haue stied so highe. Secoundelie for 215 the purginge of men, to hem that shulle than liue it shalle be purgatorie. Thridlie for more to torment the dampnid. Firthelie for more enlumininge of seintis. For aftir Seinte Basile, whan God hath made [t]his purgacioun of the fire he shalle departe the light fro the

191 the] om. H2   hym] add for L   193–4 to afferme/bi scripturis] trs. L
194 and] add shalle nye A2   195 feythe] om. L   195–8 Dauid . . . wickid lawe/
Danielle . . . discomforte] trs. and omit and before Danielle A2   196 aboue hem] trs.
H2A2   hem] hym L   197 it is . . . that] om. A2   the] þis L   199 And] As H2   as
. . . time] in þe tempill L   201 bi] add fals A2   meraclis werkinge] myraclous werkis L
204 large] fals A2   205 yeue] haue H2   207 submitte^1] turne A2   errour]
erroures L   dreede] add and by yeftis A2   210 strengthe] tempestis A2
211 sende] make A2   frist/this fire] trs. L   renue] add in H2, runne þorowe A2
213 right so] om. L   216 men] add for L   217 more/to torment] trs. L
219 this] his H2   of] with A2

220 heete, and he shalle sende alle the hete to the regioune of thoo that
shulle be dampned to be the more turmentid, and he shal sende the
brightnesse into the regioun of [the blessid] to encrese her ioie.

The thingis that fellishippen the iugement shulle be many. The
frist shal be the vnagreabulte of the iuge. The iuge shal discende into
225 the Vale of Iosephat and he shalle putte the goode on the right honde
and the wickid on the lifft honde. And it is to bileue that he shal be in a
place apperinge so that alle mowe se hym. And it is nat to vndirstonde
that alle shulle be enclosid in that vale, so as Ierome seith thei shulle
be in placis aboute, for in litille londe mai be men without noumbre,
230 and namelie whan thei be streight. And perauentur the goode shulle
be in the eire for the lightnesse of her bodies, and the dampned also
perauenture bi vertue of the Godhede. And than the iuge shalle
biginne to repreue the wickid and putte ayenst hem the werkis of
mercie that thei had nat doo, and than shulle thei alle wepe on
235 hemself, afftir that Grisostome seith vppon Mathewe: 'The Iewes
shulle waile and plaine whan thei shulle se Ihesu Criste livinge and
H2 f. 253ᵛᵇ yevinge life, the whiche thei wende that he had be a deedelie | man,
and thei shulle be ouercome whan thei shulle se hym woundid in his
bodie and thei mowe nat denye her felony. And also the paynemes
240 shulle wepe for that bi her veine dispeticiouns of philosophris thei
were disseiued and wenden that it had ben a folie vnresonable to haue
worshippid the God crucified. The synfulle cristen puple shulle wepe
for that thei loued, seruid and worshippid more the worlde than Ihesu
Crist allemyghty God. And alle the kinredis of the [erthe] shulle
245 wepe, for than shalle there be noo vertue [to] withstonde ayenst hym,
and to hide hem it is impossible and to flee thei haue noo leisere, ne
place of penaunce, ne time of satisfaccion. There shalle be anguisshe
of alle thingis, ne noothinge shalle abide that shalle plese hem.

The secounde thinge shalle be the difference of the ordenaunce, for
250 as Seint Gregorie seith that there shal be foure ordres atte iugement,
the tweine of the party of the repreued and tweine of the partie of the

222 the blessid] blisse H2A2   225 honde] side L   226 and . . . honde] *om.* A2
the²] his L   honde] side L   And] *add* as L   that] *om.* L   227 mowe] men A2   to]
add be L   230 streight] set streyte togeders A2   232 perauenture] *om.* L
235 hemself] *add* for there wrecchidnes of synne A2   237 wende] *add* were dede A2
that he had] for to have L   239 her] *add* folyes and A2   also] *om.* L   240 wepe]
waile L   veine dispeticiouns] voyde disputyngis A2, disputacions veyn L   philosophris]
philosophy L   242 puple] *om.* L   243 seruid, worshippid] *trs.* L   244 erthe]
worlde H2A2   245 to] *om.* H2, þat maye A2   246 leisere] *add* for þer is A2
248 abide . . . shalle] *om.* A2   shalle] shuld L   hem] the synfulle A2   249 the¹] *om.* L
251 of the⁴] *om.* L

chosen. The toone shalle be iugid and perissh, [tho] to whom it shal be
seide: 'I had hungur and ye yafe me noo meete, I thristid and ye yafe
me noo drinke.' The tothir shul nat be iugid | but þey shull perissh as   L f. 418ᵛᵇ
tho of whom it is seide: 'He þat levith nat is forthewiþ iugid,' for they   255
wolde not perseyve þe wordis of þe iuge ne wolde nat kepe his feith.
That oþer party of þat chosyn shall be iuged and reigne as þey | to   L f. 419ʳᵃ
whom it shall be seide: 'I had hunger and ȝe ȝave me meete *etc.'* Other
shall not be demyd and shall | regne as parfite men that shulle iuge   H2 f. 253ᵛᵇ
othir, naught that thei shulle yife the sentence but thei shulle accorde   260
with the iuge, for that apperteyneth to God allone. And that
accordaunce shalle be frist in the worshipp of seintis, for it is a
grete worshipp to seintis to haue a seete with the iuge, afftir that he
bihotith hem seienge: 'Ye shulle be aboue the seetis.' Secoundelie to
the confirmacioun of the sentence, for thei shulle approue the   265
sentence of the iuge right [as] some time thoo that be with the iuge
approue and escriue to preue it, and of that seith Dauid: 'Thei shul
make ayens h[e]m a iugement written.' Thridli to the condempna-
cioun of the wickid, the which thei shulle dampne bi the werkis of her
life.   270
    The thrid thinge that shalle be with the iuge shulle be the signes of
his passioun, that is the naylys of his hondis and the woundis of his
bodie. And these | thingis shulle be to shewe frist his glorious   H2 f. 254ʳᵃ
victories, and thei shulle appere in an excellente glorie, as Grisostome
seith vppon Mathewe: 'The crosse and the woundis shul be more   275
brighter than the beemes of the sonne.' And hit is to vndirstonde and
to considur howe moche the vertue of the crosse is grete. For the
sonne shalle wexe derke and the moone shalle yeue noo light for that
thou shalt knowe that the crosse is more shininge than is the moone
and more clerer than the sonne. Secoundeli in shewinge of his grete   280
mercie, and be these thingis he sheweth howe the goode be saued of
his mercie. Thridli for the shewinge of his rightwisnesse so that
therebi be shewed howe that the reprouid be rightwislie dampned, for

252 perissh] perisshid H2   tho] *om.* H2A2   254–9 þey . . . shall] *om.* H2A2
261 that¹] *add* iugement A2   263 to seintis] for L   264 bihotith] promysed A2
aboue] *add* þe sentence of the iugement in high A2   seetis] segis L   266 as] so H2A2
267 approue] *add* his sentence L   escriue] subscribe L, ascribe *or* ascrive A2   preue]
approven L   268 hem] hym H2A2   269 the werkis of] þer synful levyng here in A2
271 the²] *add* crosse þe L   272 is] *add* þe crosse L   his²] *add* feet and L
273 shulle be] be for L   frist his glorious] to wyckid in reprove and to the gode to ioye and
glorye and gracious A2   victories] victory L   276–7 vndirstonde and to] *om.* L
281 sheweth] *add* to you H2A2   281–2 of his] by þe grete L   283 rightwislie]
rightfullye A2

thei dispisid God that was the price and the ayennebienge of her
285 synnes bi his bloode, wherefor he reproueth hem bi these wordis as
Grisostome seith vppon Mathewe: 'I am made a man for you and
bounden and dispisid and betenne and crucified. Loo here howe that I
[haue] yeue the price of my bloode for the redempcioun of your
[soulis]. Where is the seruice that ye haue doo for me for the price of
290 my bloode for the redempcioune of youre soulis? I had you more dere
than glorie, for as I was Godde I become man and ye made me the
moost vile of alle othir thingis, for ye loued the more vile thingis of
alle the [erthe] than my right and my feithe.

The fourthe is the cruelte of the iuge, for he may nat be turned bi
295 noo powere for he is allmyghti, nor bi noo yiftis for he is alle riche,
and thereof seith Seint Bernarde: 'That daie shalle com whan the pure
hertis shul be more worthi than the proude woordis, and goode
conscience bettir than fulle [pursis]. Hit is he that mai nat be deceiued
bi woordis nor he mai nat be bowed bi yifftis.' And Seint Augustine
300 seith: 'The daie of doome is abiden and there shalle [be] the rightfulle
iuge that wille nat receiue the persoone of noo myght of whom the
paleis be of goolde and of siluer, nor no bisshoppe nor no abbotte nor
H2 f. 254rb prince mai nat | corrupte hym bi goolde nor siluer.' Nor bi hate, for he
is alle goode. And for that he is alle goode, he mai nat falle into hate,
305 wherof it is seide in the boke of Sapience: 'Lorde, thou hatist neuer
thinge that thou madist.' Nor bi loue for [he is] mooste rightfulle, for
he wille nat deliueren his bretheren the fals cristen men. And so seith
Dauid: 'The brothir shal nat [by] his brothir.' Nor bi errour, for he is
right wis. And thereof seith Seint Leon the pope: 'This is the sentence
310 of the soueraigne iuge, he hath right dredefulle and tremblinge
biholdinge, to whom alle stabulle thingis ben litille, and alle secrete
thingis apperen to hym, and alle derkenes is clere to hym, and
doumbe thingis aunswere to hym, and thoo that mowe [nat speke]
confesse hym, and thought spekith to hym without vois. And for that
315 his wisdome is so hugie and so grete, the alleageaunce of aduocatis be
naught so grete nor so worthi as his wisdome is, nothir the argumentis

284 ayennebienge] ayenbyer A2   285 his] add precious H2A2   288 haue] om.
H2   289 soulis] folies H2   289–90 soulis . . . youre] om. A2   291 than] add
my L   292 othir] om. A2   more] mooste L   293 erthe] worlde H2, worlde better
than me A2   297 proude] add hertis and grete L   298 pursis] processe H2, add of
golde and syluer A2   300 be] om. H2   the] that L   302 paleis] paleicis H2   be]
ben H2L   306 thinge] add of thyne L   he is] thou art H2   308 by] L, be E
brothir²] add &c L   309 right wis] mooste wis L, fulle of rightwysnes A2   pope]
erased L   312 hym¹] add opynlye A2   is clere/to hym] trs. L   313 nat speke] trs.
H2   314 confesse] add to L   and] add also H2, add also eueri A2

of philosophris, nothir the right faire spekinge of maistris, nothir the
pride of fooles.' And of these foure thingis seith [also] Seint Ierome:
'How moche shulle thei be more blessid bifore hym thoo without
spekinge [than] the faire spekeris, and this for the frist. For 320
the secounde howe moche more shul the shepperdis than the
philosophres, and to the thrid howe moche more thoo that be
vnkunnynge in spekinge to [the] argumentis of Seint Citerioun.'
    And as to the fourthe [how moche] the accusacioun is horrible, for
there than shalle be four accusours ayens the synfulle. The frist is the 325
feende, whereof Seinte Augustine seith: 'Than shalle the feende be
there [alle] redi recordinge the wordis of oure professioun and
apposinge us of alle that we haue done, and what [houre] we haue
synned, and what good we myght haue done. And than shulle [that]
aduersarie seine: "Right rightfulle iuge, iuge h[y]m to [be myne] for 330
[his] synnes that wolde nat be thine bi grace. He is | thine bi nature but H2 f. 254ᵛᵃ
he is myne bi [his] wickidnesse: he is thine bi thine passioune but he is
myne bi fulfillinge of my werkis; he hath disobeied to the and obeied
vnto me; he tooke of the the stoole of inmortalite and of me this pore
coote wherewith he is clothid; and he hath lost thi cloothinge and is 335
come hidir clothid in my clothinge and condempned with me." Allas,
allas, how mai he openne his mouthe that is founden in this plight that
be right is ordeined to the feende?'
    The secounde accusour shalle be his owne propur mysdeedis. For
his propur synnes shalle accuse thoo that haue doo hem, whereof the 340
wise man seith: 'The iniquitees,' that is to seie the wickidnessis of
hem, 'shulle come dredefulli in her myndis and be contrarie to hem.'
And Seinte Bernard seith: 'The werkinges spekinge togidirs shulle
seie: "Thou hast doo us, we be thi werkis and we shulle goo with the
to the iugement and accuse the of multiplienge of myssedeedis."' 345
    The thridde accusour shalle be the worlde, whereof Seinte

    318 also] *om.* H2A2   319 thoo] *add* that be A2   320 than] or H2A2   spekeris]
add as to hym alle is on A2   321 secounde] *add* and L   shul] *om.* L   than] speche or
A2   322 philosophres] *add* to hym alle is one A2   more] *om.* L   323 in spekinge]
om. A2   the] *om.* H2   Seint] *om.* L   324 how moche] the which H2A2   accusacioun]
accusaciouns H2A2   is] shal be þan fulle A2   327 alle] *om.* H2A2   328 apposinge]
opposyng L   houre] *om.* H2A2   329 good] goodis L   that] alle the H2, the A2
330 aduersarie] aduersaries H2A2   hym] hem H2A2   be myne] me H2   331 his] her
H2A2   332 his] *om.* H2A2   333 bi] *add* þe L   336 clothid] *om.* L   clothinge]
add wherfor O moost rightwis iuge deme hym to be myn L   and] *add* to be L   337 he]
the synner A2   339 owne] *om.* L   propur] *add* synnes and A2   340 his] the L
thoo] hem L   341 The . . . seie] *om.* A2   343 werkinges] workis L   345 to the]
in L   multiplienge of myssedeedis] þy grete and ful wyckyd dedis A2   of²] *om.* L

Gregorie seith: 'Yif thou aske who shalle accuse the, I seie alle the worlde.' For [whan the creature shal be wrothe, alle the worlde shalle] be wrothe,' whereof Grisostome seith vppon Mathewe: 'Atte that daie
350 there is noothinge that we mai aunswere there, for heuen and erthe, sonne and moone, daie and nyght and alle the world shalle be ayens us in wittenesse of oure synnes. And yif alle these thingis holde her pees, oure thoughtis and oure werkis shalle be specialie ayens vs in accusinge us bifore God.'
355   The fourthe thinge that shalle be there shal be the [vn]desseiuable wittenesse, for than the synfulle shulle haue three witnessis ayens hym. The toone aboue hym, and that is God that shalle be iuge and wittenesse, whereof Seint Ierome seith: ' "I am iuge and wittenesse," seith oure Lorde.' Anothir wittenesse shalle be within hym, and that
360 is his propur conscience, whereof Seinte Augustine seith: 'Who that
H2 f. 254vb euer drede the | iuge [to] come, correcte his owne conscience. For the worde of thi mouthe is wittenesse of thi conscience.' The thrid wittenesse shalle be bysidis hym, and that shalle be thi propur aungelle ordeyned to thi kepinge, that shalle bere wittenesse ayenst
365 hym as he that knoweth alle that that he hath doone. So as Iob seith in the .xx.^ti chapiter: 'The heuen,' that is to seie the aungellis, 'shulle opene the iniquitees of hym.'
The .vij.^the thinge that shal fellishipp the iuge shalle be the constreinte of [the] synner, and thereof seith Seint Gregorie: 'O
370 howe the weies be fulle streite to the synneris. For the iuge fulle of wrath shalle be aboue, the dredefulle con[fus]ioun of helle shalle ben vndir, the synnes accusinge on the right side, and on the liffte side feendis without noumbre traueile and turment; within his conscience shalle brenne hym, and without alle the worlde brenninge. And the
375 wrecchid synner thus ouerleide on eueri side, whidir he shalle flee? Where [shalle he] hide hym? To hide hym hit is impossible and to appere it is intollerable.'
The .viij.^te thinge is the sentence nat ayenne callinge. For she may

---

348 whan . . . shalle] than shalle the creature H2A2   350 for] as L
352–3 thingis . . . pees] were stylle neþeles L   353 oure¹] add owne L
355 vndesseiuable] desseiuable H2A2   358 Seint] om. L   359 Anothir] the
.ij.^de A2   360–1 whereof . . . conscience] om. A2   361 to come] come and H2
correcte] add he L   363 and] om. L   thi] his A2   369 the] a H2   synner] add and
shalle fellishipp the iuge H2   370 weies] add shulle þan L   fulle] om. L   371 the]
this shal be a A2   confusioun] conclucion H2A2   of] and A2   ben] add opyn A2
373 noumbre] add And A2, add to L   375 whidir] where L   he shalle] trs. L
376 Where . . . hym¹] om. A2   shalle he] trs. H2   hym¹] add For L

neuer be callid ayenne. And in the causis of iugementis the appele is
nat receiued for three causis. First for the excellence of the iuge, for a 380
man mai nat repelle fro the kinge that yeueth sentence in his rewme
for he hath noo soueraine ouer hym. And also there mai noone repele
from the pope nor from the emperour. Secoundelie for the evidence
of the myssedeede, for whan it is knowen opunlie it mai nat be repelid.
Thridlie for that the thinge be nat prolongned, for perauenture yif she 385
were prolonged she sholde perisshe. And for that men appele nat from
these three sentencis, right so thei mowe nat appele from [this
sentence]. First [for] the excellence of the [k]inge, for there is none
aboue hym, but he surmountith alle othir bi euerlastingenesse, bi
dignite, and bi pouste. For from the em|perour and the pope men H2f.255ra
myght in some wise appele to God, but fro God thei mowe nat appele 391
to noone othere. Secondelie for the evidence of the missedeede, for
alle the wickid synnes of wickid doeris shulle appere and ben opene,
whereof Seint Ierome seithe: 'In that daie shulle alle oure deedis
appere right as the poyntis in a table.' Thridli the thinge shalle nat be 395
prolongid, for thinge that is done there shalle haue noo dilacioun, for
alle shalle be done in a moument as lightelie as the twynkelinge of an
ey3e.

Here endith the holie Aduente, and biginnith the Concepcioune of oure blessid Ladie, Capitulo .C°.lxxv[ij.^mo]

The concepcioun of the blessid Virgine Marie was founde bi Seinte
Ierome in his youthe within a litille booke, and sithen longe time aftir
atte praier of man[y] he wrote it oute in this manere.

   Ioachym was borne in the cite of Nazareth in Galilee and toke to his
wife Seinte Anne that was of Bedeleme, and boothe were fulle 5
rightwisse and without repreue, and in alle her werkis thei fulfillid
the commaundementis of God. And her goodis thei devidid in three

379 iugementis] iugement L, *add* and of A2   381 repelle] appele A2   382 mai]
add he A2   383 pope] *erased* L   385 the thinge] þe kyng L, it A2   prolongned]
enloyned L   386 prolonged] proloyned L   387 thei] the synfulle A2
387–8 this sentence] these three sentencis H2   388 First] *om.* A2   for¹] *om.* H2
kinge] thinge H2   389 but] For L   euerlastingenesse] everlastyngis L   390 pope]
erased L   393 appere . . . opene] þan appere opynly before þem and the iuge A2
394 whereof] wherfor L   395 poyntis] *add* doon A2   a table] the tables A2
396 prolongid] pleggid A2, proloynyd L   398 ey3e] *add Deo gracias* A2

H2L; D resumes at 163 *eueri yere*   *Rubric* endith . . . and] *om.* L   blessid] *om.* L
Ladie] *add* seynt Marye L   .C°.lxxvij.^mo] .C°.lxxv.^to H2   2 aftir] *om.* L   3 many]
mane H2   4 in¹] of L   5 and] *add* alle H2   fulle] *om.* L   7 commaundementis]
comaundement L

parties, and the too parte thei yafe to the Temple and to the seruauntis
thereof, the secounde thei departid amonge pilgrimes and pore men,
10 and the thrid parte thei withhelde for hemselff and her seruauntis.
And in this degree thei liueden the space of .xx^{ti}. wynter withouten
hauynge any frute of her bodies, and than eche of hem made a
solempne vowe to God that yf bi his grace he wolde sende hem any
frute thei wolde fulli yeue it to hys seruice.

15   So hit fille as thei were wonte to goo to Ierusalem atte three
principalle feestis, hit fille that Ioachym went with his kinrede to
Ierusalem and neyghid hym to the autier to haue offrid his offringe
with othir. And whan the preeste of the lawe saugh hym, with grete
indignacioun he refusid his offringe and askid hym howe he durst
H2 f. 255rb presume | [to] nyghe the autier and repreued hym gretelie, seienge
21 that it was [nat] resonable that he which was cursed in the lawe of
God, [and had no frute of his body ne encresid nat the puple of God,]
shulde be with hem that hadden frute of her bodie. Whan Ioachym
saugh hym thus rebukid, he was [so] confused with shame that he had
25 nat turned to his owne hous to that eende that he wolde nat be scorned
ne shamed of his neightbours that had herde these wordis, but turned
to his shepperdis that were in the feeldis.

And whan he had be there a litille, on a daie as he was allone an
aungelle of heuen apperid to hym with grete light, and he was gretelie
30 merueilid with this vision. And than the aungelle bad hym that he
shulde be nat afferde and seid to hym: 'I am the aungelle of God
which hath sent me to the to anounce to the that thi praieris and thine
almes be enhauncid and lift vp bifore God. I haue herde thi shame and
seene th[e] velanye of thi bareynnesse which haue be seide to the
35 without cause. But sometime oure Lorde through his plesaunce
closeth the wombis of wommen fro beringe of frute, and sithen
afftir meruouslie he sheweth his vertues in token that the frute
procedith nat of the wickid delectacioun of luxurie ne of con-
cupiscence of the flesshe but bi a specialle yifft of God.

40   'Sarra the frist moodir of moch puple, was she nat bareine into .iiij.
score yere and .x., and natwithstandinge that she conceiued Isaak to
whom the blessinge of God and of alle men was youen? Rachelle, was
she nat bareine bi longe time and natwithstondinge she bare Ioseph

9 amonge] *add* the H2   15 three] *om.* L   16–17 with . . . kinrede/to Ierusalem]
trs. L   20 to] so H2   seienge] and seide L   21 nat] *om.* H2L   22 and . . . God]
om. H2   24 so] *om.* H2   24–5 had nat] wolde nat have L   28 litille] *add* tyme L
daie] tyme L   29 apperid . . . hym/with . . . light] *trs.* L   30 with] of L   31 I
am] þat he was L   34 the^1] thi H2   41 conceiued] *add* and bare L

that gouerned alle the reame of Egipte? Who was euere strenger than
Sampsoun or holier than Samuelle that boothe moodris, doughtris 45
and kinrede were bareine? Wherefor bi these resouns and ensaumplis
be verie trewe, but to shewe more meruouslie the [bryngynge] forth of
children of bareine wommen. And I lete the wite that oure Lorde wille
that thi wiffe shalle bere a doughtir, the which thou shalt calle Marie,
and knowe it welle that she shalle be hallowid within the wombe of hir 50
moodir and fullie sacrid to God. And | she shalle be fulfillid with the H2 f. 255va
holye gooste and she shalle nat be conuersaunt amonge the puple but
abide alleweie in the Temple of oure Lorde so that none euelle
suspecioun be had of hir.

'And right as she shalle be borne of a bareine womman, right so shal 55
be borne of hir the sone of the right high euerlastinge that shalle be
callid Ihesu, and bi hym shalle be youen hele and saluacioun to alle the
puple. And in tokenne hereof, whan thou commyst to Ierusalem atte
gilden gate, thou shalte mete with thi wiffe Anne that hath grete desire
of [thi] retournynge ayenne, and whan she shalle se the shc shalle haue 60
grete ioie.' And whan the aungelle had seide this to hym he vanisshid
aweie.

And on the tothir side Anne went continuelli and cowde fynde no
comforte, for she wist neuere where hir husbonde was bicome. Than
that same aungelle apperid to hir and anouncid to hir in the same wise 65
that he had done to hir husbonde, and seide to hir that she sholde goo
into Ierusalem to the gilden gate and there shulde fynde her husbonde
that was come ayenne. And so afftir the worde of the aungelle thei
mette togidirs. And of the visioune that they had seine thei were fulle
of gladnesse and thei were certeine of the promesse that was made 70
hem. And whan thei had worshippid our Lorde thei turned ayenne to
her owne hous and gladlie abode the biheste made to hem as it is seide
bifore.

Than Anne conceiued and brought forth a doughtir named Marie.
And whan three yere were fulfillid she was take fro the brest, and 75
[thei] ledde hir and offrid the blessid Virgine to the Temple of God
with her othir offringis. And the Temple was on an high hille and
therefor men myght nat eselie gone but bi degrees, whereof there were

44 than] *add* was L   45 moodris] *add* and L   46 kinrede] *add* þat L
ensaumplis] *add* to L   47 bryngynge] beginnins H2   51 she . . . be] *om.* L
56 right] *om.* L   60 thi] the H2   she²] yee L   61 had] *om.* L   this] þus L
63 And] *om.* L   fynde] nat take L   64 neuere] not L   67 there] *add* she L
71 And] *om.* L   75 And] *om.* L   fulfillid] *add* þat L   76 thei] *om.* H2   hir] *om.* L
offrid] *add* hir H2   blessid] *om.* L   77 And] *om.* L   78 gone] *add* vp L

.xv. And the Virgine Marie was sette on the lowest degree, but anone
80 allone without helpe of any creature, seenge alle the puple, she stied
vp .xv. grees as lightelie as though she had be of parfite age. And when
H2 f. 255ᵛᵇ hir offringis were fulfillid, thei lefft | hir doughter Marie in the
Temple amonge othir virginnes and turned ayenne to her hous.

This holie Virgine Marie profitid euerie daie in holinesse and was
85 continuelli vesitid with aungellis, the which serued hir with spirituelle
foode of heuenlie consolacioun. Seint Ierome seith in a pistille to
Cromacien and to Eli[o]dre that she toke on hir this rule, that fro the
morowetide into the Tiers she was in hir praieris, and from Tiers into
the Houre of None she [wounde] and wrought silke werke, and from
90 None she went ayenne to hir praieris vnto the tyme that an aungelle
come fro heuen and brought hir refeccioun. And thus she abode tille
she was [.xiiij.] yere of age, and than she was weddid vnto Ioseph as it
is shewed in the legende of our blessid Ladie.

And it was fulle longe time or any bodie hallowed this feeste of the
95 Concepcioun of oure Ladie, but that blessid Virgine Marie wolde that
hit sholde be halowid, as it sheweth bi manie notable meraclis. Frist bi
Seinte Ancelme in a pistille that he wrote to the bisshoppis of
Engelonde, where he tellith [of] an abbot that was callid Helsyn the
which was sent to the rewme of Denemark fro the kinge of Engelonde
100 to make a treete of pees, for thoo of Denemarke had ordeined a grete
noumbre of men of armes to putte Engelonde in subieccioun as her
propur heritage. And whan he made the pees, in his turnenge ayenne,
whan he had passed the grettest partie of the see, the tempestis and
the turmentis come so grete within the see and so feerefulli that the
105 shipmen cowde no remedie for to saile, and the kables and alle her
ordenauncis alle tobrake and the shippemen bigan to perissh.

And than thei alle togidirs biganne deuoutlie to praie to oure Ladie
the moodir of God. And the abbot Helsyn sawe come amonge the
wawes of the see a semelie prelate reue[st]id *in pontificalibus*, the
110 whiche neyghid to hem and biganne to seie vnto hem: 'Wille ye turne
sauff and hole into youre contre and escape this presente perile of the

79 And] *om.* L   80 seenge] *add* to H2   81 grees] degrees L   though] *om.* L
of] *add* a L   86 of] and L   to] of L   87 Eliodre] Elicidre H2   the] *om.* L
89 wounde] went H2   92 .xiiij.] .xvij. H2   93 is shewed] shewith L   blessid] *om.* L
94 And] *om.* L   97 Ancelme] Auselyne L   98 of] that H2   101 in] *add* her L
102 And] *om.* L   he] *add* had L   103 tempestis] tempest L   103–4 and the
turmentis] *om.* L   105 to saile] þe saylis L   the] *om.* L   105–6 and alle her
ordenauncis] *om.* L   106 tobrake] tobrast L   shippemen] ship L   108 the¹] *om.* L
come] comyng L   109 semelie] worthy L   revestid] reuersid H2   110 hem¹]
hym L   vnto hem] to hym L   Wille ye] wolte þow L   111 youre] þy L

see wherein ye are nowe?' And than Helsynne seide: | 'Allas there is no H2 f. 256ra
resonable thinge but that I fayne wolde doo it to escape this pereile
that I am inne nowe.' Than seide this prelate: 'Yiff thou wilte make
the Concepcioun of oure Ladye to be hallowid ouer alle, thou shalt 115
escape froo this perelle.' And than the abbot Helsynne askid hym in
what daie and what seruice, and the prelate seid the [.viij. daie of
Decembre he shulde halowe hir feest, and thei shulde do the same]
seruice of the Natiuite, sauff there as is seide 'Nativite' ye shalle [seye]
'Concepcioun.' And than the abbot Helsynne bihighte deuoutelie that 120
fulle gladlie he wolde doo it with alle manere reuerence. And anone
whan alle this was done thei founde hemselff sauff on the costis of
Engelonde and there arriuid graciouslie. And anone aftir the abbot
Helsyn ordeined that the Concepcioun of oure Lady shulde be yerelie
reuerentlie hallowid ouer alle on the daie abouc seide and in the 125
manere aboue written.

Of anothir notable meracle we reede also of a certeine preeste that
come on a time fro the fulfillinge of a foule synne of aduoutrie in a
shippe by the ryuer of Sayne. And as he was in seienge the Oures of
oure Ladie he perisshed sodeinliche and anone the feendis toke hym 130
and turmentid hym wondir greuouslie. And [the thridde daie] the
blessid [Virgine Marie come into the place where thei turmentid hym,
and she] seide to hem in this manere wise as hit followith: 'Yee
feendis, whi turment ye so the soule of my seruaunte?' And than the
feendis aunswerid and seid: 'We turmente hym thus skilfullie for as 135
moche as we fonde hym in oure seruice, and therein wee toke hym.'
Than aunswerid the blessid Virgine Marie: 'Alleweie notwithstan-
dinge that, he died and is deede in my seruice seienge the Matenes
and Houris of me fulle deuoutelie.' And than anone alle the feendis
his enemies fledden aweie from hym. 140

And than oure Ladie put the soule within his bodie ayenne and
anone arerid hym fro dethe to life. And than she toke hym bi the arme
and drowe hym out of the botome of the watir and brought hym to the

112 ye are] þowe art L 113 that] om. L this] þe L 114 this prelate] he to
hym L 116 the abbot] om. L 117 ins. in margin daie of decembre not in hand of
Ricardus H2 the prelate] he L seid] add to hym L 117-18 .viij. . . . same] om. H2
119 seruice] add he shuld make L of the] that L Natiuite] add is L seye] om. H2
121 fulle gladlie] om. L it] add gladly L anone] add sodenly L 122 sauff] in safte L
124 Helsyn] om. L the] add feest of þe L 125 aboue] afore L 127 we reede/
also] trs. L 128 on] in L a²] þe L 131 the thridde daie] om. H2
132-3 Virgine . . . she] ladie than H2 136 as] add þat L 137 aunswerid/the . . .
Marie] trs. with lady for Virgine Marie L 139 and] add þe L 141 than] om. L
142 anone] om. L than she] om. L

H2 f. 256rb ryuer side hoole and sounde. And than the preeste fille doun | to her
145 feete, [and seide] full deuouteli and mekeli: 'O blessid Ladi, what
maner seruice mai I offre to your high and worthy goodenes for this
grete grace and benefete that ye haue done nowe to me, that yif ne
ye had be I had be dampned and deuourid with the cursed feendis.'
And than aunswerid the blessid Virgine Marie moodir of God and
150 seide in this wise to the preeste: 'Thou shalt in the worshipp of me
and of my name and for the loue of me hallowe the Feeste of my
Concepcioun and to alle thi powere make it to be hallowid ouer alle
the .viij. daie of Decembre.'

Anothir ensaumple of a dekenne that was brothir to the kinge of
155 Hungrie, the whiche bi councelle of his specialle freendis shuld be
maried alle thinge to leue, and so it happid that in the mene time on a
daie while that the forseide dekenne seide the Houris of oure Ladie,
while he seide this anteme: *Pulchra es decora filia Iherusalem,* sodeinlie
than apperid to him oure blessid Ladie and seide to hym in this
160 maner: 'Yif it be so that I am so faire as thou seist, whi wilt thou than
forsake me for any other?' And than this yonge man seide: 'My blessid
Ladye, telle me what I shalle doo to thi worshipp and plesaunce.' And
D f. 157ra than she aunswerid hym and seide: 'Yif thou wilt | eueri yere as it
commyth about hallowe deuoutelie the Feest of my Concepcioun on
165 the .viij^{te}. daie of the moneth of Decembre, thou shalt be crowned in
the kingdome of heuen. And anone he lefft and forsoke alle the worlde
and the busines thereof and bicome a [preest, and afftir he was made a]
monke. And afftir þat it felle so þat he was made patriark of Aquile
and than he hallowid and made to be hallowid the forseid Feeste of the
170 Concepcioun of oure Ladie.

A solempne clerk of devinite that was callid Alizaundre tellith þat
whan he redde in þe vniuersite of the toune of Oxunforde in the
rewme of Engelonde and euery daie he redde on the daie of the
concepcioune of oure Ladie and he repugned gretelie ayenst that
175 feeste, but [as] he telleth in a sermon that biginnith ⟨*Fiat lux*⟩, alle
thoo yeeris whan he sholde haue redde he was smeten with a sodeine

144 side] *add* alle L   145 and seide] *om.* H2   147 done nowe] *trs.* L   yif] els L
148 ye had] had yee ne L   the] þoo L   149 aunswerid/the . . . God] *trs.* L
150 the worshipp of me] in my worship L   151 of my] *om.* L   152 alle] *add* in L
153 daie] *add* in the monthe L   157 forseide] seide L   158 es] *add* et L
159 apperid/to him] *trs.* L   blessid] *om.* L   to hym] *om.* L   163 than] *om.* L.
164 deuoutelie] *om.* L   165 the moneth of] *om.* L   166 lefft and] *om.* L
167 preest . . . a] *om.* H2   168 afftir þat] *om.* L   169 than he] *om.* L   hallowid] *add*
solemply L   172 of¹] in L   173 euery daie] ever L   175 as] *om.* H2   *Fiat lux*]
illeg. D

sikenesse þat he myght nat rede. And from thens forwarde he prechid to alle folke þat thei shulde holde the solempne feeste of þe Concepcioun of oure Ladie, wherefor Seinte Ancelme in a solempne pistille that he wrote to the kinge of Engelond seith in concludinge, 180 'He is nat vereie seruaunte of þe blessid Virgine Marie þat refuseth to hallowe þe Feeste of the Concepcioun of oure Ladie.'

Here endith the feste of the Concepcion of oure Ladie, and biginnith the life of Adam and of Eve, Cap°. .C°.lxxv[ii]j.°

⟨No⟩w take hede that whan oure ⟨Lor⟩de God had made heuen and erthe and alle the ornamentis ⟨of⟩ hem, God sawe that thei were ⟨g⟩oode and seide: 'Make we man ⟨vnto oure ymage and⟩ liknesse, and be he soueraine to the ⟨fishis of t⟩he see and to the volatiles of heuen and to ⟨the vn⟩rcsonable beestis of the eerthe and to eche crea⟨ture⟩ 5 and to eche reptile which is meued in the erthe.'

⟨And⟩ God made of naught man to his ymage and lik⟨nesse⟩, God made of nouȝt man to the ymage ⟨of⟩ God, [God] made of nought [hem] male and female. And [God] blessid ⟨he⟩m and seide: 'Encrece yee and be ye multiplied and felle ⟨ye⟩e the erthe, and make ye it 10 sogette, and be ye lordis ⟨to⟩ the fisshis of the see and to the volatilis of heuen and to alle livinge beestis on erthe.' And [God seide]: 'Loo, I haue youen to you eche herbe beringe seede on erthe and alle trees that haue in hemselff seede in her kinde, that thei be into meete to you and to alle livinge beestis on erthe, and to eche bridde of heuen and to 15 alle thingis that ben meued on the erthe [and] in which is a livinge soule, | that [thei] haue to ete.' And hit was done so, and God sawȝ alle Df. 157ʳᵇ thingis which þat he made, and thoo were fulle good.

Than oure Lorde God fourmed man of the slyme of the erthe and

181 Virgine] *add* seynt L

DHEA2LHbWhDoHc; E is legible with some losses up to 324 *hym* (E *hcm*), and thereafter largely illegible through rubbing and losses, breaking off after 500 *doun*. The text in Wh (ed. Mabel Day, EETS OS 155) is close to that of E, so the whole chapter is here based on D, and where D is defective on H2. D breaks off after 273 *þat* and resumes at 414 *and herdist* and has losses caused by excisions in 1–11, 63–6 and 107–21; Hc breaks off after 34 *went* and resumes at 270 *beynge*   Rubric .C°.lxxviij.°] .C°.lxxvj.° D   1 God] *om.* L 1–2 and erthe] *om.* HbWhDo   7 made] *om.* Hc   8 of¹ . . . made] *om.* E, hem L of¹] *add* man D   nouȝt] *add* and D   God²] *om.* DHb   9 hem¹] *om.* DL   God] *om.* D 11 ye] *add* the D   12 beestis] *add* þat ben HbWhDoHc   God seide] *om.* D   I] *add* am he þat L   13–14 on . . . seede] *om.* E   14 meete to] *om.* Do   15 and to eche] *om.* Hc   16 and] *om.* D   a] þe L   17 thei] ye D   ete] ȝete Hb   18 good] *add* Gen .J.° EHb   19 the¹·²] *om.* E

20 spired into the face of hym an entre of brethe of life, and [made is]
man into a soule yevinge liffe. Adam was made of oure Lorde God
in the vale of Ebronne, and there of foure corneris of the worlde
Adam[es bodi] was made, and aungel[es] brouȝt þat erthe fro thoo
foure parties, the which aungellis ben clepid Michaelle, Gabrielle,
25 Raphaelle and Vrielle. And the erthe þat these aungellis broughten
was bright and shininge as þe sonne, and þat erthe was brought out of
foure floodis, þat is to seie Geon, Phison, Tigres and Euffrates. Than
is man like the ymage of God made, and God blewȝ in his face
enspiringe of life, þat is to seie his soule. And so he was made of .iiij.
30 parties of the erthe, and also of .iiij. manere of wyndis of the
firmament he was enspired.

Than oure Lorde God whan Adam was made [had] youen hym [no]
name as yit, and than God seide to the .iiij. angellis that thei shulde
seche hym a name. And than Michaelle went forth into the este, and
35 there he sawȝe þe sterre that hight Annotalum, and he toke the frist
lettere þereof. And Raphaelle went forth into the southe and fonde
there the sterre of the southe that hight Dises, and he toke the frist
letter þereof. And Gabrielle went into the north, and fonde there the
sterre of the north that hight Arthos, and he toke the frist letter
40 thereof. And than Vrielle went into the west and fonde there the sterre
[of the west] that hight Memsembrion, and he toke the frist letter
thereof. And than these lettris were brought to oure Lorde, and he
bad Vrielle rede hem, and he radde hem and seide: 'Adam.' And than
oure Lorde seide: 'So shalle his name be callid.' *Vnde versus: Annotale*
45 *dedit A, Disis D, [A] contulit Arthos, M Memsembrion; collige fiet Adam.*

And ye shulle vndirstonde that Adam was made of .viij. thingis. Oo
partie was made of þe slyme of the erthe, whereof his flesshe was, and
thereof he is slowe. Anothir parte was of the see, whereof his bloode
was, and thereof he is couetous and busie. The thrid parte was of
50 stoones of the erthe, and thereof he is harde and bitter. The fourþe

20 brethe of life] life and brethe L　　made is] made his HbDo, *trs.* D　　　　21 soule] *add*
lyving DL　　made] *add* in þe same place Wh　　　　22 in the vale of Ebronne] where þat
Ihesu Crist was born ynne, þat is in þe cytee of Bethleem which is in þe myddil of þe erþe
Wh　　　　23 Adames bodi] Adam D　　aungeles] an aungelle D　　　　24 clepid] *om.*
EHbWhDoHc　　　28 made] *add* of god L　　　30–1 of the firmament] *om.* EHbWhDoHc
32 had] and D　　no] a D　　　33 as yit] *om.* EHbWhDoHc　　　36–40 Raphaelle . . .
þereof/And Gabrielle . . . thereof] *trs.* L　　　36 went] *add* forthe EL　　　41 of the west]
om. D　　　42 thereof] *om.* L　　　44 *Vnde*] *om.* HbWhDo　　*Vnde versus*] *om.* L　　*versus*]
Iersus E　　　45 *A²*] *om.* DEL　　*contulit*] *add A* L　　*Adam*] *om.* Wh　　　46 .viij.] .iiij. L
47 made] *om.* EHbWhDo　　　47–8 and . . . slowe] *om.* Do　　　48 Anothir] And a E
49 thereof . . . and] *om.* L

parte was of the clowdis, whereof be his thynkingis | wrought, and D f. 157ᵛᵃ
thereof he is lecherous. The .v.ᵗᵉ parte was of the winde, whereof is
made his brethe, and thereof he is light. The .vj.ᵗᵉ parte was of the
sonne, and there[of] ben his ey3en, and thereof he is faire and clere.
The .vij.ᵗᵉ parte is of the light of the worlde, whereof he is made 55
gladde, and thereof he hath his vndirstondinge. The .viij.ᵗᵉ parte is of
the holie gooste and thereof is [mannis] soule, and thereof ben these
holie prophetis and alle [Goddis chosen].

Forsothe [þe] Lorde `God´ hath plantid paradis of delite from the
biginnynge, in the which he sette man whan he had fourmed hym. 60
And oure Lorde God brought forth of the erthe ech a tree faire of
sight and swete to eete, also the tree of life in the myddille of paradis,
and he toke man and putte hym in paradis and ⟨he plantid⟩ the tree of
knowinge good and eville. ⟨Than oure⟩ Lorde toke man and putte him
in parad⟨is of delite⟩ that he shulde worche and kepe it. And he 65
⟨comman⟩did hym seienge: 'Of eche a tree of paradis eete of, sauff of
the tree of knowinge goode and euelle eete thou nou3t, and what daie
that euer thou eete thereof, with deeth thou shalt die.'

Also the Lorde God forsoth seide: 'It is nat good to a man to be
allone. Make we to hym an helpe like to hym.' The Lorde God 70
fourmed of the mooste erthe alle thingis of the erthe havinge soule and
alle volatilis of heuen, and oure Lorde God brou3t hem to Adam þat
he shuld se what he shuld clepe hem. Alle thingis forsothe of soule
livinge afftir the kinde and propirte of it he yafe it name, and right as
Adam cleped hem is [such] the name of hem. But vnto Adam forsothe 75
was nought founde an helpe [like] to hym.

Then sent the Lorde God sleepe vnto Adam, and whan he was
asleepe, he toke oone of his ribbis and fulled flesshe for it, and than
our Lorde God edefied that ribbe the which he toke from Adam into a
woman, and brou3t hir to Adam. Than Adam seide: 'This is nowe a 80
boone of my boones and flesshe of my flesshe, this shalle be clepid
mannes deede, for she is taken of man. Wherefor a man shalle forsake

51 was] add made E   thynkingis] thingis Hb   52 was] add made E   53 was]
add made E   54 thercof] there D   ben] he E   55 worlde] word Do
57 mannis] made his D   58 Goddis chosen] goodis D, Goddis children Wh
59 þe] om. D   63 he¹] a tree of knowinge of good and yuel thanne the lord Do   he
plantid the] a EWh   63-5 and³ . . . paradis] om. LDo   65 it] om. Hb   66 of
sauff] om. EHbWhDo, but L   67-8 what . . . euer] what euere day EHbWh, what
euery day Do   71 mooste erthe] erthe þat was moyst L   72 volatilis] volatile
HbWh   73 shuld²] add kepe hem and L   74 right] suche L   75 such]
alleweie sith D   forsothe] om. L   76 helpe] helpere HbWhDo   like] om. D
78 fulled] fulfelled ELHbDo

fadir and moodir and drawe to his wiffe, and thei shulle be twoo in oo
flesshe.' And eithir of hem forsothe was nakid, and þat was Adam and
85 Eve his wiffe and thei shamed nat.

But the adder was feller than any livers of the erthe which the
Lorde God made, whiche addere seide to þe woman: 'Whi
D f. 157vb commaundid | God to you that 3e shulde nat eete of eche tree of
paradis?' To whom the womman aunswerid and seid: 'Of the frute of
90 the trees þat ben in paradis wee ete off, [but of the frute] of þe tree þat
is in the myddis of paradis commaundid God vs that we shulde nat
eete, ne that we shulde nat touche hit, lest perauenture we deie.'
'Forsothe,' quod the addere to the woman, 'throu3 dethe ye shulle nat
deie, but God wote welle forsothe that what daie ye eete þerof youre
95 ey3en shulle be opened and ye shulle be as goddis, knowenge goode
and eville.' Than the woman sawe welle that the tree was goode and
swete [for to ete] and faire to the ey3e and delectable to the sight, and
she toke of the frute and eete þereof and yafe to [her] man, the which
eete þereof also. And than the eyen of hem boþe were opened, and
100 whan thei knewe hemselff to be nakid, thei sowed togedirs leves of
figge trees and made hem breches.

And whan thei hurde the vois of þe Lorde God goynge in paradis
and the shininge afftir middaie, Adam and his wiffe hidde hem from
the face of the Lorde God in the myddis of the trees of paradis. And
105 than the Lorde God cleped Adam and seide to hym: 'Where art thou,
Adam?' And than he aunswerid and seide: 'Lorde, I hurde thi vois in
paradis, but I dradde therethrou3 [that] I was nakid, and ⟨hidde⟩ me.'
To whom the Lorde God seide: 'Who f⟨orsothe⟩ shewed the that thou
were n⟨akid, but that thou ete⟩ of the tree of which I comma⟨undid the
110 that thou shold⟩ist nat eete?' And than Ada⟨m seide: 'The womman
that⟩ thou yafe me to fellawe yafe ⟨to me of the [tree], and⟩ I ete
thereof.' And oure Lorde ⟨God seide to the womman⟩: 'Whi didist

85 nat] add Gen. .iij°. EHbWh   86 livers] liberd is L   87 addere] om.
ELHbWhDo   þe] add yonge D   89 and seid] om. ELHbWhDo   90 but . . . frute]
sauff D   93 quod the addere] the eddre saide ELHbWhDo   94 welle] om.
ELHbWhDo   what] what euer EHbWhDo, every L   96 sawe welle] seithe E, sawe
LHbWhDo   97 for to ete] om. D   delectable] delitable HbWhDo   98 frute] add of
it ELHbWhDo   and eete] om. Wh   þereof] om. ELHbWhDo   her] the D
99 þereof also] om. ELHbWhDo   101 breches] add þereof to hide þerewith her preue
membris D   103 and¹] add yn Hb   104 the trees of] om. Do   106 Adam . . .
and] whiche ELHbWhDo   Lorde] om. ELHbWhDo   107 but] and EHbWhDo, om. L
therethrou3] the thorugh E, þe`re´ þorow L   that] for D   109 nakid] add no E, add
nat L   111 yafe¹] made L   me to fellawe] felowe to me LWh   tree] frute H2, excised D
I] om. L   112 thereof] om. ELHbWhDo

thou soo?' And than ⟨the womman aunswerid⟩ and seide: 'The adder begilid me and I eete ⟨þereof.' And⟩ than the Lord God seide to the serpent: 'For tha⟨t thou⟩ hast doo this thinge, þou shalt be cursid 115 amonge ⟨alle⟩ the soul[e hauers] and beestis of þe erthe, and v⟨ppone⟩ thi brest thou shalt goo and erthe thou shalt e⟨te⟩ alle þe daies of thi live, and enemytees I shalle p⟨utte⟩ bitwene the and [the] woman and thi seede and hir ⟨seede; she⟩ shalle treede thine heede and thou shalt espie to ⟨hir⟩ hele.' 120

And also to the woman [forsothe] God sei⟨de⟩: 'I shalle multiplie thi deseses and thi conceivingis and in sorowe thou shalt bere thi childrenne, and thou shalt be vndir the powere of man and he shalle haue lordeshippe ouer the.' And than [to Adam forsothe God seide]: 'For þat þou hast herde þe voice of thi wiffe and þat þou hast etennc 125 of þe tree of which I | commaundid þat þou sholdist nat eete, cursid is Df.158ᵃ þe erthe in thi werke and in traueile þou shalt eete of it alle the daies of thi life; and it shalle [burione to] the thornes and breris, and þou shalt ete the herbis of the erthe in [the] swote of thi chere [or] face, and thou shalt ete thi brede vnto the time þat thou shalt turne ayenne vnto 130 the erthe of which thou art take and imade of. Forsoth, poudir þou art and to poudir thou shalt turne.'

And Adam cleped the name of his wiffe Eve, tho[r]uȝ [þat þat] she was moodir of alle thingis livinge. Also forsothe the Lorde God made to Adam and to his wiffe letheren cootes and clothid hem and seide: 135 'Se, Adam is made as oone of vs, knowinge goode and eville; nowe perauenture he puttith out his honde and takith also of the tree of life and ete and liv[e] euermore.' And the Lorde God sent hym out of paradis of delite that he shulde werche in the erthe of the which [he was] take and made of, and he threuȝ out Adam and sette cherubyn 140 bifore paradice of delite and a flawmynge swerde and a pliaunt to [the weie of the tree of live to be kept].

116 soule hauers] soulis heiris D, soulis of heven L   118 enemytees] enemyes L, Vnreste Wh   thc²] om. D   119 she] om. L   121 forsothe] oure Lorde D   seide] add Forsothe D   124 to Adam . . . seide] the lord god seide to Adam forsothe D 126 commaundid] add the E   127 in¹] and Hb   and in] in LHbWhDo, is E 128 burione to] bere vnto D   129 in the] in D, and þe Hb   chere, face] trs. Wh   or] and D   and] twice D   131 and imade of] om. EHbWhDo, and made L   Forsoth] for HbWhDo   133 thoruȝ þat þat] thouȝ D   135 his wiffe] Eve L   136 vs] om. L 137 takith] toke E   of²] add his   138 live] livid D   hym] om. Do   139–40 he was] om. D   140 and made of] om. ELHbWhDo   141–2 the weie . . . kept] kepe the weie towardis the tree of live D

This þat followeth was done afftir that Adam was cast
out of paradis into this woofulle place.

145   Afftir that Adam and Eve were cast out of paradis, thei went into
the west and made hem there a tabernacle, and thereinne thei dwellid
.vij. daies, wepenge, louringe and crienge in moost tribulacioun. And
afftir thoo .vij. daies thei begonne to hungre and sought mete and
founde noone that thei myght eete of. And than seide Eve unto Adam:
150   'My lorde, I hungre sore. Whi goo ye nat to seche some thinge þat we
myght ete and therebi live, yif perauenture oure Lorde God wille loke
on vs and haue mercie on vs and clepe vs ayenne to the steede þat we
woned inne friste?'
Than aroos Adam afftir thoo .vij. daies and yede about the londe
155   .vij. daies and fonde noo such mete as thei had in paradis. Than seide
Eve vnto Adam efte: 'A, my lorde, I deie for hungre. Wolde God þat I
myght deie or ellis be slaine of the, my lorde, for whi for me God is
wrooth with the.' And than seide Adam: 'Grete is in heuen and in
erthe his wrath, whethir it be for me or for the I note.' And eft seide
160   Eve vn[to] Adam: 'My lorde, slee me, that I mai be done aweie fro the
face of God and fro the sight of his aungellis, so þat oure Lorde God
foryete to be wrothe with the, so that he myght lede the ayenne into
paradis, for whi for the cause of me thou art put out thereof.' Than
seide Adam: 'Speke no more so, lest oure Lorde God sende his
165   malisoune on us. Howe myght it be þat I shulde putte myne hond |
Df.158rb   into my flesshe, þat is to seie, howe myght it be that I myght slee my
flesshe? But arise and goo we and seche we wherewith to live, ne stent
we nat to sech it.'
Than thei went forth and sought .ix. daies, but þei fonde nat such
170   as thei had in paradis, but neuertheles thei founde such as beestis
etenne. Than seid Adam to Eve: 'Oure Lorde God deliuerid [mete to
beestis but to vs he deliuerid] mete of aungellis, wherefore make we
sorowe and doo penaunce bifore the sight of oure Lorde that made vs

143 followeth] suithe EHbDo, suwiþ now aftir Wh   144 woofulle] *add* vale and Do
place] worlde L, *add* of sorowe and of wrecchidnesse Do   147 louringe] lorwing E,
sorwyng HbWhDo   moost] gretest HbWh   150 seche some] suche L, seche HbWhDo
153 inne] *om.* EHbWhDo   154 londe] *add* oþere Wh   156 A] *om.* ELHbWhDo
157 be] that y were ELHbWhDo   my lorde] *om.* ELHbWhDo   160 vnto] vn D
161–2 oure . . . so that] *om.* Hb   162 with the] *add* for me L   the²] *om.* L
164 Adam] *add* Eue EHbWhDo, *add* to Eue L   166 howe . . . be] *om.* L   169 forth]
om. ELHbWhDo   171–2 mete . . . deliuerid] vs D   172 wherefore] but
ELHbWhDo   173 and doo penaunce] *om.* HbWh

.xl. daies, yif happelie oure Lorde God þat made vs foryeue vs and
ordeine vs wherewith to liven.'   175
   Than seide Eve to Adam: 'My Lorde, what is penaunce or howe
shuld we doo penaunce, lest happelie þat we take on vs that we mai
nat fulfille, and oure praieris be nat herde and God turne his face from
vs, yif we fulfille nat that we haue bihote? Thou, my lorde, whi seidist
þou so? Whi thoughtist thou to doo penaunce, for I haue brought the   180
to tribulacion?' Than seid Adam to Eve: 'Myghtist thou nat suffre as
many daies as I mai? Suffre [as many] and thou shalt be sauff. I shal
suffre .xl. daies and .vij., for alle thingis were made, confermed and
blessid in .vij. daies. Arise and goo thou to the floode of Tigree, and
bere a stoone with the and stonde thou thereon in the watir vp to the 185
necke, and let noo worde come out of thi mouþe, for we ben vnworthi
to praie to God, for oure lippes ben vnclene for we etenne of the
forboden tree. Be thou there .xl. daies, and I shalle goo into flome
Iordan and be there .xl. daies and .vij., yif happelie oure Lorde God
wille haue mercie on vs.'   190
   Than Eve went to the watir of Tigree as Adam bad hir, and Adam
went to the flome Iordane and leide his stoone and stoode thereon vp
to the necke in the floode, and the heere of his hede was spred abroode
on the watir. Than seide Adam: 'I seie to the, Iordan, gedre togidir thi
wawes and alle livinge beestis within the and com about me and make 195
sorowe [with] me, but for youreselff make ye noo sorowe but alle for
me, for ye haue nat synned, but I wickidlie ayenst my Lorde haue
synned; nothir ye did noo defaute, ne ye were nat begilid from your
sustenaunce ne from youre meetis ordeined for you, but I am begilid
fro my sustenaunce the whiche was ordeined for me.'   200

   See here how that alle thingis [livinge] sorowedene with Adam.

   Whane Adam had made alle this lamentacion | with sighynge and D f. 158ᵛᵃ
sorowefulle teeris, than alle livinge thingis on erthe, fisshe, foule and
beeste, come aboute hym in makinge sorowe with hym, and also the
watir stode stille in þat tyme of praienge. Than Adam with   205

176 Lorde] add saie me ELHbWh   howe] om. Do   176–7 or . . . penaunce] om. L
177 doo] be E   179 seidist] seyst HbWh   180 Whi] þow Hb   thou] ins. Hb   182 as
many] om. DL   183 thingis] add that D   188–9 I . . . and¹] om. Hb   191 went] yede
EWhDo   192 went] yode EHbWhDo   stoone] add in þe botme of þe watir Wh
195 wawes] waters E   within the] with thine eighe E   196 with] om. D   but] not
ELHbWhDo   make] made E   noo] om. EHbWhDo   198 from] for HbWh   199 from]
for HbWh   200 fro] for Wh   201 See here how that] om. Hb   here] om. EDo, now Wh
livinge] om. D, add vpon erthe Do   sorowedene] add togedre HbWh   202 alle] om. Do
204 also] om. ELHbWhDo   205 watir] add soruyngly Wh   stille] full E

teeris crie[d] to the Lorde God fro daie to daie, so that his voice waxe
hors.

And whan .xix. daies of his sorowe were fulfillid with Adam and
alle livinge thingis þat sorowed with hym for his synne, than his
210 aduersarie the feende, stered with wrath and envie to hym warde,
transfigurid hym into an aungelle oþere to a faire ymage, and went to
the floode of Tigre there Eve was sorowinge, and he come to hir and
wepte with hir. And than the feende seide to hir: 'Come out of the
floode and wepe noo more, for þou art dischargid of alle thine othir
215 penaunce; for God hath seene youre sorowes and hath foryeuen to you
your trespas atte praier of me and of alle othir aungellis. Com out, for
Adam is out. And God sent me to the to lede Adam and the vnto your
sustenaunce ayenne the which yee hadden in paradis and lost for your
synne. Therefor come out, þat ye were at youre mete that is made
220 redie for you.'

Than Eve come out of the watir, and hir flesshe was grene as gres
for coold of the watir. And whan she come to londe, she fille doune for
febilnesse and laie there stille as deede allmoost a daie. And than the
feende toke hir vp and comfortid hir and brought hir to Adam.

225 And whan Adam saw3 hir, he cried wepenge: 'O Eve, where is the
werk of thi penaunce? Howe is it that oure enemye hath begilid the,
the which begilid vs from oure dwellinge place in paradis and fro oure
goostelie ioie?' And whan Eve hurde this [she knewe herselff] begilid
throu3 þe feende [and] fille grouelinge to þe erthe, and than was hir
230 sorowe doublid. And than Adam fille doun, and his sorowe was
doublid, and cried and seide: 'Cursid be þou, feende. What eylith the
at vs or what haue we doo to the? Whi dost thou suche malice to vs?
Haue we ought binome the thi ioie or thine honoure? Whi fightist
thou ayenst vs, thou envious deville and wickid feende?' Than
235 aunswerid the deville and seide sorowfullie: 'O Adam, alle myne
enevie, malice and sorowe is throu3 the, for throu3 the I am kepte fro |

206 cried] crienge D   208 his sorowe] soruinge ELHbWhDo   Adam] add and of
Eue Wh   209 hym] hem Wh   his] her Wh   210 hym] hem Wh   211 an
aungelle oþere to] om. HbWhDo   213 the feende] cam þe feend to Eue and Wh
215 to you] om. Hb   216 othir] om. Do   Com out] add come oute D, þerfore come
now out Wh   217 Adam¹] add þi lord Wh   219 synne] om. Hb   220 for you]
om. HbWh   221 come] went ELHbWhDo   223 there stille] downe L
224 feende] deuel ELHbWhDo   comfortid hir, brought . . . Adam] trs. Hb
225 wepenge O Eue] spitously and seide L   226 hath] add thus ELHbWhDo
228 she knewe herselff] þat she was D   229 and] she D   231 feende] deuel
ELHbWhDo   eylith] eiled EHbWhDo   232 or] om. ELHbWhDo   233 or] and L
234 thou¹] add thus ELHbWhDo   deville] om. L   feende] om. EHbWhDo

my ioie and cast out of my heritage þat I had in heuen amonge Df. 158ᵛᵇ
aungellis, and for [the] I am cast out into th[e] erthe.' Than aunswerid
Adam: 'What haue I doo to the or wherefor blamest thou me? Thou
were vnknowen to me ne I wist nat of the.' 240
    Than the feende seide to Adam: 'Thou wotist nat what thou seiest,
for in þat daie þat thou were made I was cast adoune fro heuen, and
whan God blew3 in the the spirite of life and thou were made to the
liknesse of God, and Mighelle the aungelle lad the bifore God, and
God said: "Loo, I haue made Adam as oone of vs," Migell went forthe 245
and cleped alle þe aungellis and seide to hem: "Worshipp yee the
ymage of God, as God hath comaundid." And þat same Mighelle first
honourid hym and clepid me and seide to me: "Honour thou þe image
of God." And I aunswerid and seide: "Nay, 1 haue naught to doo to
worshipp Adam." And whan Mighel chargid me to worshipp the, I 250
seide to hym: "Wherefor chargist thou me? I wille nat worshipp a
foulere than I am, for I am fairere than he, and I was afore alle
creaturis, and or he was I was made, and þerefor [he shalle worship
me and] I shalle nat worshipp hym." And also othir aungellis þat
herde and knewe this wolde nat worshippe hym. And than seide 255
Mighel: "Worshipp thou the ymage of God or els God wolle be
wrothe with the." And I seide to hym: "Yif so be that God be wrothe
with me, I shalle sette my seete aboue the sterris of heuene and be like
to hym that is althir highest."
    'And than God was wrothe with me and commaundid that I shuld 260
be driven out of heuen and out of my ioie, and with me alle the
aungellis þat consentid with me that wolde nat worshippe the. [And
so] bicause of the we be put out of oure dwellinge place and cast into
þe erthe. And anone I was brought into sorowe and angir, for I was
put out of alle my ioie, and þou were put into alle manere of merthis 265
and delitis, and therefor I beganne to be envious to the ward, for I

238 the¹] that D   the²] this D   238–9 Than . . . Adam] Adam answeride and seyde
to þe deuel Wh   239–40 Thou . . . me/ne . . . the] trs. E   241 feende] deuel
ELHbWhDo   243 the²] om. HbDo   244 the aungelle] om. ELHbWhDo
245 Adam] man L   vs] add And than D   247 þat same] thilke EHbWhDo, þan L
first] om. L   248 me¹] om. HbWh   to me] om. ELDo   249 to doo] doun Hb
251 Wherefor] Where with ELHbWhDo   253–4 he² . . . and] om. D   254 shalle
nat worshipp] not EHbWhDo   255 and knewe] om. EHbWhDo   256 els] om.
ELHbWhDo   257 so be that] om. EHbWhDo   258 sette] make Do   aboue] on
HbWh   261 me] om. HbWh   alle the] myn HbWhDo   262 þat . . . worshippe the]
om. HbWh   262–3 And so] Also D   263 put] cast Wh   place] om. HbWhDo
cast] put here Wh   265 manere of] om. EHbWhDo   265–6 merthis, delitis] trs.
HbWh

myght nat suffre the to be in so grete ioie and merthis as thou were
inne. But than I went and begilid the woman, and with hir I begilid
the fro alle the delicis, ioies and merthis þat þou were inne, right as I
270 was put out fro my glorious beynge.'
    And whan Adam had hurde alle this he cried wepingeli and seide:
'Lorde God, my life is in thine hondis. Make þat this wickid
H2 f. 260ᵛᵇ aduersarie be ferre fro me, for he sechith [euer] in alle þat | he may
to spille my soule. Lorde, graunte me the ioie that [he les].' Than
275 when Adam had thus longe made his lamentacioun, the feende
vanisshid aweie from his sight. And than Adam treulie fulfillid
there his penaunce .xl. daies and .vij. in grete sorowe and anguisshe
in the flome Iordan.
    And than Eue seide to Adam: 'My Lorde God l[i]ueth; to the is
280 grauntid liffe, and my life is grauntid to the. For atte frist time nor atte
last thou were nat cursed, but I am cursed and begilid, for bicause that
I kepte nat the commaundementis of God. Wherefor nowe departe me
fro the light of this life, for I wolle be departid fro the sight of the, for
I am nat worthi to se the nothir to haue comforte ne merthe of the for
285 my wickidnesse. But I wolle wende as ferre as that I may into the west
and dwelle there tille that I deie.'
    And so than anone she went forth into the west with right grete and
passinge sorowe, and there she made [hir] a woninge place to dwelle
inne, and therein she wepte fulle bittirlie. And in that time she had
290 gone with childe three moonethis. And whan the time [come] of the
childis birthe, that she sholde be deliuerd, she was traueilid gretelie

267 in so grete] so in ELHbWhDo   267–8 and . . . inne] ne lyue in so moche mirthe
EHbWhDo   268 inne] *om.* L   269 fro] for LWh   the²] *om.* E, þy LWhDo   ioies,
merthis] *trs.* HbWh   þat . . . inne] *om.* EHbWhDo   271 had hurde alle] herd
HbWhDoHc   this] þese seyinges L   wepingeli] weping HbWhDoHc   272 my] thi
Do   273 sechith] techit Hc   euer] *om.* DL   may] canne Hc   274 he] I D   les]
lost DL   275 thus longe] *om.* HbWhDoHc   his] this EHbWhDoHc   feende] deville
LHbWhDoHc   276 his] hym out of L   treulie] *add* þer Hb   277 there] the Hc
his penaunce] *om.* ELHbWhDoHc   in grete . . . anguisshe] in penaunce EHbWhDoHc,
om. L   278 flome] water of EHbWhDoHc, water of flom L   279 God] *om.* Do
liueth] leueth H2   the] *add* grace and H2   is] and hath E, his L   280 grauntid¹] *add* to
the H2, þe E   281 bicause that] *om.* EHbWhDoHc   282 commaundementis]
heestis Wh   Wherefor] and ELHbWhDoHc   283 fro the/light] *trs.* L
284 comforte, merthe] *trs.* E   comforte ne merthe of the] myrþe of the ne comford
HbWhDo, of the no comfort Hc   286 tille . . . deie] vnto I ende my life L   286–
7 and dwelle . . . west] *om.* Hc   287 right] *om.* EHbWhDoHc   287–8 and passinge]
om. EHbWhDoHc   288 hir] vntore H2, vnto her L   place] stede ELHbWhDoHc
289 therein . . . fulle] wepte there inne EHbWhDoHc   290 come] *om.* H2
290–1 the childis] *om.* EHbWhDoHc, her L   291 that . . . deliuerd] *om.* EHbWhDoHc
gretelie] *om.* ELHbWhDoHc

with many diuers sikenesses. And than she mette with oure Lorde and seide to hym: 'Lorde God, haue mercie on me and help nowe me.' And God wolde nat hire hir ne he had noo mercie on hir. And than Eue seide to hirselff with mornynge chere: 'Who shalle nowe doo my 295 lorde Adam to wite and to knowe of my | woo? [The] lightis [in] H2f.261ra heuene, whan ye turne ayenne into the este, shewe ye my sorowes and dissesis vnto Adam myne husbonde.' And also sone as she had thus ipraied, her dissesis were iopened and shewed vnto Adam.

And whan Adam vndirstode and knewe hir sorowes and tribula- 300 ciouns, he seide than: 'The deses[e] of my wife Eve [is] come vnto me, and therefor lest the wickid addir the feende come and fight with hir, I wolle goo nowe and vesite hir.' And he went longe time forth and vesitid hir, and fonde hir in grete sorowe and dissese. And anone as euer Eve saugh hym she seide to hym: 'My soule and my life is welle 305 refresshid through the sight of Adam my lorde.' And than seide Eue vnto Adam: 'Nowe, good lorde, praie for me, that I myght be deliuered of these werst penauncis.' And than Adam praied for her vnto God ful ententifflie. And there come anone .xij. aungellis and two vertues, that is to seie twoo othere ordris of aungellis, stondinge 310 alle about hir bothe on the right side and also on the left side. And Michael stode on the right side and touchid hir face and [hir] brest and seide to hir: 'Eue, thou art blessid for Adam that is for the in penaunce and in praieris [of hym], for through his praieris we bene sent to the that thou myght vndirstonde helpe and socoure of godis 315 aungellis. Wherfor arise thou nowe and make the redie to the birthe, for the time is nyghe.' And she anone made hir redie thereto, and than she childid and brought forthe a sone with grete sorowe and traueile.

293 nowe] om. EHbWhDoHc   294 wolde . . . noo] herd her not neyþer (ne there E) hadd EHbWhDoHc, herde nat her askyng neþer he had noo L   295 nowe] om. Hb 296 Adam] om. ELHbWhDo   and to knowe] om. EHbWhDoHc   woo] add I preye Wh The] Ye H2   in] om. H2   297–8 and dissesis] om. EHbWhDoHc   298 thus] om. L 299 iopened] open Do   and shewed] om. EHbWhDoHc   300 vndirstode and] om. EHbWhDoHc   300–1 and tribulaciouns] om. EHbWhDoHc   301 desese] desesis H2L   is] be H2L   come] comen H2L   303 nowe and] om. EDoHc, and HbWh longe time] om. EHbWhDoHc, long L   303–4 and vesitid hir] om. EHbWhDoHc 304–5 as euer] whanne EHbWhDoHc   305 to hym] om. EHbWhDoHc   my] om. HbWhDoHc   is] add wondir L   306 refresshid] add nowe L   my lorde] om. EHbWhDoHc   307 vnto Adam] om. HbDoHc   Nowe] om. Hc   308 penauncis] peynes LHbWhDoHc   309 ful ententifflie] om. HbWhDoHc   anone] om. HbWhDoHc 311 also] om. LHbWhDoHc   312 hir²] the H2   313 in] om. ELHbWhDoHc 314 in] om. L, þe HbWhDoHc   of hym] for the H2   316 nowe] om. EHbWhDoHc 317 the] thy HbWh   anone] om. ELHbWhDoHc   318 and brought forthe] om. EHbWhDoHc   grete] om. EHbWhDoHc   and traueile] om. EHbWhDoHc

And anone the childe roos up and ranne forth and toke gras in his
320 hondis and yaffe to his moodir. And thei clepid his name Cayme. And
than Adam toke Eue and hir childe and ledde hem into the este. And
oure Lorde God sent Michael the archaungelle to sowe diuers seedis
and yafe hem vnto Adam, and taught Adam to worche and to tilie the
lond for to haue frute to live bi, and alle othere generacions afftir hym.
325 Than afftir, Eue conceiued and bere a son that hight Abelle. And
Cayme and Abelle woned togidir. And Eve seide to Cayme: 'My dere
H2 f. 261rb sone, | as I slept, me thought in my slepe that I saugh the bloode of
Abelle thi brother fallen into thine hondis.' And this same thinge Eve
tolde vnto Adam. And when Adam herde this, he seide: 'I drede
330 gretelie lest Cayme slee Abelle his brothir, and therefor thei shulle be
departid and dwelle assondre.' And than [thei] made hem dwellinge
placis, the toone ferre from the tothir, and Cayme was made a tiliere
of the erthe, and Abelle was made a shepperde. And yit afftirwarde
Cayme slough Abelle. And in that tyme that Cayme slough Abelle,
335 Adam was an hundrid and .xxx.^{ti} yere oolde, [forsothe] Abelle was
slaine of Cayme in the yeeris of his age an hundrid and twoo yere. And
afftir that knewe Adam Eve his wife and bigate a sone that hight Seth.
Than seide Adam to Eue: 'I haue begoten a son for Abelle which that
Cayme sloughe.' Than livid Adam afftir that he bigate Seth .viijC.
340 yere and bigate in alle .xxxiij.^{ti} sones and .xxxij. doughtris, so that alle
his childrene in oo noumbre were .lx. and .v., the whiche multiplied
gretelie vppon the erthe.

This that followith here tellith howe Cayme slow3 Abelle his
brothir, and of the veniaunce that God toke of Caym, as is
345 in Genesis in the .iiij.^{the} chapiter.

Afftir that many daies, Cayme shulde offre of the frutes of the erthe

321 hem] him Hb   322 oure Lorde] *om.* Hb   324 for] and ELHbWhDoHc
othere] the EHbWhHc, *om.* Do   hym] hem EHbWhDo   325 afftir] *om.* HbWhDoHc
327 in my slepe] *om.* HbWhDoHc   328 thinge] *om.* EHbWhDoHc   329 when . . .
he] Adam EHbWhDoHc   330 gretelie lest] that EHbWhDoHc   his brothir] *om.*
EHbWhDoHc   331 thei] Adam D   332 Cayme was made] made Caym
EHbWhDoHc   333 was made] *om.* ELHbWhDoHc   334 And . . . Abelle] *om.* L
335 yere] wynter L, *om.* Do   forsothe] for sith H2   335–6 forsothe . . . yere] *om.*
HbWh   336 yere] *om.* EDoHc   337 Eve] *om.* Hc   340 in alle] *om.*
EHbWhDoHc   .xxxiij.^{ti}] .xxx.^{ti} HbWhHc   so that] *om.* EHbWhDoHc   alle] and Hc
341 in oo noumbre] *om.* EHbWhDo   oo] *om.* LHc   343–5 This . . . chapiter] *om.* Hc
343 followith here] suithe EHbWhDo   343–4 his brothir] *om.* EHbWhDo   344 is]
it is write L   334–5 as is in] *om.* EHb   as is . . . chapiter] for þe deþ of Abel Do, *om.*
Wh   345 .iiij.^{the}] .iij. HbWh   346 that] *om.* EHbWDoHc   daies] *add* þat L

and of his yifftis to the Lorde God, and Abelle his brothir offrid and
vsed to offre the frist bigotenne thing of his flok and of the fat[nes] of
hem. And our Lorde hymselff behelde to Abelle and to his yifftis, and
also vnto Cayme and his yifftis forsothe he behelde naught, and for 350
this cause Cayme was gretelie wrothe with his brothir and felle with
his chere. And than oure Lorde God seide to hym: 'Caym, whi art
thou wrothe and what is the cause [also that therewith fallith thi
chere]? Shalt thou nat [resseyue] good if thou haue doo welle? And
elles forsothe anone euelle, and in the yatis thy synne shalle be atte 355
the. But vndir the shalle be the appetite of hym and thou shalt haue
the [lord]shipp of hym.' | And than Cayme seide to Abelle his brothir: H2 f. 261va
'Goo we out.' [And whan thei were] in the feelde, Cayme aroos with
envie ayens Abelle his brothir and slough hym. And than oure Lorde
seide to Caym: 'Where is Abelle thi brothir?' And Caym aunswerid 360
and seide: 'I note nat where. Whan was I the keper of my brothir?'
And than God seide to hym: 'Caym, what hast thou doo? Loo, the
voice of the bloode of thi brothir crieth to me fro the erthe. Wherefor
nowe thou shalt be cursed on the erthe, which opened his mouthe and
toke the blood of thi brother [of] thine hondis. And whan thou 365
werchist the erthe, [it] shalle nat yeue to the his frute; va[g]aunt and
ferre fugitiff thou shalt be on the erthe alle the daies of thi life.' And
than Cayme seide to the Lorde God: 'More is my wickidnes than I
des[eru]e foryeuenesse. [Se], thou cast me out this daie fro the face of
the erthe, and fro thi face [I shall] be hidde, and I shalle be 370
vagabounde and ferre fugitiff in the erthe. Alle than that shalle

347 of his] *om.* EHbWhDoHc   his brothir] forsothe EHbDoWhHc   347–8 and vsed
to offre] *om.* EHbWhDoHc   348 vsed] *add* allewey L   thing] *om.* EHbWhDoHc
fatnes] fattest H2Hc   349 hymselff] *om.* EHbWhDoHc   350–1 for this cause] *om.*
EHbWhDoHc   351 was] wax Hc   with his brothir] *om.* EHbWhDoHc   felle with]
therwith felle EHbWhDoHc, fill L   352 Caym] *om.* EHbWhDoHc   whi] what L
353 what . . . that] whi EHbWhDoHc   therewith] *om.* Hc   353–4 also . . . chere] Abelle
thi brother with fallith his chere and malice *with punct. before* Abelle H2   354 nat] *om.*
DoHc   resseyue] haue H2   good] *om.* EHbWhDoHc   haue doo] do L, doest
EHbWhDoHc   355 the] þi Wh   356–7 and thou . . . of hym] *om.* Hb
357 lordshipp] worshipp H2   358 And . . . were] *om.* H2, *add* oute L   358–9 with
envie] *om.* EHbWhDoHc   360 to] *om.* Wh   361 nat] ncre HbWh   where] whe/ther
E, *add* he is L   Whan was I] I am EDo, I am not L, am I HbWhHc   362 hym] Cayme L
Caym] *om.* ELHbWhDoHc   Loo] *om.* HbWhDoHc   363 the bloode of] *om.* L   fro] out
of Hc   363–4 Wherefor nowe] Now thanne ELHbWhDoHc   365 of²] in H2   hondis]
honde ELHbWhDoHc   366 it] *om.* H2, he Wh   vagaunt] but be vacaunt H2, dagaunt (?)
Do, vangaunt (?) Hc   367 ferre fugitiff] forgetyn Hc   368 than] *add* þat HbWhHc
369 deserue] desire H2   Se] Sith H2, *om.* Hc   370 fro thi] for Hc   I shall] thou shalt H2
hidde] *add* fro me H2   371 vagabounde] vagaung Hb, vagaunt WhDo, vengeaunt Hc
Alle than] alle the daies of my life and than who H2

fynde me shalle slee me.' And than the Lorde seide to hym: 'Hit shalle
nat ben don so, but alle thoo that shalle slee Caym shalle .vij. foolde be
ponysshid.' And than oure Lorde God sette a signe in Caym that alle
375 thoo that fyndith hym shalle nat slee hym. And than Caym passid
thens out fro the face of oure Lorde and dwellid ferre fugitiff in the
erthe atte este [place] of Edon.

Than Cayme forsoothe kneugh his wiff, the which conceiued and
bere hym Ennok, and this Ennok [bilded a cite and cleped the name of
380 it Ennok]. And Ennok bigate Irade, and Irade bigate Manianelle, and
Manianelle bigate Mat`er´sale, and Matersale bigate Lameth, the
which toke twoo wifis, and the name of the too wife was Ada and
the name of the tothir Sella; and he bigate Iabelle, that was fader of
duelleris in tentis and of sheppardis. And the name of his brother was
385 Tuballe, and he was fadir of syngeris in harpe and organ. And Sella
gate Tubal[caym], that was an hamersmyth and a smyth to alle werkis
of bras and of irenne, and the sust[er] of [Tubalcaym], Neoma. And
H2 f. 261vb Lameth seid thus to his | wifis Ada and Sella: 'Hire ye my voice, wifis
of Lameth, and herkene ye my worde, for I slough a man into a
390 wounde, a litille wexinge man into my wa[n]nesse. Veniaunce shalle
be youen [of] Caym .vij. foolde, and of Lameth forsothe .lxx. times
.vij.'

Yit forsothe Adam knewe his wife, and she conceiued and bare a
sone and clepid the name of hym Seth, and Adam seide: 'God hath
395 sent to me anothir [seed] for Abelle whom Cayme slough.' But vnto
Seth is borne a sone whom he clepid Enos, and this biganne
[inwardly] to clepe the name of the Lorde. And Adam seid to Seth:
'Sone, hire thou me nowe and I shalle telle the what I saugh and hurde

372 Hit] y Hb   375 alle thoo] everich L, eche EHbWhDoHc   shalle] shulde
EHbWhDo   376 thens] om. EHbWhDoHc   dwellid] add þens L, dwellith Hc
377 este] laste L   place] partie H2   379 hym] by her L, om. HbWhDoHc   this] þat
same L   this Ennok] he EHbWhDoHc   a cite] om. Hc   379–80 bildid . . . Ennok¹] om.
H2   380 Ennok¹] after þe name of his sone ennok Hb, so omitting ennok Wh
382 the too] his oo L   wife was] om. HbWhDoHc   383 he] om. LHbDoHc
384 in] add the templis H2, add templys L   385 organ] organus H2
386 Tubalcaym] Tuballecaan H2   387 suster] sustris H2   Tubalcaym] hym wer
Taym and H2   388 thus] om. EHbWhDoHc   his] add two Hc   Hire] add nowe L
389 a²] om. EhbWhDoHc   390 litille] 3onge Wh   wannesse] warinesse H2L, vannesse
Hb   391 of¹] to H2, to of Hc   times] sythe HbWh, sithes Do   391–2 and . . . .vij.]
om. Hc   .lxx. .. vij.] seventifolde seven tymes L   392 .vij.] seuenfolde EDo
393 conceiued and] om. ELHbWhDoHc   393–4 a sone] hym a child L, a childe
EHbDoHc   394 name] add there Hc   and Adam seide] seiynge ELWhDoHc, om. Hb
395 seed] sone H2   397 inwardly] in worde H2   Lorde] add god almi3ti Do, add Gen.
.iiij. c° EHb   398 nowe] om. EHbWhDoHc   I²] we Hc

afftir that thi moodir and I weren [caste] out of paradis. I and thi
moodir [as we] were in orisoune, Michaelle the archaungel, Godis 400
messangere, come to me and y saugh the ordris of aungellis as thikke
as winde beynge in a faire sercle, and I saugh a chare and the wheles
thereof were as fire. And than I was rauisshid into paradis, and there I
saughe oure Lorde, and his semblaunce and chere was as fire
brenninge and his vesa[g]e and chere was so bright that I myght 405
nat in noo manere wise endure ne suffre to loke therevppon, and a
grete multitude of aungellis were euer there about the brennynge
beemes of [the] brightnes of his semblaunt and chere. And than also I
sawe anothir wondirfulle companie of aungellis beynge on his right
side and also on his lefft side. 410

'And bicause of alle these sightis I was in grete drede, an than I
made my praier to God in erthe. And than my Lorde God seide to me:
"Wite it welle that thou shalt deie, for thou foryate and were
vnobedient and that thou brakist my commaundement | and herdist Df. 159ᵃ
and tokist hede of the wordis of thi wiffe, the whiche wiffe I yauc to 415
the to be thine vndirlinge and sogette to thine owne wille, and thou
obeiedist to hir and nought to me." And whan it was so þat I hurde
these woordis I fille anone doun to the erthe and seid thus: "A, Lorde
that art moost myghtyfulle and most merciable, God bothe blessid
and meke, ne foryete thou nat the worshipfulle name of thi dignite but 420
comforte thou, Lorde, my soule, [for] I die and my spirite passeth out
of my mouthe. Ne cast me nat, Lorde, aweie fro thi face, which thou
hast made of slyme of the erthe, ne put thou hym behynde that thou
hast norisshid with thi grace. Biholde howe that thi wordis brenne
me." And than oure Lorde seide to me: "For thine herte is such that 425
thou lovist science and konnynge and goodenes and repentest nat that

399 thi moodir and I] we HbWhDoHc   caste] passid H2   400 as we] om. H2
402 in] and Hb   404 and chere] om. EHbWhDoHc   405 vesage and] vesase and
H2, om. HbWhDoHc   406 in noo manere wise] om. HbWhDo   ne] to L   ne suffre]
om. HbWhDoHc   407 euer there] þere L, om. HbWhDoHc   brennynge] om.
HbWhDoHc   408 the] his H2L   brightnes] add and H2   and chere] om.
HbWhDoHc   411 bicause . . . sightis] om. HbWhDoHc   in] add fulle L
413–14 and . . . brakist] om. EHbWhDoHc   415 and tokist hede of] om. HbWhDolIc
416 owne] om. EHbWhDoHc   417 And whan] thanne seyde Adam now whanne Wh
it was so þat] om. EHbWhDoHc   418 anone] om. EHbWhDoHc   thus] om.
HbWhDoHc   A] om. LHbWhDoHc   419 that art] om. HbWhDoHc   moost] add of D
420 thou] om. EHbWhDo, ye Hc   thi dignite] deynte Hc   421 comforte] conuerte
HbWh   Lorde] om. EHbWhDoHc   for] Whan D   422 Lorde] om. EHbWhDoHc
424 Biholde] add on me Lord Wh   425 to me] om. Wh   426 and konnynge] om.
HbWh   repentest] add þe EHbWhDo, repentaunce ne Hc   426–7 nat . . . shalt] þou
shalt not HbWhDoHc

thou shalt be done aweie fro thi connynge, therefor the seede that
comyth of the and that wille serue me shalle neuer be lorne." And
whan I had herde alle these woordis, I honourid hym lowelie on þe
430　erthe and seide to hym: "Thou art God without begynnynge and
endinge and euery creature owith to worship þe and loue the, for thou
art aboue alle lightis shinynge, thou art the uerreie light of life, thou
art suche that noo tonge mai telle ne comprehende in noo manere
witte. O thilke grete and meruelous vertue of God, alle creaturis to the
435　yeuen honoure and preisinge, whom thou hast made mankinde
through thi gret vertue."

'And anone as euer I had praied thus, Michaelle the archaungelle of
God toke me bi the honde and cast me out of paradis in the
visitaciouns fro the sight of God. And Michaelle helde a yerde in
440　his honde with the which he touchid the watris that went in [the]
circuite of paradis, bi the which touchinge of þe forseide yerde the
watris congelid togidirs into ise, and I went on hem. And Michaelle
went with me and ladde me ayenne into the place of paradis fro the
which he rauisshid me, and efft ayenwarde he lad me to the lake there
445　he ravisshid me.

'Nowe, my sone Seth, hire thou me, and I shalle shewe to the `þe´
priuetees that beth to come and the sacramentis that ben shewed to
me, for whi I vndirstonde and knowe thingis that ben to come in this
worlde temporalle the which God made for mankinde, that is to seie, I
D f. 159rb　had my knowinge and vndirstandinge of þingis | þat be comminge bi
451　etenge þat I ete of the tree of vndirstandinge that was forbode me.
Also I vndirstond þat God shalle shewe hym in the fourme of fire and
goo out of the [sete] of his mageste, and he shalle yeue men of his
heestis and make hem holie in the hous of his mageste, and God shalle
455　shewe to hem a meruelous place of his mageste on which thei shulle
make dwellinge placis in erthe and there thei shulle bigge an hous in
erthe to her God. And thei shulle breke his commaundementis, and

428 neuer] *add* more L　　　429 alle] *om.* EHbWhDoHc　　　433 that noo tonge] as
nothyng Hc　　noo manere] *om.* EHbWhDoHc　　　434 thilke] þat L　　and meruelous] *om.*
EHbWhDoHc　　　435 whom] whan HbWhDoHc　　　436 vertue] *add* it bihoueþ þee to
be worschipid Wh　　　437 euer] *om.* ELHbWhDoHc　　　thus] þis þis Wh, this HbDoHc
437–8 of God] *om.* L　　　438 me bi the] myn ELHbWhDoHc　　　in] into D
440 went] weren Wh　　the³] *om.* D　　　441 bi] and with LHbWhDoHc　　　441–2 the
watris] thei HbDoWhHc　　　443 the¹] a L　　　447 to come] to me Hc
448 vndirstonde and knowe] vndirstode and knewe LHbWhDo　　　in] into D
449 worlde] *om.* Hc　　　451 that . . . me] *om.* EHbWhDoHc　　　452 vndirstond]
understode ELHbWhDo　　　453 sete] Cite D　　men] me Hb　　　453–4 and . . .
mageste] *om.* Hc　　456 there] þe erth Hc

her holie place shalle be brent and her lande shalle be forsaken, and
eche of hem shalle be driven from othir bicause thei wolle wraþe her
Lorde God. 460
'And the .vij.^te daie God shalle make hem sauff and bringe hem
ayenne togidirs, and efft thei shulle beginne newe housis to her God,
and than shalle the last hous of God be better saued than the frist.
And yit efftsones shalle shrewednesse ouercome rightwisnes, and than
shalle God dwelle in erthe with men to be seene, and than shalle 465
rightwisnesse biginne to shine, and enemies than shulle haue noo
more powere to noye noo man that trowith in God. And he shalle saue
his folke, and the wickid men shulle be ponisshid and departid [from]
God, for thei wolde nau3t kepe his commaundementis ne kepe his
lawe ne his wille. And God shalle than areise a [sauff] puple to be 470
made withouten eende, and wickid men shulle put Adam out of his
kingedome, and afftir that whoo that wille [of that] kingedome loue
heuen and erthe night and daie, and alle manere creatures be
worshippinge to the Lorde, and thei shul nat breke his commaundementis ne thei shulle nat chaunge his werkis. And thoo men that 475
foryeten the commaundementis of God thei shull be chaungid, for
God shalle put out wickid men, and rightwis men shulle dwelle as
rightwisnesse askith in the sight of God, and in þat time men shulle be
purified of her synne bi watir of cristendome, nau3t willinge to be
purified bi watir. Wise is that man that amendith his soule, for whi 480
there shalle be a grete daie of iugement amonge synfulle men and her
deedis shulle be enquerid of the rightwis God her iuge.'
    And whan that Adam was of .ixC. and .xxx.^ti yere oolde he wist
welle that his life daies shortid and neighid fast and sone shul[d]e
eende. And than he seid to Eve: 'Gadre togidir nowe alle my children, | 485
þat thei mowe com before me and þat I mai speke my fille vnto hem Df.159va
and yife hem my blessinge or that I deie.' And than thei come togidir

459 bicause] for EHbWhDoHc   461 .vij.^te] .viij.^te D   462 beginne] bigge Wh
housis] housyng Hc   464 yit] om. EHbWhHc   than] eftesones ELDo, efte HbWhHc
466 enemies] deuelles Hc   467 noye] om. HbHc   468 from] bifore D
469 wolde] will Hc   commaundementis] heestis Wh   kepe^2] om. EHbWhDoHc
470 ne his wille] om. EHbWhDoHc   sauff] faire D   472 of that] haue the D
473 manere] om. HbWhDoHc   be] om. EHbWhDoHc   475 thoo] om. EHbWhDoHc
475-6 that foryeten] foryetinge EHbWhDoHc   476 for] fro god and Hc
477 rightwis] rightwismen D   shulle] add aske to D   478 askith] om.
HbWhDoHc   482 enquerid] requyrid L   her iuge] heringe Do   484 shortid
. . . fast and] om. EHbWhDoHc   shulde] shulle D   485 nowe] om. ELHbWhDoHc
486 þat . . . com] om. EHbWhDoHc   my fille] om. HbWhDoHc   487 yife hem my
blessinge] blesse hem EHbWhDoHc

in three parties bifore his praienge place where þat Adam had praied
to oure Lorde God. And thei come togidir with oo voice seienge:
490 'What seie ye to us, Fadir, whi be we hidir gaderid togidir bifore you,
and whi list thou in thi bedde? Seie to vs what is thi wille that wee mai
doo it.'

Than Adam aunswerid and seide: 'My children, me is fulle woo
and with sorowes I am turmentid and traueilid.' And than his children
495 seide to hym: 'Fader, what is it to haue eville and with sorowes to be
traueilid othir tormentid?' Than seide his sone Seth: 'Lorde, Fadir,
thou desirist happelie to eete of the frute of paradis of the which
sometime thou eete, and therefor þou liest thus in sorowes. Wolt thou
þat I goo and ney3 to the yatis of paradis and doo duste on myne hede
500 and falle doun to þe erthe bifore the yatis of paradis and crie in grete
lamentacioun, praieng to oure Lorde God, and happelie he wille hire
me and sende his aungelle to me to bringe me that thou desirist.' And
than Adam aunswerde and seide: 'Sone, I desire noothinge, but þat I
am woxen fulle sike and I haue grete penaunce in my bodi.' And Seth
505 aunswerid: 'I wote nat what sorowe is, therefor seie what it is and hile
it nou3t to me.'

Than seide Adam: 'Herkeneth nowe, alle my childrenne, whan
God made me and youre moodir and putte vs in paradis, and yafe to
vs alle þe trees beringe frute to eete whan wee wolde, but oonelie of
510 the tree of goode and eville that stondith in the myddis of paradis.
Thus God put vs than in paradis, and yafe me powere in the este and
in the parties ayens the northe, and to youre moodir he yafe from the
southe into the west, and yaffe twoo aungellis to kepe vs. The time
come that these aungellis went to the sight of God, hym to honour,
515 and than the feend anone fonde a place in youre moodir and
counseilid hir to eete of the forbooden tree, and she eete and profrid
me to eete, and I eete. And anon oure Lorde was wroth with vs. Than

490 hidir] *om.* L   bifore you] *om.* EHbWhDoHc   491 bedde] bedis Hb   mai] *om.*
EHbWhDoHc   492 it] *om.* Hc   494 turmentid and] *om.* HbWhDoHc
495 sorowes] *add* other L   496 traueilid, turmentid] *trs.* E   othir tormentid] *om.*
HbWhDoHc   his sone] *om.* Wh   Seth] *add* to Adam his fadir Wh   Lorde] *add* my Wh
497 desirist] desirid L, hast desirid EHbWhDoHc   498 therefor] *add* I suppose Wh
thus] *om.* ELHbDoHc   499 doo] *om.* L   499–500 and doo . . . paradis] *om.* Hc
502 aungelle] angels Hc   503 Sone] *om.* Hb   503–4 þat I am woxen] I wexe
HbWhDoHc   505 aunswerid] *add* Fadir Wh   506 to me] *om.* LHbWhDoHc
507 Herkeneth nowe] herith HbWhDoHc   510 of¹] *add* knowynge Wh, *add* lyff
knowing Hc   eville] ill Hc   stondith] stode Hc   511 and²] *om.* L   512 parties]
add þat is L, partie þat ys HbWhDoHc   513 yaffe] *add* us Wh   514 these] *add* .ij.
LDoHc   went] came L   515 in] and Hb

he seid to me: "For thou hast forsake my commaundementis, and þat
I ordeined to the thou hast nat kept, se nowe I shalle cast into thi bodie
.lxx. woundis of diuers sorowes and maladies fro the coroune | of thine D f. 159ᵛᵇ
hede into the soole of thi foote, and alle the diuers membris of thi 521
bodie be thei turmentid." Loo, sones, many sondrie sikenessis God
hath ordeined vs for oure trespas and to alle oure kinrede afftir vs.'

Thus Adam se[iynge] to his sones, he [is] itake with grete sorowis,
and he cried with a grete vois and seide: 'What shalle I wrecche nowe 525
doo, that am put into suche sorowes and tribulaciouns?' And whan he
had alle this iseide and Eve had hurde alle this, she biganne to wepe
and seid: 'Lorde God, put these sorowes in me, for whi I haue
trespacid, and nought he.' And than Eve seide to Adam: 'Good Sir,
yeue me parte of thi desesis and of þi sorowes, for my defautis make 530
the to haue these sorowis.' And than Adam seide to Eve: 'Arise and
goo with thi sone Seth and ney3 the to the yatis of paradis, and castith
erthe on youre heedis and fallith doun and makith sorowe in the sight
of oure Lorde God, that happelie he wille haue mercie on vs, and
happelie he wille commaunde an aungelle to the tree of mercie fro þe 535
which tree renneth oile of life, and happelie he shall [take] you of that
medicine, so that ye may anointe me therewith, that I myght be lissed
of my sorowes þat I suffre, in the which I brenne and am fulle werie off.'

Than Seth and Eve his moodir went toward paradis. And while thei
yoode bi the weie, sodeinlie þer come vppon hem a foule adder 540
without pete and a foule beeste, right as it were [a] feende, and he
boote Seth wickidli in the face. And whan Eve saw3 that, she biganne
bittirlie to wepe and seid: 'Allas to me, wrecch, for I am cursed, and
alle that kepe nat the commaundementis of God.' And than Eve seide
to the adder with a grete voice: 'O thou cursed beeste, whi dou3tist 545

518 forsake] broke Hc   and] om. Hc   519 kept] add me D   520 .lxx.] .vij. Hc
and maladies] om. HbWhDoHc   521 and] om. HbWhDoHc   membris] add 'lay' in
Hand B Hc   522 sones] om. Wh, add how Hc   sondrie] sones Hb, om. Wh   523 for
. . . trespas] om. HbWhDoHc   kinrede] kinde DoHc   kinrede afftir vs] ofspringe HbWh
524 seiynge] seid D   is] om. D   525 nowe] om. HbWhDoHc   526 am] add nowe D
into suche] in þese HbWh   and tribulaciouns] om. HbWhDoHc   526–7 he . . .
and] om. HbWhDoHc   527 alle] om. HbWhDoHc   this] add sorowe of hir husbonde
Wh   528 put] om. with laye ins. in Hand B Hc   these] þi Wh   530 thi . . . þi] your
LHbWhDoHc   defautis make] defaute makid Hc   531 these] om. Wh   532 the¹]
3e HbWhDoHc   535 to] add go to LWh   536 of¹] add and del. mercie D   take] om.
DHb, 3eue Wh   537 ye] he Hb   lissed] blessid L   538 þat I suffre] om.
HbWhDoHc   539 paradis] add in haaste Wh   540 yoode] came Hc   weie] add
þederwarde L   sodeinlie] om. Hc   vppon . . . foule] an HbWhDoHc   541 without
pete and] right L   right] om. LHbWhDoHc   a²] the D   543 to²] is Wh
543–5 and alle . . . cursed] om. Hc

thou nat to hurte and to noie thus cruelli the ymage of God? And
howe art thou so hardie and so boold to fight with it, or that thi teethe
shulde greue so worthi a creature?' And than the addre aunswerid and
seide with a grete voice: 'O thou Eve, wheþere oure wrecchidnes be
550 nat afore God, ne hath nat God steerid oure woodenesse ayens you?
Seie thou, Eve, howe were þou so hardie to eete of the tree the which
oure Lorde forbedde and commaundid to eete nat of? For biforehande
we had no right ne power ouer yowe, but afftir that time that ye had
ones broken Goddis biddinge and his commaundement we hadden
555 powere anone in yowe.' And than seide Sethe to the worme: 'Cursed
D f. 160ʳᵃ be thou of God. Goo | aweie fro þe sight of men and close thi mouthe
and wexe thou doumbe, cursed enemie and distroier of rightwisnes.
Goo from the sight of the Lord Godis image tille the time þat God
calle the ayenne to be preued what thou art.' And than the worme
560 seide to Sethe: 'I mai nat withstonde thi biddinge, but nowe I goo
aweie from þe image of God.'

And Seth and Eve his moodir wenten to the yatis of paradis. And
thei toke the dust of the erthe and kest it on her heedis and on her
facis, and thei fillen doun grouelinge to the eerthe and made grete
565 sorowis, and praieden to God to haue merci on Adam, and that he
wolde sende an aungelle to bringe hem of the oile of the tree of mercie
to hele with Adam. Than the aungelle Michaelle appered to hem and
seide: 'I am the archaungelle Michaelle that am ordeined of God
keper[e] of mannys bodie. I seie to the, Seth, wepe no more ne praie
570 nat for the oile of mercie to anoynte with the bodie of thi fadir Adam,
for thou maie nat haue of that oile tille .vM.CC. and .x[x]viij. yere be
eendid. Than shalle come on erthe Ihesu Criste, Goddis sone, and
shalle ben baptisid in the flome Iordane, and he shalle deie and rise
ayen and goo to helle and anointe there Adam thi fadir, and bring hym
575 and alle feithfulle deede men with [hym], whiche annointinge shalle

546 thus cruelli] *om.* HbWhDoHc   547 so¹] *om.* HbWhDoHc   and so boold] *om.*
HbWhDoHc   with it] with hi3t Hb, þerwith Hc   549 wrecchidnes] schrewidnesse
HbWhHc   552 forbedde and] bad and L, *om.* HbWhDoHc   commaundid] *add* þe
HbWhDoHc   biforehande] byfore HbWhDoHc   553 right ne] *om.* LHbWhDoHc
ouer] at alle in L, in HbWhDo, of Hc   time that] *om.* HbWhDoHc   554 ones] *om.*
HbWhDoHc   and his commaundement] *om.* HbWhDoHc   hadden] *add* dewe L
555 anone] *om.* HbWhDoHc   the] þat cursid Wh   556 Goo] *add* we D   558 the
time þat] *om.* HbWhDoHc   558–9 God calle the] þou be called Hc   564 doun] *om.*
HbWhDoHc   565 praieden] preyinge HbWhHc   566 of¹] to Hc   of³] *add* lyfe
and L   567 hele] help Hc   569 kepere] kepers D   569–70 ne praie nat] preyng
LHbWhDoHc   571 nat] *add* nowe LDo   of that oile] þerof Hc, *add* of mercy
LHbWhDo   tille] vnto the tyme þat L   .xxviij.] .xviij. D   574 hym] *add* to blisse *del.*
'of' Wh   575 alle] *om.* Hc   deede] *om.* Hc   hym] *om.* D, hem Hc

endure withouten eende. Than shalle Ihesu Criste sti3e vp, and he wille lede thi fadir into paradis to his tree of mercie. And goo thou nowe to thi fadir and seie to hym the time of his life daies ben doone, for afftir .vj. daies his life daies shall passe. And than thou shalt se grete wondris in heuen and in erthe amonge the brighte aungellis of 580 heuen.' And whan Michaelle the archaungelle had seide alle this, anone he vanisshid aweie.

And than Eve and Seth turned ayenne homewarde, and toke with hem swete oynementis [odoramenta, þat is], nardum, cro[c]um, calamynt, synamom and canelle. And whan thei come home to 585 Adam, [thei] tolde howe the serpent had betenne Seth his sone. And than [Adam seide to his wife]: 'Biholde what thou hast done to vs. Thou hast brought to vs grete dissesis and synnes to alle oure kinrede. Wherefor alle that thou hast done vs and alle thingis that is done shewe to my children afftir my dethe, that thei that shulle come 590 of vs hereafftir ne shulle nat be wroothe to bere the dissesis þat thei shull haue, nor the sorowis. Than thei shalle curse towarde vs and seie: "These | dissesis hath oure fadris and moodris brought to vs that D f. 160ʳᵇ were in the biginninge afore vs."'

And whan Eve had hurde alle this she biganne to wepe and make 595 grete sorowe and doole. And as Michael the archaungelle had seid bifore, afftir .vj. daies Adam [d]eide. And bifore that he deied, he seide to his children: 'Biholde, for nowe I deie, and the noumbre of my yeris in this worlde ben .ixC. and .xxx. yere. And wha[n] I am deede, burie me ayens Godis yerd[e] in the feelde of his dwellinge 600 place.' And whan he had seide this, he yelde vp the spirite. And than the sonne wexe derke and the mone and the sterris, .viij. daies lastinge afftir his dethe. And whan Seth and his moodir Eve had leide forth

578 daies] *om.* LHbWhDoHc   581 alle] *om.* HbWhDoHc   584 odoramenta/þat is] *trs.* D   odoramenta] adoramenta D, ordoramenta HbWhHc, Odoramenta Do   nardum] vardoune Hc   crocum] Crotum D, crocrum Hc   586 thei] Eve D   tolde] *add* vnto hym L 587 Adam/seide ... wife] *trs.* D   588 Thou ... dissesis] a gret disease þou hast broute vs in Hc   grete dissesis] a grete disese LHbWhDo   synnes] synne LhbWhDo   589 kinrede] kynde LHbWhDoHc   Wherefor] but sothely LHbWhDoHc   590 shewe] shall be shewed Hc   my¹] oure HbWhDoHc   591 of vs] *om.* L   wroothe] worth Hc 593 fadris] fore fadris L, former fader HbWhDo, forne faders Hc   moodris] modyr HbWhDo   595 alle] *om.* HbWhDoHc   596 grete sorowe and] *om.* HbWhDo, gret Hc Michael the archaungelle] seynt mighelle L, Mighel HbWhDoHc   597 deide] seide D bifore²] *add* or L   bifore that] heer Hb, eer Wh, or DoHc   deied] dide Hb   598 Biholde] *add* 3e now on me, my children Wh   for] *om.* HbDoHc, and seeþ Wh   nowe] *add* how Wh 599 yeris] dayes Wh   in this worlde] *om.* Hc   yere] *om.* LHbDoHc   whan] wham D 600 yerde] yerdis D   601 this] *add* word Wh   602 lastinge] *om.* L   603 afftir his dethe] *om.* HbWhDoHc   his moodir/Eve] *trs.* Wh   Eve] *om.* LHbDoHc

Adame his body, thei soroweden on it, and thei lokid toward the erthe
605 clappinge her hondis on her hedis, and thei put doun her heedis on
her knees sore wepinge, and alle her childrenne also.

And than Michael the archaungelle appered to hem stondinge at
Adames heede and seide to Seth: 'Arise vp fro the bodie of thi fadir
and come to me, that thou mai se thi fadir and the ordenaunce wh[ich]
610 oure Lorde purposed to doo with hym, for he ha[th] mercie on hym
atte this time.' And than alle aungellis tromped vp seienge: 'Blessid be
God of thi makinge, for þou art nowe merciable on hym.' Than saw3
Seth the honde of God hold[en] vp [and helde his fadris] soule, and
toke it to Seint Michaelle and seide: 'Lete this soule be in thi kepinge
615 in tormentis into the last day of dispensacioun, and than shalle I
deliuer hym of his sorowes. Forsothe than he shalle sytte on his
ioiefulle throne, he þat hath cast hym so lowe.' And yit God seide
ayenne to Michaelle: 'Bringe to me thre clothis of sendelle [and
besmes], and leie oone ouer Adam and anothir ouere his sone Abel.'
620   And alle the ordris of aungellis wenten bifore Adam and blessid the
slepe of his last eende of his dethe. And archaungelis buried the bodie
of Adam in the vale of Ebronne, as the Maistir of Stories tellith. And
Seth and his moodir Eve saw3 what the aungellis diden, and thei
meruelid gretelie. And than seide the aungellis to hem: 'Loke howe ye
625 haue seene these bodies buried, and in þe same manere burie ye youre
D f. 160ᵛᵃ   dede bodies here afftirward forth in time commyng.'

And than .vj. daies afftir that Adam was thus deede and buried, Eve
knewe than that deth was commynge to hir fast, and she gadrid togidir
alle hir sones and doughtris and seid to hem: 'Hire ye me, my sonnes
630 and doughtris, what I telle you. Afftir the time that youre fadir and I
passid Godis biddinge, Michaelle the holie archaungelle seide to vs:

604 Adame his body] the deed body of Adam Wh   body] add and HbDoHc, add þanne
þei kneliden adown oon tyme and saten anoþir tyme and Wh   thei¹] add greetly Wh   it]
þat deed body Wh   and] om. HbHc, add euere Wh   lokid] add downward Wh
607 appered to hem] spak to Seeth and to Eue his modir as þei weren Wh   609 which]
what D   610 purposed] purposiþ L   hath] had D   613 holden . . . soule] holdinge
vp the soule of his fadir Adam D   617 ioiefulle throne] trone fulle of ioy L
618 thre] the Hc   618–19 and besmes] om. D   619 Adam] add anoþir ouer Eue Wh
his] her Wh   621–2 the bodie of Adam] his body Hc   622 in . . . tellith] on þe body
of his sone Abel in paradys Wh   624 Loke howe] as HbWhDoHc   625 and] om.
HbWhDoHc   626 here] om. HbWhDoHc   afftirward] add alwey L   forth in time
commyng] om. HbWhDoHc   time] add to D   627 afftir] add þis L, om. Hc   and
buried] om. HbWhDoHc   Eve] se now how Eue EWh   628 to hir] to hir ward
HbDoHc, towardis hir Wh   629 me] om. LDo   630 I¹] add schal Wh   I²] add
hadden Wh   631 biddinge] comaundementis Wh   holie] om. HbWhDoHc   seide]
add þus Wh

"For youre synne God wolle distroie youre kinde, first bi watir and afftir be fire, and in these twoo alle mennes kinde be of God." Therefor hire, my sone Seth: make tablis of stone and also tablis of shininge claie or erthe, and write þereinne the livis of youre fadir and 635 me and alle thoo thingis that ye haue herde and seen of vs. For atte that time whan God shalle iuge alle oure kinde bi watir, the tablis of erthe wille lose and melte aweie with sokinge and drinkinge of the watris, but thou shalt vndirstonde and knowe welle þat the tablis of stoone wille dwelle and abide. And forsothe, whan God wille iuge 640 mankinde bi fire, than wille the tablis of [erthe] abide and endure.'

And whan Eve had seide alle this to hir children, she spradde hir hondis abrode and lokid vpwarde to heuen, knelinge on the erthe praienge to God. And whilis she praied hir spirite passed. And than alle hir childrenne wepte bittirlie and buried hir. And while thei made 645 sorowe for her moodir foure daies [l]astinge, Michael the archaungelle apperid [to hem and seid]: 'M[a]n of God, make no sorowe for the deth of [thi] fadir ne of [thi] mooder noo lenger than .vj. daies, ne for noone that deien, for the .vij. daie is tokenne of oure vprisinge and rest that is to comen of þis worlde, and in the .vij.ᵗᵉ daie he toke rest of alle 650 his werkis.' And than [Seth made] tablis of stone and of erthe, and also he wrote in hem bothe þe livis of his fadir Adam and of his moodir Eve, and leide the same tablis in his fadris oratorie where he was wonte to worship God. And afftir Noes floode th[o] tablis were founden and seen of many oone, but thei were nat redde ne declarid. 655

And than afftirward come Salamon, the wise kinge, and saw₃ these tablis wretenne, and he deuoutelie praied to God that he myght vndirstonde the writinge of thoo tablis. And than apperid to hym an

632–3 and afftir] aftirward Wh   634 make] add þou tweyne Wh   tablis²] om. Wh
635 claie or erthe] erthe of cley L, cley (clery Do) erþe HbWhDoHc   636 alle] om.
HbWhDoHc   636–7 atte that time] om. HbWhDoHc   638–9 melte . . . welle þat] om.
HbWhDoHc   638 drinkinge] dryvyng L   640 and abide] om. HbWhDoHc
641 erthe] stone D   abide and] om. LHbWhDoHc   642 alle] om. HbWhDoHc
644 praienge] preiede Wh, praysyng Hc   645 and] add so with greet moornynge Wh
wepte bitterlie, buried hir] trs. L   646 lastinge] fastinge D   archaungelle] add of God
Wh   647 to hem/and seid] trs. D   Man] Men D   make] add ye D, add þou Wh
648 thi¹] youre D   thi²] youre D, om. Hc   650 that is] om. HbWhDoHc   651 Seth
made] trs. D, add tweyne Wh   and] add tables Hb   651–2 also . . . bothe] wrote þerinne
HbWhDoHc   653 and] add þen Hb, add whanne tho weren maad he Wh, add þan he Hc
the same tablis] hem HbWhDoHc   he] hys fadir HbWhHc   654 wonte] add or vsyd Wh
worship] add almy₃ty Wh   tho] þe D   655 ne declarid] om. HbWhDoHc
656 afftirward] aftir L, add by longe processe of tyme Wh   657 wretenne] and the
wrytynge þereynne Wh, writyng Hc   deuoutelie] om. HbWhDoHc   658 to hym] om.
Hc   an] the Wh

aungelle of God, [seienge: 'I am the aungelle] that helde the honde of
Df. 160ᵛᵇ Seth whanne he wrote this with irenne in his tablis. Thou shalt | knowe
661 the scripture thereof, and these tablis were in the place where Adam
and Eve were wont to praie to God, and therefor hit bihoueth to the to
make a praienge place to God.' And than Salamon clepid these lettris in
the tablis Archiliates, that is to seie without techinge of lippes iwreten
665 with the fynger of Seth, the aungelle of God holdinge his honde.

Than made Salamon an hous [in the name] of God menne to praie
inne. And [in] th[o] tablis were founde iwrittenne that was prophecied
of Adam .vij. sythes, and Ennok spak of Noes floode and of the
cominge of Criste Ihesu. 'Loo,' he seid, 'Oure Lorde shalle come in
670 his holie knyghthode to make iugement of men and to distroie alle
wickid men of her werkis and of alle the spekinge of hem with
synners. Wickid men and grucchers thei seke to speke afftir her owne
couetinge, thei entrid and spak proudelie.'

This is the boke of the generacioun of Adam. Adam in that daie in
675 the which God made man of nought to the ymage and liknesse of God
and he made of hem both male and female and he made hem of
nought, and than he blessid hem and clepid the name of hym Adam in
that daie the which he was made of nouȝt. Adam forsothe livid [an
hundrid yere] and .xxx.ᵗⁱ or he gate a sone, and than he gate a sone to
680 the liknesse of his ymage and callid the name of hym Seth. And the
daies of Adam be made, afftir that he had bigote his sone Seth, .viijC.
yere, and he bigate sones and doughtres many oone. And alle the time
that Adam livid here in erthe was markid and imade and it commeth
to .ixC. and .xxx. yere, and alle the sones of Adam were in noumbre
685 .xxxiij. and the doughtris of hym were in noumbre .xxxij.

659 seienge . . . aungelle] om. DHc   aungelle²] add of God LDo   660 his] this Hb,
thise DoHc, these two Wh   tablis] add and seide D, add haldynge it in his riȝt hond. And yn
these two tablis weren wryten manye wondirful profecyes and I sey to thee Salamon Wh
661 thereof] þat is wryten in these tablis Wh   663 make] add þe L, add þer HbWhDoHc
praienge] dwellynge Wh   665 fynger] add of the riȝt hond of Wh   his honde] it Wh
666 in the name] om. D   God] add for LHc   667 in tho] the D   668 spak] also profecyede
Wh   669 of] add oure Lord Wh   670 knyghthode] kyngdome Hc   671 men] om.
HbDoHc   of³, with] trs. L   674 Adam²] And L   675 ymage] add of god Hc   676 both]
om. HbWhDoHc   677 clepid] called HbWh   hym] hem HbWh   677-8 in that . . . was]
And þe day in þe whiche þey were L   678 he was] þey weren HbWhDoHc   678-9 an . . .
.xxx.ᵗⁱ] .ixC. and .xxx.ᵗⁱ yere D, a .C. yere Hc   679 or . . . sone¹] om. HbWhDoHc
680 liknesse . . . ymage] ymage and his liknes Wh   of¹] and Hb   681 his sone] om.
HbWhDoHc   682 many oone] om. HbWhDoHc   683-4 that . . . commeth to] ys made in
whiche Adam lyued HbWhDoHc   684 yere] add Genesis .v. cᵒ Hb   in noumbre] om.
HbWhDoHc   685 the doughtris . . . .xxxij.] and .xxxij.ᵗⁱ douȝttres HbWhDoHc   in
noumbre] om. L   .xxxij.] add and so alle hise children weren þre score and fyue. Blessid be oure
Lord God. Amen. Thus eendith thys blessid tretys of oure Fadir Adam Wh

Here endith the life of Adam and of Eve, and biginnithe
the Fyve Wilis of Kinge Pharao the which he vsid ayenst
the childrenne of Israelle to kepe hem in his londe, [Cap°.
.C°.lxxix.°]

The frist wile was that Kinge Pharao grauntid þat Goddis puple
shulde goo to doo sacrifice to her God, so þat thei wolde dwelle stille
in the londe of Egipte. So the deville wille that men doo outward
penaunce, [as] shrifft of mouthe and penaunce enioined of the preeste,
so that thei dwelle stille and contenue in her synne.   5

The secounde wyle is that Kinge Pharao grauntid to Goddis puple
to goo out of his londe and make sacrifice to her god, so that thei goo
nat ferre out thereof. Thus the deville wille suffre that men leve her
synne for a tyme for drede and shame of þe worlde, so that thei putte
nat aweie the ny3e occasiouns | thereof, for herebi he trustith sikirlie to   Df.161ʳᵃ
bringe hem ayen to synne deppere than thei were [bifore].   11

The thrid wile is that Kinge Pharao grauntid to Godis puple to goo
ferre out of his londe and doo sacrifice vnto God, so thei lefft her
children in the londe of Egipte. Thus the deville wille suffre þat men
doo outward penaunce and good werkis of kinde so þat thei be done in   15
ypocrise and in veineglorie.

The fourthe wile is þat Kinge Pharao grauntid to Godis puple to
goo [ferre] out of the londe of Egipte and make sacrifice to God and to
take her childrenne with hem, on that condicioun that thei shuld leve
her shepe and her beestis in the londe of Egipte. Thus the deville wille   20

DH2EA2LCbHbHaCaYaDo; E runs from about 48–148, but this last surviving folio of
the text is damaged, rubbed and mostly illegible, legible variants being recorded below; D
breaks off after 311 *deede*, and resumes at 445 *and service*, the missing passage being
supplied from L, and has excision damage from 466–75 and 543–5; H2 breaks off after 98
to goo; Hb breaks off after 83 *vse* and resumes at 121 *his mercie*; Ha breaks off after 126
deedlie; Ca consists of two passages in reverse order with a linking sentence, 36 *Hit is
nedefulle* to 92 *synne* and 6 *The secounde* to 35 *dampnacioun*; Ya consists of two separated
passages, 1–35 *dampnacioun* and 271 *goode vertues* to 344 *worchynge*   1 The frist . . .
Pharao] This is þe first he HbYa   wile] *om.* L   was] is CbHa   Kinge] *om.* Ha
2 her] *om.* Ha   so þat] but HbYa   3 that] *add* synfull CbHbHaYaDo
3–4 outward/penaunce] *trs.* L   4 as] of DCb   5 dwelle] wole stonde HbHaYa
stille] *om.* Cb   and] to HbYaDo, *om.* Ha   6 is] *add* this Ha   7 her] *om.*
LCbHbHaCaYaDo   goo²] yeede LCbHbHaCaYaDo   8 nat] *om.* Ha   thereof] of
his contrey A2   deville] fend Ha   9 tyme] while L   drede and] the A2
10 sikirlie] *add* she D   11 were] did A2   bifore] *om.* D   15 and] of A2
16 and in] of Do   17 is] *om.* Hb, *add* þis Ha   18 ferre] free D   the londe of
Egipte] Egipte CbHbHaYaDo, his lond Ca   make] do A2   make . . . and to] *om.* Ca
18–20 and to . . . Egipte] by so þei left her childre and her bestis still in his lond Ha
19 on that condicioun] so CbHbCaYaDo   20 shepe] godis Ya   and] *add* all HbCa

suffre that Goddis puple doo outward penaunce and many good werkis of kinde, so þat thei parfourme her bodilie wittis in sewinge of lustis of hem and doo nouȝt þe werkis of resoune and of discrecioun with heuenli desiris that shulde plese God.

25 The fyffte wile is þat King Pharao grauntid þat Godis puple shuld goo ferre out of Egipt and doo sacrifice to God and that thei shuld take with hem her childrenne and her beestis, so that thei wolde speke good of hym and of his londe. Thus the deville wille suffre þat Godis puple doo outward penance and leve her synne outward and the nyȝe 30 occasioun[s] thereof and doo good werkis of kinde and chastice her flesshelie wittis, so that thei be glad to thinke and speke of her oolde synnes and delite hem thereinne. For th[u]s thei lese alle her good werkis of kinde and the mede that shulde sewe hem. Therefor Ihesu through his grace deliuere vs fro the snaris of the fende and out of the 35 welle of dampnacioun. [Amen.]

Hit is nedefulle to vndirstonde howe the feende disseiueth many men and hath hem vndir his gouernaile principalie whan thei wene that thei were out of his thraldome. And so whan thei wene that thei be out of synne than be thei in the myddis thereof. But howe and in 40 what maner this shulde be knowen hit mai welle be shewid bi the .v. wilis þat Kinge Pharao vsed ayens Godis puple, the which were the childrenne of Israelle. Bi the which Pharao and his wilis is vndir-stonde the feende of helle, the which vseth to founde ayenst mennes soulis in the londe of Egipte, the which is interpreted derkenesse of

21 Goddis puple] men Ha   doo] *add* go to schrift and do Ya   many] *om.* CbHbHaCaYaDo   22 bodilie wittis] *trs.* Ya   in] and Hb   sewinge] shewyng L, synne Ca   of²] and Ca   25 wile is] *om.* L, *add* þis Ha   28 and of] in Ha   his] *add* pepille and his L   29 the] eschew Ca   nyȝe] nyce Cb, *om.* Ca   30 occasiouns] occasioun D   werkis] deedis Do   31 flesshelie] *add* lustis and þer A2   flesshelie . . . so] flessh with L   glad] *add* and ioyfulle A2   32 and] *add* to reioyse them and A2   thereinne] *add* And D   thus] this D, so Ca   lese] lesse Ha   alle] *om.* Cb   32–3 good werkis] goodis Ha   33 shulde sewe hem] thaye shulde haue thereof A2   sewe] *add* of LHaCaYaDo   Therefor] *om.* LHbCaDo   33–4 Therefor/Ihesu . . . grace] *trs.* Cb   33–5 Therefor . . . Amen] *om.* Ha   35 welle] wilis Cb, weie HbCaYaDo   of] *add* evir lestyng Ca   Amen] *om.* DA2   36 is] *add* fulle A2   feende] deville L   37 men] *add* and women Ha   gouernaile] gouernaunce and A2   principalie] *om.* CbHbHaCaDo   38 his] þis Hb   38–9 thei be] þei weryn Ca   39 thereof] þerin LCbHbDo, *om.* Ca   39–40 and . . . maner] *om.* CbHbHaCaDo   40 welle] *om.* CbHbHaCaDo   be²] *add* knowen and L   41 þat] of A2, of þat þe Hb, of þe Ha   vsed . . . puple] *om.* HbHa   were] bytoneþ þe fende dede to Hb, þe fend þat he did to Ha, dede to Ca   42 and] as by A2   Bi . . . wilis] Pharrao Ca   Pharao . . . wilis] Pharoys wiles Cb, *om.* HbHa   his] *om.* Do   43 feende of helle] feendis wilis Cb   feende] deville L   of helle] *om.* CaDo   the feende . . . ayenst] *om.* HbHa   the which . . . ayenst] and be þe children of israel Ca   which] *add* he CbDo   to founde] to fyght A2, *om.* CbDo   44 is interpreted] is vndirstonde the A2, betokeyth Ca   derkenesse] *add* and þat is HbCa

synne throu3 the which a man commeth to derkenes of euerlastinge 45
peine. The whiche .v. wilis Kinge Pharao vsed ayenst the childrenne
of Israelle bi a sleight that God shulde nat haue hem out of his londe
and so out of [his] thraldome.

For whanne he was dryve bi nede throu3 the wirchinge of [the
honde of] allemyghti God doynge .x. gret veniauncis on hym and on 50
his londe to þat entente to dryve hym to lete the children of Israelle to
goo, Pharao vsed þereayens .v. wiles, | wenynge to hym to haue Df. 161rb
disseiued God and þe childrenne of Israelle and so to haue had hem
stille vndir his bandon, the which .v. wilis and othir wrenchis ben
written in the secounde boke of Goddis lawe in Exodi in the .viij.te 55
and .xij. chapitres.

The first wile is in the .viij.te chapitre, where he telleth þat God did
mani veniances to this kinge Pharao for þat he wolde nat deliuere his
puple out of his londe, but whan nede drofe hym he seid: 'Goo yee
and doth sacrifice to [your] God in this londe', and þis was but a wile 60
as thou3 he had seide: 'I consent gladli that ye doo sacrifice to your
God so that yee doo it in this londe that I am kinge off, and so ye
shulle abide stille vndir my powere, for it is litille lettinge to me thou3
ye doo sacrifice to youre God so that ye alleweie dwelle stille in my
londe vndir my powere, lordship and thraldom. For I am sekir of you 65
as longe as ye be in my londe that ye shulle be vndir my powere and
[at] my commaundement and wille.' So than the deuelle, kinge of the
londe of derkenesse that is synne, whan that nede dryueth hym bi the

46 Kinge Pharao] he HbCa   46–7 vsed . . . Israelle] dide to hem HbHaCa
47 hem] þe (his Ha) children of israel HbHaCa   48 so] *om.* Ca   his] *om.* D
49 he was] wee were L   wirchinge] wrecch A2, power and þe hand Ca   49–50 the
honde of] *om.* DA2   50 allemyghti] *om.* HaCb   God] *add* his honde D   doynge]
he sende vpon hym A2   on hym] *om.* A2   51 to þat entente] for EHbCaDo, *om.*
CbHa   to þat . . . hym to] that he shulde not A2   hym] hem Hb   52 goo] *add*
and D, *add* in to þe londe of beheest and kyng A2   Pharao] He ELCbHbHaCaDo
þereayens] ECbHbHaDo, his Ca   wenynge to hym] *om.* HbHa   52–4 wenynge
. . . wrenchis] and þay Ca   53 and so] *om.* HbHa   haue had] kepe A2, haue HbHa
54 bandon] bondage A2   wilis and othir] *om.* CbHbHaDo   and othir] other E, or L
55 Goddis lawe] *add* þat ys clepid HbCa, holy write Ha   55–6 in³ . . . chapitres] *om.*
CbDo, .viij. Ha   56 and] *add* .x. and Hb   57 the] exodi HaDo   .viij.te] *om.* L
God] *om.* Ca   58 mani] *add* grete D   59 londe] hond Cb   drofe] drowe L,
compellyd Ca   hym] *add* thereto than A2   59–61 Goo . . . seide] *om.* E
60 your] *om.* DA2, *add* lord Ca   and²] *add* thus Do   62 so that yee] but HbHaCa
off] *add* so that ye do it in none other E   63–5 for it . . . powere] *om.* L
64 alleweie] *om.* ECbHbHaCaDo   65 powere . . . and] *om.* HbHaCaDo   lordship]
om. E   lordship and thraldom] *om.* Cb   66 be¹] dwel Ha   67 at] *om.* DA2
my] *om.* A2   commaundement and] *om.* EA2CbHbHaCaDo   deuelle] *add* the D
kinge] *add* Pharo kyng L   68 is] *add* vnderstonde bi DA2L

passioune of oure Lorde Ihesu Criste and bi the sacrament of penance
70 to deliuere mannes soule out of his londe þat is the brode weie to helle
and so oute of his powere, to doo sacrifice of a contrite hert to
allemyghti God and so to be saued fro dampnacioun, than the feende
graunti[th] vndir this wile of falsenes that man shulde knowelich his
synne and offre hymselff to God and to doo penaunce enioined of the
75 preeste, and also offre to God othir goode deedis as almesse deedis and
deedis of mercie and such othir which þat ben goode deedis in her
owne kinde, yif it be so that man goo nouȝt out of his londe of
derkenes that is synne, þat is soo þat man leve naught his synne that
he hath done.
80   In this disseite of the feende dwelle many men þat thenken þat it is
ynowȝ to be saued that thei be shreven of her synnes and that thei doo
penaunce þat is boden hem of the preeste [and] othir good deedis of
kinde so thei dwelle stille in [þe] vse of the same synne þat thei were
inne bifore. This is but a fals and a sotille wile of þe feende to haue
85 h[e]m stille vndir his powere in the state of dampnacioun. For it is but
litille greuaunce to the feende, thouȝ men fast or goo wollewarde or
þat [thei] doo allemesse [deedis] and so of othir good deedis, so that
thei dwelle stille in the londe of derkenesse, that is to seie deedelie
D f. 161va synne [and] in þe state of dampnacioun. | For the fende wote welle þat
90 it is written in holie writ that þe offringe or sacrifice of the wickid man
is abhominable to God, and þat is vndirstonde of hem that forsaken
nought ne goo nat out of deedelie synne. Noo doute that the kinge of
wickidnesse, that is þe deville, wote welle þat man plesith nat God ne
gete any grace of merci ne of foryeuenesse but yif þat a man frist

69 oure Lorde] *om.* A2   sacrament] sacramentis L   71 of²] with Ca
73 grauntith] grauntid DA2, *add* it HaCa   74 and¹] *add* so CbHbHaCaDo
75 almesse deedis and] *om.* L   deedis²] dede Hb, *om.* Ca   75–6 and deedis of]
and Hb, of Ha   75–7 as almesse . . . goode deedis/in her owne kinde] *trs.* Cb   77 yif
it] *om.* ECbHbCaDo   be so] by so EHbHaDo, so Cb, *trs.* A2   that] *om.* Ha   nouȝt] *om.* L
78 is¹] *add* oute of A2   þat is] *om.* HbCaHaDo   leve] love Ca   80 is] *add* not A2
81 ynowȝ] now Hb   be shreven . . . thei] *om.* Ha   82 and] or of any DA2, *add* bi schriue
of here synne Ha   othir] *om.* A2   83 so] þowh LCbHbHaCaDo   in] into Hb   þe]
om. D   vse of the] *om.* Ha   83–4 þat . . . inne] vsing it as þei didyn Ha   84 fals,
sotille] *trs.* L   fals . . . sotille] *om.* CbHaCaDo   85 hem] hym DA2Cb   in] into Ha
but] *om.* CbHaCaDo   86 or¹] and Cb   goo] *add* barefote and A2   87 þat thei] þat
day D, *om.* CbHaCaDo   deedis¹] *om.* D   and so of] or Cb   88 thei] he Cb   that is] *om.*
Ca   to seie] to mene L, of CbCaDo, *om.* Ha   89 and] *om.* D, *add* so LCbDo   and . . .
dampnacioun] *om.* HaCa   90 writ] scripture A2, *add* Prouer xxj c⁰ EHaCaDo   or] of A2
wickid] vnholy L   91 þat] *add* it A2   is] *add* to L   92 nought] *om.* Ca   ne goo nat]
to be A2   deedelie] þe lond of Ca   synne] *add* for no prechinge nor techinge but contynuyn
in here synne Ca   Noo] ne A2   doute] *add* but A2   92–5 Noo . . . synne] *om.* L
93 deville] *add* for þe fent Ha   94 yif . . . frist] he Cb   frist] *om.* EHaDo

forsake his deedeli synne and so goo out of the londe of Egipte, þat is 95
deedeli syn.

For it is wreten in holie writte þat it is an holie sacrifice to yeue
entente to the commaundementis of God and to goo from alle
wickidnesse. And a noble praiere it is for synne to goo aweie fro
falsenesse. It is fulle moche plesinge to the Lorde God to torne aweie 100
fro wickidnesse, and a good praiere to torne aweie fro [falsenesse and]
vnrightwisnesse. And therefor yif thou wilt haue foryeuenes of thi
trespas, goo thou out of synne and take hede of the commaundementis
of God, and than offrist thou a noble praier and sacrifice [ye] aboue
goolde or any worldelie thinge, sith that noothinge þat man mai doo 105
shalle plese God without this. Therefor than doo thou [þy] besinesse
and aske help of God, for Seint Augustine seith: 'He that made the of
nou3t, he makith the nat rightfulle without the.'

And therefor lete nat this sleight of the fende disseiue the to make
the trowe þat thou sholdist be saued thou3 thou doo many good deedis 110
to see too, so that thou vse stille thi life in deedelie synne. For Seint
Gregorie seithe in his Pastorallis: 'He that yeueth mete to the hungry
and cloothinge to the nakid, and [yit] is diffoulid also with wickidnes
of synne in his soule or in his bodie, that [that] is of lesse value he
yeueth it vnto rightwisnesse, and þat that is of more value he yeueth to 115
synne, and his goode he yeueth to God, and hymselff to the deuelle,
and so the deuelle is fulle siker of hym.' But yit it is full nedefulle
thou3 a man be in deedelie synne to doo almesse deedis and othir good
deedis as Seint Gregorie seith, and it is put in þe canon *De penitencijs*
distinctione quinta, and the chapiter biginnith *Fallas*. For þis cause, as 120

95 deedeli] *om.* Ha   96 deedeli] *om.* ECbDo   97 in holie writte] ecclesiastici
xxxv HbDo   holie²] holsom CbHaDo   yeue] *add* to þe L   98 entente] entendaunce
A2   to¹] of L   99 noble] *om.* L   it is] *om.* LCbHaDo   for] to do awey A2   synne]
add is CbHaDo   goo aweie] turne L, go A2   100 falsenesse] *add* of þi trespasse and
vnri3tfulnes Ha   fulle] wel Do   It . . . moche] for it is grete A2   100–1 It . . .
falsenesse] *om.* L   100–2 It . . . vnrightwisnesse] *om.* Ha   101 and¹] *add* also it is A2
good] *om.* ELCbDo   aweie] *om.* LCbDo   falsenesse and] *om.* DA2Cb
102 vnrightwisnesse] vnry3tfulnes Cb   wilt] wit Ha   104 and²] *add* a D   and
sacrifice] *om.* Cb   ye] *om.* DA2   aboue] *add* all E   106 þy] *om.* D   107–8 of nou3t]
wiþowt þe LCbHaDo   110 trowe] beleue A2   saued thou3] made saue when L, saued
whan CbHaDo   111 to see too] in the sight of the people A2, *om.* Cb   so that] þowh
LCbHaDo   stille . . . in] forthe þy L   112 seithe] *om.* Ha   Pastorallis] *add* in þe xliiij
c° seiþ Ha, *add* .xlij. Do   113 yit] *om.* D   114 bodie] *add* or in boþe Ha   that²]
om. D   114–15 he yeueth] temporal A2   117 fulle] *om.* Cb   118 deedis] *om.* Ha
and] or Do   118–19 and . . . deedis] *om.* A2, *add* for twey skyls Ha   119–20 *De*
penitenciis . . . chapiter] *om.* CbDo   120 *distinctione quinta*] þe fifþe distinccion Ha   For
þis cause] one cause is Ha

[he seith, that] God through his mercie makith mannes hert þe
sonnere to haue light throuȝ grace to be turned to penaunce.

Also anoþere skille is this, and is put in þe lawe in the place that is
D f. 161ᵛᵇ seide bifore | in the thrid distinccion, and the paraffe biginnyth *Potest*,
125 where it is seide that a man that dothe goode deedis þat is inne
deedelie synne and shalle be dampnid, yit the euerlastinge turment of
helle shalle be [made] to hym the more fauorable. So it is nedefulle to
doo good deedis in what state þat a man be inne, and also to be ware of
þe wyle of the feende that wille make a man to trust [þere that no
130 trust] is, to wene that whan a man is in þe state of deedelie synne and
þereto in purpos to abide þereinne, [that] he shuld doo worshippfullie
sacrifice to God and acceptable and worthi mede. For Moyses the
prophete seith: 'Hit mai nat be sothe that we shalle offre abhomina-
ciouns of Egipte, that is of deedelie synne, vnto the Lorde God,' as
135 though he seid: 'Hit mai nat be acceptable to the Lord any good deede
that is defoulid with deedelie synne, but vs must goo out of the londe
of Egipte.' He seith that is out of deedeli synne, which is the londe of
[the feende], wherefor late vs doo sacrifice vnto the Lorde God.

[The secounde wile.] And whan Kinge Pharao herde this aunswere
140 that he shulde bi nede graunte that the childrenne of Israel must
needis goo out of his londe and so out of his powere, than he
bithought hym of anothir cursid wile, that is the secounde disseite,
and seid to Moyses as it is written: 'Yif yee goo out of my londe to doo
sacrifice to the Lorde God, goth nauȝt ferre,' as thouȝ he [seid] or
145 ment: 'Sith yee wolle naught doo sacrifice to the Lorde God in my
londe but þat ye woll goo oute thereof, yit I graunte thereto so that yee

121 he seith that] seith he for D   mannes hert] many mennys hertis L
121–2 makith . . . light] man to haue syȝt þe sunnere Hb   122 light] siȝte
CbHaDo   123 skille] cause L   lawe] lawes D   the] *add* same Ha   124 in . . .
distinccion] *om.* CbDo   paraffe] *add* thereof D, *add* .iij.ᵈ Do   biginnyth] *add* þus Hb
125 goode] *om.* L   126 yit] ye A2, *om.* Cb, in Do   127 made] *om.* DA2
128 what] *add* ever L   man] *add* euer DA2   129 wyle of the feende] feendis wyle Cb
that wille] to CbHbDo   make] *om.* L   129–30 þere . . . trust] *om.* D   130 to wene
that] that is A2   131 abide] laste LHbDo, reste Cb   that] whan D   132 to God/
and acceptable] *trs.* CbHbDo   and¹] *add* an L, *add* to hym A2   mede] *add* of hym A2
133 prophete] *add* Exod .viij°. LHbDo   sothe] sith A2, so Hb   134 that is . . . synne]
om. CbHbDo   136 that is] *om.* HbDo   136–7 the londe . . . Cb
137 of Egipte] *om.* HbDo   seith] *add* he A2   deedeli] *om.* HbDo   138 the feende]
Pharao D, the devylle A2   wherefor late vs] and þan LCbHbDo, *add* forsake hym and A2
139 The secounde wile] *om.* DHb   142 cursid] *om.* LCbHbDo   143 written] *add*
Exod viij° LHbDo   144 seid or] thought or D, *om.* A2   144–5 or ment] *om.*
CbHbDo   145 Sith] *add* than D, *add* þat L   146 but . . . thereof] *om.* Cb   þat ye
woll] *om.* HbDo   thereof] *om.* HbDo

goo nauȝt ferre but þat ye mowe come sone ayenne to dwelle vndir my powere.'

This same wile worchith the feende with man, for he wolle graunte that a man bi the sacrement of penance goo out of his londe that is 150 derknesse of synne so that he goo nat ferre but that he come sone ayenne; as som there ben þat live in synne alle the yere tille it be Estir and than thei morne, for that nede driueth hem more for shame of the worlde than for the loue of go[o]d l[i]vinge, and than thei goo and shriue ham and doo penaunce a litille, but thei goo nat ferre out of the 155 londe of Egipte that is synne, for thei come sone ayenne whan þei torne sone ayenne to synne.

And so through disseite of the feende thei wene that it were ynowȝ to haue grace of foryefenesse and mercie for þat thei be shrewen, thouȝ thei turne anone ayenne to þe same synne þat thei did bifore. 160 That man that dothe thus is foule begilid throuȝ the wile of the | feende, for Seint Augustine seith in a boke that is iclepid Df. 162ra Soliloquiorum, and it is put in the Canon de penitencijs the thrid distinccion and the chapiter beginnith thus: 'Inanis. Shriffte and penaunce,' he seith, 'is but void whan deedeli synnes followinge 165 [defoulith] it. Noothinge profitith, nothir wepenge ne murnynge for synnes yif dedelie synnes be fordone and ben vsid ayenne. Ne it availith nat to aske forgiffnesse of syn and efftsones to doo ayenne the same synne. And nat ooneli he that turneth ayenne to synne and endith therein shalle haue no foryeuenesse of [þat synne that he 170 endith his life in, but also he getith no foryeuenesse of] noo synne [þat euer he did] thouȝ he were shreuen thereof and did some penance.'

And that this is sothe shewith the Maistir of [Sentence] in the

147 but] om. CbHbDo   ayenne] add ye so for L, add and ȝe so CbHbDo   vndir] in Cb
149 worchith] vsith L, norischiþ Hb   150–1 out . . . goo] om. Cb   151 he²] ye A2
152 there] oþer A2   it be] at A2, add nere CbHbDo   153 morne] om. Cb   for that . . .
hem/more] trs. and om. that Cb   hem] add thereto A2   153–4 more . . . worlde] om.
CbHb   of the worlde] om. LDo   154 good livinge] God levinge her synne D, God that
thaye leve A2, god leuyng Hb   and . . . goo and] om. CbHb   155–6 out . . . synne] om.
CbHb   156–7 whan . . . ayenne] om. Cb   158 feende] deville LCbHbDo   ynowȝ]
add to hem CbHb   159 of] and A2   160 ayenne] om. Cb   þat . . . bifore] afore doo
CbHb   161 that . . . thus] om. A2   begilid] add þat A2   wile] wiles Hb
162 feende] devil Cb, add so doyth A2   is iclepid] he clepyth Cb   163 Soliloquiorum]
add ad deum A2   164 Shriffte and] om. L   and²] or CbHbDo   165 followinge] om.
A2, add on CbHb   166 defoulith] followith DA2   nothir] om. LCbHbDo   ne] and
LCbHbDo   167 be fordone] be for done D, be forbodyn A2   and ben vsid] be
renewed LCbHbDo   170 shalle haue no] noþer he getith A2   170–1 þat synne . . .
foryeuenesse of] om. DA2   171 also] om. Cb   171–2 þat . . . did] om. DA2
173 Sentence] Stories DA2L

.iiij.^{þe} boke of Sentencis, the [.xxij.^{de}] distinccion, þe frist and the
175 secounde chapitris, bi diuers auctoritees on this wise: 'Seint Ambrose
vppon Poulis epistelis [vnto the Ephesios seith]: "Foryeueth togidir
that any man hath trespacid to othir or ellis God [reuoketh] that þat
he hath foryouen. For but yif it be done, without doute God shalle
reuoke his sentence throuȝ which he yafe mercie, as it is redde in the
180 gospelle of þe wickid seruaunte which was founde without mercie to
his fellawe seruaunt." And R[a]banus on the same texte seith: "The
lorde did þe wickid seruaunte to turment tille that he [had] paied eueri
dette. Nouȝt oonelie the synnes that he did afftir his bapteme shulle be
are[tt]ed to hym to peyne, but also origenalle synnes which that were
185 foryouen in bapteme." Also Seint Gregorie seith in the thrid boke of
his Morallis of the worde of þe gospelle: "Hit folowith that if we
foryefe nat of alle oure hert that þat is trespacid vnto vs, than shalle
that be renued on vs which we were ioiefulle [of that throuȝ penaunce]
was foryouen vs." And Seinte Augustine seith in an omelie on a worde
190 þat Criste spekith in Luke: "Foryeve and it shalle be foryouen to
you," and [he] seith on this manere wise: "Foryeue. Yif thou foryevist
nat I shalle [clepe] the ayenne, and whatsoeuer I haue foryeve the I
shalle turne it ayenst the. For whosoeuer foryete the goode yifftis of
God, God wille venge his owne wrongis. Nouȝt [only] of synnes to
195 come he shalle disserue noo mercie, but also of the synnes passid
whiche he wende had be foryeuen to hym [shalle be] turne[d] ayenne
to hym bi vengeaunce." And also Bede vppon Luke seith: "Whoso
that affter bapteme whethir shrewdnesse of eresie or of worldlie
199 couetice falle on, anone hit berith hym doun into the depeth of
D f. 162rb synnes." | And Seint Augustine also in the frist boke that is clepid *de*

174 of Sentencis] of Sentence A2, *om.* CbHbDo   .xxij.^{de}] .xij.^{þe} DA2L   175 wise]
add sayeth A2   176 epistelis] epistel HbDo   vnto . . . Ephesios/seith] *trs.* DL
177 hath trespacid] trespassith L   reuoketh] rekneth DA2   that^2] not A2, *om.* CbHb
178 without doute] *om.* Cb   180 gospelle] *add* of mathewe the .xviij. chapitre CbHbDo
181 fellawe] fellawes DA2   Rabanus] Robanus D   182 had] *om.* D   eueri] alle þe A2
183 Nouȝt oonelie] *add* for LDo   184 aretted] arekened D, ordeinede A2   186 his]
om. CbHbDo   the worde of] *om.* A2   187 alle] *om.* CbHb   that . . . trespacid] trespace
done A2   þat] *om.* CbHb   188 renued] rerid Hb, reysid Cb   ioiefulle] wilfulle Cb   that]
add þat Cb   of that/throuȝ penaunce] *trs.* D   189 seith] *om.* A2LCbHbDo   in an
omelie/on a worde] *trs.* Cb   190 þat Criste] *om.* Cb   spekith] saide A2   Luke] *add* þe
sixte chapitre CbHbDo   191 he] *om.* D   manere] *om.* CbHbDo   Foryeue] for L, *om.* Cb
192 clepe] *om.* D   the^1] *om.* A2   193 foryete] forȝetyng LCbHbDo   194 God^2] *om.*
CbHbDo   only] *om.* DA2L   195 mercie] merite Cb   196 shalle be turned] but turne
D, but thaye shalle turne A2   197 bi] to LCbHbDo   Luke] *add* the .xj. chapitre CbHbDo
198 whethir] *add* it be A2   of^1] or L, *om.* Cb   eresie] erroure Cb   200 the . . . is] his boke
A2   de] *om.* Cb   200–1 de . . . paruulorum] *Soliloquorum anime ad deum* A2

baptismo paruulorum seith that synnes foryeuen shalle turne ayenne where brothirlie charite is nat.

'Oure Lorde techeth opunlie in þe gospelle of that seruant of whom the lorde askith ayenne the dette foryouen in as moche as he wolde nat foryeue the dette to his fellaw[e] seruaunt. Men myght seie ayenst 205 this, yiff a man shulde be ponisshid efftsoone for that synne þat he was sorie fore and did penaunce for it, hit wolde seme nat rightfulle that God sholde ponisshe twies for oo synne and double tribulacioun reise þerefor, which is ayenst the scripture in þe frist chapiter of Na[um] the prophete. But vnto this mater,' seith the Maistir of Sentenc[e], 'it 210 mai be aunswerd thus, that nothir double tribulacioun riseth nothir God ponisshith twies for oo thinge, that is to seie where that worthi satisfaccioun and sufficiaunt penaunce is fulfillid. But he made noo worþi satisfaccioun ne sufficiant that had noo goode perseueraunce in good livinge, for he ought to haue had a customable mynde on his 215 synne nouʒt for to doo it ayen but [for to flee] it. He ought also nat to haue foryete alle the grete yifftis and good beneficis of God, which yifftis, as Seint Augustine seith vppon the psalme, be many as be these foryeuenesse of diuers synnes. He ouʒt therefor to thenke on as many yifftis of God as he had doo synnes, and for thoo foryevenessis to doo 220 vnnumerable thankingis to oure Lord God vnto the last endinge of his life. But for he, as an vnkinde hounde, turned ayenne to ete that he had cast or spowen, and as a sowe that is faire wasshe waloweth hir ayenne in a foule slowgh, as it is written in þe secounde epistille of Seint Petire the seconde chapiter, there he slowgh alle the goode 225 deedis þat he had done bifore and reuokid to hym the synne that was

203 of¹] in LCbHbDo   204 the lorde] he A2   askith] asked CbHb   the dette] *om.* Cb   205 fellawe] fellawis DA2   207 for it] *om.* LCbHbDo   208 synne] þyng LCbHbDo   208–9 reise þerefor] *om.* Hb   209 scripture] scriptures Cb   chapiter] book Do   Naum] Naman DA2, Naym CbHb   210 mater] *om.* CbHbDo   of] add the Cb   Sentence] sentencis and D, add and A2   211 that] add a DA2   riseth] *om.* Cb   212 that¹ . . . seie] *om.* Do   that . . . that] For that were sothe if after CbHb   213 sufficiaunt] *om.* A2   is fulfillid] he (*om.* Hb) shuld efte sonys ponysshe CbHb   fulfillid] add sufficiauntlye A2   214 worþi . . . sufficiant] satisfaccioun worthy (vttirly Cb, worthily HbDo) and sufficyauntly LCbHbDo   goode] *om.* DoCbHb   215 for] *om.* Cb   had] *om.* Hb   216 ayen] *om.* LCbHbDo   for to flee] leve D   also] add or he nedyd Cb   217 and good beneficis] *om.* CbHbDo   218 the] a Cb   be¹] add as HbDo   be . . . be] he was by A2   these] *om.* CbHbDo   219 to thenk on] for Cb   220 doo¹] *om.* LCbHbDo   thoo foryevenessis] the foryevenes of þem A2   221 vnnumerable] *om.* CbHbDo   last] *om.* CbHbDo   endinge] day L, ende A2CbHbDo   222 turned] turnyth L   that] add þat CbHb   223 cast or] *om.* LCbHbDo   that is] *om.* CbHbDo   wasshe] add turnyth hir and Cb   224 ayenne] *om.* Cb   slowgh] add that she came oute of or many oþer suche A2   225 there] therfor CbHbDo   slowgh] distroyed Cb

frist foryouen to hym, so that to what buxome man and lowe and meke
þat God foryafe synne, afftir to þat same man beynge prowde and
vnkinde God shalle are[tt]e ayenst hym þe same synne. And so for the
230 vnkindenesse he is as synfulle as he was tofore.' Alle these woordis
biforeseide seith the Maistir of Sentence.

   Syth he than that synneth deedelie sleethe alle his goode deedis that
he did bifore, so that thei shulle nat be thought on bifore God, as it is
D f. 162ᵛᵃ written bi þe prophete, but yif he haue grace of amendinge, | and [yif]
235 he amende [hym] bi penance and doo afftir the bidding of God, alle
his synnes shulle nat be thought on but goode life he shal live. And
thereto [he shalle queken ayenne] alle his goode deedis that were
bifore throuȝ synne slayne. [Right so he þat synneth deedelie sleethe
alle his goode deedis and quekeneth ayenne alle his evelle deedis þat
240 were bifore slayne.] And so hit shewith the last eende of man wers
than the former eende, as it is written in the gospelle.

   Therefor it is nedefulle to hym that wille goone out of synne to be
fulle ware of the feende, and to goo so ferre fro synne þat he come noo
more ayen and so doo worþi frutis of penaunce, as Seint Iohn Baptist
245 biddith, which, as Seint Gregorie seith, is for to wepe so and [morne]
for synne þat he hath done, þat he doo no more synne to wepe fore
and so to be ware of þe wile of þe feende.

   [The thrid wile.] But whan the feende mai nat haue man stille in his
londe, that is [to] vndirstonde in deedelie synne bi these twoo cursed
250 and disseiuable wylis that haue here beforne [be] rehercid, than wille
he cast the thridde wile as Kinge Pharao did, and that was this. Whan
Moises seide to hym: 'Vs must needis goo out of thi londe and also we

227 that] *add* this Do, *add* þat L   man] *om.* CbHbDo   227–8 and meke þat] *om.*
CbHbDo   228 beynge] *om.* CbHbDo   229 arette] arere DA2, areyne Cb   ayenst]
om. L, to Cb   230 Alle] And A2   231 Sentence] Sentencis L   234 bi] in
CbHbDo   prophete] *add* ezechiel the .xviij. chapitre CbHbDo   yif¹] that A2
amendinge] amendment Cb   yif²] þat DA2   235 amende] haue grace of amendyng
Do   hym] *om.* D   236 goode life] by lyfe CbHb   237 he shalle/queken ayenne] *trs.*
DA2   shalle queken] hath quykened LCbHbDo   237–8 were/bifore . . . synne] *trs.*
LDo   were bifore/throuȝ synne] *trs.* CbHb   238–40 Right so . . . bifore slayne] *om.*
DA2   241 as] and A2   gospelle] *add* (of Luk Hb) the .xj. chapitre CbHb, *add* of luk .x.°
Do   243 fulle] *om.* CbHbDo   so] *om.* Hb   244 Baptist] *add* sayeth and A2
245 biddith] *add* do ye worthye penaunce the A2, *add* in the gospel of Mathewe the thridde
(.ix. Do) chapitre CbHbDo   seith] *add* it D   is for to] *om.* A2   morne] many D
246 hath . . . he] *om.* CbHbDo   247 and so] but whan the feende sterith vs to synne A2
wile] wylys Cb   þe feende] hym A2   248 The thrid wile] *om.* DA2   249 londe]
honde Do   to] *om.* D   vndirstonde in deedelie] *om.* CbHbDo   249–50 cursed and
disseiuable] *om.* CbHbDo   250 haue] *add* nowe L   that haue here] *om.* CbHbDo   be]
om. D   rehercid] seyd CbHbDo   251 was this] *om.* CbHbDo

must goo ferre, for wee must goo three daies iourneie to doo sacrifice
to the Lorde,' thoo Kinge Pharao bithought hym on anothir wile and
seide as it is wreten in Exodi the .x.^{þe} chapiter: 'I wille nat lete you goo 255
and youre children also, for noo doute yee thinke fulle euelle ayens
me; but I wolle that men shul goo and doo sacrifice and that the
children shalle abide at home,' as thou3 he had seid and mente: 'I
graunte that yee goo out of my londe to doo sacrifice to the Lorde God
and also to goo ferre, vppon this condicioun, that yee leve youre 260
children at home in my londe.' And he seid thus vndir this wile and
entente þat he wist welle, yif the children of hem þat went out were
lefft at home, thei that went oute shulde thenke on her childrenne and
for þe loue of hem come þe rathir ayenne and so to abide stille vndir
his powere and dominacioun. This same fals wile vseth the feende to 265
mannes soule, for whan þat nede driueth hym he wille graunte þat
man goo out of his londe of derkenes, that is synne, and also he will
þat he goo ferre out of his londe, þat is to seie beynge in purpos to
torne no more ayenne, so þat he leve his children at home vndir his
powere.   270
    And what ben oure children? Nought but goode vertues which we
conceiue in oure hert throu3 þe worde of God, and growith forth bi
goode willis and [goode] thou3tis | and be borne of oure soule and Df. 162vb
bodie through goode werchenge and good deedis doynge, and so be
norisshid forthe in the worlde through goodenesse bathed in tribu- 275
lacioun and wasshen in wepenge and in penaunce and taught throu3
the drede of God and welle cloþid in þe condiciouns of charite. These

253 must^1] add nedis A2   doo] om. L   255 in . . . chapiter] om. Do   257 I . . .
that^1] om. CbHbDo   that the] þat her L, lete your A2, hir Do, om. CbHb   258 as] And
CbHb   seid and] om. A2   and mente] om. CbHbDo   258–9 I graunte] ignorant Cb
260 vppon this condicion] by so CbHbDo   261 And] 3itt Cb   thus] that A2   this] a
A2   and] to the A2   261–2 and entente] om. CbHbDo   262–3 the children . . .
childrenne] þere children at home in his londe that thaye shulde þynke alweye vpon them
A2   264 for . . . ayenne and] om. Cb   abide] be CbHbDo   stille] om. A2   265 and
dominacioun] om. CbHbDo   fals] om. CbHbDo   to] ayenste A2   267–8 of derkenes
. . . londe] om. L   267 he will] om. CbHbDo   268 out . . . londe] om. CbHbDo
271 And . . . but] We chul vndirstond þat we must leue 3oure synnes and not delite in hem
but be war of hem and of þe .v. soteltes of þe fend as it chewith in þe last ende of þe boke in
þe last lef and vse Ya   Nought] om. A2CbHb   vertues] werkes Cb   272 conceiue]
conserve L, conseyuyde HbYa   þe worde of God] goddes grace and be his holi worde Ya
growith] growid Hb   bi] in Ya   273 goode^1] add werkis D   goode^2] om. DCb
thou3tis] thou3tis//thou3tis D   273–4 be . . . through] om. Ya   and bodie] om. Cb
274 and^1] om. Ya   so] om. LCbHbYaDo   275 in the . . . goodenesse] by gode willis
and gode thoughtis A2   276 taught throu3] by A2   277 drede] deede Cb   of God]
om. CbHbYaDo   cloþid] yclad DoYa

children shulle helpe a man welle at nede whan he wexeth oolde and
mai nat helpe hymselff, and þat is whan he shalle goo out of this
280 worlde. Than wille thei folowe hym, as holie writte seith in the
Apocalips in the .xiiij. chapiter, and than shulle thei helpe hym and
[susteyne] hym as Thobie did his fadir, wherefor he was clepid of his
moodir þe staffe of hir oolde age.

And whoso wille wite þe names of hem, some I shalle reherce and
285 biginne atte eldest frist, which that is lowenesse, buxomnesse,
mekenes, rightwisnes, mercie, pete, almesse deedis doynge, for
synne morninge, goode hope and sadde feith holdinge, pouerte of
spirite, dispite of hymselff, quik in goodnesse, slowʒ in euelle, stronge
in good deedis, faint to doo amysse, harde in holinesse and fulle
290 cowarde in malice, lover [of] vertue and hater of synne, deuoute in
praieris and foryeuere of wronges, pacient in sikenesse and in
aduersite, perseueraunte in goodnes, ioiefulle of goodnesse hiringe
and hevie of euelle spekinge, his neightbouris nouʒte denienge and to
the better alleweie drawinge, demynge hymselff to [be] werst of alle
295 othir atte his owne knowynge and anothir holiere than hymselff bi his
semenge redie to goodnesse, lernenge and the worde of God nauʒt
foryetenge, his enemies the feende, the flesshe [and] the worlde
dispisinge and afftir h[e]uenlie thingis longinge, badde life of
neightbores forsakinge and holinesse of seintis followinge, pees
300 sewenge, discorde hatinge, wise and ware of [the] wilis of the
feende and spedie of vertue l[ern]inge, trewe with his neightbour in
[delynge] and for goode loue flee begilinge, the name of God praisinge

278 children] *om.* A2   helpe] kepe Hb   man] *add* wondir L   oolde] cold Hb
279 goo] passe Cb   280 wille] when Hb   holie . . . seith] it is seide in holy writte L, it
is sayd CbHbYaDo   281 chapiter] *om.* Do   282 susteyne] socoure D   285 frist]
om. CbHbYa   which that is] with L   lowenesse] lowlynes Cb   286 mekenes] *add* and
mildenesse HbYaDo   deedis] *om.* CbHbYa   287 sadde] *om.* CbHbYa   pouerte] pore
A2   288 dispite] *om.* L   hymselff] *add* holdynge CbHbYaDo   quik] swifte Ya
goodnesse] *add* and full CbHb   slowʒ] slouʒful Ya   289 good] wele doo Cb   harde]
hardy A2CbHbYa   fulle] foule Ya   290 of¹] in DA2   hater] batere Hb
291 wronges] *add* to hym done CbHbYa   and²] *om.* LDo   292 goodnes] *add* and not
faylyng CbHbYaDo   293 nouʒte] *add* evyl A2   denienge] demenyng L, demyng A2Cb
294 be] the DA2   alle] *om.* CbHbYaDo   295 atte . . . knowynge] that he knowith A2
hymselff] he A2   296 to goodnesse lernenge] euer to lerne godenes A2   297 his] *add*
.iij. gostely A2, *add* thre CbHbYaDo   feende] devylle A2   and] *om.* D   flesshe, worlde]
trs. and add euer A2   298 and] *add* euer A2   afftir] *om.* CbHbYa   heuenlie] houenlie D
longinge] desiryng A2, lovyng CbHb   of] *add* thy A2   299 neightbores] *add* euer A2
seintis] *add* euer A2   300 hatinge] *add* and to be A2   wise and] *om.* CbHbYa   the¹]
om. D, *add* sotylle A2   301 spedie] spedyng L   lerninge] livinge D, euer levynge A2
trewe] trulye A2   in] *om.* CbHbYa   302 delynge] diligence D   goode] goddys Cb
loue] *add* to A2   begilinge] *add* and euer A2

and hym as [mercy]fulle fader worshippyng, his fader and his mooder
honouringe and doo alle her leefulle biddinge, of soulis in her [peynes
rewthe] having and some goodnesse doo to her deliueringe, noo man 305
disseiuenge, trewelie and rightfullie alle thinge worchinge, alle dettes
welle paienge, extorcion and wronge euere fleynge, in housolde faire
berenge, his wife, childrenne and meyne welle gouerninge, his sogettis
in [goodnesse] lerninge, buxome and lowelie to hem þat ben aboue
in hiȝe berenge, fellawe to hem þat ben binethe in conninge, weight, 310
noumbre and mesure in [thought], worde and deede, | chaste feith and Lf. 434 ᵛᵃ
beleve in soule to God kepyng and clennes in hert havyng, and wiþ a
ioyful sperite in contemplacioun ioiyng, and so synge to God in
iubilacioun lowing. But þe beste, richest and wisest to rewle hem alle
with is charite nat feyned.   315
   These and meny mo be children of þe sowle, [but] for febilnes of
witt þey fallen nat all to mynde. And whoso hathe but þese fewe, all
baren is he nat. And also þe body wele rewlid shuld [nat] be all
wiþowte but bryng forthe som goode froite to his owen profite, of
whiche þe names shull be clepid as þey sewen heraftir forthwith: 320
chastite, sobirnes, goode occupacioun, penaunce and trewe laboure,
mesure and goode rule in eetyng and drynkyng, wakynge and slepyng,
to the reson of þe soule lowly subiectyng, for no lust ne peyne [þe]
biddyng of God brekyng, and þe lawe of God buxomly fulfillyng, all
temptaciouns of lustis lawefully wiþstondyng, peynes and sikenes þat 325
be nat evermore lastyng settyng at nought, þe reward of þe peyne þat

303 as] add moost A2, add all Do   mercyfulle] worshippfulle DA2   and²] om. Ya
303–4 worshippyng, honouringe] trs. Cb   304 honouringe] worshippyng L   alle] at
CbHbYaDo   304–5 peynes rewthe] praieris right D, paynes pety A2   305 doo to] trs.
Ya   deliueringe] deluyuerance A2   307 euere] om. CbHbYa   308 his wife . . .
gouerninge] om. CbHbYa   welle] trewly and goostly L, truli and goodli Do
309 goodnesse] buxom DA2L, add godly CbHbYaDo   lerninge] add abydyng and to be
A2   and lowelie] om. A2   lowelie] lowe LCbHbYaDo   310 in hiȝe] in L, Esy of
CbHbYaDo, of Do   binethe] add the A2   in conninge] in comenyng LDo, om. CbHbYa
311 thought] trouthe DA2   chaste] chastite A2   312 kepyng] wepyng for þi synne A2
313 sperite] herte A2   ioiyng] om. CbHbYa   so] add euer to A2, om. Cb   synge] singyng
DoYa   in²] om. A2   314 lowing] lovyng A2, om. CbHbYaDo   þe . . . wisest] thye laste
wysenes and riches A2   beste richest] cherefullest Cb   richest] richesse Ya   richest/and
wisest] trsp. with richesse for richest Do   hem alle] alle thes aforesayde Cb   315 is] his A2
316 but] om. L   317 all¹] om. A2CbHbYa, in Do   And] But Cb   whoso] who Hb   but]
om. A2Cb   fewe] add children A2   318 nat²] om. L   319 som . . . froite] om. A2
owen] sowle Cb   320 as . . . forthwith] om. CbHb   heraftir] after A2   forthwith] The
furste is A2, om. Do   321 goode] and A2   occupacioun] add watch in mesure holily (hooli
Do) occupied CbHbYaDo   322 wakynge, slepyng] trs. A2   323 subiectyng]
submyttyng A2   323 þe²] ne L   325 of] and A2   lawefully] lowly A2   wiþstondyng]
withsitting HbDo, withsettynge Ya   326 settyng] haue them Cb   settyng/at nought] trs.
Ya   þe¹] to HbYaDo   þe reward] to the regarde Cb

hathe noon endyng and suffir hem gladly for þe love of ioy þat is and
evermore shall be duryng, in goode life deeth nat dredyng for ioy of
þyn aȝeen vprisyng, in all þe lymes of þy body to God gladly bowyng
330 in goode will to do at his biddyng, his wittis wele rewlyng and þe
L f. 434ᵛᵇ outragiousnes | of hem by reson of þe soule withsittyng.

Meny moo goode children of þe body þer been, but fewe folk have
hem in vsyng. And he þat hathe suche a nobill meyne off soule and of
body to fight wiþ the feende is myghty inowe at fulle, and namely yf
335 Goddis grase be hym nyȝe þan dare hym in noo wise drede. These
children than coveite[þ þe devyll to haue] still in [his] lordship þough
þat a man go fro hym by þe sacrament of penaunce. These children
been in þe lond of þe feende þat is in þe lond of derkenes of dedely
synne when they be doone or brought forthe þorowe veynglory and
340 ipocrisy. In every goode dede goodely doon þere be .ij. personys
entremetynge, þat is to sey God þorowe his grace vertu ȝevyng, [and
man þorowe þat grace goodely worchynge, wherefor in every goode
dede be othir .ij. thingis, that is worshipp and glory to God for his
grace ȝevyng] and profite to man in blisse for his wele worchynge. But
345 when man, lower þan God, takith awey fro God his glory þat shuld
longe to hym and his worshipp þat oonly longith to God and to noon
other, as he seith hymself Isay .xlij°. cap°: 'My glory I shall ȝeve to
noon other,' right so þe devill, lower þan man, takiþ awey fro man þe
profite of his goode worchyng þat he shuld have had in blisse, and [he]
350 þat hathe þe profite of eny worke he hathe [the] worke. But þe feende
thorowe veynglory and ipocrisy hathe [aweie] fro man þe profite of his

327 suffir] suffring HbYa   and²] om. A2   328 shall be duryng] enduryng A2   life] add
and A2   for] add love of CbHbYa   328–9 of þyn] om. Hb, in CbYa   329 þe] thye A2,
om. CbHb   gladly] lowlye A2, om. CbHb   330 his²] and thy A2   þe] thye A2
331 outragiousnes] ouȝtragenes Ya   333 nobill] om. CbHbYaDo   334 wiþ] add ayenst
A2   is] add euer A2   at fulle] at the falle to withstonde hym A2, om. CbHbYaDo
335 hym¹] hem Hb   in noo wise] not CbHbYaDo   335–6 These . . . his] the children þat
holde togedir in the A2   336 coveiteþ] coveiten L   þe devyll/to haue] trs. L   his] her A2L,
om. Hb   lordship] add and power of the feend A2   337 go] add ferre A2   hym] hem Ya
338–9 þat is . . . synne] om. CbHbYaDo   339 doone or] om. Cb   be . . . þorowe] done there
dedis in A2   forthe] om. Cb   340 dede] add that shulde be A2   goodely doon] godlye thaye
do it so A2   doon þere] om. Cb   þere] om. HbYaDo   341 þat is . . . sey] om. CbHbDo, and
þat is Ya   341–4 and man . . . ȝevyng] om. L   342 grace] add and A2   goodely] gode Cb
343 that is] om. CbHbDoYa   344 to man/in blisse] to the blysse of man A2, trs. CbHbDo,
so with and for in Ya   wele] good Cb   345 lower þan God] is slowe to do gode than he A2
his] om. CbHbDo   345–6 þat shuld . . . hym/and . . . worshipp] trs. and om. his Cb
346 his] om. CbHbDo   346–7 God . . . other] hym CbHbDo   347 seith/hymself] trs.
and add by A2, add by CbHb   Isay] add the prophete in the A2, add the prophete the CbHb
348 right . . . devill] but as the feend that is A2   man²] hym A2   349 he²] om. DL
350 þat] om. A2   he] that A2   the] to DL   351 and] or CbHb   aweie] allwey L

werkis þat been his children, for þey were defoulid as it is write in þe
gospell. And þe briddis of the [eir] þat be devillis eete hem vp, | þat is   L f. 435ra
to sey, devourid hem and lost hem at her wille. þan muste nedis his
children, þat been his workis þat been overleide and ovircome with 355
synne, be vndir þe feendis power, for allþough þey were good werkis
in kynde, ȝit þey were nat godely wrought ne kepte sith þat þey were
lost þorowe veynglory and lefte behynde þorowe ipocrisy.

þe .iiij. th wile. But Moyses seide to þe kyng Pharo, as it is wreten
and declared in Exodi capᵒ .ix.ᵒ: 'Vs muste go to do sacrefice to þe 360
Lord with olde men and yong men and with men children and with
wommen children and with beestis of shepe and of neete, for it is a
grete solempnyte to the Lord.' And Kyng Pharo wolde nat graunte it
till þat God dr[of]e hym therc by grete veniauncis. And when he was
dryven by nede, he grauntid it vndir þe fourth wile thus and seide: 365
'Goith and doythe sacrefice to þe Lord, and lette youre children go
with yowe, and oonly letith your beestis of shepe and nete be at home,'
as þowgh he had seide: 'Yee desire þat youre children go wiþ yowe
and I graunte therto so þat yee leue your beestis at home.' For he
wiste it wele þat all her lijfloode stode moste by bestys, and þerfor if 370
they had lefte hem behynde þey wolde haue comen home aȝeen for
love of her housholde and lijfeloode, and so [to] be stylle vndir his
power. Right so | and in liche maner wise dothe þe fals feende vndir L f. 435rb
[a] wile, for when he seeth þat he may noon otherwise do but þat man
woll go out of his londe, þat is synne, be penaunce, and also þat he go 375
ferre by purpose not for to turn aȝeen to synne, and þat he have his
children with hym þat been his goode vertues by so þat he leve his
beestis in his lond.

þese beestis been his .v. wittis bodely, whiche, when þey be fedde

353 gospell] add of luke the viij chapitre CbHbDo   eir] erthe A2L   354 devourid]
they devoure Cb, deuouren Do   355 children . . . his] ther Cb   and ovircome] om.
CbHbDo   356 allþough] thouȝe alle Cb   358 þorowe¹,²] by A2   359 But] as A2
seide] om. A2   360 and declared] om. CbHbDo   go] add oute Cb   361 and with¹]
om. Cb   362 wommen] woman and Cb   363 graunte it] om. Hb   it] thereto A2,
om. CbDo   364 drofe] drewe L   there] om. CbHbDo   by] add þe L   365 dryven]
add þereto A2   thus] om. CbHbDo   seide] add to þem A2   367–8 and oonly . . . yowe]
twice with lettith and ȝowe second time L   367 be] abide A2, dwelle CbHbDo
370 þerfor] add he thought A2, om. CbHbDo   372 housholde and] om. CbHbDo   to]
þey L   stylle] om. Cb   372–3 stylle/vndir his power] trs. Hb   373 Right so and]
om. CbHbDo   maner] om. A2   wise] om. CbHbDo   fals] om. CbHbDo   374 a] þe
.v. L   for when . . . þat¹] he grauntith when CbHbDo   otherwise] oþer wile Hb   but] om.
CbHbDo   375 woll] om. CbHbDo   þat is] of CbHb, add oute of dedely A2
376 not for] neuer A2   377 vertues] warkes Cb   leve] haue A2   378 beestis] add
stylle A2   379 bodely] om. CbHbDo

380 at her lustis and wandryn abowte at her wille in Egipt, þat is synne,
þey make men as beestis, of the whiche þe gospell spekith, þat he þat
hadde bought .v. 30kkis of oxen excusid hym to come to Goddis feest.
þese .v. 30kkis of oxen þat been beestis, as Ianuensis seith and
Gregory also on þe gospell þe .xxxvj. chaptir or omely, bene
385 mannys .v. wittis. And as Austyn seith, þey be callid .v. 30kkis of
oxen, for alwey .ij. be knette togeder, as .ij. eien, too eren, .ij.
nostrellis, .ij. in þe mouth as savour and speche, and .ij. hondis or
.ij. felyngis, as felynge in all þe body and an other felyng in
distruccioun of þe .iiij. wittis. Yf þese wittis be lefte behynde and
390 goon at her wille abroode as beestis in þe londe of synne at her lustis
and likyng, þey shull make hem to turne a3een and be but as beestis
whiche be rewlid nat aftir þe sperite of resoun but after þe wille of þe
wittis of þe flessh. Of whiche men þus rewlid aftir þe wille of her
L f. 435ᵛᵃ bodely wittis folowynge þe lustis | of hem, or ellis let her wittis wander
395 at her will and nat rewle hem by þe sperite of resoun and of grace of þe
holi gost, spekith Iude in his Epistill, clepyng hem beestly men and
nat havynge sperite, þat is to sey nether off reson ne of grace, whom
God reprovith by the prophete Dauid in the Sawter, seiyng: 'Will 3ee
nat to be made as [a] hors and [a] mule in whom is noon vndir-
400 stondyng,' for they have nat þe sperite of resoun. And þe apostill
seith: 'Whosomevir have nat þe sperite of Crist, he is nat Cristis,' þat is
to sey, he þat is nat rewlid aftir the sperite of resoun and he hathe nat þe
sperite of grace with hym dwellyng, but he folewith aftir þe lustis of his
beestly wittis, he is nat Cristis, and þan muste he nedys be the devilles.
405   Wolte þowe se howe þe wittis of man þat be not wele rewlid be
made as beestis þorowe þe vnlawfull heryng of the eere þat our modir
Eve 3ave to the serpent, as it is writen in the first boke of Goddis lawe

---

380 and] *add* also for to A2   her²] *add* owne A2   381 spekith] *add* in luke the fourtenthe
chapitre CbHbDo   þat²] *om.* Do   384 also] *om.* CbHbDo   chaptir or] *add* in the A2, *om.*
CbHbDo   385 mannys] namyd A2   .v.¹] *om.* Hb   callid] clepyd CbHb   388 and] *add*
þer is A2   389 distruccioun] discrecion CbHb   þe] *add* other CbHbDo   þese] *add* .v. A2
390 abroode] as broode L   391 and likyng] *om.* CbHbDo   hem] men CbHb
392 resoun] *add* and of grace of the hooli goost Do   394 folowynge] and folowe A2
395 of¹] *add* very A2   grace] *add* and Cb   396 spekith] as sayeth A2   Epistill] *add* the
seconde chapitre CbHb   397 grace] *add* to whom powle acordythe in the first corintheos þe
.ij.ᵈᵉ chapitre and saythe sothly a bestely man perceyueth not tho thynges that been of god.
Verily it is foly to hym and he may not vnderstond what the wayes be of vertu and of grace Cb
whom] the which people A2   398 Sawter] *add* the .xxxj. psalme CbHb   Will] Be Cb
399 to be] *om.* Cb   a¹] *om.* LDo   and] or Hb   a²] þe LCb, *om.* Do   400 apostill] *add* to the
romayns seythe in the .viij. chapitre CbHb   401 Cristis] of cristis floke Cb   402 he
hathe] thaye haue A2, hath CbHbDo   403 hym] them A2   405 þat be not wele] not
CbHbDo   be ... rewlid] wylle not be rulid thaye A2   405–6 be made] made man CbHb

in Genesis .iij.°, and þe sight nat refreyned þat she let goo to the
forboden tree and þe froyte þereof, and þe towchyng of þe felynge of
the honde þat she toke þe froyte of þe tree with, and þe taste of þe 410
mouthe þorowe whiche she eete of þe froyte nat leefull to here and
þan ȝafe it to her husbond Adam, and boothe eete þereof and made
man to be caste owte of paradise as beestis vnto þe erthe and þere to
eete herbis | and corne in labour and traveill as beestis, [and also to Lf.435vb
suffre hete and colde, hungir and thurste, werynes and sikenes, and at 415
the laste sterve as beestis] done. And all þis shulde nat haue befall but
þat Adam and Eve lefte reson and folowid the luste of her bodely
wittis. And aftirward þe bodely flesshely sonnes of men þorowe þe
bodely sight of her eyen sawen þe doughtres of men that þey were
feyre, and chasyn hem wifis aftir þe lustis of her wittis, as it is writen 420
in þe boke of Genesis 6. And þey þan vsynge hcr lustis as beestis
corruptid þe erth before God þorowe synne and fulfillid it with
wickidnes. And þan God, seyng þat man levid but as beestis or worse,
distroyed þorowe a floode of water for þe synne of man all þe beestis
of þe erthe, and with hem mankynde þat lived as beestis, owtake a 425
fewe þat were savid in Noes shipp. Lo, all þese veniauncis God did to
man for þat man folowid þe lustis of his wittis whiche made hem but
as beestis. And aftir, Noe folowyng þe luste of his taaste of his mowthe
in drynkyng wyne, brought in thraldom, as it is writen Genesis 9°.
And Loothe þorowe þe same synne was made witles as an vnresonabill 430
beeste doyng lechery with his owen doughtres, hymselfe nat wetyng
ne vndirstondyng þereof. All þis is writen in þe boke aforeseide.
   Therefor man rewlid þorowe his bodely wittis, lesyng þe will of the
resoun of þe soule, is likened to witles beestis by þe prophete Dauid
where he seith: 'For he is liche to hem'. And Salamon seith þat 'God 435

408 in Genesis .iij°.] om. Do   nat refreyned/þat she let goo] trs. with refreynynge for
refreyned Cb   refreyned] restreyned as correction Hb   to] om. Cb   409 of¹] or A2
409–10 felynge . . . honde] the handys felynge Cb   413 caste] chacyd Cb, cacched Hb
414 also] om. CbHbDo   414–16 and also . . . beestis] om. L   416 done] om. CbHbDo
417–18 bodely wittis] fleshlye apetytes A2, add as beestis CbHbDo   418 aftirward] aftir
Hb   bodely] add and the A2, om. CbHb   flesshely] add lustis of þe A2   419 sight] om. Hb
þey] om. A2Do   420 and] om. CbHb   421 6] om. A2Do   423 but] om. A2
424 þorowe . . . water] by water in Noes flode A2   425–6 mankynde . . . fewe] excepte tho
A2   426 Noes shipp] the arke with Noe that were but .viij. personys Cb   þese veniauncis]
this veniaunce CbHbDo   427 his] add bodyly A2   429 thraldom] chirledom Hb
Genesis 9°] om. A2   430 an vnresonabill] a CbHbDo   432 þereof. All] om. CbHbDo
boke aforeseide] add the xix chapitre CbHb, add .ix°. Do   433 bodely] dedelye A2
434 likened] made lyke A2   by] as sayeth the A2   435 where he seith] þe xlvij psalme
CbHb   where . . . is] for he is lyke to vnwyse beestis and is made A2   is] add made CbHb
Salamon] add in the ecclesiastes the thridde chapitre CbHb

L f. 436ra hath previd þe sonnes of men þat þey be nat | rewlid after þe resoun of
þe sperite and hathe shewid hem to be liche to beestis'. But ȝit [yif]
þese beestis be nat lefte behynde in þe lond of syn to wandir at her
owne will in lust and likyng, but dryven owt by resonabill chastysyng
440 and had forthe by reson of þe soule, than may be made of hem to God
an holy sacrifice and a worshipfull offryng. And for to preve þis
soothe, Moyses seide to Kyng Pharo by a figure, as it is wreten:
'Offryng and sacrifice wee muste offir to owre Lord God, and all our
beestis shull go with vs, forsoothe þer shall noon leve behynde of hem
D f. 163ra o clawe that is necessary [to the] worshipp | and se[r]vice of oure
446 Lorde.' For mannys bodilie wittes that be but as beestis must be
hadde forthe bi resoune of the soule to goodnesse and to vertue, and
shette fro synne þe eeris of harde hiringe and of badde thingis, the
mouþe fro euelle spekinge, as God biddith bi the wise man, seyenge:
450 'Hegge vp thine eeris with thornes which ben dreedis of the [doome of
God] prikkinge, and ne wille thou nat to hire a wickid tonge, and
make þou dores to thy mouthe and lockes to thine eeris, and weie thi
wordis, sith man shalle [yeelde] rekeninge of euerie idelle woorde atte
daie of dome,' as Criste seith in the gospelle. And Seinte Gregorie
455 seith that a worde [is] spoken in idelle whan it wantith profite of
rightwisnesse or els resoun of iust neede. Also the eyȝen shul[d]e be
turned fro vanite, as the prophete David praied fore vnto God and
made a covenaunte with h[e]m that thei shulde nauȝt loke ayenne
afftir synne, as Lothes wife did whan that she went out of Sodome, as
460 it is written, but as the holie man Ioobe did, seienge: 'I haue made
couenaunt with myne [eyen] that thei shulde nat thinke on a virgine.'

437 yif] of L, and A2, om. Cb   439 owne] om. Do   owne will in] om. CbHb   and
likyng] om. CbHbDo   but] add ben A2   440 had] add with þem A2   reson] add and
vertue A2   soule] add kepyng CbHb   than] add yet þere A2   442 wreten] add in Exodi
the .x. chapitre CbHb   443 offir] doo Cb   444 of hem] not A2   445 to the] and L
and . . . of] om. L   service] sevice D   447 of the soule] om. CbHbDo   and to vertue] om.
CbHbDo   448 þe eeris of harde] and the A2   harde] evylle Cb, badde HbDo   of² . . .
thingis] om. CbHbDo   449 wise man] add Ecclesiasticus the .xviij. chapitre CbHb
seyenge] add thus CbHb   450 doome] doumbe D   450–1 of God] om. DA2
451 prikkinge] add vs to remembre oure wrecchidnes A2   and ne] anoon L   and²] add loke
A2   452 weie] weies to D   453 wordis] add or thaye passe thye mouthe A2   sith] for
A2   yeelde] yeve D   euerie] eny Hb   454 the gospelle] Mathew þe xij chapitre CbHbDo
455 is] om. DL   profite] perfite A2   456 els] om. A2   Also . . . shulde] So þerto shuld þe
yȝes Hb   shulde] shulle DL   be] add also Hb   457 God] add þe hundryd and xviij
psalme CbHb   458 made] make LHb   hem] hym D, om. A2   460 written] add in
genesis the xix chapitre CbHb, add Gen^s .ix°. Do   but] add we shulde do A2, bycause þat
aȝenst the commaundment of god she lokid backward she turnyd into a salt stone. Wherfor be
ware man and turne not from the commaundementys of god and make a comnaunt wyth thyn
eyen Cb   did seienge] sayth Cb, add the .xxxj chapitre CbHbDo   461 eyen] om. D   thei]
I CbHb   thinke on] loken vppon L   a virgine] vanyte A2, add in eville thought L

And like as I haue seide of these three wittis, so vndirstonde þou of
alle othir to haue hem out of the londe of Egipte, that is synne, and
leve nouʒt oone behinde nat so moche as oo clawe of hem, as Moyses
seide, that is nat so moch as a litille purpos to turne ayenne to synne 465
but cha⟨s⟩tice hem as the appostulle did, as it is written, and bringe
hem into seruage and drive hem with the yerde of chastisinge þat is
drede and penaunce into the mounte of God that ben good vertu⟨es,
as⟩ Moises did the beestis that he kepte, as ⟨it is written⟩, and offrid
hem to God in good vertue of ⟨lyuyng⟩, a more worshippfulle sacrifice 470
and offringe than was the sacrifice and offringe of beestis in the oolde
lawe. Than sith it is bettir, holier and of gretter value a man to offre
hymselff brennynge in loue of alle his herte, of alle his soule, of alle his
mynde and of alle his strengthis, than be his bodilie and goostelie
wittis better than is any offringe of beest⟨is⟩. Wherefor the prophete 475
David spekith in the persoone of the rightful man to God and seithe:
'Lorde God,' he seith: 'thou askist nat offringe that is done of doumbe
beestis for synne, but I seide: "Loo, I come myselff a resonable
offringe", for it is written, Lorde God, þat I shulde doo thi wille in
kepinge of thi lawe; I wolde hauc it in the myddes of myne hert. | 480
[The fyfte wile.] Bvt the feende is fulle lothe þat man shuld make Df. 163ʳᵇ
this offringe to God, for he wote welle than þat man is clene deliuerid
fro hym but yif it so be þat the [fyfte] wile mai helpe that Kinge
Pharao did to the children of Israelle in Egipte, as it is written where it
shewith þat God did so grete veniauncis to Kinge Pharao and to his 485
puple that he was drive bi neede to lete hem goo. And than he seide to
hem: 'Goothe and doth sacrifice to the Lorde God as ye seide, and
takith with you youre children and youre beestis as ye askid frist, and
yee goynge out of my londe blesseth me,' as thouʒ he had seid

462 wittis] *add* before Cb   þou] *om.* Hb, 3e Cb   464 oone] *add* beest A2
465 turne] walke CbHb   ayenne] *om.* CbHbDo   466 written] *add* in (þe first pistel to
Hb) the corinthijs the .ix. chapitre CbHb   467 hem¹] thy wittis Cb   þat is] *om.* CbHb
468 vertues] *add* and A2, *excised* D   469 written] *add* in exodo the .iij.ᵈᵉ chapitre CbHb
offrid] offir LHb   470 of] and Cb   a] and Do   471 and²] or LCbHbDo
472 lawe] *add* nowe A2   473 hymselff] his herte in L   474 than] þat CbHbDo
be] *add* in Cb   and goostelie] *om.* Do   475 better] *om.* CbHbDo   476 spekith]
spekyng CbHb   and] *om.* CbHb   seithe] *add* in the xxxix psalme CbHb   477 he seith]
om. A2   479 in] and Cb   480 kepinge of] *om.* CbHb   lawe] *add* therfor Cb
wolde] wylle Cb   it] *om.* CbHb   481 The fyfte wile] DA2CbHb   fulle] weol Hb,
wel Do   482 this] his L   clene] than CbHb, *add* oute of his clowe A2   483 fro
hym] clene fro hem Hb   fyfte] frist DA2   Kinge] *om.* A2   484 did] *om.* Hb   written]
add in the .xij. chapitre of exodi CbHb   485 to²] *add* all CbHb   486 goo] *add* The
.v.ᵗʰ chapitre Cb   487 as ye seide] *om.* A2   seide] sey Cb   488 children and youre]
om. CbHb   and²] but as A2   489 goynge] go A2

490 or mente: 'Sith that it mai noone othir be but that ye wolle goo out of my londe to doo sacrifice to the Lorde God and thereto goo ferre, and also to haue youre childrenne with you and eke youre beestes, I graunte thereto so that whan ye goo ye blesse me.' In Latyn it is seide: *Benedicite michi, benedicite.* In Englisshe it is for to seie welle. So

495 Kinge Pharao wolde that thei shuld speke good of hym and of his londe, allethouȝ it were þat he did hem moche harme, for þat in time followinge thei shulde haue mynde on her lustie fare that thei had in his londe, and þat thei shulde loue hym the bettir and holde hym for her kinge and to be in the bettir wille to come to hym ayenne yif thei

500 myght. And th[i]s followith affter in deede, as it is written where he telleth þat the childrenne [of Israelle], allethough it were that God fedde hem with manna havinge alle maner ⟨o⟩f swetnesse and alle maner of delicis, yitte thei grucchid ayenst God and seid as it is written: 'Who shalle yeve vs flesshe [to eete]? Wee haue mynde of the

505 flesshe that we eete f[r]essheli in Egipte,' which preisinge is clepid blessinge. Wherefor thei were in wille yiff thei had myght to torne ayenne into Egipte to haue ben vndir Kinge Pharaoes powere. For thouȝ thei were out of Egipte with her bodies, yit thei were þereinne with her hertis, wille and speche, and so thei were stille liegemen to

510 Kinge Pharao.

Suche a wile worchith the feende with cristen men whan he mai nat holde hem, but that thei wolle bi þe sacrament of penaunce allegate

D f. 163ᵛᵃ goo froo hym, and þereto goo bi a fulle purpos | no more to turne ayen to synne, and haue with hem her childrenne þat be her goode werkis

515 and vertues out of veinglorie and ypocrisie, and her beestis that ben her bodilie wittis welle irulid. Yit the feende wolde that thei shulde blesse hym, that is to [sey] speke gladlie good of hym and of his londe,

490 or] and L   or mente] *om.* CbHbDo   othir] *add* wyse A2   491 thereto] *add* to D
492 eke] also A2, *om.* Cb   493 ye²] þe L, *om.* Cb   seide] to sey Cb   494 *benedicite*]
benedicere HbDo   it] *om.* LDo   is] *add* saide A2   495 shuld] *add* do Do   500 this]
thus D   followith] folwid CbHb   written] *add* in the boke of numeri the .xj. chapitre
CbHbDo   501 of Israelle] *om.* D   503 delicis] *add* as it is writen in the boke of
wisdom the .xvj. (.xvij. Hb) chapitre CbHb, *add* as it is writen Sap. .xvj°. Do   as] *om.* L
503–4 as . . . written] *om.* CbHbDo   504 vs] his L   to eete] *om.* D, for nowe A2
505 flesshe] flesshis Hb, fisshes Cb   fressheli/in Egipte] *trs.* LCbHbDo   fressheli]
flessheli DA2, right fresschely L, frely CbHb   clepid] callid A2   506 were] *add* ofte
CbHb   had] *om.* A2   torne] have turnyd LCbHbDo   507 Kinge] *om.* Cb
508 thouȝ] alle thouȝe it be þat CbHb   of] *add* pharaoys power and oute of Cb
509 were] abode A2   510 Pharao] *add* and at his wille L   511 wile] wille Cb   men]
folke LHbDo, folke nowe Cb   512 allegate] *om.* CbHbDo   513 goo²] *add* awey A2,
add far CbHbDo   no] neuer A2   ayen] *om.* LCbHbDo   515 of] *add* alle A2
517 sey] *om.* DDo   gladlie] *add* of hym and to speke A2   of hym] *om.* A2

þat is to reherse her synnes of her yonge life reioisinge hem þereof and
be merie whan thei thinke or speke thereof, and thenke that thei were
lustie and likinge and inwarde merie whan thei dwelle`d´ thereinne 520
and howe it was `a´ merie world than, or in such manere preise her
euelle livinge othir reherse it for preisinge or for lust. And so thei be
iocounde and merie whan thei thenke þereon, as it is written: 'Thei be
merie whan thei before han done euelle, thei be ioiefulle of the worst
thingis, and yif thei hire speke of God and so of goodnesse thei ben 525
hevie and tedius thereof. And yif thei speke or hire speke of synne that
men clepe merthe and harlotrie, and yit some clep[e it] good sporte,
than þ`e´i wille throuȝ ioie seie þat it was good game, and so blesse and
praise the feende whan thei praise and blesse that thinge þat is synne
and contrarie to holincs.' And alletliouȝ it be so that [thei] be clepid 530
cristenne bi the vertue of the sacramentis of holie Church, yit thei ben
in her wille and in her hert liegemen to þe feende of helle, wherefor,
yif thei durst, for drede of peine or for shame thei wolde turne ayenne
to her oolde myschieff and so to be stille vndir þe feendis powere. But
the puple of God blessen oure Lorde and praise hym, and doone good 535
vertues that longen to hym, [and] be welle ware of the wilis of the
feende, and praise nat the werkis of hym ne be nat ioieful of her
myssedeedis, but be sorie whan thei thenke on hem. And thei speke
nat of her synnes throuȝ lustie merthe, but whan thei hire of hem loke
that thei be inwardlie sorie and put it aweie fro her lustie speche, as 540

518 reherse . . . life] saye of þer synnes done in þer yong age and A2   518–19 and be . . .
thereof] *om.* L   519–20 that . . . and¹] howe mery and lustye in A2   520 inwarde]
inwardly Do, *om.* CbHb   merie] *add* thaye were A2   521 and howe it] or þat is L   or]
add any suche penaunce were vsid and so A2   preise] praysing A2   522 reherse]
rehersid A2   523 iocounde and] *om.* Hb   written] *add* Prouer 2° LCbHbDo
524 whan . . . before] of that they Cb   before . . . done] be in mynde of þe olde A2   euelle]
add and after A2   525 and so of goodnesse] of gode þyngis anon A2, *om.* Cb
526 tedius] wery A2   thereof] *om.* CbHb   speke¹] thynke Cb   527 men] they Cb
and yit] *om.* A2   and yit some] þat men Hb, they Cb   clepe it] clepid D   it good] *om.*
CbHb   529 praise², blesse] *trs.* I.CbHbDo   and blesse] *om.* A2   530 contrarie]
contrariouse CbHbDo   allethouȝ] alle thought L, yett though A2   thei] ye D
531 cristenne] cristen men CbHb   sacramentis of/holie] *trs.* A2   532 feende] devyll
CbHbDo   533 or] and A2   wolde] *add* anone A2   534 stille] *om.* LCbHbDo
535 God] *add* euer A2   blessen, praise] *trs.* A2L   oure] there CbHb   Lorde] god Cb
doone] *om.* LHbDo, the Cb   536 and] wherefore DA2   welle] *om.* CbHb   wilis] wile
LHbDo   537 hym . . . nat] hem that be Cb   her] your A2   538 myssedeedis] evylle
dedis A2   but] *add* euer A2   thei¹] *add* torne into youre mynde to A2   on hem] þeron Hb
And] *add* that DA2   thei²] *om.* CbHb   speke] reioyse them A2   539 nat] *om.* L   of her
synnes] therof CbHb   hire] *add* speke Cb   of hem] therof CbHb   539–40 loke that
thei] to A2, they L, *om.* CbHbDo   540 inwardlie] *om.* CbHb   aweie . . . speche] oute of
þer mynde suche lustye spekyng in fleshlynes A2

God biddyth bi the prophete A[nne] seienge: 'Lete oolde synnes goo
aweie from youre mouthe, for the Lorde is God of knowinge and to
hym mennes thoughtis ben made openne.' Also the ⟨aposte⟩lle biddith
that 'fornicacioun or vncl⟨enesse or ava⟩rice or couetice, let nought
545 he⟨m be named⟩ nor spoken amonge you, nothir foule speche, nothir
folie speche, nothir harlotrie whiche perteineth nouȝt to profite, but
Df. 163ᵛᵇ rathir doynge | gracis or thankingis to God that hath brought vs out of
Egipte, that is synne, bi the sacrementis of holi Church, and
principaliche by the passioune of oure Lorde Ihesu Criste that
550 ledeth vs [through] the deserte of penance for synne and tribulacioun,
and shalle bringe vs to the londe of biheeste, that is the blisse of
heuen, through his grace and goodness.' Amen.

Here endithe the .v. wilis of Kinge Pharao whiche he vsed
ayenst the childrenne of Israelle.

And also here endith the lives of seintis that is callid in
Latynne *Legenda Aurea* and in Englissh the Gilte Legende,
the which is drawen out of Frensshe into Englisshe the
yere of oure lorde a .Mˡ. .CCCC. and .xxxviij. bi a synfulle
wrecche whos name I beseche Ihesu Criste bi his meritis of
his passioune and of alle these holie seintis afore written
that hit mai be written in the boke of everlastinge life.
Amen.

541 biddyth] sayeth A2   prophete] prophetesse Hb   Anne] Amy D, Amos A2L,
dauid Cb, *add* in þe firste book of kingis Do, *so and add* the seconde chapitre CbHb
seienge] *om.* A2   542 aweie] *om.* Cb   knowinge] kunnyng LCbHbDo   543 made]
add fulle Cb, *add* wel Hb   Also] *om.* CbHb   apostelle] *add* to the ephesies the .v. chapitre
CbHb   544 that] What *preceded by paraph* Do   545 nor spoken amonge] in Hb
546 folie speche, harlotrie] *trs.* Cb   perteineth . . . profite] profitith nat L, perseiueþ not
profite Do   profite] the profite of the body and soule A2   547 or] and A2   548 is]
add to saye oute of A2   549 the] *add* gracious LDo, his graciful CbHb   of . . . that] and
Hb, and his glorious blode shedynge oute he wasshythe vs from oure synnes and he Cb
550 through] to DA2L   for] fro Cb   552 grace and goodness] gracious and eendles
mercy L   and goodness] *om.* HbDo, that it may be so praye we alle therfor to oure almyȝty
fadyr that ys in heuenys that by his mercy he bryng vs alle to his blisse. Amen. Here endithe
the .v. wyles of kynge pharao Cb